AVIATION IN CRISIS

T0361922

For Vishesh, success in high school.

Aviation in Crisis

RUWANTISSA I.R. ABEYRATNE

LONDON AND NEW YORK

First published 2004 by Ashgate Publishing

Reissued 2018 by Routledge
2 Park Square, Milton Park, Abingdon, Oxon OX14 4RN
711 Third Avenue, New York, NY 10017, USA

Routledge is an imprint of the Taylor & Francis Group, an informa business

Publisher's Note
The publisher has gone to great lengths to ensure the quality of this reprint but points out that some imperfections in the original copies may be apparent.

Disclaimer
The publisher has made every effort to trace copyright holders and welcomes correspondence from those they have been unable to contact.

A Library of Congress record exists under LC control number: 2002025861

ISBN 13: 978-1-138-70974-4 (hbk)
ISBN 13: 978-1-138-70971-3 (pbk)
ISBN 13: 978-1-315-19816-3 (ebk)

Contents

Foreword

This work, the latest in a series of impressive treatises by Dr Abeyratne, will not fail to enlighten any lawyer or executive concerned with the current challenges facing the international airline industry. Focusing, from a primarily regulatory and aeropolitical perspective, on the crisis facing the airline industry, both before and after 11 September 2001, Dr Abeyratne has drawn together, in typical thoroughness and eloquence, a broad diversity of topics of *fundamental significance to the industry*. These *include the implications* of the depressed state of the industry for security, commercial transactions (including leasing and financing), insurance, environmental issues and air carrier liability.

Since the response of the world community to the crises in airline security, commercial transactions and insurance has been largely voiced through the medium of the International Civil Aviation Organization (ICAO), Dr Abeyratne's vantage point, as a senior legal officer in ICAO, makes him peculiarly qualified to address the *topics considered in this work*.

The reader will be impressed by the ability of the author to write with first-hand knowledge and experience on matters of both public and private international law, while at the same time considering the issues in numerous municipal jurisdictions, including the United Kingdom, United States and Canada.

This carefully researched and well-written book, which draws on the author's vast experience in the airline industry at both the governmental and private levels, represents a significant contribution to the literature in the field. I commend it to all who have an interest of any kind in the legal issues affecting the airline industry.

Rod D. Margo
Los Angeles

Preface

The events of 11 September 2001 defy modern economic theory when addressed in aviation terms. Economic theory would suggest that, once the impact of such events are a thing of the past, and economies are restored to their *status quo ante*, a rise in the gross domestic product of states to earlier levels would almost inevitably result in increased consumption. This in turn would mean that the demand for air travel would rise to earlier proportions and consumption in terms of air transport services would be restored to normality. However, the September attacks on United States property introduced a unique characteristic through the fear factor that directly effects the future development of air transport. As a result, the grim task of restoration of passenger confidence stands in the way of economic revival of the air transport industry.

In a manner of speaking, aviation was always in crisis. The air transport industry, even prior to 11 September 2001, although seemingly a glamorous, exciting and prosperous business, never enjoyed sustained periods of profitability. Even among the large carriers, a short bout of profitability would inevitably be followed by a period of downturn in real income. There is nothing arcane about this situation. It is simply that this fluctuation in fortune is an ineluctable characteristic of air transport, whose fortunes are dictated by rigid regulation, competition and technological change. For this reason, it would be doing the air transport industry an injustice if an analysis of the situation it is faced with should be strictly bifurcated into pre- and post-September 2001 segments. However, this by no means suggests that the tragic events of September did not gravely aggravate the fortunes of an industry already at a disadvantage. They placed issues in a strictly realistic perspective, making one realize that, if a sustained analysis were to be made of air transport, plain economic theory would no longer be the exclusive discipline for consideration. Rather, all relevant factors have to be taken in context and emerging issues should be analysed as possible threats to the economic well-being of the air transport industry.

Any study of present-day aviation would incontrovertibly involve viewing issues from both an economic and a legal perspective in addition to other relevant factors. In the field of aviation security, these two disciplines are intertwined with the regulatory regime, calling for a wide discussion of legal and regulatory regimes in the role played by states in ensuring security in aviation within their territories. In a parallel dimension, the importance of economic issues can be viewed as predominant in the field of insurance, particularly in the inquiry as to whether states should be establishing an aviation reinsurance pool to support airlines in crisis, thus giving states much more control over the running of their national airlines. Therefore, in an overall sense, the question arises as to whether increased state involvement in both security and insurance issues would not bring back rigid state control over national carriers. If this question were to be answered in the affirmative and day-to-day state control made a comeback, one would unavoidably have to inquire into the continued validity of gradual liberalization of market access, bringing the commercial angle into play and forming an interlinked triangle. When this phenomenon occurred, the necessary corollary – the question as to whether absolute competition would no longer be a collective goal among states, and whether the need for added capacity would therefore no longer arise in the volumes earlier required – would inevitably obviate the earlier compelling necessity for airlines to order new aircraft. They could continue using aircraft already in use to their maximum capacity. This added dimension would introduce environmental considerations, making the entire study a complex fabric woven with different but symbiotic threads.

This book not only addresses issues in a rigid post-September 2001 context but also analyses issues past and present, with the intent of looking at the future. This will be attempted by taking four major areas into consideration which were in crisis but are truly affected by the events of September 2001. These areas relate to crises in the commercial, security, insurance and environmental protection fields. Of these the first and fourth areas are inextricably intertwined, as aircraft noise regulations in various states have a direct impact on aircraft financing, which in turn is linked to demand for air services. A drop in demand for air services would essentially mean that the demand for lease or purchase of new aircraft would drop. When this occurred, air transport enterprises would be more inclined to cut costs and therefore concentrate on using the aircraft already at hand, upgrading them to conform to the more demanding noise and emissions regulatory standards. It therefore becomes necessary to view all these factors separately, in the multitude of issues they provide, with a view to understanding the course which the air transport industry will be taking in the future.

The purpose of this book is to view the overall picture of an aviation industry – comprising air transport and other aviation-related industries – in crisis, through issues that continue to affect the economic viability of air transport, particularly as a result of the events of 11 September 2001.

Ruwantissa Abeyratne

Table of Cases

Chapter 1

Introduction

At best, the air transport industry's fortunes have been irregular. The airline industry, despite its glamour and perceived commercial power, has experienced marginal profitability and cyclical fiscal growth in the long term, with periods of growth and profit being watered down by less successful periods that follow. One of the reasons for this fluctuating pattern is that the airline industry is driven by variable factors such as operational and technological changes as well as regulatory control. To add another dimension of unlawful interference with civil aviation to this list would almost certainly break the industry's back.

It is an incontrovertible fact that the sad and tragic consequences of the events of 11 September 2001 affected first and foremost the victims of those terrible attacks, and their families. It is equally unchallengeable that the second casualty in this horrendous series of events was aviation. Aeronautically speaking, aviation paid the irrecoverable cost of having aircraft used as weapons of vast destruction. Commercially speaking, the closure of airspace, as an immediate measure throughout the United States and some parts of Europe, and its subsequent opening amidst restricted commercial activity of airlines, not only affected the air transport industry during the first few days of the catastrophe, but also continues to portend grave commercial implications for the airline industry in the years to come. This chapter will outline these implications, with particular focus on insurance and security considerations which were considered in some depth by the 33rd Assembly of the International Civil Aviation Organization, which concluded its deliberations on 5 October 2001.

AERONAUTICAL IMPLICATIONS

The International Civil Aviation Conference, convened at the initiative of President Roosevelt of the United States, was held in Chicago, Illinois from 1 November to December 1944. The delegates at this conference, in the words of President Roosevelt, 'met in a high resolve that ways and means be found, and rules may be evolved, which shall permit the healing processes of peace to begin their work as rapidly as the interruptions resulting from aggressive war can be cleared away'.[1] The resultant consensus, the Convention on International Civil Aviation,[2] begins by stating that the development of international civil aviation can greatly help to create and preserve friendship and understanding among the nations and peoples of the world, yet its abuse can become a threat to the general security.[3]

The Chicago Convention identifies its scope as being applicable to international civil aviation, thus presumably leaving us with the assumption that at least technically, the Convention may not apply to local or domestic aviation. If this were to be accepted without further debate, one could argue that the attacks on the United

States, carried out with aircraft flying domestic routes within the country, would not come within the purview of the Chicago Convention. The situation, however, is not that simple or straightforward. The Chicago Convention does not state anywhere that the Convention will apply only to international civil aviation. On the contrary, the Convention, in Article 4 provides: 'Each Contracting State agrees not to use civil aviation for any purpose inconsistent with the aims of this Convention.'

Although the provision itself is contextually irrelevant to the events of 11 September 2001, the use of the words 'civil aviation' links domestic or local aviation to the Chicago Convention and therefore to the work of the international aviation community, in pursuing safe and orderly development of international civil aviation. The ICAO Council, at its 141st Session in 1994, in addressing the subject of aircraft accident investigation, noted that, although Article 26 of the Chicago Convention, which requires a state to institute investigations upon an aircraft of another state which meets with an accident in the territory of the first state, and that what was seemingly described by Article 26 was an accident occurring during international air transport, the Foreword to Annex 13 specifies that the annex may also deal with accidents of a kind which do not fall within the purview of Article 26. Accordingly, the Council, in 1944 considered an amendment to the annex which ensured some uniformity in investigation procedures regardless of whether an accident involved an international or domestic flight.[4]

Annex 13[5] has incorporated the above-mentioned amendment by stating in its Foreword:

> Article 26 does not preclude the taking of further action in the field of aircraft accident investigation and the procedures set forth in this Annex are not limited solely to an inquiry instituted under the requirements of Article 26, but under prescribed circumstances apply in the event of an inquiry into any 'aircraft accident' within the terms of the definition herein.

The annex defines an 'accident' as an occurrence associated with the operation of an aircraft which takes place between the time any person boards the aircraft with the intention of flying until such time as all such persons have disembarked.[6] The definition does not mention that the accident has to occur during an international flight.

Annex 17 to the Chicago Convention,[7] on the subject of aviation security, defines 'security' as a combination of measures and human and material resources intended to safeguard international civil aviation against acts of unlawful interference. This would mean that any measure taken, including one following the occurrence of an accident caused as a result of domestic aviation, would, if such an event affects or threatens to affect international civil aviation, fall within the provisions of Annex 17.

INSURANCE IMPLICATIONS

Following the events of 11 September 2001, the international insurance market gave notice on 17 September that, effective from 24 September, third party war risk liability insurance, covering airline operators and other service providers against losses and damages resulting from war, hijacking and other perils, would be cancelled.[8] As an immediate response to this measure, the President of the ICAO Council, Dr Assad Kotaite, issued a State Letter[9] to all ICAO contracting states, requesting that they take effective measures to preclude aviation and air transport services from coming to a standstill. This letter also appealed to contracting states to support airline operators and other relevant parties, at least until the insurance market stabilized, by committing themselves to cover any risks to which airline operators and others might become exposed by the cancellation of insurance cover.

The 33rd Session of the ICAO Assembly, held in Montreal from 25 September to 5 October 2001, considered as an urgent priority the insurance issue by adopting Resolution A33-20.[10] This resolution, while recognizing that the tragic events of 11 September had adversely affected the operations of airline operators globally as a result of war risk insurance cover no longer being available at levels which are practical and accessible to airline operators, prima facie urges contracting states to work together to develop a more enduring and coordinated approach to the important problem of providing assistance to airline operators and other service providers. The resolution, basing itself on the fundamental premise enunciated in Article 44 of the Chicago Convention, which refers to the objective of ICAO to ensure safe, regular, efficient and economical air transport, directs the Council of ICAO to establish urgently a Special Group to consider issues emerging from action taken in the insurance market regarding third party war risk insurance coverage.

One must of course appreciate that war and associated risks, including hijacking and acts of terrorism, pose an extremely high risk exposure to insurers. Aviation hull and liability policies therefore usually contain an express exclusion in respect of such risks. The war risk exclusion used in the London market, known as AVN 48B,[11] excludes the risks of war, invasion, hostilities, civil war, rebellion, revolution, insurrection, martial law, hostile detonation of atomic weapons, strikes, riots, civil commotions or labour disturbances, acts of a political or terrorist nature, sabotage, confiscation, nationalization, seizure and hijacking.

In practical terms, war risk insurance is required to cover three eventualities: to protect an airline operator from potential financial liability that could jeopardize its existence; to justify operations into territories of states by assuring those states that they and their citizens would be financially compensated in the event of damage; and to protect the financial interests of airlines, their owners, financiers or lessors. It is usual for an aircraft, depending on its type, to be covered for any amount up to US$750 million to US$1 billion on aggregate (as against per single occurrence). As against this figure, it is significant that the underwriters permitted coverage for only up to US$50 million aggregate consequent upon their issuing notice of withdrawal of third party war risk insurance on 17 September 2001.

Many contracting states, following the State Letter of the President of the ICAO Council, stepped in to address issues regarding cancellation of insurance. It is therefore relevant to discuss steps taken by these various ICAO contracting states in responding almost immediately to the difficulties posed to their airline operators and other service providers. In the United States, the administration proposed a plan to have taxpayers cover most of the losses that insurance companies would suffer in future terrorist attacks. The administration viewed its proposal as an alternative to legislation drafted by lawmakers from both parties in Congress at the behest of the insurance industry. The industry plan recommends a new government-backed insurance company that would manage a pool of premiums and payouts for terrorism policies. Once losses exceeded the amount of money in the pool, the government would cover the difference – which could total much more than taxpayers stand to pay under the administration's proposal. The administration was wary of the industry approach, fearing the creation of a new federal bureaucracy that is insensitive to costs.[12]

The White House was reported as planning to propose that the federal government relieve insurance companies of 80 per cent or more of the cost of damages from any terrorist attacks over the next year. The proposal would leave the government vulnerable to huge losses if there were large-scale attacks, but administration officials said they thought it was the most workable plan at a time when the industry and others that depend on insurance need a quick fix. Experts estimate that about 70 per cent of the insurance contracts covering terrorist attacks will expire by the end of the year, and reinsurers, who essentially offer insurance to the insurers, have said they plan to drop such coverage.[13]

In Europe, the member states of the European Union recognized that the terrorist attacks exposed the vulnerability of the air transport sector, with damage exceeding all rational estimates. The EU member states have asked the Commission to draw up guidelines to ensure an efficient and coherent response in such cases. Possible responses could include the establishment of a 'mutual fund' for risks in order to avoid the cost of national measures. In addition, the Commission proposes harmonizing the amounts and conditions of insurance required for the issue of operating licences.[14]

The European Commission announced, on 10 October 2001, that it would allow member states to help European airlines recover from the turmoil after the attacks on 11 September. The Commission, which in the past has been critical of government assistance to airlines, was urging governments to extend compensation to cover the rise in premiums until the end of 2001, and has proposed setting up a fund to cover the higher premiums.[15]

In the context of European States, it must be borne in mind that the European Civil Aviation Conference (ECAC) had, during a special Plenary Meeting held in Paris on 13 December 2000, adopted a resolution[16] setting certain third party liability limits for airline accidents involving carriers of ECAC member states. The action of the European Union of 10 October 2001 would be presumed to apply, at least temporarily, notwithstanding the earlier ECAC resolution.

Japan's government stepped in to help the struggling airline industry as companies tried to cope with rising insurance costs and falling demand in the aftermath of the suicide attacks on the United States. The Ministry of Land, Infrastructure and Transport said the government would guarantee third party insurance up to $2 billion for Japan's airline carriers to cover any shortfall in claims after insurers reduced coverage to $50 million following the September 11 attack.[17]

Colombia's airlines pleaded for government aid on 3 October 2001, after their insurance costs rose by 6300 per cent, to $32 million, following the 11 September attack in the United States. Colombia's Association of Colombian Air Transporters (ATAC) said the Andean nation was hit especially hard, since it had already faced a high premium due to its 37-year guerrilla war. Colombia's government stated that it would authorize an increase in passenger ticket prices to help offset the added costs, but did not offer further details.[18]

Almost immediately after the withdrawal of coverage, Singapore gave the assurance that it will extend third party war risk liability coverage to various approved aviation service providers for their operations in the city state. The government had earlier decided to provide third party war risk liability coverage to Singapore Airlines, SilkAir, SIA Cargo and the Civil Aviation Authority of Singapore. 'A commercial charge will be levied for this insurance cover but this will be waived for the first 30 days,' the statement said.[19]

Royal Air Maroc (RAM)'s insurance has almost quadrupled, from 28 million dirhams to 120 dirhams, since 11 September. The government of Morocco agreed to offer RAM war insurance guarantees following the insurance companies' decision to cap airlines' third party war and terrorism insurance at $50 million in the expectation of potential record payouts.[20]

Hong Kong's Civil Aviation Department on 4 October 2001 gave the green light for 15 airlines to levy insurance surcharges on passengers on Hong Kong routes. The 15 airlines that have secured approval from the Civil Aviation Department to impose insurance surcharges include the two locally based passenger carriers, Cathay Pacific Airways Ltd and Hong Kong Dragon Airlines Ltd (Dragonair). Table 1.1 lists the 15 airlines and the proposed surcharges.[21]

Air Transat joined its Canadian rivals on 5 October 2001 by announcing it would charge passengers C$3 extra per one-way trip to cover soaring insurance costs following the 11 September attacks on the United States. The company said that the surcharge would be applied on all its domestic, transborder and international fights, starting on 8 October 2001.[22] Air Transat is the last major Canadian carrier to impose such a surcharge. Air Canada, the country's dominant carrier, and no-frills airlines WestJet and Canada 3000, each imposed a C$3 fee.

KLM said, on 22 September 2001, that it had reopened bookings for that week after the Dutch government agreed to grant war risk insurance.[23] KLM announced it was adding a US$5 a flight surcharge to fares immediately to help cover the cost of additional safety procedures being taken since the US aircraft attacks. 'It's a safety surcharge; we have taken a lot of measures to boost safety, and that incurs costs,' said a KLM spokesman.[24]

The Spanish government and domestic airlines agreed to implement the Ecofin accord, according to which Insurance Compensation Consortium (ICC) will pay insurance premiums for the airlines' risk against war and terrorism for a period of one month.

On 28 September 2001, the International Air Transport Association (IATA) hosted a meeting of air carriers, financiers, national governments, freight forwarders, insurers and other industry participants to review the current war risk insurance situation and discuss proposals for dealing with the current difficulties resulting from the 24 September 2001 withdrawal by insurers of third party war risk insurance coverage. IATA proposed that the participants from this meeting should encourage states to use model or uniform text with respect to the provision of indemnities or guarantees, and that such guarantees must be for a period greater than 30 days, preferably in the order of 90 days.

In face of the dramatic recession of insurance coverage, states began to take measures to provide excess insurance cover to carriers, in most cases up to the previous policy limit, for war and terrorism-related third party risk. Provision of such coverage meant that at least some air carriers would not be in violation of domestic and international regulations and lease covenants respecting war risk cover. However, there was concern expressed at the fact that a considerable number of countries in Latin America, Asia and Africa, while having taken steps necessary to ensure continued coverage, have not provided the necessary guarantees and indemnities in the same amount as states in Europe and North America.

Table 1.1

Airlines	Proposed insurance surcharges
Cathay Pacific	US$4 per flight coupon
Dragonair	US$4 per air segment
Asiana Airlines	US$1·25 per sector
KLM Royal Dutch	US$5 per ticket coupon
Gulf Air	US$5 per sector
Singapore Airlines	US$1·25 per sector
Emirates Airline	HK$39 per sector
Philippine Airline	US$6 per sector
Thai Airway International	US$1·25 per flight coupon
Korean Air	HK$10 per flight sector
Myanmar Airway	C$1·25 per flight sector
Air New Zealand	US$3·10 per flight coupon
Malaysian Airlines	US1·25 per flight sector
Air Canada	C$3 per one way
China Airlines	US$2·50 per flight sector

More recently, insurers in the United States envisaged an insurance pool along the lines of Britain's 'Pool Re', a government-backed, mutually-owned company, set up in 1993 after the planting of a series of bombs in mainland Britain by Northern Irish terrorists. Through such a scheme, insurers collect premiums for terrorism insurance and the government promises to chip in if claims exceed the pool's premiums plus reserves. So far, there have been no settlements by the government, although the important feature was the guarantee that it would have honoured its commitment if a situation calling for settlement had arisen. This proposal has not been accepted by the American administration, which takes the position that the insurance industry will meet the first $10 billion of a terrorist loss and the federal government will pick up 90 per cent of larger losses, up to $100 billion in the first year. The insurers would not be required to repay the government.

Action taken by ICAO contracting states in responding to the insurance crisis has legal legitimacy in two international conventions: the Rome Convention of 1952[25] and the Montreal Convention of 1999.[26] Article 15 of the Rome Convention provides that any contracting state may require that the operator of an aircraft registered in another contracting state shall be insured in respect of his liability for damage sustained in its territory for which a right to compensation exists. The operative clause, in the context of indemnities offered by the several ICAO contracting states as discussed earlier, is contained in Article 15.4 of the Rome Convention which provides that, instead of insurance, inter alia, a guarantee given by the contracting state where the aircraft is registered, shall be deemed satisfactory if that state undertakes that it will not claim immunity from suit in respect of that guarantee.[27] The Montreal Convention of 1999, which is yet to come into force, provides in Article 50 that states parties shall require their carriers to maintain adequate insurance covering their liability under the Convention. This provision further stipulates that a carrier may be required by the state party into which it operates to furnish evidence that it maintains adequate insurance covering its liability under the Convention.

SECURITY IMPLICATIONS

Integral to implications for air transport of enhanced security measures are issues of privacy and the rights of the airline passenger. Simplified Passenger Travel (SPT) is a process introduced largely to alleviate the usual long-drawn-out process of passenger clearance at airports that has become characteristic of air travel. The system anchors itself on the use of a smart card holding relevant information of the passenger, that can be swiped through a machine, giving instant clearance.[28]

Hand-in-hand with the smart card is the practice of the exchange of Advance Passenger Information (API), which has already proved the usefulness of providing immigration and customs authorities of a state in whose territory a passenger disembarks with that passenger's information in advance of his arrival, particularly to be used for deciding whether that passenger would be admissible to the state concerned or not. The notion of an API system was conceived and introduced by the customs services of certain states. They identified the need to address the increased risk posed by airline passengers in recent years, especially in regard to drug trafficking and other threats to national security. It was pointed out in compelling terms that in some locations this need to enhance controls, combined with the growth of air passenger traffic, had begun to place a severe strain on the resources of customs and immigration authorities, resulting in unacceptable delays in the processing of arriving passengers at airports. A system in which identification data on passengers could be sent to the authorities while the aircraft was in flight, to be processed against computer databases before the passengers arrived, was therefore envisioned as a means of addressing the twin objectives of better compliance and faster clearance of low-risk passengers.

The regulatory foundation of customs and immigration clearance lies in Article 29 of the Chicago Convention,[29] which requires every aircraft engaged in international navigation to carry certain documents, including, for passengers, 'a list of their names and places of embarkation and destination'. Annex 9 to the Convention, on facilitation of air transport, specifies, in Standard 2.7, that *presentation* of the passenger manifest document shall not normally be required, and notes that, if the *information* is required, it should be limited to the data elements included in the prescribed format; that is names, places of embarkation and destination, and flight details.

This standard contemplates the passenger manifest as a paper document which would have to be typed or written and delivered by hand. Nonetheless, the concept of a limitation on the amount of information to that which is essential to meet the basic objectives of safety, efficiency and regulatory compliance is applicable to modern electronic data interchange systems such as API, in which additional (but not unlimited) data may be transmitted to the authorities in exchange for a more efficient clearance operation. It is widely recognized that, in any system involving the exchange of information (automated or not), it is the collection of data which is the major expense. Increases in data collection requirements should result in benefits which exceed the additional costs.

As the airlines and control authorities progress in their refinement of the system and improvement of the system performance, passenger clearance times for trans-oceanic flights (which, prior to use of API, frequently involved delays in excess of two hours) have been reduced to averages well below the recommended goal of 45 minutes, stipulated in Annex 9. In addition to this improvement in productivity, the control authorities have realized an enhancement of their enforcement efforts, owing to the fact that receipt of information in advance gives them more time to process the information on the passengers and make better decisions regarding their inspection targets and the appropriate level of control.

The data included in the transmissions between the airlines and the immigration and customs authorities of recipient states consist of details contained in the machine-readable zone of a passport of the passenger concerned,[30] plus specific data concerning the inbound flight, such as airports of departure/arrival, flight number and date. An Electronic Data Interchange for Administration, Commerce and Transport (EDIFACT) message format is used to transmit the data by electronic data interchange (EDI). The system works well but is very demanding in terms of requirements for high levels of completeness and accuracy of data provided. Unlike cargo shipments, each of which is processed for clearance on its own track, passengers must pass through immigration customs as a 'flight' and are interdependent with respect to the time it takes to clear them. If data on too many passengers are missing, the whole group is slowed down, and so are the flights of passengers arriving behind them.

There is currently a tug-of-war between the airlines and immigration/customs over airline system performance standards versus short clearance times (facilitation benefits) provided by the authorities. But the reality is that, the higher the data quality, the faster the clearance can be accomplished. So the airline has to meet a certain standard in order to get 'blue lane' treatment. One of the issues that emerge as important in the API process is that the data required must be collectable by machine or already contained in the airline's system. Manual collection and data entry at the check-in desk for a scheduled flight is time-consuming and prone to errors, and therefore is not acceptable. Most travellers now hold machine-readable passports (MRPs); as a result, manual input need only be done on an exception basis. Participation in API must be compensated with a measurable improvement in facilitation. The authorities concerned must also aim at achieving improvements in the ensuring of security with the use of these measures.

At its 33rd Session, held in September/October 2001, the ICAO Assembly, while acknowledging that new measures should be taken to enhance security, observed that such measures should not impede ICAO's current work on improving border control systems at airports and ensuring the smooth flow of passengers and cargo. Consequently, the Assembly stressed that ICAO's work on these issues should continue on an urgent basis.[31] The machine-readable travel document was among specific areas mentioned by the Assembly as requiring urgent continuing work, in keeping with UN Security Council Resolution 1373 of 23 September 2001, which reaffirmed the need for continuing work to ensure the integrity and security of passports and other travel documents.[32] In this context. the Assembly agreed that all contracting states should be urgently encouraged to issue their travel documents in machine-readable format and enhance their security in accordance with ICAO specifications, while introducing automated travel document reading systems at their international airports.[33]

These measures of the ICAO Assembly bring to bear the essential link between aviation security and facilitation and the fact that one cannot be ignored while the other is given some prominence, as is the case with aviation security at the present time.

COMMERCIAL IMPLICATIONS

In broad terms, an immediate, if not short-term, recession and a drop in the gross national product of States is a probable consequence of the attacks on America. With regard to the airline industry, the first few days of inactivity and following weeks, if not months, of reduced operations, coupled with delays caused by security enforcement, would be devastating. 'Downsizing' and layoffs would be common not only among the smaller operators, but also among the major international operators, including domestic airlines in states whose air carriers operate air services in Europe and the Americas in particular.

Code sharing, which is a prolific commercial tool used by air carriers to maximize market access and make full use of providing capacity to meet demand, presents special challenges from the perspective of aviation security. A code share is not successful from a marketing point of view if there is no seamless customer service. Thus code share partners have to ensure that security measures adopted by all partners are consistent and smooth flowing. This would particularly prove to be a challenge in the present context, where governments may issue mandatory standards for security on their airlines which may not necessarily be consistent with standards imposed on those airlines' code share partners by the latters' governments. In addition, an air carrier itself may, in view of its particular exigencies, impose security measures on its passengers that cannot be enforced on another carrier's passengers. The difficulty of arriving at a common security system in code sharing essentially lies in the fact that, while the 'operating' carrier is ultimately responsible for security of a flight, the 'marketing' carrier who sells a passenger his air ticket implicitly warrants that the passenger will be assured of the quality of security usually applied by the marketing or selling carrier.

Recent events have brought to bear the threat of risk transfer from one airline to another. In other words, if one airline were to carry a greater risk of damage than others in a code share (or other airline alliance situation), the risk would be shared by all partners to the agreement. Specific instances that may cause delays could well include the following: a passenger needing to be off-loaded from a code-shared flight where that passenger had been accepted earlier according to the security procedures of another carrier under a code share agreement; the carriage of escorted prisoners in various sectors involving code share flights; carriage of security sensitive personages such as VIPs in several sectors of code-shared flights; and the challenges of information sharing between code share partners with a disruptive passenger.

Outsourcing of services, another entrenched commercial practice in the airline industry, would also come under special scrutiny from a security perspective. Airlines would have to give serious consideration to the quality of services they receive from private entities offering security services. Carriers would, as of necessity, be compelled to rethink their quality assurance systems in security, with particular emphasis on security training and evaluation of implementation.

Security audits, imposed either by government or by other entities which have governmental approval, may be a mandatory feature for airlines in the future with consistent requirements for the real assessment and comparative 'note sharing' with other carriers. These measures would indeed have an impact on the timely despatch of aircraft, requiring passengers to lengthen their check-in times and procedures.

Enhanced costs incurred by carriers, both in providing for improved and more stringent security measures and in absorbing delays caused by the implementation of such measures, may have to be met, one way or another. Increased airfares could be one mode of recovery. The imposition of security charges on passengers could be another. Guidance with regard to the imposition of security charges is already available in documentation of the International Civil Aviation Organization.[34]

The bilateral requirement of *substantial ownership and effective control*, which is based on the fundamental postulate that a majority ownership provision would effectively preclude foreign ownership from taking major control of a national carrier, has not been easy to enforce or put into practice in all situations. Although a blanket provision might require majority national ownership and control, airlines and states have had to contend in many instances with complex issues of nationality of members of a board of directors, the powers of a board and the powers of directors of such boards.[35] Often states have attempted to circumvent these difficulties by establishing a safeguard to ensure for the government concerned a 'golden share' which accords the owner government a greater voice in the decision-making process on issues of importance and significance to the carrier concerned.[36]

Although airline alliances may offer a way round the market access constraints that may be presented by bilateral air services agreements, such alliances are not usually effective against the inhibiting qualities of the traditional ownership and control provisions of the typical agreement, particularly in the context of facilitation of cross-border investment, which is essentially regulated by the bilateral air services agreement. In order to find a practical and legitimate way out of this seemingly impossible situation, ICAO has devised a proactive approach based on making the 'principal place of business' and 'permanent residence' of the carrier the operative criteria for purposes of devolution of control.

Both the United States and member states of the European Union have protected their domestic markets from external operators by preserving these markets for their flag carriers or at least carriers that were owned by the state concerned or nationals of that state. In the European Union, in keeping with Article 4 of Court Regulation 2407/92, national authorities are vested with the power of granting operating licences based on the criteria that the principal place of business of the carrier applying for the licence must be located in the licensing member state; the carrier must be involved in air transport as its main occupation; the holder of the licence must be under direct or majority ownership of nationals of the European Union; and the licencee must be effectively controlled by such nationals. Effective control essentially means the power and ability to exercise a decisive influence on an air transport undertaking, including but not limited to the use, enjoyment and alienation of movable and immovable property of that undertaking. One of the reasons, at least from the perspective of the European Union, for retaining the ownership and control criteria within its territory is to safeguard the interests of the member states of the Union and to preclude carriers of non-EU states from capitalizing on a liberalized European Union Market.

United States law too contains explicit requirements pertaining to nationality in terms of management of airlines,[37] in some contrast to Regulation 2407/92 of the EU, which does not expressly address issues regarding nationality of management. Arguably, the EU addresses external control by stockholders of a company, and not particularly, as envisaged by the United States law, management control of the administration and running of the air transport enterprise. Be that as it may, both the United States and the European Union have shown, by their legislation, that the issue of ownership and control still remains for them a critical consideration in the overall picture of liberalization of and competition in air transport. Under the present circumstances, both the United States and the European Union may wish to review their positions on whether it would now be prudent to retain existing standards of ownership and control.

One of the most critical issues in the ownership and control equation is the impact of commercial civilian airlines on military interests. As an example, one can cite the Civil Reserve Air Fleet Programme (CRAF) of the United States, where US carriers have pledged a substantial number of their aircraft to the United States Department of Defense for defence purposes. If any other state were to have a similar system, the issue of foreign nationals' ownership and/or control of aircraft that may be used for defence purposes could be a critical one which the state concerned would be compelled to consider.

From a regulatory perspective, it is worthy of note that ICAO's Worldwide Air Transport Conference (Montreal, 1994), which examined the present and future regulation of international air transport, recommended that ICAO proceed with studies and develop recommendations on a number of important issues, including the review of the traditional air carrier ownership and control criteria with a view to their broadening. Following this trend, ICAO's Air Transport Regulation Panel has noted that, at the conference, the principal objections to broadening the traditional airline ownership and control criteria for the use of market access by using a criterion based on 'headquarters, central administration or principal place of business' were its possible use as an unacceptable means of gaining market access, abuse from differing interpretations of the terms involved, and the fact that it might lead to 'flags of convenience' with lack of regulatory control and social 'dumping'. The panel concluded that a criterion based on a combination of 'principal place of business' and 'permanent residence' could be used to further broaden the traditional ownership and control criteria, thereby providing a third option to those two involving groups of states which had been adopted at the conference. In the panel's view, the principal place of business/permanent residence criterion would result in a firm link to the designating state which would not result in a degradation of safety, while meeting the concerns expressed at the conference. The panel recommended that states wishing to accept broadened criteria for air carrier use of market access in their bilateral and multilateral air services agreement agree to authorize market access for a designated air carrier which has its principal place of business and permanent residence in the territory of the designating state; and has and maintains a strong link to the designating state.

In judging the existence of a strong link, states should take into account elements such as the designated air carrier establishing itself, and having a substantial amount of its operations and capital investment in physical facilities in the designating state, paying income tax and registering its aircraft there, and employing a significant number of nationals in managerial, technical and operational positions. Where a state believes it requires conditions or exceptions concerning the use of the principal place of business and permanent residence criterion based on national security, strategic, economic or commercial reasons, this should be the subject of bilateral or multilateral negotiations or consultations, as appropriate. The above guidelines were approved by the Council of the ICAO on 30 May 1997 for the guidance of states.

At the time of writing, ICAO was receiving responses from contracting states to a questionnaire sent to them by the organization seeking their views on and details of practices of ownership and control of airlines in their territories. It will be interesting to find out, once all responses are received, whether states have veered towards more state control of air carriers, particularly in terms of the element of control a state would retain in such areas as employment of trained public servants in ensuring security at airports and in the sky and overall government shareholding in airline companies. Trends in ownership and control will be a critical issue to be addressed at the ICAO 5th Air Transport Conference to be held in Montreal in March 2003.

THE ROLE OF CIVIL AVIATION IN SECURING PEACE AMONG NATIONS

The attacks of 11 September 2001 inevitably highlighted the strategic position of civil aviation both as an industry vulnerable to attack and also as an integral tool in ensuring peace and security in the world. The modernist view of civil aviation, as it prevailed when the Convention on International Civil Aviation[38] was signed at Chicago on 7 December 1944, was centred on state sovereignty[39] and the widely accepted postwar view that the development of international civil aviation can greatly help to create and preserve friendship and understanding among the nations and peoples of the world, yet its abuse can become a threat to general security.[40] This essentially modernist philosophy focused on the state as the ultimate sovereign authority which can overrule considerations of international community welfare if they clashed with the domestic interests of the state. It gave way, in the 1960s and 1970s to a post-modernist era of acceptance of the individual as a global citizen, whose interests at public international law were considered paramount over considerations of individual state interests.

Civil aviation in the modernist era

In 1944, at the height of the modernist era of social justice and commercial interaction, the Chicago Convention was drafted within 37 calendar days[41] and was the result of consensus reached only by 52 states which attended the Chicago Conference. However, as Milde says: 'It is in the first place a comprehensive codification/unification of public international law, and, in the second, a constitutional instrument of an international inter-governmental organization of universal character.'[42] Be that as it may, the real significance of the Convention, particularly as a tool for ensuring political will of individual states, lies in the fundamental philosophy contained in its Preamble. If one examines the Preamble carefully, the Convention enunciates a message of peace through aviation. It makes mention of the future development of international civil aviation being able to help preserve friendship and understanding among the nations of the world, while its abuse (that is abuse of future development of international civil aviation) can become a threat to 'the general security'. By 'general security' the Chicago Conference presumably meant the prevention of threats to peace. These words have been interpreted in the widest possible sense by the Assembly of the International Civil Aviation Organization (ICAO) to cover instances of social injustice such as racial discrimination as well as threats to commercial expediency made possible by civil aviation. For example, the 15th session of the ICAO Assembly adopted Resolution A15-7 (Condemnation of the Policies of Apartheid and Racial Discrimination of South Africa) which urged South Africa to comply with the aims and objectives of the Chicago Convention, on the basis that apartheid policies constitute a permanent source of conflict between the nations and peoples of the world and that the policies of apartheid and racial discrimination are a flagrant violation of the principles enshrined in the Preamble to the Chicago Convention.[43]

The Preamble was also quoted in Resolution A17-1 (Declaration by the Assembly) which requested concerted action on the part of states towards suppressing all acts which jeopardize safety and orderly development of international civil aviation. In Resolution A20-2 (Acts of Unlawful Interference with Civil Aviation) the Assembly reiterated its confidence that the development of international civil aviation can be an effective tool in bringing about friendship and understanding among the peoples of the world.

When one looks at the discussions that took place during the Chicago Conference, one gets a general view of the perspectives of each state, particularly in terms of what they expected out of the Convention concerning the role to be played by civil aviation with regard to ensuring peace, security and economic development in the world in the years to come.

The Chicago Conference and peace initiatives

The Chicago Conference was initiated on 11 September 1944, when the government of the United States of America, on its own initiative, sent a letter of invitation to 53 states and two dignitaries[44] whose governments were in exile, inviting them to a conference that would lead to the development of international air transport as a post-war measure. This letter also informed the invitees that the United States had conducted numerous bilateral discussions with states who had shown a special interest in this measure, especially in the fields, inter alia, of rights of aircraft in transit and non-traffic stops, the non-exclusivity of international operating rights, the application of cabotage to air traffic and the use and operation of airports and facilities. The letter stated:

> The approaching defeat of Germany, and the consequent liberation of great parts of Europe and Africa from military interruption of traffic, sets up the urgent need for establishing an international civil air service pattern on a provisional basis at least, so that all important trade and population areas of the world may obtain the benefits of air transportation as soon as possible, and so that the restorative processes of prompt communication may be available to assist in returning great areas to processes of peace.[45]

The US government suggested that the proposed international conference consider, inter alia, the establishment of provisional world route arrangements by general agreement which would form the basis for the prompt establishment of international air transport services by the appropriate countries. There was also a suggestion to set up a permanent international aeronautical body, and a multilateral aviation convention dealing with the fields of air transport and air navigation, including aviation technical subjects.[46]

Over the past 50 years the Chicago Convention has proved to be one of the most intrepid international agreements adopted by man, rendering immeasurable service to international civil aviation, which is undoubtedly one of the most vital and dynamic human endeavours in international relations. Milde, in assessing the significance of the Chicago Convention at its fortieth anniversary, said of the Convention:

> The fortieth anniversary of the adoption of the Chicago Convention is a good opportunity to draw a balance sheet. The Organization (ICAO) has accomplished

remarkable achievements in the technical, economic and legal fields; the technical activities, the regulatory work in the adoption of standards and recommended practices and their implementation on regional and national levels through regional plans and technical assistance represent the true backbone and *raison d'être* in the life of the Organization. Throughout the years, the Convention proved to be a reliable and suitable legal framework for the work of a technical agency performing practical work of immediate practical application by States. Even after forty years, the Chicago Convention continues to provide a firm legal basis for cooperation of States in the field of international civil aviation and represents an acceptable balance of interests among States.[47]

After 55 years of its being in force, the Convention, through ICAO, still serves to ensure collaboration between states and international harmony through issues pertaining to civil aviation. The Chicago Conference was inaugurated with the reading of a message to the Conference from the president of the United States. In his message, President Roosevelt, referring to the Paris Conference of 1919 which was designed to open Europe to air traffic, but unfortunately took years to be effectively implemented, stated:

I do not believe that the world today can afford to wait several years for its air communications. There is no reason why it should.

Increasingly, the aeroplanes will be in existence. When either the German or Japanese enemy is defeated, transport planes should be available for release from military work in numbers sufficient to make a beginning. When both enemies have been defeated, they should be available in quantity. Every country has its airports and trained pilots; practically every country knows how to organize airlines.

You are fortunate to have before you one of the great lessons of history. Some centuries ago, an attempt was made to build great empires based on domination of great sea areas. The lords of these areas tried to close the areas to some, and to offer access to others, and thereby to enrich themselves and extend their power. This led directly to a number of wars both in the Eastern and Western Hemispheres. We do not need to make that mistake again. I hope you will not dally with the thought of creating great blocs of closed air, thereby tracing in the sky the conditions of future wars. I know you will see to it that the air which God gave everyone shall not become the means of domination over anyone.[48]

Thus President Roosevelt urged states to eschew protectionism, while encouraging them to avoid dominance over one another. Ever since, the fate of economic regulation of international air transport has been relegated to the status of an obdurate dilemma which posed the question as to how states could avoid dominance by others without protecting themselves. The elusive delicate balance between the two is still being vigorously sought, as will be seen in discussions to follow.

The chairman of the Conference, Adolf A. Berle Jr, endorsed the president's comments by observing:

There are many tasks which our countries have to do together, but in none have they a clearer and plainer common interest than in the work of making the air serviceable to mankind. For the air was given to all; every nation in the world has access to it. To each nation there is now available a means of friendly intercourse with all the world, provided a working basis for that intercourse can be found and maintained.[49]

At the Conference, the United States took the position that the use of the air and the use of the sea were both common in that they were highways given by nature to all men. They were different in that man's use of the air is subject to the sovereignty of nations over which such use is made. The United States was therefore of the opinion that nations ought to arrange among themselves for its use in such manner as would be of the greatest benefit to all humanity, wherever situated. The United States further asserted the rule that each country has a right to maintain sovereignty of the air which is over its lands and its territorial waters. There was no question of alienating or qualifying this sovereignty. This absolute right, according to the United States, had to be qualified by the subscription by states to friendly intercourse between nations and the universal recognition of the natural rights of states to communicate and trade with each other. This right could not be derogated by the use of discriminatory measures.[50] The fact that the United States required states to exchange air traffic rights reciprocally is clearly evident in the statement: 'It is therefore the view of the United States, that, without prejudice to full rights of sovereignty, we should work upon the basis of exchange of needed privileges and permissions which friendly nations have a right to expect from each other.'[51]

The privilege of communication by air with friendly countries, according to the United States, was not a right to wander at will throughout the world. In this respect, it was contended that traffic by air differed materially from traffic by sea, where commerce need have no direct connection with the country from which the ship may have come. The air routes were analogous to railroad lines and the right to connect communication links between states was to establish a steady flow of traffic, thereby opening economic routes between countries. According to the United States, it was too early to go beyond this concept, and states should accept the fact that what the Chicago Conference would accomplish was to adopt a Convention that would establish communication between states.[52]

With regard to the establishment of an international organization, the United States was of the view, that in the purely technical field, considerable power could be wielded by such an organization, while in the economic and political fields only consultative, fact-gathering and fact-finding functions should be performed by this organization. The United States concluded:

> the United States will support an international organization in the realm of air commerce having power in technical matters and having consultative functions in economic matters and the political questions which may be directly connected with them under a plan by which continuing and collected experience, widening custom, and the growing maturity of its counsel may establish such added base as circumstances may warrant for the future consideration of enlarging the functions of the consultative group.[53]

It is worthy of note that, in 1944, the United States government had envisioned greater scope for the proposed international organization in economic issues.

The United Kingdom, in its statement of position, strongly advocated a plan that would provide the services needed between states, serve the interests of the travelling public and would be fair between states. It was further recognized that each state had a fair share in the operation of air services and carriage by air of traffic, giving as an example the prewar proposals by the United Kingdom and the

United States of opening a transatlantic service on a fifty–fifty basis. The United Kingdom further contended:

> While recognizing national interests we want to encourage enterprise and efficiency which are indeed themselves a national as well as an international interest. And we want therefore to encourage the efficient and to stimulate the less efficient; only by common action on some such lines as indicated can we reduce and gradually eliminate subsidies, thereby putting civil aviation on an economic footing and incidentally very considerably relieving the tax payer. Unrestricted competition is their most fruitful soil.[54]

The United Kingdom seemed to have adopted a balanced approach that supported the establishment of air services to serve the needs of the travelling public, while not unduly affecting the rights of states to have a fair share of traffic for themselves.

Canada suggested the establishment of an international air authority to plan and foster the organization of air services internationally. This authority would, according to Canada, ensure inter alia that, so far as possible, international air routes and services were divided freely and equitably between the various member states, and afford every state the opportunity of participating in international airline operations, in accordance with its need for air transportation service and its industrial and scientific resources.[55]

India, while believing that it was essential for air services to develop rationally, with a certain degree of freedom of the air being the inherent right of every state, went on to say:

> We believe that the grant of commercial rights – that is to say, the right to carry traffic to and from another country, – is best negotiated and agreed to on a universal reciprocal basis, rather than by bilateral agreements. We think that only such an arrangement will secure to all countries the reciprocal rights which their interests require. But the grant of any such freedoms and rights must, in our opinion, necessarily be associated with the constitution of an authority which will regulate the use of such freedoms. It will be the function of such authority ... to ensure that the interests of the people, both of the most powerful and of the smaller countries, are secured.[56]

India's position, therefore, has been to recommend a liberal approach of universal reciprocity within the parameters of control by an authority which could ensure that the smaller nations were protected from being swamped by larger states.

France, too, strongly supported the establishment of an international organization which could act as a 'watchdog' against predatory practices by states in the operation of international air services. In its statement of position, France stated:

> As the President of the United States of America recommended yesterday in his message, we must endeavour to avoid the future formation of rival blocs.
>
> To escape this danger, of which we were so justly warned, all the nations invited here must have a reasonable share in air transportation. The international organization, which we are to consider, seems to us the only means of reaching this goal and of affording to international air transportation the unlimited development to which it is entitled.[57]

The incontrovertible fact that emerges from the views of the states that were discussed above is that there had been general consensus that competition for air traffic rights, based on the concept of state sovereignty, should be fair and equitable. It is for this reason that some states even went to the extent of suggesting the creation of an 'umpire' to determine and rule on whether fair competition was being practised when states commenced seriously operating commercial air services between each other's territory.

As a first measure, the contracting states to the Convention recognize the complete and exclusive sovereignty of every state over the air space above its territory,[58] a pre-eminent tenet of international air law that had been recognized from the time of the Roman Empire[59] and carried over to the Paris Convention of 1919.[60] While each contracting state agrees that aircraft of the other which are not engaged in scheduled international air services shall have the right, subject to the observance of the terms of the Convention, to make flights into or in transit non-stop across its territory and make stops for non-traffic purposes without having to obtain permission of the grantor state for such operations, such aircraft are also generally given the right of taking on or discharging passengers, mail and cargo, provided the aircraft are engaged in the carriage of such traffic and the rights of a state concerned are not derogated by such operations.[61]

The most significant modernist construction of the role of civil aviation in securing world peace and security comes from language used in the letters of invitation issued by the United States to the participant states to the Chicago Conference, to the effect that, consequent to the war, the restorative processes of prompt communication may greatly facilitate the return to the processes of peace, However, the conscious awareness of the parties to the Convention, that in securing this peace, prudent economic and business principles must not be compromised, should not be forgotten, particularly in the context of the discussion to follow, on the role of civil aviation in the post-modern era.

Civil aviation in the post-modern era

Post-modernism was a characteristic of the 1960s and 1970s which progressed steadily towards the twenty-first century. Post-modernist thinking was geared to accepting that human culture, as we knew it from a social and economic perspective, was reaching an end. This school of thought associated itself with the momentum of industrial society, drawing on an image of pluralism of cultures and a multitude of groups. The interaction between political modernism, which brought to bear the globalization of nations and deconstruction of separatism of human society, while at the same time ascribing to the individual rights at international law that transcended natural legislation parameters and civil aviation, has been symbiotic and essentially economic. In the post-modernist era, the fundamental modernist philosophy of state sovereignty and peace gave way to an industrial culture that emphasized economic coexistence for the betterment of the global citizen.

In view of the importance of globalization and economic integration, civil aviation went through a metamorphosis in regulatory approaches to commercial aviation in the 40 years leading to the twenty-first century. Peace and understanding among nations was achieved through the post-modernist imperative of citizens' needs.

Emphasis on commercial and economic issues

The commercial bottleneck created by arguably the most contentious provision of the Chicago Convention – Article 6 – where a scheduled international air service may not operate air services into the territory of a contracting state, except with the special permission or other authorization of that state, and in accordance with the terms of such permission or authorization, became a stumbling block to globalization of air transport, which was the essence of post-modernist thought. As a response to this impasse, commercial competition transcended the past era, where dominant markets protected their established market shares. Most mega commercial activity was then the purview of governmental control under instrumentalities of state which were mostly cumbersome bureaucracies at best. Perhaps the best analogy is the biggest commercial market – the United States – which had, until recently, extensively regulated larger commercial activities pertaining to energy, transport and telecommunications.

The modernist trend towards achieving mutual understanding through economic globalization of the air transport industry has its genesis in the Chicago Conference, where several delegates underscored the importance of international harmony through economic symbiosis. Ever since President Roosevelt, in his letter of invitation to States, urged them to eschew protectionism, while encouraging them to avoid dominance over one another, the fate of economic regulation of international air transport has been relegated to the status of an obdurate dilemma which posed the question as to how states could avoid dominance by others without protecting themselves.

Issues of security and peace

Economic integration was not the only concern of post-modernist aviation in its quest for peace among nations. A series of unlawful acts against civil aviation in the 1960s and 1970s left the aviation world in urgent need of unification of law to find common ground between nations in eradicating the spate of offences committed against aircraft and those on board. The international aviation community took cognizance of the fact that the maintenance of international peace and security is an important objective of the United Nations,[62] which recognizes one of its purposes as being, inter alia:

> To maintain international peace and security, and to that end: take effective collective measures for the prevention and removal of threats to the peace, and for the suppression of acts of aggression or other breaches of peace, and to bring about by peaceful means, and in conformity with the principles of justice and international law, adjustment or settlement of international disputes or situations which might lead to a breach of the peace.[63]

It was clear that the United Nations had recognized the application of the principles of international law as an integral part of maintaining international peace and security and avoiding situations which may lead to a breach of the peace.[64] Under the aegis of the International Civil Aviation Organization, three international conventions were adopted to combat this series of offences. The first – The Tokyo Convention of 1963 on Offences and Certain Other Acts Committed on Board Aircraft – referred to any offence committed or act done by a person on board any aircraft registered in a contracting state, while the aircraft is in flight or on the surface of the high seas or of any other area outside the territory of such state. The aircraft is considered to be in flight from the moment power is applied for the purpose of take-off until the moment when the landing run ends.[65] In addition, the Tokyo Convention mentions acts of interference, seizure of or other wrongful exercise of control of an aircraft, implying its concern over hijacking.[66]

The Hague Convention of 1970[67] which followed, in Article 1 identifies any person who, on board an aircraft in flight, unlawfully by force or threat or by any other form of intimidation seizes or takes control of such aircraft, or even attempts to perform such an act, as an offender.[68] Anyone who aids such an act is an accomplice, and is included in the category of the former.[69] It is clear that the Hague Convention by this provision has neither deviated from Article 11 of the Tokyo Convention nor offered a clear definition of the offence of hijacking. It merely sets out the ingredients of the offence: the unlawful use of force, threat or any other form of intimidation and taking control of the aircraft. The use of physical force, weapons or firearms or the threat to use such modes of force are imputed to the offence in this provision. The words 'force', 'threat' or 'intimidation' indicate that the element of fear would be instilled in the victim. It is an interesting question whether these words would cover an instance where the use of fear as an implement to execute the offence of hijacking covers non-coercive measures such as the drugging of food or beverages taken by the passengers or crew. The Hague Convention does not ostensibly cover such instances. In this context, many recommendations have been made to extend the scope of its Article 1.[70] It is also interesting that the Convention does not envisage an instance where the offender is not on board the aircraft but remains on the ground and directs operations therefrom after planting a dangerous object in the aircraft. According to Article 1, the offence has to be devoid of a lawful basis albeit that the legality or illegality of an act is not clearly defined in the Convention.

It is also a precondition in Article 1 that the offence has to be committed in flight, that is while all external doors of the aircraft are closed after the embarkation of the passengers and crew.[71] The mobility of the aircraft is immaterial. Furthermore, Article 1 is rendered destitute of effect if an offence is committed while the doors of the aircraft are left open.

The Convention for the Suppression of Unlawful Acts Against The Safety of Civil Aviation, signed at Montreal on 23 September 1971,[72] also fails to define in specific terms the offence of hijacking, although it circumvents barriers placed by Article 1 of the Hague Convention.[73] For instance, it encircles instances where an offender need not be physically present in an aircraft; includes instances where an aircraft is immobile, its doors open; and even draws into its net any person who disseminates false information which could endanger an aircraft in flight.[74] None of the three conventions, however, have succeeded in identifying the offence of hijacking or advocating preventive measures against the offence itself.

The failure of all attempts at identifying the offence of hijacking and formulating a cogent system of preventive criteria attains its culmination in a political terrorist act. Such offences underscore the significant fact that, not only is political terrorism treated subjectively under different social and political contexts, but also that so far the only attempts at recognizing the threat of terrorism have been made on an intrinsic approach, more to condemn the offence than to find a cure for the deep-seated social and political factors which form the permanent breeding grounds for terrorism. The inevitable continuity of the commission of this offence cannot be stopped if serious consideration is not given to

a) the reasons for the perpetration of terrorist acts,
b) the universal definition of such acts,
c) the fact that such acts transcend national boundaries and affect the entirety of the civilized world, and
d) the fact that every act of terrorism brings a political advantage to certain nations.

Civil aviation in a neo-post-modernist era

Until 11 September 2001, the link between civil aviation and world peace was somewhat conceptual and intellectual. However, when four civilian aircraft on US domestic services were destroyed by terrorist acts, and crews, hundreds of passengers and thousands of innocent victims in buildings located in New York City and Washington, DC were killed, civil aviation ceased to be isolated from the world peace efforts and became immediately inextricably linked to overall endeavours of the world community towards achieving peace and economic sustainability.

The neo-post-modernist era for civil aviation was signalled by United National Resolution A/RES/421(XIV) which referred to the immediate consequences of the attacks of 11 September 2001 as the closure of civil airports in the United States and disruptions of air services. The Resolution also referred to A/RES/145(V) which concerned the safety of civil aviation in relation to tourism. The new era brought about by the paralysis experienced in terms of world trade brought in both states and their instrumentality, together with the private sector to join in finding solutions to keep the trade machine of the world functioning.

Sustainability of air transport

It is incontrovertible that the most critical challenge facing international civil aviation at the present time is to sustain the air transport industry and assure its consumers of continuity of air transport services. The Air Transport Association (ATA), in its 2002 State of the United States Airline Industry Statement, advises that, in the United States, the combined impact of the 2001 economic downturn and the precipitous decline in air travel following the 11 September 2001 attacks on the United States has resulted in devastating losses for the airline industry which are likely to exceed $7 billion and continue through 2002.[75] Of course, the overall picture, which portends a certain inevitable gloom for the air transport industry, is not the exclusive legacy of US carriers. It applies worldwide, as was seen in the abrupt decline of air traffic globally during 2001. The retaliation by the world community against terrorism, which is a continuing feature of world affairs, has increased the airline passenger's fear and reluctance to use air transport. In most instances in commercial aircraft purchasing, air carriers have cancelled or postponed their new aircraft requisition orders. Many carriers, particularly in developing countries, are re-examining their cost structures and reducing their human resource bases.

The ripple effect brought to bear on the aviation insurance industry, which has compounded airlines' operational costs, is a critical issue to contend with. To counteract problems, the US and European governments have pumped subsidies of billions of dollars into their national carriers notwithstanding the fact that most of these carriers are private entities. The rationale behind these state subsidies is that air transport is strategic and vital to the economy of every country. However, state subsidies and aid are not a permanent solution to the sustainability crisis faced by the global airline industry in the present context. A wider, more profound approach is necessary, calling for a reconsideration of overall air transport policy. Of course this does not mean that states, particularly those in the developing category, need coerce their carriers to run head on towards privatization, participate in alliances or enter into regional agreements on a multilateral basis. A certain sustained but restrained strategy appears to be the most prudent approach.

The operative phrase which binds civil aviation to world peace and security still remains in the Preamble to the Chicago Convention which recognizes that the abuse of the development of civil aviation can become a threat to the general security. The critical words in this phrase pertain to the reference to the abuse of the development of civil aviation, imputing importance to economic and commercial aspects of the industry. When the events of 11 September 2001 are placed in perspective, the offences concerned were not only aimed at destruction of human life and property, but were also calculated to disrupt global commercial activity. This link brings to bear a compelling and intrinsic role which civil aviation can play as a key consideration for self-defence by the world community within the parameters of the United Nations umbrella.

Civil aviation and the United Nations Charter

The Preamble to the Chicago Convention unequivocally imparts to civil aviation sufficient status as a key consideration that could be vulnerable in being the target of disruption of world peace and security. The Tokyo, Hague and Montreal conventions already referred to are some tools that have been introduced in this regard. United Nations Security Council Resolution 1269,[76] adopted by the Security Council on 19 October 1999, reflects the concern of the world community with regard to the increase in international terrorism which endangers the lives and well-being of individuals worldwide as well as the peace and security of all states. The resolution goes on to condemn all acts, methods and practices of terrorism as criminal and unjustifiable, regardless of their motivation, and in all their forms and manifestations, wherever and by whomever committed, in particular those which could threaten international peace and security. With this declaration, the United Nations Security Council has widened the scope for combating terrorism, particularly to encompass such instances as the 11 September events, which could expand to economic paralysis of global commercial activity through attacks aimed at the aviation industry.

The principle of state responsibility with regard to world peace and security lies primarily in Article 24 of the United Nations Charter,[77] which calls upon all members to refrain in their international relations from the threat or use of force against the territorial integrity or political independence of any state, or in any other manner inconsistent with the purposes of the United Nations. Furthermore, Article 51 of the Charter preserves the right of individual or collective self-defence if an armed attack occurs against a member of the United Nations, notwithstanding any right granted by the Charter that would preclude any member state from interfering in the affairs of another member state, particularly with regard to matters of state sovereignty.

International terrorism purportedly committed by private individuals could none-theless be brought within the preview of the above-mentioned provisions of the United Nations Charter, particularly from the neo-post-modernist approach of collective involvement. This principle is embodied in recent work of the International Law Commission, through Article 2 of the Draft Articles on Responsibility of States for Internationally Wrongful Acts,[78] which provides that international responsibility of a state, which is referred to in Article 1, is attributable to that state if conduct of the state constitutes a breach of an international obligation of that state. The document also provides that the wrongfulness of an act of a state is precluded if the act constitutes a lawful measure of self-defence taken in conformity with the Charter of the United Nations.[79] The state responsible for an internationally wrongful act is under an obligation to compensate for damage caused, including reparation for financially assessable damage such as loss of profits.[80]

In addition to state responsibility for conduct attributable to that state, the International Law Commission has established that a crime against the peace and security of mankind entails individual responsibility, and is a crime of aggression.[81] A further link drawing civil aviation into the realm of international peace and security lies in the Rome Statute of the International Criminal Court, which defines a war crime, inter alia, as intentionally directing attacks against civilian objects; attacking or bombarding, by whatever means, towns, villages, dwellings or buildings which are undefended and which are not military objects; employing weapons, projectiles, and material and methods of warfare that cause injury.[82] The statute also defines as a war crime any act which is intentionally directed at buildings, material, medical units and transport, and personnel using the distinctive emblems of the Geneva Conventions in conformity with international law.[83]

The vulnerability of civil aviation against acts of terrorism remains in the possibility of potential offenders being domiciled in certain jurisdictions which may lay themselves open to acts of self-defence by states that are threatened. An explicit political interpretation of the role of the United Nations Charter was given in 1986 by the then United States Secretary of State. George Shultz said: 'The Charter's restrictions on the use or threat of force in international relations include a specific exception on the right of self-defense. It is absurd to argue that international law prohibits us from capturing terrorists in international waters or airspace.'[84]

The inherent nature of civil aviation, in its dependance on national and international regulation and control, calls for ineluctable state involvement and responsibility in ensuring world peace and security in relation to matters pertaining to civil aviation. In other words, if states were to take action in the field of civil aviation through which self-defence can be achieved, any threat to civil aviation must be linked to a state to which can be attributed or imputed some relationship with actual or possible offenders. In the *Nicaragua* case,[85] addressed by the International Court of Justice in 1986, the court accepted the premise that self-defence could involve responses to counter groups who have either been sent by a state or are acting on behalf of that state with its explicit or tacit acquiescence. Therefore an 'armed attack' could be definitively sustained within the text of the United Nations Charter only when the link between the state and the non-state factor is sufficiently close, and the attack could be tantamount to an attack by that state.

Relief flights

There is specific provision in Annex 9 to the Chicago Convention for provision by the state of relief flights. Contracting states are required, by Standard 8.8 of Chapter 8 of the Annex, to facilitate the entry into, departure from and transit through their territories of aircraft engaged in relief flights performed by or on behalf of international organizations recognized by the United Nations or by or on behalf of states themselves and to take all possible measures to ensure their safe operation. The relief flights referred to should be undertaken to respond to natural and man-made disasters which seriously endanger human health or the environment. An emergency is acknowledged in the Annex as 'a sudden and usually unforeseen event that calls for immediate measures to minimize its adverse consequences'. A disaster is described in the Annex as 'a serious disruption of the functioning of society, causing widespread human, material or environmental losses which exceed the ability of the affected society to cope using its own resources'.[86]

The Charter of the United Nations, which was signed on 26 June 1945 and came into force on 24 October 1945, lists the achievement of international cooperation in solving international problems of an economic, social, cultural or humanitarian character as one of the purposes of the United Nations.[87] The problems that the United Nations is mandated by its Charter to solve should therefore be necessarily of an international nature. Article 2(7) of the Charter expands the scope of this philosophy further when it provides that the United Nations is not authorized to intervene in matters which are essentially within the domestic jurisdiction of any stare, without prejudice to the right of the United Nations to intervene in matters which are within the domestic jurisdiction of any state, and apply enforcement measures where there is an occurrence of acts of aggression, a threat to the peace or breach thereof.[88] Therefore, *stricto sensu*, the United Nations cannot intervene in instances where natural disasters such as famine, drought or earthquakes render the citizens of a state homeless, destitute and dying of starvation unless invited by the states concerned. The principle, however, cannot be too strictly interpreted, as natural disasters may lead to breaches of the peace. In such instances the United Nations Security Council may take such actions by air, sea or land as may be necessary to maintain or restore international peace and security.[89] For such instances, Article 43 of the Charter provides:

> All members of the United Nations, in order to contribute to the maintenance of international peace and security, undertake to make available to the Security Council,

on its call and in accordance with a special agreement or agreements, armed forces assistance and facilities, including rights of passage necessary for the purpose of maintaining international peace and security.

Here again, action can only be taken for the maintenance of international peace, effectively precluding any direct intervention in a domestic issue.

Resolutions adopted by the United Nations Security Council relating to Somalia[90] and Bosnia-Herzegovina[91] clearly demonstrate the parameters of the scope of UN intervention under its Charter.[92] In the case of Somalia, the United Nations Security Council recognized the unique character of the situation in the country, where conflict and violence demanded that all concerned take all necessary measures to facilitate the measures of the United Nations, its specialized agencies and humanitarian organizations to provide humanitarian assistance to the affected population in Somalia. In the case of Bosnia and Herzegovina, the Security Council recognized in its resolution that the situation in the two states constituted a threat to international peace and security. In both resolutions, the Security Council had to function within its mandate of intervention only in instances of conflict and breaches of the peace.

The Geneva Conventions

The Geneva Conventions of 12 August 1949 for the Amelioration of the Wounded and Sick in Armed Forces in the Field contain provisions for facilitation of aircraft for the removal of the wounded and sick and for the transport of medical personnel and equipment.[93] The thrust of the Conventions is that relief operations by air in the case of removing wounded and sick soldiers and civilians in instances of armed conflict are protected from attack and facilitated. The Conventions also provide that medical aircraft of parties to the conflict may fly over the territories of neutral powers, land thereon in case of necessity, or use them as ports of call.[94] Medical aircraft are required by the Conventions to give neutral states previous notice of their passage through such states.

At the Diplomatic Conference on the Reaffirmation and Development of International Humanitarian Law Applicable in Armed Conflicts, held in Geneva between 1974 and 1977, two protocols to the Geneva Conventions of 1949 were adopted – the first relating to the protection of victims of international armed conflicts and the second relating to the protection of victims of non-international armed conflicts. Article 27 of Protocol 1 provides:

1. The medical aircraft of a Party to a conflict shall continue to be protected while flying over land or sea areas physically controlled by an adverse Party, provided that prior agreement to such flights has been obtained from the competent authority of the adverse Party.
2. A medical aircraft which flies over an area physically controlled by an adverse Party without, or in deviation from the terms of, an agreement provided for in paragraph 1, either through a navigational error or because of an emergency affecting the safety of the flight, shall make every effort to identify itself and to inform the adverse Party of the circum-stances. As soon as such medical aircraft has been recognized by an adverse Party, that Party shall make all reasonable efforts to give the order to land or alight on water, referred to in Article 30, paragraph 1, or to take other measures to safeguard its own

interests, and, in either case, to allow the aircraft time for compliance, before resorting to an attack against the aircraft.[95]

Paragraph 1 concerns medical aircraft which will only fly through the air space of the adverse party without landing in its territory, except when the aircraft contends with technical difficulties, or if ordered to land. The purpose of paragraph 2 was to prevent accidents: the shooting down of medical aircraft. The paragraph has also taken into account legitimate fears of the parties to the conflict with regard to their security.[96]

Article 28 of the Protocol prohibits parties to a conflict from using medical aircraft to attempt to acquire any military advantage over an adverse party. They should not use medical aircraft in attempts to render military objects immune from attack.[97] The provision further requires that medical aircraft not be used to collect or transmit intelligence data or carry any equipment intended for such purposes. Medical aircraft are also prohibited from carrying any persons or cargo not included within the definition of Article 8, sub-paragraph (f).[98] The article does not, however, prohibit the carrying on board of personal effects of the occupants or equipment intended solely to facilitate navigation, communication or identification.[99] According to Article 28, medical aircraft should not carry any armament except small arms and ammunition taken from the wounded, sick and shipwrecked on board and not handed to the proper service, and light weaponry that might assist those on board to defend themselves should the need arise.[100] Article 28(4) provides that, while carrying out relief flights, medical aircraft should not be used in the search for the wounded, sick and shipwrecked, unless previously agreed upon by the parties concerned.

Article 29 specifies notification requirements of medical relief flights. Article 30 specifies that medical aircraft flying over areas that are physically controlled by an adverse party, or over areas the physical control of which is not clearly established, may be ordered to land or to alight on water, as appropriate, to permit inspection. If such inspection discloses that the aircraft is in fact a medical aircraft as defined in Article (f); is not in violation of conditions applicable to medical aircraft and is operating with a permit or prior agreement between parties concerned, the aircraft will be authorized to proceed on its way.[101] If, on the other hand, the inspection discloses that the aircraft is in breach of any of the three conditions above, the aircraft may be seized and its occupants treated in conformity with the relevant provisions of the Conventions and the Protocol.

Article 31 provides that except by prior agreement, medical aircraft should not fly over or land in the territory of a neutral or other state which is not a party to the conflict. If such an agreement has been entered into, the aircraft should be respected as a medical relief flight throughout its flight. Recognition of relief flights is indeed an important requirement in the facilitation of relief flights. Relief actions undertaken under the auspices of the International Committee of the Red Cross (ICRC) and consequently enjoying the protection of the Red Cross emblem should preclude them from being escorted by members of the armed forces. When there is a risk of a lack of discipline or knowledge of the emblem by the armed forces of a party, it is obligatory on the party concerned to undertake a major effort of dissemination of information to ensure simultaneously that the significance of the protective emblem is understood and that the Red Cross mission is accepted. Finally, in instances of banditry or riots, which may be brought about by the operation of relief missions, the relief operations should be able to rely upon the local police or armed forces for support. There is also an obligation which devolves upon the parties who benefit from their relief operations to facilitate the rapid distribution of relief supplies.

The legality of relief operations may also encompass logistics concerning the dissemination of relief. The coordination of relief in armed conflicts or natural or man-made disasters raises very real problems. In many instances, the lack of coordination in relief operations often results in an imbalance in consignments, foodstuffs perishing in large warehouses and the lack of adequate transport to provide relief in areas which need assistance. Paragraph 5 of Article 70 of Protocol 1 to the Convention lays down the principle of *effective* international coordination of relief. This provision lays down obligations of all parties concerned: donors, transit countries and beneficiaries.

In 1969, the XXIst International Conference of the Red Cross adopted a resolution whereby states were requested to exercise their sovereign and legal rights so as to facilitate the transit, admission and distribution of relief supplies provided by impartial international humanitarian organizations for the benefit of civilian populations in disaster areas when disaster situations imperil the life and welfare of such populations.[102] The United Nations subsequently announced that this resolution would also apply to situations arising from armed conflict.[103]

Although the suffering and needs of a civilian population are much the same in any disaster situation, it is incontrovertible that an armed conflict that brings about destitution and suffering is a more complex situation, and a more rigid legal control is necessary for the implementation of relief operations in such instances. Article 18 of the second Protocol to the Geneva Conventions addresses this concern and sets out the fundamental principles governing relief operations. The provision also lays down the conditions under which victims of conflicts may be assisted and protected within the parameters of non-intervention. Article 18 consists of two paragraphs, each of which has a separate scope, while they complement each other. The first paragraph deals with humanitarian assistance within the territory of a state where an armed conflict is taking place, while the second paragraph provides for the possibility of organizing international relief operations there.

The above discussion is not intended to obfuscate the fact that the provisions of the Geneva Conventions and the United Nations Charter do not admit of the operation of relief flights at the will and pleasure of the benefactor, without the permission of the recipient state. Nor is it intended to circumvent the fact that states are primarily responsible for organizing relief. Relief societies such as the Red Cross and the Red Crescent organizations are merely called upon to play a supplementary role by assisting the authorities of the states concerned in their task.

Since it is clear that the intervention of the United Nations Security Council in a matter lying within the domestic jurisdiction of a state can only be justified in instances where there is a threat to international peace and security, a breach of the peace within a state or an act of aggression, a question which arises when a relief flight is operated as a part of a humanitarian project is whether the operation of such a flight could form a legitimate ground for unilateral action by states. The question would essentially be grounded in a legal analysis of the principles of humanitarian law and state sovereignty. On the one hand, everyone has the right to life, liberty and security of person[104] and the right to a standard of living adequate for the health and well-being of himself and of his family, including food, clothing, housing and medical care.[105] On the other, there is overall recognition of the fact that every state has complete and exclusive sovereignty over the airspace above its territory.[106] Except for the Paris Convention of 1956,[107] which provides for civil aircraft registered in a member state of the European Civil Aviation Conference (ECAC) to fly freely into member states for the purposes of discharging or taking on traffic where such aircraft are engaged, inter alia, in non-scheduled flights for the purpose of meeting humanitarian or emergency needs,[108] there is no multilateral or bilateral agreement that admits of unilateral intervention of a state in another for humanitarian purposes, where the intervening state does not obtain permission of the recipient state. In fact, the United Nations General Assembly at its 46th Session in December 1991 adopted Resolution 46/182, which explicitly provides in the Annex to the Resolution that the sovereignty, territorial integrity and national unity of states must be fully respected in accordance with the Charter of the United Nations and that, in this context, humanitarian assistance should be provided with the consent of the affected country and in principle on the basis of an appeal by the affected country.[109] These conflicting principles, although not bestowing legal authority on the United Nations to intervene in a state with relief flights, at least give some degree of justification to the United Nations' efforts to mediate with states concerned in the promotion of relief operations and to seek the support of other states, with the concurrence of affected states.

Since, under general law, no one can intervene unilaterally in a state to provide relief flights to that state, the question is whether there are any special circumstances that the law may construe as an exception to the rule. The answer would seem to lie in what legal commentators call 'humanitarian intervention', which is considered to be a basic moral response of one human being to another, to save the latter's life. One definition identifies humanitarian intervention as 'the proportionate transboundary help, including forcible help, provided by governments to individuals in another State who are being denied basic human rights and who themselves would be rationally willing to revolt against their oppressive government'.[110]

Generally, courts have insisted that the principle of state sovereignty is *jus cogens* and is inviolable under any circumstances. In the *Corfu Channel Case*,[111] where British warships had, as a response to having been fired at on 15 May 1946, and being damaged by Albanian mines later in the year, swept for mines in November of the same year in Albanian waters without the consent of the government of Albania, the International Court of Justice (ICJ), although holding Albania responsible for the explosions and the ensuing damage to the British warships, held the United Kingdom responsible for having violated Albanian sovereignty by attempting to carry out activities of mine sweeping in Albanian waters without the consent of the government of Albania. In the *Barcelona Traction Case*,[112] where the Belgian government instituted action against the government of Spain on behalf of shareholders of Belgian nationality of the Barcelona Traction and Light Company – a Canadian company running its business in Spain and affected by executive action of the Spanish government – the ICJ held: 'Belgium would be entitled to bring an international claim if it could show that one of its rights had been infringed and acts complained of involved the breach of an international obligation arising out of a treaty or a general rule of law.'[113] The court denied that injury to the economic interests of a state through prejudice to the investments of its nationals constituted a violation of that right. It is therefore logical to follow the principle that courts in this context would insist on the breach of an obligation by one state to another – such as the breach of the principles of state sovereignty – to be the only criterion to award judgment in favour of an aggrieved state.

Humanitarian assistance *per se* is by no means contrary to the principles of international law. In *Nicaragua* v. *USA (Merits)*,[114] the International Court of Justice (ICJ) held that 'there can be no doubt that the provisions of strictly humanitarian aid to persons or forces in another country, whatever the political obligations or objectives, cannot be regarded as unlawful intervention, or in any way contrary to international law'.[115] However, when the recipient state does not grant permission to a state or organization to operate relief flights into its territory, the status quo becomes different, and the legality of the relief flight becomes prima facie questionable. In such an instance, a relief flight would ipso facto be an intervention. The fact that such a flight does not obtain permission to fly over or into the recipient state would clearly be tantamount to a forcible entry. The question which emerges in this scenario is when, if at all, does a unilateral humanitarian intervention, such as a relief flight operated unilaterally, become legally justifiable?

The Court in the *Nicaragua* case, having concluded that the activities of the United States in assisting the *Contras* against the wishes of the Nicaraguan government constituted prima facie acts of intervention, held that the principle of non-intervention derives from customary international law, and a mere request for assistance by a person or group of persons or organization in a state would not justify at international law the unilateral intervention of one state in the affairs of another.[116] The court relied heavily on the paramount authority of treaty provisions over the other sources of international law and applied the principle that the use of force or threat thereof by one state on another – to render assistance to the latter, without the latter's consent – was contrary to existing treaty law and therefore unacceptable. Judge Sette-Camara quoted the International Law Commission and observed: 'the law of the Charter concerning the prohibition of the use of force in itself constitutes a conspicuous example of a rule of international law having the character of *jus cogens*'.[117] The court in this case has therefore clearly arranged legal priorities in such a manner that the United Nations Charter takes overall paramountcy over any other moral or ethical argument on humanitarian assistance.

Principles relating to sovereignty in airspace were first recognized formally in the Paris Convention of 1919,[118] which provided: 'the high contracting Parties recognize that every Power has complete and exclusive sovereignty over the airspace above its territory'.[119] This Convention also provided that during peacetime, aircraft of contracting states may fly over territories of other contracting states provided the provisions of the Convention were followed in the course of the flight.[120] There was also a provision that for military reasons, a contracting state could prohibit aircraft of other contracting states from flying over certain areas of its territory.[121]

The Chicago Convention of 1944 which replaced the Paris Convention also provides that contracting states recognize that every state has complete and exclusive sovereignty over the airspace above its territory.[122] The Convention defines a territory for its purposes as the land areas and territorial waters adjacent thereto under the sovereignty, suzerainty, protection and mandate of that state.[123] The Convention, which is applicable only to civil aircraft and does not apply to state aircraft, that is aircraft used in military, customs and police services, explicitly extends its prohibition by Article 3(c) to these aircraft from flying over, or landing in the territory of a contracting state without authorization of that state or special agreement therewith.

Article 9 of the Chicago Convention provides for contracting states to prohibit, for military reasons or reasons of public safety, aircraft of other contracting states from flying over certain areas of their territory. While these prohibited areas have to be notified to all states and the ICAO, the prohibition under this provision has to be applied without distinction of nationality to aircraft of all other states.[124]

Article 5 of the Chicago Convention provides for aircraft that do not operate scheduled international air services to make flights into or in transit non-stop across a state's territory without obtaining permission, *subject to the observance of the terms of the Convention* (my emphasis) and the right of the state flown over to require landing. The fact that this provision is subservient to the concept of state sovereignty and the requirements of Article 9 of the Convention has made it a mere cosmetic gloss on an otherwise rigid regulatory regime. Practically, Article 5 has been rendered nugatory of effect, since non-scheduled flights are usually required to inform states whose territories they fly over or land in, prior to the operation of the flights, and the grantor state has the right to refuse such requests.

The Convention recognizes in its Preamble that the future development of international civil aviation can greatly help to create and foster friendship among nations. Professor Bin Cheng addresses the principles governing post-World War II sovereignty over airspace as enunciated in Article 1 of the Chicago Convention and concludes: 'The now firmly established rule of international law that each State possesses complete and exclusive sovereignty over the airspace above its territory means that international civil aviation today rests on the tacit acquiescence or express agreement of States flown over.'[125]

Shawcross and Beaumont define sovereignty in international law as the right to exercise the functions of a state to the exclusion of all other states in regard to a certain area of the world.[126] In international aviation, the concept of sovereignty is the fundamental postulate upon which other norms and virtually all air law are based.[127] Post-1944 attitudes towards the concept of sovereignty in airspace and the philosophy of air law range between the unlimited public law right of a state to exercise sovereignty over its airspace and the idea of free movement of air traffic. Professor Goedhuis identifies the idea of 'free traffic' as opposed to the exclusivity of the sovereignty principle as being considered by jurists as a constructive element of aviation which assists in preserving life and raises it to a higher level.[128] This view is supported by the claim that general principles of international law demand that sovereignty of states be limited by the principle of freedom of peaceful traffic.[129] Be that as it may, a view advocating the free use of airspace of a country by aircraft of foreign nationalities would give rise to a dichotomy: that there should be freedom of aviation with a minimum of restrictions or none at all, or that international air traffic should be firmly regulated. Professor Lissitzyn analyses the concept of sovereignty in its modern development as having three basic principles: each state has exclusive sovereignty over its airspace; each state has complete discretion as to the admission of any aircraft into its airspace; and airspace over the high seas and other areas not subject to a state's jurisdiction is *res nullius* and is free to the aircraft of all states.[130]

One can therefore observe that air law has developed from being a series of exclusive rights – first in private law and then in public law – and has also set parameters within which a host of other progressive objectives may be attained. The concept of sovereignty now entails for each state the responsibility of being conscious of its obligations to the international legal community. The sovereignty principle has therefore evolved to become a cohesive system of coexistence in the air by states which respect the exclusive rights of each state to sovereignty over its airspace. Mutual obligations have sprung up between states bringing as their corollary a deep respect for the principles of international law and the rights of individual states.

COMMENTS

One way in which civil aviation can play a role in ensuring peace among the nations of the world is primarily through its key role of facilitating international discourse and communication. This has been achieved to a large extent through ICAO, which is charged by Article 44 of the Chicago Convention to work toward assisting the global community in developing civil aviation in an orderly, economic and safe manner. ICAO's initiatives in ensuring peace and harmony in the field of aviation is largely achieved through its Council, which has its genesis in the Interim Council of the Provisional International Civil Aviation Organization (PICAO).[131] PICAO occupied such legal capacity as may have been necessary for the performance of its functions and was recognized as having full juridical personality wherever compatible with the constitution and the laws of the state concerned.[132] The definitive word 'juridical' attributed to PICAO a mere judicial function, unequivocally stipulating that the organization and its component bodies, such as the Interim Council, were obligated to remain within the legal parameters allocated to them by the Interim Agreement[133] and that PICAO was of a purely technical and advisory nature. A legislative or quasi-legislative function could not therefore be imputed to the Interim Council of PICAO. It could mostly study, interpret and advise on standards and procedures[134] and make recommendations with respect to technical matters through the Committee on Air Navigation.[135] Under the Interim Agreement[136] the PICAO Council was required to act as an arbitral body on any differences arising among member states relating to matters of international civil aviation which may be submitted to it, wherein the Interim Council of PICAO was empowered to render an advisory report or, if the parties involved so wished, give a decision on the matter before it.[137] The Interim Council, which was the precursor to the ICAO Council, set the stage therefore for providing the Council with unusual arbitral powers which are not attributed to similar organs of the specialized agencies of the United Nations system.[138] *A fortiori*, since the ICAO Council is permanent and is in almost constant session, contracting states could expect any matter of dispute brought by them before the Council to be dealt with, without unreasonable delay.[139]

Chapter XVIII of the Convention formalizes the arbitral powers of the Council by stating: 'If any disagreement between two or more contracting States relating to the interpretation or application of this Convention and its Annexes cannot be settled by negotiation, *it shall* [emphasis added], on the application of any State concerned in the disagreement, be decided by the Council.'[140] This provision reflects two significant points: the first is that contracting states should first attempt to resolve their disputes by themselves, through negotiation;[141] the second is that the word shall in this provision infuses into the decision-making powers of the Council an unquestionably mandatory character. Furthermore, a decision taken by the Council is juridically dignified by Article 86 of the Convention, when the article states that, unless the Council decides otherwise, any decision by the Council on whether an international airline is operating in conformity with the provisions of the Convention shall remain in effect unless reversed on appeal. The Council also has powers of sanction granted by the Convention, if its decision is not adhered to. Schenkman states: 'The power of sanctions in this field is an entirely new phenomenon, attributed to an aeronautical body ... none of the pre-war instruments in the field of aviation had the power of sanctions as a means of enforcement of its decisions.'[142]

Most contracting states have, on their own initiative, enacted dispute-settlement clauses in their bilateral air services agreements wherein provision is usually made to refer inter-state disputes relating to international civil aviation to the ICAO Council, in accordance with Chapter XVIII of the Convention. In this context, it is also relevant to note that the president of the Council is empowered by the Convention to appoint an arbitrator and an umpire in certain circumstances leading to an appeal from a decision of the Council.[143]

A most interesting aspect of the ICAO Council is that one of its mandatory functions is to consider any subject referred to it by a contracting state for its consideration,[144] or any subject which the president of the council or the secretary general of the ICAO secretariat desires to bring before the Council.[145] Although the Council is bound to consider a matter submitted to it by a contracting state, it can refrain from giving a decision, as the Council is only obligated to consider a matter before it.

There seems to be an unfortunate dichotomy in terminology in the Convention since, on the one hand, Article 54(*n*) makes it mandatory that the Council shall merely *consider* any matter relating to the Convention which any contracting state refers to it, while on the other, Article 84 categorically states that any disagreement between two or more states relating to the interpretation or application of the Convention and its Annexes that cannot be settled by negotiation shall be decided by the Council. The difficulty arises on a strict interpretation of Article 54(*n*) where even a disagreement between two states as envisaged under Article 84 could well be considered as 'any matter' under Article 54(*n*). In such an instance, the Council could well be faced with the dilemma of choosing between the two provisions. It would not be incorrect for the Council to merely consider a matter placed before it, although a decision is requested by the applicant state, since Article 54(*n*) is perceived to be comprehensive as the operative and controlling provision that lays down mandatory functions of the Council. It is indeed unfortunate that these two provisions obfuscate the issue which otherwise would have given a clear picture of the decision-making powers of the Council. A further thread in the fabric of adjudicatory powers of the Council is found in Article 14 of the Rules of Settlement promulgated by the Council in 1957,[146] which allows the Council to request the parties in dispute to engage in direct negotiations at any time.[147] This emphasis on conciliation has prompted the view that the Council, under article 84, would favour the settling of disputes rather than adjudicating them.[148] This view seems compatible with the proposition that the consideration of a matter under Article 54(*n*) would be a more attractive approach *in limine* in a matter of dispute between two states.

Dempsey points out that in the four decades since the promulgation of Chapter XVIII, only three disputes had been submitted to the Council for formal resolution:[149] the first involved a dispute between India and Pakistan (1952), where India complained that Pakistan was in breach of the Convention by not permitting Indian aircraft to overfly Pakistani airspace on their way to Afghanistan; the second was a complaint filed by the United Kingdom against Spain (1969), alleging the violation by Spain of the Convention by the establishment of a prohibited zone over Gibraltar; and the third was a complaint by Pakistan against India (1971), concerning a hijacking of Indian aircraft which landed in Pakistan. India unilaterally suspended Pakistan's overflying privileges five days after the hijack

The other area through which civil aviation could contribute to peace and security among the nations of the world is, as already mentioned, through humanitarian flights operated to and from places of conflict and disaster. Legal scholars hold divergent views on whether unilateral intervention by one state in another to render humanitarian assistance is legally justified; judicial opinion favours an adherence prima facie to treaty provisions which prohibit unilateral intervention unless the exceptions provided for in such treaties admit of such intervention; and an aircraft cannot fly over or into the territory of another state without first obtaining the permission for such flight from the state concerned.

The question which would finally emerge from the above propositions is whether a relief flight could, on moral grounds and purely for humanitarian purposes, disregard the need to obtain permission from the recipient state and fly over or into that state. The answer is entrenched in the law and is clearly in the negative. Besides the Chicago Convention, which recognizes the inviolability of sovereignty of states over their airspace, the recognition by the ICJ that high-altitude overflights for reconnaissance purposes by US aircraft over Nicaraguan airspace was a violation of the law[150] establishes clearly the inviolability of a state's sovereignty in its airspace. The curious position of the relief flight at humanitarian law remains therefore torn between morality and legitimacy and, unhappily, the quality of mercy that an unsolicited and unpermitted relief flight may bring with it will not outweigh the illegitimacy that taints it at law. One can only hope that, in view of modern exigencies which give rise to the need for the international community to help in refugee situations with monotonous regularity, and the liberal approach that is now being taken to the concept of sovereignty, states will view humanitarian assistance and relief flights with less suspicion. The international community could then consider a review of sovereignty in airspace to accord with its modern setting.

WORK OF ICAO

Aviation security

The 33rd session of the Assembly and the high-level ministerial conference

At the 33rd Session of the Assembly, ICAO adopted Resolution A33-1 entitled 'Declaration on misuse of civil aircraft as weapons of destruction and other terrorist acts involving civil aviation'.[151] This resolution, while singling out for consideration the terrorist acts which occurred in the United States on 11 September 2001, and, inter alia, recognizing that the new type of threat posed by terrorist organizations requires new concerted efforts and policies of cooperation on the part of states, urges all contracting states to intensify their efforts in order to achieve the full implementation and enforcement of the multilateral conventions on aviation security, as well as of the ICAO Standards and Recommended Practices and Procedures (SARPs) relating to aviation security, to monitor such implementation and to take within their territories appropriate additional security measures commensurate to the level of threat in order to prevent and eradicate terrorist acts involving civil aviation. The resolution also urges all contracting states to make contributions in the form of financial or human resources to ICAO's aviation security mechanism to support and strengthen the fight against terrorism and unlawful interference in civil aviation; calls on contracting states to agree on special funding for urgent action by ICAO in the field of aviation security; and directs the Council to develop proposals and take appropriate decisions for a more stable funding of ICAO action in the field of aviation security, including appropriate remedial action.

Resolution A33-1 also directed the Council to convene, at the earliest date, an international high-level ministerial conference on aviation security in Montreal with the objectives of preventing, combating and eradicating acts of terrorism involving civil aviation; of strengthening ICAO's role in the adoption of SARPs in the field of security and the audit of their implementation; and of ensuring the necessary financial means to strengthen ICAO's AVSEC mechanism, while providing special funding for urgent action by ICAO in the field of aviation security.

The effects of this resolution, which have been far reaching, can be seen in certain concerted efforts made in both the United States and Europe to take immediate measures to strengthen aviation security. The European Transport and Telecommunications Council, at its meeting in Luxemburg on 16 October 2001, welcomed the proposal by the Commission for a Regulation establishing common rules in the field of civil aviation security.[152] The Council invited member states and the European Commission to contribute to the preparation for the ICAO high-level/ministerial conference as referred to in Resolution 13/1.

In the United States, Jane Garvey, FAA administrator, stated on 17 October 2001, at a meeting in Washington, that the United States will start using new technology called the 'Computer Assisted Passenger Pre-screening System', which would introduce new technologies to detect plastic weapons, and greater use of explosive detection equipment.[153] Ms Garvey further added that Transportation Secretary Mineta had created a $20 million dollar fund to explore new technologies to improve aircraft security. These grants could be used to test any new technology that leads to safer, more secure aircraft.[154]

At its meeting of 1 October 2001, the Rapid Response Team on Airport Security, which was formed under the Department of Transportation of the United States, recommended the following measures for the reform of the nations's aviation security system:

- establishment of a new federal security agency, housed within the Department of Transport;
- integration of law enforcement and national security intelligence data with airline and airport systems, including passenger reservation;
- designation by all airlines and airports of a senior-level security officer who should possess a security clearance required to act on sensitive intelligence information;
- adoption of new technologies for the positive identification of passengers, airport workers and crews, detection of explosives, and more effective passenger and baggage screening to be incorporated in airport security programmes as soon as practicable;
- establishment by the FAA of an Aviation Technology Consortium;
- application of the Computer Assisted Passenger Pre-screening System (CAPPS) to all passengers.[155]

On 19 and 20 February 2002, in keeping with the requirement of Assembly Resolution A33, a high-level ministerial conference on aviation security was held in the headquarters of the International Civil Aviation Organization, Montreal. In the words of Dr Assad Kotaite, president of the ICAO Council, who opened the Conference (and later served as the chairman of the Conference), the Conference was being held 'at a critical juncture for civil aviation and for society at large ... and would review and develop global strategy for strengthening aviation security with the aim of protecting lives both in the air and on the ground, restoring public confidence in air travel and promoting the health of air transport in order that it can renew its vital contribution to the world economy'.[156] Dr Kotaite stated that this was a historic moment in the evolution of civil aviation.

At this Conference, attended by member states of the International Civil Aviation Organization, some 714 participants from 154 contracting states and observers from 24 international civil aviation organizations endorsed a global strategy for strengthening aviation security worldwide and issued a public declaration at the conclusion of their two-day meeting. A central element of the strategy is an ICAO Aviation Security Plan of Action, which includes regular, mandatory, systematic and harmonized audits to enable evaluation of aviation security in place in all 187 member states of ICAO. An indicative cost of the security oversight programme is US$17 million, of which more than 15 million will have to come from new contributions. The programme will cover initially the period 2002 to 2004 and serve to identify and correct deficiencies in the implementation of ICAO security-related standards. Dr Kotaite called upon all members of the world aviation community to give their full and unconditional support to the Plan of Action and to all elements of their global strategy, in terms of human and financial resources, so that air transport remains the safest and most efficient mode of mass transportation there is. The Plan of Action also includes the following:

- identification, analysis and development of an effective global response to new and emerging threats, integrating timely measures to be taken in specific fields, including airports, aircraft and air traffic control systems;
- strengthening of the security-related provisions in the Annexes to the Convention on International Civil Aviation, using expedited procedures where warranted and subject to overall safety considerations, notably to provide for protection of the flight deck;
- close coordination and coherence with audit programmes at the regional and subregional level;
- processing of the results by ICAO in a way which reconciles confidentiality and transparency; and
- a follow-up programme for assistance, with rectification of identified deficiencies.

The Conference called for the Council of ICAO to develop the Plan of Action for adoption not later than 14 June 2002 and implementation commencing immediately thereafter within the shortest feasible time frames.

A declaration adopted at the conclusion of the Conference reaffirms condemnation of the use of civil aircraft as weapons of destruction as well as of other acts of unlawful interference with civil aviation wherever and by whomsoever and for whatever reason they are perpetrated, while being mindful of the need for strengthening measures to prevent all acts of unlawful interference with civil aviation. It emphasizes the vital role which civil aviation plays in economic development; stresses the pre-eminence of safety and security as underlying fundamentals in civil aviation which need global address; and reaffirms the responsibility of states for the security and the safety of civil aviation, irrespective of whether the air transport and related services concerned are provided by government, autonomous or private entities.

Among the salient features of the declaration is that it notes the significant improvements in aviation security recently initiated in a large number of states; recognizes that a uniform approach in a global system is essential to ensure aviation security throughout the world and that deficiencies in any part of the system constitute a threat to the entire global system; and affirms that a global aviation security system imposes a collective responsibility on all states. The declaration also notes that the additional resources which will be required to meet enhanced aviation security measures may create an undue financial burden on the already limited resources of developing countries.

Through the declaration, the states participating in the Conference commit themselves to achieving full implementation of the multilateral conventions on aviation security and the ICAO Standards and Recommended Practices (SARPs) and Procedures for Air Navigation Services (PANS) as well as ICAO Assembly resolutions and Council decisions relating to aviation security and safety; applying within national territories appropriate additional aviation security measures to meet the level of threat; fostering international cooperation in the field of aviation security and harmonizing the implementation of security measures; ensuring that security measures are implemented in a most cost-effective way in order to avoid undue burden on civil aviation; ensuring to the extent possible that security measures do not disrupt or impede the flow of passengers, freight, mail or aircraft; ensuring that security measures are implemented in a manner which is objective and non-discriminatory on the basis of gender, race, religion or nationality; enhancing the quality of human resource functioning within aviation security, including application of sustained education and training; and to restore public confidence in air travel and revitalize the air transport industry. As referred to above, the declaration also endorses the establishment of a comprehensive ICAO Aviation Security Plan of Action for strengthening aviation security worldwide.

Several states pledged financial and human resource assistance towards the implementation of the action plan proposed by ICAO. The Conference was a singular success, not only because it achieved its objective of reaching consensus among 154 states as to the compelling need for an aviation security oversight audit programme to be conducted on contracting states by ICAO, but also because it proved to be an exemplary post modernist attempt at a global proclamation against acts of terrorism that threaten the security of the world community. The Conference underscored the need for an integrated management structure that could combat unlawful interference with exigencies of day-to-day social and commercial intercourse. It amply demonstrated, through the various deliberations that took place during the two days, that there was no room for any doubt that, in international civil aviation management, international and domestic civil aviation should not be considered in mutual exclusivity when it comes to matters of aviation security.

Perhaps the most significant message sent out by the high-level ministerial conference is that the world community would now have to establish a carefully synchronized and thoughtfully orchestrated plan of action and system of progressing towards achieving substantial enforcement of aviation security. Also highlighted at the Conference was the fact that, on a more short-term level, and of no less critical importance, there are the insurance and security implications that require urgent actions.

The outcome of the Conference was clear evidence that, although monuments to power can be shaken by acts of unlawful interference, the foundations of a family of nations and their civilized discourse on solidarity and comity among nations cannot ever be destroyed. Also evident was that long-term resolution was an essential supplement to short-term retaliation, if an enduring solution was to be pursued against terrorism. In this case, there is no room for the rhetoric of war, as there are no boundaries to encroach upon and no soldiers to fight. Global terrorism transcends frontiers of state authority. The dialogue of civilized nations eventually triumphs over individual response.

In achieving the above-mentioned management objectives, the Conference sent a clear message that the aviation community should start by attaining a full appreciation of the potential social and economic advantages of restoring confidence in air travel worldwide. The starting point should ineluctably be in the area of regulatory management, where ICAO should be called upon to identify and analyse new emerging and potential threats to civil aviation and formulate appropriate practical strategy to address the threats. Once threat identification is completed, effective management follow through should involve modular application of technological tools. Available technology, such as biometric identification equipment and machine-readable travel document readers, should be put to wider and more effective use. Management databases containing personal information relevant to ensuring safety should also be used extensively on the basis that the international use of these databases in providing advance passenger information is essential as a preventive management tool.

Another important preventive measure is the immediate revision of existing regulatory guidelines, including Annex 17 to the Convention on International Civil Aviation, which lays down Standards and Recommended Practices for states to follow in the field of aviation security. With regard to state responsibility, the Conference was unreserved in recognizing that states should reaffirm their responsibility for effective security management. They should ensure integrated management, through partnerships between aviation and other authorities, between government and industry, spreading out to global, regional and interregional cooperation. Critical to this exercise would be the conduct by ICAO of aviation security audits, along the lines of aviation safety audits already carried out by the organization. Procedures for assisting states in taking remedial action have to be in place with the necessary follow-up and technical assistance. It is only then that an effective preventive security management system could be developed.

Conclusions and recommendations of the Conference

The high-level ministerial conference came to several conclusions and adopted numerous recommendations containing guidance for follow-up action. The Conference concluded that the events of 11 September 2001 have had a major negative impact on world economies and an impact on air transport which is unparalleled in history, and that restoration of consumer confidence in air transport and assurance of the long-term health of the air transport industry are both vital, and many states have already initiated a range of measures to this effect. It was also the view of the Conference that the effective application of enhanced uniform security measures, commensurate with the threat, will help to restore confidence in air transport, but these measures will need to be passenger and cargo user-friendly and not overly costly for the industry and its consumers if traffic growth is to be regenerated. Accordingly, the Conference recommended that, consistent with Assembly Resolution A33-1, states should intensify their efforts to achieve the full implementation and enforcement of the multilateral conventions on aviation security as well as of the ICAO SARPs relating to aviation security, and take within their territories appropriate additional security measures which are commensurate with the level of threat and are cost-effective. Since restoration of confidence in air transport is a collective responsibility, the Conference called upon states to enhance international cooperation in aviation security and assist developing countries to the extent possible.

With regard to the compelling need to strengthen aviation security worldwide, the Conference concluded that a strong and viable aviation security (AVSEC) programme was indispensable and that a global uniform approach to the implementation of the international aviation security standards is essential, while leaving room for operational flexibility. It was also considered useful to establish regional and subregional approaches which could make a significant contribution to ICAO's aviation security activities. The Conference concluded that aviation security was a responsibility of contracting states, and states which outsource aviation security programmes should therefore ensure that adequate governmental control and supervision are in place. The Conference also observed that, since gaps and inadequacies appear to exist in international aviation security instruments with regard to new and emerging threats to civil aviation, further study was needed in this regard. There was a need for a comprehensive ICAO Aviation Security Plan of Action for strengthening aviation security, through a reinforced AVSEC mechanism, an ICAO aviation security audit programme, technical cooperation projects, promotion of aviation security quality control functions and appropriate performance indicators.

On the basis of the above conclusions, the Conference recommended that states take immediate action to lock flight deck doors for aircraft operated internationally, while maintaining measures on the ground to provide the highest level of aviation security. States were also requested to share threat information actively in accordance with standards in Annex 17 and employ suitable threat assessment and risk management methodologies appropriate to their circumstances, based on a template to be developed by ICAO, and ensure that aviation security measures are implemented in an objective and non-discriminatory manner.

As for ICAO's role in this process, the Conference recommended that the organization, as a matter of high priority, develop amendments to the appropriate Annexes to require protection of the flight deck door from forcible intrusion; continue its efforts to identify and analyse the new and emerging threats to civil aviation with the purpose of assisting in the development of security measures and to collaborate actively with other associated agencies; carry out a detailed study of the adequacy of the existing aviation security conventions and other aviation security-related documentation with a view to proposing and developing measures to close the existing gaps and remove the inadequacies, including amendment where required, so as to deal effectively with the existing, as well as the new and emerging, threats to international civil aviation; develop and take action to deal with the problem of aviation war risk insurance; and develop and implement a comprehensive Aviation Security Plan of Action and any additional actions approved by the Council, including a clear identification of priorities.

One of the key conclusions of the Conference was that, in order to further enhance safety and security and to ensure the systematic implementation of the critical elements of a state's aviation security system, there is an urgent need for a comprehensive ICAO programme of aviation security audits and that such a programme should audit national-level and airport-level compliance with Annex 17 and with aviation security-related provisions of other Annexes on a regular, mandatory, systematic and harmonized basis. It was the view of the Conference that the ability to determine whether an airport or state is in compliance will require that auditors have a solid aviation security background and be sufficiently trained and certified by ICAO to ensure that auditing is conducted in a consistent and objective manner. The Conference was strongly convinced that such an audit programme should be undertaken under the auspices of ICAO's AVSEC mechanism, which could be guided by proven and successful concepts used in viable programmes already developed by the European Civil Aviation Conference (ECAC), the United States and other states in the development of the framework for a security audit programme.

It was considered that the regional approach has many benefits and is to be considered as supplementary to local initiatives, in particular by promoting regional partnership and the activities of the ICAO Regional AVSEC Training Centres. The AVSEC Panel should assist in the development of technical requirements and guidance materials needed to administer the audits and assist in the development of an effective quality assurance programme to maintain standards of audit performance; and since an audit programme could provide only security levels of audited airports at the time of the audit, a permanent mechanism based on quality control and the regular conduct of exercises and inspections could guarantee the continuity and improvement of security levels determined by the audits.

Arguably, the most significant and seminal recommendation of the Conference was that ICAO establish a comprehensive programme of universal, regular, mandatory, systematic and harmonized aviation security audits, with implementation beginning in 2003, based on the final work plan established by the Council. In order to be effective, the programme should be based on an audit process that uses ICAO-trained and certified audit teams which are headed by an ICAO staff member and which consistently apply fair and objective methods to determine compliance with Annex 17 by observing measures at airports and assessing the state's capabilities to sustain those measures.

The Conference was of the view that of singular importance to the audit process was the need for the audit programme to be established under the auspices of ICAO's AVSEC mechanism. It recommended that, in developing the audit programme, which should be transparent and autonomous, ICAO should ensure the greatest possible coordination and coherence with audit programmes already established at a regional or subregional level, taking into account aviation security situation in these states. For this to be a reality, a compliance mechanism has to be built into the programme, which will distinguish between minor and serious areas of improvement, ensure that immediate corrective action is taken for serious deficiencies and provide developing states with the necessary assistance to improve security measurably.

With regard to funding an aviation security audit programme to be run by ICAO, an adequate and stable source of funding has to be sought for the AVSEC mechanism through increased voluntary contributions until such time that an allocation of funds can be sought through the regular programme budget, which should be as soon as possible. It was recommended that all states be notified of a completed audit, that ICAO Headquarters be the repository for full audit reports and that the sharing of audit reports between states take place on a bilateral or multilateral basis. States were required, under such a programme, to commit themselves to provide the ICAO with national AVSEC findings based on a harmonized procedure to be developed by ICAO as early as possible. Of course, those states, in particular developing countries, should be provided with technical and financial assistance under technical cooperation, so that they may take remedial actions to rectify the deficiencies identified during the audit. States should also utilize the ICAO audits to the maximum extent possible and could always approach ICAO with regard to the audit findings for other states.

The Conference also concluded that, in order to execute the ICAO Aviation Security Plan of Action, an indicative additional funding requirement is for a minimum of US$15·4 million through voluntary contributions for the current triennium 2002–4, these figures to be used as a basis for further study by the Council. However, for the longer term a more stable means of funding the ICAO Aviation Security Plan of Action would be either through an increase of the assessment to the ICAO General Fund for the following triennia or by a long-term commitment, on a voluntary basis, of systematic contributions according to an approved suggested level of contribution, to be determined by the Council, by all states. With regard to recouping policies of states, the Conference observed and confirmed that ICAO's policy and guidance material on cost recovery of security services at airports in ICAO's *Policies on Charges for Airports and Air Navigation Services* (Doc. 9082/6) and the *Airport Economics Manual* (Doc. 9562) remained valid, although there was a need for development of additional policy and guidance material on cost recovery of security measures with regard to air navigation services complementary to that which already exists with respect to airport security charges. There was also a need for further improvement of human resources, utilizing the existing training centres and the standardization of instruction materials, where appropriate based on ICAO's TRAINAIR methodology.

On the above basis, states were called upon by the Conference to commit themselves to providing adequate resources, financial, human and/or otherwise in kind, for the time being on a voluntary basis through the AVSEC mechanism, for the ICAO Aviation Security Plan of Action for the triennium 2002–4 as a matter of priority, and to be aware of the continuing needs for subsequent triennia. They were also called upon to agree to remove the existing ties they individually impose on the expenditures of AVSEC mechanism contributions in order for ICAO to utilize immediately all funds available in the AVSEC mechanism trust funds. The Conference observed that states might wish to use the Technical Cooperation Programme of ICAO as one of the main instruments to obtain assistance in advancing implementation of their obligations under relevant international conventions, SARPs of Annex 17 – Security, and related provisions of other Annexes, as well as adherence to ICAO guidance material.

As for ICAO's involvement and contribution, the organization was requested to establish an ICAO Aviation Security Follow-up Programme and seek additional resources, similar to the USOAP Follow-up Programme of the Technical Cooperation Bureau, to enable states to obtain technical cooperation in the preparation of necessary documentation and in resource mobilization for aviation security. One of the ways in which this could be achieved was by ICAO promoting the use of the ICAO Objectives Implementation Mechanism as a means for states to obtain technical cooperation, as required for the rectification of deficiencies identified during aviation security evaluations and audits and urgently pursuing the development and implementation of an International Financial Facility for Aviation Safety (IFFAS),[157] to encompass not only safety but also security. Another significant function of ICAO was to elaborate on its policy and guidance material on cost recovery of security services, notably to include development of policy and guidance material on cost recovery, through charges, of security measures with regard to air navigation services and explore the issue of using security charges as a means of recovering the cost of ICAO assistance when it is provided to states for security development projects.

Post-conference work

In furtherance of the recommendations of the Conference, the ICAO secretariat initiated an aviation security plan of action which is aimed at reviewing legal instruments, in particular the enhancement of Annex 17 – Security – Safeguarding International Civil Aviation against Acts of Unlawful Interference – to the Convention on International Civil Aviation (the work undertaken by the AVSEC Panel and the latest Amendment 10 to Annex 17) and introduction or strengthening of security-related provisions in other Annexes to the Convention (Annex 1 – 'Personnel Licensing', Annex 6 – 'Operation of Aircraft', Annex 8 – 'Airworthiness of Aircraft', Annex 9 – 'Facilitation', Annex 11 – 'Air Traffic Services', Annex 14 – 'Aerodromes'; and Annex 18 – 'The Safe Transport of Dangerous Goods by Air'). The plan of action also envisions reinforcing AVSEC Mechanism activities, notably in the preparation of security audits and in undertaking immediate/urgent assistance to states, and expediting work on improving technical specifications relating to and further implementing the use of machine-readable travel documents (MRTDs), biometric identification and travel document security and improving border security systems. The reviewing of certain Procedures for Air Navigation Services (PANS) and revision of relevant ICAO manuals and other guidance material including further development of Aviation Security Training Packages (ASTPs), training programmes, workshops and seminars, as well as assistance to states through ICAO's technical co-operation programme, are also on the programme of implementation.

ICAO considers the development and execution of a comprehensive and integrated ICAO AVSEC Plan of Action as its highest priority. The success of this Plan of Action will be measured over a long period, as the improvements expected in contracting states will require an intensive and continuous worldwide commitment. The full and active participation of all contracting states, as well as all technical and deliberative bodies of ICAO, is essential for the achievement of concrete results within an acceptable period of time.

The aviation security plan of action of ICAO will focus on the development of new training and guidance material on national quality control (NQC), system testing, auditors, audit guidelines and forms, including urgent distribution to all states, and training and certification of international auditors through the existing ICAO Aviation Security Training Centres (ASTCs) network, which will be reinforced and expanded where required. It will also include undertaking universal, mandatory and regular AVSEC audits to assess the level of implementation and enforcement by states of SARPs contained in Annex 17, together with the assessment of security measures undertaken and, on a sample basis, at airport level for each state. ICAO would maintain an ICAO AVSEC findings database. The creation of Aviation Security Regional Units (ASRUs) functionally linked to the AVSEC mechanism, to be urgently implemented in Africa, the Middle East, Eastern Europe, the Americas, Asia and the Pacific, in order to coordinate the execution of AVSEC mechanism activities and provide direct assistance to states would also be a feature of the plan.

Third party war risk insurance

In the light of the dramatic recession of insurance coverage following the withdrawal of third party war risk liability insurance and its partial reinstatement with lower limits and higher premiums, states began to take measures to provide excess insurance cover for carriers, in most cases up to the previous policy limit, for war and terrorism-related third party risk. Provision of such coverage meant that at least some air carriers would not be in violation of domestic and international regulations and lease covenants respecting war risk cover. However, there was concern expressed regarding the fact that a considerable number of countries in Latin America, Asia and Africa, while having taken steps necessary to ensure continued coverage, have not provided the necessary guarantees and indemnities in the same amount as states in Europe and North America.

Action taken by ICAO contracting states in responding to the insurance crisis has legal legitimacy in two international conventions, the Rome Convention of 1952[158] and the Montreal Convention of 1999.[159] Article 15 of the Rome Convention provides that any contracting state may require that the operator of an aircraft registered in another contracting state shall be insured in respect of his liability for damage sustained in its territory for which a right to compensation exists. The operative clause, in the context of indemnities offered by the several ICAO contracting states as discussed earlier, is contained in Article 15.4 of the Rome Convention which provides that, instead of insurance, inter alia, a guarantee given by the contracting state where the aircraft is registered shall be deemed satisfactory if that state undertakes that it will not claim immunity from suit in respect of that guarantee.[160] The Montreal Convention of 1999, which is yet to come into force, provides in Article 50 that states parties shall require their carriers to maintain adequate insurance covering their liability under the Convention. This provision further stipulates that a carrier may be required by the state party into which it operates to furnish evidence that it maintains adequate insurance covering its liability under the Convention.

The work of the ICAO Special Group on War Risk Insurance was considered by a Council Study Group on Aviation War Risk Insurance, established by agreement of the Council on 4 March 2002. This study group had two meetings, on 16 April and 24 April 2002, respectively, wherein the group considered a draft report to Council containing the outcome of the work of the special group. This report firstly outlines coverage to be provided in respect of third party war risk liability insurance, which is up to US$1·5 billion per aircraft, per occurrence, per insured, over and above the coverage offered by the private market amounting to US$50 million, which is already in place. Special features, which are tantamount to advantages offered by this coverage, are that it would not be cancellable (which is in contrast to the current seven-day cancellation clause) and that coverage would encompass all areas of the aviation industry, including airlines, airports, ground handling agents, screening companies, manufacturers of aircraft and components lessors, air traffic controllers and other providers of air navigation services. The scope of coverage would be global.

In terms of rates, the ICAO scheme would charge 50 cents per passenger for coverage up to US$1·5 billion in excess of the private cover of US$50 million, which, as already mentioned, is available at US$1·25 per passenger. The rate of 50 cents per passenger compares favourably with the current US$1·50 excess charge currently levied in respect of excess third party insurance which goes only up to a maximum of US$1 billion in two extra layers at US$1·00 for both layers in addition to the primary cover fixed at US$1·25. The premium advantage notwithstanding, the strongest thrust of the coverage offered by the ICAO scheme is its intrinsic guarantee against cancellation, particularly in view of the existing seven-day cancellation clause.

With regard to participation, which is of course voluntary, the exposure of a participating state to risk of payment in the instance of a claim under third party war risk liability would amount to its ICAO contribution percentage of US$15 billion. To give an example, a state which participates in the ICAO scheme which contributes 3 per cent of the ICAO budget has a maximum exposure of US$450 million. Compared to state guarantees given in the aftermath of the September 2001 events, which were often unlimited, this modality should be acceptable to most states. In order to participate, an ICAO contracting state would be required to sign a participation agreement with ICAO which would be designed to fit the particular legal structure and legislative requirements of each state concerned.

An insurance entity which is proposed within the parameters of the ICAO scheme would have to be established by the ICAO Council, and thereafter be formally incorporated jointly by ICAO and the industry, consequent upon development of appropriate statutes and statutory instruments, in accordance with applicable domestic and regulatory requirements. The participation agreement would be open for signature to all ICAO contracting states. In summary, the inherent advantages of the proposed ICAO scheme are its uniqueness in terms of its global application, non-cancellability, affordability with regard to premium and exposure to claims, and its design in accordance with regulatory requirements.

The seminal consideration regarding ICAO's role in sustaining the aviation industry lies in the mandate of the organization, as contained in Article 44 of the Convention on International Civil Aviation.[161] In the context of the current discussion, the aims and objectives of ICAO, as prescribed by the Convention are, inter alia, to develop the principles and techniques of international air navigation and foster the planning and development of international air transport so as to ensure the safe and orderly growth of international civil aviation throughout the world, meet the needs of the peoples of the world for safe, regular, efficient and economical air transport, and ensure that the rights of contracting states are fully respected and that every contracting state has a fair opportunity to operate international airlines.[162] With these provisions in place, ICAO incontrovertibly becomes the foremost regulatory authority in international civil aviation charged with the responsibility of ensuring that air transport worldwide is sustained and that the consumer is assured of continuity of air services.

Quite apart from ICAO's reactive initiatives after September 2001, the organization had already taken numerous measures to ensure that its mandate in sustaining air transport is carried out. The fundamental premise upon which ICAO's current work on facilitation of passenger travel is based is contained in the Convention on International Civil Aviation (Chicago Convention),[163] Article 22 of which provides, inter alia, that each contracting state agrees to adopt all practical measures, to facilitate and expedite navigation by aircraft and to prevent unnecessary delays to aircraft, crews, passengers and cargo. Annex 9 to the Chicago Convention, on facilitation, is the operative document providing guidelines to states on alleviating the lot of the passenger.

On the subject of delays or cancellation of flights, the passenger is informed that when (owing to circumstances beyond their control) airlines cancel or delay a flight, or cause a passenger to miss a connection, most airlines accept the obligation to refund or provide alternative flight arrangements at no further cost to the passenger, but do not generally accept any further liability for any damages incurred as a result (for example, lost vacation or work time). Advice that, where major financial or other losses are incurred as a consequence of delay, passengers may wish to ascertain their rights at law is also contained in the Guidelines.

The two critical factors that will carry the sustainability of air carriers and assurance of air services in the years to come will be regulatory control and economic strategy. There is no doubt that the regulatory environment will be a certain cause for uncertainty in the near future. In early 2003, the ICAO will be convening the Fifth World Air Transport Conference (ATConf/5) which will consider this issue in its entirety. The uniqueness of the operation of air transport services as a trading practice lies in the symbiosis required for its sustenance between state and national carrier. This peculiar relationship requires that a certain responsibility devolve upon states to ensure the prosperity of its air transport industry and prevention of its collapse. Although air transport may be heavily privatized in some instances, particularly in the developed world, this does not take away the overall regulatory supervisory role of the state and its obligation to support its national carrier in remaining in service. This responsibility can only be fulfilled through active regulatory participation by states. The responsibility of sustaining air transport and ensuring continuity of services should not devolve upon ICAO alone.

THE ROLE OF AIRLINES IN ENSURING SECURITY

The new neo-post-modernist approach calls upon air carriers to be more involved with state attempts at ensuring security. One good example is the role of the airline in the application of the contract of carriage by air of persons. The ability of an airline to refuse a passenger boarding if it has reason to believe that the passenger could be a threat to the safety and security of flight transcends common law principles of offer and acceptance of a contract. This is particularly so in instances of air rage.

The term 'air rage' is an all-encompassing one aimed at identifying violence, verbal abuse and threats, assault, sexual harassment and sexual assault perpetrated by a person on another on board an aircraft.[164] One of the more insidious aspects of air rage becomes evident where the above-mentioned conduct is directed at crew members, where an interference with their duties may seriously undermine the safety of flight. In this broad context, it is not only a passenger who perpetrates an act identifiable as air rage against a fellow passenger who can be considered a threat but, *a fortiori*, a passenger who attempts to assault and incapacitate a member of the crew can also be a serious threat to air safety. In such instances, the exercise of vigilance by both regulatory and airline authorities at the point of check-in and boarding would be a necessary preventive measure. The question would be to what extent authorities can exercise their right to refuse boarding to a person who demonstrates, prior to boarding, a proclivity for misconduct on board. Below we inquire into both contractual rights of the airline to refuse boarding to such passengers and recent legislative measures adopted by some jurisdictions which may give some insight into emergent trends in the area of preventive protection of passengers and crew in flight. Common law principles of frustration of a contract become of paramount interest to this study, since contractual law principles of the United Kingdom and the United States are grounded in common law. Also important are the legislative measures adopted in the various civil codes of some European jurisdictions.

Contractual considerations

Frustration

Much has already been written on the increase of incidents pertaining to air rage[165] and it is therefore not our intent here to analyse the problem. Rather, our scope will be limited to examining the right of a carrier to refuse to take a passenger on board on the basis that he may be a threat to the safety of the flight concerned.

Generally, under common law, once a contract is concluded, that is, an offer has been made by one party and validly accepted by the other, it must be honoured. Therefore a passenger who holds a valid airline ticket having paid the full price required by the carrier is entitled to the air trip covered by the ticket he holds. Inevitably, however, there could be exceptions to this issue, when the law will be called upon to recognize that circumstances may cause an injustice to be done if strict enforcement of the contract is carried out. Called the doctrine of frustration, this area of contract law absolves parties to a contract from performance and obligations attendant upon an already concluded contract which would be deemed frustrated and accordingly brought to an end by operation of law.

The doctrine of frustration, when applied to a contract for carriage by air of a person, becomes relevant when it may be alleged that a change of circumstances after the conclusion of the contract has rendered it commercially or physically impossible to perform the contract. It is important to consider that, in the case of what is termed an 'absolute' contract, performance is mandatory, as obligations of parties are absolute. One has to consider in this instance where contract for carriage by air is 'absolute'.[166]

The real test, with regard to determining whether a contract of carriage by air is frustrated when the carrier has compelling reason to believe that the passenger concerned may not be able to discharge his obligation of not endangering the safety of flight, lies in the basic determination whether the passenger is guilty of making a radical change in his obligation. The test was first applied by the House of Lords in 1956, in the case of *Davis Contractors Ltd* v. *Fareham U.D.C.*[167] where the court held that, if the person who is called upon to discharge the obligation (in this case the airline passenger) would discharge it in a fundamentally or radically changed manner from the obligation originally undertaken, the contract would stand frustrated. Lord Radcliff observed:

> frustration occurs whenever the law recognizes that without default of either party a contractual obligation has become incapable of being performed because the circumstances in which performance is called for would render it a thing radically different from that which was undertaken by the contract.[168]

The inability of the person to perform his obligation as originally expected of him comes under the legal maxim *Non haec in foedera veni*, which means 'it was not this that I promised to do'.

This doctrine, when translated or applied to the instance of a passenger who, at the time of purchase of his airline ticket from the carrier gives an implied promise to the carrier that he would conduct himself with decorum during the flight, but appears for the flight grossly intoxicated or drugged and intimidates the staff at the check-in counter prior to boarding, would be a valid legal consideration in support of the carrier considering that the contract of carriage stood frustrated. In a well researched and meticulously documented study, Angela Dahlberg refers to the 'environmental stress model' which reveals that alcohol consumption during drug dependencies, mental instability, gambling losses, special charter groups and sports teams, seasonal workers and other types of group travel as well as certain exigencies that involve operational hazards such as delays in departure may lead to disturbances in flight.[169]

The House of Lords in the *Davis Contractors* case stressed that if the contract entered into by the parties was wide enough to apply to the new situation then the contract would remain valid. However, in its true construction, if it was not wide enough to apply to changed exigencies, it was at an end.[170] Of course, a precondition to this determination was that the first step towards arriving at a conclusion as to whether there were changed circumstances was to assess and construe the terms of the contract which should then be read in the light of the circumstances in which the contract was formed. The purchase of the air ticket by a passenger, in this context, although concluding the contract between carrier and passenger, would entail an understanding, whether explicitly stated in the contract document (the passenger ticket) or implicitly understood between the parties, that the passenger be in a fit and appropriate condition to undertake air travel under the contract of carriage. A key consideration, therefore, in frustration is that the court will construe that a contract is frustrated on the basis of the question as to whether the ultimate situation was within the scope of the contract concerned. Of course it has now been determined that whether a supervening event would prove to frustrate a contract or not would essentially be a matter of degree,[171] and ascertained in accordance with 'mercantile usage and the understanding of mercantile men'.[172]

The non-performance of a contract of carriage by a passenger owing to his incapacity to travel in the manner required is analogous to a contract of employment being frustrated because of an employee's incapacity to work. In this context a passenger who is refused carriage by air by an airline should be in a position where his inability to travel would radically reflect a deviation from the expectations of the contract.[173] Assuming that in almost every case where an air carrier may consider a contract of carriage frustrated owing to 'the passenger' being unable to undertake travel without jeopardizing the flight, it is inevitably the duty of the airline to prove that frustration is self-induced by the passenger. This devolution of responsibility on the carrier in discharging the burden of proof has been judicially recognized in the 1947 case of *Joseph Constantine SS Line* v. *Imperial Smelting Corp. Ltd*,[174] and later endorsed in 1983.[175] This principle is particularly relevant if the passenger concerned decides to sue the airline for breach of contract.

Clearly, the passenger incapacitated or unable to undertake travel in the manner envisioned in the contract of carriage cannot rely on self-induced frustration. In the 1987 case of *F. C. Shepart & Co.* v. *Jerrom*,[176] the court held that the party rendered unable to perform his part of the obligations under a contract cannot initiate a claim on the basis of frustration. Clearly, this principle is linked to the expectations of the parties at the time of formation and conclusion of the contract. This would be on the assumption that an implied understanding or term could be imputed to the parties that they would perform the contract in a manner so as not to jeopardize the interest of either party.

Prospective frustration

Largely, the refusal by an air carrier to carry a potentially unruly passenger will involve the doctrine known as 'prospective frustration' where the carrier concerned may claim that the contract of carriage has been discharged before there actually has been any interference with performance. The carrier's claim could be predicated on the ground that supervening events (such as the passenger's state of intoxication or cantankerous attitude) show that there is a high probability that there will be an interference regarding the passenger's performing his part of the obligation under the contract of carriage. In the 1914 case of *Embiricos* v. *Sydney Reid & Co.*,[177] which involved one party to the contract considering a shipping contract as having been frustrated in the anticipation that a prevailing war situation might effectively preclude the contract from being performed, although it turned out that no such circumstances prevailed, the court held that the charterer concerned was justified in considering the prospect of frustration.

The principle of prospective frustration is based on the reasoning that the exigencies are of such nature that a decision on their probable effect on the contract can be taken as soon as they occur. The principle has to be applied with caution, however, as one incident may not necessarily provide sufficient justification to the air carrier to consider refusing carriage. In a 1982 case,[178] which involved a strike by dock workers which was considered as adversely affecting the performance of a charter party agreement, the court held that the contract was not frustrated at once – as soon as the strike began. Rather, it was the court's view that it was necessary to wait upon further events that would lead a reasonable person to conclude that continued conduct would probably interfere fundamentally with performance.

The underlying principle behind the airline passenger's potential conduct while on board is that the doctrine of frustration would most certainly not protect the passenger whose own conduct would be tantamount to breach of contract. In other words, a person cannot rely on self-induced frustration to will that a contract is frustrated when he is responsible for the conduct that led to frustration. In the 1964 case of *The Eugenia*,[179] the court held that a charterer who was in breach of contract would not order a ship into a war zone with the intention of claiming consequent detention of that ship as a ground of frustration.

Legislation

European legislation

Usually, in contracts of carriage by air the price of the airline ticket is paid by the buyer prior to carriage. Therefore the question arises as to whether the passenger may claim the price of the fare if he is refused carriage by the carrier for self-induced frustration. It is arguable that, in self-induced frustration, the carrier need not be called upon to pay back monies payed by the passenger if the carrier can show that the seat allocated to the passenger could not have been sold at the last moment when the passenger's condition or threat posed by him was disclosed, thus causing loss to the airline. In the United Kingdom, the Law Reform (Frustrated Contracts) Act, 1943 provides that money already paid under the contract is recoverable, while money due ceases to be.[180] However, while the carrier will have to prove that it had compelling reasons to refuse carriage to a passenger, in the ultimate analysis, the court will have to decide on the merits of each case.[181]

Under Danish law, Article 36 of the *Contract Act* admits of a doctrine called 'failed assumptions' when a contract may be declared void if one party is aware that the other's promise was predicated upon a fundamental assumption, such as that a person will be carried in an aircraft upon contract only if that person is in a fit state to travel without endangering the safety of the aircraft. However, a seller of an airline ticket under this law will only be exonerated of his obligation to carry a person if the supervening events are of an extraordinary nature and beyond normal commercial expectation. Danish legal criteria under the Contract Act are more flexible than English law principles, in that Danish law considers as valid good faith of the parties to the contract, fair dealing and the test of reasonableness. Swedish law is similar to Danish law in this regard.

Dutch contract law on the subject of frustration is contained in Article 258, Book 6 of the Dutch Civil Code. Article 258 provides that a court may rescind or amend any contract in instances of unforeseen circumstances where certain supervening factors which are not provided for in the contract may emerge. In a 1984 case,[182] the Dutch courts decided that whether a contract was frustrated or remained valid would largely depend on the good faith principle on the basis that it would be unfair and unjust to compel performance of a contract in completely different circumstances which were not envisioned at the point of conclusion of a contract.

French law is entrenched in Article 1134 of the Civil Code which enunciates the general principle that private contracts cannot be altered unilaterally by a party to a contract or a court even if performance of the contract concerned is not consistent with the parties' expectations. This rule can usually be amended only in instances of *force majeure* (act of God) where a party's obligations can be suspended and the contract terminated. Of significant interest to a contract of carriage involving a potentially unruly passenger is an exemption to Article 1134 where courts hold public interest to be a paramount consideration.

With regard to German law, there is no principle of frustration as in the parlance of English law. German law, however, has the principle of fundamental change – *Wegfall der Geschäftsgrundlage* – when Article 242 of the Buerghesliches Gesetzbuch (BGB) applies the good faith principle to determine whether the parties to a contract can be found legally reprehensible in breaching the provisions of a contract.

Italian law on the subject is contained in Articles 1463–8 of the Italian Civil Code which plainly provide for termination of a contract which is impossible to perform. Obligations of parties in such instances are extinguished in the eyes of Italian law. On a comparative note, this is also the case in Spanish law which has no doctrine of frustration but, in accordance with Article 1105 of the Spanish Civil Code, requires a party to a contract to prove that unforeseen and inevitable circumstances (*Casa fortuito* or *Fuerza Major*) preclude the performance of a contract by either party.

United States legislation

The United States is arguably one of the most active jurisdictions in adopting recent legislation with regard to airline passengers carried into the territory of a state. On 19 November 2001, the president signed into law the Aviation and Transportation Security Act, which added a new requirement that each carrier, foreign and domestic, operating a passenger fight involving foreign air transportation into the United States must transmit to the US Customs, electronically and in advance of the arrival of the flight, a related passenger manifest and crew manifest containing certain specifically required information on such persons. Following this law, the Customs authorities of the United States published an interim rule[183] in the Federal Register on 31 December 2001 which requires air carriers, for each flight subject to the Aviation and Transportation Security Act, to transmit to Customs, by means of an electronic data interchange system approved by Customs, a passenger manifest and, by way of a separate transmission, using the same system, a crew manifest.

The passenger name record (PNR) information so required must electronically provide Customs with access to any and all PNR data elements concerning the identity and travel plans of the passenger to any flight in foreign air transportation to and from the United States, to the extent that the carrier in fact possesses the required data elements in its reservation system and/or departure control system.

Section 402 of the US Enhanced Border Security and Visa Entry Reform Act of 2002 amends section 231 of the Immigration and Nationality Act by providing that for each commercial vessel or aircraft transporting any person to any seaport or airport of the United States 'it shall be the duty of an appropriate official ... to provide ... manifest information about each passenger, crew member and other occupant transported on such vessel or aircraft prior to arrival at that port'. This new provision admits of the valid use of advance passenger information (API) to determine the admissibility of a person to the United States as well as the admissibility of a person as a passenger in an aircraft. The provision details the type of information that may be required. Section 231 is amended in (*f*) which states that no operator of any private or public carrier that is under a duty to provide information shall be granted papers until the requirements of the provision are complied with. Sub-section (*g*) prescribes penalties to be imposed on carriers who do not comply with the requirement of providing information to the authorities.

The significance of these requirements to the carrier's right in refusing a passenger's boarding is that such requirements may impose upon the carrier the added responsibility of being doubly vigilant as to the safety of flights performed by the carrier into the United States. It is therefore evident that the above legislation imposes an obligation on air carriers in the United States to be vigilant and aware of persons they have contracted to carry. This follows a sustained trend in the United States which ensures that abusive passengers who are likely to be a threat to airline employees or fellow passengers are prohibited from flying.[184] It is not only the US airlines which follow this rule. British Airways and Virgin Atlantic are reputed to have advocated a policy which bans unruly passengers from future flights.[185]

The role of the airline in screening or being vigilant of persons who may, if allowed on board, be a threat to the safety of the flight is inextricably linked to the state machinery and state authority in the United States. In other words, an airline which, with good reason and acting under colour of legislative requirement, rejects a person checking in for a flight, could be seen as a 'state actor'. In the 1973 case of *United States* v. *Davis*,[186] it was held that the United States was sufficiently linked to a search carried out by an airline employee of a passenger's bag, where the employee found a loaded revolver in the carry-on baggage of the passenger. There is also a federal statute[187] in the United States which gives legitimacy to an airline's act of refusing a passenger on its aircraft, based on anti-hijacking considerations.

However, the discretion afforded to airlines in refusing transportation to persons who contract with them, although a flexible one, is by no means absolute or unfettered. In the 1999 case of *Schaeffer* v. *Cavallero*,[188] the court held that an 'arbitrary and capricious' refusal on the part of an airline may lay it open to a claim by the person so refused for damages. In this case, the plaintiff passenger – an attorney – had loudly protested before take-off against a refusal by a member of the cabin crew to carry on board a second carry-on item of baggage belonging to the plaintiff. The trial court had originally held that 'the decision to exclude a vociferous but peaceful passenger who limits himself to complaining of the airline's treatment may in some circumstances constitute an abuse of [that] discretion'.[189]

Comments

The subject matter of this chapter involves considerations requiring a delicate balance between economic theory, contract law principles and social justice. The last consideration becomes compelling, particularly in the context of the events of 11 September 2001, where a person or persons who were passengers of aircraft used them as weapons of mass destruction. This was done through assault and violence perpetrated against the airline crew concerned. Whatever may be the terminology used in describing the perpetrators, in the original analysis, they were unruly passengers who might have been identified as potentially unruly if certain determinations were made either by the governmental authorities concerned or by airline authorities prior to boarding.

One of the issues that surface in regard to the admissibility of a person into an aircraft is the information now available to authorities in the form of advance passenger information (API). The question is whether an airline can use such information in refusing a person with a criminal record into its aircraft cabin, particularly if past records show that the offences that were committed by a person would lead the airline to believe that the person would constitute a threat to the safety of the flight. The issue as to whether an air carrier can refuse a potentially unruly passenger access to an aircraft, particularly in instances where the airline has compelling reason to fear for the safety of its passengers and property, has not been adjudicated so far in any jurisdiction. It is the author's submission that, should such an issue be addressed by the judiciary, rigid contractual principles might not always prevail, in view of the compelling social policy reasons which are now significant.

NOTES

1   *Oral Proceedings of Chicago Conference, 1944*, vol.1.
2   Convention on International Civil Aviation, signed at Chicago on 7 December 1944, ICAO Doc. 7300/8, 8th edn, 2000, hereafter referred to as the Chicago Convention.
3   Ibid., preamble.
4   C-Min 141/19, at p. 158.
5   Annex 13 to the Convention on International Civil Aviation, Aircraft Accident and Incident Investigation, 9th edn, July 2001.
6   Ibid., Chapter I, Definitions, Standard 2.1 states that, unless otherwise stated, the specifications in Annex 13 apply to activities following accidents and incidents wherever they occurred.
7   Security, Safeguarding International Civil Aviation Against Acts of Unlawful Interference, Annex 17, 6th edn, March 1997.
8   Underwriters subsequently reinstated partial coverage for war risks with drastically reduced limits at considerably higher premiums.
9   State Letter EC 2/6-01 dated 21 September 2001.
10 A33-20, Coordinated Approach in Providing Assistance in the Field of War Risk Insurance.
11 The London insurance market introduced the AVN 48B clause after the Israeli raid on Beirut Airport on 28 December 1968. This war and hijacking risk exclusion clause is now included in every aviation hull and liability policy. This clause covers a wide range of eventualities, including damage caused as a result of any malicious act or act of sabotage.
12 Jennifer Loven, Associated Press, 13 October 2001.
13 Stephen Labaton with Joseph B. Treaster, *The New York Times*, 13 October 2001.
14 BBC News, 10 October 2001.
15 Ibid.
16 Resolution ECAC/25-1 on Minimum Level of Insurance Cover for Passenger and Third Party Liability.
17 Daisuke Wakabayashi, Reuters, 5 October 2001.
18 Javier Mozzo, Reuters, 3 October 2001.
19 Reuters, 29 September 2001.
20 Reuters, 4 October 2001.
21 Ibid.
22 Reuters, 5 October 2001.
23 Air letter No. 14 835, 'World Aviation, Space & Defence Day by Day', 25 September 2001.
24 Air letter No. 14 835, 'World Aviation, Space & Defence Day by Day', 26 September 2001.
25 Convention on Damage Caused by Foreign Aircraft to Third Parties on the Surface, signed in Rome on 7 October 1952, ICAO Doc. 7364.
26 Convention for the Unification of Certain Rules for International Carriage by Air, done in Montreal on 28 May 1999, ICAO Doc. 9740.
27 See Article 15.4(*c*).
28 For more information on the use of the smart card, see R.I.R. Abeyratne, 'The Automated Screening of Passengers and the Smart Card – Emerging Legal Issues', *Air & Space Law*, XXIII(1), January 1998, 3–7.
29 *Supra*, note 2.
30 For details of the machine-readable passport and its development in the International Civil Aviation Organization, see R.I.R. Abeyratne, 'The Development of the Machine Readable Passport and Visa and the Legal Rights of the Data Subject', *Annals of Air & Space Law/Annales de Droit Aérien et Spatial*, XVII, pt II; 1992, 1–31.
31 See ICAO Assembly Documentation, *A33-WP/280*, Report on Agenda Item 28, at 28-1.

32 Ibid.
33 Ibid.
34 *ICAO's Policies on Charges for Airports and Air Navigation Services* (Doc. 9082/6) addresses security charges specifically in paragraph 29 and in Appendix 1. This policy was originally recommended by the 1981 Conference on Airport and Route Facility Economics, modified slightly by the 1991 Conference on Airport and Route Facility Management, and as such reaffirmed by the Conference on the Economics of Airports and Air Navigation Services (ANSConf 2000). In addition, the *Airport Economics Manual* (Doc. 9562) contains various guidance on financial and organizational aspects of airport security. This is covered generally, together with other issues, in different parts of the manual and specifically addressed in, for example, Chapter 1 – ICAO Policy on Airport Charges, para. 1.14; Chapter 2 – Organizational Structures of Airports, para. 2.46; Chapter 3 – Airport Financial Control, para. 3.39 and 3.72; Chapter 4 – Determining the Cost Basis for Charging Purposes, para. 4.53; and Chapter 5 – Charges on Air Traffic and Their Collection, para. 5.26 to 5.28.
35 See 'Ownership and Control, Report of the Think Tank', *World Aviation Regulatory Monitor*, Geneva, 7 September 2000, prepared by Peter van Fenema, IATA, Government and Industry Affairs Department, p. 4.
36 Ibid.
37 49 U.S.C. § 40102 (a) (15) 1994.
38 *Supra*, note 2. The Convention came into force only on 4 April 1947.
39 Article 1 of the Chicago Convention provides that the contracting states recognize that every state has complete and exclusive sovereignty over airspace above its territory.
40 Preamble to the Chicago Convention, *supra*, note 1.
41 The Conference on International Civil Aviation, which was held in Chicago from 1 November to 7 December 1944, was the forum which drafted the provisions of the Chicago Convention. See United States Department of State, *Proceedings of the International Civil Aviation Conference, Chicago, Illinois, November 1–December 7 1944*, Vols I & II (Washington, DC: US Government Printing Office, 1948).
42 Michael Milde, 'The Chicago Convention – *Are Major Amendments Necessary or Desirable 50 Years Later?*', *Annals of Air & Space Law*, XIX, Part I, 1994, p.403.
43 See Repertory Guide to the Convention on International Civil Aviation, 2nd edn, 1977, Preamble - 1. This subject was also addressed at a later session of the Assembly when the Assembly, at its 18th Session, adopted Resolution A18-4 (Measures to be taken in pursuance of Resolutions 2555 and 2704 of the United Nations General Assembly in Relation to South Africa).
44 The Danish minister in Washington and the Thai Minister in Washington.
45 *Proceedings of the International Civil Aviation Conference*, Chicago, *supra*, note 41, vol. I, p. 11.
46 Ibid., p. 12.
47 Michael Milde, 'The Chicago Convention – After Forty Years', *Annals of Air & Space Law*, 1984, IX, p. 130.
48 *Proceedings of the International Civil Aviation Conference*, *supra*, note 41, pp. 42–3.
49 Ibid., 43.
50 Ibid., at 55.
51 Ibid., 56.
52 Ibid., 57.
53 Ibid., 61.
54 Ibid., 65.
55 Ibid., 69.
56 Ibid., 76.
57 Ibid., 82.

58 Convention on International Civil Aviation, 7 December 1944, 15 UNTS 295; ICAO Doc. 7300/6, Article 1.

59 For a discussion of the legal foundation of sovereignty and air traffic rights, see R.I.R. Abeyratne, 'The Air Traffic Rights Debate – A Legal Study', *Annals of Air & Space Law*, XVIII-I (1993), p. 16. See also, by the same author, 'The Philosophy of Air Law', *American Journal of Jurisprudence*, 37, 1992, 135–44.

60 Convention Relating to the Regulation of Aerial Navigation, dated 13 October 1919, Article 1.

61 Ibid., Article 5.

62 Charter of the United Nations and Statute of the International Court of Justice, Department of Public Information, United Nations, New York, DPI/511 - 40108 (3-90), 100M at 1.

63 Ibid., at 3.

64 On 17 November 1989, the United Nations General Assembly adopted Resolution 44/23 which declared that the period 1990–1999 be designated as the United Nations Decade of International Law (the full text of Resolution 44/23 is annexed as Appendix 1 at the end of the text). The main purposes of the decade have been identified inter alia as
(a) the promotion of the acceptance of the principles of international law and respect therefor;
(b) the promotion of the means and methods for the peaceful settlement of disputes between states, including resort to the international Court of Justice with full respect therefor;
(c) the full encouragement of the progressive development of international law and its codification;
(d) the encouragement of the teaching, studying, dissemination and wider appreciation of international law.

65 Ibid., Chapter 1, Article 1(3).

66 Ibid., Chapter 4, Article 11.

67 Convention for the Suppression of Unlawful Seizure of Aircraft, the Hague, 16 December 1970, hereafter referred to as the Hague Convention.

68 Ibid., Article 1(*a*).

69 Ibid., Article 1(*b*).

70 See S. Shubber, 'Aircraft Hijacking Under the Hague Convention 1970 – A New Regime?', *International and Comp. Law Quarterly*, 1973, 692. See also the Report of the Legal Committee, ICAO, 17th Session, ICAO Doc. 8877-LC/161 p. 1, para 4.

71 Hague Convention, *supra*, note 67, Article 3, para. 1.

72 Hereafter referred to as the Montreal Convention.

73 Montreal Convention, Article 1.

74 Ibid.

75 State of the United States Airline Industry, 'A Report on Recent Trends for United States Carriers', Air Transport Association, 2002, Statement by Carol B. Hallett, President and CEO, ATA.

76 S/RES/1269 (1999), 19 October 1999.

77 Charter of the United Nations and Statute of the International Court of Justice, United Nations, New York.

78 Draft Articles on Responsibility of States for Internationally Wrongful Acts, Adopted by the International Law Commission (53rd Session, 2001).

79 Ibid., Article 21

80 Ibid., Article 36.

81 'Draft Code of Crimes Against the Peace and Security of Mankind, International Law Commission Report', 1996, Chapter II, Article 2.

82 Rome Statute of the International Criminal Court, Article 8.2 (*b*) (ii), (V) and (XX).

83 Ibid., Article 8.2(*b*) (XXIV).
84 G. Shultz, 'Low-Intensity Warfare: The Challenge of Ambiguity', Address to the National Defense University, Washington, DC, 15 January 1986, reproduced in *International Legal Materials*, 25 (1986), p. 206.
85 (1986) *I.C.J. Rep.* 14.
86 Annex 9, 'Facilitation', 10th edn, April 1997, Chapter 8, C, Standard 8.8, note 1.
87 *Charter of the United Nations and Statute of the International Court of Justice*, United Nations: New York, Article 1.3.
88 Ibid., Chapter VII, Articles 39, 41 and 42.
89 Ibid., Article 42.
90 S/RES/794 (1992), 3 December 1992.
91 S/RES/770 (1992), 13 August 1992.
92 See also the earlier Security Council Resolution 688 (1991), 5 April 1991, whereby the Security Council expressed grave concern at the repression of the Iraqi civilian population in parts of Iraq and insisted that Iraq allow immediate access by international humanitarian organizations to all parts of Iraq.
93 'Geneva Conventions for the Amelioration of the Wounded and Sick in Armed Forces in the Field', *Geneva Conventions of August 12 1949*, Geneva, International Committee of the Red Cross, 1970, Article 36.
94 Ibid., Article 37.
95 *Official Records of the Diplomatic Conference on the Reaffirmation and Development of International Humanitarian Law Applicable in Armed Conflicts*, Geneva (1974–7) Volume 1; Federal Political Department, Berne (1978) p. 135.
96 As one delegate remarked at the conference: 'Apart from the fear that the safety of medical aircraft could not be assured against attack from distances which exceeded the range of recognition of the distinctive emblem, an important factor in limitations on the protection of medical aircraft ... was the concern felt over the security threat posed by possible abuses of protected status.' See *Official Records of the Diplomatic Conference*, *supra*, note 95, p. 137.
97 Ibid., Article 28(1).
98 Article 8(*f*) defines medical transportation as a conveyance by land, water or air of the wounded, sick, shipwrecked, medical personnel, religious personnel, medical equipment or medical supplies protected by the Geneva Conventions and the Protocol.
99 Article 28(2).
100 Article 28(3).
101 Article 29(3).
102 Resolution XXVI, sub-para. (5), 'Declaration of Principles for International Humanitarian Relief to Civilian Populations in Disaster Situations, XXIst International Conference of the Red Cross, Istanbul, 1969', *International Red Cross Handbook*, 12th edn, International Committee of the Red Cross, Geneva: Martinus Nijhoff, 1987, p. 661.
103 Resolution 2675 (XXV) of the United Nations, Principle 8 wherein the United Nations declared: 'The provision of international relief to civilian populations is in conformity with the humanitarian principles of the Charter of the United Nations, the Universal Declaration of Human Rights and other international instruments in the field of human rights. The Declaration of Principles for International Humanitarian Relief to the Civilian Population Disaster Situations, as laid down in Resolution XXVI adopted by the twenty-first International Conference of the Red Cross, shall apply in situations of armed conflict, and all parties to a conflict should make every effort to facilitate this application.'
104 Universal Declaration of Human Rights, United Nations Department of Public Information, Article 3.
105 Ibid., Article 25.

106 Convention on International Civil Aviation, 1944 (Chicago Convention), ICAO Doc. 7300/6, 6th edn, 1980, Article 1.
107 Multilateral Agreement On Commercial Rights of Non-Scheduled Air Services In Europe, signed at Paris on 30 April 1956. See *Selected International Agreements Relating to Air Law*, ed. Gabriel Weishaupt, London: Butterworths, 1979, p. 409.
108 Ibid., Articles 1(*a*) and (*b*) and 2.1(*a*).
109 *Supra*, Annex 1.3.
110 Fernando R. Teson, *Humanitarian Intervention: An Inquiry into Law and Morality*, Dobbs Ferry, New York: Transnational Publishers, 1956, p. 5.
111 1949, *I.C.J. Rep.*, at 4.
112 1970, *I.C.J. Rep.*, at 5.
113 Ibid., paras 85–7.
114 *Military and Paramilitary Activities in and Against Nicaragua (Nicaragua v. US)* Merits, 1986, *I.C.J. Rep.*, p. 14.
115 Ibid., para. 242.
116 Ibid., para. 246.
117 Ibid., para. 199.
118 'Convention Relating to the Recognition of Aerial Navigation', dated 13 October 1919.
119 Ibid., Article 1.
120 Ibid., Article 2.
121 Ibid., Article 3.
122 Chicago Convention, Article 1.
123 Ibid., Article 2.
124 Ibid., Article 9(*b*).
125 Bin Cheng, *The Law of International Air Transport*, London: Stevens and Sons, 1962, p. 3.
126 Shawcross and Beaumont, *Air Law*, London: Butterworths, 1977, p. 15.
127 Ibid.
128 D. Goedhuis, *Idea and Interests in International Aviation*, (1947) quoted in Z. Joseph Gertler, 'Order in the Air and the Problem of Real and False Options', *Annals of Air & Space Law*, IV, 1979 p. 100.
129 Ibid.
130 O.J. Lissitzyn, *International Air Transport and National Policy*, Boston: Harvard University Press, 1983, p. 365.
131 Hereafter referred to as PICAO. See Interim Agreement on International Civil Aviation, for signature at Chicago, 7 December 1944, Article 3. Also in L. Hudson, *International Legislation*, vol. IX, New York: National University Press, 1942–5, p. 159.
132 Ibid., Article 1, Section 4. It is interesting to note that PICAO was established as a provisional organization of a technical and advisory nature for the purpose of collaboration in the field international civil aviation. See Article 1, Section 1.
133 *Oral Proceedings of the Chicago Conference*, vol. 1, 1944.
134 Interim Agreement, Section 6.4.*b*(1).
135 Ibid., Section 6.4.*b*(6). See also T. Buergenthal, *Law Making in the International Civil Aviation Organization*, 1969, p. 4, where the author states that PICAO's functions were merely advisory, which precludes any imputation of legislative or quasi-legislative character to its Interim Council.
136 See note 133.
137 Interim Agreement, Article III, Section 6(*i*).
138 Schenkman, *supra*, 160.
139 See statement of R. Kidron, Israeli Head Delegate, Statement of the Second Plenary Meeting of the Seventh Assembly on 17 June, 1953, reported in ICAO *Monthly Bulletin*, August–October 1953, p. 8.

140 Article 84.
141 A. Hingorani, 'Dispute Settlement in International Civil Aviation', *Arb. J.*, 14, p. 16 (1959). See also *Rules of Procedure for the Council*, 5th edn, 1980, Article 14.
142 Schenkman, *supra*, p. 162.
143 Article 85.
144 Rules of Procedure for the Council. Section IV, Rule 24(*e*). Also Article 54(*n*) stipulates that one of the mandatory functions of the Council is to consider any matter relating to the Convention which any contracting state refers to it.
145 Rules of Procedure for the Council, Section IV, Rule 24(*f*). The two additional multilateral agreements stemming from the Convention and providing for the exchange of traffic rights – the Air Services Transit Agreement and the Air Transport Agreement – also contain provisions that empower the ICAO Council to hear disputes and 'make appropriate findings and recommendations'. See Air Services Transit Agreement, Article 11, Section 1, and the Air Transport Agreement, Article IV, Section 2.
146 Rules for the Settlement of Differences, ICAO Doc. 7782/2 (2nd edn, 1975).
147 Ibid., Article 14(*a*).
148 Buergenthal, *supra*, note 135, p. 136.
149 Paul Stephen Dempsey, *supra*, p. 295.
150 *Nicaragua* v *US*, *supra*, para. 91.
151 *Assembly Resolutions in Force* (as of 5 October 2001), ICAO Doc. 9790, at p.VII-1. Also of general interest is UN General Assembly Resolution 56/88, 'Measures to Eliminate International Terrorism', adopted at the Fifty-Sixth Session of the United Nations, which calls upon states to take every possible measure in eliminating international terrorism. See A/RES/56/88, 24 January 2002.
152 Transport and Telecommunications Council, Luxemburg, 16 October 2001
153 Jane Garvey, Administrator FAA, 'The New World of Aviation', National Press Club, Washington, DC, 17 October 2001.
154 Ibid., p. 2.
155 Department of Transportation, 'Meeting the Airport Security Challenge', Report of the Secretary's Rapid Response Team on Airport Security, 1 October 2001.
156 ICAO News Release, PIO 02/2002.
157 For detailed information on the proposed International Financial Facility for Aviation Safety, see, Ruwantissa I.R. Abeyratne, 'Funding an International Financial Facility for Aviation Safety', *The Journal of World Investment*, 1(2), December 2000, pp. 383–407.
158 Convention on Damage Caused by Foreign Aircraft to Third Parties on the Surface, signed at Rome on 7 October 1952, ICAO Doc. 7364.
159 Convention for the Unification of Certain Rules for International Carriage by Air, done at Montreal on 28 May 1999, ICAO Doc. 9740.
160 See Article 15.4(c).
161 Convention on International Civil Aviation, 8th edn, 2000, ICAO Doc. 7300/8.
162 Ibid., Article 44(a), (d) and (f).
163 Convention on International Civil Aviation, *supra*, note 161.
164 See Angela Dahlberg, *Air Rage, The Underestimated Safety Risk*, Aldershot: Ashgate, 2001 p. 2.
165 See Christian Giesecke, 'Unruly Passengers: The Existing Legal System and Proposed Improvements', *Annals of Air & Space Law*, 2001, XXVI, pp. 45–75. See also J. Balfour and O. Highly, 'Disruptive Passengers: The Civil Aviation (Amendment) Act 1996 Strikes Back', *Air & Space Law*, XXII, 1997, p. 194; P.T. Reiss, 'Increasing Incidence of Air Rage is Both an Aviation Security and Safety Issue', *ICAO Journal*, 53(10), december 1998, p.13; J. Huang, 'ICAO Study Group Examines the Legal Issues Related to Unruly Airline Passengers', *ICAO Journal*, 56(2), March 2001, p.18; S. Luckey, 'Air Rage', Airline Pilot, 69(8), September 2000, p. 18, F. Kahn, 'Air Rage

Syndrome', *Aviation Quarterly*, 4(3), 2000, p. 142. R.I.R. Abeyratne, 'Unruly Passengers – Legal, Regulatory and Jurisdictional Issues', *Air & Space Law*, XXIV, 1999, p. 50.

166 In *Paradine* v. *Jane* (1646) Aleyn 26, a lessee who claimed that he was unable to pay rent under his lease, due to being prevented from obtaining certain income from his property that would have been used to pay the rent, was nonetheless held liable, on the ground that, 'where the law creates a duty or charge and the party is disabled to perform it and hath no remedy over, there the law will excuse him ... but where the party of his own creates a duty or charge upon himself, he is bound to make good his promise'. This principle was upheld in *Brown* v. *Royal Insurance Society* (1859) 1 E & E 853.

167 (1956) A.C. 696.

168 Ibid., at 729.

169 Angela Dahlberg, *supra*, p. 5. Ms Dahlberg quotes Baum, Singer and Baum (1981) who developed the 'environment stress model' which offers a framework for the relationships between human environment and human behaviours. See Dahlberg, *supra*.

170 *Per* Lord Reid, *supra*, p. 721. In 1980 and 1981, the House of Lords in two cases expressly upheld the *Davis Contractors* decision and its formulation of the test for frustration. See *National Carriers Ltd* v *Panalpina (Northern) Ltd* (1981) 2 W.L.R 45 and *Pioneer Shipping Ltd* v. *B.T.P. Tioxide Ltd* (1981) 3 W.L.R. 292.

171 *Tsakiroglou & Co. Ltd.* v. *Noblee Thorl GmbH* (1962) A.C. 93 at 118.

172 Ibid., p. 124.

173 *Marshall* v. *Harland & Wolff Ltd.* (1972) 1 W.L.R. 899. Also *Hebden* v. *Forsey & Son* (1973) 1 C.R 607; *Hart* v. *A.R. Marshall and Sons (Bulwell) Ltd* (1977) 1 W.L.R. 1067.

174 (1942) A.C. 154.

175 *The Torenia* (1983) – 2 *Lloyd's Rep.* 210 at 216.

176 (1987) Q.B. 301.

177 (1914) 3 K.B. 45

178 *The Nema* (1982) A.C. 724

179 (1964) 2 Q.B. 226.

180 Section 1.

181 *Gamarco* v. *I.C.M.* (1995) *The Times*, 3 May 1995, at 12:23.

182 *National Volksbank* v. *Helder*, NJ 1984, p. 679. See also the 1978 case of *Re Algemeen Ziekenfonds*, NJ 1978, p. 156.

183 66 FR 67482.

184 'Problem Airline Passengers; Limiting Carry on Baggage Before the Subcommittee on Aviation', 11 June 1998, quoted in William Mann, 'All the Air Rage: Legal Implications Surrounding Airline and Government Bans on Unruly Passengers in the Sky', *Journal of Air Law and Commerce*, 65(4), Fall 2000, p. 863.

185 'World News Roundup', *Aviation Wk. & Space Tech.*, 9 November 1998, p. 31.

186 482 F. 2d. 893 (9th Cir. 1973). This case must be distinguished from the decision in *United States* v. *Ogden*, 485 F. 2d. 536, at 538 (9th Cir. 1973) where the court held that the colour of state authority or support will only be given to airline screening processes authorized by statute and not to those initiated by airline employees to satisfy their own curiosity.

187 49 U.S.C.S. 44902 (b).

188 54 F. Supp. 2d. 350 at 352 (S.D.N.Y. 1999).

189 29 F. Supp. 2d. 184 at 186 (S.D.N.Y. 1998).

Chapter 2

The Commercial Crisis

COMPETITION AND LIBERALIZATION

In addition to the continuing crisis it faces, the airline industry has also to face up to a dichotomy. On the one hand, while it has been prolifically international in terms of operations, the airline industry has been unobtrusively national with regard to matters of ownership and control of airlines and interests relating to market access. The latter, brought to bear by regulatory inhibition, which does not admit of an airline freely gaining access to markets by flying at will anywhere in the world, and prevailing restrictions as to who owns and controls an airline which bears the nationality of a state, has been increasingly viewed as overtly restrictive in an expanding air transport market. This has led to a gradual liberalization of market access as well as ownership and control in many parts of the world, opening the door to increasing competition between carriers required to cater to a rapidly expanding demand for air transport services. Of course, trends of liberalization and competition have necessitated open skies and common aviation areas being identified; liberalized air services agreements entered into; and legislation enacted, while dexterous commercial tools have been introduced to implement new thinking and circumvent antiquated and counterproductive commercial practices.

In view of the current exponential growth of air transport, in response to rapidly evolving trends of demand for capacity and services, and the innovative changes in commercial practice that have taken place in the air transport field over the past decade, the Council of the International Civil Aviation Organization (ICAO) decided on 28 February 2001 to convene the Organization's 5th Air Transport Conference (AT Conf/5), with the title 'Worldwide Air Transport Conference: Challenges and Opportunities of Liberalization', to be held from Monday 24 March to Saturday 29 March 2003. The decision was taken in the belief that the convening of a worldwide air transport conference would provide a global forum for ICAO and its contracting states to examine issues and policy options in the field of air transport regulation, to consider harmonization and evolution of the various regulatory regimes, to promote understanding of the concept of full liberalization and its impact (including the benefits and the drawbacks) and to provide policy guidance for safeguarded liberalization.

The objectives of the Conference will be to develop a framework for the progressive liberalization of international air transport, with safeguards to ensure fair competition, safety and security, and including measures to ensure the effective and sustained participation of developing countries. Given the interrelated nature of the various aspects of air transport activity, the Conference will cover all relevant contemporary regulatory issues including economic, safety and consumer issues. The Conference will be structured around three integral components: (1) examination of key regulatory issues; (2) review of a template air services agreement for liberalization; and (3) adoption of a declaration of global principles for international air transport.

Current trends in air transport

In 2000, world gross domestic product (GDP) grew by approximately 4·4 per cent in real terms. The industrialized countries showed a 4 per cent increase, with North America showing a robust 5·3 per cent growth and Europe achieving 3–5 per cent. Africa's economy achieved a 3·6 per cent growth within an overall growth for developing countries which was at 5·6 per cent. Asia and Pacific countries reflected a significant 6·7 per cent and South America and the Caribbean recovered to post a healthy 4·3 per cent GDP growth.[1]

The world trade volume in goods grew by approximately 10 per cent in 2000, which was the highest rate achieved over the decade and more than twice the rate achieved in 1999. International tourism trends showed a similar growth, doubling the increase in 1999 to 7·4 per cent.[2] Seven hundred million tourists travelled in 2000, spending approximately $745 billion in US dollars, posting an increase in travel and spending of 4·5 per cent over the previous year.[3]

In the air transport sector, the total scheduled traffic carried by airlines amounted to a total of 1647 million passengers and some 30·2 million tonnes of freight. This was an 8 per cent increase over 1999.[4] Countries continued to expand the international air transport network, by concluding with each other 73 bilateral air services agreements in 2000, compared to 67 in 1999. Over 70 per cent of these agreements showed a marked trend towards liberalization, with 17 'open skies' agreements concluded, within an overall figure of 83 such agreements concluded at the time of writing.

The winds of liberalization sweeping the globe were clearly seen during the year 2000, both regionally and on a bilateral basis. Heads of states of governments coming within the umbrella of the Organization for African Unity (OAU), who met in August 2000, endorsed a regional provisional aviation agreement reached in 1999 by the African transport ministers, formally called the Yamoussoukro II Decision. This agreement is calculated to bring about gradual liberalization of African skies by 2002. In the Asian continent, five members of the Asia Pacific Cooperation (APEC)[5] concluded a new 'Multilateral Agreement on the Liberalization of International Air Transportation' in November 2000. In Europe, the transport ministers of the European Council adopted, in December of the same year, an agreement on a new European Union (EU) treaty dealing with the institutional operations of an enlarged EU. This measure will include 12 additional states, ten of which are from Central and Eastern Europe. The European Commission, in its role of representing the EU, followed through on a proposal to negotiate with the United States for a Transatlantic Common Aviation Area (TCAA).

In August 2000, the Aeronautical Authorities Council of States of the South American region participating in the Fortaleza Agreement signed in 1997 by six countries in the region, set up a commission to further study trends in liberalization options. In September of the same year, representatives of the Caribbean

Community (CARICOM) and the United States met in Jamaica to exchange views on a possible regional 'open skies' agreement.

Future trends in air transport

It is forecast that the world economy will remain moderately stable and healthy in the near future, despite a slowdown in economic growth. In the short term, inflation may hold steady and inflation rates will probably decrease gradually. The continuing upward trend in fuel prices is likely to increase airline fixed costs and aviation will increasingly be defined in trade terms. Aviation will also be a strong candidate for trade liberalization, with a firm focus on services. A compelling factor in this overall picture will be increasing pressure on governments to facilitate transnational ownership of airlines. The other key issue will be aviation and the environment in the global scenario of air transport.[6]

All the above indicators incontrovertibly point to one central driver of future air transport – competition. The issue of competition will ensure the increasing influence of global alliances and partnerships between carriers as a key element in industry strategic development where 'core' groups of airlines will provide direction and focus. Airline management, geared towards competition, will be called upon to improve coordination, and provide integration and stability to the air transport industry, resulting in the inevitable corollary of cost reduction.

The outsourcing of non-core activities will continue among airlines, encouraging fledgling carriers to emerge in a liberalized market. Larger airlines will seek franchising and code-sharing agreements with other airlines to the farthest extent possible, and will not disregard the importance of creating low-cost subsidiaries when possible, while also looking to consolidate their services with other carriers. In the process, existing distinctions between scheduled and non-scheduled (charter) carriers will be minimalized. In terms of service distribution, airlines will invest in e-commerce, while at the same time concentrating as much as possible on selling their services directly on line.

As for regulation, there is a high probability of increasing governmental regulators on safety, security and environment, with heavy focus on the importance of slot allocation for trading services. The demand for aircraft will surge ahead, in keeping with the burgeoning demand for capacity and the compelling need to retire old aircraft for environmental purposes. Very likely, the needed aircraft and engine capacity will be financed by leasing. Organizations such as the EU, OECD and WTO, whose memberships comprise states, will be called upon to play a greater role in aviation-related matters, while states themselves will focus on regulating heavily on consumer rights, environmental protection, security, safety and competition.

Today's commercial competition has transcended the past era, where dominant markets protected their established market shares. Most mega commercial activity was then the purview of governmental control under instrumentalities of state which were mostly cumbersome bureaucracies at best. Perhaps the best analogy is the biggest commercial market – the United States – which had, until recently, extensively regulated larger commercial activities pertaining to energy, transport and telecommunications.

Airline alliances

Happily, over the past decade, commercial air carriers have broken the shackles of rigid regulation to form strategic alliances among themselves. These alliances have been formed in the realization that the performance of an airline can be affected by two factors: the average performance of all competitors in the airline industry; and whether the airline concerned is a superior or inferior performer in the industry. Michael Porter[7] encapsulates these two factors in the single premise that any business achieves superior profitability in its industry by attaining either higher prices or lower costs than rivals. Curiously, in the airline industry, it is the latter – lower costs – which has been the cornerstone of strategic alliances.

The reason for airlines banding together is to share an otherwise wasted market which is still regulated by bilateral governmental negotiations. This unfortunate state of affairs has been brought about by a lacuna in the Convention of International Civil Aviation[8] (Chicago Convention) which leaves the absolute prerogative of allowing air carriers to carry passengers, cargo and mail into and out of their territories to states.[9] This privilege has encouraged the protective instincts of states to ensure that their national carriers obtain optimum market share 'belonging' to them, based on a now antiquated belief that all passengers, cargo and mail destined to a particular state, or leaving that state, is the birthright of the national carrier of that state. This stifling phenomenon has encouraged airlines to think more strategically over the past two decades, resulting in the pursuit of improved operational effectiveness in their activities.

The seminal response of most strategic airlines to the interference of governments was to 'share' each other's resources, including air traffic rights, thus gaining access to what was disallowed under bilateral governmental agreement. Recently, airlines have become more aware than ever that they are becoming an increasingly capital-intensive industry and have a compelling need to reduce costs in order to survive. The end result has been an array of commercial arrangements between airlines: from statements of common interests to block space arrangements, code sharing and coordination of frequent flyer programmes, to name just a few.[10]

Arguably, the most spectacular strategic airline alliance so far is the 'Star' Alliance, which was launched in 1997 by Lufthansa, SAS, United Airlines, Thai Airways International and Air Canada. Brazilian carrier Varig joined later, and it was expected that Ansett Australia and Air New Zealand would join the alliance in 1999. Recently, Singapore Airlines signed a commercial agreement with SAS, one of the 'Star' Alliance members, which will bring Singapore Airlines inextricably close to the alliance itself.[11] It is evident that the carriers of North America, Europe and the Asia Pacific regions, which form the Star Alliance have skilfully manoeuvred their dominance of the regions they represent. The direction in which the alliance is heading, with the possible future membership of Japan's All Nippon Airways (ANA), is incontrovertibly to assert its presence in the burgeoning Asia Pacific market, in particular the Pacific Region.

The underlying philosophy of the airline alliances, typified by the 'Star' Alliance, is not so much an emphasis on the more effective use of resources such as labour, capital and national resources (which are inevitably important factors) but rather an overall reliance on the strategy of location, where the sharing of locations represented by the various airlines has enabled them to produce their goods and services in a consistent manner, thus achieving the status equivalent to a cartel, while still retaining their individual identities.

Airlines have developed both a corporate strategy and a competition strategy to cope with competition. These strategies are becoming increasingly complementary rather than being mutually exclusive, which they were at the inception of airline competition 50 years ago. As airlines began to compete with each other across the borders, they acquired the ability to locate themselves overseas, creating a compelling need for commercial airlines to be fully acquainted with locational strategy and competitive advantages of various locations. Very early in the game, giants such as PANAM and TWA began to realize that even the strongest company with an established position in the airline industry unthreatened by competition from new entrants or smaller airlines, would start losing business if they faced a better or lower-cost product. The threat of new entrants, the bargaining power of suppliers and customers and the superior quality or low cost of substitute products were arguably the underlying reasons for established airlines to begin experiencing a downturn in the 1960s, which was exacerbated through the 1970s and 1980s. These threats could not be effectively circumvented or overcome by the established carriers, partly because of the sustained circumscription of market entry imposed by Article 6 of the Chicago Convention.

The genesis of airline alliances therefore was a contrived symbiosis or coexistence between the new entrants or new competitors – who had the clout of resources but not the dimensions of a larger carrier – and the larger carrier itself who had an established product to offer. Together, these two types of carriers could eradicate such obstacles as product differentiation (which was a distinct disadvantage to carriers which did not have an established brand); capital requirements (which again was a disadvantage faced by a smaller carrier); economies of scale (which forced a smaller carrier to compete on a large scale); and government policy (which affected both types of carriers, particularly the larger carrier which had the resources to operate air services but not the market access to a given region).

Another type of commercial alliance is the 'mega' alliance referred to earlier in analogy typified by the 'Star' Alliance. The precursor to this type of alliance could have been the modest 'pool agreement' between two carriers operating third and fourth freedom traffic, that is, traffic purely originating and ending in each others' territories. The pool agreement was written into a bilateral air services agreement between two states in order to ensure equal enjoyment of market share between their carriers in the route between their states' territories. This notion gave rise to an extension of the principle of pooling, which was to share locational traffic on a fifth freedom, that is, traffic which is picked up at intermediate or beyond points on services between two states, and, more importantly, sixth freedom – traffic to which a carrier had no right but could operate under the air traffic rights of another carrier, through a commercial arrangement such as a code share agreement signed by and between the carriers.

Airline alliances, particularly code-sharing agreements, add destinations to a route network and offer more frequencies of service to customers. With such arrangements, an airline can add on flights using its code-sharing partner's flight entitlement and operate to additional destinations without adding any resources. Of course, such an arrangement would create a duopoly, depriving customers of the benefit of competition, pricing and so on if the airlines concerned were in competition on a given route. Code sharing not only affects passenger traffic, but influences the consolidation of cargo carriage as well, as was seen in the Swissair–Delta Airlines cargo alliance across the Atlantic.[12]

In Europe, the 'open skies' concept, introduced by the European Union, as legislator, in 1977 was meant to open competition between European carriers in Europe in order to offer competitive airline services to customers. However, this has not had the desired effect, owing largely to airlines forming alliances under the umbrella of the open skies legislation. In particular, the four alliances, headed by British Airways, Lufthansa, KLM and Swissair, have vigorously entered into alliances with smaller carriers under franchising agreements in order to gain access to markets they have not obtained in their air services agreements.

Franchising

One of the more recent marketing initiatives to emerge in the airline industry is franchising. In its contemporary business garb, franchising has permeated a wide spectrum of businesses, introducing a sophisticated business relationship between two parties, thereby creating a contractual relationship. The franchisor, who develops a unique and individual way of conducting business, permits the franchisee to make use of the franchisor's business name and use his business methods in the franchisee's business, subject to controls imposed by the franchisor.

The application of the principles of franchising fits in well with the modern exigencies of airline business, where the personality developed and projected by a highly successful airline has become of increasing importance to passengers, thus making an airline's image a marketable quantity. Some major airlines have indeed capitalized on this commercial possibility by developing much-vaunted and attractive consumer-based brand personalities and using them as key marketing tools towards attracting potential franchisees, from whom they derive independent income by selling their names and business methods.

A fundamental advantage offered by franchising is the attraction for airlines to allow them to protect and extend their brand to routes (which are otherwise commercially unviable) without actually operating air services to such routes. This is done by getting a franchisee to operate on such routes while using the name and livery of the franchisor, whereby the latter skilfully avoids the risk of capital investment but still derives income in the shelter of a franchise agreement.

One of the compelling reasons for franchising to emerge as a marketing tool in the airline industry, particularly in Europe, is the European air travel market's polarization between scheduled and unscheduled (charter carriers). European charter carriers have grown prolifically in the last two decades as a backlash to increasingly high scheduled fares. In 1996, it was reported that, in the United Kingdom alone, 14 million travellers used charter flights on their vacation.[13] The growing disparity between the fares of scheduled carriers and the low package fares offered by charter carriers has released in Europe the franchisee – hybrid carriers in the form of a compromise between scheduled and unscheduled carriage – where a small airline can offer competitive fares under the ever important brand name of a large, prestigious carrier. The 'franchised' flight therefore offers the travelling public a *via media*: of a comparatively low fare for a customized flight under the brand name of a large carrier.

The major concern caused by franchising is that major airlines use the services of smaller airlines to carry out franchise services by using a mix of franchise/code share agreements in order to obviate the necessity for operating on revenue-losing routes themselves, while retaining their presence on these routes through the franchisees' operations. The European Union has claimed that, by using franchising agreements in the above manner, major airlines have retained their unprofitable routes and also the valuable slots that go with such operations.[14]

The role of the World Trade Organization (WTO)

Perhaps the most significant development, both from a regulatory and industry point of view and from perspectives concerned with changes occurring in air transport, has been the increasing involvement of the WTO in air transport. In 2000, the WTO launched a review process of its General Agreement on Trade in Services (GATS), with a possible focus on expansion of the GATS Annex on Air Transport, notably on both 'soft' rights such as airport services and 'hard' rights such as air traffic rights. There has been an awareness in the world trade community, since trade negotiations within the General Agreement on Tariffs and Trade (GATT) decided in the early part of the last decade to exclude much of air services from the scope of the WTO rules governing services, trade and investment, that a review of the various elements of trade forming air services would be timely at the present time. Hence it is quite possible that, in the years to come, the trading world will see serious consideration being given to the US $1400 billion worth of trade generated by the air transport industry within the GATS.

Although the Air Transport Annex of GATS currently includes aircraft repair and maintenance; the selling and marketing of air services; and computer reservations systems, a certain ambivalence pervades the interpretation of inclusionary elements in the Annex and their application. This is evident in the fact that while only 30 to 35 WTO members have committed themselves to the first two activities, only five WTO members have committed themselves to participating in the Annex on computer reservations systems.

One reason for the lack of clarity that permeates the issue of market access to air transport services, particularly with regard to its relation to WTO, is the proliferation of misconceptions that tend to obfuscate public policy debates on the possible role of GATS in liberalizing air transport within the parameters of the Air Transport Annex. This ambivalence may partially be due to a lack of familiarity within the aviation community with the complex web of rules governing trade practices within the purview of WTO regulations and also due to the pervading protectionism that has been exhibited by nations irrespective of their resource bases when it came to market access.

The first misconception that has to be addressed is that which pertains to the general belief that inclusion of market access-related issues of air transport in the GATS would necessarily lead to liberalization. If air transport services are covered by the Annex, it would indeed remain a voluntary domestic decision of the state concerned and coverage under the GATS Annex would not imply deregulation or any attendant obligation to revise and modify existing regulatory regimes. A commitment to provide air transport services under the GATS Annex would essentially retain for the state concerned its pristine right to enforce regulations in force that bring to bear obligations governing safety, environmental protection and security. Furthermore, committing itself to a GATS-governed market access system would not impel a state to alter or in any manner derogate from entrenched principles regarding foreign ownership of airlines.

Another misconception associated with the GATS system is that it is a rigid, inflexible mechanism that would stultify individual regulatory reform within a state or inhibit a state from initiating its own legislation in trade-related issues such as safety, security and environmental protection. The GATS offers the air transport industry, through the respective states' mechanisms, the flexibility to make choices based on material interests.[15] The GATS would offer member states the right to select opportunities and times to make sector-specific market access decisions and national treatment commitments. The GATS admits of progressive liberalization, in accordance with differing levels of development of services. Given the exponential growth of the air transport industry, this system would effectively facilitate consistency between national initiatives towards progress and predatory practices associated with excessive competition.

There has been sustained interest in the world of commerce aimed at bringing international air services within the General Agreement on Trade in Services (GATS) under the umbrella of the General Agreement on Tariffs and Trade (GATT). At its 32nd Assembly in 1998, the ICAO Assembly adopted Resolution A 32-17, entitled 'Consolidated Statement of Continuing ICAO Policies in the Air Transport Field', which reaffirms, inter alia, ICAO's primary role in developing policy guidance on the regulation of international air transport.[16] This statement reaffirms the recognition that ICAO has actively promoted an understanding by all parties concerned of the provisions of the Chicago Convention and of ICAO's particular mandate and role in international air transport. The resolution also requests the World Trade Organization (WTO) and its member states to accord due consideration to the fact that ICAO has a constitutional responsibility to international air transport which could be discharged through the results of ICAO's World-wide Air Transport Conference and ICAO's continuing work on economic regulation of international air transport.[17]

There has been some debate in the aviation world on whether air services performed by commercial airlines – operating both scheduled and unscheduled flights – should be included in GATS or GATT.[18] GATS seeks to establish a multilateral framework of principles and rules for trade in services with a view to expansion of such trade under conditions of *transparency*,[19] national treatment[20] and *progressive liberalization*.[21] The fundamental principle of GATT is its Most Favoured Nation (MFN) Treatment clause[22] whereby each party to the agreement accords immediately and unconditionally to services and service providers of any other party, treatment no less favourable than that it accords to like services and service providers of any other country. These provisions reflect the basic philosophy of GATS and play a vital role in affecting the decision of the international community on whether or not air transport services should be brought under its purview. Other features of GATS which have attracted discussion in relation to air services are provisions relating to increasing participation of developing countries within GATS[23] and dispute settlement.[24]

The issue of trade in services in general was discussed in GATT's latest round of multilateral trade negotiations launched by ministers of GATT contracting states who met in September 1986 in Punta del Este, Uruguay. The Uruguay Round was the eigth round of multilateral trade negotiations held by GATT so far,[25] and, by far, the most complex. This round of negotiations was assisted by the Group of Negotiators on Services (GNS) which the GATT established in 1986 to follow the services negotiations. The GNS had drafted a detailed agreement comprising 35 articles and five annexes, with one of the annexes comprising provisions on air transport services. The Annex on Air Transport Services applies both to scheduled and unscheduled air services and generally excludes its application to: (a) air traffic rights covered by the Chicago Convention, including the five freedoms of the air[26] and bilateral air services agreements; and (b) directly related activities which would limit or affect the ability of parties to negotiate, grant or to receive traffic rights, or which would have the effect of limiting their exercise.[27]

Notwithstanding the above provisions, however, GATS applies, inter alia, to computer reservations systems in air transport; the selling or marketing of air transport services; and transactions in aircraft maintenance.[28] The proposition, that GATS would not apply to air traffic rights covered by the Chicago Convention but apply to the selling or marketing of air transport services, creates *in limine* a dichotomy that has to be resolved. Air traffic rights that result from the Chicago Convention's provisions are the tool with which the selling or marketing of air transport services are carried out and the two are inextricably linked to each other. Confusion is worse confounded by Article 1 of GATS which defines trade in services as, inter alia, the supply of a service from the territory of one party into the territory of another party. The application of this definition to the provision of air transport services by an air transport enterprise would lead one to the inexorable conclusion that the definition of trade in services provided in GATS refers implicitly to the exercise of air traffic rights – which are obtained by virtue of the Chicago Convention. The explicit exclusion of air traffic rights in GATS is therefore ambivalent.

For the present, the overall purpose of including air transport services in GATS seems to be to apply the broad principles of market access and the MFN philosophy to the selling or marketing of air traffic services. The purview of GATS in controlling air transport services would therefore be considered only in situations where air traffic rights are exercised multilaterally or plurilaterally. GATS would not apply in instances where states elect to use Article 6 of the Chicago Convention, which governs all bilateral air services agreements and provides that the permission of a grantor state is necessary for a commercial air transport enterprise to operate air services into or out of a state. In any event, the Annex on Air Transport Services to GATS does not reflect confidence in itself by providing, in Article 6 of the Annex, that the operation of the Annex shall be reviewed periodically or at least every five years.

There are two provisions in the Annex on Air Transport Services in GATS which are also worthy of mention. One is on the access to and use of publicly available services offered by a party on reasonable and non-discriminatory terms,[29] and the other is on dispute settlement procedures which could be invoked only where dispute settlement procedures provided for in bilateral air services agreements, or under the Chicago Convention itself, have been exhausted.[30]

The main strength of the GATT approach to air transport services lies in its commitment to liberalization within a defined time scale. The discipline of GATT in accomplishing its objectives also acts as a positive factor. In a general sense, GATT is viewed with favour by those who see some merit in its role as custodian and guide of air transport services, for two reasons:

a) the modern trend of aviation towards globalization, privatization and cross-border alliances and Computer Reservations Systems (CRS) conglomerates and the overall tendency of air transport operators to seek market access, have made bilateralism obsolete. The changing structure of international civil aviation needs to consider multilateralism, which is the ideal of GATT; and
b) the Uruguay Round, which intends to envelop air transport services in the GATT concept, advocates a process of gradual liberalization (firstly only of 'soft' rights), negotiated market access and an efficient dispute settlement system.[31]

Arguments against the GATT's role in air transport services are, however, more compelling, the most basic being that aviation issues must essentially come within the purview of an organization specializing in international civil aviation, such as ICAO. The strongest objection is aimed at the principles of GATT such as the unconditional MFN treatment philosophy which is calculated to lead to competitive imbalances between airlines, and the long and tedious process of GATT which would take some time to resolve disputes, whereas under the existing bilateral system more expeditious measures are available.[32] To overcome this problem, experts have suggested that GATT's MFN rule should apply only to 'soft' trading rights in aviation (such as ground handling, CRS systems and sales), and 'hard' rights should be included in a multilateral agreement outside GATT.[33] Kasper opposes the application of the MFN philosophy to air services:

> unconditional MFN would deprive air service negotiators of essential flexibility. Trade barriers in air services vary widely in form and impact across markets, forcing even liberal nations to discriminate when granting traffic rights in order to counteract the sometimes severe restraints their carriers encounter in foreign markets. Due to the nature of this non-tariff barriers and to the fact that they often arise in ancillary markets, a universal solution, such as the elimination of the ancillary restraints by all signatories, would be exceedingly difficult to negotiate and to enforce.
>
> Under these circumstances, adopting unconditional MFN would undermine the ability of governments to tailor packages of economic rights that offset the mix of restraints in particular foreign markets. It would be especially troubling for those markets characterised by a high degree of cooperation between the national airline and the government.[34]

There is also the disturbing thought that unlike a bilateral negotiation for air traffic rights, where two states can readily analyse the economic implications of sharing air traffic rights between points of the two states, the MFN principle would create a free-for-all, the consequences of which would not be capable of being economically assessed or controlled.

IATA has suggested that ICAO adopts GATT principles with regard to all aspects of the air services agreement except in the area of air traffic rights and frequency of operations of aircraft. This suggestion has been strongly resisted by the International Chamber of Commerce (ICC) which argues that the aviation field should retain its purity of having characteristics and attributes that are susceptible to negotiation, although air traffic rights should be negotiated under a more efficient system than the prevailing bilateral system. Kasper shares a compatible view:

> To achieve true liberalization in air services, a new approach will be required, one that focuses on securing agreement among a relatively small group of liberal trading partners willing to abide by a strict condition on a reasonably level playing field.[35]

Although GATS does not seek control over air traffic rights, it is appropriate to view this subject as a future consideration of the overall GATT philosophy. It is evident that the principles of GATT are inconsistent with the present legal regime that applies to air traffic rights. The Chicago Convention is the sole legal document that governs the principle of air traffic rights and explicitly recognizes the principles of state sovereignty in Article 1. The sovereignty of a state reserves for that state the right to control activities within its territory and, *a fortiori*, the Convention strengthens this concept by requiring that special permission of a state must be obtained for the operation of air services into and out of its territory by an air transport operator of another state.

The foregoing discussion reflects the fact that, ever since the question of commercial air traffic rights arose as a corollary to the principle of sovereignty as recognized in the Chicago Convention, air transport has been viewed as a social need, run on equality of opportunity that is not a mere theoretical concept but one that can be practically enjoyed by states.[36] To these qualities have been added the view of Wassenbergh, that state policy in civil aviation must protect the integrity and identity of the national society.[37] The Chicago Convention, in its Preamble, calls for cooperation between nations and peoples so that international air transport services may be established on the basis of equality of opportunity and operated soundly and economically. The Chicago Convention further charges ICAO with the task of ensuring the prevention of economic waste caused by unreasonable competition[38] and ensuring that the rights of contracting states are fully respected and that every contracting state has a fair opportunity to operate international airlines. The critical question therefore is whether multilateral liberalization of the bilateral air services agreement would preclude some states from having a fair opportunity to operate international airlines on an equal opportunity basis. It is only logical to conclude that the answer to the question of whether multilateralism should ultimately replace bilateralism would lie in a clear perception of what is meant by the term 'multilateralism' in this context, and whether multilateralism would interfere with the states' right to the practical enjoyment of fair and equal opportunity in the operation of air services.

The genesis of competition law in trade, and, therefore, of WTO rules on competition, may well lie the United Nations Conference on Trade and Development (UNCTAD), held in Havana in November 1947. This conference laid the ground for the International Trade Organization (ITO), the charter of which had two chapters relating to competition. Chapter III of the Charter of the International Trade Organization provided that no member shall impose unreasonable or unjustifiable impediments that would preclude other members from obtaining, on equitable terms, facilities for economic development. Chapter V, which provided for the elimination of restrictive business practices, requires that each member will take appropriate measures, individually or through collective involvement, to prevent business practices from affecting international trade, thereby leading to restrained competition, limited access to markets or fostered monopolistic practices.[40] The ITO competition rules were embellished by controls over price fixing and other forms of anti-competitive practices endemic to private enterprises. However, the functioning of ITO never attained fruition and these provisions remained academic. A second attempt was made by the United Nations Economic and Social Council (ECOSOC)[41] and this effort too was destined for failure. The third attempt, made by GATT in 1959, also failed to elicit a concrete proposal. Later, the Organization for Economic Cooperation and Development (OECD) established a system of exchange of information and a procedure for consultation of competition rules among enforcement authorities.

WTO was established on 1 January 1995 and will administer the new global trade rules, agreed in the Uruguay Round, which came into effect on the same day. These rules, which are the result of seven years of negotiations among member states of GATT, establish the rule of law in international trade – estimated at $5 trillion in 1995. The WTO involvement in world trade is estimated to raise the fiscal proportions of trade to $500 billion by the year 2005.[42] The WTO has a membership of more than 150 states and is far wider in scope than its predecessor, bringing into the multilateral trading system trade in services, intellectual property protection and investment. Unlike GATT – which was a provisional treaty serviced by an ad hoc secretariat, WTO is a full-fledged international organization in its own right and administers a unified package of agreements to which all member states are committed. In other words, it is an improved version of GATT and serves as an effective watchdog of international trade and a management consultant. Its economists are required to keep a finger on the pulse of the global economy and provide studies on the main trade issues of the world.

WTO considers that the following four fundamental factors are shaping the world economy: the broader integration of the world economy, the sharply different trends in the developed and developing countries, the spread of market-oriented reforms, and the end of the cold war.[43] On the subject of market-oriented reforms WTO believes:

> If there are no rules in trade then the resulting anarchy will inevitably lead to conflict. International norms not only ensure freedom for economic agents to operate in their commercial interest across national frontiers. They also enhance the freedom of govern-ments in their trade policy interventions, by defining the scope of actions permissible within the confines of international law. The behaviour of all governments becomes more predictable when all accept the rules of the game.[44]

Obviously, WTO believes that a coherent set of rules followed in conformity with the accepted norms of international law should govern competition. This does not necessarily mean that WTO is against free trade. It merely means that free trade has to be conducted according to accepted universal norms and these norms have been explicitly laid out in the WTO Agreement. The trade in services portion of the agreement carries specific rules of competition. One of the seminal principles of the agreement requires each member state to accord, immediately and unconditionally to services and service suppliers of any member, treatment no less favourable than that it accords to like services and service suppliers of any other country.[45] Called the most favoured nations treatment (MFN) clause, this provision *in limine* establishes common ground between trading partners and creates certain parameters of activity for partners to follow. The MFN clause is the cornerstone of the WTO principles and acts as the fundamental postulate on which other WTO competition rules are based.

Transparency is another concept which has been recognized for practical applicability in the WTO rules. Accordingly, each member is required to publish promptly and, except in emergency situations, at the latest by the time of their entry into force, all relevant measures of general application which pertain to or affect the operation of the agreement.[46] There is also the requirement of publication of international agreements pertaining to or affecting trade in services to which a member is a signatory.[47] Article XVII of the agreement lays down the principle of national treatment which requires each member to accord to services and service providers of any other member, in respect of all measures affecting the supply of services, treatment no less favourable than it accords to its own like services and service suppliers. This provision is effectively tied up with the principle of elimination of all discrimination from the applicability of the agreement, as reflected in Article V, achieving the dual goal of elimination of existing discriminatory measures and prohibition of new or more discriminatory measures.

The requirement for equality of treatment is also reflected in provisions related to market access, whereby the agreement requires, in Article XVI, treatment no less favourable from any member to others than that uniformly provided under WTO rules. It is claimed that, since the primary purpose of the WTO system is to achieve trade among members as liberally and fairly as possible while retaining the essence of non-discrimination in trade practices, the WTO system should guarantee a fair and equitable opportunity for market access by enterprises of members to the national markets of other members. This is done mainly through the removal of governmental barriers to the extent possible and the convergence of national regulatory regimes such as those which relate to intellectual property rights.

One of the most serious challenges faced by WTO in this regard is the claims by some states of 'unfair trade' by others, where the claimant states feel victimized by private business practices of enterprises of other states. The corollaries of anti-dumping is one such example, where the exporter is faced with the situation in which imports to his country are precluded by his country, with a view to compelling the consumption of the exporter's goods within the country of production. This practice often leads to price hiking and protectionism within a market. The WTO rules therefore strive for fair and equal opportunity in competition, in the same way the bilateral air services agreement requires.

One of the major considerations of the WTO is the perceived incompatibility between business practices of countries and uniform competition rules which are required to be enforced globally. There is an obvious link between business systems and corporate behaviour on the one hand, and competition rules (or the lack thereof) on the other. There is also probably a functional relationship between them in that competition rules partly reflect existing business systems and corporate behaviour (a regulatory system functions well only if it is fundamentally accepted). Also business systems and corporate behaviour often adjust to, and take advantage of, the possibilities opened by competition rules.

To that extent, the disparities between competition rules, on the basis that what is permitted in one state may be prohibited in another, may influence disparities in business systems and corporate behaviour and may constitute an impediment for enterprises which seek entry into another market. Some examples are cited below.

In the European Community where governmental barriers such as tariffs and import restrictions have been removed, competition policy measures play a vital role in ensuring that the common market operates without hindrance by private restrictive business practices. In the EC, the role of competition policy has increased dramatically with the progressive integration of the common market.

In the Structural Impediment Initiative (SII) negotiated between the United States government and the Japanese government in 1989–90, business customs and corporate behaviours were the major issues. The US government has claimed that restrictive business customs and corporate behaviour were the major impediments which restricted effective market access to the Japanese market by foreign enterprises. In accordance with the SII, both governments have agreed that an increase of competition rules in Japan would increase market access to the Japanese market by foreign enterprises by removing private restrictive business practices. A number of reforms of the Japanese Anti-monopoly Law resulted from this agreement, including an increase of administrative surcharge and criminal fine to be imposed on enterprises when they engage in cartels.[48] This functional relationship between competition rules and business systems and corporate behaviour, rooted as they are in cultural, economic and political traditions, may, however, often place limitations upon possible achievements attained by the applicability of partial harmonization of competition rules. Differences in business systems and corporate behaviour are generally wide-ranging and complex, and the application of competition rules may often fail to bridge the gap between the two elements. This notwithstanding, a vigorous enforcement of competition rules in trading nations may still be able to play a useful role in preparing common rules which could be made applicable to trading nations. The adoption of common rules of conduct for enterprises may well reduce undue imbalances in different business systems and could pave the way for enterprises to compete for roles in markets of trading states outside their own market place.

WTO should also take into consideration the fact that, as globalization of national economies is achieved through the removal of governmental barriers to trade such as tariffs and import restrictions, new trade issues may arise. One such issue is the possible incompatibility between different regulatory/business systems among trading states. Differences in domestic regulatory systems and in business customs and behaviours often emerge as barriers to transnational business activities. These differences may take the form of inconsistencies between technical standards, taxation, environmental protection measures, labour standards and other barriers which hamper enterprises seeking to engage in trans-boundary trade. Such differences obviously create disparity among the states concerned.

COMPETITION

Current trends and market access

Competition in global air transport presents unique strategic issues. Global industries, such as multinational air carrier alliances, are characterized by the presence of competitors operating worldwide from home bases in different countries. The governments concerned may have deep-rooted interests and objectives relating to employment and balance of payments including other factors that may not strictly be economic but are nonetheless of critical importance to competition among airlines. Therefore, airlines will be increasingly called upon to conduct stringent competitor analysis through examination of the relationships between individual air carriers and their governments. The home country's industrial policy must be well comprehended, particularly in terms of political considerations which may be related to such issues as purchases of aircraft and the exchange of market rights.

A global industry, such as air transport, is one in which commercial entities offering their services view competition as global and build strategies accordingly. Therefore it follows that competition involves a coordinated worldwide pattern of market positions, facilities and investments. Factors to be taken into account are overlap between competitors, geographic location of carriers and defensive investments in particular markets and locations so as not to let competitors gain advantages that can be factored into their overall global posture.[49]

Competition in the air transport industry is a complex process, as there is no consensus among airline economists as to the exact nature of the industry. The demand for air services, particularly in the context of the airline passenger, is a contrived demand emerging from other demands based on activities such as business and leisure. This calls for a certain segmentation in travel where, in business travel, the passenger does not usually pay for the travel himself, whereas in leisure travel it comes out of his own pocket. Therefore the leisure market calls for a different kind of competition, primarily based on the fare, whereas in business travel, although the fare is important, other considerations, such as facilities on board, may also play a considerable role in competition.[50]

Those supporting the retention of regulation argue that the very nature of air transport, being either naturally monopolistic or interdependently oligopolistic, calls for regulation in order that fares are not arbitrarily raised and remain competitive. Another theory in support of regulation is that some form of control should be exercised over 'mushroom' airlines that may sprout up to exploit a liberalized market, thus disturbing the existing balance of an integrated network. Of course, each route is a separate market in itself and would require separate consideration. Although principles of economics of scale may apply generally to airline competition, where a fact such as larger aircraft being more efficient than smaller aircraft would apply on a general basis, individual assumptions for different markets have caused the two major aircraft manufacturers, Boeing and Airbus Industrie, to concentrate on manufacturing aircraft with strengths in speed and capacity, respectively.

The main consideration, leading up to efforts by the international aviation community to achieve a deregulated global airline industry, is involved with the question as to whether free market principles can be applied globally to air transport. What needs to be considered is whether we are ready to accept the throwbacks as consequences of free market competition in air transport, particularly in losing national prestige projected by flag carriers. One of the corollaries to industry deregulation is the introduction of free market competition when companies switch from operative performance to competitive performance. Competition therefore emphasizes the need to focus on a company's performance in relation to its competitors'. This principle can be readily apply to various industries that have already been deregulated, such as the motor vehicle industry, chemical industry and information technology industry. The operative question is, 'are these good analogies for application to the air transport industry?' Whatever the answer to this question, if the deregulated domestic air transport industry of the United States were to be considered an analogy, one could say that a deregulated system in the United States, introduced in 1978, has led to a more efficient airline sysstem in the country.[51] Whatever the case may be, access to facilities in a competitive market is essential to attaining fluidity of market forces. In the air transport industry, this can be translated to mean that, if free markets do not exist in the supply of complementary facilities, there will be no positive impact of liberalization.[52] The complementary services in the supply of air transport are airport access, computer reservation systems and airport and air regulation services.

The International Chamber of Commerce (ICC), in a policy statement issued recently, expresses the view that the efficiency of air transport would be enhanced by creating more open markets and more flexibility with regard to foreign ownership. Given air transport's capability to facilitate economic activity, its liberalization would enable the sectors that make use of it to become non-efficient.[53] ICC is in favour of a freer exchange of air services throughout the world and is convinced that it is time to move beyond the existing bilateral system, towards a genuine multilateral liberalization of air transport.[54] Of course, liberalization would give way to competition, which in turn would impel airlines to pool their resources in order that they maximize on such assets as code sharing and airport slots. However, alliances do not necessarily mean lack of competition between partners. Airlines within alliances have to do their utmost to gain market access and keep their businesses alive. In order to do this, both private enterprises and the states in which these enterprises are entrenched have to be equally competitive.

Any agreement to bring in an aspect of trade within a liberalized framework is generally a proactive measure, which brings to bear the willingness and ability of the governments to face trading issues squarely in the eye. However, any agreement for trading benefits would be ineffective without the element of competition, both between enterprises and between states. The essential requisite for success in trading relations is competition, which in turn leads to national prosperity. A free trade agreement is merely the catalyst in the process.

Anti-competitive conduct and antitrust issues

The regulation of competition within the European Community is governed by the EC Treaty.[55] Two provisions in particular, Articles 81 and 82, contain principles which outlaw anti-competitive conduct. While the former prohibits the prevention, restriction or distortion of competition, the latter makes itself applicable against abuse by one or more undertakings of a dominant position within the market. While the former essentially contains provisions for agreements, decisions or practices with anti-competitive effects, the latter concerns itself with abuses of a dominant marketing position. The aim of these two provisions in particular is to preclude distortion of competition within the Common Market by supplementing the basic principles enshrined in Articles 81 and 82 with substance. The goals of the Treaty in general and Articles 85 and 86 in particular are to promote the free movement of services, goods, persons and capital whilst effectively obviating barriers to trade within the community. Both these provisions relate generally to all sectors of transport unless explicitly excluded by the Treaty provisions.[56]

Article 81 prohibits as incompatible such agreements as directly or indirectly fix purchase or selling prices or any other trading conditions; limit or control production, markets, technical development or investment; share markets or sources of supply; apply dissimilar conditions to equivalent transactions with other trading parties, thereby placing them at a competitive disadvantage; and make the conclusion of contracts subject to acceptance by other parties of supplementary obligations which, by their nature or according to commercial usage, have no connection with the subject of those contracts. These conditions are imposed on agreements between undertakings, which are defined as independent entities performing some economic or commercial activity.

Article 82 provides that any abuse by one or more undertakings of a dominant position within the Common Market or in a substantial part of it shall be prohibited as incompatible with the Common Market insofar as it may affect trade between member states. The Article prohibits direct or indirect imposition of unfair purchase or selling prices or unfair trading conditions; limitation of production, markets or technical development to the prejudice of consumers; application of dissimilar conditions to equivalent transactions with other trading parties, thereby placing them at a competitive disadvantage; and conclusion of contracts subject to acceptance by the other parties of supplementary obligations which, by their nature or according to commercial usage, have no connection with the subject of such contracts.

In implementing these two provisions, air carriers have to exercise caution in not assuming that purely in view of a bloc exemption on air transport in the Treaty that may pertain to a particular issue, a related practice would be exempt from the prohibitions contained in Articles 81 and 82. In the air transport section of the Treaty, it is abundantly clear that bloc exemptions may apply only if abuse of dominant position is not evident in a given transaction.[57] Articles 81 and 82 are independent and complementary provisions and any exemption under Article 81 will not necessarily render the provisions of Article 82 nugatory.[58] 'Dominant position' was defined in the 1979 decision of *Hoffman-La Roche* v. *Commission*[59] as a position of economic strength enjoyed by an undertaking which enables it to prevent effective competition being maintained on the relevant market by affording it the power to behave to an appreciable extent independently of its competitors, its customers and ultimately of its consumers. Such a position may necessarily preclude some competition except in monopoly or quasi-monopoly situations. There is every indication, from existing jurisprudence and EC practice, that an assessment on an abuse of dominant position would not be predicated upon one factor alone or a single characteristic but would rather be anchored on numerous factors such as market structure, barriers to entry and conduct of the business enterprise concerned.

In the United States, the term 'antitrust laws' encompasses federal and states legislation (statutes) which regulate competition with a view to wiping out unfair trade practices and preserving competition among sellers and buyers. Needless to say, antitrust laws apply equally to international air services, and are calculated to preclude both conduct and structural changes in business enterprises. A typical example of conduct coming under antitrust laws in the United States is a merger between competitors which would unduly limit competition. These laws are also meant to prevent producers or purchasers of goods from exercising a monopoly in imposing prices which significantly deviate from expected free market competition norms.

Antitrust legislation in the United States goes back to 1890, with the enactment of the Sherman Act which makes it criminally illegal for any contract, combination or conspiracy to be formed in restraint of trade. This all-encompassing provision prohibits price fixing, anti-discounting agreements, divisions of markets by pooling agreements and capacity agreements, and exchanges of information that can be considered as competitively sensitive. The Act also prohibits monopolies and conspiracy to monopolize in Section 2.

In 1914, the United States Congress legislated the Clayton Act, primarily to supplement the Sherman Act. The Clayton Act outlaws certain types of 'exclusive dealing' and 'tied sales' and prescribes standards for determining the legality of mergers and acquisitions. Both the Acts admit of compensation to persons injured in their trade or business up to three times the amount of their loss plus attorney fees. Courts have also permitted consumer class actions on antitrust activity, allowing for significant recovery of damages.

In its role as the sole international regulatory body in the field of air transport, the International Civil Aviation Organization has issued clear policy and guidance material on the avoidance or reduction of conflicts over the application of competition laws to international air transport. ICAO has issued these guidelines to address the conflicts that may arise between states which adopt policies, practices and laws relating to the promotion of competition and restraint of unfair competition within their territories. ICAO urges states to ensure that their competition laws, policies and practices, and any application thereof to international air transport, are compatible with their obligations under relevant international agreements.[60] Within this guideline, there is a strong recommendation for close consultation between states and all interested parties in order that uniformity in practice be achieved across borders to the maximum extent possible. Accordingly, when a state is adopting laws pertaining to competition, it is expected to give full consideration to views expressed by any other state or states whose interests in international air transport may be affected. States are urged to have full regard to principles of international comity, moderation and restraint. The guidelines also provide direction on dispute resolution and problem solving.

The regulation of air transport services lies within the purview of ICAO member states which maintains in its Legal Bureau a register of all bilateral air transport agreements. The bilateral air transport agreement usually includes a reciprocal agreement between states for their carriers to have fair and equal opportunity in operating air services between their territories without unduly affecting the air services operated by each other. Under a bilateral agreement, capacity offered by carriers must bear close relationship to the needs of the people using air transport.[61] These regulatory provisions have so far succeeded in protecting carriers of less developed states by obtaining for them fair and equal opportunity to operate air services in routes that are shared by more established carriers of wealthier nations.[62]

Since GATS cannot sustain air transport services within a bilateral framework, it now remains to be seen whether the aviation community would move in the future towards placing air traffic rights in a multilateral or plurilateral system. In such an eventuality, GATS would doubtless rejuvenate its efforts at seeking to include air transport services within its purview under liberalized market access and the MFN treatment clause. In this context, the role played by ICAO – the guardian and mentor of international civil aviation – becomes relevant.

ICAO has the mandate (under the Convention on International Civil Aviation signed in Chicago in 1944), experience and expertise in a wide range of air transport matters: technical, economic and legal. Issues of operating arrangements, market access, pricing and capacity for the designated airlines of each state are the subject of bilateral air transport agreements between states, except for arrangements within the European Economic Community for mutual relations between member states. International air transport is, in effect, conducted under an extensive network of some 3000 separate bilateral agreements or treaties. ICAO has taken the position that international air transport is an economic activity in which there is a strong national interest and involvement as well as a long established, comprehensive and detailed structure of standards, principles and operating arrangements.

ICAO believes it important to draw to the attention of GATS and its member states certain critical features of international air transport which are relevant to any present or future consideration of how air transport should be treated in the context of the trade in services negotiations. The main consideration that impels ICAO to maintain steadfastly its position as the guiding force behind air transport services is that it feels that bilateralism at the operating level has, over the decades, proved to be a flexible system which allows states to pursue their objectives, whether these be open and competitive or more protective or restrictive regimes for their airlines. ICAO strongly maintains that any external multilateral framework which sought general or limited application would need to recognize and be compatible with this existing structure of air transport.

Nevertheless, multilateralism in the form of a broad-based consensus on principles and guidance to states in the conduct of their air transport activities has enjoyed renewed interest in ICAO in recent years. While seeking to develop progressively positions and guidance to assist states in their regulatory/economic activities, ICAO recognizes the sovereignty of states in pursuing their own national air transport policies and objectives. ICAO's role in this sphere is therefore merely consultative and recommendatory, without being incompatible with liberalization in this sector. ICAO has also expressed its resolve to continue to cooperate with GATT and the GNS in its trade in services discussions in order that ICAO's views and concerns and the particular features of the international air transport sector are properly taken into account by GATT and the GNS.

The organization's position on the regulation of air transport services was formally adopted at its 7th Assembly, held in June/July 1953, where Assembly Resolution A 7-15 resolved that there was no prospect at the time of achieving a universal multilateral agreement, although ICAO acknowledged that the achievement of multilateralism in commercial rights remained an objective of the organization. This resolution is still in force and reflects ICAO's commitment to achieving an acceptable multilateral basis for air transport services.

Later, at its 26th Session in September/October 1986, the ICAO Assembly adopted Resolution A 26-14, which reaffirmed that ICAO was the multilateral body in the United Nations system competent to deal with international air transport, and urged contracting states which participated in any multilateral negotiations on trade in services where international air transport was included to ensure that their representatives were fully aware of potential conflicts with the existing legal system for the regulation of international air transport. The resolution also requested the ICAO Council to promote actively a full understanding by international bodies involved with trade in services of the role of ICAO in international air transport and the existing structure of international agreements regarding air transport. This resolution helped sensitize states and GATT regarding the air transport sector. Although this resolution is no longer in force, it reflects adequately ICAO's philosophy on the subject. In view of the significant recent and possible future developments in the trade in service negotiations, the question arises, however, as to whether this policy is fully adequate to continue to serve the interests of ICAO and international air transport over the next few years, or whether it requires reassessment and additional directives from the Assembly.

Assembly Resolution A26-14 gave guidance to states and the Council and expressed certain concerns, but it did not set out an organizational view on the inclusion of international air transport in a multilateral agreement on trade in services. A future session of the Assembly may consider developing such a view for transmission to GATT and the GNS as well as to contracting states. One possible view the Assembly might consider is that air transport should not be included in a services agreement. The adoption of such a position by ICAO could be grounded on two of the concerns found in Resolution A26-14. One is the organization's concern about ICAO's role as the United Nations specialized agency responsible in air transport matters. The other is the organization's concern for the integrity of the Chicago Convention principles and arrangements and the widespread system of bilateral air transport agreements that are a consequence of those principles.

Airlines are faced with the imminent prospect of the future realm of commercial aviation being controlled by a group of air carriers which may serve whole global regions and operated by a network of commercial and trade agreements. Regional carriers will be predominant, easing out niche carriers and small national carriers whose economics would be inadequate to compare their costs with the lower unit costs and joint ventures of a larger carrier. It is arguable that a perceived justification for 'open skies' or unlimited liberalization exists even today in the bilateral air services agreement between two countries, where *fair and equal opportunity to operate* air services is a sine qua non for both national carriers concerned. This has been reinterpreted to mean *fair and equal opportunity to compete* and, later still, *fair and equal opportunity to participate effectively* in international air transport as agreed.[63] Of course, there has been no universal acceptance of this evolution in interpretation, and carriers and states whose nationality such carriers bear have maintained their own positions tendentiously.

ICAO has suggested the following preferential measures for the consideration and possible use of its member states who are at a competitive disadvantage when faced with the mega trends of commercial aviation and market access:

a) the asymmetric liberalization of market access in a bilateral air transport relationship to give an air carrier of a developing country: more cities to serve; fifth freedom traffic rights[64] on sectors which are otherwise not normally granted; flexibility to operate unilateral services on a given route for a certain period of time; and the right to serve greater capacity for an agreed period of time;

b) more flexibility for air carriers of developing countries (than for their counterparts in developed countries) in changing capacity between routes in a bilateral agreement situation; code sharing to markets of interest to them; and changing gauge (aircraft types) without restrictions;

c) the allowance of trial periods for carriers of developing countries to operate on liberal air service arrangements for an agreed time;

d) gradual introduction by developing countries (in order to ensure participation by their carriers) to more liberal market access agreements for longer periods of time than developed countries' air carriers;

e) use of liberalized arrangements at a quick pace by developing countries' carriers;

f) waiver of nationality requirement for ownership of carriers of developing countries on a subjective basis;

g) allowance for carriers of developing countries to use more modern aircraft through the use of liberal leasing agreements;

h) preferential treatment in regard to slot allocations at airports; and

i) more liberal forms for carriers of developing countries in arrangements for ground handling at airports, conversion of currency at their foreign offices and employment of foreign personnel with specialized skills.[65]

These proposed preferential measures are calculated to give air carriers of developing countries a 'head start' which would effectively ensure their continued participation in competition with other carriers for the operation of international air services. Furthermore, improved market access and operational flexibility are two benefits which are considered as direct corollaries to the measures proposed.

While the 'open skies' policy sounds economically expedient, its implementation would undoubtedly phase out smaller carriers who are now offering competition in air transport and a larger spectrum of air transport to the consumer. Lower fares, different types of services and varied in-flight service profiles are some of the features of the present system. It is desirable that a higher level of competitiveness prevail in the air transport industry and, to achieve this objective, preferential measures for carriers of developing countries would play a major role.

In addition to addressing the preferential measures proposed by ICAO, which would be of immense assistance to carriers of developing countries if implemented, it would be prudent for the international aviation and trading community to consider the larger issue of funding, whereby long-term low-interest loans could be made available to carriers of developing countries through such institutions as the World Bank and the International Monetary Fund. Some consideration could also be given to a balanced distribution of aircraft throughout the world, whereby developing countries could have access to aircraft which have been discarded by their more affluent counterparts. An equitable system of leasing these aircraft is a possibility that could be considered in this regard.

The exemption of aircraft operated by carriers of developing countries from technological standards (to the extent possible) which may apply to modern aircraft is another useful tool which could be addressed under the umbrella of preferential measures. Aircraft engine emission standards and noise regulations are some examples which could be examined in this regard.[66]

Preferential measures may also be considered on a collective basis whereby air traffic rights could be used by a carrier of one country on behalf of another carrier representing another country. This would help, particularly in the event of a developing country not being able to launch its own airline or its being unable to allocate its national carrier on a particular route for economic reasons. This principle could also be extended to cover instances where airlines from developing countries could combine their operations by using their collective air traffic rights. For example, airlines of countries A and B who have been granted air traffic rights to operate air services from their countries to countries C and D, respectively, would be able to operate one joint service to countries C and D in one flight, using their collective traffic rights under this scheme.

It could be argued on behalf of the airlines that, as far as possible, developing countries should be released from the obligation to own and control their air carriers or to have their carriers substantially owned and controlled by their nationals. It is only then that countries which cannot fully finance their carriers could maintain them and provide well-rounded competition in the air transport industry.

Ownership and control of airlines

For a long and sustained period of time since the formal regulating of civil aviation, many countries have owned and controlled their national carriers, partly for national prestige and symbolism, and partly because of a traditional requirement in the standard bilateral air services agreement, that a designated carrier should be substantially owned and effectively controlled by nationals of a country which designated that carrier to operate air services under bilateral agreements entered into by that country. This requirement, although tolerable in the first decades of commercial aviation when demand for capacity was manageable, gradually evolved into being an inhibitor in the provision of air transport services. Many states were left with unprofitable state-owned airlines that largely required subsidization. The circumscribing nature of an inflexible ownership and control requirement has prompted many states to permit privatization of air carriers, with a reduction in the percentage of government-held shares. For example, British Airways and Lufthansa have been completely privatized, while Air France, Alitalia, Sabena and Iberia have been partially privatized. Across the Atlantic, the United States deregulated its domestic carriers in 1978 in order to meet capacity demands efficiently and equitably, offering lower prices and improved services to customers.

Although liberalization of air transport is sweeping the globe with its various attractions, offering more capacity and competitive services, it is claimed that the bilateral air services agreement is still preventing proactive measures of airlines to merge with each other and enter into other strategic alliances, through antiquated requirements of national ownership.[67]

In order to face the exponential growth of the air transport industry, it is inevitable that competition and liberalization of the industry should be given serious consideration as a current and future trend in the aviation field. What is needed, first and foremost, to improve international cooperation towards achieving a well meshed and overall competitive policy, is to consider the various possible options available. One of the options to promote competition and facilitate trade in air transport lies indisputably in combating and eliminating anti-competitive practices. State responsibility for achieving this goal is a key factor. One way of ensuring collective state action in this regard and enforcing the duties of states towards the international community is to establish an international entity charged with ensuring the implementation of a global competition code. States may also enter into under-standings or agreements towards combating restrictive trade practices, either bilaterally or plurilaterally. Along with a plurilateral framework of competitive policy, there should also be a concomitant bilateral structure of individual agreement between states to monitor anti-competitive conduct stringently.

As for liberalization of air transport, there has so far been no indication whatsoever that any state favours total liberalization calculated to open up its domestic market. Strategic alliances between airlines, be they through mergers or other arrangements, will be viewed with caution and objectivity by individual airlines and states so as to preclude the total overrunning of local interests. It is this consideration that would make liberalized ownership and control criteria less attractive to local entrepreneurs, who would not encourage foreign ownership to encroach upon the local control that airlines have of their own markets.

Finally, although liberalization of air transport cannot be dismissed as a viable prospect for the future, particularly in trading terms, the players concerned must necessarily view air transport in its entirety, as a service composed of critical factors that are inherent in safe and efficient air transport.

E-commerce

Cyberspace has opened up virtual product development in the air transport industry, giving commercial air carriers the opportunity to conduct business through the Internet. The Internet explosion, occurring largely in the last three years of the 1990s, was due to three fundamental drivers: deregulation of telecommunications globalization and the acceptance of an Internet protocol as a de facto standard.[68] When the concept of e-commerce is applied to the average contract of carriage between the airline and the passenger, what immediately comes to mind is concerns related to the centuries-long practice of the exchange of paper-based documents which have been the predominant means of recording commercial information pertaining to contracts between parties.

Ironically, the Internet explosion which resulted in e-commerce brings to bear a certain 'back to basics' approach from a legal perspective. For centuries before a documented form of contract was formally recognized as a valid means of recording a contract, the world frowned upon the somewhat widespread practice of entering into oral contracts, particularly in the case of certain types of agreement. This difficulty was obviated under English law with the enactment of the Statute of Frauds.[69] This legislation established the basic requirement of a contract having to be established in writing, at least in the instance of particular contracts. Although the statute was repealed in 1954, its principles still subsist in some common law jurisdictions. The requirement of 'writing', as envisioned in the Statute of Frauds, was arguably a stipulation for words and figures written in ink on paper (the prevalent means of putting things on paper at the time) and therefore left a perceived lacuna in the law on the issue of telegraphic contracts which became popular in the mid-nineteenth century. When faced with the question as to whether a telegraph message containing an offer and another reflecting accepting would constitute 'writing' as required by statutes, common law jurisdictions[70] were consensual in assuming that a telegram constituted a written agreement.

Courts even went to the extent of accepting a telephone message, conveyed by one of the parties to the contract to a phone clerk at the telegraph company, and later transcribed by the clerk into telegraphic form, as satisfying the criterion for a 'written' agreement. In the seminal American case of the *Selma Sav Bank*[71] decided in 1918, the court, dismissing as unimportant the mechanical means of making and signing the writing as a determinant, followed the principle enunciated in an earlier case which held:

> When a contract is made by telegraph, which must be in writing by the Statute of Frauds, if the parties authorize their agents either in writing or by parol, to make a proposition on one side and the other party accepts it through the telegraph, that constitutes a contract in writing ... because each party authorizes his agents; the company or the company's operator, to write for him; and it makes no difference whether that operator writes the offer or acceptance in the presence of his principal and by his express direction.[72]

This approach reflects a strong judicial predilection, even at that early stage, to accommodate new developments in technology. It is encouraging that, with the acknowledgment of the first dynamic of computer law – that technological advancement would be purposeless without due recognition of its efficacy – courts have pioneered a sensible approach with predictable ramifications.

The telecopier followed the telegram, and the courts followed the path cleared through the telegraph cases. In a 1988 ruling, Canadian courts ruled:

> the law has endeavoured to take cognizance of, and to be receptive to, technological advances in the means of communication. The conduct of business has for many years been enhanced by technological improvements in communication. Those improvements should not be rejected automatically when attempts are made to apply them to matters

involving the law. They should be considered and, unless there are compelling reasons for rejection, they should be encouraged, applied and approved.[73]

A subsequent case, which pertained to a fax transmission, endorsed the above view, urging encouragement and approval of contracts made through the electronic media.[74] This commonsensical approach may well be extended all the way to instances of computer-to-computer transactions (popularly called electronic data interchange) involving e-commerce conducted through e-mail.

In the case of the carriage of passengers and cargo by air, e-commerce is becoming an increasingly popular medium of transaction. However, air carriage raises esoteric issues of liability brought about by a complex web of legal requirements pertaining to the delivery of the document which evidences the contract of carriage. Some of those legal issues will be examined in the discussion to follow.

The contract of carriage by air

Encryption

When a contract of carriage by air is entered into through e-commerce, the most fundamental process of an electronic contract – encryption – has to take place. In this context, an e-commerce contract for carriage by air is not dissimilar to any other e-commerce transaction. Without encryption, e-commerce is not only nearly impossible, but also insecure at best. When one buys something online such as an air ticket using a 'secure server', one's private information will be encrypted before it is sent over the Internet. Similarly, when one conducts Internet banking, the bank concerned uses encryption to make private financial information unreadable to anyone but that bank.

'Encryption' is a set of complex mathematical formulae that permit anyone transmitting electronic information to scramble the message so that only the intended recipient can decode and thus understand it. Encryption is essential for e-commerce because e-commerce largely takes place over the Internet, which is an open network. As a practical matter, this means that somebody other than the intended recipient of information can intercept it and read it. Encryption protects such information as credit card numbers and all other private information sent through the Internet.

There are several ways to learn whether a browser used for an e-commerce transaction is encrypting information. For example, when one purchases something online using Netscape's browser, if the picture of a lock in the lower left-hand corner is in the locked position with a glow around it, proper encryption is being ensured. One can also look at the Internet address of where one's browser is. If, for instance, it starts with 'https' instead of just 'http', it means that the browser is using a secure server that uses encryption.

The basic concept of how one encrypts information is simple. One uses a computer program, which uses an encryption algorithm (essentially a mathematical equation). This algorithm or equation converts the intended data (confidential files, credit card number, and so on) into an encoded message using a key (think of the 'key' as your password for decoding or deciphering the message). The result of the encryption process is that the plain text message comes out the other end unreadable because it looks like gibberish.

Encryption comes in two basic forms. One uses a single key (or password) and the other uses dual keys. With single key encryption, the key to encode information is used, which is then sent to the intended recipient. The recipient then uses this same key to decipher the encrypted message. This means that the sender of information has to share the secret key with the recipient. A grave concern with this process is that the sender will need a secure way to share the key. This limits the usefulness of single key encryption in e-commerce because it is rarely practical to whisper the key into someone's ear when one is conducting business online.

On the other hand, dual key encryption is the prominent player in e-commerce. This system gives two mathematically related keys to work with. One key is called the 'public key' and the other key is called the 'private key'. The public key is a key that the sender of information can and should announce to the world. He can post it on his web site and put it in an advertisement in a newspaper if he so wishes. It is a public document and therefore is not a secret. When someone wishes to send a confidential message that only an intended recipient should read, the sender could encrypt it using his public key. For instance, if he wants to send his credit card number to *Utopiaairlines.com*, his browser might encrypt it using *Utopiaairlines.com*'s public key.

The interesting part of this two-way process is that, if a thief intercepts a credit card number over the Internet and tries to decode it using *Utopiaairlines.com*'s public key, it will not work. The advantage of a dual key system is that the public key is a one-way key. It encrypts information, but it will not decrypt it. That is the reason it is not important for a sender of information to keep the public key a secret. When Utopia Airlines is ready to read the credit card number sent, its software will use *Utopiaairlines.com*'s private key to decrypt or decode the information. The private key is the key that must remain absolutely secret. It is the one that lets somebody read messages intended only for them that were encrypted using their public key.

Offer and acceptance

Usually, a contract is concluded when, in response to an offer made by an offeror, the offeree indicates acceptance to the offeror. In cases of simultaneous communication of the offer and acceptance, made face-to-face by the offeror and offeree, the essentials of a contract are clear. However, when parties are not in close proximity to each other and communicate their dealings over the telecommunications medium, the process may become slightly more complicated, in that it may not always be clear as to what constitutes an offer or an acceptance. In such instances, it largely becomes a matter of interpretation as to whether both the offeror and the offeree had the intent to conclude the contract.

The element of intention to contract and to conclude the process on the part of both the offeror and the offeree is initial to the formation of the contract. Courts have insisted that proof of an offer to enter into legal relations upon definite terms must be followed by the production of evidence from which the courts may infer an intention by the offeree to accept that offer. Thus the statements made by the parties in the process of negotiations are of extreme importance in the determination of a concluded contract. The 1840 case of *Hyde* v. *Wrench*[75] offers the seminal principle that a series of communications from either party may impinge upon an original offer. In the *Hyde* case, the defendant, on 6 June, offered to sell an estate to the plaintiff for £1000. On 8 June, in reply, the plaintiff made an offer of £950, which was refused by the defendant on 27 June. However, on 29 June, the plaintiff wrote to the defendant that he was now willing to pay £1000.

The importance of the *Hyde* decision lies in the fact that the court held that no contract existed. The plaintiff had, by rejecting the offer made on 6 June, precluded himself from reviving the offer later. In other words, once an offer is rejected by the offeree, he cannot go on on the basis that the offer would still stand in its original form.

In the instance of a sale carried out over the Internet, it is important to note that, by placing its seats for sale on the Internet, an airline is placing itself on the same footing as a shop owner who displays his goods for sale in his shop, with price tags marked on the goods. By doing this, the shop owner is merely making an 'invitation to treat'. The buyer who walks into the shop and selects an item for purchase is making the offer, which the shop owner is entitled to accept or reject. Similarly, it is the purchaser of the airline ticket over the Internet who makes the offer, making him the offeror and the airline then becomes the offeree.

The primary issue at stake in the determination of a contract is whether the parties intended the contract to be concluded. For instance, if a person offers to buy an airline ticket over the Internet and the airline gives him a reference number, the allocation of that number may not necessarily indicate acceptance of the offer by the airline. The 1989 United States case of *Corinthian Pharmaceutical Systems Inc.* v. *Lederle Laboratories*[76] is a good analogy. In the *Corinthian* case, a person dealing in medicinal drugs on a wholesale basis ordered a consignment of drugs through a computerized telephone ordering system. The order was placed strategically a day before a price increase was to take effect. The wholesaler ordered through the manufacturers' automated telephone order system, and after the order message was placed by him, he was allocated a 'tracking number' by the manufacturer's computer system. There was absolutely no human interaction in the transaction. Subsequently, when the manufacturer refused to sell the consignment of drugs as ordered by the wholesaler at the pre-increase price, the court held with the manufacturer's position that the tracking number issued by the manufacturer's computer was not an acceptance of the offer, but merely an acknowledgment of the receipt of the order – or offer in contractual law terms. The court concluded that no contract had been concluded, and the wholesaler was denied purchase of the goods at the lower price.

The early case of *Henkle* v. *Pape*[77] brings out another difficulty that might arise from contracts transacted through the Internet. The *Henkle* case, decided in 1870, concerned a transaction carried out through telegraphic messages for the sale of up to 50 rifles. The offeror sent the offeree a telegraphic message offering to buy three rifles but the message was transcribed to the offeree as 'the' instead of 'three' rifles. Accordingly, the offeree held the offeror liable for the purchase of all 50 rifles. The court held that the offeror could not be held liable for the error of the telegraph clerk who had wrongly deciphered the message and therefore no contract had been concluded.[78]

The 1870 principle of the *Henkle* decision still holds water in the instance of a contract transacted through the Internet, in that the latter instance, like the *Henkle* case, involves a contract negotiated through electronic means where there is always the risk that messages intending to create contractual obligations may not reach their destination, or even perhaps, more ominously, are received by the recipient in a form other than the one sent originally by the sender. In the seminal Canadian case of *Kinghorne v. The Montreal Telegraph Co.*[79] decided in 1859, the court subsumed the reasons behind the determination of an electronic contract which may still apply:

> We must look, I think, in the case of each communication, at the papers delivered by the party who sent the message, not at the transcript of the message taken through the wire at the other end of the wire, with all the chances of mistakes in apprehending and noting the signals, and in transcribing for delivery.[80]

Of course, compared to early telegraph systems that caused numerous problems, the modern Internet is more reliable and errors such as those encountered in the *Henkle* and *Kinghorne* cases may not be commonplace. However, there is of course the possibility of garbled messages flowing through the Internet, where courts would have no hesitation in determining the real intent of the parties to conclude a contract as the preliminary issue.

The above concerns are by no means intended to suggest that contracts through the Internet are questionable in general terms. In fact, current computer-based technologies are more effective than earlier technologies at assisting parties to the contract to conclude their agreement unambiguously. For example, electronic data interchange (EDI) as a commercial medium has evolved in Canada to the extent that the EDI Council of Canada's Model TPA encourages parties to be extremely precise in identifying particular messages as constituting an order (or offer) by introducing a two-phased process: the first using a functional acknowledgment of the offer (such as the tracking number in the *Corinthian* case); and the second using a purchase order acknowledgment.

Time and place of contract

There is no doubt as to when and where the contract comes into being, when parties sign a contract simultaneously in a face-to-face setting. It is often not a trivial legal task to determine when and where, when either an offer, or an acceptance, or both, are sent by telegraph, telex, fax, EDI, e-mail or via the Internet, or are communicated by telephone. The uncertainty began even before the advent of the telegraph, with the mail delivery system. The general contract law principle is that an offer is not considered accepted until the acceptance of the offer is received by the offeror. In England in the nineteenth century, an exception to this rule was developed by judges for offers and acceptances sent by the mail. The so-called 'post box rule' or expedition theory prescribes that, where an offer is made in the mail, the contract takes effect immediately at the time acceptance is posted in the mail (rather than when the acceptance is actually received by the offeror) where use of the mail is reasonable in the circumstances or expressly contemplated by the parties. This rule effectively precludes the need to hold the offeree responsible for delays in communications and places the burden of uncertainty of the waiting period on the offeror; that is, the offeror does not know that it has earlier concluded a binding contract until it receives the offeree's acceptance in the mail, whereas the offeree knew the contract came into existence the moment it posted its reply letter. Shifting this risk to the offeror, and giving the concomitant assurance to the offeree, was reasonable because of the increased reliability of the Royal Mail in the late nineteenth century, to the point where multiple deliveries a day in larger urban centres were the norm. The expedition theory is a good example of a legal doctrine being firmly grounded in the communication environment and commercial processes of its day.

As the telegraph, telephone and other new communications technology evolved into widespread use, cases established principles as to when and where contracts were concluded. In *Carow Towing*, an early Canadian case, courts held that a contract entered into by telephone should be treated like a letter and should follow the expedition theory, with acceptance occurring at the place where the acceptance is spoken and not where the offeror hears the acceptance.[81] By contrast, in the *Entores*[82] case, a later British decision, Lord Denning concluded that, for simultaneous communications like the telephone, the place where the contract is concluded is where the offeror hears the acceptance, and thus, if the line goes dead during the telephone conversation, the onus is upon the offeree to call back the offeror to ensure the words of acceptance had been communicated to the offeror. Subsequent cases in Canada have followed the decision in *Entores*, rather than the approach in *Carow Towing*,[83] with the exception of Quebec where, until recently, the preponderance of case law has followed the principle that telephone contracts arise when and where the offeree speaks its acceptance;[84] since the enactment of the current Civil Code of Quebec in January 1994, Article 1387 explicitly provides that in respect of telephone contracts acceptance occurs when and where the acceptance is received. It is interesting to note that the *Entores* decision was also followed in two fax cases, one in Nova Scotia[85] and one in New Zealand,[86] where each held that a contract made by fax arises when the offeror receives by fax the acceptance of the offeree.

Courts in the *Entores* case also held that telex technology results in instantaneous communications, with the result that acceptance occurs when the message is received by the offeror. This approach was confirmed in a decision by the House of Lords in the *Brinkibon* case,[87] in which the court held that, although telex communications should be categorized as simultaneous, in each case the specific constituent elements and factors in the communications system concerned need to be carefully considered:

> The senders and recipients may not be the principals to the contemplated contract. They may be servants or agents with limited authority. The message may not reach, or be intended to reach, the designated recipient immediately; messages may be sent out of office hours, or at night, with the intention, or on the assumption, that they will be read at a later time. There may be some error or default at the recipient's end which prevents receipt at the time contemplated and believed in by the sender. The message may have been sent and/or received through machines operated by third persons. And many other variations may occur. No universal rule can cover all such cases; they must be resolved by reference to the intentions of the parties, by sound business practice and in some cases by a judgment where the risks should lie.[88]

The recognition of the above facts in the *Brinkibon* case raise a number of emerging issues in respect of EDI, e-mail and Internet communications. Certain EDI transmissions, for example, will fall into the simultaneous communications category. Much of EDI is effected, not between the trading principals, however, but by use of intermediaries, so-called 'value-added networks' (VAN) or service providers. An EDI message could likely go through the message sender's VAN, then through the recipient's VAN, and finally to the recipient. Similarly, e-mail messages over the Internet may be routed to electronic mailboxes from which the recipient has then to download. In such instances, it may be more difficult to conclude that the simultaneous communication rules should apply. Also it may be difficult to determine when exactly an electronic message arrives at the recipient's location for purposes of being recognized as legally effective: for instance, an early British case held that a letter sent in a sealed envelope is not considered received until it is opened by the addressee personally.[89] Whether such a rule should apply in the case of e-mail, or whether an e-mail message should be deemed received when it is available to be viewed by the intended recipient, regardless of the time at which the recipient actually reads the message, is a moot point. Another question is: when should a telex or fax be deemed to have arrived at a workplace? In one case,[90] the answer pointed to the time when the message was received by the recipient's machine (on a Friday after business hours and not three days later on a Monday morning when a person actually reads the telex).

Given these ambiguities, prudent users of electronic commerce should try to avoid having to refer these issues to a judge by providing, in their EDI Trading Partner Agreement or other similar document, precisely what electronic message must be received by which computer (that is the recipient's or the recipient's VAN) in order for a contract to arise, thereby bringing clarity to the questions as to when and where the electronic contract arose. As to the 'where' question, the parties to the TPA would be well advised to select a governing law in advance, and to make sure the VAN agreements contain the same jurisdiction, so that there is no question of which law would apply if it were ever considered necessary to resort to adjudication. This is particularly true for EDI and Internet transactions, where each trading party's VAN, or Internet service provider, may be in a jurisdiction different from the customer, and therefore possibly the laws of four different jurisdictions may apply if the parties remain silent on the governing law question. In such circumstances, as Lord Denning observed in the *Entores* case concerning two parties in different jurisdictions, the problems arise since the laws of the respective jurisdictions are different. Therefore, predicting a court's probable response is difficult, given that the court will invariably try to seek the most just remedy under the circumstances, but in some cases this is truly a difficult task. As an example, see the court's commentary in the *Export Packers* case where the judge recommended that the various rules developed by the law over the years, such as the simultaneous communication rule in the *Entores* case, should not be applied in a rigid fashion:

> When the common law rules relating to offer and acceptance were under development the telephone did not exist. At that time agreements were made by two or more persons getting together and reaching a common understanding. As the postal system came into being elaborate rules were made by the courts covering the mechanics of reaching a bargain by mail. Today a person ordinarily resident in British Columbia may telephone

from Japan where he is on a business trip to a person ordinarily resident in Ontario but who is also then visiting Italy. They may agree to the same kind of contract which is the subject-matter of this writ. It does not necessarily follow the place where the contract was made was Japan and that Japanese law governs its interpretation. Alternatively, it would be hard to argue the place where the contract was made was Italy and the law of that country ought to apply to its interpretation.[91]

This dictum clearly confirms the benefit accrued to users of electronic commerce in crafting their own rules for dealing with issues of formation of contract. Making commercial relationships more secure and predictable through contract, however, can be a costly and time-consuming exercise. Therefore this may be an area for law reform. In the United States, the National Conference of Commissioners of Uniform State Law are already working towards establishing new rules under the Uniform Commercial Code that would take the view that Internet communications are instantaneous in nature and that therefore a contract comes into existence when the sender of the offer receives an electronic message signifying acceptance. This does not, however, answer the question as to when the acceptance is effective if the offeror was not present before the computer; in other words, does receipt require a human intervention and acknowledgment? In resolving this question, the following should be observed: the purpose and function of the rule; who would be prejudiced by a particular holding; what are the reasonable expectations of the parties; and on whom it is reasonable to place a burden for helping to 'fix' the system, if indeed it needs it.

Delivery of the airline ticket

The Warsaw Convention of 1929[92] states that, for the transportation of passengers, the carrier must deliver a passenger ticket which shall contain certain details.[93] The Convention also says that the absence, irregularity or loss of the passenger ticket shall not affect the existence of the validity of the contract of transportation which shall nonetheless be subject to the rules of the Convention. Nevertheless, if the carrier accepts a passenger without a passenger ticket having been delivered, he shall not be entitled to avail himself of those provisions of the Convention that exclude his liability.[94] Article 3 of the Convention provides that the information contained in the ticket delivered to the passenger must contain the place and date of issue; the place of departure and destination; agreed stopping places; name and address of the carrier or carriers; and a statement that carriage is subject to the liability provisions of the Convention.

The issue of 'delivery' of an airline ticket to a person who contracts with an airline for travel is significant at air law. The two cases of *Lisi* v. *Alitalia*[95] and *Chan* v. *Korean Air*[96] clearly demonstrated that the meaning of 'delivery' in relation to the Convention is indeed important. The important issue is not the 'physical' delivery of the document of carriage, but the 'purpose' of delivery of the ticket to the passenger. In this sense, the two cases contain similar facts, and in both cases the respective tickets were 'delivered' to the passengers. The issue, however, was whether the ticket served its purpose as envisaged by the courts, *vis-à-vis* Article 3 of the Convention. A very important point in this connection is that both cases, and indeed the precedent *cursus curiae*, were subject to judicial 'surgery' in the interpretation of the meaning and purpose of Article 3 of the Convention and that a discussion of the two decisions would be meaningless if their history, albeit very briefly, were not outlined.

Miller succinctly sums up the purpose of Article 3 when she says:

> Delivery is no longer the physical delivery of the ticket by the carrier. The requirement is qualified in such a way that the delivery must allow the passenger (I) to realize that the carrier's liability is greatly limited and (II) if he so wishes, to buy additional insurance. In other words, there must be adequate notice of the liability limitations.[97]

The judicial arguments in the United States (where both these cases were decided) are based on the fact that courts have imputed to the carrier the breach of the Convention by 'non-delivery' of the ticket in the case that the ticket is physically delivered but does not give the passenger the opportunity to read its contents, although Article 3(1)(*e*) expressly provides that 'a statement that the carriage is subject to the rules of the Convention' must be included in the ticket, thereby precluding any need for imputation of liability. By bringing the case under 'non-delivery' under Article 3.2, the courts effectively veer the case into the realm of sanctions, which entails the all-important question of unlimited liability of the carrier.[98]

The predecessors to the *Lisi* and *Chan* decisions held that failure to give adequate notice (of the liability limitation), amounting to the absence of delivery of the ticket, has been addressed and recognized in instances either where the ticket was not physically delivered at all, or where the passenger receives his ticket, but does not have the opportunity to read the contents therein, in order that he has sufficient time to take necessary action (such as obtaining additional insurance coverage for himself).[99] These cases involved instances where the passenger ticket was handed over to the passenger at the stairs to the aircraft, just before boarding, and after the passenger had boarded the aircraft, respectively.

The *Lisi* case added a new twist to the circumstances by challenging the United States Court of Appeal to address the issue of the ticket being delivered under normal circumstances, but the passenger being precluded from reading its contents, owing to the very small print used in the ticket. The Court of Appeal, recalling its decision of *Mertens* v. *Flying Tiger Line Inc.*,[100] stated:

> We read Article 3(2) to require that the ticket be delivered to the passenger in such a manner as to afford him a reasonable opportunity to take measures to protect himself against the limitation of liability ...[101] The convention's arbitrary limitations of liability... are advantageous to the carrier, but the quid pro quo for this one-sided advantage is delivery of the passenger ticket ... which gives him notice that on the air trip he is about to take, the amount of recovery ... is limited very substantially.[102]

MacMahon J, criticizing the small print in the ticket, stated that the conditions of carriage were 'camouflaged in Lilliputian print in a thicket of conditions of contract'[103] and unequivocally decided that the ticket had not been delivered to the passenger in the context of Article 3 of the Convention. Moore Circuit J, dissenting, on the other hand called the pronouncement by the majority 'judicial treaty making' where the judges have attempted to 'rewrite' the Convention. According to Justice Moore, the language of the treaty was clear and its parameters were clearly stated. *Chan* v. *Korean Air*[104] took a diametrically opposed stance by stating:

> All that the second sentence of Article 3(2) requires in order to avoid its sanction is the 'delivery' of a passenger ticket. Expanding this to mean ... a passenger ticket in compliance with the requirements of the Convention is rendered implausible by the first sentence of Article 3(2) which specifies that irregularity ... shall not affect the validity of the contract.[105]

The court in this instance followed a previous decision[106] and held that there exists a contract even if the ticket is absent or 'irregular' and that the contract was still governed by *all* the provisions of the Convention.[107]

It must be noted that, while the *Lisi* case dealt with a ticket with a 4 type print, the *Chan* case dealt with an 8 type print, making it imaginable that the majority in the former case would have been influenced by the minuscule print. It is also noteworthy that the 10 point print prescribed for the passenger ticket, which was authoritatively considered by the court in the latter, was set by the Montreal Agreement of 1966, a private agreement between airlines and not an international treaty. Valerie Kaiser criticizes the *Chan* decision on the grounds that the court was inconsistent in terminology[108] and used an interpretation of the treaty while claiming to follow strictly the provisions of the Convention. While citing a subsequent case,[109] she concludes that courts should not indulge in 'judicial treaty or law making' (presumably implying that treaties have to be adhered to *stricto sensu*). It is indeed relevant in this instant to inquire whether the principles of *contra proferentem* have any place in this debate, since, after all, Warsaw considerations are contractual considerations. As for the question of judicial law making, it could well be arguable that the role of the judiciary has been rather simplistically dismissed, being relegated to the background.

The new Convention[110] aimed at replacing the Warsaw Convention, done at Montreal on 28 May 1999, in Article 3 provides that the travel document must contain information, inter alia, of the places of departure and destination. However, it does not insist on physical delivery of the airline ticket. Instead the Convention provides that any other means which preserves the information in the ticket may be substituted for the delivery of the document, provided the carrier offers the passenger a written statement of the information so preserved.[111] This provision has obviously been designed to accommodate electronic ticketing and therefore is relevant to the commercial exigencies pertaining to current marketing practices and the airline product where carriers would offer different services in apprising their customers of information contained in an airline ticket.

Issues of jurisdiction

Perhaps the single most important issue in cyber contracts is that which pertains to jurisdiction. Given the World Wide Web and its global application, the most compelling question in this regard would pertain to the trans-boundary applicability of an Internet contract. In this regard, the most convenient analogy comes from the two jurisdictions of Canada and the United States. Would an offeror in Canada, who offers $500 over the Internet for a round trip between Toronto and Miami, be able to enforce an agreement concerning a sale against a United States airline at its home base in Florida? In a case decided in 1952, in Canada,[112] where the plaintiff brought a case to the Ontario High Court against an American radio broadcasting station which was broadcasting, from across the border, allegedly libellous statements which could be heard over the air waves in Canada, the defendant radio station brought up a motion of dismissal, alleging that the Ontario Court in Canada had no jurisdiction to hear a case against a party to the action which was an enterprise based in the United States. The court disagreed, and held:

> A person may utter all the defamatory words he wishes without incurring any civil liability unless they are heard and understood by a third person. I think it a 'startling proposition' to say that one may, while standing south of the border or cruising in an aeroplane south of the border, through the medium of modern sound amplification, utter defamatory matter which is heard in a Province in Canada north of the border, and not be said to have published a slander in the Province in which it is heard and understood. I cannot see what difference it makes whether the person is made to understand by means of the written word, sound-waves or ether-waves in so far as the matter of proof of publication is concerned. The tort consists in making a third person understand actionable defamatory matter.[113]

In the more recent case of *Pindling* v. *National Broadcasting Corporation*[114] in respect of an American television broadcast received in Canada, the Ontario High Court held that the prime minister of the Bahamas was held entitled to bring the case to Canada, instead of the United States. The *Pindling* decision illustrates well the principle of 'forum shopping' which can be culled from the television context and be held applicable to the analogous situation of a contract transacted over the Internet.

The above principle may be derogated only in an instance where the court seized of the case could invoke the principle of 'forum non convenience' which allows the transfer of a suit from an originally filed jurisdiction to some other jurisdiction which is better placed to hear the case concerned. In the 1996 case of *National Bank of Canada* v. *Clifford Chance*,[115] the Canadian courts which were charged with hearing a case where a Toronto-based firm which had contracted with a law firm in the United Kingdom transferred the case to the United Kingdom although the contract was concluded in Toronto, on the grounds that the contract concerned a UK-based project and the legal advice obtained had been UK law given by lawyers in the United Kingdom. On the basis of the *Clifford Chance* principle, it would not be unusual for a common law court to determine that in the sale of an airline seat, where the offer emanates from, say, Canada over the Internet for a seat out of the United Kingdom on a UK-based carrier, the applicable jurisdiction would lie with the courts in the United Kingdom, although the contract itself may have been concluded in Canada.

There is a dichotomy in the judicial thinking with regard to cases involving contracts concluded over the Internet. On the one hand, courts are refusing to bring a person into a jurisdiction purely because he contracted with a business entity which is based in that jurisdiction. This approach is illustrated by the 1994 US decision in the case of *Pres-Kap, Inc.* v. *System One, Direct Access Inc.*,[116] where the court refused to grant jurisdiction to Florida where a resident in New York had used a Florida-based online network information service merely to gain access to a database. Similarly, the court in the famous 1997 *SunAmerica* case[117] refused to find jurisdiction in a trademark case solely on the basis of the defendant's operation of a general access web site:

Plaintiffs ask this Court to hold that any defendant who advertises nationally or on the Internet is subject to its jurisdiction. It cannot plausibly be argued that any defendant who advertises nationally could expect to be haled into Court in *any* state, for a cause of action that does not relate to the advertisements. Such general advertising is not the type of 'purposeful activity related to the forum that would make the exercise of jurisdiction fair, just or reasonable'.[118]

Similarly, in the 1997 case of *Hearst Corporation* v. *Goldberger*,[119] where the defendant operated a passive general access web site, the courts were of the view that to open worldwide jurisdiction merely because the Internet offered worldwide access would be iniquitous:

Where, as here, defendant has not contracted to sell or actually sold any goods or services to New Yorkers, a finding of personal jurisdiction in New York based on an Internet website would mean that there would be nationwide (indeed, worldwide) personal jurisdiction over anyone and everyone who establishes an Internet web site. Such nationwide jurisdiction is not consistent with traditional personal jurisdiction case law nor acceptable to the Court as a matter of policy.[120]

The *Hearst Corporation* decision seems to have followed the observation of a case[121] decided one year earlier where the court held:

Because the Web enables easy worldwide access, allowing computer interaction via the Web to supply sufficient contacts to establish jurisdiction would eviscerate the personal jurisdiction requirement as it currently exists; the Court is not willing to take this step. Thus, the fact that Fallon has a Web site used by Californians cannot establish jurisdiction by itself.[122]

The second line of judicial thinking is the converse to the above approach, where courts have imputed to the non-resident defendant the responsibility for complexities brought about by the Internet in its universal applicability. Therefore, in *Compuserv Incorporated* v. *Patterson*,[123] the courts held a Texas-based computer programmer legally responsible for his Ohio-based computer network online service, and found him to be under Ohio law. Although the defendant had never visited Ohio, he was nevertheless found to be subject to Ohio law on the basis that an electronic contract had been concluded in Ohio where the defendant was distributing his product.

The principle of universal application of jurisdiction has been invoked in other instances, where courts have accepted jurisdiction on the basis of sales made to customers through the defendant's web site,[124] or based on soliciting donations,[125] or based on subscribers signed up by the defendant for services delivered over the Internet,[126] or for having follow-on contacts, negotiations and other dealings in addition to, and often as a result of, the initial Internet-based communication.[127] The common thread which runs through the fabric of judicial thinking in this regard is that parties who avail themselves of technology in order to do business in a distant place should not then be able to escape that place's legal jurisdiction. These cases are all embracing, from contract breach claims to tort, including trade libel; in several cases, courts have even found jurisdiction in trademark infringement matters merely on the basis of a defendant's general access web site,[128] or linking to a national ATM network through a telephone line indirectly through an independent data processor in a third state.[129]

An overall evaluation of the US civil cases discussed above concludes that, while the general trend is for courts to assert jurisdiction over non-residents based on their Internet activities, there are still a few situations where some courts may not apply jurisdiction.

Although the choice of forum may extend universally, it does not necessarily mean that enforcement from a judgment would automatically follow. In the case of *Bachchan v. India Abroad Publications Incorporated*,[130] the plaintiff, who was a national of India who had won the right to have his case heard in the United Kingdom, was unable to enforce judgment in New York. The New York courts held that the UK law applicable to the case did not accord with US law and therefore the decision could not be recognized as enforceable in the United States.

A distinct advantage of using e-commerce in the sale of airline tickets is the facility afforded to airlines to caution possible clients of the hazards of air travel through the Internet. For instance, when a detailed contract of carriage is posted in the Internet, constituting effective delivery of the contract of carriage in accordance with established law, airlines could at the same time bring to the attention of the passenger such hazards of travel as the aerotoxic syndrome (the causing of blood clots in the human body through sustained seating in restricted spaces) and turbulence, by explicitly cautioning travellers of these dangers through their web sites and through web sites dedicated to such specific issues. This would not only ensure that adequate notice is given to air travellers of such hazards, but would also effectively preclude possible actions against airlines for non-disclosure of material facts in personal injury cases.

On the minus side, operators of web sites have to exercise caution in order to avoid being hauled into any jurisdiction in the event of adjudication. The airline which sells its seats over the Internet is no exception. The first thing airlines must address is the need to establish with their possible clients over the Internet an explicit agreement prescribing applicable or governing law with regard to the agreement and an agreed jurisdiction in case of dispute. The airlines must also set out, as a condition, the types of persons it will not enter into contract with (such as persons whose geographic location may not offer the airline benefit from the contract). The bottom line is that airlines which advertise their seats for sale on the Internet should have well-thought-out, well-drafted conditions of contract which the offeror would have to read carefully and indicate that he agrees with them, before he makes his offer.

FINANCING OF AIRCRAFT AND EQUIPMENT

The two leading aircraft manufacturers, Boeing and Airbus Industrie, have forecast exponential growth in air traffic in the long term, necessitating a steadily increasing need for capacity and services. While Airbus Industrie has estimated that 13 000 new aircraft will be needed, at a value of US$1·2 trillion, by the year 2020,[131] Boeing has made a more liberal estimate of 18 406 new aircraft valued at US$1·25 trillion over the same period.[132] The International Civil Aviation Organization has forecast an annual growth rate in air transport in excess of 5 per cent over the next ten years. This expected growth will involve larger investment requirements not only in air navigation and airport infrastructure but also in fleet financing and leasing, including the financing and leasing of aircraft equipment. Consequently, funding requirements relating to the acquisition of new aircraft and equipment are expected to accelerate and reach higher levels in the next few decades, placing major challenges on both aircraft operators and states who finance such operators.

The compelling needs for the replacement of aircraft are essentially brought to bear by environmental factors, in the case of aircraft and equipment purchase, and the need to retain acceptable levels of safety in air transport, in the case of leasing of aircraft. These issues will be discussed below, along with the financial aspects of asset-based financing and leasing of aircraft.

Asset-based financing

The philosophy of asset-based financing admits of aircraft operators pledging as collateral the assets inherent in the aircraft or aircraft equipment they decide to purchase in order to seek financing independently of state support. This fundamental principle, which veers from sovereign-backed financing, is an initiative calculated to promote international trade and financing in this area. Inherent to such an initiative is the inevitable significance of an appropriate legal and regulatory regime that would primarily maintain a certain control of commercial activity, while at the same time safeguarding the interests of the financiers and the operators alike.[133]

Aircraft by nature are highly movable objects that are capable of crossing political boundaries within a relatively short period of time. They are also high-value assets having great economic value and therefore represent valuable collateral as a basis for extending aviation credit.

The economic problems of aircraft financing are multifarious and form a complex web of international commercial activity, which brings to bear a compelling need for some flexibility in investment management to cope with internationalization, and the huge growth of the air transport industry has made financing of high-value assets such as aircraft become heavily reliant on multiple sources of funding. Consequently, the financing of aircraft can involve trans-boundary activity where parties of different countries can be major players. The quality inherent in aircraft, as highly movable property, lends itself to the regular practice of using aircraft as collateral, thereby leading to a worldwide distribution of assets. An essential corollary to this situation is the regular occurrence of greater geographic distances between the actual location of the aircraft and its registered owner.[134]

One of the pre-eminent considerations with investments in fleet financing concerns the fact that the legal remedies available to a financier regarding recoverability of collateral in the event of default by the borrower may differ substantially from jurisdiction to jurisdiction. Each legal system may have its own regulations and legislation concerning the treatment of rights in property over aircraft, including the legal enforcement measures applicable.

It is an incontrovertible fact that, depending upon the location of the aircraft at the time remedies are sought, the laws of certain jurisdictions may lend themselves more easily to accommodating foreign creditors, where prompt recourse to the value of the asset could be readily available. There are instances, however, where, in certain jurisdictions, the treatment of security can be approached in a hostile manner and legal enforcement may take several years. Hence reliance on the *lex situs* or law of the location has usually been regarded with apprehension by aircraft financiers.

The economics of credit dictate that extensions of credit should, in essence, be profitable for both the debtor and the creditor. For the borrower or debtor, credit is presented as a fund-generating mechanism which is critical for investment pertaining to fiscal arrangements concerning operations and expansion. In general terms, assets composing credit facilitate economic growth and present to the creditor a viable tool to enhance sales and earn interest at the same time.[135]

One of the fundamental postulates of asset-based and sovereign financing is that not all credit represents itself as being profitable. While, on one hand, a creditor will be benefited only in instances where the borrower fulfils his obligations, and a defaulting borrower will inevitably represent a loss of profits for the creditor, on the other hand, a borrower may find himself enjoying gains from the loan if the return on investment is greater than the interest paid. The borrower will usually not profit from a transaction if the creditor charges a high interest rate.

A regulatory initiative was undertaken by the International Civil Aviation Organization (ICAO), in cooperation with the International Institute for the Unification of Private Law (UNIDROIT), which culminated in a Diplomatic Conference to Adopt a Mobile Equipment Convention and Aircraft Protocol, held in Cape Town, from 29 October to 16 November 2001. The Convention sought to address issues concerning the compelling need that exists to acquire and use aircraft equipment of high value or particular economic significance and to facilitate the financing of the acquisition and use of such equipment in an efficient manner, while ensuring that interests in such equipment are recognized and protected universally. With these goals in view, the Convention provided for the constitution and effects of an international interest in aircraft objects and associated rights and be applicable when, at the time of the conclusion of an agreement creating or providing for the international interest, the debtor is situated in a Contracting State.[136] The Convention entitled any person to assert rights and interests under the Convention if he should enter into an agreement or a sale, and register an international interest in, or a sale of, an aircraft object,[137] in an agency, trust or other representative capacity. An interest is constituted as an international interest under this Convention, where the agreement creating or providing for the interest is in writing; relates to an object of which the charger, conditional seller or lessor has power to dispose; enables the object to be identified in conformity with the Protocol; and, in the case of a security agreement, enables the secured obligations to be determined, but without the need to state a sum or maximum sum secured.

In the event of default, the chargee may, to the extent that the charger has at any time so agreed, exercise any one or more of the following remedies: (a) take possession or control of any object charged to it; (b) sell or grant a lease of any such object; (c) collect or receive any income or profits arising from the management or use of any such object, or apply for a court order authorizing or directing any of the above acts.

Any remedy under the Convention shall be exercised in a commercially reasonable manner. A remedy shall be deemed to be exercised in a commercially reasonable manner where it is exercised in conformity with a provision of the security agreement, except where such a provision is manifestly unreasonable.

At any time after default, the chargee and all the interested persons may agree that ownership of (or any other interest of the charger in) any object covered by the security interest shall vest in the chargee in or towards satisfaction of the secured obligations. The court may on the application of the chargee order that ownership of (or any other interest of the charger in) any object covered by the security interest shall vest in the chargee in or towards satisfaction of the secured obligations. The court is, under the Convention, empowered to grant an application under the preceding paragraph only if the amount of the secured obligations to be satisfied by such vesting is reasonably commensurate with the value of the object after taking account of any payment to be made by the chargee to any of the interested persons. At any time after default and before sale of the charged object or the making of an order, the charger or any interested person may discharge the security interest by paying in full the amount secured, subject to any lease granted by the chargee under Article 8(1). Where, after such default, the payment of the amount secured is made in full by an interested person other than the debtor, that person is subrogated to the rights of the chargee.

Ownership or any other interest of the charger passing on a sale or otherwise is free from any other interest over which the chargee's security interest has priority under the provisions of Article 27. As for remedies of conditional seller or lessor, in the event of default under a title reservation agreement or under a leasing agreement the conditional seller or the lessor, as the case may be, may terminate the agreement and take possession or control of any object to which the agreement relates; or apply for a court order authorizing or directing either of these acts.

The debtor and the creditor may at any time agree in writing as to the events that constitute a default or otherwise give rise to the rights and remedies specified in the Convention. In the absence of such an agreement, 'default' would mean a substantial default. Any additional remedies permitted by the applicable law, including any remedies agreed upon by the parties, may be exercised to the extent that they are not inconsistent with the applicable mandatory provisions of the Convention.

One of the most compelling flexibilities pertaining to relief is found in provision making it obligatory on a a contracting state to ensure that a creditor who adduces evidence of default by the debtor may, pending final determination of its claim and to the extent that the debtor has at any time so agreed, obtain from a court speedy relief in the form of such one or more of the following orders as the creditor requests: (a) preservation of the object and its value; (b) possession, control or custody of the object; (c) immobilization of the object; and/or (d) lease or management of the object and the income therefrom.

The Convention also provides that, in making any order under the preceding paragraph, the court may impose such terms as it considers necessary to protect the interested persons in the event that the creditor, in implementing any order granting such relief, fails to perform any of its obligations to the debtor under this Convention or the Protocol; or fails to establish its claim, wholly or in part, on the final determination of that claim. Before making any order, the court is given the discretion to require notice of the request to be given to any of the interested persons.

With regard to the registration of interests, the Convention provides for an International Registry to be established for registrations of international interests, prospective international interests and registrable non-consensual rights and interests; assignments and prospective assignments of international interests; acquisitions of international interests by legal or contractual subrogation; subordinations of interests; and sales or prospective sales of objects to which the Convention makes reference by a Protocol; and notices of national interests.

The Convention provides for a Supervisory Authority and a registrar. The Supervisory Authority is empowered to establish or provide for the establishment of the International Registry; except as otherwise provided by the Protocol, appoint and dismiss the registrar; after consultation with the contracting states, make or approve and ensure the publication of regulation pursuant to the Protocol dealing with the operation of the International Registry; establish administrative procedures through which complaints concerning the operation of the International Registry can be made to the Supervisory Authority; supervise the registrar and the operation of the International Registry; at the request of the registrar provide such guidance to the registrar as the Supervisory Authority thinks fit; set and periodically review the structure of fees to be charged for the services and facilities of the International Registry; do all things necessary to ensure that an efficient registration system exists to implement the objectives of this Convention and the Protocol; and report periodically to contracting states concerning the discharge of its obligations under the Convention and the Protocol. The registrar is empowered by the Convention to ensure the efficient operation of the International Registry and perform the functions assigned to it by the Convention, the Protocol and regulations; and implement directions given by the Supervisory Authority.

A registration shall be valid only if made in conformity with Article 20 and shall take effect upon entry of the required information into the International Registry database so as to be searchable and will be searchable for the purposes of the preceding paragraph at the time when the International Registry has assigned to it a sequentially ordered file number; and the registration data, including the file number, are stored in durable form and may be retrieved at the International Registry. If an interest first registered as a prospective international interest becomes an international interest, the international interest shall be treated as registered from the time of registration of the prospective international interest. These principles may apply with necessary modifications to the registration of a prospective assignment of an international interest. A registration shall be searchable in the International Registry database according to the criteria prescribed by the Protocol.

An international interest, a prospective international interest or an assignment or prospective assignment of an international interest may be registered, and any registration amended or extended prior to its expiry, by or with the consent in writing at any time of the debtor or assignor or intending debtor or assignor. The subordination of an international interest to another international interest may be registered by or with the consent in writing at any time of the person whose interest has been subordinated. A registration may be discharged by or with the consent in writing of the party in whose favour it was made and the acquisition of an international interest by legal or contractual subrogation may be registered by the subrogee. It is also notewothy that, under the Convention, a registrable non-consensual right or interest may be registered by the holder thereof and a notice of a national interest may be registered by the holder thereof.

The registration of an international interest remains effective until discharged or until expiry of the period specified in the registration and any person may, in the manner prescribed by the Protocol or regulations, make or request a search of the International Registry concerning interests registered therein. Upon receipt of a request therefor, the registrar, in the manner prescribed by the Protocol or regulations, is empowered to issue a registry search certificate with respect to any object: stating all registered information relating thereto, together with a statement indicating the date and time of registration of such information; or stating that there is no information in the International Registry relating thereto.

Leasing of aircraft and equipment

Leasing has become a strategic commercial manoeuvre of airlines only in the past 20 years. Of these, the first decade – the 1980s – saw a boom in commercial aviation and therefore a corresponding upsurge in aircraft manufacture, and the 1990s saw a downturn of this trend, contributed to in part by vacillations of the world economy which brought to bear regional economic crises such as the Asian slump in the late 1990s.

The downturn of the 1990s and the ensuing money market crisis has underscored the value of juggling the most expensive singular asset of the aviation industry – the aircraft. Aircraft financiers are quick to offer flexible investment options to airlines to obviate the burden of outright purchase of aircraft. Apart from traditional loans available, two of the most effective financial tools now available to the airline industry for the procurement of aircraft are finance leasing and operational leasing.[138] These leasing options are particularly beneficial to small airlines which are at high risk because of their limited asset bases.

Leasing of aircraft has effectively extended the operational life of aircraft to encompass second and third operators. The magnitude of this financial option is well borne out by the fact that at least 25 per cent of aircraft being used in the airlines are leased.[139] Essentially, the three most basic benefits bestowed to the lessor and lessee by a lease are reduction and spreading of risk of the asset, attendant tax benefits and flexibility of operation. In terms of the nature of operation of a lease, the leasing process may either take the form of a wet lease – a lease where the air crew of the lessor is an integral part of the lease agreement – and a dry lease, where the lessor transfers possession of the aircraft without crew.

Very simplistically put, leasing is the transfer of possession without ownership. Legally speaking, however, the definition becomes somewhat longer, in that a lease at law is essentially a commercial arrangement whereby a lessor (or equipment owner) conveys to the lessee (or operator of the equipment) for valuable consideration in the form of rentals over a period of time specified in the lease agreement, the right to use the equipment.[140] The lessee is legally obligated to return to the lessor the equipment he leases at the expiration of the term of the lease,[141] in reasonably good order, leaving a margin for wear and tear of normal usage.[142]

Donald Bunker, in his most informative treatise[143] on aerospace financing, cites the 1960s paradigm of IBM and XEROX leases which typifies the principles of the modern lease. Both companies utilized the lease of their equipment as a tool of marketing strategy which was calculated to maximize their profits over a standard sale, by amortizing the capital costs of the equipment and earning a profit over the sustenance of the lease period. Over and above this fundamental benefit, a lease effectively demarcates the market pricing between new and used equipment, thus allowing the resale market to flourish on its own by removing obsolete equipment from the market place. The blend of new and used equipment pricing policies balances an enterprise's cash flow and asset base while ensuring a more orderly growth of reported profits.[144] To the consumer, or operator, a lease offers maximum flexibility for selective use of a product, which, in lay terms, would be the equivalent of walking into a baker's shop and being able to buy a slice of pie to allay one's hunger, without having to buy the whole pie. In the context of aircraft leasing, this financial principle is of paramount importance, since leased aircraft can meet seasonal demand for additional capacity without the operator having to incur the capital outlay involved in the outright purchase of an aircraft. Additionally, leased aircraft can be selected to fit into routes and meet specific measurements and requirements of certain routes for which an operator obtains air traffic rights but does not own the equipment to enjoy the rights. This is particularly applicable in the case of smaller air carriers who have traffic rights to operate on certain routes but do not have the appropriate equipment for the purpose.

The registration of the airline is a paramount legal consideration which has to be addressed when an airline uses leased aircraft. The basic postulate of law which currently applies to the legal identity of aircraft lies in Article 17 of the Chicago Convention,[145] which states that aircraft have the nationality of the state in which they are registered. The Convention further provides that an aircraft cannot be validly registered in more than one state, but its registration may be changed from one state to another.[146] With regard to the registration or transfer of registration of aircraft, the Convention provides that such has to accord with the applicable national laws and regulations of the states concerned.[147]

The most fundamental characteristic of an aircraft at international law is its nationality. Both the Paris Convention of 1919[148] and the Chicago Convention provide that the nationality of an aircraft is governed by the state in which such aircraft is registered. The Tokyo Convention on Offences Committed on Board Aircraft (1963)[149] provides that the state of registration has jurisdiction over offences and acts committed on board.[150] Therefore it is reasonable to conclude that the national status of an aircraft would depend on the fact of its registration and to this extent is not dissimilar to the maritime law concept of nationality of ships. The most explicit pronouncement on nationality of vessels was given by the International Court of Justice in the famous *Nottebohm* case,[151] where the court held:

> The character thus recognized on the international level as pertaining to nationality is in no way inconsistent with the fact that international law leaves it to each State to lay down the rules governing the grant of its own nationality. The reason for this is that the diversity of demographic conditions has thus far made it impossible for any general agreement to be reached on the rules relating to nationality, although the latter by its

very nature affects international relations. It has been considered that the best way of making such rules accord with the varying demographic conditions in different countries is to leave the fixing of such rules to the competence of each State. On the other hand, a State cannot claim that the rules it has thus laid down are entitled to recognition by another State unless it has acted in conformity with this general aim of making the legal bond of nationality accord with the individual's genuine connection with the State which assumes the defence of its citizens by means of protection as against other states.

... According to the practice of states, to arbitral and judicial decisions and to the opinions of writers, nationality is a legal bond having as its basis a social fact of attachment, a genuine connection of existence, interests and sentiments, together with the existence of reciprocal rights and duties. It may be said to constitute the juridical expression of the fact that the individual upon whom it is conferred, either directly by the law or as the result of an act of the authorities, is in fact more closely connected with the population of the State conferring nationality than with that of any other State. Conferred by a State, it only entitles that state to exercise protection vis-à-vis another State, if it constitutes a translation into juridical terms of the individual's connection with the State which has made him its national.[152]

In the particular instance of aircraft, the concept of registration and nationality has evolved with changing conditions of civil aeronautical activities relating to the development of airline contracts concerning the use of aircraft which brought in fiscal advantages to airlines. Specific contacts, such as leases, charters and interchange of aircraft, are now assisting air carriers to obviate the need to find money to buy new aircraft. More carriers are now entering into short-term lease agreements to keep their operations afloat and such dry or wet lease agreements necessitate a closer look at the requirements of registration and nationality as dictated to by the Chicago Convention.

In order to accord with commercial exigencies relating to lease and charters in the air transport industry, The International Civil Aviation Organization (ICAO)[153] has introduced Article 83*bis* to the Chicago Convention, which provides, inter alia, that, when an aircraft registered in a contracting state is operated pursuant to a contract for the lease, charter or interchange of the aircraft by an operator who has his principal place of business or, if he has no such place of business, his principal residence in another state, the state of registry of the aircraft concerned may, by agreement with such state, transfer all or part of its duties as state of registry to such other state.[154] Technically, this means that a state may lease aircraft registered in another state, and, by mutual agreement, take over responsibilities of the state of registration in respect of that aircraft. Under these circumstances, it may be reasonable to assume that, in the event of an aircraft leased by a state performing functions of a military nature for the lessee state, such state could be considered the state of registration if an agreement to that effect had been put into effect between the lessor and lessee.

Article 83*bis* of the Convention was timely, in that it was adopted at a time when trade barriers were being rapidly obviated and many industries were being globalized. Instances of as many as nine multinational partners in one industry are not uncommon in today's commercial world. In particular, commercial trends in the United Sates and United Kingdom show new emergent large airlines with the participation of more than one nationality.

Although the current bilateral regulatory structure calls for substantial ownership and effective control of airlines by nationals or companies of a designating state –

which essentially means that for Country A to designate its airline to operate commercial flights the airline must be substantially owned and effectively controlled by nationals or companies of Country A – this requirement is increasingly becoming impracticable to fulfil in various instances. In recognition of one such circumstance, the ICAO Assembly, at its 24th Session, adopted Resolution A24-12 which recognized the political reality of regional groupings of states into composite economic entities, forming a community of interest. The Assembly recognized that such a community of interest, when applicable to groups of developing states, would require their airlines to be identified on a common basis with regard to their substantial ownership and effective control in the context of bilateral regulation of air traffic rights. Therefore the ICAO Assembly urged contracting states by its resolution to accept the designation of, and allow an airline substantially owned and effectively controlled by one or more developing state or states (or its or their nationals) belonging to a regional economic grouping to exercise the route rights and other air transport rights of any developing state or states within the same grouping under mutually acceptable terms.

There are other instances, such as when airlines have multinational ownership (involving ownership of one airline by several states, as in the instances of Gulf Air, Air Afrique, SAS and LIAT), have ownership registered in one country but being accepted as airlines of another (such as Britannia and Monarch, whose ownership rests in Canada and Switzerland, respectively, but operate air services as designated carriers of the United Kingdom), and are owned by legal persons whose businesses are not domiciled in the country in which the carrier has its place of business (such as Cathay Pacific Airlines).

The 'Third Package' of the European Union, which allows for airlines within the Union to be owned by nationals or companies of any member state, gives further credence to the compelling need to consider the element of designation of airlines outside the purview of the conventional philosophy of 'substantial ownership and effective control' as required by the current bilateral regulatory regime. In view of the above developments, the dictates of aircraft financing require financiers to be aware of the multitude of possibilities of litigation for ownership and control of aircraft financed by them and also the legal implications of aircraft leasing in the modern context. Donald Bunker states:

> The concept of registration has now developed such that financiers of commercial aircraft for use internationally must be well aware of the effect that the country of registration could have on their rights. The relatively liquid world market in used aircraft makes aircraft financing quite attractive to many investors. However, most prudent financiers like to be assured of being able to obtain possession of their equipment, free and clear of a defaulting debtor's rights and deregistered by the operator's country so that an efficient realization of their security could be achieved.[155]

From the point of view of the airline which leases aircraft and sustains damage to the aircraft and to its passengers, the legal relationship between lessor and lessee of property would apply in common law jurisdictions. The lessor of the aircraft would usually be covered by his own insurance or by an indemnification agreement between the lessor and lessee. In a typical financial lease agreement of aircraft, the position of the lessor could be that of a lender at common law, and to that extent he would be protected from the mere presumption ipso facto that he is liable by virtue of his ownership of the aircraft. However, this is not strictly an inflexible rule and different jurisdictions may impose strict liability in certain situations.[156] There is also the possibility that rules of negligence may apply in certain jurisdictions where an injured party – the lessee – may seek redress from the lessor of the aircraft. Such claims are often prompted by the favourable financial circumstances that lessors are in usually.

The protection of the lessee in instances of damage is usually assured by the liability insurance obtained by the lessee. The lessee could also qualify the indemnity agreement he signs with the lessor that the lessee's liability would be valid and effectual only in instances when the lessor is not negligent or in default of his agreement. The lessee would therefore be protected against such acts as arbitrary seizure of property by the lessor. Other legal measures available to the lessee are his capacity and legal right to insert a clause in the lease agreement that the leased property is accepted by the lessee on condition of warranty as to the quality of the property; and his ability to obtain warranty direct from the manufacturer.

The formation of a lease contract is like that in any other contract involving the offer of the offeror and acceptance by the offeree. However, unlike the contract of sale when possession and ownership of the article in issue passes to the offeree, the lease contract passes only possession. In other words, the lessee obtains from the lease contract the rights to use and enjoy the property concerned but is precluded from having the right to alienate (or sell) it. Of course, the lessee is required, in exchange for the above rights, to pay the lessor a periodic rental.

Usually, as in any contractual agreement, the parties to the agreement have to place their signatures on the document of contract to conclude the deal and activate performance of the contract. There are exceptions to this rule, however, which may, albeit unusually, apply to an aircraft lease. An agreement would be enforceable without signature. In the 1988 Australian case of *Empirnall Holdings Pty Ltd* v. *Machon Paull Partners Pty Ltd*,[157] where a building contract required the signature of the client with the architects and the client refused to sign the contract form, the New South Wales Court of Appeal held that, since the project went through with the knowledge of the client and without his formal objection, the contract was valid. Analogically, if by practice or habit and repute a lease arrangement is sustained by the lessor and lessee, common law courts may presume that the offer by the lessor was accepted by the conduct of the lessee.

There is also the possibility of courts imputing to the parties their intent to implement a contractual agreement if the parties negotiate for some time and start to act as though a deal has been made. In the 1988 case of *Integrated Computer Services Pty Ltd* v. *Digital Equipment Corporation (Australia) Pty Ltd*,[158] where the parties concerned negotiated for some time and slid into implementing the terms of their negotiation without a formal contractual document, the court said:

> Moreover, in an ongoing relationship, it is not always easy to point to the precise moment when the legal criteria of a contract have been fulfilled. Agreements concerning terms and conditions which might be too uncertain or too illusory to enforce at a particular time in the relationship may by reason of the parties' subsequent conduct become sufficiently specific to give rise to legal rights and duties. In a dynamic

commercial relationship new terms will be added or will supersede older terms. It is necessary therefore to look at the whole relationship and not only at what was said and done when the relationship was first formed.

It may well be that a lessee airline may need an aircraft on lease urgently and therefore negotiate with the lessor on terms which, before they are enshrined in a contractual agreement, are put into practice to provide urgent air transport services. In such cases, the *Integrated Computer Services* case[159] may be seen as a persuasive judicial pronouncement. An extension to the principle of performance of a contract without formal agreement lies in the principle of estoppel where, even though a contract is not signed, it is considered to be legally binding on the basis of the conduct of the parties whereby one party may be estopped from regarding the contract as voidable on the grounds of lack of formal documentation or signature. For the doctrine of estoppel to operate the following criteria have to be satisfied: there must be a definite assurance or representation by words or conduct (which can include doing nothing); there must be reasonable detrimental reliance by the other party; and there must be unconscionable conduct by the party estopped.[160]

If the lease is put up for tender by the lessee, the tenderer or prospective lessor may make an offer, to be accepted by the lessee. In such an instance, courts no longer find the tendering process mutually exclusive from the contractual process in that the tendering process is called the 'pre-contractual' process which itself may be governed by common law principles of contract. The Canadian Supreme Court, in 1981, pronounced that there are two contractual processes which run parallel to each other: the tendering process and the contractual implementation process.[161] Therefore, according to this principle, one cannot argue that the tendering process or period covering tendering negotiations were not covered by enforceable obligations.

Frustration of a lease, or non-performance of the lease contract owing to intervening circumstances such as the outbreak of war, is indeed a realistic circumstance that has to be considered on the subject of aircraft lease. On the question as to what recourse either party has to a lease if, after the execution of a lease agreement for the lease of an aircraft the contract cannot be performed because of the outbreak of war, both parties to the agreement may find the contract frustrated at least temporarily. In such an instance, the court invested with the case would inquire as to whether the lease could have been carried through on a long-term basis and the 1945 *Cricklewood*[162] principle, established by the House of Lords – that a temporary event such as the outbreak of war would not strike at the root of a lease transaction if such transaction could have been executed in the long term – would apply. However, it has since been established in certain circumstances that the doctrine of frustration can affect a lease, particularly before the lessee takes possession of the leased property.[163]

The lessor usually opts for the law of his domicile as choice of law in the event of a dispute or adjudication, or even for the administration of the lease. Often the lessee negotiates this issue by suggesting another form, particularly if the lessee's choice does not adversely affect the lessor's rights. The lessee gains the right to 'quiet use and enjoyment' of the property through a fundamental covenant of aircraft lease, which essentially guarantees the lessee uninterrupted and untrammelled use of the leased aircraft. Margo[164] points out that, in some instances, a lessor may attempt to preserve for himself residual rights with regard to uninterrupted and untrammelled use, by hedging the absolute covenant. This hedging process could take place particularly in instances where the leased property comes with a lien or rights of a head lessor or financier.[165]

One of the critical factors of an aircraft lease, particularly from the perspective of the lessee, is the date of delivery of the aircraft. This is yet another area where lessees have to be cautious about exclusionary language in the lease transaction allowing a lessor to have unreasonable flexibility with regard to the delivery date. A security deposit of an advance of rental is usually requested by the lessor and this condition is usually incorporated in the memorandum of understanding or letter of interest which forms the base document of the lease transaction. The memorandum, which is the precursor to a formal agreement, usually covers the fundamental terms of the agreement and records the fact that the parties will, at a future date, enter into a formal lease agreement. Obviously, the lessee will exercise caution as to the terms of the contract, which could be heavily weighted in favour of the lessor in the usual instance of the letter of intent and formal agreement being drafted by the lessor's lawyers.

Maintenance of the leased aircraft is another issue which has to be addressed by the lessee with caution, particularly in the event of an operational lease. The lessor, in this instance, would insist on stringent maintenance terms, at least in accordance with the lessee's approved maintenance standards, prudent airline industry practice and pertinent manufacturer's manuals. The lessor is also usually cautious in avoiding the possibility of the lessee surrendering possession of the leased aircraft during the time of the lease to a third party for maintenance purposes. The lessee usually has options such as sub-leasing – particularly when it becomes necessary to be consistent with the demand faced by the lessee for air transport – and pooling of aircraft components with other carriers. The interchange of aircraft components within the lessee's aircraft fleet is another option that the lessee may wish to negotiate.

Leasing of aircraft has far-reaching consequences in the regulatory field, in that several provisions of the Chicago Convention affect the commercial activity of leasing. As discussed earlier, Article 17 of the Convention provides that aircraft have the nationality of the state in which they are registered, which, prima facie, means that a leased aircraft would be considered as bearing the nationality of the state in which it is registered. There is no dual registration under the Convention as per Article 18. Furthermore, each contracting state is obligated by Article 12 to ensure that every aircraft entered in its register complies with the laws and regulations in force therein, wherever the aircraft may be at any given time. There are three other relevant provisions: Articles 30, 31 and 32(*a*) of the Convention which prescribe that the state of registry shall be responsible for the certification of aircraft's airworthiness, licensing of radios and the licensing of operating crew. Such certificates are required to be issued and validated according to the relevant Annexes to the Convention, that is Annex 1 (Personnel Licensing) and Annex 8 (Airworthiness of Aircraft). In addition, Annex 6 pertains to the operation of aircraft which devolves the responsibility of compliance with the rules of the annex on the state of the operator.

A later development in the annals of the Chicago Convention is the formal adoption by ICAO contracting states of Article 83*bis* on 20 June 1997, where the 98th instrument of ratification of the article was received by ICAO. Article 83*bis*, which was approved by the ICAO Assembly on 6 October 1980 at its 23rd Assembly, essentially provides that, notwithstanding the above-mentioned provisions of the Convention, when an aircraft registered in a contracting state is operated in pursuance of an agreement for the lease, charter or interchange of the aircraft or any similar arrangement by an operator who has his principal place or business or if he has no principal place of business, his permanent residence in another contracting state, the state of registry may, by agreement with such other States, transfer to it all or part of its functions and duties as state of registry and the state of registry shall be relieved of responsibility in respect of the functions and duties so transferred.[166]

According to guidelines of the ICAO Secretariat[167] on the application of Article 83*bis*, states should not enter into a transfer agreement if the state of the operator concerned is not capable of adequately performing the duties and functions which are envisaged for transfer. The aircraft concerned should be clearly identified in the agreement by including reference to the aircraft type, registration and serial numbers.

Any type of commercial arrangement for cross-border lease, charter or interchange of aircraft, or any similar arrangement, may give rise to a transfer agreement. The ICAO Secretariat guidelines also provide that wet-leased aircraft may be subject to a transfer agreement between the state of registry (normally the state of the lessor) and the State of the lessee or sub-lessee, provided that they are operated under the air operator certificate (AOC) of the lessee or, in the case of a sub-lease, under the AOC of the sub-lessee. The issuance of an AOC, as required by Annex 6 for (international) commercial operations, is not a precondition for such a transfer agreement, whose object may be general aviation aircraft as well.

It is also recommended that the duration of the agreement on the transfer should not exceed the period covered by the corresponding commercial arrangement (for example, the lease). Accordingly, the period of validity of the transfer should be mentioned in the agreement, taking into consideration that the registration of the aircraft concerned will not be changed. The level of authority for signing transfer agreements should be equivalent to that required for administrative arrangements between aeronautical authorities.

The ICAO guidelines note that, pursuant to Article 83, as referred to in Article 83*bis* paragraph (b), the 'Rules for Registration with ICAO of Aeronautical Agreements and Arrangements' (Doc. 6685) apply to any agreement or arrangement relating to international civil aviation. Implementation of Article 83*bis* can be made through agreements between civil aviation authorities, usually signed at the level of Director General, that is, which do not require diplomatic credentials for signature; nor do they require ratification.

Any transfer agreement signed between states parties to Article 83*bis* will be binding upon the other states parties thereto, on condition that it has been formally registered with the Council of ICAO and made public in accordance with Article 83 of the Chicago Convention, or that any third state concerned has been officially advised by way of direct notification, normally by the state of the operator. Consequently, the state of registry shall be relieved of responsibility (and, where applicable, of liability) in respect of the functions and duties duly transferred to the state of the operator, and the latter shall comply with them in accordance with its own laws and regulations. States are required to ensure that, as state of registry, their legislation enables them to divest themselves of the functions and duties which are the object of a transfer agreement. Furthermore, as state of the operator, states should ensure that their legislation will apply to foreign-registered aircraft subject to a transfer agreement.

States which have ratified Article 83*bis* should ensure that, in order to be consistent with the provisions of Article 33 of the Convention, their legislation recognizes the validity of certificates of airworthiness, as well as of radio licences and crew licences, issued or validated by the state of the operator in accordance with Article 83*bis*. Furthermore, states which ratify Article 83*bis* should ensure that the information they have received concerning the existence of transfer agreements relating to aircraft operating to/from their territory is promptly relayed to the authorities involved in inspection. For the purpose of identifying the responsible states during the verification process, a certified true copy of the transfer agreement should be carried on board the aircraft at all times while the transfer agreement is in force.[168]

In the instance of an aircraft under an Article 83*bis* agreement entering the airspace of contracting states which are not parties to the provision, or which are parties but have not been duly advised about a transfer agreement in accordance with this provision, the certificates and licences on board the aircraft should be issued or rendered valid by the state of registry as the latter would in this case remain fully responsible in regard to Articles 30, 31 and 32(*a*) of the Convention despite the transfer agreement with the state of the operator.

The European Civil Aviation Conference (ECAC) in July 1997, issued its policies and practices of states on aircraft leasing.[169] According to these policies, it is recommended that, before granting approval for a lease, authorities should obtain the following information:

- type of lease;
- names of the parties to the agreement;
- start date and duration of lease;
- number and type of aircraft, registration mark(s) and country of registration, noise certificate(s) where appropriate;
- evidence of passenger and third party insurance;
- name of air carrier under whose AOC the aircraft will be operated and maintained;
- name of air carrier with commercial control of the aircraft.

ECAC has recommended that member states may also require additional information, for example concerning the reason for the lease and the planned operations, to the extent that such information is necessary to ensure compliance with their national rules and international obligations.

On the subject of transfer of functions and duties in a leasing situation, the ECAC recommendation is that, in the case of a dry lease, all or part of the functions and duties in respect of the leased aircraft under Articles 12, 30, 31 and 32(*a*) of the Chicago Convention should normally be transferred to the authorities of the lessee in accordance with Article 83*bis*. For this purpose it is recommended that all member states ratify this article as soon as possible to enable it to enter into force.

In the case of a wet lease the ECAC recommendations are as follows:

a) Before granting approval to an air carrier to lease in an aircraft, an aeronautical authority shall be satisfied, if necessary by means of an audit, that the lessor meets safety standards equivalent to those which its own airlines are required to meet under their AOC.

b) Furthermore, an air carrier shall only be permitted to wet lease in an aircraft of a type not included in its own AOC if the authority considers that this will not affect the maintenance of safety standards equivalent to those which the lessee is required to meet under its own AOC.

c) A lessor may not fulfil its obligations towards the lessee with capacity wet leased in from a third carrier unless this has been approved by the aeronautical authority of the lessee.

d) Approval for the use of wet-leased aircraft should not be given for an unlimited period of time.

e) The information listed in paragraph 2 should also be obtained before approval is granted for short notice leases. However, alternative arrangements for the prior approval of such leases may be implemented by the appropriate aeronautical authorities. Such alternative arrangements might include, for example, the establishment of a list of air carriers approved by its national aeronautical authorities from whom an air carrier may lease an aircraft at short notice to meet an unforeseen need for a short period.

f) The use of wet-leased aircraft should not be used as a means to circumvent applicable laws, regulations or international agreements.

g) Aeronautical authorities should respond promptly to requests from their counterparts in other Member States for information about leases.

h) Consumers should be informed, as soon as practicable and in any event prior to boarding, of the actual operator if a flight is to be operated with a wet-leased aircraft.

i) Member States may also, for safety and/or economic reasons, and where this is compatible with national and international regulations, choose to ensure that air carriers are not excessively dependent on wet-leased aircraft registered in another State.

ECAC urges member states to cooperate in the provision of information concerning leases, in particular in connection with the ECAC Action Programme for the Safety Assessment of Foreign Aircraft (SAFA).

Technically, Article 83*bis* is calculated to tighten and ensure the more efficient operation of aircraft in terms of both safety and commercial expediency by attaching responsibility to the state of the operator since it is the state of the operator which is immediately concerned with the operation of the aircraft concerned, rather than the state of registry, which may be far away from the actual operational site. However, this transfer of functions and duties does not take effect automatically, but has to be given affect through bilateral accord between the state of registry and state of operation. The transfer shall only have effect upon states which ratify the Protocol implementing Article 83*bis*. The particular transfer of functions and duties must be registered with ICAO.

The worlds 'any similar arrangement' in Article 83*bis* widens the scope of commercial activity envisaged from lease, charter or interchange to any other arrangement of a similar character.

Safety issues

The basic postulate in determining the safety aspects of the use of leased aircraft in international air transport lies on the fact that responsibility for safety should devolve on clear and identified states parties in the context of the use of leased aircraft. The questions as to which state (state of registry or state of the operator) is responsible for ensuring compliance with applicable safety standards provided by the Chicago Convention and its annexes, and which operator (air carrier or company) is responsible for complying with the relevant international safety standards which have been incorporated into the applicable national laws and regulations, become compelling and relevant.

Although the Chicago Convention devolves responsibility for ensuring compliance with applicable safety standards primarily upon the state of registry of the aircraft, it also assigns responsibility to the state of the operator on certain aspects of a lease agreement. This bifurcation is to take into consideration contingencies where traffic rights are exchanged on a bilateral/regional basis, and national laws and regulations which may be applicable to the registration of aircraft, where, in most cases operators which are designated or authorized by a state for international commercial service use aircraft registered in that state. In these circumstances, responsibilities with regard to safety on the part of both the state and the operator become eminently clear.

Whether it be a dry or wet lease, safety considerations are equally significant and important. In the case of a dry lease, where the leased aircraft is registered in the state designating or authorizing the lessee operator for international commercial services, essentially the same principles would apply from a safety standpoint as when that operator uses its own aircraft. Accordingly, when an airline takes on a dry lease of an aircraft from another airline domiciled in the same state and uses such aircraft for international air transport, there is no change in the state's safety oversight responsibility, although the responsibility for air carrier compliance rests with the lessee. Where an airline enters into a wet lease of an aircraft with another airline of the same state, the safety responsibilities remain at status quo ante, that is, with the lessee who operates the aircraft, but compliance with other responsibilities such as certification generally remain with the lessor.

Safety problems may also arise where a leased aircraft is registered in a state other than that of the operator who uses the leased aircraft in international commercial services. For this reason, approval of dry and wet leases should clearly stipulate the scope of responsibilities and liabilities of parties with respect to safety standards undertaken by each of them.

The issue of crew competence, or capability, which is a critical factor in aviation safety oversight, arises particularly in instances where a dry-leased aircraft is not registered in the state of the operator. It is noteworthy that, in this regard, Article 32 (*a*) of the Chicago Convention requires that the pilot of every aircraft and the other members of the operating crew of every aircraft engaged in international navigation shall be provided with certificates of competency and licences issued or rendered valid by the state in which the aircraft is registered. As discussed earlier, the application of Article 83*bis* and ICAO Secretariat guidelines require an agreement between the two states which sets forth the specific responsibilities to be transferred and the particular aircraft to which they will apply.[170] Any transfer agreement signed between states parties to the Protocol relating to Article 83*bis* legally binds all other states parties to the Protocol, on condition that any such transfer agreement has been formally registered with the Council of ICAO and made public in accordance with Article 83 of the Chicago Convention. This principle would also apply in instances where any third state concerned has been officially advised by way of direct notification, normally by the state of the operator.

An incentive for states in considering whether or not to conclude an agreement under Article 83*bis* lies in the assurance that the state to which safety responsibilities are to be transferred has the capability of fulfilling its safety oversight responsibilities with respect to the specific aircraft involved. Of a particularly persuasive stature in this regard is the fact that states parties to Article 83*bis* can also use the results of audits carried out under the ICAO Safety Oversight Audit Programme which are available to states through summary reports.

The aircraft noise issue has entered a phase where trading and environmental issues are at a delicate balance. On the one hand, competition issues pertaining to the sale of hush-kits and other equipment calculated to reduce aircraft engine noise to levels prescribed by ICAO are quite significant from the perspective of international trade, and, on the other hand, environmental issues that have been addressed by the ICAO Council through its Committee on Aviation Environmental Protection (CAEP) and also by the Assembly should also be given careful consideration. As discussed in Chapter 5, ICAO Assembly Resolution A32-8 urges states to give consideration to the economic difficulties that some states may have to face in phasing out Chapter 2 aircraft by the year 2002. However, the resolution does not leave room for states to claim that pure economic factors would effectively preclude them from phasing out Chapter 2 aircraft by the date stipulated in the resolution.

The dichotomy presented by the aircraft noise issue has to be viewed in the broader perspective of trade and the environment. The symbiosis of trade and the environment emerged as a critical issue for trade negotiators in the last stages of the Uruguay Round of discussions. At these discussions the focus remained on two approaches to the issue. The first approach was from the essentially pro-environment groups, who considered that those involved in international trade are primarily interested in the movement of their goods and therefore were not concerned about the environmental implications of their trading activities. The second approach was based on the belief that increased trading activity enhanced possibilities of solving environmental problems.

The key issue in the developments taking place in aircraft noise legislation must essentially be that economic progress through international trade and the conservation of the environment should not be viewed as mutually exclusive, but rather as inseparably linked and mutually supportive streams of activity. The international profiles of these two prolific considerations have unfortunately been perceived and developed in isolation. While free traders advocating trade liberalization have been represented by some as being ideologically opposed to environmentalists who are allegedly in favour of trade restrictions in favour of environmental protection, environmentalists, in some quarters, have been portrayed as purely one-sided and anti-development. These perceptions are somewhat extreme and colour the necessary balance between the two activities.

Although free trade is seemingly the antithesis to environmental protection, it is a fact that the two interact in a complex manner. The possibility that free trade would increase incomes, give access to more resources and education, thus creating more opportunity for environmental protection, should be viewed with the counterargument that trade liberalization would reduce prices and increase demand, leading to an overexploitation of natural resources and free trade across barriers which would, in turn, encourage the movement of environmentally hazardous material. The most pragmatic view seems to be that free trade and the environment are equally crucial for sustainable economic development.[171]

Multilateral lending institutions such as the World Bank and the International Monetary Fund are beginning to lay more emphasis on the environmental impact of projects funded by them. However, in the ultimate analysis, both international trade and environmental protection are key issues for development, and they should be viewed as tools that could result in a win–win situation for the parties concerned. This principle takes an interesting turn where, in this particular context, the introduction of new aircraft and the increase in trade in aircraft is a by-product of the environmental consciousness of the world community.

The popularity of a lease contract lies essentially in the fact that both the lessor and the lessee gain optimum ownership and possessary benefits, respectively, from a lease, which may not accrue from a straightforward sale. For instance, the lessor retains ownership of the property, which is still considered by most financiers to be the most substantial security for the purpose of transacting. Another great benefit of a lease is that it may provide and attract substantial fixed funding over a sustained period of time. From the lessee's perspective, his taxes would decrease in comparable terms from the lessor's rates through the benefits of manufacturing and processing credits, and also through delivery and installation costs, insurance premiums and professional fees.

Another benefit of a lease is that a lease could be structured to be as flexible as the parties wish it to be. While leasing companies have more pliant policies in constructing lease contracts, they may also be willing, in most instances, to vary lease payments. Above all, a lease may allow the lessee a much needed 'stopgap' measure to fill in its airline operations with a few more aircraft, while not tying itself down to commit itself to the purchase of a new or second-hand aircraft. A lessee airline could use a lease to run its operations to an optimum level, while retaining the option to update its airline fleet from time to time. This remains the most fundamental benefit of the lease agreement and makes it the most flexible tool in airline fleet management.

On the negative side, parties to an aircraft lease have to exercise extreme caution with regard to the safety consequences which a lease may entail. It is prudent to determine and arrive at a legally binding understanding between parties as to the specific states which will be responsible for regulatory aspects of safety in a lease and which airline operators are responsible for complying with safety standards, be it the lessor or lessee. Other key areas for consideration are what measures are necessary for safe operation of the leased aircraft (crew familiarization, licence validation, and so on); what factors are necessary for compliance with Article 83*bis* for the provision to be effective and efficiently implemented; the specific states involved; the safety functions to be transferred; and the aircraft to be included.

States concerned should establish the types of leases which can be approved or need not be regulated, such as financial and operating leases of non-airline entities; leases of aircraft owned by air carriers of parties to relevant bilateral agreements if any are applicable; and wet leases in short-term, unforeseen situations, using a list of potential lessor airlines as approved sources. Another need is to establish criteria for the approval of wet leases of aircraft from airlines of third countries, taking into consideration such factors as the right to use air traffic rights involved, the aspect of reciprocity of enjoyment of air traffic rights and the attendant benefit with regard to the traffic carried or in the use of particular routes.

Aircraft and equipment leasing is now a common practice in the airline industry and a rigid approach to leasing would indeed be counterproductive. At the same time, it would be distinctly detrimental to the future of the airline industry if one were to make the leasing agreement and arrangements between carriers pertaining to leases overly flexible, resulting in the impingement of safety. The two aspects have to be addressed harmoniously so that a cautious balance of the elements of freedom and compulsion is maintained.

RIGHTS OF THE PASSENGER

In 2020, there will be no more stressed passengers. There will be more routes to choose from and more flights to more destinations. Flying will become a customized experience with greater seat pitch, more leg room, quieter interiors and cleaner cabin air quality. Ninety-nine per cent of aircraft will arrive on time and depart within 15 minutes of the published schedule. Electronic check-ins will ensure steady passage through the terminal building and advanced automated baggage handling will ensure that you will sleep in your pyjamas in the hotel, after landing.

Called the 2020 vision, the above reflects how European aerospace personalities see the future.[172] This glowing picture is somewhat tainted by the innumerable complaints which now seem to be arising out of the carriage of passengers by air. In December 2000, an Australian law firm reportedly announced that it would launch a class action suit against several airlines over failure to warn passengers about the risk of health hazards associated with air travel.[173]

The ICAO records that, during the year 1999, 1558 million passengers were carried by 721 air carriers.[174] Even if this figure may not prove to be spectacular in the face of the exponential growth of air traffic, estimated to grow well above the 5 per cent mark during the years 2000–2001,[175] it provides some stimulus for reflection as to the enormity of passenger carriage by air that will occur over the next few decades. It also begs the question as to whether we should be returning to the commercial aviation philosophy of the mid-1980s, explained so eloquently by the then president of SAS, Jan Carlson, that 'everyone needs to know and feel that he is needed; everyone wants to be treated as an individual'.[176]

The main thrust of aviation at the dawn of the twenty-first century, at least from the perspective of air law, lies in the consideration of the abiding moral, if not legal, responsibility of the airline industry to take steps in converting the contract of carriage from a mere exchange of rights and liabilities to an extended relationship of 'give and take' between the carrier and the airline passenger. On the one hand, emerging trends of commercial aviation reflect the fact that, in view of increased competition, airlines have to woo the passenger now more than at any time before, with promises of an enchanted journey. On the other, the passenger has to conduct himself better while in the custody of the carrier throughout the journey.

In the new millennium, individual airlines will be compelled to remain competitive, just to survive. They will need to flow with the tide of such commercial trends as privatization, the use of information technology, removing infrastructure constraints and governmental restraints and, most importantly, changing travel patterns. These trends have given rise to the new phenomenon in the global aviation scene that survival (if not success) of airlines is now dependent, not on pricing, but on service. This new phenomenon calls for the airline product to be similar to one from the entertainment industry, bearing in mind that a passenger spends 70 per cent of his total travel time in the aircraft on long-distance flights. To counter strong alliances between countries and airlines, the smaller carriers (as well as the big ones) are now going in more for glamour and in-flight luxury to score on the 70 per cent in flight time. Personal video screens for every seat, satellite-assisted telephone facilities and tele-conference services are some of the luxuries offered. Indeed, as David Shoenfeld, International Marketing Vice President of Federal Express, said: 'If you view your services as flying between terminals, you miss the point.'

The view that 'marketing is determined from the view of the customer' is becoming more valuable now than ever before. To survive, airlines have to build 'brand recognition'. In this context, the International Travel Market Research (INTRAMAR) study is one of the best indicators of the key strategic factors in achieving passenger satisfaction. INTRAMAR usually measures for each airline a PAX/SAT (passenger satisfaction) index that correlates closely with the major indicators of airline performance. An INTRAMAR study, conducted on 44 of the world's most profitable and financially successful airlines, reveals that Singapore Airlines received an extremely high PAX/SAT index rating, coming second among all airlines of the world. The first was Swissair.

According to the INTRAMAR survey, there are 12 important factors influencing passenger choice: flight punctuality, excellence of in-flight service, superiority of aircraft, comfortable seats, clean cabin seats and washrooms, good food and beverages, superior first class, superior business class, efficient reservations systems, pricing, good check-in service, and attractive frequent flyer programmes. At least seven of these factors are entirely dependent on the quality of the aircraft. The foremost important factor – punctuality – cannot, indeed, be achieved with aged aircraft. The matter becomes more crucial to a relatively small airline, running a small fleet of aircraft where, if one aircraft was grounded for reasons of repair or maintenance, the entire flight schedule of the airline would be in disarray, leading to delays down the line. Connecting services would be disrupted and passengers stranded. It is needless to envisage the effect this catastrophe would have on the airline's good name. No amount of superior in-flight service would atone for a six-hour delay where a connecting passenger has to sit inside an unknown airport terminal. It is therefore necessary for any airline to consider seriously removing one of its most burdensome infrastructural constraints – its ageing aircraft.

For the passenger's part, he has to refrain from being disruptive of the flight, in that he should respect the rules of conduct on board an aircraft. In a recent survey conducted by the International Air Transport Association, to which 62 airlines responded, it was revealed that 1132 cases of unruly passenger conduct were reported in 1994, which figure rose to 2036 cases in 1995, 3512 cases in 1996 and 5416 cases in 1997.[177] A Secretarial Study Group established by ICAO to address issues of unruly passenger conduct, at its fourth meeting in October 2000, developed draft model legislation on offences committed on board civil aircraft by unruly passengers.[178] The delicate balance between airline and passenger brings to bear the core issue concerning the ultimate consumer in the air transport industry, the passenger. Is the passenger entitled to specific rights and attendant treatment in pursuance of the contract of carriage? The following discussion will examine this issue in some detail.

The passenger

There is no existing definition of 'passenger' in cohesive terms. The closest definition, formulated at a stage when commercial air transport was incipient, can be culled from the British Air Navigation Order of 1960 which lists a passenger, inter alia, as a person carried for hire or reward given or promised in connection with a flight, whether wholly or partly therefor and irrespective of the person by or whom the consideration has been or is to be given.[179] The definition also includes a person carried gratuitously by an air transport undertaking, excluding certain categories.[180] At its Ninth Session, held in 1997, the ICAO Statistics Division recognized that, for the purpose of reporting statistics to ICAO, a revenue passenger would be a passenger for whose transport an air carrier receives commercial remuneration.[181] This definition included passengers travelling under publicly available promotional offers or loyalty programmes (for example, redemption of frequent flyer programmes) passengers travelling as compensation for denied boarding, passengers travelling at corporate discounts, and passengers travelling on preferential fares. The definition excluded passengers travelling free, those travelling at a fare or discount available only to employees of air carriers or their agents or only for travel on the business of the carriers, and infants who do not occupy a seat.[182]

ICAO, by implication, identifies a passenger within its definition of 'passenger aircraft' contained in the 'International Civil Aviation Organization Vocabulary' which provides:

> A passenger aircraft is an aircraft that carries any person other than a crew member, an operator's employee in an official capacity, an authorized representation in an appropriate national authority or person accompanying a consignment or other cargo.[183]

For purposes of discussion within the parameters of this chapter, a passenger would be considered as a person who corresponds to the characteristics contained in the ICAO vocabulary, irrespective of financial considerations flowing between the carrier and the carried or the necessity for a contract of carriage.

ICAO initiatives

The fundamental premise upon which ICAO's continuing work on facilitation of passenger travel is contained in the Convention on International Civil Aviation (Chicago Convention),[184] Article 22 of which provides, inter alia, that each contracting state agrees to adopt all practical measures, to facilitate and expedite navigation by aircraft and to prevent unnecessary delays to aircraft, crews, passengers and cargo. Annex 9 to the Chicago Convention, on facilitation, is the operative document providing guidelines to states on alleviating the lot of the passenger. Annex 9 derives its authority from Article 37 of the Chicago Convention, which vests authority in ICAO to adopt and amend from time to time international standards and recommended practices dealing with facilitation. Numerous provisions of the annex require states to provide services and facilities that would obviate delays and other procedural impediments that would otherwise act to the detriment of the passenger's journey by air.

Chapter 3 of the Annex commences with the general requirement in Standard 3.1 requiring regulations and procedures applied to persons travelling by air not to be less favourable than those applied to persons travelling by other means of transport. This provision establishes, *in limine*, a certain parity of status between air transport and surface transport, particularly in relation to passenger clearance at border crossings and entry points. Standard 3.4 requires that contracting states shall not require from visitors travelling by air any other document of identity than a valid passport. Although this provision could be perceived as unduly restrictive on the sovereign prerogative of a state to require specific entry documentation from individuals, it is not intended to discourage states who wish to be more liberal from accepting official documents of identity other than passports in lieu of valid documents of identity. The annex also contains provisions calculated to simplify travel documents, to provide open access to facilities to obtain a passport, to improve quality of passports, visas and other travel documents, to make easier the visa obtaining process, to expedite entry to and exit from states visited, to obviate difficulties of transit through states not intended to be visited and to ensure the rapid return of baggage which becomes separated from the owners in the transportation process.

In support of these objectives, numerous specifications and guidelines have been published by ICAO for the issuance of machine-readable travel documents,[185] including circulars containing guidance material on access to air transport by people with disabilities, dynamic flight information displays at airports and standardized signs for passengers at airports.

ICAO has also included valuable guidelines for passengers in its *Manual on the Regulation of International Air Transport*.[186] This guidance material was issued by decision of the Council to assist states in publishing or encouraging the publication of booklets intended to inform air transport users of their rights and obligations. The material was developed having regard to the increasing complexity of tariff rules and conditions and the need expressed by states to ensure that the public is fully informed of the rules and conditions when purchasing air transport services.

In 1992, the Latin American Civil Aviation Commission, a regional intergovernmental aviation organization, produced for the guidance of its members a 'Charter of Rights for the Air Transport User' which included many of the items in the inventories developed by ICAO. In considering whether information booklets should be developed in their own countries, states are invited by ICAO to take into account the various means by which such booklets might be developed and disseminated, bearing in mind the need to ensure an appropriate balance of public interest and to ensure that any guidance material is brief, readily comprehensible and widely available.

In some countries, such documents have been developed and published as a public service by the government transport or consumer protection agency concerned, while in other cases independent consumer action groups have been responsible for the documents, funded by government subsidy and/or public donations. All of these publications are made available on request, free of charge, to the general public. Government publications generally make it clear that they are for information only, are not binding and do not override airlines' approved tariff rules or conditions of carriage.

In some other cases, documents have been developed by individual airlines or freight forwarders and made available free of charge on their own aircraft and/or in their sales outlets. Further means of development and distribution are through user groups, such as business associations or associations of shippers, and through commercial publishers.

Guidelines of ICAO[187] relating to economic policy provide advice that on most routes two or more classes of travel and a wide range of fares are available, with descriptions indicating the advantages of normal fares (for example, unlimited stop-overs/transfers, indirect routing allowances, no charge for cancellation/change of flight) and of 'restricted' normal economy fares in some markets which retain most of the characteristics historically associated with normal economy fares but have restrictions, for example, on the availability of stopovers or, in some cases, on the ability to interline as well as the price advantages and restrictive conditions attached to special fares (for example, circle trip/round trip requirements, seasonal application, stopover/transfer limitations, minimum and maximum stay periods, advance reservation and payment provisions, cancellation charges and forfeits, group require-ments, ground purchase or other additional purchase requirements). There is also a description of varying availability of discounts for infants, children, students/youth, and so on, and of preferential fares.

There is also advice on conditions that may apply to checking in advance of purchase and, where charges or forfeits apply for change in ticket validity or for ticket change/cancellation, advice to check whether exceptions are granted (for example, in cases of illness or death) and whether insurance against unforeseen changes of plan is available through the airline and/or directly from the insurance company (and, if so, what it covers). The following guidelines are also provided in the ICAO Manual:

a) advice that in many areas certain taxes and/or charges (for example, airport service charges) are not included in the price of the ticket; in such cases, they may be added at the time of purchase and/or collected at the airport prior to departure;
b) advice that the air ticket is the passenger's evidence of his or her contract with the air carrier or charterer;
c) advice regarding implications of purchase of irregularly issued tickets;
d) brief explanation of the main elements of notation on the ticket (for example, boxes showing passenger's name, airports, airlines, flight numbers, code-shared flights

and their significance for the traveller, class of travel, departure dates and times, status, validity, and so on);

e) advice that a file reference number should be obtained and noted when making a reservation or reconfirmation;

f) advice that most airlines have established deadlines by which tickets must be paid for in full (and in some cases collected) failing which the reservations concerned are subject to cancellation, and that tickets are issued at fares subject to government approval;

g) advice that in many countries fares may be advertised and tickets sold at fares which have yet to receive government approval; that such advertisements and tickets should be clearly annotated to the effect that the fares are 'subject to government approval'; and that purchasers of such tickets should ensure that they are aware of the potential consequences of the unapproved status of the fares (for example, possible non-applicability, possible surcharge, rights to refund);

h) advice that, as a general rule, tickets paid for may be subject to surcharge where a fare increase is subsequently approved, but that exceptions to this rule exist in a number of countries;

i) advice concerning rights to refunds and procedures to be followed to obtain refunds;

j) description of differences between 'voluntary' and 'involuntary' refunds and refunds for lost or stolen tickets, service charges, periods within which applications must be made, and expectation of delays in processing;

k) with regard to check-in, advice concerning airline check-in requirements and consequences of failure to observe them, such as cancellation of the reservations for that and any subsequent flights on the itinerary; and

l) on the subject of free baggage allowances and excess baggage charges, there is advice on the existence of different methods of establishing free baggage allowances and excess baggage charges under the so-called 'piece and weight systems', on airline variations under both systems, and on the possibility that different allowances may apply on different sectors of an interline journey or on the return journey.

The Manual also provides valuable information on how best to advance from the airline or its agent the detailed allowances which apply throughout the intended journey, both for carry-on baggage and for checked baggage, cautioning that an airline, at its discretion, may accept excess baggage at charges related to the system being applied and according to its regulations. Attention of passengers is also brought to the fact that passengers travelling together may pool their free baggage allowances.

Often the passenger is unaware that personal effects may be shipped as cargo, generally at lower cost than for shipment as excess baggage, but under more onerous circumstances. One of the most useful items of information could prove to be advice on the existence of limited liability by the airline for lost or damaged baggage, levels of which may be ascertained from the carrier or its agent. Advice on the liability exclusions regarding checked baggage (for example, for certain perishable and valuable items), on the available option of declaring a higher value for baggage on payment of an additional charge and/or, where available, taking out insurance, is also made available to the passenger.

Under certain circumstances, airlines may refuse carriage, in relation to the conduct, age or mental or physical state of the passenger. This brings to bear important exigencies such as 'no-shows', overbooking and compensation for denied boarding.

ICAO guidance which includes a description of a 'no-show' and how to avoid being a 'no-show' includes advice that to compensate for no-shows most airlines often overbook flights, that as a result passengers with confirmed reservations are occasionally denied boarding because of non-availability of seats, and that in certain countries and for certain airlines compensation for such denied boarding is available. Passengers are also informed that they may wish to ascertain, before accepting compensation, their rights at law where major financial or other losses are incurred as a consequence of denied boarding.

On the subject of delays or cancellation of flights, the passenger is informed that when (owing to circumstances beyond their control) airlines cancel or delay a flight or cause a passenger to miss a connection, most airlines accept the obligation to refund or provide alternative flight arrangements at no further cost to the passenger, but do not generally accept any further liability for any damages incurred as a result (for example, lost vacation or work time). Where major financial or other losses are incurred as a consequence of delay, passengers may wish to ascertain their rights at law.

In case of delay to passengers, most airlines customarily provide certain amenities, such as the free provision or reimbursement of the cost of communications, meals, refreshments, transit taxes and, usually in circumstances of prolonged delay during the night hours (at points which are not origin, destination or stopover points), hotel accommodation and ground transport. In this context, the passenger is provided with advice that, in the case of delayed baggage, airlines may, in certain circumstances, provide or reimburse passengers for the purchase of personal necessities.

On reconfirmation of flights, many airlines require reconfirmation of an onward reservation wherever a journey is broken for more than 72 hours, and failure to comply may result in cancellation of the reservation in question, together with those for any subsequent flights in the journey. This is a crucial issue for most passengers, particularly regular travellers who may neglect reconfirmation of flight. Advice as to complaint procedures and avenues for action, including information on differing time periods within which formal claims must be made, is also a key piece of information recommended by ICAO that States disseminate to passengers.

An essential prerequisite for the passenger is his awareness of the conditions of carriage, and ICAO strongly recommends that passengers (and air carriers or charterers) are made to understand that they are bound by conditions appearing on the ticket, by tariff conditions, by carrier or charterer regulations and, outside Canada and the United States, by conditions of carriage, all of which should be readily available from the carriers or charterers for reference. Also of importance is the fact that all these conditions may vary for different segments of a journey, if provided by more than one airline.

On the issue of liability, a brief summary of limits of liability as provided for by international treaty (supplemented in some instances by other arrangements) and available for reference in summary on the ticket coupon and in detail in air carrier conditions of carriage (air carrier tariffs in Canada and the United States) is considered essential information for the passenger. ICAO also recognizes the need for, and recommends strongly that states concerned make available to the passenger, a glossary of descriptions of commonly used air carrier terms and abbreviations.

Also considered critical to the passenger is a checklist of non-tariff matters and advice regarding the following:

- travel documentation: passports (including information on machine-readable passports, where applicable), visas, medical certificates, driving licences, diplomatic/consular representation in foreign countries, and so on;
- health: vaccination requirements, medical treatment, health risks and protection.
- insurance;
- foreign currency and currency restrictions, traveller's cheques, use of credit cards;
- general customs requirements and duty-free purchase allowances, dual-channel clearance system;
- facilities, conditions and procedures for carriage of unaccompanied minors, pregnant women, the obese, and sick and/or handicapped persons;
- carriage of pets;
- hotel reservations and car hire;
- in-flight services (meals, including availability of special meals, drinks, entertainment, and so on);
- seat reservation and selection, smoking regulations;
- how to pack and label, what to pack in carry-on baggage, what to wear;
- carriage of dangerous goods;
- control of illicit traffic in narcotic drugs;
- facilities available at airports;
- key to flight displays and standard signs at airports;
- check-in and boarding procedures, including security arrangements;
- safety on board;
- procedures to be followed in the event that baggage is lost;
- effects of alcohol;
- jet lag.

Other initiatives

The Air Transport Association (ATA) has taken several measures to initiate, among the member carriers of the ATA, a commitment to provide the best level of service to customers. There has been an increasing recognition of the need to improve airline passenger service. As a result, ATA carriers, working with members of Congress, have developed an Airline Customer Service Commitment, and each carrier will develop its individual Customer Service Plan to demonstrate its continuing dedication to improving air travel. ATA carriers are committed to offering the lowest fare possible, in that each airline will offer the lowest fare available for which the customer is eligible on the airline's telephone reservation system for the date, flight and class of service requested. In addition, carriers are required to notify customers of known delays, cancellations and diversions by each airline giving customers at the airport and on board an affected aircraft, in a timely manner, the best available information regarding known delays, cancellations and diversions. Also each airline will establish and implement policies for accommodating passengers delayed overnight. A clear and concise statement of airlines' policies in these respects will also be made available to customers.

With regard to on-time baggage delivery, each airline will make every reasonable effort to return checked bags within 24 hours and will attempt to contact any customer whose unclaimed, checked luggage contains a name and address or telephone number. Each airline will allow the customer either to hold a telephone reservation without payment for 24 hours or (at the election of the carrier) to cancel a reservation without penalty for up to 24 hours, in order to give customers an opportunity to check for lower fares through other distribution systems, such as travel agents or the Internet. Also airlines will issue refunds for eligible tickets within seven days for credit card purchases and 20 days for cash purchases, and will disclose its policies and procedures for handling special needs passengers, such as unaccompanied minors, and for accommodating the disabled in an appropriate manner. Airlines are also required to meet customers' essential needs during long on-aircraft delays by making every reasonable effort to provide food, water, restroom facilities and access to medical treatment for passengers aboard an aircraft that is on the ground for an extended period of time without access to the terminal, as consistent with passenger and employee safety and security concerns. Each carrier will prepare contingency plans to address such circumstances and will work with other carriers and the airport to share facilities and make gates available in an emergency. Airlines will handle bumped passengers (those who have been denied boarding) with fairness and consistency. Each airline will establish and disclose to the customer policies and procedures, including any applicable requirements (such as check-in deadlines), for managing the inability to board all passengers with confirmed reservations.

Airlines will also disclose travel itinerary, cancellation policies, frequent flyer rules, and aircraft configuration. Each airline will disclose to the customer: (a) any change of aircraft on a single flight with the same flight number; (b) cancellation policies involving failures to use each flight segment coupon; (c) rules, restrictions and an annual report on frequent flyer programme redemptions; and (d) upon request, information regarding aircraft configuration, including seat size and pitch.

Another aspect of customer protection and service that ATA recommends is service from code-share partners. Each airline is required to ensure that domestic code-share partners make a commitment to provide comparable consumer plans and policies. Airlines are also expected to be more responsive to customer complaints in that each airline will assign a Customer Service Representative responsible for handling passenger complaints and ensuring that all written complaints are responded to within 60 days.

Airlines are expected to develop and implement a Customer Service Plan for meeting its obligations under the Airline Customer Service Commitment. Customer Service Plans will be completed and published within 90 days and will be fully implemented within six months. Airline implementation will include training for airline reservation, customer service and sales personnel to enhance awareness of the responsibilities involved in implementation of the Customer Service Commitment and Plans. The airlines will publish and make available their Customer Service Plans on airline Internet web sites, at airports and ticket offices (upon request) and to travel and reservation agents.

Upon completion and publication of the Customer Service Plans, the airlines will notify and provide copies to Congress and the Department of Transportation. The airlines expect and will cooperate fully with any request from Congress for periodic review of compliance with the Customer Service Commitment.

At the 56th IATA Annual General Meeting, held on 4–6 June 2000, IATA airlines endorsed a global customer service framework.[188] To this end, IATA adopted a Resolution on Customer Service which endorsed the IATA Customer Service framework as a guide for airlines in developing their own individual or alliance customer service commitments and plans. IATA endorsed the view that the air transport industry is one of the most complex and interdependent industries in the world. The member airlines of IATA were committed to providing a high level of service to their customers. As essential elements of its global customer service framework, IATA airlines recognize the following.

a) Airlines will use their best efforts to offer, through their telephone reservations service, the lowest fare available for the dates and classes of travel requested, for which the customer is eligible. Lower fares may be available through other channels.

b) Airlines may offer passengers an 'option period' during which the passenger may determine whether they wish to purchase a promotional fare or non-refundable ticket. The duration of this option period will be determined by each individual airline and may vary depending on the special fare to be applied and whether the airline has an agreement with any other carriers involved in the journey. Passengers can use this period to confirm that the fare and conditions attached to it meet their needs and are acceptable to them. A passenger has the right to cancel this reservation within the option period without any penalty. The passenger wishing to 'confirm' this reservation must do so within the option period or the reservation may be cancelled by the airline.

c) Airlines will endeavour to process passenger refunds as quickly as possible. In publishing their individual customer service commitments and plans, airlines should establish specific performance targets for processing refunds.

d) Airlines will adopt clear policies regarding denied boarding compensation. These policies will always reflect any legislation or other government-imposed requirement on the carrier. This information will be made available to the passenger upon request.

Airlines will also have available for their passengers the following information relevant to their journey:

1) any change of aircraft on a single flight with the same flight number, that is, change of gauge;
2) their refund and cancellation policies;
3) regulations regarding their frequent flyer programme, if any;
4) the aircraft type scheduled to be operated on a route, the cabin configuration and services normally offered on board (audio/video systems);

5) their alliance or code share partners, and any effect this might have on the passenger's journey;
6) language that makes it clear that the passenger's contract is with the marketing airline (the airline whose designator appears on the flight coupon next to the flight number) and that it is that airline's standards and conditions that apply;
7) whether the ticket purchased can be endorsed for travel on another airline; and
8) other relevant conditions of carriage.

Airlines will have available for the passenger information concerning their liability for death and injury in the event of an accident.

Airlines will endeavour to keep the passenger informed of any significant delay, cancellation or diversion as soon as this information is known to the carrier. Airlines will do all possible to find accommodation and provide appropriate meals in the event of a prolonged delay. If the passengers are already on board an aircraft which will remain on the ground for an extended period, and do not have access to the terminal, the airline will make every reasonable effort to meet essential needs, such as providing food, water, restroom facilities and medical treatment.

Airlines will make their best efforts to accommodate passenger seating requests, except in the case of flights without pre-assigned seating. In the interest of the safety and comfort of all passengers and crews, airlines will implement policies, including involvement of law enforcement agencies, aimed at preventing disruptive passenger behaviour and at protecting the safety of the crew and passengers.

Airlines will endeavour to deliver all checked baggage as quickly as possible following an aircraft's arrival at an airport. In their individual customer service commitments and plans, airlines should establish performance targets for baggage delivery times. In the case of 'mishandled' checked bags, the airline will make every reasonable effort to return them on the next available flight. The airline will endeavour to keep passengers informed of the status of their 'mishandled' baggage. Airlines will have available for passengers information concerning the airlines' liability limits for baggage lost, damaged or delayed.

Airlines will respond quickly and responsibly to any passenger complaint. Each airline will establish a convenient point of passenger contact for all complaints and the address, phone number and departmental name of this customer service function will be provided in timetables, on web sites and any other appropriate public information source. This information will also be available at all travel agents accredited by the airlines. Airlines will develop a clear policy on customer service which specifies that all written complaints will receive a reply and the maximum length of time for processing this correspondence.

Airlines will disclose their policies and procedures for handling special needs passengers, such as unaccompanied minors, and for accommodating the disabled in an appropriate manner. Airlines will endeavour to accommodate all special needs passengers, both in the airport and on board the aircraft, if informed in advance of the passenger's special need or condition and if this need or condition can be accommodated in a safe manner on board the aircraft and at the airports concerned. Airlines will take reasonable measures to accommodate the requirements of special needs passengers during an extended delay.

The European Commission, in early 2000, issued a comprehensive consultative document on consumer protection in Air Transport.[189] This statement introduced a common air transport policy and raised a number of issues such as the contractual rights of passengers, tariffs, and comfort and health. This document provides an inventory of passenger rights, including the following:

- Information about flights and reservation of tickets. Any passenger has the right to neutral and accurate information.
- Check-in and boarding. European Community rules require that passengers must receive fair treatment and proper compensation when they are denied boarding.
- Liability in case of an accident. Passengers travelling with a European Community airline will receive full compensation in the case of an accident.
- Data protection. Passengers reserving their tickets in the EC have the right to know what personal details about them are being stored on the computerized reservation systems.
- Air travel as part of a package holiday. Air passengers travelling as part of a package tour or holiday bought in the EC must receive clear and precise information from the organizer about their trip. They also enjoy clear rights concerning the performance of the contract.
- Enforcing passenger rights. The passenger rights set out above are laid down either directly in EC law or in national laws which have been made to implement EC directives. Therefore airlines, travel agents, tour operators and all other business involved in the provision of air transport services must observe them. In turn, passengers should stand firm in demanding that their rights are respected and complain when they are not.

Harold Caplan, who analyses this document, concludes: 'although several parts of the Green Paper cite US initiatives, it would be a mistake to regard this as a pale reflection of what the US DOT already does better'.[190] Caplan further suggests an air passenger's charter and defines a charter as 'a binding declaration of basic principles, which is one of the modern methods of redressing the unequal bargaining power between users and providers of public services'.[191] He then identifies a number of elements as integral to a present-day charter of passenger rights. Regulators should ensure that, at each airport licensed for public air transport, adequate arrangements are in force regarding the following:

- If checked baggage fails to arrive on the same flight as the passenger and there is no reasonable prospect that the baggage will be delivered to the passenger within one hour of passenger arrival, the aircraft operator shall thereupon issue to the passenger an appropriate claim form including a summary of the passenger's rights in respect of delayed, lost or damaged baggage.
- A non-refundable advance in local currency not exceeding 100 Euro in value which may be taken into account when the passenger's claim is finally concluded.
- Aircraft and airport operators shall develop and practise at irregular intervals comprehensive contingency plans for dealing with major accidents.
- Aircraft operators shall use their best endeavours to avoid adverse weather conditions, including forecast turbulence.

- Employees of aircraft and airport operators who come into contact with passengers shall be trained to recognize the most common medical emergencies and take appropriate action.
- On routes where it may be impossible to land at a suitable airport within 30 minutes of discovering acute medical emergency in flight, at least two members of the aircraft crew shall be trained and equipped to provide appropriate first aid until professional assistance can be obtained.
- To ensure health, comfort and convenience of passengers, the possibility of an orderly exit within 90 seconds in actual or simulated emergency condition must be met.
- All publicly available fares and charges by aircraft and airport operators and by states shall be notified to the public in accordance with the passenger information protocol (PIP).
- Fares and charges by aircraft and airport operators and by states which are not determined by competition shall not exceed the levels prescribed by the regulator.
- States shall devise and promote convenient and cost-effective modes of dispute resolution to supplement existing modes of resolution for the exclusive benefit of air passengers.

As a general requirement, Caplan suggests that the rights of passengers in accordance with this charter should be in addition to and not in substitution for all other rights and remedies and that all rights as stipulated in a charter may be directly enforced by passengers.

Commercial issues involving passenger rights

The utility of air travel is often diluted by the apprehension an airline passenger feels when he approaches the check-in counter to obtain his seat allocation. On the other side of the counter are the check-in staff of the airline, with their computers, waiting to punch the passenger's name into their machines, take over his baggage for the flight and issue him with his boarding card. However much a passenger reconfirms his seat long before the flight, he could, in some circumstances be 'bumped' (denied boarding) on the flight and would have to wait for the next flight … or the next … or the next … whenever that might be. Worse still, most airlines include a condition in their passenger tickets and baggage checks indicating that they do not guarantee dates and times of departure and arrival that are given in the documents of carriage.

One of the unpleasant side-effects of being deprived of an opportunity to board an aircraft that one believes holds a confirmed seat for one, is the ensuing disagreement between the passenger and airline staff. Usually, instances of denied boarding are unpleasant both to the passenger and to the airline check-in staff. Some jurisdictions, such as the United States, have envisaged circumstances wherein a passenger could arbitrarily be denied boarding, leading to the imputation of discrimination on the part of the airline. These jurisdictions have incorporated statutory provisions for remedies in instances of discriminatory 'bumping'.

Admittedly, denied boarding is not a regular feature in commercial aviation any more. Airline reservation systems are now more streamlined and booking profiles of most airlines are conservative and prudent. Unfortunately, however, there are still instances where airlines overbook (accept reservations for more passengers than a flight could actually take) or oversell, on the expectation that a certain percentage of passengers would be 'no-shows' (fail to turn up for the flight). As one commentator observed :

> Although most airlines deliberately overbook, it is often not done with the intent to defraud passengers or to deny advertised and contracted services, but rather for the purpose of limiting losses due to the failure of passengers to use their reservations. The effect on passengers of overbooking and overselling may be similar, in that harassment, mental anguish, distress, discrimination and material damages are likely to arise. However, the expectations of the parties to the contract and the legal implications are in the end clearly different.
>
> Booking is generally defined as the process by which a reservation is made for the passenger until the passenger confirms at a later date that reservation with a contract of carriage. The carrier confirms the reservation and guarantees the seat only when the passenger pays the price and is given the ticket, that is, when the seat on the aircraft has been sold to the passenger. An airline reservation for a seat on a flight, therefore, merely amounts to a promise of future performance, on the condition that the number of bookings and sales is not greater than the seating capacity of the aircraft. However, in a widely-adopted international airline practice, the number of bookings often exceeds seating capacity, with the promise of future performance becoming void upon entry into the contract, that is, at the time when the passenger discovers that his or her reservation cannot be confirmed. From the outset, therefore, the intent of the carrier may seem less than well-meaning. Overbooking, as well as the logical consequence of possible over-selling, implies that a passenger, who believed he or she was going to fly, will necessarily be bumped.[192]

In the 1976 case of *Nader* v. *Allegheny Airlines Inc.*,[193] Justice Powell, addressing the problem of overbooking, observed:

> Such overbooking is a common industry practice, designed to ensure that each flight leaves with as few empty seats as possible despite the large number of 'no-shows' – reservation-holding passengers who do not appear at flight time. By the use of statistical studies of no-show patterns on specific flights, the airlines attempt to predict the appropriate number of reservations necessary to fill each flight. In this way, they attempt to ensure the most efficient use of aircraft while preserving a flexible booking system that permits passengers to cancel and change reservations without notice or penalty. At times the practice of overbooking results in oversales, which occur when more reservation-holding passengers than can be accommodated actually appear to board the flight. When this occurs, some passengers must be denied boarding, that is, they are 'bumped'. The chance that any particular passenger will be bumped is so negligible that few prospective passengers aware of the possibility would give it a second thought.[194]

A last-minute aircraft change from a larger aircraft to a smaller one (mostly due to unforeseen technical problems or aircraft scheduling difficulties) is another reason for a passenger to be denied boarding. The good news, however, is that 'bumping' is often a 'democratic' process where a busy airline executive, an even busier lawyer and a footloose tourist may all get 'bumped' together from the same flight.

Of course, delinquent airlines do their best to make amends. Some even offer cash gifts and plush hotel accommodation (with full board) on the house. Although this mode of 'conciliation' sometimes proves to be an unexpected 'bonus' to a tourist who would rather leave his holiday resort the next day (or better still three days later), the airline executive and the lawyer, who are both tightly scheduled for their overseas meetings the same day, would lose immensely if they did not find accommodation on the flight that they thought they had obtained 'confirmed' reservations for well in advance. Would these hapless passengers have a legal remedy against the errant airline? What damages could they claim?

The contract of carriage

Places of departure and destination

The contract of carriage by commercial airlines of airline passengers is governed by the Warsaw Convention of 1929,[195] which applies to all international transportation by air, of persons, baggage and goods, performed by aircraft for hire. Article 1.2 of the Warsaw Convention provides:

> For the purposes of the Convention the expression 'international transportation' means any transportation in which, according to the contract made by the parties, the place of departure and the place of destination, whether or not there be a break in the transportation or transshipment, are situated either within the territories of the two High Contracting Parties or within the territory of a single High Contracting Party, if there is an agreed stopping place within a territory subject to the sovereignty, suzerainty, mandate or authority of another power, even though that power is not a party to the Convention. Transportation without such an agreed stopping place between territories subject to the sovereignty, suzerainty, mandate or authority of the same High Contracting Party shall not be deemed to be international.

Accordingly, the Warsaw Convention would apply to a passenger only if his journey was between two countries or within the same country where, during the journey, the aircraft stops at another country previously agreed upon and stipulated in the timetable published by the carrier (for example, where the place of departure is Lyons and the place of destination is Paris, with an agreed stopping place in Brussels).[196] In the 1936 case of *Grein* v. *Imperial Airways Ltd*,[197] the Court of Appeal defined an 'agreed stopping place' as:

> a place where according to the contract the machine by which the contract is to be performed will stop in the course of performing the contractual carriage, whatever the purpose of the descent may be and whatever the rights the passenger may have to break his journey at that place.[198]

Although this definition has been generally accepted in later cases, the question arises as to when the stopping place is 'agreed to'. An American case decided in 1954[199] (reflecting the common law approach) and a French decision of 1959[200] (reflecting the civil law approach) have both agreed that an agreed stopping place is one that is published in the tariffs and timetables of the carrier.

Judicial determination of the nature of 'international carriage' has been consistent with the terminology used in the Warsaw Convention. In the *Grein* case,[201] the Court of Appeal in England determined that a round trip from London to Antwerp was considered to be one contract of carriage on the basis that the place of departure and the place of destination was in the same country (London, in this instance) although the agreed stopping place was in Belgium. The court in this case overruled the King's Bench judgment in the same case, which had held that there were two contracts of carriage: between London and Antwerp and between Antwerp and London. Greene L J observed:

Once the contract is ascertained to be a contract for the class of carriage described, it matters not that the journey is broken. Thus, if the contract were for carriage of a passenger from Paris to Madrid, it would make no difference if the passenger was entitled under the contract to break his journey at Toulouse; he might be entitled to remain at Toulouse for a week or a month and then resume his journey, the carriage would nonetheless satisfy the definition. The reason for this is clear once it is appreciated that the contract is the unit, not the journey. Such a traveller, speaking without reference to the Convention, might well say, if asked by a fellow passenger on leaving Paris what his place of destination was, that it was Toulouse; but this would not alter the fact that his place of 'destination' for the purpose of para. 2 of art.1 would be Madrid, since it is to Madrid that the carrier agrees to carries him. The fact that the contract between the parties is the primary matter to be regarded is made even clearer when para. 3 is examined. Under this paragraph the conception of the contract as being what I have called the unit, is extended to include the case where there is a series of contracts, provided the parties have regarded the carriage as a 'single operation'. In that case, the series of contracts is treated as the unit and the justification for so doing lies in the fact that the parties have regarded the carriage to be performed thereunder as a single operation, a justification which has its basis in reason and good sense.[202]

Greene L J also referred, inter alia, to the fact that the geographical restriction of Article 1.2 is clarified in Article 1.3 which deems air carriage performed by several successive air carriers to be one undivided transportation, if it has been regarded by the parties (the airline and the passenger) to be a single operation. The Warsaw Convention, by this provision, recognizes the international character of a journey even if a dispute were to arise when successive carriers are involved and the passenger's journey involves one or more stopping places within a country in which the damage is caused.

Elements of the agreement

Drion[203] analyses the contract of carriage of passengers by air to mean the following:

1. the carriage must be by aircraft;[204]
2. the carriage must be performed pursuant to some agreement (thus the carriage of a stowaway is not governed by the Warsaw Convention but by applicable national laws); and

3. the contract must be one relating to the carriage by air of the passenger, between
    agreed points.[205]

The nature of the contract of carriage of passengers by air was discussed in 1967
by Circuit Judge Wisdom in the case of *Block* v. *Compagnie Nationale Air France*,[206]
when he said:

> The applicability of the Convention undeniably is premised upon a contract, but on a
> contract of a particular kind. It is based on a contract of carriage that arises from a
> relationship between a 'carrier' and the passenger. This contractual relationship
> requires only that the carrier consents to undertake the international transportation of
> the passengers from one designated spot to another, and that the passenger in turn
> consents to the undertaking.[207]

The *Block* case also underscored the incompatibility between the common law
concept of consideration – which prompted most common law jurisdictions to
interpret the Convention as calling for the passing of consideration between the
parties – and the civil law concept of gratuitous carriage. Miller[208] concludes that
there need be no such divergence, since the Convention applies to all international
carriage, whether performed gratuitously or for reward.

Although tickets are traditionally used as evidence of the conclusion of a contract
of transportation – whether it be by air, road or sea – there is now the awareness that
the cost of production of such tickets can be obviated by such measures as the
introduction of magnetic strips that are machine-readable. The ATB1 ticket, which
is designed on the lines of a machine-readable card, has now gained acceptance as a
device which would effectively preclude the hassle of printing, issuance, checking
at control points and the tedium of going through a revenue collection process for air
carriers.

Although the Warsaw Convention in Article 3(2) requires that a ticket be delivered
to the passenger containing specified information, in order that the limitation of
liability provisions of the Convention be not jeopardized as far as the carrier is
concerned, the Guatemala Protocol of 1971 envisages ticketless travel in its Article
3(2). Peter Martin attributes the modern trend in popularity of the computerized and
mechanized ticket to the increasing popularity of automation, where reservations for
airline seats are made, paid for and confirmed electronically.[209] Martin says of the
advent of the electronic airline passenger ticket and baggage check: 'At long last,
Chan will come into its own as the champion of bare delivery and the perceived
restrictions of *Mertens* and *Warren*[210] will be buried at last; but delivery remains of
critical importance.'[211]

However, Martin quite validly cautions against inherent dangers in the electronic
ticketing system on such aspects as the evidential validity of such a document; the
possibility of including conditions of carriage in the document: problems of security
and identification: the practical and legal liability aspects of baggage registration;
and, more importantly, the commercial significance of this breakthrough *vis-à-vis*
the agent, who would be rendered useless in the process.

Warsaw provisions

Article 19 of the Warsaw Convention provides: 'The carrier shall be liable for damage occasioned by delay in the transportation by air of passengers, baggage and goods.' Legally, the notion of delay implies a discrepancy between the time when one party is entitled to expect the performance of the carrier's duty and the time when the duties are actually performed.[212] Thus, when a passenger is denied boarding on a flight he has contracted with the airline to board, the airline becomes prima facie liable for the damage caused by the delay, provided the passenger was subsequently carried by that airline after some delay. Therefore, in an instance where an airline fails to carry a passenger at all, it is not envisaged that Article 19 of the Warsaw Convention would apply.

One of the perceived inadequacies of the Warsaw Convention is the absence of a definition of 'delay'. The lapse is aggravated by the words of Article 18(2) which implicitly provide for a definition of 'delay' in relation to the carriage by air of baggage and goods. The 'delay' referred to is one envisaged to be caused when the baggage or goods are in the carrier's charge. Therefore, even if Article 18(2) is to be applied analogically to passengers, it would be regarded only to cover cases where a passenger had already been accepted for carriage. Most instances of denied boarding which cause a delay in the passenger's transportation occur when the passenger is not checked into the flight at all. The latter instance is not alluded to by the Warsaw Convention. Even Article 19 can directly be applied only to instances where a passenger is accepted for a flight and delayed in the process of being carried to his destination. It may, however, still be arguable that liability as referred to in Article 19 can be imputed to the carrier in cases of denied boarding, since, anyway, the act of denial of boarding results in a delay in the carriage of a passenger.

In a 1956 decision,[213] which discussed the carriage of goods by air, the courts interpreted Article 19 to mean that the carrier was bound to deliver goods quickly to shippers, since shippers resort to carriage by air only because it allows quick delivery. By analogy, therefore, the decision would show early tendencies of the courts to be supportive of enforcing passengers' rights under Article 19 to the speed inherent in air transport. In a later case,[214] the courts articulated this attitude by laying down the law to be stringent in the requirement that airlines cannot be exonerated when they cause long delays, flight cancellations or postponement of flights.[215]

Early common law attitudes were seemingly compatible with the early civil law attitude discussed above. In the case of *Bart* v. *British West India Airways Ltd*,[216] the court held that the carrier cannot be left to deliver passengers and goods as he pleases and has to ensure delivery within a reasonable time having regard to all the circumstances of a particular case.

Assessment of damages

The Warsaw Convention, as could be expected, is silent on the question of damages caused by the delay in the carriage of passengers. The determination of damages therefore devolves upon the *lex fori* – the court seized with jurisdiction to hear the case. Accordingly, it is evident that damages in each case would be assessed in accordance with the internal laws of the country in which a case is heard. The carrier can exonerate himself in certain circumstances, where he shows that he took all the necessary precautions to avoid the delay,[217] or that the contributory negligence of the plaintiff was a causative factor of the delayed carriage.[218] The court is empowered by the Warsaw Convention to exonerate the carrier totally or partially from liability. Article 25 of the Warsaw Convention precludes the carrier from availing himself of the limitation of liability provisions of the Convention[219] if the damage is caused by the carrier's wilful misconduct or by such default on his part as, in accordance with the law of the court to which the case is submitted, is considered to be equivalent to wilful misconduct. Similarly, the carrier is not able to seek the exclusions and limitations of liability under the Warsaw Convention if the damage is caused under the same circumstances by any agent of the carrier acting within the scope of his employment. Any action grounded on damages arising from delay in the carriage of passengers, however founded, can only be brought subject to the conditions and limits set out in the Convention.

Whenever an airline issues a ticket to a passenger in return for the payment of money, the airline undertakes to carry the passenger to the destination given on his ticket with reasonable care and within a reasonable time.[220] Courts have accordingly followed the principle that the airline is professionally bound to carry a passenger who has been issued with a passenger ticket[221] and that the airline is bound by the following legal parameters:

1. the airline is bound to carry any person, without the imposition of any un-reasonable conditions, if he is not in an unfit condition, and has paid his fare;
2. the airline has to carry the passenger safely;
3. the passenger has to be treated with due care throughout his flight; and
4. the airline has to ensure that the passenger is given the benefit of the speed inherent in air transport.

Of course, the parties to a contract of carriage of passengers may generally incorporate in the contractual document (the airline passenger ticket) any terms and conditions upon which they agree, as long as such conditions are not contrary to the provisions of the Warsaw Convention.[222]

The terms and conditions in an airline ticket are not binding upon the passenger unless he consents to them either expressly or impliedly.[223] Although, generally, if a passenger accepts his ticket without objection, he will be taken to have accepted the conditions in his ticket, a court would be very reluctant to accept strictly a condition in a ticket that totally exonerates an airline where it fails to carry a passenger with reasonable dispatch. Also, as the *Lisi* case held, the passenger cannot be taken to have assented to conditions of carriage incorporated in his ticket if he has no opportunity to examine his ticket or dissent from the provisions thereof,[224] although the airline could, in its defence, prove that the passenger knew of the condition in the ticket even though he did not read the provisions incorporated in his ticket or that the passenger was given notice of the existence of the conditions in the ticket.[225]

Clearly, 'bumping' of passengers by airlines is therefore not an eventuality that the Warsaw Convention has considered *stricto sensu*. It would be largely left to the courts to interpret the Convention on this point with the help of Article 19, the analogous case law and the general principles of the law of contract.

Courts in the United States have in recent times had occasion to view denied boarding in its various contexts. In March 1995, in the case of *Azubuko* v. *Varig Airline*,[226] the trial court had to determine an instance where transportation was refused to a validly ticketed passenger because of an erroneous belief by the carrier's employee that the passenger was required to have a visa to his destination. The air carrier sought dismissal of the plaintiff's claim for breach of contract amounting to $35 million in damages for alleged loss of business as a result of the denied boarding on the ground that the claim was based upon a refusal to transport and was pre-empted by the Airline Deregulation Act of 1978.[227] The court held that the plaintiff was seeking only to enforce a private agreement for transportation and that the case did not involve any enlargement or enhancement of the agreement based on state laws or policies external to the terms of the contract of transportation. The reasoning in this case arguably has its genesis in the rationale of the PANAM adjudication relating to the Lockerbie case, where the court held that the Warsaw Convention pre-empts all state law causes of action falling within the purview of the Warsaw Convention.[228] One court has distinguished between a claim arising as a result of a delay in transportation and a claim arising from total non-performance of the contract of transportation where, for instance, after being denied boarding, the passenger does not travel at all. In the latter instance, the court held that the claim is not covered by the Warsaw Convention and the passenger may pursue a remedy based on local law rather than under the Convention.[229] A clear distinction has to be made, however, between non-performance and subsequent transportation of the passenger, where, in the latter case, the delay in transportation would clearly come under the Warsaw Convention's Article 19, thus pre-empting local law on the subject in the United States.[230]

In the case of *Lathigra* v. *British Airways PLC*,[231] it was alleged that the issuing carrier (British Airways) neglected to inform the passenger that one of the reconfirmed connecting flights operated by another carrier had been discontinued. As a result, the passengers were stranded en route for five days. British Airways applied to remove the plaintiff's claim to a federal court on the ground that it fell within the purview of the Warsaw Convention. The plaintiff applied to the Court of Appeal on the ground that the claim did not arise under the Warsaw Convention. In addressing the question of whether the claims arose under Article 19 of the Warsaw Convention, the Court of Appeals held that they did not, because the damages claimed did not arise from the delay in transportation by air for purposes of Article 19. The court accepted the argument of the plaintiff that the alleged negligence of British Airways did not occur during performance of the contract of carriage but rather days before, when the airline mistakenly reconfirmed the reservations of a non-existent flight. The court also recognized that British Airways, in confirming a non-existent flight of another carrier was acting as the latter's agent. The court concluded:

> We emphasise that BA's liability here is based upon its negligent act of reconfirming appellant's reservation days before departure in a situation where the 'carrier' no longer served the route in question. Once the passenger presents herself to the carrier of its agents as ready to begin the air journey, the Convention generally governs liability for delays in the carrier's performance, and its provision apply until completion of disem-barkation at the destination airport.[232]

In an interesting case indirectly arising out of the 1990 Gulf War, which concerned a British Airways flight which arrived in Kuwait on 2 August 1990, shortly after the war had broken out, resulting in some of its passengers being detained by the Iraqi government, an action for damages was brought against British Airways by one of the passengers in a Scottish court. The court, addressing the question of 'delay' which the passenger experienced while being detained by the Iraqi government, was of the view that any loss experienced by the passenger detained by the Iraqi government after arrival in Kuwait could not in any reasonable sense be said to have been caused by any 'delay' in the flight in question.[233]

In *Jamil* v. *Kuwait Airways Corporation*,[234] an airline passenger sued the airline under the Warsaw Convention, claiming that a four-day delay in transportation resulted in the passenger's failure to finalize crucial documents to secure funding for a government project with the Pakistani government. The United States District Court for the District of Columbia held that, under the Warsaw Convention, a four-day delay in transportation suffered by the passenger was not a proximate cause of his failure to finalize crucial documents related to his contract as claimed. The court further held that the airline could not reasonably have foreseen that a four-day delay would result in an intervening government coup that would in turn affect that passenger's chances of finalising his contract. Sporkin D J held:

> The chain of events which has led to Mr. Jamil's alleged loss is as long as it is unlikely. Tracing the claim of this disappointed traveller takes this court over three continents, through the policies of at least two foreign governments and one election, and involves a time period spanning over a year ... Mr. Jamil would have the court trace this entire causal chain and land the blame for his lost project squarely at the feet of KAC (*sic*). I decline, however, plaintiff's invitation to find causation in the air. Such a determination would fly in the face of common sense and legal notions of proximate cause.[235]

Mahaney v. *Air France*,[236] which was decided in 1979, is an interesting case where a claim for delay in transportation caused by denied boarding was combined with the claim that the plaintiff was subjected to unjust discrimination or was unduly or unreasonably placed at a disadvantage by the airline.[237] Pierce D J, citing precedent,[238] observed that 'bumping', which often occurs as a result of overselling by the airline, may be considered in certain circumstances as an economic necessity for an airline in view of inevitable cancellations or 'no-shows'. His honour observed, however, that when a flight is thus oversold, the airline must fill the plane in a reasonable and just manner: 'To establish that a preference or discrimination has occurred, it suffices that the passenger is able to prove that he possessed a confirmed reservation and a resultant right to a seat, and that this priority was not honoured.'[239] In this instance, the court recognized the applicability of Section 404(*b*) of the Federal Aviation Act,[240] which provided that a passenger is entitled to recover compensatory and punitive damages under the Act for bumping in a discriminatory manner from the airline concerned.

The provision relating to delay in the carriage of passengers by air, as imputed to Article 19 of the Warsaw Convention, is rendered ineffective in the face of the Convention's two-year statute of limitations as stipulated in Article 29. While Article 24 of the Warsaw Convention stipulates that, in the cases covered by Articles 18 and

19 of the Convention, any action for damages, however founded, can only be brought subject to the conditions and limits set out in the Convention, Article 29(1) of the Convention provides:

> The right to damages shall be extinguished if an action is not brought within two years, reckoned from the date of arrival at the destination, or from the date on which the aircraft ought to have arrived, or from the date on which the transportation stopped.

The *Mahaney* decision brought to bear an interesting fact relating to judicial interpretation of this provision. Since the plaintiff had brought two concurrent actions – one for delay in transportation, and the other for discriminatory bumping – the court held that had the plaintiff's action been only for the delay in transportation, Article 29(1) of the Warsaw Convention might have applied. However, the court recognized the claim against discriminatory bumping as coming under the purview of section 404(*b*) of the Federal Aviation Act, thereby excluding the purview of Article 29(1) of the Warsaw Convention from this case.[241] Eight years after the *Mahaney* decision, a similar case, (*Wolgel* v. *Mexicana Airlines*)[242] considered the dual question of delay and discriminatory bumping and concluded that if a plaintiff claimed damages for bumping itself, rather than incidental damages due to delay in carriage, the Warsaw Convention would not apply, as the Convention's purview was limited in Article 19 to instances of delay in carriage. On the question of whether Article 19 extended to cases of discriminatory bumping, Flaum C J held:

> Treaties are construed more liberally than private agreements, and to ascertain their meaning we may look beyond written words to the history of the treaty, the negotiations, and the practical construction adopted by the parties...The history of the Warsaw Convention indicates that the word 'delay' in Article 19 is intended to extend to claims, such as the Wolgels', that arise from the total nonperformance of a contract.[243]

In the 1991 decision of *Sassouni* v. *Olympic Airways*,[244] the United States District Court of New York had no difficulty in identifying a rather uncomplicated instance of denied boarding as coming within the purview of Article 29(1) of the Warsaw Convention. The plaintiff, who had a round-trip ticket from New York to Athens and return through Tel Aviv, had been denied boarding at Athens, on his way to Tel Aviv. The issue was one of delay in transportation, and Haight D J held: 'Very few courts have confronted the issue of the application of Article 19 to being 'bumped' from an airline flight. However, those that have, hold uniformly that damages arising from a delay in transportation caused by being bumped are governed by Article 19.'[245] The court, while endorsing the *Wolgel* decision, reiterated that Article 19 does not cover claims for damages arising from actually being bumped, such as discriminatory bumping or intentional infliction of emotional distress.

Legal liability of the carrier

A somewhat delicate balance is called for in determining whether, in the absence of cogent evidence that a restricted seat pitch in the economy class of an aircraft would inevitably cause venous thromboembolism in passengers (an exigency involving the affliction of a passenger would be considered 'unexpected' and therefore an accident) or whether the carrier knows or ought to know of the risk and takes necessary measures to avoid the danger or risk, in which case absence of such measures would impute to the carrier a certain intent, proving his wilful misconduct. An accident is purely an 'inappropriate and unexpected happenstance'[246] which does not happen as a matter of course. Sudden turbulence, or the sounding of a smoke alarm in the cabin which is unexpected, are typical profiles of an accident. If such were to be the case, would it be reasonable to consider the infliction of a passenger by venous thromboembolism an accident?

A probable approach that a common law court may adopt is to treat a proven instance linked to air travel as an accident in the same way as in instances of turbulence. Of course, in similar vein, the carrier may be expected to issue prior warning and advice as to how to cope with the risk. In such circumstances the analogy of an accident and possible negligence that would take the issue beyond a mere accident would be a distinctly logical sequence.

The new Montreal Convention of 1999,[247] in Article 17, provides that the carrier is liable for damage sustained in case of death or bodily injury of a passenger upon condition only that the accident which caused the death or injury took place on board the aircraft or in the course of the operations of embarking or disembarking. Liability of the carrier is limited on the basis of strict liability at 100 000 Special Drawing Rights (SDR). Furthermore, this limit cannot be exceeded if the carrier proves that he and his servants or agents were not negligent or did not commit a wrongful act or omission in connection to the injury or such damage was solely caused by the negligence or wrongful act or omission of a third party.[248] The Montreal Convention, which is yet to come into force, seemingly makes provision to recognize carrier negligence both in terms of the provision of abnormally small seat pitches in his aircraft and in regard to its neglect in warning passengers of potential hazard of prolonged air travel in restricted areas and not advising passengers of ways and means to mitigate possible risk of venous thromboembolism.

The currently operative legal regime in this area is governed by the Warsaw Convention of 1929,[249] which provides that the carrier is liable for damage sustained in the event of death or wounding of a passenger, or any other bodily injury suffered by a passenger, if the accident which caused the damage so sustained took place on board the aircraft or in the course of any of the operations of embarking or disembarking. Of course, on the face of the provision, the words 'wounding' and 'bodily injury' do not necessarily lend themselves to be associated with infection. *A fortiori*, according to the Warsaw Convention, the wounding or injury must be caused by 'accident', which is not typically a synonym for 'infection'. However, the recent decision in *El Al Israel Airlines Limited* v. *Tseng*[250] introduced a new dimension to the word 'accident' under the Warsaw Convention by giving it pervasive scope to include such acts as security body searches performed by the airlines. In this context, the word 'accident' loses its fortuity and it becomes applicable to an expected or calculated act. Thus, if an airline knows or ought to have known that an infected passenger was on board its flight, causing others on board to be infected, it may well mean that the act of the airline will be construed by the courts as an accident within the purview of the Warsaw Convention.

Liability under the Warsaw Convention

It is an incontrovertible principle of tort law that tortious liability exists primarily to compensate the victim by compelling the wrongdoer to pay for the damage he has done.[251] The second international conference on private international law,[252] which led to the introduction of the Warsaw Convention,[253] obviously followed this basic principle but deviated to align the provisions of the Warsaw Convention on existing exigencies of civil aviation. The Conference based its approach towards air carrier liability on the fault theory of tort, which has its genesis in the Industrial Revolution, when common law adopted the principle that a wrongdoer or tortfeasor must be at fault for him to be compelled to compensate the injured. The fault theory was introduced as a solution to the problems caused by injury to persons by the proliferation of machinery during the Industrial Revolution and on the basis that those responsible for introducing faulty machinery should pay those who are injured by them.

One of the fundamental deviations from the fault liability principle in the context of the Warsaw Conference was that, instead of retaining the basic premise that the person who alleges injury must prove that the injury was caused by the alleged wrongdoer, the Conference recognized the obligation of the carrier to assume the burden of proof. This was done seemingly to obviate the inherent difficulties which are posed in situations of air carriage where it would be difficult, if not impossible, to determine fault from evidence which is reduced to debris and wreckage after an aircraft accident.

The Conference succinctly subsumed its views on liability through the words of its reporter:

> These rules sprang from the fault theory of the liability of the carrier toward passengers and goods, and from the obligation of the carrier to assume the burden of proof. The presumption of fault on the shoulders of the carrier was, however, limited by the nature itself of the carriage in question, carriage whose risks are known by the passenger and consignor. The Conference had agreed that the carrier would be absolved from all liability when he had taken reasonable and ordinary measures to avoid the damage ... one restriction on this liability had been agreed upon. If for commercial transactions one could concede the liability of the carrier, it did not seem logical to maintain this liability for the navigational errors of his servants, if he proves that he himself took proper measures to avoid a damage.[254]

The Conference went on to suggest that, if the damage arises from an 'intentional illicit act' for which the carrier was liable, he should not have the right to avail himself of the provisions of the Convention.[255] The words 'intentional illicit act' were later changed to 'wilful misconduct' by the Conference at the request of the British delegate Sir Alfred Dennis and the Greek delegate Mr Youpis.[256]

Deeming that it was not equitable to impose absolute liability upon the carrier, the Conference admitted that the carrier's responsibility would be limited to liability limits of monetary *value* and, furthermore, he could be freed of all liability when he had taken the reasonable and normal measures to avoid the damage.[257]

The Conference obviously based the Warsaw Convention on tort law principles of liability, where tort duties are primarily fixed by law in contrast to contractual obligations which can arise only from voluntary agreement.[258] Sixty-six years after the Warsaw Convention was introduced, however, there was a palpable shift towards introducing a contractual element by the 1995 IATA Inter-Carrier Agreement which, although not having the legal status of a Convention but remaining an agreement among air carriers, retains the basic presumption of air carrier liability of the Convention but rejects the liability limitations of the Warsaw Convention and its Protocols by recognizing that the compensatory amount that a carrier should pay for personal injury or death may be contractually agreed upon by the carrier and claimant according to the law of the domicile of the claimant.

Admittedly, this is not what the Conference envisaged. However, it must be borne in mind that the Conference recognized that the Warsaw Convention applied only to the unification of 'certain' rules, as proposed by the delegate of Czechoslovakia. Also the underlying purpose of the IATA initiative – which is to allow for greater flexibility for insurance underwriters on the one hand, and more leverage for airlines in their risk management on the other – is fundamentally consistent with the views of the Warsaw Conference. At the same time, the Convention does not preclude the right of a carrier to enter into agreement with a claimant on the issue of compensation. The Warsaw Conference itself recognized that:

> in reality, this Convention creates against the air carrier an exceptional system, because in the majority of the countries of the world, contracts of carriage are concluded under a system of free contract. The carrier is free to insert in the contract clauses which exclude or reduce his liability, as much as for goods as for travellers.[259]

The Inter-Carrier Agreement, which was approved by IATA carriers at their Annual General Meeting in Kuala Lumpur in October 1995, claims to preserve the Warsaw Convention, but carriers agree to take action to waive the limitation of liability on recoverable compensatory damages in claims for death, wounding or other bodily injury so that recoverable compensatory damages may be determined and awarded by reference to the law of the domicile of the passenger. This provision in effect introduces a contractual element to an otherwise pure tortuous liability regime. The agreement attacks the monetary limits of liability of the Convention and retains all other provisions of liability – which are essentially the presumption of liability of the carrier and his defences against such a presumption.

With the rejection of the liability limits, the provision relating to breaking such limits in instances where the carrier is guilty of wilful misconduct has also been rejected. Therefore, effectively, certain elements of tortuous liability that the Convention had have been expunged. In the final analysis, the principle of fault which the architects of the Warsaw Convention entrenched into the Convention has been rejected by the IATA agreement. Lee Kreindler observes:

> The fault system is extremely important to the public. It is a public protection. It has improved aviation safety and security. While I don't profess to understand what the international airlines are now up to, it is clear to me that one of their purposes is to put an end to the tort system, in international airline transportation, at least as between the passenger and the airline, and that I oppose.[260]

Kreindler points out the ambivalence of the IATA agreement in designating the law of the domicile of the passenger as being applicable for the award of compensatory damages, while it retains the provision of the Warsaw Convention which designates jurisdictions.[261] Sean Gates picks up the issue of 'domicile' and observes that the IATA agreement refers to Article 28 of the Warsaw Convention which it claims relates to 'domicile' but in actual fact does not. In fact, Gates questions whether 'domicile' would cover personal or corporate domicile and holds that this is another area where the IATA agreement has not shown clarity.[262]

When there is incontrovertible evidence of a person contracting a disease such as tuberculosis as a result of being infected in an aircraft while on board, liability issues pertaining to the airline arising from the incident may involve principles of private air carrier liability. The new Montreal Convention of 1999,[263] which emerged consequent to the Diplomatic Conference on Private Air Law of the International Civil Aviation Organization held from 10 to 28 May 1999, provides that the carrier is liable for damage sustained in the event of death or bodily injury of a passenger upon condition only that the accident which caused the damage so sustained took place on board the aircraft or in the course of any of the operations of embarking or disembarking.

Later in this discussion, liability issues under the Montreal/Warsaw regime will be addressed with a view to determining whether, in general terms, the infection of a passenger with tuberculosis could be considered an 'accident' if the negligence of the carrier can be shown.

General principles

Generally in law an accusation has to be proved by the person who alleges it. Therefore a presumption of innocence applies to an accused person until he is proved guilty. However, in the instance of carriage by air of passengers, the airline is presumed liable if a passenger alleges personal injury or if his dependants allege his death as having been caused by the airline.[264] Of course the airline can show in its defence that it had taken all necessary measures to avoid the damage[265] or that there was contributory negligence[266] and obviate or vitiate its liability. This curious anomaly of the law imposing on the airline a presumption of liability is contained in the Warsaw Convention, Article 17 of which states:

> The carrier shall be liable for damage sustained in the event of the death or wounding of a passenger, if the accident which caused the damage so sustained took place on board the aircraft or in the course of any of the operations of embarking or disembarking.

To control the floodgates of litigation and discourage spurious claimants, the Convention admits of certain defences the airline may invoke and above all limits the liability of the airline to passengers and dependants of deceased passengers in monetary terms. The Warsaw system therefore presents to the lawyer an interesting and different area of the law which is worthy of discussion. Article 17 of the Warsaw Convention needs analysis in some detail in order that the circumstances in which a claim may be sustained against an airline for passenger injury or death be clearly identified. Further, the defences available to the airline and the monetary limits of liability also need to be discussed.

Defences available to the airlines

The foregoing discussion involved two key factors which govern the civil liability of airlines. They are the presumption of liability that is imposed upon the airline and the liability limits that apply to protect the airline from unlimited liability and spurious claimants. There are two other factors which operate as adjuncts to the initial concepts. They are that the airline may show certain facts in its defence to rebut the presumption and that, if the airline is found to be guilty of wilful misconduct, it is precluded from invoking the liability limits under the Warsaw Convention. Viewed at a glance, the said four concepts seem to be grouped into two sets of balancing measures. The end result is that, whilst on the one hand the airline is subject to stringent standards of liability, on the other, it is protected by two provisions which limit its liability in monetary terms and allows a complete or partial defence in rebuttal of the presumption.

Article 20(1) of the Warsaw Convention provides that the airline shall not be liable if it proves that the airline and its agents had taken all necessary measures to avoid the damage or that it was impossible for the airline and its agent to take such measures. Shawcross and Beaumont are of the view that the phrase 'all necessary measures' is an unhappy one, in that the mere happening of the passenger injury or death presupposes the fact that the airline or its agents had not in fact taken all necessary measures to prevent the occurrence.[267] The airline usually takes such precautions as making regular announcements to passengers on the status of a flight, starting with instructions on security and safety measures that are available in the aircraft. These measures are taken by the airline to conform to the requirement of the Warsaw Convention that the airline has to take all necessary measures to prevent an accident in order that the presumption of liability is rebutted. Thus, in a case decided in 1963,[268] it was held that a passenger who leaves her seat when the aircraft goes through turbulent atmosphere is barred from claiming under the Warsaw Convention for personal injury. Here it was held that an admonition of the airline that the passengers were to remain seated with their seat belts fastened during the time in question was proof of the airline having taken the necessary measures as envisaged in the Warsaw Convention.[269] This case also established the fact that 'all necessary measures' was too wide in scope and that a proper interpretation of the intention of the Warsaw Convention would be to consider the airline to require taking all 'reasonably necessary measures'. In a more recent case, Chapman J imputed objectivity to the phrase 'reasonably necessary measures' by declaring that such measures should be considered necessary by 'the reasonable man'.[270] A similar approach was taken in a subsequent case where the court held that the airline should show more than the fact that it was not negligent in order to invoke Article 20(1) of the Warsaw Convention.[271] The United States also follows this approach of objectivity. In *Manufacturers Hanover Trust Co.* v. *Alitalia Airlines*,[272] it was emphasized that the airline must show that all reasonable measures had been taken from an objective standpoint in order that the benefit of the defence be accrued to the airline. Some French decisions have also approached this defence on similar lines and required a stringent test of generality in order that the criteria for allowing the defence be approved.[273]

The airline which has the burden of proof cannot seek refuge in showing that normal precautions were taken. For example, taking normal precautions in attending to the safety of the passengers prior to a flight is not sufficient. If, therefore, the airline cannot adduce a reasonable explanation as to why the accident occurred despite the reasonably necessary precautions being taken, it is unlikely to succeed in its defence.[274] Insofar as the requirement of impossibility to take precautions is concerned, the courts have required clear evidence of the difficulties faced by the airline in avoiding the disaster. In one case of a crash landing, the court required that it was insufficient for the airline to show that the aircraft was in perfect condition and that the pilot took all steps to effect a good landing. The airline had to show that the weather conditions were so bad that the aircraft could not land in another airport.[275] In *Haddad* v. *Cie Air France*,[276] where an airline had to accept suspicious passengers who later perpetrated a hijacking, the court held that the airline could not deny boarding to the passengers who later proved to be hijackers. In that instance, the airline had found it impossible to take all necessary precautions and was considered sound in defence under Article 20(1). A similar approach was taken in the case of *Barboni* v. *Cie Air France*,[277] where the court held that, when an airline receives a bomb threat while in flight and performs an emergency evacuation, a passenger who is injured by evacuation through the escape chute cannot claim liability of the airline since it would have been impossible for the airline to take any other measure.

If the airline proves that the damage was caused by or contributed to by the negligence of the injured person, the court may, in accordance with the provisions of its own law, exonerate the carrier wholly or partly from his liability.[278] Contributory negligence under the Warsaw Convention has been treated subjectively as and when cases are adjudicated. The courts have not set an objective standard as in the earlier defence. For instance, in *Goldman* v. *Thai Airways International Ltd*,[279] it was held that a passenger is not guilty of contributory negligence if he keeps his seat belt unfastened through the flight and suffers injury when there is no sign given by the aircraft control panel to keep the seat belt on. However, if a passenger removes a bandage or brace that he is required to keep on for an existing injury and he suffers injury in flight due to the removal of the support he would be found to have contributed to the negligence resulting in his injuries.[280]

Article 25(1) of the Warsaw Convention states that the airline shall not be entitled to avail itself of the provisions of the Warsaw Convention which excludes or limits its liability, if the damage is caused by the wilful misconduct or by such default on the part of the airline as, in accordance with the law of the court to which the case is submitted, is considered to be equivalent to wilful misconduct. Article 25(1) extends this liability to acts of the agent of the airline acting within the scope of his employment and attributes such wilful misconduct to the airline. Such action as the failure of the technical crew of the aircraft to monitor weather conditions and the failure to execute a proper approach in adverse weather conditions are examples of wilful misconduct of the airline.[281] Similarly, the failure of a crew which is going off duty to inform the incoming crew of a defect in the aircraft or any such relevant issue which would affect the safety of the aircraft could be construed as an act of wilful misconduct on the part of the airline.[282]

The effect of Article 25 is that the plaintiff becomes entitled to lift the limit of liability of the airline as prescribed in Article 22 of the Warsaw Convention if he proves that the airline was guilty of wilful misconduct. Thus the burden of proof falls on the plaintiff and if he succeeds he may claim an amount over and above the prescribed limits of airline liability.

The limitation of liability of the carrier that the Warsaw Convention imposes could be circumvented by the plaintiff proving that the carrier was guilty of wilful misconduct in causing the injury. Wilful misconduct as an exception to the limitation of liability rule appears in all three air law conventions that admit of liability limitations.[283] The original French text of the Warsaw Convention states that, if the carrier causes the damage intentionally or wrongfully or by such fault as, in accordance with the court seized of the case, is equivalent thereto, he shall not be entitled to claim the limitation of liability.[284] Drion[285] maintains that the English translation inaccurately states that the liability limitations of a carrier will be obviated if the damage is caused by his *wilful misconduct* or by such *default*.[286] The contentious issue in this question is what kind of misconduct is required: Drion is of the opinion that, by approaching the issue in terms of conflicting concepts, the question whether *faute lourde* as proposed originally in the French text and for which there was an English equivalent of 'gross negligence' was in fact more appropriate than the word *dol*, which now occupies the document and for which no accurate English translation exists, and this has emerged as a critical question which needs resolution with regard to standards that may be used in extrapolating the words *dol* or 'wilful misconduct'.[287] Miller[288] takes a similar view when she states that the evils of conceptualistic thinking that had pervaded the drafting of Article 25, which rendered it destitute of coherence, have now been rectified by the Hague Convention which has introduced the words 'done with intent to cause damage or recklessly and with knowledge that the damage would probably result'.[289]

This confusion was really the precursor to diverse interpretations and approaches to the concept of wilful misconduct under Article 25 of the Warsaw Convention. The French government took steps by its Air Carrier Act of 1957 to rectify ambiguities in this area by interpreting *dol* in the Convention as *faute inexcusable*, or deliberate fault, which implies knowledge of the probability of damage and its reckless acceptance without valid reason,[290] making a strong analogy with the Hague Protocol's contents. This interpretation, needless to say, brought out the question whether such reckless acceptance would be viewed subjectively or objectively.

The Belgian decision of *Tondriau* v. *Air India*[291] considered the issue of Article 25 of the Convention and the Hague interpretation. The facts of the case were usual, involving the death of a passenger and a consequent claim under the Convention by his dependants. The significance of the case lay, however, in the fact that the Belgian court followed the decision of *Emery and others* v. *SABENA*[292] and held that, in the consideration of the pilot's negligence under Article 25, an objective test would apply, and the normal behaviour of a good pilot would be the applicable criterion. The court held:

> Whereas the plaintiffs need not prove, apart from the wrongful act, that the pilot of the aircraft personally had knowledge that damage would probably result from it; it is sufficient that they prove that a reasonably prudent pilot ought to have had this knowledge.[293]

The court rationalized that a good pilot ought in the circumstances to have known the existence of a risk and no pilot of an aircraft engaged in air transport ought to take any risk needlessly. The Brussels Court of Appeal, however, reversed this judgment and applied a subjective test, asserting that the Hague protocol called for 'effective knowledge'. Professor Bin Cheng seems to prefer the objective test in the interpretation of 'wilful misconduct' in Article 25, on the grounds that a subjective test would defeat the spirit of the Convention and that judges would be 'flying in the face of justice in search of absolute equity in individual cases'.[294]

Peter Martin, analysing the Court of Appeal decision in *Goldman* v. *Thai Airways International Ltd*,[295] agrees with Bin Cheng and criticizes the lower court decision which awarded Mr Goldman substantial damages for injuring his hip as a result of being thrown around in his seat in turbulence, in an instance where the captain had not switched on the 'fasten seat belt' sign.[296] Martin maintains that Mr Goldman failed to prove that the pilot knew that damage would probably result from his act, as envisaged in the Hague Protocol principle. Being an aviation insurance lawyer, Martin is concerned that, while the English courts have a proclivity towards deciding Article 25 issues subjectively, insurance underwriters could view the breach of the limits stringently. Both on the count of the need for objectivity and on the count of the adverse effects on insurance, it is difficult to disagree with Cheng and Martin.

The question of air carrier liability and the approach taken in its context by the Warsaw Convention has seen the emergence of the scholarly analysis of two issues: should liability of the carrier be based on fault and consequently on the principles of negligence and limited liability, or should liability be based on strict liability? Drion, in his 1954 treatise on liability,[297] inquires into the various rationales and scenarios that may come up in an intellectual extrapolation of the subject. He examines the fact that an insurance system for liability, which would be inextricably linked to a strict liability concept, would be desirable, as a plaintiff would be able to claim compensation from an impecunious defendant through the latter's insurer, on the deep pocket theory,[298] and that insurance underwriters may, in their own interest, be impelled to formulate aviation accident preventive schemes, strengthening the effects of accident prevention.[299] Drion also puts forward eight rationales for the rebuttable limitation of liability presumption that appears in Article 17, quantified by Article 22 of the Convention: maritime principles carry a limitation policy; the protection of the financially weak aviation industry; the risks should be borne by aviation alone; the existence of back-up insurance; the possibility of the claimants obtaining insurance; limitation of liability being imposed on a *quid pro quo* basis on both the carrier and operator; the possibility of quick settlement under a liability limitation n regime; and the ability to unify the law regarding damages.[300]

These rationales, and whatever else may form considerations of policy in the assessment whether a liability system should be based on negligence or strict liability, should be addressed with the conscious awareness that, while the Convention imposes a rebuttable presumption of limited liability on the carrier, the contributory negligence of the plaintiff can exculpate the carrier and obviate or apportion compensation. More importantly, wilful misconduct of the carrier transcends liability limits and makes the liability of the carrier unlimited. Strict liability, on the other hand, as proposed in Montreal Protocols 3 and 4, does not admit of breaking liability limits, sets a maximum limit of compensation that the carrier has to pay, and makes this limit unbreakable by such extraneous factors as the carrier's wilful misconduct.

The ultimate question therefore is, does one keep the Warsaw–Hague concept of fault and limited liability, or does one embrace a system of strict liability which assures the aggrieved party of pecuniary or reipersecutory recompense, while obviating the need for lengthy determinations of who was at fault after the fact. In other words, does one point a finger at the carrier in the first instance, then limit his liability and again break the limit if he is at fault, or does one make the carrier pay a sum of money, the maximum limits of which have been set, with the assurance that such limits would not shoot up unconscionably if the carrier was negligent?

The Convention unified legal principles relating to air carrier liability, thus precluding the application of scores of differing domestic laws.[301] However, it did not succeed in presenting to the world unequivocally objective and quantified rules of liability. This precludes a plaintiff from knowing that he would, as a rule, be compensated if he was injured in an air accident, since the Convention admits of challenge on the grounds of the plaintiff's conduct before, during or after the accident. The strict liability principle introduced by the Guatemala City Protocol and carried through by the Montreal Protocols, on the other hand, has been applauded on the following grounds:

> First, it gets money into the hands of the passengers much more quickly. Second, it saves transaction expenses which include legal fees and other substantial litigation costs. Third, it provides compensation to passengers in those factual situations where no responsible party is at fault, such as in an act of terrorism.[302]

Alexander Tobolewski points out very validly that actual aviation practice in terms of aviation insurance by the airlines has nothing to do with limitation of liability and claims, since airlines insure their fleets and liabilities for colossal amounts in the insurance market.[303] He suggests, therefore, the harmonization of the law and actual practice (presumably by infusing more specific quantum in damages) and simplification of the system of recovery inter alia, both of which strongly suggest a regime such as the one envisaged in the Montreal protocols.[304] Werner Guldimann concludes:

> The most important and urgent matter in the present decade is the continuation of the efforts undertaken by ICAO to re-establish the former universality and uniformity of the Warsaw system by having the Montreal Protocols No 3 and 4 rapidly ratified by the greatest possible number of contracting States.[305]

Although Professor Bin Cheng considers that the Montreal Protocols are heavily weighted towards the carrier, that the limits therein are inadequate and that the unbreakability of the limit of the SDR value is undesirable,[306] the view that strict liability should be embraced seems more sensible, in view of the inconceivable number of passengers carried every year by air, the possible eradication of legal contingency fees and, above all, giving teeth to the meaning and purpose of law – that it should be an instrument of solace, not an opportunity for debate. In an evaluation of the Warsaw System,[307] it was said in 1979 that, during the first 25 years of the existence of the Warsaw Convention, it had served the aviation community satisfactorily.[308] Peter Martin bases this observation on the argument that, when the Hague Protocol was being drafted in 1955, it was recorded that only 55 Warsaw cases had been adjudicated, and that is a very small number of cases for an instrument of the stature of the Warsaw Convention.[309] The unifying process of the liability of an air carrier, started by the Warsaw Convention, dealt with liability concepts, quantum of compensation, exceptions on liability, jurisdictional issues and prescription of action. It is sad, however, that, together with the original Warsaw Convention, there are now seven other international agreements, few of which have ever seen the light of day. This means that the unification process started by the Warsaw Convention had been criticized and found wanting at various stages of its chequered history. The original document has been excoriated so many times, prompting Professor Cheng to call it the 'Warsaw shambles',[310] although it remained, when these comments were made of it, the most widely implemented private international law convention.[311]

Ex facie, from a strictly practical standpoint, it would appear that many facets of unification of the Warsaw Convention have come under interpretation by different philosophies, presumably because of the lack of specificity of the principles of unification and, *a fortiori*, the language used. For instance, the delivery of the passenger ticket and the attendant carrier liability came under a series of confounding judicial thought processes, where in two cases[312] the courts decided that the ticket had to be delivered in such a manner as to afford the passenger a reasonable opportunity to take measures to protect against liability insurance, only to decide in *Chan* v. *Korean Airlines*[313] that the only requirement of Article 3 of the Convention was that a ticket be delivered. *Goldman* v. *Thai Airways International Limited*[314] was another case where two confusing issues were decided upon. The first involved the question whether the concept of 'wilful misconduct' as reflected in Article 25 of the Convention was to be interpreted objectively or subjectively. The second issue concerned compensatory limits which were so confusing to both the courts and the parties to litigation that an outside settlement was effected on a mutually acceptable basis.[315] The issue regarding compensatory limits for death or personal injury has had a consistent evolution, starting from the Warsaw Convention at approximately 8300 US dollars, increased twofold by the Hague Protocol 1955, increased again by the Guatemala City Protocol to 100 000 special drawing rights (SDR) (about 130 000 US dollars) with the Montreal Protocols going even higher. The currency conversion to gold value has been another source of contention of many parties to litigation, and the case of *Franklin Mint* v. *TWA*[316] left the situation in fiscal anarchy by deciding that, in the United States, the Poincaré gold franc has to be converted to the last official price of gold before the United States left the gold market, and not the free market price of gold. This not only made the overall American attitude towards seeking enhanced compensation turn 360 degrees, but also awarded unrealistically low compensation to the plaintiff. Further, a case in Australia has given a new interpretation to the notion of carrier negligence in the carriage of cargo,[317] and a New Zealand case has decided that any interested party can now claim compensation under a cargo claim.[318]

The Montreal Agreement of 1966, a private agreement between carriers plying the United States, was also the result of failure by contracting states to reach an international solution to the problem of unifying principles of liability, particularly insofar as the quantum of damages was concerned. The Montreal Agreement amply demonstrates, as an ICAO document[319] points out, that a private agreement between air carriers, sponsored by IATA, can unhinge and question the credibility of a multi-lateral international treaty between sovereign states. Mankiewicz attributes this chaotic state of disagreement to the stand taken by the United States:

> Indeed, there is real irony in the history of the Warsaw Convention. For more than thirty years, the United States of America have steadily and successfully fought for, and obtained and signed six protocols to amend the Warsaw Convention as well as a 'Convention Supplementary to the Warsaw Convention'. But they have ratified not one of these Warsaw instruments. In spite of the huge amounts of time and money spent all these years by ICAO and its member States, the US judiciary is still saddled with the awkward task of applying, construing constructively or destructively, misinterpreting and circumventing a convention which is now 60 years old.[320]

There is only one viable alternative to rectify this anomaly and to preserve the unification efforts of the Warsaw Convention, and that comes in the nature of ratifying the Montreal Protocols 3 and 4. As Michael Milde states:

> There is hardly any viable alternative to a determined effort to bring the Montreal Protocols Nos. 3 and 4 into force. If that aim is not accomplished in the very near future, we may witness a trend to denunciation of the Warsaw System by several States with the ensuing chaotic conflicts of laws, conflicts of jurisdiction, unpredictably high compensation claims and skyrocketing increase in insurance premiums.[321]

The civil liability of an airline for the causing of death or injury to passengers has been established by international treaty and entrenched in law by judicial interpretation. The courts have attempted to balance the interest of both the airline and the passenger, as indeed has been the perceived intention of the Warsaw Convention. The predominant feature of this area of civil liability is that air transport in terms of the commercial transportation of passengers is incontrovertibly the mode of transport that involves the highest levels of technology. Therefore courts may find difficulty in ascertaining negligence, wilful misconduct and the overall liability of the airline in the face of complex technical arguments and defence. However, this reason alone should not justify obviating the tortious element that has so carefully been entrenched in the Warsaw Convention by its founders and used by courts for more that 70 years. As the foregoing discussions reflect, liability issues under the Warsaw Convention have been consistently addressed by the courts on the basis of their interpretation of negligence, wilful misconduct and contributory negligence, all of which are exclusively issues involving principles of tort law.

Relevance of 'accident' to the illness of the passenger

It is clear that the conventional interpretation of the term 'accident' in tort liability has been extended in aviation cases under Article 17 of the Warsaw Convention where the courts have imputed intention to the carrier in certain instances. To this extent, as the *Seguritan*[322] case – which addressed the issue of the carrier's liability in not being able to provide regular medical assistance when necessary – and the *O'Leary* case[323] – more liquor than he could consume in flight – perforce prove the courts have interpreted the Warsaw Convention to enforce liability of the carrier on the principles of intention. Wilful misconduct, therefore, has played an important role in establishing that, in certain circumstances at least, there could be justification in considering that the extent of the carrier's fault is a valid consideration in the award of damages.

Fault liability as enforced by the Warsaw Convention may also be adequately reflected in intentional negligence, where the carrier intentionally breaches the duty of care he owes the passenger. Determination of a breach of a duty or care as a distinct evidentiary tool by the courts would act towards accident prevention in that instances of carrier liability which emerge from accident investigations could then be used as admissible evidence.

The new trend introduced by the Montreal Convention of 1999 in doing away with fault liability and introducing a system of liability that may apply irrespective of fault, but aligned on monetary compensation based upon subjective assessments of jurisdictional liability, has its genesis in the decade from 1960 to 1970. During this period civil law liability in tort entered a new phase, effectively superannuating the existing system of liability and replacing it with a system of liability insurance. Tortious liability was no longer considered cost-effective, and was no match for less expensive insurance. Jurists thought it more equitable and, above all, practical to embrace a legal system that espoused loss distribution, which acted as the national precursor to liability insurance. This system of liability was helped along the way by three reasons which militated against fault liability and acted as catalysts for the successful launch of liability insurance. Firstly, a tort system based upon fault was expensive to administer, when compared with any system of insurance; secondly, litigation was fraught with delay, which a plaintiff could often ill afford; thirdly, the unpredictability of the result of cases based upon fault liability often put plaintiffs under pressure to settle their claims for amounts less than they would receive if their claims went successfully to trial.

Wilful misconduct of the carrier

Of the two instances in which the Warsaw Convention provides that the carrier's liability is unlimited, one relates to the absence of documentation (absence of the passenger ticket and baggage check or air waybill) on the grounds that the document of carriage evidences the special regime of limited liability as prescribed in the Warsaw Convention. The other, which has turned out to be contentious, deals with instances where the damage is caused by the carrier's wilful misconduct, or such default on his part as, in accordance with the law of the court which exercises jurisdiction in the case, is considered to be the equivalent of wilful misconduct. Article 25 of the Warsaw Convention provides:

> The carrier shall not be entitled to avail himself of the provisions of this Convention or exclude or limit his liability, if the damage is caused by his wilful misconduct or by such default on his part as, in accordance with the law of the court seized of the case, is considered to be equivalent to wilful misconduct.[324]

The provision further stipulates that the carrier shall not be entitled to avail himself of the above provisions if the damage is caused as aforesaid by any agent of the carrier acting within the scope of his employment.[325]

The primary significance of Article 25 is that it addresses both wilful misconduct and the 'equivalent' (my emphasis) of wilful misconduct. The authentic and original text of the Warsaw Convention, which is in French, uses the words 'dol' and 'faute ... equivalente au dol'. There is a palpable inconsistency between English translation of the original text and the original text itself in that the French word 'dol' connotes the intention to inflict an injury on a person, whereas the English words 'wilful misconduct' require the defendant carrier to be aware of both his conduct and the reasonable and probable consequences of his conduct, in the nature of the damage which may ensue from the carrier's act. Wilful misconduct, therefore, may not necessarily involve the intention of the carrier, his servants or agents and remains wider in scope as a ground of liability.

Most civil law jurisdictions have equiperated 'dol' with 'gross negligence'. Drion[326] dismisses the element of intention by citing examples such as the theft or pilferage of goods or baggage (which are more frequent in occurrence than aircraft accidents) which may not necessarily always occur with the concurrence or knowledge of the carrier, and cites a list of possible instances where gross negligence would form more justification for the invocation of Article 25. Notable examples are assault or indecent behaviour by personnel of the carrier, accidents caused by conduct of personnel, serving bad food, bumpy rides causing passenger injury and failure to instruct passengers of rough weather and so on.[327] Drion also makes the valid point of citing delay in carriage as having many dimensions which may be accommodated within the purview of Article 25 without warranting the consideration of intention.[328]

Common law jurisdictions, on the other hand, have separated 'wilful misconduct' from 'negligence' and insisted that the conduct of the carrier has to be 'wilful' or intentional for a successful case to be grounded on Article 25 of the Warsaw Convention. This approach is consistent with the original contention of the British delegate to the Warsaw Conference, who claimed that wilful misconduct should pertain to 'acts committed deliberately or acts of carelessness without any regard for the consequences'.[329] In the 1952 British case of *Horabin* v. *British Overseas Airways Corporation*, the court held:

> To be guilty of wilful misconduct the person concerned must appreciate that he is acting wrongfully, or is wrongfully omitting to act and yet persists in so acting or omitting to act regardless of the consequences, or acts or omits to act with reckless indifference as to what the result may be.[330]

In the same year, in the United States, the New York Supreme Court appellate Division held that wilful misconduct was

> dependent upon the facts of a particular case, but in order that acts may be characterized as wilful there must be on the part of the person or persons sought to be charged, a conscious intent to do or to omit doing the act from which harm results to another, or an intentional omission of a manifest duty. There must be a realization of the probability of injury from the conduct and a disregard of the probable consequences of such conduct.[331]

The above approach has been followed by subsequent American decisions which have classified wilful misconduct as requiring 'conscious intent to do or omit doing an act from which harm results to another'[332] and 'wilful performance of an act that is likely to result in damage or wilful action with a reckless disregard of the probable consequences'.[333]

As to the second limb of Article 25.1, which provides that the equivalent of wilful misconduct would suffice to impose liability, the Convention leaves the scope of the provision wide open to include an instance of the carrier knowingly providing small seats and not advising the passenger of the inherent dangers related thereto.

Judicial decisions on wilful misconduct

Arguably, the watershed decision on the notion of wilful misconduct in recent times was contained in the case *In re Korean Airlines Disaster of September 1, 1983*,[334] where the trial court considered wilful misconduct to be 'The performance of an act with knowledge that the act will probably result in an injury or damage, or in some manner as to imply reckless disregard for the consequences of its performance'. This pronouncement was used by the American courts, in the 1994 decision of *Pasinato v. American Airlines, Inc.*,[335] who concluded that the act in question of a flight attendant did not constitute wilful misconduct within the purview of Article 25.2 of the Warsaw Convention. In the *Pasinato* case, a passenger of an American Airlines flight which was bound for Chicago from Italy was struck on the head when a heavy totebag fell from an overhead bin in the cabin. The incident was the outcome of an initial request by the passenger for a pillow immediately after take-off, where the flight attendant, in a bid to open the overhead bin above the passenger to retrieve the pillow, was unable to prevent a totebag falling from the bin onto the passenger's head. The passenger and her husband sued American Airlines under Article 25 on the grounds of wilful misconduct. The trial court was of the view:

> there is no dispute that the flight attendant opened the overhead bin to get a pillow for another passenger. The flight attendant's disposition indicates that she opened the bin with one hand, in her customary manner, with the other hand placed defensively above her head near the bin to prevent an object from falling upon her or a passenger sitting below. Further, the flight attendant stated that she tried to catch the totebag that fell from the bin (and may have touched it as it fell), but that it fell too quickly.[336]

The court took cognizance of the contention of American Airlines that the technical and cabin crews give reported warnings to passengers of the dangers of opening overhead bins, both over the public address system of the aircraft and by personal messages. The evidence of the flight attendant – that incidents of objects falling from overhead bins were infrequent and generally harmless – based on her experience, was also considered relevant. The court found difficulty in applying the criterion of the *Korean Airlines Disaster* case,[337] in that it was difficult for the court, if not impossible, to envision how the flight attendant's actions could amount to wilful misconduct. It was of the view that the pivotal criterion for determining the existence of wilful misconduct – knowledge that the act would probably result in an injury or damage – was absent. *A fortiori*, the court observed that the other criterion established in the *Korean Airlines* case – that of an act which is performed in a manner indicating reckless disregard for the consequences – was also missing in the *Pasinato* case.

In the 1994 case of *Baba* v. *Compagnie Nationale Air France*,[338] involving damage to cargo, a Federal trial court in Washington found for the plaintiff and awarded damages against the act of the defendant carrier for improperly packing and storing hand-woven Persian carpets, as a result of which some of the carpets were damaged owing to the seepage of rain water when the carpets were kept outside by the carrier pending their loading onto the aircraft. The court in this instance followed the bench in *Pasinato* by reiterating the criteria for the proof of wilful misconduct as established by the *Korean Air* litigation. A compelling piece of evidence which enabled the court to arrive at its conclusion in the *Baba* case was the fact that the air carrier had disregarded its own cargo handling regulations in storing the carpets outdoors, in the rain. In its findings the court held:

> In short, through a series of acts, the performance of which were intentional, the carrier has demonstrated a reckless disregard of the consequences of its performance, This disregard is emphasized by the fact that no damage report was ever produced.[339]

The court, while waiving the liability limits of the Warsaw Convention in the *Baba* case, noted that a combination of facts can, taken together, amount to wilful misconduct. It was sufficient, in the court's view, for an act to be intended, and not necessary for the resulting injury or wrongfulness of the act to reflect intention or knowledge. It was also significant that the court further observed that a finding of wilful misconduct was appropriate when the act or omission constituted a violation of a rule or regulation of the defendant carrier itself.

Courts in the United States have been cautious to determine the parameters of 'scope of employment' as envisaged in Article 25.2 of the Warsaw Convention, which imputes liability to the carrier with regard to acts of its employers acting within the scope of their employment. In the 1995 case of *Uzochukwu* v. *Air Express International Ltd.*,[340] where a New York Federal trial court had to decide on a case of theft by two airline employees of cargo of the two carriers, it was held that the fact that the employees had used forged documents to perpetrate the offence of theft was sufficient to conclude that the act was outside the scope of employment and that the carrier could not be held liable under Article 25.2. It is arguable that the conclusion of the court was based on the fact that, generally, in the United States, 'wilful misconduct' is regarded as the intentional performance of an act with knowledge that the performance of that act would probably result in injury or damage, or the intentional performance of an act in such a manner as to imply reckless disregard of the probably consequences.

In *Robinson* v *Northwest Airlines Inc.*,[341] a case decided in March 1996 and involving circumstances similar to the *Pasinato* case, the United States Court of Appeals dismissed the appeal of the plaintiff who had lost judgment in the trial court against the carrier. The trial court had allowed a motion of the carrier that the plaintiff's claim in relation to her being injured by a piece of hand luggage falling from an overhead bin while the plane was taxiing, and additional injuries caused to her by a passenger striking her on the head with the latter's baggage, were valid at law. The Court of Appeals, in affirming the dismissal of the action of the plaintiff, noted that, while a common carrier (a carrier who opens itself to the world to conduct business in the carriage by air of passengers, baggage and goods) owes a high degree of care to its passengers, it cannot be considered an insurer of the passenger's safety. The court found that the plaintiff failed to raise an issue of fact regarding the carrier's breach of duty towards her. The court was of the following view:

> Short of physical constraint of each passenger until each is individually escorted off the plane, we fail to see what Northwest could have done to prevent this accident. At best, that is precisely what the plaintiff has established; the fact that an accident occurred. However, as noted above, common carriers are not insurers of their passenger safety.[342]

A similar approach can be seen in the contemporaneous case of *Bell v Swiss Air Transport Co. Ltd*,[343] where an Intermediate Appellate court in New York State refused to allow the plaintiff's claim that the loss of his laptop computer during a security check of the airline was due to the airline's wilful misconduct. In the court's view, the plaintiff had failed to prove that the airline intentionally mishandled his baggage with knowledge or reckless disregard for the probable consequences of its conduct. The court also noted that it was the local police, and not the airline, who had required the carrying out of the security check.

The case of *Singh v. Pan American World Airways*,[344] decided in May 1996, offers a helpful insight into the rationale for determination of wilful misconduct. In wrongful death and personal injury actions arising out of the 1995 hijacking of a PANAM flight between Bombay and New York, the jury concluded that the carrier had been guilty of wilful misconduct on the reasoning that the management of the carrier knew, or ought to have known, of serious lapses in its security programme. In fact, there had been representations made by the carrier's staff to the management on several occasions prior to the hijacking. Furthermore, the jury was influenced in its conclusion by the fact that the carrier was aware of terrorist activity at European, Middle Eastern and Asian high-risk airports and that very little had been done by the carrier to provide enhanced security at these airports.

In the case of the crash of *Thai Airways Flight TG-311 near Katmandu, Nepal in July 1992*,[345] the question at issue was whether the air crew had been guilty of wilful misconduct in flying into terrain. The fatal crash occurred during approach to Katmandu airport – an airport known to be one of the most difficult in the world in which to land.[346] Evidence had revealed that the captain had given the bearings of the aircraft to the control tower shortly before the crash, and that such were inconsistent with instruction previously given by the tower to the crew in the cockpit of the aircraft. The court concluded that the plane had veered towards terrain surrounding the airport owing to the crew's conscious failure to monitor their navigational instruments. The court held:

> the captain and the first officer knew or should have known that failing to perform their duty to continuously monitor the aircraft's navigational instruments would create a grave danger under the circumstances ... both the captain and the first officer were well aware that their duty to consciously monitor navigational instruments was an act

necessary for safety ... their duty to perform this crucial act was so obvious under the circumstances that failing to perform it was *reckless in the extreme*.[347]

The *Thai Airways* case therefore marks an instance where the elements of wilful misconduct were imputed to the crew on the basis that, because of their expertise, they knew or ought to have known the reasonable and probable consequences of their act.

A further dimension to the notion of wilful misconduct was added in the *Northwest Airlines Air Crash Case*[348] of August 1996, where the Court of Appeals of the Sixth Circuit added that a finding of wilful misconduct may be based upon consideration of a series of actions or inactions. The court was of the view that, since many complex safety systems interact during an air plane flight, an air disaster would usually require multiple acts. In other words, the court held that it was permissible for a jury to consider an airline's individual errors or a series of errors and not restrict itself to the only act which seemingly caused an accident.

If one were to analyse the rationale of wilful misconduct in the light of the *cursus curiae* so far discussed, one would conclude that wilful misconduct hinges itself on knowledge of the perpetrator that damage would result, or reckless disregard for consequences of an act on the part of the perpetrator. The question which then arises is whether an instance of the carrier knowingly providing small seats and not advising the passengers of the dangers of prolonged air travel in confined spaces would subscribe to the notion of wilful misconduct as it is perceived at the present time.

'Accident' in air law

In commercial aviation, the word 'accident' is sometimes given as broad a definition as those just considered. The Chicago Convention of 1944 defines accident as 'occurrence associated with the operation of an aircraft'.[349] The Montreal Convention of 1999, in Article 16, refers to 'the accident which caused the death or injury' and the Warsaw Convention in Article 17 speaks of the 'the accident which caused the damage' – both Conventions reducing the accident to the cause rather than to the death or injury.[350] The United States Supreme Court has held that *in limine* an accident must be unexpected and external to the passenger.[351] It is not sufficient that the plaintiff suffers injury as a result of his own internal reaction to the usual, normal and expected operation of the aircraft.[352] Such incidents as hijackings, terrorist attacks and bomb threats have been considered to be accidents, together with aircraft crashes.[353] An accident could even involve such lesser incidents as tyre failure on take-off[354] and the supply of infected food causing food poisoning of passengers.[355]

In the *Seguritan v. Northwest Airlines* case, decided in 1982, the allegation against the airline was that, as a result of the failure on the part of the airline to provide assistance, a passenger travelling from New York to Manila suffered a massive coronary seizure in flight, resulting in death. Responsibility devolved upon the court to fit this incident to that of an 'accident' within the meaning of the Warsaw Convention. The court readily did this by deeming that the word 'accident' in air law in this instance was not the heart attack itself but the failure on the part of the airline to render medical assistance in flight. The court said: 'After all, it is no different from an airline's liability in a hijacking incident where the accident is not the acts of the hijackers but the alleged failure on the part of the carrier to provide adequate security'.[356] The airline was accordingly found liable for damage so sustained by the deceased passenger.

In a contemporaneous case, a passenger brought action in the US District Court of Puerto Rico for a hernia sustained by the lifting of a heavy suitcase from the conveyor belt. A baggage handler of the defendant airline had refused to carry the suitcase and the plaintiff had solicited aid from her relatives who were not allowed to enter the baggage area by a guard on duty. The action against the airline was dismissed by the court primarily on the grounds that the plaintiff did not suffer an unexpected injury as she had previously undergone a gall bladder operation and would have known her condition to be delicate.[357]

In 1983, a medical practitioner suffering from a head cold and respiratory infection boarded an aircraft. He disembarked completely deaf. The plaintiff averred that he suffered discomfort in his ears at descent probably due to sudden pressure changes that occurred. He alleged that the airline knew or ought to have known that passengers suffering from head colds would risk losing their hearing. In addition, it was alleged that the airline owed a duty to warn the passenger that it was dangerous to travel with a head cold. The airline denied the existence of such a duty. The US District Court for the Southern District of New York reasoned that it would be incongruous to impose a duty on an airline to envisage all possible human afflictions and assess their effect on air travel and warn passengers accordingly. In any event, the airline was in this instance not aware that the passenger was suffering from a head cold. In this decision the court clearly indicated that the presumption of liability imposed by the Warsaw Convention on airlines and the highest-degree-of-care doctrine applicable thereto should not be taken advantage of by plaintiffs.[358] Similarly, there would be no cause of action against an airline where a passenger's ill-health is aggravated owing to acceleration at take-off or deceleration at landing.[359]

In April 1984, an intermediate Appellate Court in New York was faced with the task of deciding whether an airline can be held liable for the death of a passenger who chokes to death owing to his own intoxication. The decision was in the affirmative and the court in enforcing judgment against the airline drew the analogy between a dispensing druggist and an airline. The airline serves its passengers with drink and thus undertakes the responsibility not to serve in excess and to exercise reasonable care for the safety of passengers. In addition, in the event of excessive intoxication of a passenger, the airline is under a legal duty to render such medical assistance as is necessary to revive the passenger or in any event to keep him out of danger. In the light of this principle, the airline has a further duty to protect others from a drunken passenger who gets out of control.[360]

In *Air France* v. *Saks*,[361] the United States Supreme Court interpreted the word 'accident' in the context of the Warsaw Convention to mean an occurrence whereby a passenger is injured owing to an unexpected or unusual event or happening that is external to the passenger,[362] and that where the injury results from the passenger's own internal reaction to the normal exigencies of air travel such injury would not be construed as having resulted from an accident. In this case, the plaintiff was a passenger on an Air France flight from Paris to Los Angeles. During the descent, the plaintiff suffered severe pain in her left ear which was aggravated thereafter. The plaintiff – who consulted a doctor after the plane landed – was informed that she was rendered completely deaf in her left ear. The plaintiff brought an action in a California State court on the grounds that her hearing loss was due to the negligent maintenance by the airline of the pressurization system of the aircraft which transported her. Air France moved that the allegation of the plaintiff could not be sustained within the meaning of the word 'accident' of Article 17 of the Warsaw Convention, which was meant to be an unusual and unexpected happening. Further, the airline alleged that at all times the pressurization system of the aircraft had been normal. The District Court granted summary judgment to the plaintiff on the basis that 'accident' in Article 17 was meant to be an unusual and unexpected happening. The Supreme Court rejected the rationale adopted by the lower court on the ground that Article 17 refers to an accident which causes an injury and therefore it is the cause and not the effect that is the determinant. Accordingly, the Supreme Court held that air carriers would be liable only if an accident caused the passenger injury. Thus an injury that was in itself an accident was insufficient to satisfy the requirements of Article 17 of the Warsaw Convention.

There will be no accident if in a normal flight free of turbulence a passenger suffers discomfort from a condition he suffers from, such as a hiatus hernia[363] or thrombophlebitis.[364] In *Abramson* v. *Japan Airlines*, an airline passenger suffered an aggravation of a pre-existing hiatus hernia shortly after take-off from Anchorage on a flight to Tokyo. The passenger, who had been under medication for his condition for six years, had not informed the carrier prior to boarding. The passenger, however, claimed that, had he been given occupation of a few empty seats, he could have massaged his stomach to normality. The airline had claimed that there were no empty seats in flight, contrary to the passenger's claim that there were in fact nine empty seats in flight in the first class section of the aircraft. The passenger claimed that his hernia attack constituted an 'accident' within the provisions of Article 17 of the Convention. The court rejected this claim and held that the plaintiff's difficulty was not in any way related to his transportation by air and, accordingly, there was no accident under Article 17.

It would have been interesting if the court had applied the principle of *Seguritan*'s case,[365] where failure to render medical assistance by the airline was construed as falling within the purview of the word 'accident'. After all, the airline did not make any attempt at rendering assistance to the passenger in *Abramson*'s case. The court's reasoning in the latter case contradicts the earlier decision and leads to a logical absurdity. The intention of the Convention was seemingly to provide a uniform system of compensation for passengers bringing claims against airlines operating international air services. To suggest that the failure of an airline to render required assistance is excusable under the Convention is completely at odds with earlier decisions and also arguably with the intention and purpose of the Convention itself.

Insofar as the word 'wounding' of a passenger in Article 17 is concerned, courts initially held that such would only be in instances of 'bodily injury' and consequently would be palpably conspicuous physical injury.[366] This excluded mental injury. However, a later decision[367] held that types of injuries enumerated should be construed expansively to encompass as many types of injury as are colourably within the ambit of the enumerated types, including mental and psychosomatic injuries. This decision has been followed consistently in a strong line of cases.[368] In the United States, mental injury is now entrenched in most jurisdictions as an independently compensable head of damages,[369] as indeed Burnett C J said in *Medlin* v. *Allied Investment Co.*:[370]

> Memory and empathy tells us that 'hurt' perceived through sensory media other than that of touch may be just as painful if not more than the hurt perceived by the tactile sense. Moreover, physicians tell us that the consequences of invasion of the person accomplished through the perceptory media of sight and sound may be also as damaging if not more damaging than invasions of the persons accomplished through the sense of touch.[371]

Therefore mental anguish or injury would now be recognized by most jurisdictions as falling within the purview of 'wounding' of a passenger under Article 17 of the Warsaw Convention.

It is apparent from the *cursus curiae* that a stringent standard of proof of the nature of the occurrence is insisted upon by the courts if liability of the carrier is to be established under Article 17 of the Warsaw Convention. In *Salce* v. *Aer Lingus Airlines*,[372] the District Court for the Southern District of New York required of the plaintiff to show that the landing of the aircraft in which the plaintiff travelled was anything other than a normal landing. The plaintiff averred that he had received personal injuries due to the hard landing of the aircraft. In the absence of clear evidence of a hard landing, the court would presume that the landing performed by the aircraft in this instance was not an unexpected or unusual event that would satisfy the requirements of an 'accident' under the Warsaw Convention.

However, when facts are self-evident, as in the case of *Salerno* v. *Pan American World Airways*,[373] the courts would not hesitate to award damages to a plaintiff passenger. In this case, the District Court for the Southern District of New York held that knowledge of a bomb threat which subsequently caused a miscarriage to a passenger came within the meaning of scope of the word 'accident'. The plaintiff and her two children were passengers aboard a PANAM flight from Miami to Uruguay. The cockpit crew, after take-off, instructed the cabin crew to look for a bomb which the former had been informed by air traffic control to be on board. The crew notified the passengers, including the plaintiff. She suffered a miscarriage 24 hours after being informed of the alleged bomb on board and having watched the cabin crew looking for the object. The court held that an 'accident' within the meaning of the Warsaw Convention caused the plaintiff's injuries because a bomb threat is 'external to the passenger' and is an unexpected and unusual event outside the usual, normal and expected operation of the aircraft.[374]

The above discussion highlights the salutary principle that the word 'accident' is considered far more liberally in modern air law than is done under other areas of common law. It also underscores the fact that courts would be more inclined to treat acts of omission on the part of airlines as an 'accident', as was shown in *Seguritan*'s case.[375] The airline is presumed liable for an 'accident' where a drunken passenger assaults another, or where a passenger suffers a heart attack and is not given the necessary medical attention in flight as is possible, just to name two instances. Of course, the claimant has to adduce clear evidence of the event and the ensuing injury.

Embarking and disembarking

Both Conventions provide that the accident which causes the damage should take place on board the aircraft or in the course of any of the operations of embarking or disembarking. The first alternative – that of being on board – is self-explanatory and does not require discussion. The second, which involves the operations of embarking or disembarking, has been subject to sustained judicial discussion and analysis. Although, *ex facie*, the words 'on board the aircraft' are not problematical, the phrase has been interpreted at least once to engulf time spent by passengers in a hotel consequent to a hijacking.[376] The argument in this case was that the passengers would have been on board if not for the hijacking. This is an extreme interpretation which seems to say that the airline is liable for all accidents within that period of time from the start of the embarkation process to the end of the disembarkation.

Current law on the subject seems to favour the test known as the *Day–Evangelinos* test which was developed as a consequence of a series of terrorist acts on passengers in airport departure lounges. This is a tripartite test which has the three elements of consideration: the location of the passenger, the nature of his activity at the time of the accident and the degree of control exercised by the airline at the relevant time. A number of US cases have accepted this test.[377] This test clearly establishes the fact that, unless the passenger is under the control or direction of the airline at the terminal, there is no liability for injury or death caused to the passenger under the provisions of the Warsaw Convention. A case which brings out the significance of this test is *Adler* v. *Austrian Airlines*, where a passenger slipped on some ice and fell when travelling between the terminal building and the aircraft by bus. The bus was operated by the airport staff and not by the airline. A Brussels court, applying a test similar to the *Day–Evangelinos* test, held that the passenger was not under the control of the airline and was thereby precluded from invoking the provisions of Article 17 of the Convention.

The test itself obviates the need to go through every possible exigency painstakingly in the light of the requirement that the accident should occur during the process of embarkation or disembarkation. Prior to the adoption of this test, there was no uniformity in the judicial reasoning behind the definition of embarkation and disembarkation. It was left to each individual court to determine whether a given situation would fall within the scope of chronology of these two extremities. Now the tripartite test has made the task of the courts much easier.

It would be extremely difficult for an airline to determine latent illnesses such as tuberculosis of its passengers. Therefore instances of negligence pertaining to an airline accepting for travel a person infected with the TB bacterium may be rare. However, it would not be uncommon to evaluate critically the conduct of an airline after the fact, by an assessment of the quality of air in the cabin and assistance offered to those infected in flight. Airlines have to follow carefully the guidelines issued by the World Health Organization, and take initiatives on their own, such as those discussed earlier, so that they can convince a court that they acted like prudent, caring business enterprises in the face of a calamity.

As for considering infection an accident, particularly where it is established that the airline knew or ought to have known of the risk involved, it is highly arguable that, on the strength of the broad interpretation of the *Tseng* case,[378] courts may be inclined to treat the contracting of tuberculosis or any disease as an accident. Also relevant to this issue is the 1996 Supreme Court decision in *Zicherman* v. *Korean Air Lines*,[379] which ruled that it was quite evident that the English word 'damage' or 'harm', which was reflected in the official French text of the Convention as 'dommage', has a wide application and was, in fact, used by the Warsaw Convention drafters in its classical French law sense of 'legally cognizable' harm.

It must be emphasized that, in selling an airline ticket for travel by air, an airline offers a composite service, not only to carry a passenger from point A to B, but also to ensure that transportation is accomplished in a safe and sanitary manner. Therefore the services offered by the airline in the area of clean air in the cabin become extremely relevant and critical to the issue.

Admittedly, it would be extremely difficult for an airline to determine the proclivity of their passengers to latent illnesses such as venous thromboembolism. Therefore instances of negligence pertaining to an airline accepting for travel a person who could possibly be afflicted with the disease may arguably be difficult to determine. However, it would not be uncommon to evaluate critically the conduct of an airline, which, knowing full well that the seat pitch in the aircraft would cramp an average-size passenger, and being cognizant of the medical evidence which identifies prolonged air travel in confined spaces as a risk factor for deep vein thrombosis, does not take any precautions for the prevention of the occurrence. The cases of *Seguritan, Horabin, Thai Airways* and the *Korean Airlines Disaster* strongly suggest the need for vigilance on the part of airlines to follow scientific and medical developments related to air transport and passenger safety.

As for issues of liability under the Warsaw Convention, although the *Tseng* case[380] widened the scope of the word 'accident', the case itself addressed a personal security check on a passenger and it remains to be seen whether courts would interpret negligence on the part of the airline to warn the passenger of inherent dangers and advise him of the appropriate precautions as wilful misconduct under the Convention. It certainly could be argued that, in the light of the varied inter-pretations emerging from the *cursus curiae*, an accident under the Convention, although not explicitly defined in any past instance, could be considered as 'any incident unexpected and external to the passenger which is avoidable by the airline and which causes death, wounding or injury to a passenger'. Therefore, although no conclusive medical evidence has been released distinctly and conclusively linking venous thromboembolisms to the so-called 'Economy Class Syndrome', since there is strong evidence to suggest a risk factor in air travel, the airline could be expected to take or be seen to take some precaution against the danger.

Airlines would be well advised to apprise passengers that, in order to minimize risk of venous thromboembolism, some of the guidelines are that they should not place baggage in the space under the seat, as it may reduce the ability to move the legs; should exercise legs at regular intervals while seated, in order to improve blood flow; change positions regularly; take a stroll down the aisle every once in a while; avoid sleeping in a cramped position; avoid using alcohol, tobacco, narcotic drugs and hypnotic drugs; and consume as much water and other fluids during the flight as possible.

The aerotoxic syndrome cannot be addressed in isolation, but should be considered as one more health-related occupational hazard for cockpit and cabin crew. Together with sleep loss-induced fatigue, and substance-abuse cabins which permit smoking, the aerotoxic syndrome should be addressed within a composite health-related problem. To counter the collective problem, an airline has to adopt a safety culture which addresses issues of contamination in the aircraft with inherent difficulties related to crew resource management as common problems. Individual case studies and 'brainstorming' should regularly be carried out to address potential problems and an efficient internal audit process should monitor progress made. A deficiency rectification system should be in place to remedy lapses without loss of time.

Airlines should strictly enforce the ICAO resolution on smoking[381] in the cabin which quotes World Health Organization resolutions and those of the International Labour Organization to the effect that occupational health and safety are interrelated, and apply the same principle to air quality in general, supporting further research on the effects of contaminants on passengers and crew, particularly in relation to anoxia and hypoxia. Both cabin crew and technical crew should be encouraged to report instances of contamination and experiences of sick feeling within the cabin and cockpit without the risk of reprisals from management. If these precautions are taken and measures adopted accordingly, an airline need not be concerned about being found guilty of reprehensible conduct.

Airline management

The Independent Working Group on the Future of the United Nations, which was convened in late 1993, gave its overall approval to the Group's Final Report at its final May 1995 meeting. The working group was of the view that, as we enter the twenty-first century, the prospects ahead are at the same time forbidding and promising. If promise is to triumph, the nations of the world need to bind themselves together in forging a new order of human rights that will call for assistance from the powerful to the helpless. This would enable people to pursue, in common purpose, a world of equity and justice, a world of shared economic progress, a world in which future generations can live in security and god health, at peace with themselves and with the environment on which their very survival will depend.

One starts from a positive assumption and sees that human creativity and invention have made the conditions of life across a good portion of this planet far better than they were 50 years ago. A majority of people today enjoy a standard of living considerably superior, in material terms at any rate, to that of their grandparents. The regions of the world and their peoples, still widely separated only yesterday, face the future as a community drawn ever closer by shared ideas, by communication, by economic exchanges and, we believe, by a common yearning for freedom and peace.

These transformations are related to the unprecedented revolution in communications and to an emerging global economy that, despite its regional, cyclical and structural anomalies, is far more open than it was when the UN Charter first called for international cooperation to resolve economic problems. World output over the past half-century has grown faster than in any comparable period in history.

According to the *United Nations Human Development Report* and other leading global social indicators, this is the kind of world we will be living in during the coming decades:

- increased global income and consumption (and greater inequality in their distribution);
- a growing population (but, with smaller families, levelling out by the middle of the twenty-first century);
- an ageing population (more than a doubling of over 60s by 2030) and a higher proportion of dependent to productive people, but the wealthier segments having increased disposable income and leisure time;
- increased urbanization;
- increased migration;
- further globalization of markets and liberalization of trade rules;
- further shifting of taxation from progressive to regressive and from direct to indirect;
- increased strains on the environment;
- a continuing information revolution (which will, inter alia, redefine the nature of white-collar work through tele-working and outsourcing – towards the 'virtual office').

All these factors are indicative of increasing demands on air transport, the provision of which will have to be weighed carefully between conflicting interests of economic demand and social justice. Both the public and the private sector enter-prises offering air transport to a future world will be required to come to grips not only with supplying demand but with fulfilling a moral obligation that necessarily entails enhanced care when one's client is being hurtled through the atmosphere 35 000 feet up in the air. The inherent vulnerability of the passenger, not only in flight, but throughout the airport check-in process, calls for a greater degree of care on the part of the airline manager.

Theories of management

Contrary to popular belief in some quarters, that good aviation management is achieved only through experience, and that as long as a passenger is transported from one point to another on time the customer is satisfied, research conducted[382] through a questionnaire shows differing attitudes and approaches to aviation management, particularly between Europe and North America. The purpose of the survey was to gain insight into managers' attitudes on various items related to the management of a new entrant airline. Significant similarities and differences between European and American management attitudes emerging from the survey included the following:

- European managers agreed strongly, on average, that the board of directors is highly involved in the airline's affairs. Their US counterparts averaged considerably lower.
- European managers felt more strongly that it was necessary to improve market share, which indicates that they assume that market share is important in a competitive environment.

- Airline managers from both Europe and the United States disagreed that emphasis is placed in their profession on diversification into other industries.
- US managers had stronger feelings than their European counterparts regarding their airlines providing incentives to employees to encourage extra commitment.
- US managers carriers felt that long-term prospects in their airlines' primary markets were excellent.
- US managers agreed more readily that important information should be communicated to employees to enable effective decision making.

One of the distinctive differences between a highly deregulated American and less deregulated European market concerned influencing government policy on aviation. In a fully regulated economic environment, influencing government policy was a major part of senior management's function if resources and market position were to be secured. A higher proportion of European airports is congested than in the USA, this being an explanation for the greater importance accorded by European airlines to acquisition of airport slots.

Alliance with the incumbents was viewed as important by many European airlines as a preparation for increased competition stimulated by the liberalization process.

The importance of delegation was rated more highly in the USA and the likely explanation for this trend is the necessity to empower employees in order to maintain the highest possible efficiency level. Also in the USA, incentive programmes are important to motivate employees and to maximize their worth to the organization. According to the findings of the survey, US carriers have placed much less importance on staff reduction than European carriers.

Looking at the significant differences where European managers scored more highly, one can see that managers of US new-entrant carriers appear to be more inclined towards focusing on their staff's welfare than their European counterparts.

The following are some current airline management techniques:

a) use strategy to place responsibility for ideas, decisions and actions with the people who are the faces of the airline: ticket agent, flight attendants, baggage handlers and all the other front line employees;
b) in a customer-driven company, the distribution of roles is radically different. The organization is decentralized, with responsibility delegated to those who until now have comprised the order-obeying bottom level of the pyramid;
c) have an effective and efficient market survey department: however, once responsibility is successfully passed on to the front line, reduce the number of market surveys conducted, as they are no longer needed;
d) strategy should ensure that airlines are custom-driven companies. The classic production-oriented company produces or invests by purchasing an aircraft and adapting its operations to equipment; a customer-driven philosophy is usually more successful.

In general, in-flight service, which is one of the most important indicators of successful airline management, is an intangible. Airlines should not spend an inordinate amount of time researching what passengers think of in-flight offerings, but, rather, be aware of what the competition is offering. Airlines also have to realize that they are a hospitality provider who need to create very strong brand experiences not just for the premium passenger.[383]

The business passenger offers the most profit to an airline. Although airlines have put enormous investment and effort into providing adequately for this segment, most airlines do not seem to have fully appreciated that a fast-growing segment of the market, almost 28 per cent and 22 per cent, respectively, of North American and European air travellers, are female.[384] It is not sufficient to woo the passenger with an attractive package of hospitality. The passenger must be made to feel comfortable and, above all, that she is cared for from the time she makes her reservation. On the face of it, this is a blanket statement with seemingly no specificity. Upon deeper analysis, however, one realizes that the airline industry, like the motor industry, has to make publicly known its philosophy towards the client and actively demonstrate its philosophy in practice.

Human aspects of airline management traverse the hinges of two key issues for management: economic theory and social justice. Economic theory essentially reflects competitiveness of an airline and how to keep ahead of others in the business, whereas social justice requires that the passenger be cared for in a manner befitting the travel and entertainment business. As the foregoing discussion revealed, branding and identity are important factors.

Corporate prosperity is created, not inherited. Although corporate resources are a company's assets, the prosperity of a company does not necessarily emerge solely from the natural endowments of the company concerned, nor from its labour resources, but rather from a certain localized process which engulfs economic structures, values, culture and institutions. The essential catalyst to trade is corporate competitiveness.

Competitiveness is one of the most critical drivers of successful industry. Some see competitiveness as a macroeconomic phenomenon, driven by variables such as fluctuations in markets, change of demand and airline passenger flow trends. Others may argue that competitiveness is a function of cheap and abundant labour. This is not an absolute argument in the face of some airlines which are phenomenal successes in places of business where labour is expensive and in short supply.

More recently, the argument has gained favour that competitiveness is driven by corporate policy. A final popular explanation for competitiveness is differences in management practices, including management–labour relations. The problem, however, is that different industries may require different approaches to management. Practices governing small, private and loosely organized Italian family companies in footwear, textiles, and jewelry, for example, would produce a management disaster if applied to German chemical or motor companies, Swiss pharmaceutical makers or American aircraft producers. Nor is it possible to generalize about management–labour relations.

Clearly, none of these explanations is fully satisfactory; none is sufficient by itself to rationalize the competitive position of industries. Each contains some truth; but a broader, more complex, set of forces seems to be at work. The lack of a clear explanation signals an even more fundamental question. What is a 'competitive' airline in the first place? Is a 'competitive' airline one where every segment or department is competitive? No airline meets this test.

The only meaningful concept of competitiveness at the airline level is *productivity*. The principal goal of an airline is to produce a high and rising standard of service to its clients. The ability to do so depends on the productivity with which an airline's labour and capital are employed. Productivity is the value of the output produced by a unit of labour or capital. Productivity depends on both the quality and features of products (which determine the prices that they can command) and the efficiency with which they are produced. Productivity is the prime determinant of an entity's long-run standard of business practice. The productivity of human resources determines employee wages; the productivity with which capital is employed determines the return it earns for its holders.

When economic theory relating to competitiveness is blended with social justice, which is the human element of commercial aviation practice, the picture becomes somewhat more subdued from a competition perspective but brings out the importance of social consciousness in commercial practice. Airlines could play a role in being moral watchdogs of the global community in such present-day threats which manifest themselves as abduction of children by air, abusive conduct of unruly passengers and the smuggling of humans across borders. To achieve this objective, it is necessary for modern aviation management practice, as discussed earlier, to merge with a clear statement on the rights of the passenger.

THE CARRIAGE OF AIR FREIGHT

Like any other growing industry, the air freight[385] industry is expanding exponentially. The issues faced by the industry are complex ones and its impact on other business operators is tangible. Transportation, which is an essential service relied upon by the air freight industry, makes it inevitable that this industry affects almost every other business and brings to bear its relevance and interest to business management. Air transport is the most expensive of all modes of transport (road, rail, air and sea) to operate in terms of per kilogram of mass carried.[386] This essentially means that commercial air transport is predominantly offered to the high-value/high-yield end of the market, that is to the business community, the tourism industry and the time-critical freight industry dealing with overnight documents and high-value/highly perishable items.

The total scheduled traffic (domestic and international) carried by the airlines of contracting states of ICAO in 1999 is estimated to have been at about 369 billion tonne-kilometres performed, an increase of about 6 per cent over 1998.[387] The airlines of these states carried a total of 1558 million passengers and some 28 million tonnes of freight in 1999. The freight figure compares with 26 million tonnes carried in 1998,[388] an increase of 9 per cent.

The ICAO records that, between 1989 and 1998, the reported number of commercial aircraft in service increased by about 60 per cent, from 11 253 to 18 139 aircraft. In 1998, 1463 jet aircraft were ordered, compared with 1309 in 1997, and 929 were delivered, compared with 674 aircraft in 1997. In 1998, the total scheduled traffic carried by airlines of the 185 contracting states of ICAO amounted to a total of about 1462 million passengers. In the years 1988–99, the total tonne-kilometres performed, or in other words, total scheduled airline traffic, grew at an annual rate of 5·2 per cent.[389] Passenger kilometres growth during this decade was 4·6 per cent and freight tonne-kilometres growth was 6·6 per cent for the same period.[390]

These figures[391] are reflective of the rapidly increasing frequency of aircraft movements at airports, calling for drastic management of airport capacity. Scheduled and chartered freight tonnage is expected to grow by an average 5·3 per cent per year over the period 1998–2002, according to the latest freight forecast of the International Air Transport Association (IATA). At a regional level, the high-growth regions (those likely to experience an average annual growth rate in excess of 6 per cent between 1998 and 2002) will be Central America, South Asia, the South Pacific, lower South America and Southern Africa.[392] Over the past two years, the world has come out of recession. Trade has picked up and the pressure on airports to facilitate better and faster cargo handling and clearance is greater than ever. But there are other factors, apart from economic growth, in the ever-growing attraction of airfreight, since more and more wide-bodied aircraft are being used for passenger traffic and more freight can be carried on these flights. To cope with the demand, airlines are forming strategic alliances among themselves by utilizing such commercial tools as franchising, leasing and interchange of aircraft.

Competent airline managers now need to know that, in the foreseeable future, there will be a few mega-carriers operating in America, Europe, Asia and the Pacific Rim and that these carriers will probably be composites of strong strategic alliances between powerful airlines and powerful regional states. They will be well equipped to offer the quality of service and punctuality that modern glamour requires of air travel. To compete with these carriers for a fair share of the market, a smaller airline will have to offer a comparable product.

At the Fourth Air Transport Conference of ICAO held from 23 November to 6 December 1994 at ICAO Headquarters in Montreal, it was observed that, in terms of tonnes of international cargo loaded and unloaded at airports, 15 airports in 12 countries accounted for 50 per cent of the total amount of international cargo loaded and unloaded worldwide,[393] and 30 air carriers from 25 countries accounted over the same year for 76 per cent of total international passenger-kilometres performed worldwide by 365 air carriers. The market share of the largest 30 carriers had increased slightly over the period between 1982 and 1993 while the market share of the largest 10 carriers had increased by 2 per cent. This tendency towards concentration of international passenger services in a few air carriers also manifested itself in international cargo, where 30 scheduled service air carriers from 26 states were responsible for the carriage of 75 per cent of the total tonne-kilometres performed in 1993.[394] Many air carriers had concluded bilateral agreements relating to special commercial arrangements such as code sharing, pooling, block space, yield management and schedule coordination, making themselves stronger in the market place. These arrangements, although having the ability to strengthen existing commercial potential of air carriers, would also be calculated to obtain for them indirect market access, thus causing concern among those air carriers who depended entirely on their bilateral air services agreements for the carriage of commercial traffic between states.

Another consideration that influenced the deliberations of the conference was the ICAO traffic forecast up to the year 2003. According to this forecast, total world airline scheduled passenger traffic in terms of passenger-kilometres is expected to grow at an annual rate of 5 per cent over the period 1992 to 2003, compared with 5·6 per cent per annum over the period 1982 to 1992. Freight traffic growth over the same period is forecast to be stronger, at 6·5 per cent per annum in terms of freight tonne-kilometres. International traffic is expected to continue to grow faster than total traffic, at 6·5 per cent per annum for passenger-kilometres and 7 per cent per annum for freight tonne-kilometres.[395] Over the 1992-2003 period, the annual total number of domestic and international aircraft departures on scheduled services is forecast to rise by nearly a quarter (to 18 million), the number of passengers carried by over half (to 1835 million) and the number of freight tonnes carried also by over a half (to 27 million).[396] These figures show a sustained trend of growth over the past decade in the carriage of passengers and freight by air.

Current trends in the carriage of air freight

It is incontrovertible that air cargo is an important revenue generator. In 1992, about 12 per cent of the world's total traffic revenue earned on scheduled services came from cargo. A more recent development that adds importance to air cargo is the huge expansion of the courier and express/small package business, which offers door-to-door air service for time-sensitive documents or small packages, usually with the delivery guaranteed within specified time limits but subject to size or weight limitations. Some airlines have also become more involved in door-to-door services, rather than limiting themselves to provision of the air transport component.

A major problem experienced by all cargo operators is the lack of flexibility in market access rights under bilateral agreements in which air cargo is treated as part of passenger service. In such agreements, the limitations usually imposed on passenger service in respect of routes, traffic rights, frequency and so on may also apply to all-cargo service. Other regulatory problems all-cargo operators may encounter include airport curfews and limitation on airport slots.[397]

Many economies are becoming increasingly dependent on air cargo because of changes in the way that multinational companies are organized. They are looking for ways of cutting their working capital by reducing their stocks and working on the basis of just-in-time delivery. The air freight industry has received a lot of attention lately with the change of global industry and, owing to its particular characteristics, is in a much better position than most to appreciate the reality of the global economy. It has, by definition, an international view. As the world's economies mesh more and more with each other, the community of interests made up of the airport authorities, the customs, the handling agents and the airlines have found it more important than ever to pool information.[398]

Cargo revenue makes a strong contribution to airline profits and is often the difference between profit and loss. Blue chip researchers forecast tripling of revenues within the next 20 years, a faster growth than the passenger side of business. Economic integration is the catalyst for global markets. Air cargo will benefit dramatically, growing at three times the rate of the global economy. As the air cargo industry grows significantly, some reasons for concern arise, since, although air cargo is a US$200 billion industry, only 20 per cent of this revenue actually accrues to air transport. The rest stays in distribution.

One of the problems of growth in air transport is that, unless initiatives are taken, airlines, major passenger airports, handling agents and forwarders will be left with lower-yielding consolidation. This is because integrators are both expanding the total market and carving out an increasing share of what was enjoyed by the traditional market players. With the growth of service industries, and process taking over from 'batch', these integrators of cargo anticipate the triumph of delivery over dispatch.

The catalyst behind the current business paradigm relating to air freight was the advent of the 747. Whilst its effect on the passenger business was well known, what is not generally appreciated is its effect on reshaping the cargo business. The 747 and other wide-bodied jets altered the capacity ratio between what was carried in bellyholds and what was carried in freighters. Airlines, in order to fill the additional space, gave control of the distribution system to a middleman, the forwarder. When the forwarder took over, the airlines assumed that they would only have one master airway bill and that freight space would be filled. However, forwarders, instead of reinvesting the enhanced margins from consolidations into new service options, used their newly found muscle to deepen discounts from airlines.

Another problem for the traditional industry is that Express[399] will continue to grow both in its own right and at the expense of general cargo. Express will become the prime source of cargo revenues. Equally, integrators will continue to increase both their revenues and their own discrete aircraft fleets. As the Express traffic migrates the traditional industry – airlines, airports, handling agents and forwarders – will be left with the remaining lower-yielding traffic. The opportunity lies in the huge potential market that Express offers the traditional industry, which does have many cards to play, including the Internet. The Internet has already been the means of survival for many small and medium forwarders and cut the costs of the large ones.[400]

It is also noteworthy that a new system of air cargo, called GFX, has been introduced recently. The system is a global Internet-based trading system for air cargo capacity and was tested in early 2001. It promises to bring air cargo all the benefits of e-business: reduced transaction costs, speedy quotes and a wealth of transaction data that will enable airlines and forwarders to implement more effective pricing. GFX also overcomes the perceived wisdom in air cargo that electronic-capacity trading would never work because airlines would never reveal commercially sensitive information on the web site. On GFX, it is up to airlines how much capacity they reveal.[401]

The most striking development among leading players in the scheduled airline industry is a new tendency to take cargo departments and reconstitute them as stand-alone entities, operating as independent profit centres. All carriers with any ambitions in international air cargo have moved away from the concept of simply filling their mainline's spare belly space in passenger aircraft. In 1998, the German airline Lufthansa created Lufthansa Cargo as a separate company within the group, operating as an independent unit. The wider role proposed by Lufthansa will rely on closer cooperation between carrier and forwarder. The German carrier says it does not want to develop new skills that already exist among forwarders. The carrier will work with forwarders as partners instead of competing against them, which has been the standard practice in the industry.[402]

Air service providers are still highly restricted in their ability to develop the supply of services on the basis of technological and commercial considerations. There are differences between countries and regions as to the availability of cargo-relevant traffic rights, but, as a general rule, the international design of cargo carriage consists of different categories of carriers. The rules restrain their corporate and business structures, notably their ownership and control structures, the possibility to contract freely with domestic/local carriers abroad, and to diversify into complementary services such as trucking. In addition, in certain instances, freight forwarding, in order to develop seamless transport services for domestic and international customers and to clear air cargo in airports that erode the advantage of the air mode, often has to overcome quality and costs problems in the ground handling of their cargo and problems of access to airport runways at cargo-relevant periods of the day, notably because of airport curfews and noise restriction.

Currently, the air transport aspect of cargo services is predominantly governed by bilateral aviation agreements prevailing in all countries limiting air carriers' ability to respond to market developments and to exploit the market potential. As a result, carriers cannot plan international route structures and develop services in full competition with each other. From a strictly economic point of view, all categories of air carriers should be allowed to make use of the full range of traffic rights and have the same opportunities for unimpeded route design and network operations.

All cargo operators and, where consistent with existing bilateral air service agreements, combination carriers, should enjoy full operational flexibility in order to exploit business opportunities and to enhance competition among air transport providers. Leaving pricing to be set by the market place without any governmental intervention would certainly be the ideal economic solution. However, given the long history of direct and indirect governmental involvement in pricing of air transport, a widespread agreement to such a provision may prove very difficult to obtain.

There are other factors to the air cargo industry, such as intermodal transport, which bring to bear issues that need consideration. Virtually all sectors of transport rely on intermodal transport services. Air cargo in particular depends to a large extent on other modes of transport since goods are transported from the producers airport-to-airport and are then channelled via different modes of transport to their final destination. Air cargo transport serves as one piece in the logistical chain to ensure relatively new services, such as time-definite deliveries and door-to-door integrated services, which are in high demand by shippers. The operation of intermodal transport services is therefore a unique feature of the air cargo industry.

Industry experts have noted that customs clearance procedures account for as much as 20 per cent of average transport time and 25 per cent of average transport costs of imports in many states. While expedited customs clearance is a crucial issue for the express delivery services industry, reductions in the time and cost of customs clearance will benefit all air cargo service providers.[403]

Liberalization of air freight market access

One of the proposed future regulatory arrangements at the 4th ICAO Air Transport Conference was that parties would grant each other full market access (unrestricted route, operational and traffic) rights for use by designated air carriers, with cabotage and so-called 'seventh freedom' rights exchanges optionally. Of course, each party would have the right to impose a time-limited capacity freeze as an extraordinary measure and in response to a rapid and significant decline in that party's participation in a country pair market. The latter measure, called the 'safety net', was intended to form a buffer against a total swing towards favouring unregulated commercial operations of air carriers. The market access and 'safety net' principle was designed to award to each party's air carrier unrestricted basic market access rights to the other party's territories for services touching the territories of both parties (to the exclusion of cabotage rights, that is rights to operate commercial air services within points in the territory of another party) optionally, for so called 'seventh freedom' services (services touching the territory of the granting party without touching the territory of the designating party); and/or optionally, with cabotage rights. To these rights, the 'safety net' brought in the caveat that each party would have the right to impose a capacity freeze as an extraordinary measure, under six conditions that called for such a freeze:

a) to be implemented only in response to a rapid and significant decline in that party's participation in a country pair market;
b) to be applied to all scheduled and non-scheduled fights by the air carriers of each party and any third state which directly serve the affected country pair market;
c) to be intended to last for a maximum finite period of, for example, one year, two years, or one year, renewable once;
d) to require close monitoring by the parties to enable them to react jointly to relevant changes in the situation (for example, an unexpected surge in traffic);
e) to be responsible for creating a situation in which any affected party may employ an appropriate dispute resolution mechanism to identify and seek to correct any underlying problem; and
f) to be aimed at requiring mutual efforts to ensure the earliest possible correction of the problem and removal of the freeze.[404]

It is worthy of note that the above framework of future regulatory arrangements was intended to function in different structures and relationships, for example bilaterally, between two states, between a state and a group of states and between two groups of states, and multilaterally, with a small or large number of states. It was expected that this structure would also respect all rights, existing and newly granted.[405]

Airlines are therefore faced with the imminent prospect of the future realm of commercial aviation being controlled by a group of air carriers which may serve whole global regions and operated by a network of commercial and trade agreements. Regional carriers will be predominant, easing out niche carriers and small national carriers whose economies would be inadequate to compare their costs with the lower unit costs and joint ventures of a larger carrier. It is arguable that a perceived justification for 'open skies' or unlimited liberalization exists even today in the bilateral air services agreement between two countries, where, *fair and equal opportunity to operate* air services is a *sine qua non* for both national carriers concerned. This has been re-interpreted to mean *fair and equal opportunity to compete* and, later still, *fair and equal opportunity to participate effectively* in the international air transportation as agreed.[406] Of course, there has been no universal acceptance of this evolution in interpretation, and carriers and states whose nationality such carriers have have maintained their own positions tendentiously.

ICAO has suggested the following preferential measures for the consideration and possible use of its member states who are at a competitive disadvantage when faced with the mega trends of commercial aviation and market access:

a) the asymmetric liberalization of market access in a bilateral air transport relationship to give an air carrier of a developing country more cities to serve; fifth freedom traffic rights[407] on sectors which are otherwise not normally granted; flexibility to operate unilateral services on a given route for a certain period of time; and the right to serve greater capacity for an agreed period of time;

b) more flexibility for air carriers of developing countries (than for their counterparts in developed countries) in changing capacity between routes in a bilateral agreement situation, code-sharing to markets of interest to them, and changing gauge (aircraft types) without restrictions;

c) the allowance of trial periods for carriers of developing countries to operate on liberal air service arrangements for an agreed time;

d) gradual introduction of developing countries (in order to ensure participation by their carriers) to more liberal market access agreements for longer periods of time than developed countries' air carriers;

e) use of liberalized arrangements at a quick pace by developing countries' carriers;

f) waiver of nationality requirement for ownership of carriers of developing countries on a subjective basis;

g) allowance for carriers of developing countries to use more modern aircraft through the use of liberal leasing agreements;

h) preferential treatment in regard to slot allocations at airports; and

i) more liberal forms for carriers of developing countries in arrangements for ground handling at airports, conversion of currency at their foreign offices and employment of foreign personnel with specialized skills.[408]

These proposed preferential measures are calculated to give air carriers of developing countries a 'head start' which would effectively ensure their continued participation in competition with other carriers for the operation of international air services. Improved market access and operational flexibility are two benefits which are considered direct corollaries to the measures proposed.

While the open skies policy sounds economically expedient, its implementation would undoubtedly phase out smaller carriers who are now offering competition in air transport and a larger spectrum of air transport to the consumer. Lower fares, different types of services and varied in-flight service profiles are some of the features of the present system. It is desirable that a higher level of competitiveness prevail in the air transport industry and, to achieve this objective, preferential measures for carriers of developing countries would play a major role.

ICAO initiatives

The carriage of air freight has no spectacular history or particular milestones in the annals of air carriage. It grew as a necessity, to transport merchandise which was needed for air transport. Earlier records show that the first instances of the carriage of air freight were in transporting mail by balloon or dirigible from city to province, for example during the siege of Paris in 1870.[409] Air cargo has been defined *a contrario* from the definition of baggage contained in Article 4 of the Warsaw Convention[410] simply to mean 'goods transported which are not baggage'.[411] Annex 9 to the Chicago Convention defines cargo as 'any property carried on an aircraft other than mail, stores and accompanied or mishandled baggage'.[412] Magdelenat makes the valid point that air cargo carries with it the advantage of being transported more quickly than by other modes of transport and therefore frequently consists of articles of high value, urgently needed merchandise and extremely perishable goods.[413]

A milestone, if ever there were one for air freight, would be Chapter 4 of Annex 9 to the Chicago Convention,[414] which opens with the initial requirement that regulations and procedures applicable to goods carried by aircraft shall be no less favourable than those which would be applicable if the goods were carried by other means.[415] In order to serve best consignors who send their urgently needed or perishable goods with expediency, the Annex, in Standard 4.3, impels contracting states to examine with operators and organizations concerned with international trade all possible means of simplifying the clearance of goods carried inbound and outbound by air.

Another positive requirement of the Annex, in keeping with the electronic age and its requirements, is that contracting states, when introducing electronic data interchange (EDI) techniques for air cargo facilitation, should encourage international airline operators, handling companies, airports, customs and other authorities and cargo agents to exchange data electronically, in conformance with UN/Electronic Data Interchange for Administration, Commerce and Transport (UN/EDIFACT) international standards, in advance of the arrival of aircraft, to facilitate cargo processing.[416] The Annex is supported in these proactive measures by its parent document, the Chicago Convention, which, in Article 22, provides that each contracting state agrees to adopt all practicable measures, through the issuance of special regulations or otherwise, to facilitate and expedite navigation by aircraft between the territories of contracting states, and to prevent unnecessary delays to aircraft, crews, passengers and cargo, especially in the administration of the laws relating to immigration, quarantine, customs and clearance. Article 23 of the Convention opens the door for Annex 9 to require of states, from time to time, to keep abreast with developments in the carriage of air freight when it provides:

> Each Contracting State undertakes, so far as it may find practicable, to establish customs and immigration procedures affecting international air navigation in accordance with the practices which may be established or recommended from time to time, pursuant to this Convention. Nothing in this Convention shall be construed as preventing the establishment of customs-free airports.

The overall aim of Annex 9, through its Chapter 4, which addresses entry and departure of cargo and other articles, is to retain the advantage of speed inherent in air transport. However, the Annex makes provision for recognizing the need for Contracting States to adhere to application regulations relating aviation security which are incorporated in Annex A to the Chicago Convention. For example, in Standard 4.2, Annex 9 requires that contracting states shall make provisions whereby procedures for the clearance of goods carried by air and for the interchange of cargo with surface transport will take into account applicable regulations which address issues of aviation security. For its part, Annex 17 recommends that each contracting state should, whenever possible, arrange for the security measures and procedures to cause a minimum of interference with, or delay to, the activities of international civil aviation.[417]

Yet another ICAO initiative in the carriage of air freight is Annex 18 to the Chicago Convention, on 'The Safe Transport of Dangerous Goods by Air', which was developed by the Air Navigation Commission of the Organization in response to a need expressed by states for an internationally agreed set of provisions governing the safe transport of dangerous goods by air. The Annex draws the attention of the states to the need to adhere to 'Technical Instructions for the Safe Transport of Dangerous Goods by Air',[418] developed by ICAO, according to which packaging used for the transportation of dangerous goods by air shall be of good quality and shall be constructed and securely closed so as to prevent leakage[419] and labelled with the appropriate labels.[420]

The Second Facilitation Panel Meeting, which took place in Montreal from 11 to 15 January 1999, had, as its primary incentive, the updating and revision of the provisions of Annex 9 for air cargo and was influenced by recent work which has been substantially completed by the World Customs Organization on the comprehensive revision of the Kyoto Convention. However, the scope of the revision process was broader than the alignment of the Annex with Kyoto Convention principles.

The facilitation strategy as reflected in the SARPs which were developed during the first 25 years of ICAO contemplated a business environment of manual inspection and clearance procedures in which all information exchanges were dependent on the preparation and movement of paper documents. International airlines and airports were largely owned and often administered by governments; hence facilitation of cargo clearance activities was viewed as essentially a government responsibility.

The concept of an integrated transaction depends entirely on risk management, and is particularly important for air freight because it is focused on those controls which are exercised by Customs during the relatively short time that goods are in their physical possession. It is a very powerful example of a premium procedure because it offers very valuable benefits to both Customs and declarant. The Customs get an unambiguous single price and value statement, together with complete origin–destination information for control purposes, and therefore are privy to more than the export or import half of any transaction.

During the 1970s, with the entrance of wide-body aircraft and the emergence of computers and other new technology, states began to find ways to rationalize their inspection process. Today, issues related to information requirements are more significant than the number and type of paper documents which are exchanged among the parties to an import/export transaction. As computerization capabilities are almost universally available to both governments and industry, it is now possible to be more positive about advocating the use of information technology by all parties.

The revision of the Kyoto Convention[421] is aimed at a broad-front harmonization and improvement of basic Customs procedures, with an eye to primary Customs responsibilities for control as well as a growing sensitivity to the economic advantages of facilitation. Premium procedures are a means of bringing market forces to bear by linking specific facilitation advantages directly to prescribed-control improvements. The integrated transaction is an advanced premium procedure, in which the emerging concept of the 'authorized trader' is applied in such a way that a single submission of minimal, standardized data, by such a declarant, will suffice for all Customs export/import purposes.

It is difficult to see how such concepts as premium procedures or the integrated transaction could be worked into the Recommended Practices/Standards structure of the existing Annex. The revision of Kyoto will, of course, lend itself very well to this process of provision-by-provision adjustment and numerous panel delegates can be expected to produce detailed proposals.

Legal aspects

Liability of a carrier in loss of or damage caused to air freight is contained in Article 18 of the Warsaw Convention, which provides that the carrier is liable for destruction or loss of or damage to the cargo by air over the period during which the goods are in the carrier's charge. What the time span is during which the carrier is in charge of the goods remains a contentious issue. René Nankiewicz offers one view:

> The liability of the carriers ends when the control of the cargo passes to a person authorized to receive it and who is not one of his servants or agents, e.g. when they are delivered to a successive or actual carrier ... to the consignee or his broker or agent designated in the air waybill; and, in any event, when the cargo is put at the disposal of the consignee or his agent, because this act of the carrier completes the performance of the contract of carriage.[422]

Article 18(1) provides that liability of the carrier can be enforced for damage sustained in the event of destruction to air freight if the damage occurred during transportation by air. Article 18(2) identifies 'transportation by air' as the period during which the goods are in the charge of the carrier, whether in an airport or on board an aircraft or, in the case of landing outside an airport, in any place whatsoever. Whatever the criteria be regarding control, there is a fundamental difference in burden of proof issues with regard to injury or damage caused to persons in transportation by air and air freight. Whereas, in the former case, liability of the carrier is presumed, in the case of air freight it is the claimant who has to prove that damage occurred to freight during transportation by air. It is claimed that there is no prima facie evidence that damage to cargo occurred during transportation by air,[423] based on an evidentiary construction of Article 11(2) of the Warsaw

Convention which provides that statements related to quantity, volume and condition of the goods are prima facie evidence only in instances where the carrier checks the cargo in the presence of the consignor and a stipulation to this effect appears to have been made in the air waybill. This principle has been supported by judicial decisions.[424]

These are clear demarcations attributing the element of control of goods on the part of the carrier. For instance, even though goods are eventually meant to be carried by air, if they are lost while being transported to the carrier under a composite transport agreement, the carrier's liability is deemed to be non-existent. This was firmly established in the case of *Railroad Salvage of Conn., Inc.* v. *Japan Airfreight et al.*,[425] where the Warsaw Convention's provisions were not applied to damage caused to goods while in charge of a trucking company. In this context, warehouse cases are of critical importance to liability issues pertaining to air cargo. In 1995, a California case[426] brought to bear the principle that, when goods are lost while being stored in a cargo facility outside the airport premises, such an instance cannot be deemed to be considered within the provisions of the Warsaw Convention. Another exigency common to air freight – Customs clearance – has also been settled in judicial terms to mean that, while cargo is in the process of Customs clearance in a warehouse, the carrier cannot be deemed to be in charge of the cargo. In the 1997 Italian case of *Cristofari* v. *Aeroport de Roma*,[427] the court applied the widest possible interpretation to Article 18 of the Warsaw Convention where, in considering the theft of a shipment of Rolex watches from an airport warehouse while they were under Customs' inspection and under the control of the Customs' authorization, the court held that, when an air carrier hands over the goods to a handling agent, the responsibility for the safety of the goods is taken away from the carrier. This is particularly so, according to the court, in instances where the handling agent was not the appointee of the carrier concerned but a monopoly that offered ground handling services to the airport. However, the overall applicability of this principle, in a global sense, can be questioned, in the light of the principle established in the United States in the earlier case of *Jaycees Paton* v. *Pier Air Intl.*,[428] where in instances similar to the *Cristofari* case, the court held that the Warsaw Convention was indeed applicable since the period of carriage was considered to last until the goods were delivered to the consignee.

Multimodal transport features prominently in modern exigencies of air freight transportation where a composite and singular contract of carriage may involve surface transport and air transport. In such instances, one has to construe Article 11 of the Warsaw Convention, particularly in terms of evidentiary construction, in accordance with the circumstances under which damage caused to goods could be attributable to the air carrier. Miller suggests that, if the carriage by surface transport is incidental to the carriage by air, the damage will be presumed to have occurred during the carriage by air. However, if the carriage by road is not incidental to the carriage by air, a plaintiff who sues a carrier on the basis of liability provisions of the Warsaw Convention would first have to establish that the damage occurred during the carriage by air.[429]

The Montreal Convention of 1999[430] has skilfully done away with the somewhat cumbersome Warsaw Convention provision regarding the place in which the goods are located: that is, in an airport or on board an aircraft or, in the case of landing outside an airport, in any place whatsoever, as provided in Article 18. Article 18(3) of the Montreal Convention provides: 'The carriage by air within the meaning of paragraph 1 of this Article comprises the period during which the cargo is in charge of the carrier.' According to the Rapporteur to the Montreal Convention proceedings Article 18(3) makes a blanket statement, that the operative period of the carrier's liability is when the cargo is in the carrier's charge, to ensure that the Convention applies whenever or wherever the cargo is in the possession, custody or charge of the carrier, whether on or off the airport premises.[431] Although the Montreal Convention falls short of identifying which carrier is responsible – whether it is the actual carrier or contracting carrier – nonetheless, it improves upon the Warsaw Convention by bringing in the elements of possession, custody and charge, thus removing geographic imponderables from the equation of liability. Article 18(3) of the Montreal Convention ensures that, when cargo is handed over by a consignee to an agent of the carrier, whether it be a trucking company or another carrier, liability can be imputed to the carrier for damage caused to the goods when they were in the possession of such agent, but that liability of the carrier cannot be enforced when goods were not in the charge of the carrier, such as when they were in a Customs warehouse.

The Montreal Convention also provides for determination of liability in instances of substitutive carriage. Article 18(4) stipulates that, if a carrier, without the consent of the consignor, substitutes carriage by another mode of transport for the whole or part of a carriage intended by the agreement between the parties to be carriage by air, such carriage by the other mode of transport is deemed to be within the period of carriage by air. This provision has been introduced to ensure that the carrier cannot unilaterally decide to replace the whole or part of the carriage by air by other means of transportation and at the same time exclude the application of the Montreal Convention to issues pertaining to his liability.

In the instances covering interlining of air freight or carriage in code-shared flights, considerations of liability of the actual carrier of the goods, as against liability of the carrier who contracts with the consignor to carry the goods, has to be carefully considered.

The actual carrier

An actual carrier can be broadly identified as the person who actually transports goods from one place to another. The phenomenon of the actual carriage has been highlighted comparatively recently to accommodate the complexity of a modern commercial transaction where a contracting carrier employs another to actually convey the goods.

A typical instance of the creation of an actual carrier in carriage-by-air trans-actions is where a contracting carrier (so termed since he contracts with the consignor to carry the consignor's goods on his air waybill) accepts for carriage from the consignor and places such goods in the charge of another carrier so that the latter carrier performs the carriage of goods by air.

The genesis of the concept 'actual carrier' is seen in the typical maritime contract[432] which preceded the carriage by air contracts in the nineteenth century. However, the term 'carrier' was first used in definitive terms in the United States in the Carriage of Goods by Sea Act (1936) where an inclusive provision considered an owner or charterer who enters into a contract of carriage as a carrier for shipper.[433] It is a curious fact that this early reference to a carrier in the shipping contract did not mature into full bloom until as recently as 1978,[434] thus leaving for a sustained period of time a hiatus in the modern shipping contract with regard to the definition of the term 'actual carrier'.

The UN Conference on the Carriage of Goods by Sea (1978) which assembled in Hamburg, made a successful attempt for the first time in the history of the shipping contract to define the actual carrier as: 'Any person to whom the performance of the carriage, of the goods, or part of the carriage has been entrusted by the carrier, and includes any other person to whom such performance has been entrusted'.[435] Thus 'actual carrier 'is distinguished from a 'carrier' who is a person by whom or in whose name a contract of carriage of goods by sea has been concluded with a shipper or consignor. The attempt at defining an actual carrier clearly surfaces the fact that a separate category of carrier has been acknowledged by the international community together with his rights and liabilities.

The definition of 'actual carrier' by air is stipulated in the Guadalajara Convention of 1961[436] which states, inter alia, that an actual carrier is 'A person other than the contracting carrier, who, by virtue of authority from the contracting carrier, performs the whole or part of the carriage'.[437] The actual carrier therefore contrasts in function with the contracting carrier who is a person who makes an agreement with a passenger or consignor or with a person acting on behalf of the passenger or consignor.[438]

The air waybill is the contractual document evidencing the contract of carriage of goods by air and is a product of the Warsaw Convention of 1929.[439] The Warsaw Convention requires that 'Every carrier of goods has the right to require the consignor to make out and hand over to him a document called an "air waybill"; every consignor has the right to require the carrier to accept this document.'[440] It is noteworthy that the Warsaw Convention does not make specific reference to an 'actual carrier'. It is therefore presumable that the reference to a 'carrier of goods' implies the contracting carrier who obtains the air waybill from the consignor. It is also significant that at no place in the Convention do the words 'actual carrier' appear. However, as may be seen in the discussion to follow, the liability of the actual carrier does not go unnoticed in the face of the law.

It is a platitude to say that an agreement for the carriage of goods is usually a simple instance of a contract which involves the moving of goods from the seller to the purchaser in exchange for the purchase money which moves conversely. However, a contract for the carriage of goods, although in its genesis it is a simple contract with its accepted principles, involves a carrier – a notion unknown to a simple instance of a sale of goods. The role of the carrier coupled with the fact that carriage of goods involves a transnational element makes dispute resolution in terms of the liability of parties more complicated.

Prior to a discussion of the nature of a transnational contract in areas where it affects the liability of the actual carrier, it is necessary to analyse *in limine* a contract in general as it is the principles of the latter which the former derives and attenuates. To determine the position of an actual carrier in a contract it is necessary to analyse the concept and examine its development. The following discussion is founded on the basic premise that the liability of an actual carrier can be considered only in instances where he is privy to the contract with any party concerned.

A subjective identification and definition of a contract has always been considered difficult.[441] It is simply an agreement which does not lay down justiciable rights and duties in the form of a list but manifests itself in a few restrictive principles recognizable by the law which the parties to a contract from a chronological perspective originated from the common law practice which dates back to the twelfth century[442] where courts resolved disputes between parties who had entered into a contract. However, for clearer identification, it is traced back to the sixteenth-century action of Assumpsit.[443] The ingredients of a contract are laid out as (a) an actionable promise or promises involving two parties, and (b) an outward expression of common intention to fulfil the assurance contained in the promise, and (c) the moving of consideration from one party to another as accepted by English common law principles.

Although legal writing and judicial pronouncements have reached the sophistication of identifying the complexities arising out of a contractual agreement, the notion of contract still remains an enigma. By nature it is illusory and cannot be definitively discussed. This obscurity in the nature of a contract as a definable legal concept prompted Atiyah[444] to say that there is no such thing as a typical contract at all. Be that as it may, the courts have never encountered difficulty in definition as a positive hindrance to determining the liability of a party to a contract which arises as a natural corollary to an agreement. What the courts have considered in such instances is, inter alia, the nature of the agreement itself. In pursuance of this objective, the courts have always examined what the parties actually said in contracting, whether orally or in writing. The point of significance of the principles of contract law in this discussion is the actual statement of the parties. The question that should be asked repeatedly in modern commercial transactions is whether the intention of the parties can be imputed from what the parties actually said at the point of agreement or whether the expectation of the parties, whatever be the actual words used in the agreement, should be the primary consideration. In other words, should the courts rigidly follow the exact words of the contract and infer the intention of the parties or should they view the entire concept of offer and acceptance more subjectively and look for what the parties expected to gain from the contract irrespective of the rigid restrictive principles so far set?

This discussion is only concerned with what the actual carrier stands to gain or lose in an instance where his liability is examined by the courts. In this context, what matters in a modern contract is not solely a *consensus ad idem* or a meeting of the minds but the legal expectations aroused by the conduct of the parties. This approach precluded the undue reliance upon the necessity to determine whether a promise reflects the intentions of the promisor.

It is now clear that to say an agreement revolves round the intention of the parties is fictional and, to say the least, trite. This becomes apparent with the complexities of modern commercial transactions. The parties to a contract can no longer be held rigidly to the subject matter of contractual negotiation jeopardizing their expectations. Perhaps the best illustration of this principle is the statement by Viscount Dilhorne,[445] who dismissed the general principle enunciated by Atkin L J, to the effect that 'to create a contract there must be a common intention of the parties to enter into legal obligations, mutually communicated expressly or impliedly'.[446] According to Viscount Dilhorne, the express or implied communication of the parties to a contract cannot be relied upon strictly to denote their expectation. When the broad proposition of expectation rather than intention alone is applied to the widening spectrum of business contracts and commercial transactions in the nature of agreements for the transportation of goods, it becomes apparent that, in the present context, the business community operates with very little regard for established legal rules.[447] Although the various documents used still have standard form stipulations, in an instance where a multimodal transport document[448] is issued, in which routes, time factors and the general condition of the goods transported are relevant factors, the courts should veer from the path of rigid interpretation of a contractual document's provision, especially as in the modern world a contractual document does not often envisage all eventualities of the contractual carriage of goods.

The basic difficulty in relating the notion of 'contract' in its present form to a transaction for the carriage of goods lies in the dichotomy of treating a complex transaction involving the carriage of goods with principles of contract law established through the ages. For instance, contract law is and always has been concerned with what parties intend and not what they expect to do. This approach from the perspective of an actual carrier who contracts with a carrier to transport goods is undesirable as the notion of 'contract' is not compatible with the needs of a complex document issued in the transportation of goods.

As in the instance of a contract, a transnational contract does not have an identifiable definition. However, it is different in many aspects. Speaking in the context of an international contract for the carriage of goods, there are more than two parties involved. They are the shipper (who is the exporter or seller), the consignee (who is the buyer or importer) and the carrier who agrees to transport the goods. Further, parties to an international contract cannot place reliance solely on domestic law as attempts at unification of rules for the conduct of parties bind them to principles which are internationally acclaimed. This proposition has been judicially acknowledged in the statement, 'We cannot have trade and commerce in world markets and international waters exclusively on our terms governed by our laws and resolved in our courts.'[449] Unlike a domestic contract, this statement reflects a multitude of problem areas in the conflict of laws which, though not relevant to the present work, signifies the proportions to which the problems arising out of the basic principles of contract can be distended. The above dictum clearly surfaces the point that the parties to a transnational contract are free from the shackles of domestic law[450] as domestic law is usually not constituted to accommodate the demands of international relations. This principle was discussed as early as 1934, when a court said:

> The international character of a transaction does not depend upon the location of the place of performance, but upon its nature and the varied elements to be taken into account, whatever the domicile of the parties, to give to the transfer of funds that are inherent to it a character beyond the limits of domestic economy.[451]

The initial transaction in an export–import negotiation is the contract of sale itself. This contract is further extended by subsequent contracts relating to the carriage by air, sea, rail or road.[452] The carriage of goods from one country to another can take the form of either a unimodal agreement or a multimodal agreement whereby the carrier agrees with the shipper to transport the goods by way of two or more transport systems such as by sea, air and so on. Usually such a contract involves a single transaction even though the carrier contracts with another carrier to transport goods for him. The latter is the actual carrier whose responsibility is usually towards the carrier who originally transacts with the shipper.

The contract of sale itself can be utilized by the parties to it to demarcate the various risks and burdens which devolve upon each other. The variations of a contract of this nature arise when the shipper's intentions are to be absolved of responsibility once the goods leave the factory and the consignee prefers to be considered immune to responsibility until the goods have been actually examined by him. In pursuance of the shipper's objectives, a number of conditions attach to a transport document which are denoted by terms such as 'ex works', 'ex dock', 'c.i.f.' and so on,[453] which are broadly identified as price terms of the contract. The main purpose of these conditions is, inter alia, to denote the point of time at which the shipper receives payment for the goods. There are other conditions such as risk shifting on the force majeure and the remedies for a breach of contract all of which effectively obviate any principles of national laws. The contract for the sale of goods in an export–import situation therefore stands self-reliant.

The Lex Mercatoria which applies to commercial transactions has its sources in two areas of established legal principles. They are customary contractual rules which, after practical application, have come to be accepted as norms of practice in international transactions, and international conventions. The former not only rules out any flavour of domestic law but also sets out uniformly one accepted practice of shipping, banking and insurance throughout the world. Academically, the autonomy of such practices has been subjected to much controversy where one view taken is that such practices are not forceful enough to dispel the need for national laws,[454] and the other clearly states the Lex Mercatoria is authentic and acceptable enough to be viewed independently of any national laws.[455] However, in the ultimate analysis that the Lex Mercatoria has been accepted in modern practice and conventions have attempted to unify most problem areas regarding liability provisions in the international sale and carriage of goods, they can be applied by a forum only if the convention in question has been ratified nationally. In addition to these two sources, the elements of the contractual document itself govern the ultimate adjudication of a dispute concerning the liability of a carrier. A contractual clause stands to bind the parties independently of any source of law accepted as common practice. In this context, a discussion of the position of the carrier and the actual carrier in the face of the notion of transnational contract becomes a necessity.

The multimodal transport document is issued instead of segmented documents, mentioned above. It contains information regarding the exact movement of the goods and the conditions of contract. Issued by the multimodal transport operator (the carrier), it need not contain information on the actual carriers. If the carriers are not mentioned in the document, they cannot be held to have privity of contract with the shipper. The actual carrier's liability is contractual as far as the shipper is concerned.

For expediency, even the multimodal transport document is dispensed with in most commercial transactions and is replaced by automatic data processing, which replaces the standardized document by passing information through a print-out. To ascertain the liability of the actual carrier in this instance becomes difficult. In most cases, the actual carrier will be liable to the shipper or the consignee in tort unless the parties are actually mentioned in the print-out. Usually, the courts in such an instance will go back to the common law of contract if there is privity between the parties. In other instances the liability of the actual carrier will be in tort.

The conclusion that can be reached from the above discussion is that an actual carrier is not contractually linked to the shipper or the consignee in an air waybill or any other document discussed earlier. The only exception to the rule is evidenced in the instance where, on the construction of a through air waybill, the carrier acts as the actual carrier's agent under authority or ratification. *Non obstante*, the actual carrier can be held liable for loss, delay or damage to the goods under the general principle of tort law.

In furtherance of the emphasis placed on the complexities of transaction leading to the carriage of goods by air, the United Nations Convention on International Multimodal Transport of Goods emerged in 1980 to provide for the unification of multimodal transport. The Convention deals with only one person, the multimodal transport operator who, on his behalf or through another person acting on his behalf, concludes a multimodal transport contract, assuming responsibility for the performance of the contract.[456] When such a multimodal transport contract is concluded according to the scope of the application of the Convention, its provisions become mandatorily applicable. The multimodal transport executed in pursuance of such a contract does not require the inclusion of an actual carrier as a part to the contract.[457] It requires only the journey route and the modes of transport and the places of trans-shipment. The multimodal transport operator is responsible for the goods from the time he takes over the goods until he hands the goods over to the consignee.[458] Article 15 states explicitly that the multimodal transport operator is liable for the acts or omissions of any person whose services he makes use of where such person acts in the performance of this contract.[459] This clearly makes him liable for any act or omission of an actual carrier or his servants which occurs from the time the goods are taken over from the consignor until they are handed over to the consignee. Such liability is presumed unless the multimodal transport operator can indicate the acts or omission of the actual carrier or his servants.[460] The liability arises both in contract and in tort.[461] In any action against the servant or agent of the multimodal transport operator, such servant or agent can rely upon the limitation of liability provisions set out in Article 18 of the Convention if such person acted within the scope of his employment.[462] By virtue of this provision, an actual carrier can avail himself of the limitation of liability provision in this Convention if an action is brought against him. Any action under the Convention is limited to a period of two years.[463]

The liability of the actual carrier under this Convention is clear. Generally, he is not liable for his acts or omissions or those of his servants as the multimodal transport operator takes responsibility throughout the transaction. However, if the multimodal transport document cites him as a party to the contract, he can claim the same limitation provision included in Article 18 of the Convention. All the same, the Convention in no way removes his liability in tort which is open to any party connected with the transaction.

The relationship between the actual carrier and the carrier occurs quite independently of the main contract between the shipper and the carrier. The contractual relationship between the carrier and the actual carrier setting out the latter's liability depends mainly on the contractual document which passes between the two parties. The agreement itself can take the form of an ordinary offer and acceptance, although it is not unreasonable to assume that in most commercial transactions an air waybill passes from the actual carrier to the carrier. If this be the case, the liability of the actual carrier will be governed by the terms of the air waybill. However, even under any ordinary document setting out the contract, the liability of the actual carrier will be governed contractually by the terms of the contract laid therein. The liability of the actual carrier towards the carrier becomes more involved and extended if there are no liability provisions set out in the document or the air waybill. In a simple case where an actual carrier contracts to transport goods for and on behalf of a carrier with no specific liability provisions, the courts, in determining the actual carrier's liability, would go back to the principles of common law. Lawyers in such an instance would have to return to the simplicity of a contract. The contract becomes a simple instance of bailment where the actual carrier acts as bailee in possession of the goods until they are transported by him. As a multimodal transportation process may involve numerous transport operations by land to port, by air from port to port, transit storage and air carriage to the consignee, the actual carrier in each segment acts as a bailee so that, in terms of liability, the entire transportation process can be divided into unconnected and individual segments.

Palmer on *Bailment* states that bailment is created by contract and enforceable in tort.[464] However, later he states that bailment may arise in the absence of contract[465] and that, historically, bailment is older than contract. One of the qualities of bailment, as laid down by Lord Holt C J,[466] is that it entails the carrying of goods or the performance of some service pertaining to such goods for reward. Although the operative criterion regarding bailment is 'custody', where the bailee is considered liable in tort until the goods are in his custody,[467] it may arise even without delivery, without a contract and without the consent of the bailor.[468] Therefore, even in an instance where the actual carrier receives the goods through a person other than the carrier, he would still be a bailee to the carrier. The conclusion that can be reached is that, while an actual carrier is liable to the carrier for loss, delay or damage caused to the goods by him under the common law principles of bailment in the absence of a contract between the parties, he is liable in contract if there passes a document between him and the carrier.

The liability of the actual carrier is demarcated in the four areas discussed above, although some vagueness and inadequacy prevails in the areas of documentation, statute and convention. This is mainly due to a lack of specificity in isolating the actual carrier. Until the advent of the Guadalajara Convention of 1961, no specific mention of the actual carrier was made at all, leaving the courts to isolate his liability by constructing and implying the application of statutory provisions and international convention.

In common law, an actual carrier is liable for any loss, damage or delay, either in contract or in tort, the former applying when there exists privity of contract and the latter applying both with or without privity of contract. In determining contractual liability the courts should not be too objective and should not decide strictly on the verbal construction of the contract. For instance, if an actual carrier contracts to deliver the goods via a specified route but takes another and delivers the goods without damage or delay, such digression should not be considered grounds for enforcing liability. The basis should be the ultimate expectation of the parties and not what was initially expressed by the parties to the contract. In the area of documentation it is clear that an actual carrier does not issue an air waybill to the shipper. However, he may issue an air waybill to the carrier, in which case he is contractually liable to adhere to the terms of the document as far as the carrier is concerned. The shipper or consignee may sue the actual carrier in tort notwithstanding the absence of privity between the parties.

Any segment of air carriage performed by the actual carrier is attributed to the actual carrier. Responsibility thereof would then naturally devolve upon the actual carrier. However, the contracting carrier would remain liable for the totality of the contracted journey together with the portion of travel undertaken by the actual carrier. Thus one sees a joint liability requirement operating in the segment of carriage performed by the actual carrier both in contract and in tort, the former being valid only if there is privity between the actual carrier and another. This principle is even extended to instances of acts or omissions of the contracting carrier or his servants which occur during the segment of transport undertaken by the actual carrier where the actual carrier is held prima facie liable.[469]

Originally, only the consignor or consignee could sue the carrier (whether actual or contracting) for the loss, damage or delay to goods. Now, however, it has been established that any person interested in a particular consignment of cargo (such as the owner), can sue the carrier for damage to cargo.[470] This decision has certainly widened the spectrum of claimants who can hold the carrier liable for mishandling of cargo.

It is not easy to prove that damage or loss of goods occurred during a particular carrier's segment. However, delay can be attributed to an actual carrier with ease. Further, international conventions of this nature are always conceived with emphasis on economic factors and not on justice or equity. For that reason it becomes difficult to view conventions from a lawyer's standpoint. Also it is not surprising that there is inadequate risk distribution and that liability falls squarely on the carrier in most instances merely to make sure that an aggrieved person can be compensated by some person who is easily accessible and who takes responsibility for the carriage of goods at the outset of the contractual agreement. However, there is no reason for not dealing with an actual carrier more clearly than was done in the Guadalajara Convention. It is hoped that any future attempt at unification of the rules pertaining to the international carriage of goods will lay down the actual carrier's liability more clearly and in a more detailed manner.

Multimodal transportation of freight

With international trade evolving steadily in the 1950s and 1960s, when the maritime sector in particular was in high demand, there was an increasing need to overhaul the already sluggish cargo handling system. An innovation in the cargo transportation system was seen in the 1960s and 1970s, when structural units forming an integrated rigid shell within a container could consolidate the handling of a number of heterogeneous individual packages as a single item. Called 'containerization', this collective system of freight handling and transportation made multimodal freight transportation easier. Container transport brought with it the need for regulation of all modes of transport into a standardized regime. In response to this need, the International Standards organization adopted single standards for uniform dimensions of cargo to be carried in all forms of transport.[471] The development of international containerized carriage has also brought to bear the desirability of unifying the rates used in various modes of transport into a single rate. Nonetheless, variances were seen in liability regimes relating to surface and air transport. There were also differences in rates used by maritime transport and rail transport. For the development of efficient multimodal transport services, a conference was held under the auspices of the United Nations Conference on Trade and Development (UNCTAD), resulting in the adoption in 1980 of the United Nations Convention on International Multimodal Transport of Goods (hereinafter referred to as the Montreal Convention of 1980).[472]

The Montreal Convention of 1980 established a new liability regime applicable to a new player in the transportation field – the multimodal transport operator (MTO). The MTO undertakes full responsibility, under a single multimodal transport document, for the international transportation of goods by various operators of various modes of transport. The MTO was responsible under the multimodal transport contract as principal, to both consignor and consignee. The multimodal transport contract was modelled on the Hamburg Rules[473] applicable to the carriage of goods by sea, in view of the extensive usage of maritime transport for the carriage of freight at that time.

Multimodal transport liability provisions, under the Montreal Convention of 1980, often created some ambiguity when considered against unimodal transportation systems. Although the Warsaw Convention of 1929 stood on its own for purely air transport freight transactions, there was an element of doubt as to which regime would be applicable in instances of damage or delay caused in the transportation of cargo. Article 19 of the Montreal Convention of 1980 somewhat settles the question by introducing a national system for localized damage. In other words, the Montreal Convention of 1980 admits of the applicability of mandatory national or international law when damage or delay can be attributed to a particular mode of transportation only if, as per Article 18 of the Montreal Convention of 1980, these legal systems provide a higher quantum of damage than the 1980 Convention itself. This was not entirely satisfactory to the air transport industry, given the highly capital-intensive nature of air transport and the security and safety implications that go with transportation of air freight.

It is arguable that the Warsaw Convention would prevail upon a claim for damage caused to air cargo, however founded, if it could be proved that the air transportation involved in the overall carriage of goods concerned had caused the damage, even if the contract of carriage was effected through a multimodal contract document under the Montreal Convention of 1980. The Warsaw Convention applies to different legal systems, as was demonstrated in the 1993 Italian case of *Odino Valperga Italeuropa* v. *New Zealand Ins*. In this case, an action was brought against a freight forwarder acting as custodian of goods. The court held that the action was sustainable under the Warsaw

Convention and not under the law of contract notion of bailment as claimed, since the damage occurred while the goods were in charge of the air carrier, before the cargo was delivered to the consignee. Massey supports this view, asserting that the liability of the carrier for loss or damage to the goods will essentially come under the purview of the international convention or other law relating to the mode of transport in question and that, each time the goods are transferred from one mode of transport to another, so will be the liability regime pertaining to those goods.[474] The Warsaw Convention, by Article 31, provides that, in the case of combined carriage, the provisions of the Warsaw Convention shall apply only to the carriage by air, provided that the carriage by air falls within the terms of Article 1 of the Convention. All conventions pertaining to transportation of goods are, however, agreed that, when the stage of transport during which the loss or damage to goods occurred is not known, the liability of each carrier will be determined by rules of liability prescribed by the convention applicable to the multimodal transport operator or a carrier who issued the contract of carriage. In such an instance, the carrier who pays compensation shall be entitled to recover compensation from the other carriers who take part in the carriage.[475]

In addition to the liability standards already adopted regarding multimodal transport operations, there are other documents purporting to provide for standardized provisions for multimodal transport. In 1973, as a precursor to the UNCTAD Conference of 1979, the International Chamber of Commerce initiated uniform rules for a combined transport document which contained minimum standard rules for use in documents issued by operators. Revised in 1975,[476] they form the basis of the Combidoc (Combined Transport Document) or Combined Transport Bill of Lading. The Combidoc is issued and signed by the combined transport operator (CTO) and reflects a contract for combined transport. Under agreement and per the Combidoc, the CTO agrees to perform carriage of freight whether by one single mode of carriage or by combined modes of carriage. Both the Combidoc and the Combined Transport Bill of Lading, together with documentation under the Montreal Convention of 1980, bring to bear a compelling need to evaluate expedient means of contracting for services of freight forwarders and carriers. The air waybill under the Warsaw System also plays a key role in adding to the mass of documentation involved in the modern freight contract.

The Warsaw Convention of 1929[477] states that, for the transportation of freight, the carrier may require the consignor to make out and hand over to him an air consignment note which shall contain certain details.[478] The Convention also says that the absence, irregularity or loss of the air consignment note shall not affect the existence of the validity of the contract of transportation which shall nonetheless be subject to the rules of the Convention. Nevertheless, if the carrier accepts a passenger without an air consignment note having been delivered, he shall not be entitled to avail himself of those provisions of the Convention that exclude his liability.[479]

The air freight business has a palpable impact on the world of business and, like any other business, must follow basic economic rules. As markets open out and globalize, they must, as a necessity, begin to concentrate around fewer players. Strategic airline alliances are a first step in this equation, and it is inevitable that, over time, just a few players will dominate the world air transport market. The US market, arguably the world's most mature, will seek to mesh with the broadly deregulated intra-European market and make the North Atlantic the most powerful air transport market on an inter-regional basis. The Asia–Pacific region, often misconstrued as a purely homogeneous market owing to its geographic connotations, has shown that the region's strongest international traffic flows are between inter-regional sectors. This notwithstanding, Asia–Pacific carriers should immediately focus on strengthening their positions in local and regional markets, while at the same time emphasizing the need to enter into strong strategic alliances with carriers of other regions and those within the Asia–Pacific region.

As for aircraft manufacturers, their role in providing much-needed freight capacity for the future is a critical one. The large aircraft planned by Boeing and Airbus Industrie, the 747 XF and A 380F, respectively, were expected to offer the world's major cargo airlines a 25 per cent increase in payload. In this context, the aviation industry has voiced its concern over the cancellation by Boeing of the development of the 747 XF.[480]

The operative criterion for the provision of capacity in the carriage of air freight is whether carriers choose to band together through alliances or to operate independently, and this will depend on how competitive they are. It is incontrovertible in this context that the information revolution plays a major role as a determinant. The success story in air freight carriage, particularly in view of its link to various other aspects of business, will hinge on the operators' will to achieve dramatic reductions in the cost of obtaining, processing and transmitting information. The management of new information technology is the key to warding off competition. E-commerce, as was demonstrated earlier, is a major player in marketing air freight services.

In the air freight business, information technology is more than fast computers. It broadly encapsulates information created by the business concerned, and uses a broad spectrum of convergent and linked technologies that process such information. The information revolution is rapidly changing industry structure and altering rules of competition, offering operators new and more innovative ways to outperform their competitors. Information, deftly and strategically used, may also spawn whole new business opportunities from existing operations.

The ultimate in providing total service in the air freight business world lies in the successful combination of using information that is available to deliver a unique mix of value. Operators should be able to attract consignors with a total package rather than with fragmented services. For example, a freight carrier could offer up-to-the-minute information on the whereabouts of a consignor's freight, which improves coordination between the consignor, consignee and the carrier. It is critical in this process that managers assess the information intensity applicable to the air freight industry, determine the role to be played by information technology in their industry structure, identify and rank the way in which information technology might create competition advantage and develop a plan for taking advantage of information technology.

In terms of strategy implementation, information technology could prove to be a useful tool in tracking progress towards milestones and success factors through efficient reporting systems. By using these systems, operators could measure their business activities more precisely and help managers motivate themselves towards implementing their strategies successfully.

Basic economic principles of the twenty-first century dictate that the global player is the winner in any international business enterprise. Competitive advantages of a global strategy usually rest with the pre-eminent stratagem of location of the business. Every global strategy usually begins with some kind of advantage in location, which plays a critical role in the business penetrating the international market. The successful air freight manager will therefore use information technology and location of his business as key factors in his marketing strategy.

With regard to legal issues that may arise from the modern exigencies of air freight carriage, particularly in instances where carriage is affected through a carrier who is not a contracting carrier, the subtleties of commercial alliances between the carriers concerned should be carefully evaluated. The various nuances of the law pertaining to air freight, as discussed here, could all be relevant considerations in this regard.

NOTES

1   *Annual Report of the Council 2000*, International Civil Aviation Organization, Doc. 9770, p. 1. Also 'Airline Financial Results Remain Positive in 2000 Despite Soaring Fuel Prices', ICAO News Release P10 05/01.
2   Ibid.
3   Figures culled from World Tourism Organization reports, as reflected in the *Annual Report of the Council 2000*, *supra*, note 1, p. 2.
4   Ibid.
5   Brunei Darussalam, Chile, New Zealand, Singapore and the United States.
6   See generally *International Airlines Industry outlook 2001–2003*, International Air Transport Association, January 2001, p. 1.
7   Michael E. Porter, *On Competition*, Harvard Business Review Series: USA, 1996, p. 4.
8   Convention on International Civil Aviation, signed at Chicago on 7 December 1944, hereafter referred to as the Chicago Convention. See ICAO Doc. 7300/8, 8th edn, 2000.
9   Article 6 of the Chicago Convention provides:
    No scheduled international air service may be operated over or into the territory of a Contracting State, except with the special permission or other authorization of that State, or in accordance with the terms of such permission or authorization.
10 See Russel Miller, 'International Airline Alliances – A Review of Competition Law Aspects', *Air & Space Law*, XXIII(3), 1998, p.125.
11 *ITA Press*, 16–31 October 1998, p.4.
12 Robert Koenig, 'Swissair; Delta Raise Trans Atlantic Cargo Status', *Journal of Commerce*, 2 June 1998, p. 8A.
13 'Never the Twain', *Air Transport World*, 10/96, p. 67.
14 'EC Concerned that Franchising is Blocking New Entrants', *World Airline News*, 17 April 1995, p. 6.
15 See, generally, 'Market Access: Unfinished Business, Post Uruguay Round Inventory and Issues', World Trade Organization, *Special Studies 6*, 2001, pp. 99–105.
16 'Assembly Resolutions in Force', Doc. 9730, ICAO, Montreal , III-4.
17 Ibid.
18 GATT was a multilateral body established in Geneva on 1 January 1948 on coming into force of the General Agreement on Tariff, and Trade (GATT) negotiated and signed by 23 countries. GATT functions as the principal international body concerned with negotiating reduction of trade barriers and with international trade relations. While being an organization to which member states belong, where they could use it as a forum in which they can discuss and overcome their problems and negotiate to enlarge world

trading opportunities, GATT is also a code of rules which is calculated to liberalize world trade. GATS is an Annex to the Final Act of the Uruguay Round agreement and has a special segment on air transport services as trade in services.

One of the agreements contained in the Final Act of the Uruguay Round (*infra*, note 45) establishes a World Trade Organization which will serve as single institutional frame-work for the GATT as well as all the agreements and arrangements concluded under the Uruguay Round. This permanent organizational framework, which replaces the GATT structure, will be headed by a Ministerial Conference, least once every two years and will include a General Council to oversee the operation of the agreement and to act as both a dispute settlement body and a trade policy review mechanism. Therefore all references to GATT in this chapter will infer references to the World Trade Organization.

19 Article III of GATS requires each party to publish promptly all relevant laws, regulations, administrative guidelines and all other decisions, rulings or measures of general application, by the time of their entry into force.

20 GATT's national treatment philosophy provides foreign services and services suppliers with treatment no less favourable than that accorded to a country's own services and service suppliers.

21 Since GATS is an Annex to the GATT agreement, it should be noted that the provisions of GATS are governed by those of GATT and that the two documents incorporate the same basic principles.

22 Article II of GATS. Article XVI extends the MFN principle to market access.

23 Article IV of GATS provides that the increasing participation of developing countries in world trade shall be facilitated through negotiated specific commitments by different parties. It also requires developed member states to establish contact points within two years from the entry into force of the GATS agreement to facilitate the access of developing states' service providers to information related to their respective markets concerning commercial and technical aspects of the supply of services; registration, recognition and obtaining of professional qualifications; and the availability of service technology. The provision also states that special priority would be given to the least developed states in the implementation of Article IV and particular account would be taken of the difficulties experienced by developing states in accepting negotiated commitments in view of their special economic situation and their development, trade and financial needs.

24 Article XXIII on dispute settlement is considered to be well balanced and equitable and provides that if, any party should consider that another party fails to carry out its obligations or commitments under the agreement, it may make written representations or proposals to the other party or parties concerned and the latter should give sympathetic consideration to the representations or proposals so made. If no satisfactory settlement could be arrived at, the GATT agreement provides for a formal dispute settlement procedure in Articles XXII and XXIII.

25 There have been six rounds of trade agreements so far: 1947 in Geneva; 1949 in Annecy, France; 1951 in Torquay, United Kingdom; 1960–62 in Geneva (the Dillon round); 1964–67 in Geneva (the Kennedy round); 1973–9 in Geneva (the Tokyo round) where negotiations were launched at a ministerial meeting in September 1973 in Tokyo. The Tokyo round produced the most comprehensive agreements of the round of negotiations, where 99 member states participated. Negotiations of the Tokyo round were concluded in November 1979 with agreements covering an improved legal framework for the conduct of world trade (including recognition of tariff and non-tariff treatment in favour of and among developing countries as a permanent legal feature of the world trading system); non-tariff measures (subsidies and countervailing measures); technical barriers to trade; government procurement; customs valuation; import licensing procedures; a revision of the 1967 GATT anti-dumping code; bovine meat; dairy products; tropical

products; and an agreement on free trade in civil aircraft. The agreements contained special and more favourable treatment for developing countries.

26   The five freedoms of the air were created, the Chicago Conference of 1944 and comprise the following:
     1) the right to fly over the territory of a state without landing;
     2) the right to land in the territory of a state for non-traffic purposes;
     3) the right to put down passengers, mail and cargo taken on in the territory of the state whose nationality the aircraft possesses;
     4) the right to take on passengers, mail and cargo destined for the territory of the state whose nationality the aircraft possesses; and,
     5) the right to take on passengers, mail and cargo destined for the territory of any other contracting state and the right to put down passengers, mail and cargo coming from any such territory.

27   Annex on Air Transport Services, General Agreement on Trade in Services, MTN. TNG/W/FA, Article 2.

28   Ibid., Article 3.

29   Ibid., Article 4.

30   Ibid., Article 5.

31   Geoffrey Lipman, 'Is GATT just another Four Letter Word?', *Aerospace World*, IV, September 1990, 98. See also Daniel M. Kasper, 'The GATT approach – Applying the GATT to Air Services: Will it Work?', *ITA Magazine*, November/December 1989, 9–12.

32   Kathryn B. Creedy, 'Should Air Transport be in or out of GATT?', *Interavia*, 9/1990, 717.

33   Ibid.

34   Daniel M. Kasper, *Deregulation and Globalization: Liberalizing International Trade in Air Services*, Cambridge, Mass.: Ballinger, 1988, p. 96

35   Ibid., Preface.

36   See John C. Mc Carrol, 'The Bermuda Capacity Clauses in the Jet Age', *Journal of Air Law and Commerce (JALC)*, 29 (2), Spring 1963, 119, where the author says: 'fair and equal opportunity ... to operate should mean ... equality of practical capability to operate'. See also P. Van Der Tuuk Adriani, 'The Bermuda Capacity Clauses', *JALC*, 22(406), Autumn 1955, 413.

37   Dr H.A. Wassenbergh lists seven objectives of a state's policy in respect of modern civil aviation. They are:
     a) to contribute to the functioning of the international community of states as a total legal order by upholding and further developing the rule of international law;
     b) to protect the integrity and identity of the national society;
     c) to promote the nation's participation in man's activities in the air and space;
     d) to create the best possible conditions and opportunities for use by the public of aviation and space activities;
     e) to increase the benefits to be derived from the use of the air and outer space for its nationals;
     f) to promote the further development of technology and the knowledge of man;
     g) to cooperate with other states on the basis of equal rights in order to bridge conflicting national interests and achieve the aims mentioned above.
     See H.A. Wassenbergh, 'Reality and Value of Air and Space Law', *Annals of Air and Space*, III, 1978, 352.

38   Chicago Convention, *supra*, note 8, Article 44(*e*).

39   Ibid., Article 44(*f*).

40   For a detailed discussion of the ITO, see Robert R. Wilson, 'Proposed ITO Charter', *American Journal of International Law*, 41(4), October 1947, pp. 881, 882.

41   'U.N. Economic and Social Council, Official Records', 134th Session, 546th meeting

(5/SR.546 11 September 1951). See also Report of the ad hoc Committee on Restrictive Business Practices (E/2380, 30 March 1953).

42 *Focus Newsletter*, Geneva: WTO, January/February 1995, p.2.

43 See speech of Peter D. Sutherland, Director General of WTO, *World Trade Organization Press Release*, PRESS/1, 27 January 1995 (95-0156), 1.

44 Ibid., p. 5.

45 General Agreements on Tariffs and Trade, Multilateral Trade Negotiations Final Act Embodying the Results of the Uruguay Round of Trade Negotiations (done, Marrakesh, 15 April 1994), 33 *I.L.M*. 1125 (1994), Annex 1B, Part II Article II.

46 Ibid., Article III.

47 Ibid.

48 See B. Matsushita, 'The Structural Impediments Initiative: an Example of Bilateral Trade Negotiation', *Michigan Journal of International Law*, 12(2), Winter 1991, 436–49.

49 See Michael E. Porter, *Competitive Strategy*, New York: The Free Press, 1980, 291–8.

50 *Deregulation and Airline Competition*, Paris: OECD, 1988, pp. 20–21.

51 Pieter Bouw and Wendy Hall, 'Global Competition in the Airline Industry', *ICC World Business & Trade Review*, 1999, p.147

52 David Banister, Bjorn Andersen, Joseph Berechman and Sean Barrett, 'Access to Facilities in a Competitive Transport Market', 1993, vol. 17, p. 341.

53 'The Need for Greater Liberalization of International Air Transport', ICC Policy Statement, Doc. 310/504 Rev. 3, p.1.

54 Ibid., p. 9.

55 The EC Treaty, also called the Treaty of Rome, was concluded in 1957 to forge 'an even closer union among the people of Europe'. See Jeffrey Goh, *European Air Transport Law and Competition*, New York: John Wiley and Sons, 1997, p.15.

56 Case 167/73, *Commission v. French Republic* [1974] E.C.R. 359, 370.

57 See Bernardine Adkins, *Air Transport and E.C. Competition Law*, European Competition Law Monologues, London: Sweet and Maxwell, 1994, p. 81.

58 Case T-51/89, *Tetra Pak Rausing SA v. Commission* [1990] II E.C.R. 309, [1991] 4 C.M.L.R. 334 para. 31.

59 Case 85/76 *Hoffman-La Roche & Co. A.G. v. Commission* [1979] E.C.R. 461.

60 *Policy and Guidance Material on the Economic Regulation of International Air Transport*, Doc. 9587, 2nd edn, 1999, Appendix 2, A2-2. See also *Manual on the Regulation of International Air Transport*, Doc. 9626, 1st edn, 1996, Appendix 5, 'Guidance Material for Users of Air Transport', at A5-1.

61 These conditions are the result of an agreement reached on 11 February 1946 by the United States and the United Kingdom in Bermuda. For a clear analysis of the Bermuda Agreement see Ramon de Murias, *The Economic Regulation of International Air Transport*, McFarland, 1989, pp. 52–72.

62 See, generally, R.I.R. Abeyratne, 'The Air Traffic Rights Debate – A Legal Study', *Annals of Air & Space Law*, XVIII, pt 1, 1993, p. 3.

63 Henri Wassenbergh, 'De-Regulation of Competition in International Air Transport', *Air & Space Law*, XII, 2 November 1996, p. 80.

64 The right to uplift or discharge passengers, mail and cargo in a country other than the grantor state.

65 See *Study on Preferential Measures for Developing Countries*, ICAO Doc. AT-WP/1789, 22/8/96, A-7–A-9. For a more recent revision of guidelines, see, *Policy and Guidance Material on the Economic Regulation of International Air Transport*, ICAO Doc. 9587, 2nd edn, 1999, Appendix 3, A3-1–A3-3.

66 For a detailed discussion of regulations on aircraft noise and engine emissions, see R.I.R. Abeyratne, *Legal and Regulatory Issues in International Aviation*, New York: Transnational Publishers, 1996, pp. 271–313.

67 See Kirsten Bohmann, 'The Ownership and Control Requirement in U.S. and European Union Law and U.S. Maritime Law – Policy; Consideration; Comparison', *Journal of Airlaw and Commerce*, 66, 2001, 690.

68 See Ian Shepphard, 'Cyberspace', *Aerospace International*, May 2000, p. 24.

69 The original Statute of Frauds, passed in 1677 as Charles II C.3, was intended as an act for the prevention of frauds and injuries. See Douglas Stollery, 'Statute of Frauds', *Alberta Law Review*, 14, 1976, 222.

70 For Canadian law, see *Kinghorne* v. *The Montreal Telegraph Co.* (1859) 18 U.C.Q.B.R., p. 60. For British law, see *McBlaine* v. *Cross* (1871) 25 L.T. 804; *Coupland* v. *Arrowsmith* (1868) 18 L.T. 755. For United States law, see *Howley* v. *Whipple* 48 N.H. 487 (1869). For general reading, see S. Walter Jones, *A Treatise on the Law of Telegraph and Telephone Companies*, 2nd edn, Kansas City: Vernon Law Book Co., 1916.

71 *Selma Sav Bank* v. *Webster County Bank* 206 S.W. 870, 872 (Ky. App. 1918).

72 See *Howley* v. *Whipple*, *supra*, note 70, p. 872.

73 *Beatty* v. *First Explor. Fund 1987 & Co.* (1988) 25 B.C.L.R. (2d) 377 (S.C.).

74 *Rolling* v. *Willann Investments Ltd* (1989) 70 O.R. (2d) 578, 581.

75 (1840), 3 Beav. 334.

76 724 F. Supp. 605 (S.D. Ind. 1989).

77 (1870), 23 L.T. 419.

78 See also, *Harper* v. *Western Union Telegraph Co.*, 130 S.E. 119 (S.C. 1925); *Postal Tel. Cable Co.* v. *Schaefer*, 62 S.W. 1119 (Ky. App.1901).

79 (1859) 18 V.C.Q.B.R. 60.

80 Ibid., 64.

81 *Carow Towing Co.* v. *The 'Ed. McWilliams'* (1919), 46 D.L.R. 506 (Ex. Ct.).

82 *Entores Ltd.* v. *Miles Far East Corporation* [1955] 2 All E.R. 493 (C.A.).

83 See, for example, *McDonald & Sons Ltd* v. *Export Packers Co. Ltd* (1979), 95 D.L.R. (3d) 174 (B.C.S.C.). See also *Re Viscount Supply Co. Ltd* (1963), 40 D.L.R. (2d) 501 (Ont. S.C.); and *National Bank of Canada* v. *Clifford Chance* (1996), 30 O.R. (3d) 746 (Gen. Div.).

84 *Rosenthal & Rosenthal Inc.* v. *Bonavista Fabrics Ltd*, [1984] C.A. 52 (Que. C.A.).

85 *Balcom (Joan) Sales Inc.* v. *Poirier* (1991), 288 A.P.R. 377 (N.S. Co. Ct.).

86 *Gunac Hawkes Bay (1986) Ltd* v. *Palmer* [1991] 3 N.Z.L.R. 297 (H. Ct.).

87 *Brinkibon Ltd* v. *Stahag Stahl und Stahlwarenhandelsgesellschaft mbH* [1982] 1 All E.R. 293 (H.L.).

88 Ibid., 296.

89 *Arrowsmith* v. *Ingle* (1810), 3 Taunt. 234.

90 The *'Pendrecht'* [1980] 2 *Lloyd's Rep.* 56 (Q.B.).

91 *McDonald and Sons Ltd* v. *Export Packers Co. Ltd* (1979), 95 D.L.R. (3dl 174 B.C.S.C.), at 180.

92 Convention for the Unification of Certain Rules Relating to International Carriage by Air, signed, Warsaw on 12 October 1929. Hereafter referred to as the Convention.

93 Ibid., Article 3.1.

94 Ibid., Article 3.2.

95 9 Avi. 18 374 (U.S.C.A. 1966).

96 21 Avi. 18 228 (U.S.S.C. 1989).

97 Georgette Miller, *Air Carrier's Liability Under The Warsaw System*, The Hague: Martinus Nijhoff, 1980, p. 84.

98 Ibid.

99 *Mertens* v. *The Flying Tiger Line Inc.*, 9 Avi. 17 187 (S.D.N.Y. 1963) and *Warren* v. *The Flying Tiger Line Inc.*, 9 Avi. 17 621 (S.D. Cal. 1964).

100 Ibid.

101 *Lisi* v. *Alitalia*, *supra*, note 95, at 18 376.

102 Ibid., 18 377.
103 Ibid., 18 378.
104 *Supra*, note 96.
105 *Supra*, note 96, at 18 231.
106 *Ludecke* v. *Canadian Pacific Airlines Ltd*, 98 D.L.R. 3d. 52 (1979).
107 Ibid.
108 Valerie Kaiser, '*Chan* v. *Korean Airlines*, Case Comment', *Annals of Air & Space Law*, 15, 1990, 507.
109 *In re Air Crash Disaster Near New Orleans, Louisiana, on July 9 1982*, 22 Avi. 17 370 (U.S.C.A. 5th Cir.).
110 Convention for the Unification of Certain Rules for International Carriage by Air, done, Montreal on 28 May 1999, ICAO Doc. 9740, Montreal, 1999.
111 Ibid., Article 3.2.
112 *Jenner* v. *Sun Oil Co. Ltd* (1952) 16 C.P.R. 87 (Ont. H.C.J.).
113 Ibid., 98–9.
114 (1984) 49 O.R. (Ed) 58 (H.C.J.).
115 (1996) 30 O.R. (3d) 746 (Gen. Div.)
116 636 So. 2d. 1351 (Fla. App. 1994).
117 *IDS Life Insurance Co.* v. *SunAmerica, Inc.*, 958 F. Supp. 1258 (N.D. Ill. 1997), aff'd in part, vacated in part, 1998 W.L. 51350 (7th Cir.) (Westlaw).
118 Ibid., 268.
119 1997 W.L. 97097 (S.D.N.Y.) (Westlaw).
120 Ibid., para. 1. For a similar result, see, *Cybersell, Inc.* v. *Cybersell, Inc.*, 44 U.S.P.Q. 2d. 1928 (9th Cir. 1997); and *Blackburn* v. *Walker Oriental Rug Galleries*, No. 97-5704 (E.D. Pa., 7 April 1998), reported in *Computer & Online Industry Litigation Reporter*, 21 April 1998, p. 4.
121 *McDonough* v. *Fallon McElligott Inc.*, 40 U.S.P.Q. 2d. 1826 (S.D. Cal. 1996).
122 Ibid., 1828.
123 89 F. 3d. 1257 (6th Cir. 1996).
124 *Digital Equipment Corporation* v. *AltaVista Technology, Inc.* 960 F. Supp. 456 (D. Mass. 1997). See also *Cody* v. *Ward*, 954 F. Supp. 43 (D. Conn. 1997), where a court took jurisdiction based on telephone and e-mail communications that consummated a business relationship begun over *Prodigy*'s 'Money talk' discussion forum for financial matters. In partially justifying this decision, the court noted that the use of fax technology, and even live telephone conferences, can greatly reduce the burden of litigating out-of-state.
125 *Heroes, Inc.* v. *Heroes Foundation*, 958 F. Supp. 1 (D.D.C. 1996).
126 *Zippo Manufacturing Company* v. *Zippo Dot Com, Inc.*, 952 F. Supp. 1119 (W.D. Pa. 1997).
127 *Resuscitation Technologies, Inc.* v. *Continental Health Care Corp.*, 1997 WL 148567 (S.D. Ind.) (Westlaw). The court in this case was not concerned that the defendants had never visited the forum state in person and concluded, para. 5: 'Neither is the matter disposed of by the fact that no defendant ever set foot in Indiana. The 'footfalls' were not physical, they were electronic. They were, nonetheless, footfalls. The level of Internet activity in this case was significant.' See also *EDIAS Software International, L.L.C.* v. *BASIS International Ltd*, 947 F. Supp. 413 (D. Ariz. 1996). In this case the court summed up the essence of many of the Internet jurisdiction cases by stating, 420: 'BASIS [the defendant] should not be permitted to take advantage of modern technology through an Internet Web page and forum and simultaneously escape traditional notions of jurisdiction.' See also *Gary Scott International, Inc.* v. *Baroudi*, 981 F. Supp. 714 (D. Mass. 1997).
128 *Panavision International, L.P.* v. *Toeppen*, 938 F. Supp. 616 (CD-Cal. 1996); *Maritz, Inc.* v. *CyberGold, Inc.*, 947 F. Supp. 1328 (E.D. Mo. 1996); *Inset Systems, Inc.* v. *Instruction*

Set, Inc., 937 F. Supp. 161 (D. Conn. 1996). In the latter case the court observed, at 165:

> In the present case, Instruction has directed its advertising activities via the Internet and its toll-free number toward not only the state of Connecticut, but to all States. The Internet as well as toll-free numbers are designed to communicate with people and their businesses in every state. Advertisement on the Internet can reach as many as 10,000 Internet users within Connecticut alone. Further, once posted on the Internet, unlike television and radio advertising, the advertisement is available continuously to any Internet user. ISI has, therefore, purposefully availed itself of the privilege of doing business within Connecticut.

129 *Plus System, Inc.* v. *New England Network, Inc.*, 804 F. Supp. 111 (D. Colo. 1992).
130 585 N.Y.S. 2d. 661 (Supp. 1992).
131 Airbus Industrie, *1998 Global Forecast*, p. 4. (This forecast can be viewed at <http://www.Airbus.com>)
132 The Boeing Company, *1998 Current Market Outlook*, p. 42. According to the Boeing forecast, the world fleet is expected to more than double by 2020, with total fleet size growing to 32 954 aircraft. Over the 20-year forecast period, 5053 aircraft will be retired from active commercial service and will be replaced. An additional 18 406 will be needed to fill capacity demand.
133 See, generally, David Clancey and Gregory Voss, 'Facilitating Asset Based Financing and Leasing of Aircraft Equipment Through the Proposed Unidroit Convention: Manufacturers' Perspective', *Air & Space Law*, XXIII (6), 1998, pp. 287–9.
134 See R.M Goode, 'Security in Cross-border Transactions' (1998) 33 *Tex Int'l L.J*. 47.
135 See N.B. Cohen, 'Harmonizing the Law Governing Secured Credit: The Next Frontier' (1998) 33 *Tex. Int'l L.J*. 173.
136 The fact that the creditor is situated in a non-contracting state does not affect the applicability of the Convention.
137 'Aircraft objects', are defined as airframes, aircraft engines and helicopters.
138 A finance lease involves the substantial transfer of risks and rewards appurtenant to ownership, from lessor to lessee; and an operational lease keeps such risks and rewards within the lessor's scope of legal status. A finance lease is calculated to amortize the lessor's capital outlay and provide a profit, the end of the lease term with the lease payments received from the lessee. An operational lease does not amortize capital outlay, the end of the term and profits are derived usually after more than one lease term.
139 Maria Wagland, 'A new Lease of Life', *Aerospace International*, March 1999, p 22.
140 *Beecham Foods Limited* v. *North Supplies (Edmonton) Ltd* [1959] 1 W.L.R. 643.
141 *Ballet* v. *Mingay* [1943] 1 K.B. 281.
142 *Lang* v. *Brown* (1898) 34 N.B.R. 492.
143 Donald H. Bunker, 'The Law of Aerospace Finance in Canada', Institute and Centre of Air and Space Law, McGill, 1988, p. 22.
144 Ibid.
145 Convention on International Civil Aviation signed Chicago, 7 December 1944. See 15 U.N.T.S. 295, ICAO Doc. 7300, 6th edn, 1980.
146 Ibid., Article 18.
147 Ibid., Article 19.
148 Convention for the Regulation of Aerial Navigation, Paris 1919, Articles 5–10.
149 Convention on Offences and Certain Other Acts Committed on Board Aircraft, signed, Tokyo on 14 September 1963. See ICAO Doc. 8364.
150 Ibid., Article 3.
151 *ICJ Rep.* (1955), 1.
152 Ibid., at 3.

153 The International Civil Aviation Organization is the specialized agency of the United Nations responsible for the regulation of international civil aviation. ICAO has 185 member states.

154 On 20 June 1997, the 98th instrument of ratification of Article 83*bis* was received by ICAO, making the provision applicable to states of ratification.

155 Donald H. Bunker, 'The Law of Aerospace Finance in Canada', *supra*, note 6, p. 157.

156 Ibid., at p. 288.

157 (1988) 14 N.S.W.L.R. 523.

158 N.S.W.C.A., 23.12.88 at p. 16.

159 Ibid.

160 See *Waltons Stores (Interstate) Ltd* v. *Maher* (1988) 164 C.L.R. 387.

161 *The Queen in Right of Ontario* v. *Ron Engineering and Construction Eastern Ltd* (1981) 119 D.L.R. (3d) 167. Courts may also construct a collateral contract containing terms negotiated at the tendering stage, if such terms are not included in the formal lease document. See *City and Westminster Properties Ltd.* v. *Mudd* [1958] 2 All E.R. 733 (Ch.).

162 *Cricklewood Property and Investment Trust Ltd* v. *Leighton's Investment Trust Ltd* [1945] A.L. 221.

163 See *Rom Securities Ltd* v *Rogers (Holdings) Ltd* (1967) 205 *Estates Gazette* 427.

164 Rod Margo, 'Aircraft Leasing: The Airline's Objectives', *Air & Space Law*, XXI (4/5), 1996, 167.

165 Ibid.

166 Article 83*bis* admits of all or part of the duties and functions pertaining to Articles 12, 30, 31 and 32(*a*) of the Chicago Convention being transferred from the state of registry to the state of the operator. The duties and functions to be transferred must be mentioned specifically in the transfer agreement as, in the absence of such mention, they are deemed to remain with the state of registry.

167 See ICAO State Letter EC 2/82, LE 4/55-99/54, Attachment B.

168 It is also recommended that a certified true copy of the AOC under which the aircraft is operated, and in which it should be listed, be carried on board.

169 ECAC Recommendation on Leasing of Aircraft ECAC/21-1

170 Bermuda (UK) and Colombia signed on 18 December 1998 an agreement implementing Article 83*bis*, which was the first one of this sort to be registered with ICAO (No. 4171, dated 1 February 1999).

171 See the Brundtland Report, 1987: G. Brundtland et al., *Our Common Future*, London: WCED, Oxford University Press, 1987, p.13; also J. Biden, 'The Environment and World Trade', *Environmental Law*, 23, 1993, p. 688; J. Dunoff, 'Reconciling International Trade with Preservation of the Global Commons, Can We Prosper and Protect?', *Washington and Lee Law Review*, 49, 1992, p. 1407.

172 'On Track to the EU's Sixth Framework', *Interavia*, March 2001, p.15.

173 Tom Grill, 'Invisible Danger', *Airline Business*, March 2001, p. 46.

174 'The World of Civil Aviation 1999–2002', ICAO circular 279-AT/116, 26–7. A more conservative estimate is provided by Airports Council International (ACI), which records a forecast growth rate of 3·2 per cent a year globally. This information is based on a response to an ACI questionnaire by 380 airports. See *ITA Press*, 377, 16–28 February 2001, p. 6.

175 Ibid., Highlights.

176 Jan Carlson, 'Foreword', *Moments of Truth*, New York: Harper Collins, 1989.

177 Jiffang Huang, 'ICAO Study Group examines the Legal Issues Related to Unruly Airline Passengers', *ICAO Journal*, 56(2), 2001, 18.

178 Ibid.

179 Bin Cheng, *The Law of International Air Transport*, London: Oceania, 1962, p. 186.

180 Ibid.
181 'Statistics Division, Report of the Ninth Session', Montreal, 22 August–6 September 1997, Doc. 9703 (STA/9 (1997)), Recommendation 1, p.7.
182 Ibid.
183 'International Civil Aviation Organization Vocabulary', Doc. 9713, vol. 1, 1998, p. 604.
184 Convention on International Civil Aviation, ICAO Doc. 7300/8, 2000.
185 See R.I.R. Abeyratne, 'Facilitation and the ICAO Role – A Prologue for the Nineties', *Annals of Air & Space Law*, XV, 1990, 3–15; also by the same author, 'The Development of the Machine Readable Passport and Visa and Legal Rights of the Data Subject', *Annals of Air & Space Law*, XVII, Pt II, 1992, 1–31. See also Roderick Heitmeyer, 'Biometrics ID and Airport Facilitation', *Airport World* (ACI), 5(1), February/March 2000, 18–20.
186 *Manual on the Regulation of International Air Transport*, Doc. 9626, 1st edn, 1996.
187 Ibid., Appendix 5.
188 *Regulatory Affairs Review*, April/June 2000, p. 253.
189 'Air Passenger Rights in the European Union', European Commission, *Regulatory Affairs Review*, January/March 2000, p. 47.
190 Harold Caplan, 'Air passenger rights in the European Union Part I', *The Aviation Quarterly*, pt 3, July 2000, p. 204.
191 Harold Caplan, 'Air passenger rights in the European Union Part II', *The Aviation Quarterly*, pt 3, July 2000, pp. 211–15.
192 Guiseppe Guerreri, 'Overbooking, Overselling and Denial of Boarding', *Annals of Air & Space Law*, XVI, McGill, 1989, 192.
193 426 U.S. 290 (1976); 14 Av. L.R. 17, 148.
194 Ibid., 294.
195 Convention for the Unification of Certain Rules Relating to International Transportation by Air, signed at Warsaw on 12 October 1929; hereafter referred to as the Warsaw Convention. The Warsaw Convention was later amended by several protocols, none of which changed the substantive provisions of the Convention hereinafter cited in this chapter. See, generally, R.I.R. Abeyratne, 'Civil Liability of Airlines for Death or Injury to Passengers', *Colombo Law Review*, 7, 1990, 81–2.
196 Article 34 of the Warsaw Convention denies, however, the application of the Convention to all carriage, however international, that is performed by way of experimental trial by commercial air carriers as well as carriage performed in extraordinary circumstances and outside the normal course of the air carrier's business.
197 1 Avi. 622 (Ct. App. England 1936).
198 Ibid., at 635.
199 *Kraus* v. *KLM Royal Dutch Airlines*, 2 Avi. 16017 (N.Y. Sup. Ct. 1954). See also *American Smelting and Refining Co.* v. *Philippine Airlines Inc.*, 4 Avi. 17413 (N.Y. Sup. Ct. 1954) where the court held that a stopping place, for it to be agreed upon, need not necessarily be indicated in the airline ticket.
200 *Caisse régionale de Sécurité Sociale du Sud-Est c. Della Roma* (1959) 22 R.G.A.194.
201 *Supra*, note 202.
202 *Grein* v. *Imperial Airways*, at 634.
203 H. Drion, *Limitation of Liabilities in International Air Law*, The Hague: Martinus Nijhoff, 1954, p. 54.
204 An aircraft has been defined by the International Civil Aviation Organization (ICAO) as: any machine which derives its support in the atmosphere from the reactions of the air, other than the reactions of the air on the earth's surface. See ICAO Doc. 9569, 1991, 24.
205 Drion, *supra*, note 208, 54–8.
206 10 Avi. 17518 (5th Cir. 1967).
207 Ibid., at 17523.

208 Georgette Miller, *Liability in International Air Transport*, Amsterdam: Kluwer, 1977, p. 14.

209 Peter Martin, 'Ticketless (but not documentless) travel', *Lloyd's Aviation Law*, 14(6), 15 March 1995, 2.

210 The cases of *Mertens* v. *Flying Tiger Line Inc.* and *Warren* v. *Flying Tiger Line Inc.* have already been cited in note 99.

211 Ibid.

212 Miller, *supra*, note 213, p. 154.

213 *Sté Général Air fret* c. *Ste TWA Trans World Airlines* (1956) 10 R.F.D.A. 324.

214 *Sonillac* v. *Air France* (1965) 28 R.G.A.E. 15.

215 Ibid., at 17.

216 (1967) 1 *Lloyds Rep.* 239 (Guyana Ct. App. 1966).

217 Warsaw Convention, Article 20.

218 Ibid., Article 21.

219 The Warsaw Convention establishes a regime of liability where the liability of the carrier is presumed, once a plaintiff claims that he has suffered damage in the hands of the carrier. The carrier has to rebut this presumption. To balance this deviation from normal evidential rules, the Convention has set up limits on the carrier's liability in terms of monetary compensation payable to the plaintiff if the carrier is unable to rebut the presumption of liability. For a discussion of the presumption of liability of the carrier under the Warsaw Convention, see R.I.R. Abeyratne, 'Liability for Personal Injury and Death Inder the Warsaw Convention and its Relevance to Fault Liability in Tort Law', *Annals of Air & Space Law*, XI(1), 1996, 1–43.

220 John M. Corrigan, 'The Right of the Air Carrier to Refuse Carriage', *Annals of Air & Space Law*, III, 1978, McGill, 25.

221 *Clark* v. *West Ham Corp.* (1909) 2 K.B. 858; *Readhead* v. *Midland Railway Co.* (1869) L.R. 4 Q.B. 382; *Overseas National Airways* v. *C.A.B.*, 307 F. 2d. 634; *U.S.* v. *Stephen Bros. Lines*, 384 F. 2d. 118; *S.M.T. Ltd* v. *Ruch*, 50 C.R.T.C. 369, *Roussel* v. *Aumais*, 18 Que. S.C. 474; *Thibault* v. *Garneau* (1959) Que. P.R. 377.

222 Warsaw Convention, Article 32.

223 *Watkins* v. *Rymill* (1883) 10 Q.B. 178.

224 See also generally the common law decision of *Thornton* v. *Shoe Lane Parking* (1971) 2 Q.B. 163, which upheld the contractual principle that, for a contractual clause to be considered applicable, the parties to the contract should have the opportunity to read the clause and to dissent from it.

225 *Montreal Trust and Stampleman* v. *CP Air* (1976) 72 D.L.R. (3d) 282.

226 An account of this case appears in *Lloyd's Aviation Law*, 15(9), 11 May 1995, 2.

227 49 U.S. App. S. 1305 (1994).

228 See *In re Air Disaster at Lockerbie, Scotland*, 928 F. 2d. 1267, at 1273 (2nd Cir. 1991).

229 See *Wogel* v. *Mexicana Airlines*, 821 F. 2d. 442 (7th Cir. 1987).

230 *Malik* v. *Butta*, unreported. See *Lloyd's Aviation Law*, 12(21), 1 November, 1993, 1 for a discussion of this case.

231 Unreported at the time of writing. This case is discussed in *Lloyd's Aviation Law*, 13(22), 15 November 1994, 3–4.

232 Ibid., 4.

233 See *Abnet* v. *British Airways PLC*, cited in *Lloyd's Aviation Law*, 3(2), 15 January 1992, 4–5.

234 773 F. Supp. 482 (D.D.C. 1991).

235 Ibid., 484–5.

236 474 F. Supp. 532 (1979).

237 Ibid., 534.

238 *Archibald* v. *Pan American World Airways Inc.*, 460 F. 2d. 14, 16 (9th Cir. 1972).

239 Ibid., 17, cited in *Mahaney* v. *Air France*, *supra*, note 236, 536.
240 49 U.S.C.A. sec. 1374(b).
241 *Mahaney* v. *Air France*, *supra*, note 236, 534.
242 821 F. 2d. 442 (7th Cir. 1987).
243 Ibid., 444.
244 769 F. Supp. 537 (S.D.N.Y. 1991).
245 Ibid., 540.
246 *Laor* v. *Air France*, 1998 W.L. 886979 (S.D.N.Y. 18 December 1998).
247 Convention for the Unification of Certain Rules for International Carriage by Air, done at Montreal on 28 May 1999.
248 Ibid., Article 21.2 (*a*) and (*b*).
249 Convention for the Unification of Certain Rules Relating to International Carriage by Air, 12 October 1929.
250 1999 Westlaw 7724 (12 January 1999).
251 John G. Fleming, *The Law of Torts*, 6th edn, The Law Book Company, 1983, 1.
252 4–12 October, Warsaw, 1929.
253 *Supra*, note 249.
254 Second International Conference on Private International Law, 4–12 October 1929, Warsaw, Minutes (translated by Robert C. Horner and Didier Legrez), New Jersey: Fred B. Rottman & Co., 1975, 21.
255 Ibid., 58.
256 Ibid., 59–66.
257 Ibid., at 251–2.
258 Fleming, *supra*, note 251, p. 2.
259 Robert H. Horner and Didier Legrez, *supra*, note 254, p. 47.
260 Lee S. Kreindler, The IATA Solution, *Lloyd's Aviation Law*, 14(21), 1 November 1996, 5.
261 Ibid., 6.
262 Sean Gates, 'IATA Inter Carrier Agreement – The Trojan Horse for a Fifth Jurisdiction?' *Lloyd's Aviation Law*, 14(23), 1 December 1995, 2.
263 Convention for the Unification of Certain Rules for International Carriage by Air, Montreal, 1999. The Montreal Convention, which was signed by 52 contracting states of ICAO on 28 May 1999, would need 30 ratifications before coming into effect. Until then, the Warsaw Convention provisions and those of its instruments shall remain applicable for the most part in instances of adjudication relating to private air carrier liability.
264 Shawcross & Beaumont, *Air Law*, 4th edn, re-issue 1988, VII, 152.
265 Ibid., VII, 116.
266 Ibid., VII, 117.
267 Ibid, 116.
268 *Chisholm* v. *British European Airways* (1963) 1 *Lloyd's Rep.* 626; also *Grein* v. *Imperial Airways Ltd* (1937) 1 K.B. 50 C.A. at 69–71 *per* Greer L J.
269 See *Chisholm* v. *British European Airways*, *supra*, 629.
270 *Goldman* v. *Thai Airways International Ltd* (1981) 125 Sol. Jo. 413 (H. Ct.); also in (1983) 1 All E.R. 693.
271 (1986) 2 All E.R. 188.
272 429 F. Supp. 964 (S.D.N.Y. 1977).
273 *Preyvel* v. *Cie Air France* (1973) 27 R.F.D.A. 198; also *Rivière-Girret* v. *Ste-Aer-Inter* (1979) Uniform L.R. 173.
274 *Panalpina International Transport Ltd* v. *Densil Underwear Ltd* (1981) 1 *Lloyd's Rep.* 187.
275 *Mandreoli* v. *Cie Belge d'Assurance Aviation*, Milan 1972 (1974) Dir. Mar. 157.

276 (1982) 36 R.F.D.A. 342.
277 (1982) 36 R.F.D.A. 355.
278 Warsaw Convention, Article 21.
279 (1983) 1 All E.R. 693.
280 *Bradfield* v. *Trans World Airlines Inc.*, 152 Cal. Rep. 172 (Ca. C.A. 1972).
281 *Butler* v. *Aeromexico*, 774 F. 2d. 499 (11th Cir. 1985).
282 *Piano Remittance Corp.* v. *Varig Brazilian Airlines Inc.*, 18 Av. Cas. (C.C.H.) 18 381 (S.D.N.Y. 1984).
283 The Convention for the Unification of Certain Rules Relating to the Assistance and Salvage of Aircraft at Sea, Brussels, 1938; The Rome Convention, 1933; the Warsaw Convention, 1929.
284 Article 25.
285 H. Drion, *Limitation of Liabilities in International Air Law*, The Hague: Martinus Nijhoff, 1954, p. 195.
286 Ibid.
287 *Supra*, note 82, p. 200.
288 Georgette Miller, *Air Carrier's Liability Under the Warsaw System*, Sydney: Butterworth, 1979, 200.
289 Hague Protocol, 1955, Article XIII.
290 Miller, *supra*, note 288, 202.
291 *Revue Française de droit aérien* (R.F.D.A.) 1977, at 193.
292 5 December 1967; R.F.D.A. 184.
293 Transcript of judgment, p. 4.
294 Bin Cheng, 'Wilful Misconduct, from Warsaw to the Hague and from Brussels to Paris', *Annals of Air & Space Law*, II, 1977, 99.
295 (1983) *Law Society's Gazette*, 8 June 1983, 1485.
296 Peter Martin, 'Intentional or Reckless Misconduct, from London to Bangkok and Back Again', *Annals of Air & Space Law*, VIII, 1983, 145–9.
297 H. Drion, *Limitation of Liabilities in International Air Law*, *supra*, note 285, p. 7.
298 Ibid., p. 8.
299 Ibid.
300 Ibid., pp. 12–13.
301 *Reed* v. *Wiser*, 555 F. 2d. 1079 (2nd Cir.) at 1090.
302 Nicholas Mateesco Matte, 'The Warsaw System and the Hesitation of the United States Senate', *Annals of Air & Space Law*, VIII, 1983, 164.
303 Alexander Tobolewski, 'Against Limitation of Liability, A Radical Proposal', Annals of *Air & Space Law*, III, 1978, 63.
304 Ibid., 266.
305 Werner Guldimann, 'A Future System of Liability in Air Carriage', *Annals of Air & Space Law*, XVI, 1991, 93–104.
306 Bin Cheng, 'What is Wrong with the Montreal Additional Protocol No. 3?', *Air Law*, XIV(6), 1989, 232.
307 The Warsaw Convention of 1929 was amended by The Hague Protocol, 1955, the Guadalajara, Convention 1961, The Guatemala City Protocol, 1971 and the Montreal Protocols 1, 2, 3, 4 of varying dates. It should also be noted that the Montreal Agreement of 1966, a private arrangement between air carriers, also purported to amend the Warsaw Convention. Hereafter, joint references to all these instruments shall be 'the Warsaw system'.
308 Peter Martin, '25 Years of the Warsaw Convention', A Practical Man's Guide, *Annals of Air & Space Law*, VI, 1979, 234.
309 Ibid.
310 Bin Cheng, 'From Warsaw to the Hague', *Annals of Air & Space Law*, 11, 1977, 55.

Rene Mankiewicz also uses the word 'shambles' when he describes the Warsaw Convention. See Rene H. Mankiewicz, 'From Warsaw to Montreal With Certain Intermediate Stops', *Air Law*, XIV, 1989, 26.

311 Peter Martin, *supra*, note 308, 239.

312 *Warren* v. *Flying Tiger Line Inc.*, 352 F. 2d. 494 (C.A. 9 1965); *Mertens* v. *Flying Tiger Line Inc.*, 341 F. 2d. 841 (C.A. 2 1965).

313 21 Avi. 18 228 (1989).

314 (1983) 1 All E.R. 693.

315 D.A. Kilbride, 'Six Decades of Insuring Liability Under Warsaw', *Air Law*, XIV(4/5), 187.

316 18 Avi. 17 778, 1984.

317 *SS Pharmaceutical Co. Ltd* v. *Qantas Airways Limited*, 1988, 1 *Lloyd's Law Rep.* 319.

318 *Tasman Pulp and Paper Co. Ltd* v. *Pan American World Airways Inc.* and others; see *Annals of Air & Space Law*, XI, 1987, 323, for a detailed account.

319 Ref. LE 3/27, 3/28 - 91/3, 5.

320 Mankiewicz, *supra*, note 310, 259.

321 Michael Milde, 'ICAO Work on the Modernization of the Warsaw System', *Air Law*, XIV(4/5), 1989, 206.

322 *Infra*, note 356.

323 *Infra*, note 360.

324 See Convention for the Unification of Certain Rules Relating to International Carriage by Air, signed at Warsaw on 12 October 1929, reproduced in *Annals of Air & Space Law*, XVIII, 1993, pt II, 339.

325 Ibid., Article 25, 2.

326 H. Drion, *Limitation of Liabilities in International Air Law*, *supra*, note 290, para. 181, p. 212.

327 Ibid., para. 181.2, 213.

328 Ibid., paras 181.4 and 5, 213.

329 R.C. Horner and D. Legrez, *supra*, note 259, 42.

330 (1952) 2 All E.R. 1016 at 1022.

331 *Goepp* v. *American Overseas Airlines*, New York Supreme Court, Appellate Division (1st Dep) 16 December, 1952; [1952] U.S. Av. R. 486; IATA ACLR, No. 12.

332 *Grey* v. *American Airline Inc.*, 4 Avi. 17 811 (2nd Cir. 1955).

333 *Wing Hang Bank Ltd* v. *Japan Air Lines Co.*, 12 Avi. 17 884 (S.D.N.Y. 1973).

334 932 F. 2d 1475, 1479 (D.C. Cis), cert. denied, 1125.ct.616 (1991).

335 No. 93 C 1510, 1994 Westlaw 17 1522 (N.D. Ill. 2 May 1994).

336 Ibid.

337 *Supra*, note 334.

338 866 F. Supp. 588 (D.D.C. 1994).

339 Ibid.

340 1995 Westlaw 151 793 (E.D.N.Y. 27 March 1995).

341 No. 94-2392 (6th Cir. 15 March 1996).

342 Ibid.

343 25 Avi. Cas. (C.C.H.) 17 259 (Sup. Ct. App. Tm. N.Y. 1st Dept 1996).

344 920 F. Supp. 408 S.P.N.Y. (1996).

345 See *Koirola* v. *Thai Airways International*, 1996, Westlaw 402403 (N.D. Calif. 26 January 1996).

346 See 'Article 25 – Thai Airways found Guilty of Wilful Misconduct in 1992 Kathmandu Crash Litigation', *Lloyd's Aviation Law*, 15(6), 15 March 1996, 1.

347 Ibid., 2–3.

348 86 F. 3d. 498 (6th Cir. 1996).

349 Convention on International Civil Aviation signed in Chicago, 1944, Annex 13.

350 Shawcross & Beaumont, *supra*, note 264, VII, 153.

351 *Air France* v. *Saks*, 105 S. Ct. 1338 (1985).
352 Ibid.
353 *Husserl* v. *Swiss Air Transport Co. Ltd*, 485 F. 2d. 1240 (2nd Cir. 1975); *Day* v. *Trans World Airlines Inc.*, 528 F. 2d. 31 (2nd Cir. 1975); *Evangelinos* v. *Trans World Airlines Inc.*, 550 F. 2d. 152 (3rd Cir. 1976). See also *Salerno* v. *Pan American World Airways*, 19 Avi. Cas. 17 705 (S.D.N.Y. 1985).
354 *Arkin* v. *Trans International Airlines Inc.*, 19 Avi. Cas. 18 311 (E.D.N.Y. 1985).
355 *Abdulrahman Al-Zamil* v. *British Airways*, 770 F. 2d. 3 (2nd Cir. 1985).
356 *Seguritan* v. *Northwest Airlines Inc.*, 86 A.D. 2d. 658 (2d. Dept. 1982). See also *Lloyd's Aviation Law*, 1(4), 1 August, 1982, 1.
357 *Vincenty* v. *Eastern Airlines*, 528 F. Supp. 171 (D.P.R. 1982). Also *Lloyds Aviation Law*, 1(3), 15 July 1982, 2.
358 *Sprayregen* v. *American Airlines Inc.*, 570 F. Supp. 16 (S.D.N.Y. 1983). See also *Warshaw* v. *Trans World Airlines Inc.*, 443 F. Supp. 400 (E.D. Pa. 1977); *Pironneau* v. *Cie Air-Inter* (Pan C.A. 3 July 1986). Cf. *De Marines* v. *KLM Royal Dutch Airlines*, 586 F. 2d. 1193 (3rd Cir. 1978).
359 See *Warshaw* v. *Trans World Airlines Inc.*, *supra*, note 363, 408.
360 *O'Leary* v. *American Airlines*, 475 N.Y.S. 2d. 285 (A.D. 2d. Dept. 1984).
361 105 S. Ct. 1338 (1985).
362 Ibid., 1345.
363 *Abramson* v. *Japan Airlines Company Ltd*, 739 F. 2d. 130 (3rd Cir. 1984).
364 *Scherer* v. *Pan American World Airways Inc.*, 387 N.Y.S. 2d. 581 (1976).
365 *Supra*, note 356.
366 *Rosman* v. *Trans World Airlines Inc.*, 34 N.Y. 2d. 385 (1974).
367 *Husserl* v. *Swiss Air Transport Co. Ltd*, 388 F. Supp. 1238 (S.D.N.Y. 1975).
368 *Krystal* v. *BOAC*, 403 F. Supp. 1332 (D.C. Cal. 1975); *Karfunkel* v. *Cie Nationale Air France*, 427 F. Supp. 971 (S.D.N.Y. 1977); *Borham* v. *Pan American World Airways Inc.*, Avi. 18 236 (S.D.N.Y. 1977).
369 See R.I.R. Abeyratne, 'The Human Stress Factor and Mental Injury in American Tort Law – A Patchwork Quilt?', *The Anglo American Law Review*, 15(4), 1986, 338–60.
370 398 S.W. 2d. 170.
371 Ibid., 273–4.
372 19 Av. Cas. (C.C.H.) 17, 377 (S.D.N.Y. 1985).
373 606 F. Supp. 656 (S.D.N.Y. 1985).
374 Ibid.
375 *Supra*, note 356.
376 *Husserl* v. *Swiss Air Transport Co. Ltd*, *supra*, note 372. See also *People of the State of Illinois* v. *Gilberto*, 383 N.E. 2d. 977.
377 *Day* v. *Trans World Airlines Inc.*, 528 F. 2d. 31 (2nd Cir. 1975); *Evangelinos* v. *Trans World Airlines Inc.*, 550 F. 2d. 152 (2nd Cir. 1977); *Leppo* v. *Trans World Airlines Inc.*, 392 N.Y.S. 2d. 660 (AD 1977); *Rolnick* v. *El Al Israel Airlines Ltd*, 551 Supp. 261 (E.D.N.Y. 1982).
378 1999 Westlaw 7724 (12 January 1999).
379 116 S. Ct. 629 (1996).
380 *Supra*, note 378.
381 Resolution A29-15, Assembly Resolutions in Force, Doc. 9730, ICAO, Montreal (as of 20 October 1998) at pp. 1–42.
382 Sveinn Vidar Gudmundsson. 'The difference between European and US management practice: the case of new-entrant airlines', *Journal of Air Transport Management*, 3(2), 77–81.
383 See Mark Pilling (2001), 'Flights of Fancy', *Airline Business*, January 2001, p. 45.
384 Fariba Alamdari and Julien Farell, 'Marketing to Female Business Travellers', *Journal of Air Transportation Worldwide*, 5(2), 2000, 16.

385 Throughout this discussion, terms such as 'air freight', 'air cargo' and 'cargo' will be used interchangeably.

386 'The Supply of Air Freight Capacity to Asian Markets', Working Paper 42, Bureau of Transport Economics, Commonwealth of Australia, 2000, 1.

387 'The World of Civil Aviation 1999–2002', ICAO Circular 279-AT/116, International Civil Aviation Organization, Montreal, 27.

388 Ibid.

389 'The World of Civil Aviation 1999–2002', *supra*, note 392, para. 5.11.

390 Ibid.

391 The above figures were extracted from 'The Annual Report of the Council – 1998', Montreal: ICAO, Doc. 9732, p. 6.

392 'Air Cargo Growth to 2002 – Airlines Cautiously Optimistic?', *Airlines International*, 5(1), January 1999, p. 18.

393 AT Conf/4-WP/5, 8/8/94, 5.

394 Ibid.

395 ICAO News Release, PIO 10/94, 1.

396 Ibid.

397 *Manual on the Regulation of International Air Transport*, Montreal: ICAO, 1st edn, 1996, p. 4.5-1.

398 Eurof Thomas and David Gamper, 'Cargo: increasing throughput', *World Freight International*, 1996, pp. 28–9.

399 Express includes, inter alia, FedEx, DHL, Airborne Express and UPS. In many cases, the parcels were carried on board passenger aircraft by a courier. As volumes grew, to avoid gridlocking passenger terminals, many airports developed discrete express facilities. Consignments accepted under express service will usually be available to the consignee or their agent(s) at the airport of destination on the next business day.

400 Geoff Bridges, 'Air Cargo in the 21st Century', *International Airport Review*, 4(4), Winter 2000, 14–19.

401 Peter Conway, 'Cargo On-line', *Airline Business*, 16(2), February 2000, 78–9.

402 Michael Swindell, 'Cargo comes back off the floor', *Airlines International*, 3(2), March–April 1997, 26–30.

403 'OECD Workshop on Principles for the Liberalization of Air Cargo Transportation', Paris: OECD, 4–5 October 2000, 1–11.

404 AT Conf/4-WP/7; 14/4/94, 3.

405 See generally AT Conf/4-WP/16; 23/6/94.

406 Henri Wassenbergh, 'De-Regulation of Competition in International Air Transport', *Air & Space Law*, XII, 2 November 1996, 80.

407 The right to uplift or discharge passengers, mail and cargo in a country other than the grantor state.

408 See 'Study on Preferential Measures for Developing Countries', ICAO Doc. AT-WP/1789; 22/8/96 at A-7–A-9.

409 See Jean-Louis Magdelenat, *Air Cargo Regulations and Claims*, Toronto: Butterworth, 1983, p.1.

410 Convention for the Unification of Certain Rules Relating to International Carriage by Air, 12 October 1929, ICAO Doc. 7838, 137 L.N.T.S. 11, 49 Stat. 3000, T.S. No. 870.

411 Lopez Mapelli, *El Contrato de transporte aereo interncional: comentarios al Convenio de Varsovia*, Madrid: Editorial Tecnos, 1968 (Biblioteca Tecnos de Estudios Juridicos).

412 'Annex 9 to the Convention on International Civil Aviation (Facilitation)', 10th edn, April 1997, Montreal: ICAO, Chapter 1, Definitions. See also Georgette Miller, *Liability in International Air Transport*, Deventer: Kluwer, 1977, p.10, where the author states that the French term 'merchandises' and the English term 'goods' are not

the same: the French term denotes anything that can be the object of a commercial transaction, while under common law, 'goods' refer to inanimate objects only, thus excluding live animals.

413 *Supra*, note 409, p.6.
414 *Supra*, note 412.
415 Annex 9, Standard 4.1.
416 Ibid., Standard 4.4.
417 'Annex 17 to the Convention on International Civil Aviation (Security)', 6th edn, March 1997, Montreal: ICAO, Recommendation 2.2.1.
418 Doc. 9284.
419 'Annex 18 to the Convention on International Civil Aviation (The Safe Transport of Dangerous Goods by Air)', 2nd edn, July 1989, Standard 5.2.1.
420 Ibid., Standard 6.1.
421 Facilitation Panel (FALP), 'The Kyoto Convention, Premium Procedures and the Integrated Transaction', 4 January 1999, pp. 1–6.
422 R.H. Nankiewicz, *The Liability Regime of the International Air Carrier – A Commentary on the Present Warsaw System*, Deventer: Kluwer, 1981, p. 172.
423 See E. Ghemulla and R. Schmid (eds), *Warsaw Convention*, The Hague: Kluwer, 1998 para. 27, p. 17; also, L.B. Goldhirsh, *The Warsaw Convention Annotated: A Legal Handbook*, Dordrecht: Nijhoff, 1998, p.43.
424 *Boeringer-Mannheim Diagnostics Inc.* v. *Pan.Am*, 16 Avi. 18 177 (D.C. Tex. 1981) revised in 18 Avi. 18 090 (5th Cir. 1984) at 18 178; *Arkwright-Boston* v. *Intertrane Airfreight*, 23 Avi. 18 061 (D.C. Mass. 1991).
425 17 Avi 18,457 (D.C.N.Y. 1983).
426 *Leonid Igndesman* v. *Air Cargo Handling Services*, No. 694-0865 FMS, U.S. Dist. Lexis 1589 (D.C. Cal. 1995).
427 Tribunal of Rome, 28 December 1997, Decision No. 22915, *Air & Space Law*, XXIV, 1999, 41.
428 21 Avi. 18 496 (D.C.N.Y. 1989).
429 Georgette Miller, *supra*, note 288, p. 148.
430 Convention for the Unification of Certain Rules for International Carriage by Air, signed at Montreal on 28 May 1999, ICAO Doc. 9740.
431 Report of the Rapporteur on the Modernization and Consolidation of the Warsaw System, ICAO Doc. LC/30-WP/4, App. A, para. 5.4.14, p. A-14.
432 See The Harter Act (USA) 1893, Sec. 1, which includes such categories as master, agent, manager or owner of a vessel in its liability provisions as one who would have privity of contract in an agreement to carry goods by sea.
433 Carriage of Goods by Sea Act USA (1936) sec. 1(*a*). Also found in USAC Sec. 46: 1301. See also The Carriage of Goods by Sea (UK) 1924 Schedule, Article 1(*a*) for English Law. Both the USA and UK legislations have been influenced by the International Conference on Maritime Law in Brussels, 1922. See also The Carriage of Goods by Sea Act UK (1971) Schedule 1(*a*).
434 See United Nations Convention on the Carriage of Goods by Sea, which gave rise to a system of rules now identified as the Hamburg Rules.
435 Ibid., Article 1.2.
436 The Convention supplementary to the Warsaw Convention of 1929 for the Unification of Certain Rules Relating to International Carriage by Air Performed by a Person other than the Contracting Carrier, Guadalajara, 18 September 1961. This Convention has so far been signed by 70 states (and ratified by 64 states). See Shawcross & Beaumont, *Air Law*, 4th edn, 2 (reissue).
437 Ibid., Article I(*c*). See also Carriage by Air Act 1962 Sch. Art. 11 (UK).
438 Ibid., Article I(*b*).

439 See Convention for the Unification of Certain Rules Relating to International Carriage by Air, Warsaw, 12 October 1929, Article 6.
440 Ibid.
441 See *Anson's Law of Contract*, 25th Centenary edn, A.G. Guest (ed.), 1979, 5.
442 See Cheshire and Fifoot, *Law of Contract*, 10th edn, M.P. Furmston (ed.), 1981, 1.
443 'Assumpsit' was an action whereby an aggrieved party to a parole agreement could seek a remedy in law.
444 See P.S. Atiyah, 'Contracts, Promises and The Law of Obligations', 94 *L.Q.R.* (1978) 193 at 201.
445 See *Esso Petroleum Ltd* v. *Commissioner of Customs and Excise* (1976) 1 All E.R. 117 at 120.
446 *Rose and Frank Co.* v. *J.R. Crompton and Bros. Ltd*, (1924) All E.R. 245 at 252.
447 D.W. Greig, 'Expectations in Contractual Negotiations', 5 *Monash Uni. L.R.* (1979) 165 at 196.
448 A multimodal transport document is a document issued by the carrier who transacts with the seller to transport the seller's goods via multiple modes of transport. In such instances, there is usually no contractual privity between the seller and an actual carrier.
449 *M/S. Bremen & Unterweser Reederei GmbH* v. *Zapata Off-Shore Co.*, 407 U.S.I. 92 S.Ct. 1907, 32 L. Ed. 2d. 513 (1972) at 524.
450 G.P. Delaume, 'What is an International Contract? An American and Gallic Dilemma', I.C.L.Q., 28, 1979, 25. (This paper generally conveys the principle mentioned in the text.)
451 *Banque Hypothécaire Franco Argentine* v. *Bonn and Reynaud*, cited in Delaume, *Transnational Contracts* (1980), vol. I, s. 4.08.
452 See generally, C. Schmitthoff, *The Export Trade*, 7th edn, 1980, 6.
453 It is not proposed at this juncture to delve deep into the details of such conditions. A detailed discussion of price terms of a contract can be found in H.J. Berman and C. Kaufman. 'The Law of International Commercial Transactions (Lex Mercatoria)', *Harvard Int. Law J.*, 1978, 19(11), 231–64.
454 E. Langer, *Transnational Commercial Law*, London; Law Book Co., 1970, 215.
455 C. Schmitthoff, *Unification of the Law of International Trade*, Oxford: Oxford University Press, 1964, pp. 6–8.
456 See the Convention, Article 1.2, for a complete definition.
457 Ibid., Article 8.
458 Ibid., Article 14.
459 Ibid., Article 15.
460 See generally ibid., Article 16.
461 Ibid., Article 20 (1).
462 Ibid., Article 20 (2).
463 Ibid., Article 25.
464 N.E. Palmer, *Bailment*, New York: Transnational Publishers, 1979, p. 1.
465 Ibid., p. 14.
466 *Cogg* v. *Bernard*, 92 E.R. 107 at 109.
467 See C.W. O'Hare, 'The Duration of the Sea Carrier's Liability', Aus. Bus. L.R., 6, 1978, 65.
468 Palmer, *supra*, note 464, p.3.
469 Shawcross & Beaumont, *Air Law*, 4th edn (1), re-issue, 258.
470 *Tasman Pulp & Paper Co. Ltd* v. *Brambles, J.B. O'Loghlen Ltd and Pan American World Airways Inc.* (1982) N.Z.L.R. 225. See *Air Law*, VII, 1982, 64–5.
471 Philip Cross, 'Trucking Air Cargo: The Application of the Warsaw System to Bimodal Transport', LLM thesis, McGill, 1993, p. 11. See also Adeline M. Briant, 'A Critical Look at the United Nations Convention on International Multimodal Transport of Goods', (Geneva, 24 May 1980), LLM thesis, 1996, p. 21.

472 TD/MT/CONF/16, Geneva Conference (1979–80) documents; United Nations Conference on International Multimodal Transport of Goods, *Annals of Air & Space Law*, VI, 1981, 657–91.
473 Italian Court de Cassation, Judgment no. 6841, 19 June 1993, discussed in *Air & Space Law*, XIX, 1994, 288.
474 Eugene A. Massey, 'Prospect for a New Intermodal Legal Regime: A Critical Look at the TCM', *J. Marit. L. & Com.*, 3, 1972, 726.
475 Briant, *supra*, note 471, 67.
476 ICC Publication No. 298 (October 1975).
477 Convention for the Unification of Certain Rules Relating to International Carriage by Air, signed at Warsaw on 12 October 1929. Hereafter referred to as the Convention.
478 Ibid., Article 5.
479 Ibid., Article 9.
480 See Peter Conway, 'Cancelled 747 FX Leaves Cargo Void', *Airline Business*, May 2001, p. 11.

Chapter 3

The Security Crisis

INTRODUCTION OF NEW SECURITY MEASURES

Enhancement of aviation security measures would require the user to comply with the demands made by modern security equipment. As discussed in Chapter 1 of this book, such techniques as biometric identification of human features and electronic scanning of passport details will involve the rights of the airline passenger. Recent developments in trans-border data flows of private information, particularly concerning air travel, have raised the issue of the rights of the data subject in terms of his privacy. This discussion will critically analyse the legal issues involved in the right of privacy of the data subject and compare transatlantic legislative initiatives taken.

The data subject, like any other person, has an inherent right to his privacy. The subject of privacy has been identified as an intriguing and emotive one.[1] The right to privacy is inherent in the right to liberty, and is the most comprehensive of rights and the right most valued by civilized man.[2] This right is susceptible to being eroded, as modern technology is capable of easily recording and storing dossiers on every man, woman and child in the world.[3] The data subject's right to privacy is brought into focus by Alan Westin, who says: 'Privacy is the claim of individuals, groups or institutions to determine for themselves when, how and to what extent information is communicated to others'.[4]

Legally speaking, there are three rights of privacy relating to the storage and use of personal data:

1. the right of an individual to determine what information about oneself to share with others, and to control the disclosure of personal data;
2. the right of an individual to know what data are disclosed, and what data are collected and where such are stored when the data in question pertains to that individual; the right to dispute incomplete or inaccurate data; and
3. the right of people who have a legitimate right to know in order to maintain the health and safety of society and to monitor and evaluate the activities of government.[5]

It is incontrovertible therefore that the data subject has a right to decide what information about himself to share with others and, more importantly, to know what data are collected about him. This right is balanced by the right of a society to collect data about individuals that belong to it so that the orderly running of government is ensured.

Issues of privacy

The role played by technology in present-day commercial transactions has affected a large number of activities pertaining to human interaction. The emergence of the information superhighway and the concomitant evolution of automation have inevitably transformed the social and personal life styles and value systems of individuals, created unexpected business opportunities, reduced operating costs, accelerated transaction times, facilitated accessibility to communications, shortened distances and removed bureaucratic formalities.[6] Progress notwithstanding, technology has bestowed on humanity its corollaries in the nature of automated mechanisms, devices, features and procedures which intrude into personal lives of individuals. For instance, when a credit card is used, it is possible to track purchases, discovering numerous aspects about that particular individual, including, food inclination, leisure activities and consumer credit behaviour.[7] In similar vein, computer records of an air carrier's reservation system may give out details of the passenger's travel preferences, including inter alia, seat selection, destination fondness, ticket purchasing dossier, lodging preference, temporary address and telephone contacts, attendance at theatres and sport activities, and whether the passenger travels alone or with someone else.[8] This scheme of things may well give the outward perception of surveillance attributable to computer devices monitoring individuals' most intimate activities and preferences, leading to the formation of a genuine 'traceable society'.[9] The main feature of this complex web of technological activity is that an enormous amount of personal information handled by such varied players from the public and private sector, may bring about concerns of possible 'data leaks' in the system, a risk that could have drastic legal consequences affecting an individual's rights to privacy.

At the international level, privacy was first recognized as a fundamental freedom in the Universal Declaration of Human Rights.[10] Thereafter, several other human rights conventions followed the same trend, granting to individuals the fundamental right of privacy.[11] The pre-eminent concern of these international instruments was to establish a necessary legal framework to protect the individual and his rights inherent to the enjoyment of a private life.

Privacy represents different things for different people.[12] The concept *per se* has evolved throughout the history of mankind, from the original non-intrusion approach, which defended an individual's property and physical body against unwanted invasions and intrusions, then manifesting in whom to associate with, later enlarging its scope to include privacy as the individual's decision-making right,[13] and culminating in the control over one's personal information.[14] Thus the conceptual evolution of privacy is directly related to the technological advancement of each particular period in history.

The right of privacy, as enunciated by the United States Judge Thomas M. Cooley, was the right 'to be let alone' as a part of a more general right to one's personality. This idea was given further impetus by two prominent young lawyers, Samuel D. Warren and Louis D. Brandeis,[15] in 1890.[16] Before this idea was introduced, the concept of privacy reflected primarily a somewhat physical property or life. The foundations of 'information privacy', whereby the individuals would determine when, how and to what extent information about themselves would be communicated to others, inextricably drawing the right of control of information about oneself,[17] is a cornerstone of privacy. With the development of computer capabilities to handle large amounts of data, privacy has been enlarged to include the collection, storage, use, and disclosure of personal information.[18] The notion of informational privacy protection, a typically American usage, has been particularly popular both in the United States and in Europe, where the term 'data protection' is used.[19]

Self-determination in the right to protect one's privacy was first judicially embraced by the German Bundesverfassungsgericht in 1983.[20] The US Supreme court followed this trend by adopting the principle of privacy self-determination in *DOJ* v. *Reporters Comm. for Freedom of the Press*.[21]

It must be borne in mind that privacy is not an absolute, unlimited right that operates and applies in isolation.[22] It is not an absolute right, applied unreservedly, to the exclusion of other rights. Hence there is frequently the necessity to balance privacy rights with other conflictive rights, such as the freedom of speech and the right to access to information when examining individuals' rights *vis-à-vis* the interest of society.[23] This multiplicity of interests will prompt courts to adopt a balanced approach when adjudicating on a person's rights, particularly where interests of a state are involved.

Privacy issues in the United States

It would not be incorrect to recognize the fact that the right of privacy originally evolved in the United States following the appearance of an influential article written by Warren and Brandeis.[24] This article was prompted by the increasing intrusion of the newspaper media, particularly the 'yellow press', which publicly scrutinized personal issues of the Bostonian society in the late 1800s.[25] Although the article stresses the importance of protecting the individual right of privacy from the mass media invasion thereto by suggesting that an independent cause of action under tort law is necessitated, the issue remains primarily applicable to private individuals.[26]

The right of privacy brings to bear the need to identify possible scenarios when addressing issues of privacy rights. The United States has a two-pronged approach to the right of privacy: privacy rights between the individual and the state, and privacy rights between individuals themselves. The former consideration involves US constitutional law, since indirect references to privacy are enclosed in the Bill of Rights, involving federal legislation, including some specific legislation Congress has enacted.[27] The latter is addressed through the law of torts, and is hence a state matter involving specific legislation regulating certain industries.[28] It should be noted that the United States has adopted the approach of sectoral regulation in terms of privacy, as opposed to the enactment of 'omnibus data protection statutes' undertaken in Europe.[29] This makes US conceptualization of the right of the privacy to admit of as little government interference as possible. The rationale for the approach in the United States is encompassed in three factual bases. Firstly, a large number of Americans believe that their rights can be adequately protected through the implementation of industry codes, norms and business practices, company policies, proper technical network structure, good corporate citizenship through the implementation of guidelines,[30] and perhaps even through contractual arrangements, particularly on the basis that the market has matured sufficiently to be self-regulated.[31]

This attitude reflects the trust of the American people in the private sector. *A contrario*, numerous commentators, and predominantly civil liberties groups, have expressed profound concerns about whether further government intervention has become mandatory.[32] Secondly, the tremendous power of influential industry lobbying groups strongly opposes any further government intervention with business. US lobbying groups have direct access to the White House, thus representing considerably more bargaining power than the individual data subject.[33] Thirdly, the United States favours free flow of information according to the principles embraced by the First Amendment,[34] based on the premise that the availability of information will be regulated by market place ideas, hence reflecting an enormous trust therein.[35] In addition, some commentators suggest that excessive protection of personal information would inevitably distort efficient market functions.[36] Therefore it is unlikely the US Congress will enact a general comprehensive set of rules addressing privacy, as contained in the European spectrum.[37]

Commentators in the United States have identified five dimensions or categories of privacy. 'Physical Privacy' would be addressed through issues related to the physical integrity of the individual, originally protected through the tort of trespass to the person.[38] Secondly, 'Decisional Privacy' is embraced in the landmark *Roe* v. *Wade*,[39] where the US Supreme Court extended the right of privacy to make one's own decisions on activities related to marriage, procreation, contraception, abortion, family relationships and education. Thirdly, 'Communications Privacy' is related to the First Amendment's Freedom of Speech and Association, whereby an individual is granted the right to freely communicate among peers. Fourthly, 'Territorial Privacy' seeks to set limits or boundaries on intrusion into a specific space or area in one's property. Fifthly, 'Information Privacy' addresses control of handling of personal data.[40]

The US Constitution does not include any direct reference to privacy within its text. However, the Bill of Rights addresses the issue indirectly, through the First Amendment rights of Freedom of Speech, Press and Association,[41] the Third Amendment,[42] relating to the quartering of soldiers, the Fourth Amendment right to be free from unreasonable searches,[43] and the Fourteenth Amendment containing the due process clause.[44] Most constitutional issues related to privacy have been dealt with through the Fourth Amendment. All this notwithstanding, the recognition of privacy rights within the US constitutional law was somewhat late, which is surprising for a nation so involved in recognizing the protection of civil liberties. The first incidence of recognizing individual privacy rights was in the opinion of Justice Louis Brandeis in *Olmstead*,[45] which concerned the constitutional right of the individual's privacy.[46] Brandeis energetically pursued the legal ground for protection of the right of privacy against the unlawful intrusion of the state into one's personal affairs. However, in *Olmstead*,[47] the US Supreme Court upheld the ruling of the Circuit Court of Appeals for the Ninth Circuit, which had held that obtaining evidence without physically invading constitutionally protected areas, for instance through wiretapping, did not constitute a violation of the Fourth Amendment and therefore did not constitute an illegal search. The court's decision created the requisite of a physical invasion adopting the so-called 'trespass theory' of searches and seizures of tangible property, thereby enlarging the scope of government intrusion in the individual's private life.[48] The first federal constitutional case where the right of privacy was officially recognized by the US Supreme Court was

Griswold v. *Connecticut*,[49] where Justice Douglas, delivering the majority opinion of the court, observed that 'specific guarantees of the Bill of Rights have penumbras, formed by emanations from those guarantees that help give them life and substance … Various guarantees create zones of privacy'.[50] The opinion of Justice Douglas acknowledged the protection of privacy contained in the Bill of Rights, inferring the applicability of the First, Third, Fourth, Fifth and Ninth Amendments thereto. The fundamental value of this case lies in the recognition of the court that several parts of the US Bill of Rights indirectly refer to and thus protect the right of privacy. Subsequently, *contrario sensu* to its original ruling in *Olmstead*, the US Supreme Court in the landmark case *Katz* v. *United States*[51] adopted a broader interpretation of the protection of privacy rights, stating that the Fourth Amendment protects people rather than zones or areas of privacy, leaving behind the 'trespass' tangible requirement previously adopted in *Olmstead*.[52]

In the 1979 case of *Smith* v. *Maryland*,[53] the US Supreme Court had to address the issue as to whether the installation of a pen register tape[54] at a telephone company upon police request, for the purpose of listening to a phone conversation of a presumed robber, constituted a search requiring a warrant under the Fourth Amendment. The US Supreme Court held that, when the data subject does not have a 'legitimate expectation of privacy', the installation of such pen register tape for the purpose of monitoring calls does not constitute a search. The court established the 'legitimate expectation of privacy test' comprising a twofold requirement. First, the court analysed whether the individual had a legitimate expectation of privacy. If that were to be the case, the court proceeded to examine whether society is prepared to recognize that expectation as reasonable, and whether the individual is entitled to be free from unreasonable governmental intrusion. In a similar approach, Justice Breyer, in his dissenting judgment in *Bond* v. *United States*,[55] expressed his deep concern about the fact that the 'actual expectation of privacy' is of a subjective matter, but its determination must be 'objectively' reasonable.[56] It is indeed interesting that the 'legitimate expectation of privacy test' established in *Smith* v. *Maryland* places an onerous burden on the individual, who must prove not only infringement of a right, but also the reasonableness of his 'legitimate expectation' thereto. Additionally, the second component of the aforesaid test confers a significant discretionary spectrum of decision making on the courts on a case-by-case basis. Under the circumstances, it would be legitimate to consider the level of privacy protection given to the data subject by this precedent, particularly in view of various lower courts' decisions in the United States.[57]

Hitherto, all the cases examined herein dealt with general issues of privacy protection in US courts, but with no direct reference to the implementation of automation devices to collect personal data, as is the case this study pursues. In *Whalen* v. *Roe*,[58] the US Supreme Court was required to address the issue as to whether the State of New York may record in a centralized computer file the names and addresses of all persons who have obtained, pursuant to a doctor's prescription, certain drugs for which there is both a lawful and an unlawful market. The court held in favour of the State of New York and pronounced that there was no invasion of privacy, concluding that the state does have the right to collect such data for public purposes. This case has a certain compelling effect on issues pertaining to personal data by the state or any government agency.[59]

In *Iacobucci* v. *Newport*,[60] the US Court of Appeals for the Sixth Circuit held the right of the City of Newport to request compliance with the fingerprinting ordinance for all bar employees. Accordingly, in *Perkey* v. *Department of Motor Vehicles*,[61] the Californian Court was in favour of asserting the right of the state to require individual citizens to provide fingerprints prior to obtaining a licence. In *Skinner* v. *Railway Labour Executives Association*,[62] the US Supreme Court acknowledged that a state regulation compelling the collection and testing of railway employees' urine constituted a 'search subject to the demands of the Fourth Amendment'; however, applying the public interest test to the case in question, the US Supreme Court considered that the state regulation sought to achieve public safety for the benefit of society, which indeed outweighed the individual's expectation of privacy. Then, in *Vernonia* v. *Wayne Acton*,[63] the US Supreme Court held that a school district's policy authorizing drug testing of students participating in the district's athletics programmes did not violate the Fourth Amendment because the public interest was best served thereby.[64]

The foregoing cases clearly support the argument that US courts, within the public sphere of the constitutional right of privacy, show a tendency to establish the twofold test conceived in *Smith* v. *Maryland*, whereby the individual's expectation of privacy is balanced against the public interest of society. Therefore it becomes clear that, when a federal agency seeks to implement automated devices such as biometric measurement embedded in a smart card with the purpose of accelerating the passenger traffic flows, rarely will US courts find a situation where a privacy right under the protection of the Fourth Amendment has been violated, because the public interest is best served.

Privacy issues in Europe

The realm of privacy rights in Europe is diametrically opposed to that of the United States. Europe has emphasized more legislative edict in accordance with its long-standing civil law background, and followed an approach based on predicting the probable consequences of the emergence of particular phenomena, as has been reflected in the enactment of omnibus regulation, rather than letting law evolve as a consequence of judicial experiences.

The European approach to privacy protection is deeply rooted in the reference made to the right of privacy in the European Convention for the Protection of Human Rights and Fundamental Freedoms,[65] whereby Article 8 establishes it as a fundamental human right.[66] Hence Europe tends to approach privacy as a pre-eminent concern of humanity where as much foreseeable protection as possible should be enforced at law.[67] With the introduction of the Convention, numerous countries in Europe started enacting regulation addressing privacy.[68]

Later, the Council of Europe, pursuant to Resolution 73/22, adopted the Convention for the Protection of Individuals With Regard to Automatic Processing of Personal Data,[69] based on OECD model recommendation guidelines, on 28 January 1981.[70] Although the Convention included only automated processing of data, leaving manual processing out of its scope, it set forth the early goals pursued by the European authorities, identifying many of the issues that remain relevant in modern legislation nowadays. However, the main flaw of this instrument lies in the fact that it was only ratified by a small number of countries and, hence, failed to achieve a standard degree of privacy protection within Europe.[71] Therefore the European Commission acknowledged the necessity to take further action to achieve such goals by requiring states to harmonize privacy data legislation. Thus the path was set for the advent of the European Data Privacy Directive.[72]

On 24 October 1995, the European Parliament and the Council passed Directive 95/46 on the protection of the processing and movement of personal data.[73] The intention of the EC Directive's framers was to equalize the disparity of levels of privacy data protection within Europe, whereby countries such as France and Germany had very comprehensive legislation, but others like Italy and Greece had none. The EC Directive, which came into force in 1998, gives substance to and amplifies those provisions contained in the European Convention. The enactment of the directive was chosen by the European Commission in order to permit states to level their legislation with the minimum standards set within the directive's legal framework.[74] The aim of the EC directive is to harmonize the existing law of its member states.[75] It is the responsibility of each member state to develop its own privacy data legislation in accordance with the directive, which lays out the legal model to follow. However, one can reasonably foresee the emergence of numerous disparities when each country enacts its own legislation, a situation that could be aggravated when different administrative agencies and courts are called on to interpret the provisions contained therein.

The EC directive seeks to 'protect the fundamental rights and freedoms of natural persons, and in particular their right to privacy with respect to the processing of personal data'.[76] As clearly identified by Schwarz and Reidemberg, the directive has four main purposes: (1) to create norms for collecting and processing personal data;[77] (2) to provide an opportunity for affected individuals to renew information collected about themselves and to review the compiler's information practices; (3) to offer special protection for sensitive data, such as data pertaining to ethnic origins, religion, or political affiliation; and (4) to establish enforcement mechanisms and oversight systems to ensure that data protection principles are respected.[78] This thesis will proceed to analyse comprehensively the provisions relevant to the emerging trends on automation in facilitation of air transport.

The scope of applicability of the EC directive is extended to personal data wholly or partly processed[79] by automatic and manual means, as long as they form part or are intended to form part of a filing system.[80] This constitutes a major difference from its predecessor, the European Convention, which was solely intended to cover the automatic process of drawing the line between manual and automatic processing. Furthermore, the EC directive presents a twofold exclusionary approach: (1) it is not applicable to activities that fall outside the scope of Community law, and matters concerning the state, such as public and national security, defence, economic well-being of the state involved, criminal investigation and breaches of ethics in the regulated professions; and (2) it is not applicable to any data related to purely personal or household activities.[81] The exclusion from the directive's scope of issues such as defence, national security and criminal investigation *per se*, removes ambiguity for future judicial interpretations, which may clarify the application of national privacy data protection laws in a large number of cases. *A contrario*, American courts are often faced with the necessity to formulate juridical tests, in order to confront and balance those interests.

The EC directive undoubtedly establishes its jurisdiction by denoting that the law of each member state shall be applicable as long as: (1) the processing is carried out by a controller[82] in the territory of a member state; or (2) the controller is not located in a member state's territory, but, in order to process data, uses equipment that is located in the territory of a member state. In addition, the controller has to nominate a representative for cases where he does not operate directly in the territory of a member state, but rather uses equipment located therein.[83] *Ab initio*, the EC directive's jurisdiction specifications pose significant consequences for the air transport sector, particularly considering its feasible extraterritorial applications. For example, and bearing in mind the enormous amount of personal passenger information that carriers handle,[84] an international airline such as Aerolinas Argentinas may use an Amadeus Computer Reservation System (CRS), owned and controlled by a European carrier such as Lufthansa. Hence, even though Aerolinas Argentinas, the controller, is located outside the territorial jurisdiction of the European Union, the provisions contained in the EC directive will be directly applicable, because unarguably the non-European carrier is using automated equipment situated in the territory of a member state for the purpose of processing personal data.[85] One can certainly foresee that the European authorities will most likely favour the extension of such extraterritorial application to the non-European carrier, when the latter handles the personal data of member states' citizens. Furthermore, the EC directive will even be applicable to cases where a non-European airline has a frequent flyer smart card sponsored by a European bank. The possibilities and combinations are endless, but the foregoing examples remain common practices in the air transport industry.

Data subject's bill of rights

The EC directive grants a large number of privacy rights to the individual, and thus could be labelled as the 'Data Subject Bill of Rights'. Hence the individual is bestowed with the right to know the identity of the controller and his representative, and the purposes of processing for which the data are required.[86] In other words, when air carriers' employees swipe a passport through the reader device or input the data manually to comply with API procedures, they ought to inform the data subjects of the purpose for which such data are collected, which in practice does not usually happen. Similarly, in more complex situations, such as smart cards with biometrics embedded in them, the controller should tell the data subject who is handling the information and for what purposes, which could be somewhat difficult to determine owing to the large number of players involved. For instance, if various players were to handle passenger data on a 'need to know' basis, this could raise tremendous difficulties when establishing who the controller is. In an earlier article, the author has already observed that a state issuing machine readable travel documents is legally obliged to inform the bearer of the details enclosed therein.[87]

As provided by the United States, the EC directive grants the individual the right to access information handled by the controller. The main difference between the previously mentioned two legal regimes lies in the fact that the former only includes activities undertaken by the government and its agencies, whereas the latter is particularly directed at private and public organizations that happen to store, control or process the individual's personal data.[88] The data subject bill of rights permits the request for correction and erasure of any data processing, that is not in accordance with the provisions enclosed in the EC directive.[89] Additionally, the data subject may object to the processing of personal information at any time as long as he has legitimate grounds to do so.[90] It is important to note that the data subject bill of rights legally empowers the individual against possible invasions, intrusions or infringements of privacy rights, whereas the burden is placed on controllers and processors of data, a situation that is totally different in the United States.[91] Therefore one can easily expect that privacy claims will more likely succeed within the legal spectrum given by the EC directive. In addition, the person acting under the authority of the controller or the processor must assure the confidentiality of processing, responding only to the instructions and orders of the controller, making the latter responsible in the event of any infringement of privacy rights.[92] The foregoing *ab initio* has direct implications for the air transport automation context since almost all of the facilitation initiatives envision the inclusion of a large number of persons dealing with massive amounts of personal data.

Security concerns are also addressed by those in control of databases to provide appropriate technical and organizational measures and to avoid potential information leaks. The personal data protection is particularly crucial for the air transport environment.[93] One of the most noteworthy achievements of the EC directive has been the establishment of supervisory authorities, which are the bodies responsible for monitoring compliance with the provisions enclosed therein.[94]

The EC directive specifically mandates each member state to confer the necessary legal remedies against any breaches of privacy rights.[95] The data subject is entitled to receive compensation from the controller in the case where damage is sustained. Although the burden of proof is on the controller's side, he may be exempt if he proves that he is not responsible for the damage.[96] This is the pro-data subject spirit of the EC directive, which not only grants fundamental rights for the protection of privacy, but also provides the mechanisms to correct any deviation of the system. Perhaps this is one of the advantages of creating a specific legal framework to deal with an emerging problem or, where every situation has been carefully studied, of trying to envision all the possible derivatives; *contrario sensu*, in the United States the approach has been to let the existing legal system respond to each arising difficulty and develop from experience. However, the detractors of the former would argue that this type of legal framework is rather static and non-flexible, handicaps that do not allow the judiciary to adapt themselves quickly enough to emerging technological advances. The latter will always precede the enactment of legal rules and the entrepreneurial air transport sector will not favour a stationary business attitude awaiting legal regulations to solve the arising problems.

The EC directive asserts that member states, through the application of their national laws, must guarantee the directive's full implementation, and must also impose sanctions in the case of infringements.[97] This obligation placed on member states represents a risk for controllers, who will be forced to demand that insurers extend insurance coverage against any possible liability that might arise therefrom, thus swelling premium rates and thereby affecting operational costs.[98]

The data subject has a legal right to know what goes into a data bank with regard to his details. Accordingly, states that store such information are legally obligated to inform the data subject of the nature of the details that they may include in such public documents as his passport and to make arrangements to inform him of the information stored in governmental computers relating to him. Any indecipherable data should be clearly explained to the data subject so that he may: (1) determine whether such data should be disclosed to the public; (2) determine the accuracy of the details entered into the computer; (3) be informed of the specific use of his personal data that is stored in the computer; (4) be informed of the type of persons who would have access to the personal data that is stored; and (5) evaluate the quantum of personal information about him that is actually stored.

Since the data contained in such documents as are machine-readable, such as passports and visas, would be subject to trans-border storage, there is a compelling need to consider the introduction of uniform privacy laws in order that the interests of the data subject and the data seeker are protected. Although complete uniformity in privacy legislation may be a difficult objective to attain[99] (as has been the attempt to make other aspects of legislation uniform), it will be well worth the while of the international community to at least formulate international standards and recommended practices (on the lines of the various ICAO Annexes) to serve as guidelines for state conduct. After all, as Collin Mellors has pointed out:

> Under international agreements ... privacy is now well established as a universal, natural, moral and human right. Article 12 of the Universal Declaration of Human Rights, Article 17 of the United Nations Covenant on Civil and Political Rights and Article 8 of the European Convention for the Protection of Human Rights and Fundamental Freedoms, all specify this basic right to privacy. Man everywhere has occasion to seek temporary 'seclusion or withdrawal from society' and such arrangements cannot define the precise area of the right to privacy.[100]

It is such a definition that is now needed so that the two requirements of ensuring respect for information about individuals and their privacy on the one hand, and the encouragement of free and open dissemination of trans-border data flows on the other, are reconciled.

As for the use of biometric information such as hand geometry and eye scanning, such information is purely biological and should be used only for identification purposes, with an explicit undertaking by the authorities concerned who use the information that it will not be used for any purpose other than for the purposes of identification. Before a process for the collection of such information is formally put into practice, legal issues of ownership and patent should be carefully thought out, and given foremost consideration.

CONDUCT OF AIRLINE CREW AND HUMAN INTERACTION

Enhanced awareness of aviation security and the implementation of more stringent security measures inside the aircraft, both while it is on the ground and when it is airborne, become critical factors of determinacy in the conduct of airline crew and how such conduct would affect the passenger. There is also the compelling issue of interaction between the technical crew and the cabin crew on a flight. Finally, the aspect of the conduct of a passenger under stress should also be considered as a reckonable factor in the new aviation environment.

At any given time, aircraft of commercial airlines keep 1·2 million passengers aloft. In the process, these airlines carry thieves, pickpockets, drug addicts and con men, among other passengers. Most states do not have legislation to provide for crimes on board aircraft. At the time of writing (January 2001), there was concern in the airline industry about a stewardess who was critically wounded with a knife by a drunken passenger who was a British subject, on board an aircraft flying over German territory and registered in the Middle East. When the aircraft landed in its destination, the offender was only fined $1000 and released, as there were no laws in that country which would apply to the offence.

Little comfort, indeed, for the many thousands of flight attendants who attend to the slightest whim of all those people who are airborne at any given moment. One could well ask the question, if there are 'bouncers' at night clubs, railway security in trains, and hotel security in hotels to protect hapless staff who serve customers, why is there no such protection for the 'ministering angels' of the air transport industry? One would have thought that, in commercial aviation, where the tyranny of distance is obviated by the most sophisticated aircraft, and the ostentation of wining and dining in the most glamorous five star hotel in the world is made to look 'run of the mill' by delectable cuisine served by highly professional flight kitchens, there would be provision made to protect the airline staff on board who serve the passengers during a flight. After all, in a profession such as this, everyone is well cared for, from the humble 'chap' in overalls who checks out the aircraft before the flight, to the confident captain who pilots the aircraft.

Of course, as lawyers, we could always argue that there is the Tokyo Convention of 1963 which in Article 1 makes the Convention applicable to offences against penal law and acts which, inter alia, may jeopardize the safety of persons on board. We can also argue that Article 6 of the Tokyo Convention empowers the captain to impose 'reasonable measures' upon a person in order to protect persons or property in the aircraft. If the captain is of the view that a person has committed, or is about to commit, an offence on another, he is even empowered by Article 8 of the Convention to disembark the offender in a state in which the aircraft lands.

The question is, how are all these 'legal' provisions going to help a poor flight attendant who is assaulted by a drunk, a drug addict or a thief? Does the captain run into the cabin and assist his fellow crew members before an act of violence is committed on them, or does he take subsequent action as provided by the Tokyo Convention? What compensation can the poor crew member get from the complex and elaborate system of laws that apply to passengers, say, under the Warsaw System?

There is no doubt that cabin crew form an integral part of commercial aviation, and they should also come under universal training methods and codes of conduct, as do the pilots, mechanics, aeronautical engineers and other professionals who are involved with the successful operation of a commercial flight. There is a compelling need for the international aviation community to require a serious study on the feasibility of introducing a unified system of rules relating to the conduct of cabin crew, which could inter alia, include principles of protection of cabin crew and provide for compensation in the case of injury. After all, they are the only ones who deal with the 'human factor' of a flight, which could be most unpredictable at the best of times.

The lack of attention paid by the aviation community to the importance of the flight attendant's role in a commercial flight has led to recurring instances of breakdown of communication between cabin crew and technical crew. Inevitably, this anomaly may pose serious problems in the area of air carrier liability. It is heartening to note, however, that there is now a growing awareness of the status of the flight attendant in commercial aviation. For instance, in 1994, the United States officially recognized that flight attendants have demonstrated a critical role in the safety of passengers, by limiting the length of their duty times and introducing mandatory rest periods under federal law. Under Federal Aviation Administration (FAA) regulations, flight attendants must be given at least nine hours' rest for duty periods lasting up to 14 hours in any 24-hour period. For longer periods, the FAA prescribes specific rest periods and larger cabin crews. The rules also give flight attendants a full 24 hours of rest for every seven calendar days. Federal law had previously mandated minimum rest periods for air traffic controllers and technical crew.[101]

There have been innumerable complaints in the past by technical crews (pilots and flight engineers) relating to unacceptable cabin crew conduct that has allegedly jeopardized flight safety. A commentary published in March 1995 reported that, during a hectic night approach to a busy airport in the United States, a flight attendant had opened the door to the flight deck to remove dinner trays, flooding the cockpit with light and distracting the flight crew. The flight attendant had refused the captain's earlier request to bring meals forward early in the flight, and the food was brought in only after the descent had begun.[102] In his report, the captain had written that 'the approach was unsafe' and described a serious breakdown in communication between the cockpit crew and the cabin crew. Confirming a near miss with a smaller aircraft which was claimed by the captain to have occurred as a result of the commotion caused by the unfortunate entry of the flight attendant to the cockpit, the captain had gone on to record:

> The captain is helpless to plan the approach any more. The flight attendants ignore requests and directions from the captain. They work for the marketing department and don't hesitate to tell pilots they don't have to listen to them. On this flight, the flight attendant's blatant disregard of the captain's request resulted in an unsafe approach. If the flight attendant had listened to the captain's request to bring meals up, she would not have been in the cockpit at low altitude causing a distraction.[103]

There have also been instances where cabin crew members have been instrumental in causing involuntary injury to passengers. One such instance was when a passenger on board an American Airlines flight from Italy to Chicago was injured when a heavy tote bag fell on her from the overhead bin in the aircraft. This injury had been caused as a result of the flight attendant opening the overhead bin to retrieve a pillow at the request of the passenger. One of the considerations the court had to decide upon was the plaintiff's contention that American Airlines had failed to provide adequate instructions to its crew on the operation of aircraft apparatus.[104]

Clearly, the conduct of cabin crew members during the course of their employment would affect two classes of persons: passengers in the cabin and technical crew in the cockpit. In both instances, any adverse conduct on the part of cabin crew which would in turn result in claims for damages would affect the employer airline adversely, bringing to bear the intrinsic and incontrovertible link between the airline and its cabin crew members. Also any liability that would arise out of the conduct of cabin crew would involve air carrier liability on principles of vicarious liability at tort. The next section will therefore examine the role of the flight attendant and air carrier liability, with emphasis on general principles of air carrier liability as they revolve round the conduct of the flight attendant. There will also be a discussion of the relationship of the flight attendant with the passenger on the one hand, and the pilot on the other, with a view to eliciting principles of air carrier liability in both instances where the conduct of the flight attendant precipitates a claim by a passenger or the representative of the passenger for injury by the air carrier.

AIR CARRIER LIABILITY

General principles

The Warsaw Convention of 1929[105] provides that, for the transportation of passengers, the carrier must deliver a passenger ticket which shall contain certain details.[106] The Convention also says that the absence, irregularity or loss of the passenger ticket shall not affect the existence of the validity of the contract of transportation which shall nonetheless be subject to the rules of the Convention. Nevertheless, if the carrier accepts a passenger without a passenger ticket having been delivered, he shall not be entitled to avail himself of those provisions of the Convention that exclude his liability.[107]

The Warsaw Convention imposes a presumption of liability on the carrier in the case of death or injury caused to a passenger. As a precaution against the possible 'floodgates' of litigation that this presumption could give rise to, the Convention limits liability of a carrier to specified sums of money, unless it could be proved that the carrier did not take necessary precautions to avoid death or injury to its passengers or was guilty of wilful misconduct. Damage for death or injury under the Convention is linked to an 'accident'. An accident, as envisaged in Article 17 of the Warsaw Convention has sometimes been given a broader definition than in ordinary legal parlance. While, in ordinary common law usage, an accident is an event which, under the circumstances is unusual and unexpected,[108] The Chicago Convention of 1944 defines an 'accident' as an occurrence connected with the operation of an aircraft.[109] Article 17 of the Warsaw Convention speaks of liability of a carrier in the event of an accident which caused damage, reducing the accident to the cause rather than to the death or injury.[110] The United States Supreme Court has held, in *Air France* v. *Saks*,[111] that an accident must be unexpected and external to the passenger. It is not sufficient that the plaintiff suffers injury as a result of his own internal reaction to the usual, normal and expected operation of the aircraft.[112] In *De Marines* v. *KLM Royal Dutch Airlines*,[113] a case with facts identical to those of the *Saks* case, the court reasoned:

> An accident is an event, a physical circumstance, which unexpectedly takes place not according to the usual course of things. If the event, on board the airplane, is an ordinary, expected and usual occurrence, then it cannot be termed an accident. To constitute an accident, the occurrence on board the aircraft must be unusual, an unexpected happening.[114]

At air law, therefore, it is clear that an accident has to be an unexpected event, as at common law. The distinction lies in the cause, and the attendant circumstances thereupon that regard such incidents as bombings, hijacking, terrorist attacks to be considered as accidents, together with aircraft crashes,[115] more on the grounds of the conduct of the airline based on the cause of the 'accident' than on an incident itself. Arguably, the case which clearly and unequivocally brings out the contextual juridical application of the word 'accident' in air carrier liability is *Seguritan* v. *Northwest Airlines*,[116] where, in an instance where a passenger suffered a massive coronary seizure in flight, the court held that the accident was not the seizure itself but the failure on the part of the carrier to render medical assistance. The carrier's failure to render medical assistance was the accident 'which caused the damage' inasmuch as, according to the court, a carrier's failure to provide adequate security to passengers in an instance of a terrorist attack.

The *Day–Evangelinos* test,[117] or, as it is sometimes called, the 'tripartite test' evolved with the emerging difficulties of judicial interpretation of Article 17 of the Warsaw Convention.[118] The provision admits of compensation being awarded only if an accident takes place 'on board the aircraft or in the course of any of the operations of embarking or disembarking'.[119] The arcane precision with which many accidents have occurred after the enactment of this provision, and their varied nature, has given rise to notable judicial fecundity in the interpretation of the words 'embarking' and 'disembarking'. Although the words 'on board the aircraft' do not present complex issues *in limine*, there has been at least one instance where the time spent by passengers in a hotel consequent to a hijacking has been interpreted as time spent 'on board', on the basis that, if not for the *novus actus interveniens* of a hijacking that impelled the passengers to seek solace in a hotel room, they would have been on board the aircraft anyway.[120]

One can just imagine, therefore, the degree of concern the words 'embarking and disembarking' would cause the fertile judicial mind. The words clearly meant the period of time during which the passenger ascends the steps of the aircraft or descends from the aircraft after a flight.[121] The words 'any of the operations', however, extends the scope of this fundamental act and could well mean the time of check-in at the terminal, the period before of after security screening, and the time spent in the sterile area. However, courts have wavered between views, and have finally accepted the *Day–Evangelinos* test which was developed as a consequence of a series of terrorist acts on passengers in airport lounges. This is for all purposes an objective tripartite test, so called because it takes into account three key factors when considering whether a plaintiff was 'embarking' or 'disembarking', the location of the passenger, the nature of his activity at the time of his accident, and the degree of control exercised by the airline at the relevant time.

The test, while clearly establishing that, unless the passenger is under the control or direction of the airline there is no liability for the death or injury to a passenger, also demonstrates through a cogently analysed *cursus curiae* that there is a real danger of the test being subjectively applied in many circumstances. To illustrate this, a Brussels court brought in the application of a test analogous to the tripartite test and held that a passenger who slipped on some ice and fell between the terminal building and the aircraft bus was not under the control of the airline, since the bus was operated by airport staff. No question was asked whether the airport staff were the agents of the airline, or whether the bus service was part of the contract of carriage between the airline and the passenger.[122]

The significance of this test to the aviation lawyer is in an acquisition of a clear view of what 'location,' 'activity' and 'control' really mean. On the subject of 'location,' in the decision of *Buonocore* v. *Trans World Airlines*[123] the court held that TWA was not liable for the murder of a passenger by terrorists while waiting in the public area of da Vinci airport in Rome, since the murder did not come within the terms 'embarkation' or 'disembarkation' under Article 17. The deceased had checked in and approached a snack cart in the main concourse area of the airport when he was struck down by terrorist fire. The main criterion on which the courts anchored their decision was that, although Buanocore had checked in and received his seat assignment, he had not gone through security inspection. In the earlier case of *De La Cruz* v. *Domincana de Aviacion*,[124] the court had held that a plaintiff who slipped and fell while on the way to a baggage claim area was not in the disembarkation process. He had descended a flight of steps from the aircraft to the ramp and entered the arrivals building, passed through immigration control and, while walking down the hallway, had slipped and fallen.

The position of the courts on the other two elements have also been somewhat inconsistent. In the case of *Seidenfaden* v. *British Airways*,[125] the courts expressed the need for there to be a 'clear manifestation of control'[126] for compensation to be awarded. In another case,[127] the court held that an airline passenger could not claim when she fell in the immigration area which was just 300 yards away from the arrival gate. The rationale adopted by the court was that the area was not leased or under the control of the carrier, and therefore the passenger was out of the carrier's control. As for the activity of the passenger at the time of the accident, it is a fairly straightforward proposition that almost any activity that a passenger would usually be involved in would be related to his travel under the circumstances.

The ambiguities of the tripartite test can be attributed to the original case of *Day* v. *Trans World Airlines*,[128] where the court considered the activity of the passenger, the restrictions placed on the passenger's movement, the imminence of actual boarding and the physical proximity of the passenger to the gate[129] as criteria for establishing the test. It is time that a more realistic approach was taken by the courts, while taking into consideration the involvement of the airlines in today's security, the steps taken by airlines in securing their passengers, and the spirit of the Warsaw Convention in introducing a rebuttable presumption of carrier liability and attendant limitation of liability.

The more recent case of *Craig* v. *Compagnie Nationale Air France*,[130] demonstrates that courts are now likely to interpret the word 'accident' in the Warsaw Convention so as to prevent the likelihood of claims being brought for any injury that may seem to be an accident at first glance. In the *Craig* case, the United States Court of Appeal considered the claim for damages brought by a passenger who had tripped over a pair of shoes of the passenger seated next to her, while returning to her seat. The neighbour, who was fast asleep, had removed his shoes and had placed them in front of him. The plaintiff had been to the toilet and was returning to her seat at a time when the cabin crew had finished serving a meal and the main lights in the cabin had been switched off, in order that the passengers could sleep. The court observed:

It was the plaintiff's burden to demonstrate that the presence of shoes on the floor between two seats was an unexpected or unusual event ... Plaintiff did not submit or point to any evidence (such as an affidavit from a flight attendant) that finding shoes on the floor between two seats was unusual or unexpected. Nor did the plaintiff ask for a trial or further discovery to establish anything more than her own declaration.[131]

In a case decided in Canada,[132] where a 72-year-old woman, who suffered from a severe case of osteoporosis, claimed that she had suffered injury as a result of the aircraft in which she was travelling going through 'expected' turbulence, Sutherland J of the Ontario Court in Canada (General Division), dismissing the action, observed:

> Air turbulence itself is not unexpected or unusual. Up to some level of severity it is a commonplace of air travel ... I find as fact that the turbulence encountered here on the flight in question, while greater than that previously experienced ... did not amount to an 'accident' within the meaning of Article 17 of the Warsaw Convention as the term accident is defined in *Air France* v. *Saks*. The degree of turbulence encountered on the flight cannot be said to have been unusual or unexpected.[133]

This decision adds to the thrust of the recent trend adopted by courts where 'accident' under the Warsaw Convention is interpreted in order effectively to preclude frivolous claims based on a loose interpretation of the word.

Conduct of the flight attendant affecting the passenger

In the 1994 case of *Pasinato* v. *American Airlines*,[134] where the plaintiff alleged wilful misconduct on the part of the carrier when the act of opening an overhead bin by a flight attendant resulted in a tote bag falling on the plaintiff and injuring her as a result, the trial court accepted a definition of 'wilful misconduct' of a previous case which identified it as 'The performance of an act with knowledge that the act will probably result in an injury or damage, or in some manner as to imply reckless disregard for the consequences of its performance'.[135] The court applied the above definition to the facts of the case and arrived at the conclusion that the American Airlines flight attendant's actions in no way constituted 'wilful misconduct'. The court explained:

> There is no dispute that the flight attendant opened the overhead bin to get a pillow for another passenger. The flight attendant's deposition indicates that she opened the bin with one hand, in her customary manner, with the other placed defensively above her head near the bin to prevent an object from falling upon her or a passenger sitting below. Further, the flight attendant stated that she tried to catch the tote bag that fell from the bin (and may have touched it as it fell), but that it fell too quickly.[136]

The plaintiffs claimed that repeated warnings were given over the public address system of the aircraft as to the innate hazardousness of the act of opening the overhead bins, which reminded passengers of the dangers of baggage shifting in the bins during flight. The plaintiffs further claimed that the flight attendant should have known or ought to have known the nature of the contents of the baggage in the bin in question. The court, however, was more inclined to accept the fact that incidents of objects falling from overhead bins were rare and that the flight attendant in question had been involved in only six such incidents during her 17 years of tenure as a flight attendant, none of which had resulted in injury or inconvenience to passengers.

The court was also concerned with the formulation of an adequate and suitable definition of 'wilful misconduct' which was basically known to be the quality of behaviour resulting in an act committed with the knowledge that such act will 'probably result in an injury or damage'.[137] Another interpretation of 'wilful misconduct' recognized an act performed in a manner indicating reckless disregard for the consequences of the act as reflecting wilful misconduct on the part of the person committing such act. Applying the second criterion to the case in issue, the court recognized the act of the flight attendant in placing her hand in a defensive posture, and nearly catching the article of baggage as it fell, to be one which indicated the taking of sufficient care and precaution to preclude an accident from occurring.

Owing to the nature of cabin baggage which is now carried by passengers, courts place more stringent emphasis on the degree of care owed by the airline to the passenger in warning him of the inherent danger of injury from falling overhead baggage. In *Andrews* v. *United Airlines*,[138] where, upon arrival of the aircraft in which he was travelling, a passenger was hit by a piece of baggage descending from an overhead bin, it was the general view of the United States Court of Appeals for the Ninth Circuit that airlines in the present-day context had a more serious responsibility than their counterparts of the past, to warn passengers of the increasing hazards of baggage falling from overhead baggage compartments. The court anchored its view on the fact that, in the present context, passengers hand-carry much larger cabin baggage such as computers and musical instruments which barely fit in the overhead bins. Therefore the court held that the airline's duty of care in cautioning passengers and taking adequate care against the cause of accidents relating to falling overhead baggage was of a higher standard than that which had been expected in the past. However, responsibility for the storage and retrieval of overhead cabin baggage is not always the sole responsibility of the flight attendant. Courts have held that a negligent passenger who stores his baggage carelessly is also responsible for overhead baggage. In *US Air Inc.* v. *United States*,[139] the United States Court of Appeals for the Ninth Circuit, applying the law of California, held that a passenger who negligently stores baggage in an overhead bin must jointly share liability with the airline company, if such baggage causes injury to another passenger. The court further held that, regardless of whether the offending passenger sought or received assistance from a flight attendant when storing his briefcase, he had a duty to use care in placing his luggage in the overhead compartment and, in this case, he had breached that duty. As the offending passenger was travelling on the business of his employer, his negligent act occurred during the scope of his employment and his employer was, therefore, responsible for the injuries caused by his negligent act. Also, although the court was able to trace the actual act of opening of the overhead bin to a flight attendant, it held that the negligent act of the flight attendant in opening the baggage compartment was not a superseding cause of the injury and did not exonerate the negligence of the passenger (and his employer) in storing the brief case in an 'unstable' manner.

Lamkin v. *Braniff Airlines, Inc.*[140] is an interesting litigation which considered the rights of a passenger on a flight from Miami to Boston who suffered second and third degree burns when a cup of coffee spilled in to her lap. Shortly after take-off a flight attendant had served hot coffee to the passenger in a styrofoam coffee cup. The coffee spilled when the passenger placed the cup on the seat-back tray in front of her and the passenger seated in the front moved the seat backwards. The injured passenger sued Braniff Airlines, alleging negligence in the hiring and training of cabin staff, and negligence in the use of an allegedly defective coffee maker, seats, cups and trays. A claim for failure to warn against the excessively high temperature of the coffee was also laid.

The Federal Trial Court in Massachusetts which examined the case dismissed all claims alleged, holding that the passenger had failed to offer any evidence of negligence on the part of the airline with respect to the serving of hot coffee or treating the passenger's injury. The court also dismissed the claim of failure to warn on the ground that the passenger herself was aware that the coffee was hot, and, therefore, needed no warning as to that fact. Moreover, there was no showing that any of the airline's employees was aware that the coffee was hot enough to burn a passenger. Although the court had no difficulty in agreeing with the passenger that an airline was subject to a high degree of care and that the standard of care required may approach that of an insurer, it observed that, nevertheless, a carrier is not strictly liable for accidents which befall its passengers and an injured person must prove negligence on the part of the carrier in order to recover.

One of the significant findings of the court in this case was that the application of the doctrine of *res ipsa loquitur*, which permits one on the facts of a case to 'draw an inference of negligence' in the absence of a finding of a specific cause of the occurrence when an accident is of the kind that does not ordinarily happen unless the defendant was negligent, was inapplicable. The court found that neither the passenger's expert nor common knowledge supported a finding that the mere occurrence of the accident demonstrated negligence on the part of the carrier, particularly where the expert was not qualified to testify as to the cause of the injury and had no particular expertise regarding the proper functioning of a coffee machine.

Conduct of the flight attendant affecting the pilot

Several dramatic accidents have emphasized certain deficiencies which may exist in cockpit–cabin coordination and communication. The reasons for poor communication between pilots and members of cabin crew are multifarious, in that they are historical, organizational, environmental, psychosocial and regulatory. The basic problem between these two categories of airline staff who are thrust together on a flight involves the fact that the two crews represent two distinct and separate cultures, which may often inhibit satisfactory teamwork. Although the role of the technical crew in flight safety has been well documented,[141] the flight attendant's role in safety has been treated at best with ambivalence, where the flight attendant is considered as 'back-end crew' (as opposed to 'front-end crew', referring to the pilot), keeping a fairly orderly cabin and serving coffee. Of course, the flight attendant may assist in instances involving terrorism or emergency evacuation, but customarily the role of the flight attendant has been feminized and, often, trivialized. Perhaps the main reason for the perceived bifurcation of the two types of crew is their geographic locations, where the cockpit and the cabin remain as two distinct geographic and social environments.[142]

As there are different areas of responsibility which devolve upon technical crew members and cabin crew members, it is inevitable that two separate cultures will exist in the aircraft. Often, through no fault of their own, and because of their particular responsibilities, the technical crew in the cockpit may isolate itself from the cabin crew, leading to serious lapses of communication between the two. Australian accident investigator David Adams observes:

> If you look at almost any company (airline), you will usually find that the cabin attendants and the flight crew are very clearly separated. They work for different branches of the company in most cases. The culture is one of almost complete separation. Yet, the fact of the matter is, in a safety situation, these two sections of the company have to work together. And the consequences of not working together quite often means a bunch of people get killed.[143]

One commentator's study of crew members' attitudes in flight reflects significant differences between personality dimensions of US pilots and flight attendants. The study attributes these psychosocial differences to pilots being task-oriented and preferring a cognitive style of problem solving based on logic and systems-oriented reasoning. Flight attendants, on the other hand, were identified as preferring an affective cognitive style and orientation to decision making.[144]

Conduct of passengers

In March 2001, the British Court of Appeal heard the case of Kelly Morris, a 15-year-old, who had boarded the defendant's flight at Kuala Lumpur bound for Amsterdam, on 6 September 1998. Ms Morris was seated next to two men. After a meal, she fell asleep and was awakened by the groping hand of the man next to her touching her left thigh. He was caressing her between her hip and knee and his fingers dug into her thigh. Ms Morris got up, walked away and reported the incident to the cabin staff. She became very distressed as a result of the incident and sought medical advice on her return to Bolton, in northern England. The Doctor who examined her found that she was suffering from a clinical depression amounting to a single episode of a major depressive illness. Thankfully, she made a full recovery.

At the Court of first instance, Ms Morris based her claim for compensation on the basis of Article 17 of the Warsaw Convention[145] which provides as follows:

> The carrier is liable for damage sustained in the event of the death or wounding of a passenger or any bodily injury suffered by a passenger, if the accident which caused the damage so sustained took place on board the aircraft or in the course of any of the operations of embarking or disembarking.

Judge Carter gave judgment in favour of the claimant and awarded damages to be assessed based on his interpretation of Article 17 – that bodily injury included mental injury – and its applicability to the case at hand. The defendant appealed.

Lord Phillips MR, who gave judgment at the appeal stage, identified that the first issue was whether the claimant's illness was caused by an 'accident' within the meaning of Article 17. The second issue was whether her illness constituted 'bodily injury' within the meaning of Article 17. The meaning of these three words, Lord Phillips opined, had been analysed repeatedly in the context of Article 17 and on occasion at very great length, in the courts of a number of signatories to the Convention. His Lordship concluded that some of the jurisprudence consisted of detailed analysis of the architecture of what were found, at the end of the day, to constitute blind alleys.

The whole issue therefore percolated to the essential question of interpretation of the Warsaw Convention, as to what the founding fathers of the Convention meant by 'accident' and whether Ms Kelly's incident could be categorized as an 'accident' within Article 17 as was intended originally, and whether 'bodily injury' included clinical depression, again in the same context. In both instances, as a general basis, Lord Phillips seems to have anchored his reasoning on the dictum of Lord Diplock in *Fothergill* v. *Monarch Airlines Ltd*,[146] where His Lordship stated:

> The language of an international convention has not been chosen by an English parliamentary draftsman. It is neither couched in the conventional English legislative idiom nor designed to be construed exclusively by English judges. It is addressed to a much wider and more varied judicial audience than is an Act of Parliament that deals with purely domestic law. It should be interpreted, as Lord Wilberforce put it in *James Buchanan & Co. Ltd.* v. *Babco Forwarding and Shipping (UK) Ltd.* [1997] 3 All E.R. 1048 at 1052 [1978] AC 141 at 152, 'unconstrained by technical rules of English law, or by English legal precedent, but on broad principles of general acceptation'.[147]

Lord Phillips also quoted with approval the observations of Lord Diplock who had, on the subject of tracing the legislation history or 'travaux préparatoires' in order to resolve any ambiguities that may emerge in interpretation, followed the wisdom of Lord Wilberforce in the same case where His Lordship had stated:

> there may be cases where such travaux préparatoires can profitably be used. These cases should be rare, and only where two conditions are fulfilled: first, that the material involved is public and accessible, and, secondly, that the travaux préparatoires clearly and indisputably point to a definite legislative intention.[148]

with a qualifier used in the later case of *Sidhu* v. *British Airways Plc*[149] by Lord Hope of Craighead, who referred to the Warsaw Convention, observing that it was sufficient to say that cautious use of the legislative history of the Convention should be made. His Lordship added that the usefulness of such historic documentation will only be apparent if, after proper analysis, it clearly points to a definite intention on the part of the delegates as to how the point at issue should be resolved.

Lord Phillips emphasized earlier cases[150] which had pronounced that, in Article 17, there was a distinct difference brought to bear between bodily injury and mental injury, and that, in American jurisprudence, there was a distinction between an accident that is the cause of injury and an injury that itself is an accident. The British Court of Appeal seemingly preferred the former approach, which follows basic logic and the words of Article 17.

The essence of the judgment, at least with regard to the application of Article 17 of the Warsaw Convention, was therefore that a passenger could only claim in the following circumstances: (a) the passenger's injury is caused by an unexpected or unusual event or happening that is external to a passenger; and (b) the injury should not result from the passenger's own internal reaction to the usual, normal and expected operation of the aircraft. As to the latter, the court had no doubt that the 'accident' that had befallen Ms Morris exemplified a special risk inherent in air travel and that she could demonstrably argue successfully that the 'accident' which occurred was characteristic of air travel. However, the court was sceptical about the applicability of the intent of Article 17 to a mental injury that was seemingly the passenger's own internal reaction to the usually normal and expected operation of the aircraft.

The entire purport of Ms Morris' claim therefore lay on the interpretation of 'bodily injury' as explicitly provided for in Article 17 of the Warsaw Convention. Clearly, the defendant airline's claim was that 'bodily injury' in Article 17 was injury that results in some form of physical damage but which does not extend to illness of the mind. On the other hand, the claimant held that 'bodily injury' is not mere physical injury but also includes mental injury.

The Court of Appeal held that the depressive illness suffered by Ms Morris was not 'bodily injury' as intended by the Warsaw Convention on the following grounds: (a) there is a distinct difference between physical and mental injury. Physical injury involves damage to the structure of the body, whereas mental injury affects the well-being of the mind; and (b) it was not the court's role to read into the Convention modern exigencies and changes in civil aviation. The court was bound to interpret Article 17 along the lines of shared intentions of signatories in 1929.

With regard to the latter issue, the court disagreed with the circuit judge's findings, which supported an earlier Israeli Supreme Court decision[151] that the Warsaw Convention had to be given a modern interpretation. The Court of Appeal, in its recognition of recent pronouncements regarding the inclusion of mental injury within the scope of bodily injury, examined the 1999 Montreal Convention which revised the Warsaw Convention in various aspects but retained 'bodily injury' as the only element of non-terminal injury. The court noted that the travaux préparatoires of the new Convention included the possibility of 'bodily injury' being interpreted in some jurisdictions to include mental injury.

It is also interesting that the Court of Appeal rejected the judgment delivered in the Scottish case of *King* v. *Bristow Helicopters Ltd*,[152] where the claimant who suffered post-traumatic stress disorder (PTSD), chronic depression and phobic anxiety suffered as a result of experiencing a crash landing, was awarded damages under Article 17 of the Warsaw Convention. The award of damages was based on the fact that the psychological injury suffered by the claimant was a 'bodily injury' within Article 17.

There are two issues that emerge from the Morris decision: (a) the term 'bodily injury' strictly denotes physical injury affecting the structure of the human body; and (b) an international treaty, however old, should be interpreted and given effect to just the way intended by its founding fathers. In other words, a treaty should be frozen in time.

Bodily injury and mental injury

Article 17 of the Warsaw Convention states that the carrier is liable for damage sustained in the event of the death or wounding of a passenger or any other bodily injury suffered by a passenger, if the accident which caused the damage so sustained took place on board the aircraft or in the course of any of the operations of embarking or disembarking.

From its inception, this provision has proved contentious in its application as courts adjudicating a claim under Article 17 have been consistently constrained to interpret the words 'bodily injury' either as pure physical injury or as mental suffering accompanied by physical injury where the latter was a causative factor in bringing about the former. These rulings held that there could not be compensation under Article 17 for pure mental shock, psychic trauma, anxiety or mental discomfort. In the 1991 case of *Eastern Airlines Inc.* v. *Floyd et al.*,[153] the United States Supreme Court concluded that there must at least be physical manifestation of injury, if not death or physical injury, in order for a claimant to sue successfully an air carrier under Article 17. The court, however, did not address the issue as to whether mental injury accompanied by physical injury was a compensable element. The *Floyd* decision is consistent with its precursor – the 1974 case of *Rosman (and Herman)* v. *Trans World Airlines*[154] which related to a hijacking incident – holding that there have to be palpable, objective bodily injuries, including those caused by psychic trauma related to the incident, and for the damage flowing from the bodily injuries and not from the trauma *per se*. The *Rosman* decision followed in the wake of a 1973 decision[155] which held the same.

The inclination of the courts to insist on pure physical injury as an essential element of compensability is arguably due to the fact that courts took refuge in the original French terminology of the Convention which was '*lésion corporelle*' which means 'physical wound', as against '*lésion mentale*' which means 'mental wound'.[156] A diametrically opposed view emerged in a *cursus curiae* which ignored the connotations of the French language and visited the original intention of the drafters of the Convention. In *Husserl* v. *Swiss Air Co. Ltd*,[157] also a case concerning the hijacking of an aircraft, the court observed the lacuna relating to the absence of reference to emotional injury in Article 17 and deemed fit to construe the provision broadly, to include injuries other than pure physical injury.

The law, as any other human discipline, has treated the mind as an unfathomable abstraction. Through the years, this attitude has led to a blend of caution and curiosity.[158] This led to a compromise, that is,. to giving legal recognition to an injury to the human mind[159] only when it was accompanied by some physical attribute perceptible to the senses. To the lawyer, it remains a mere legal platitude which still exerts a strong influence on the attitude of the courts towards tortuous liability.

Although it can be seen that this attitude has acted as a pervasive influence in restricting the award of damages for pain of mind, a closer study of recent trends reveals an interesting development. Legal writing, sociological change and scientific development have prompted the courts in the United States of America[160] to show signs of recognizing the infliction of mental distress as being compatible with the legal definition of a tort. Mere pain of mind has hitherto been recognized as being abstract and indefinable in terms of visual assessment. It is this quality which has cautioned the courts against fraudulent and frivolous actions. However, it is clear that mental distress, once identified and defined, can be considered a damage for the purpose of the law of torts.

It is a curious fact that the courts in the United States and the United Kingdom have been used to recognizing a set of torts as actionable wrongs. Had they pondered over a suitable definition of a tort, they would have realized that defining a tort is as difficult as defining mental distress. Conceptually, a tort remains a breach of duty which grounds an action for damages. This excludes contractual or quasi-contractual duty. Thus far, the courts have not been overtly concerned about the question 'what is a tort?' Rather, they have been seeking an answer to the question 'what are torts?' A treatise on tort says: 'A "tort" is simply the Norman word for "wrong", but "torts" have typically been distinguished from wrongs identified with contractual relations. Tort law, then, is concerned with civil wrongs not arising from contracts.'[161]

Normally, definitions of tort refer to harm or damage caused to the injured as a requirement for the award of damages. As mentioned earlier, generally, the courts have been hesitant to consider mental distress as damage, as it has been considered to be incapable of assessment. In sharp contrast is the view, taken by some early writers,[162] that mental suffering is indeed damage and an injury upon the human being and therefore should be considered a tort. It is submitted that such a view is more acceptable as it is based on both scientific and sociological studies.

The society we live in today is far more complex and variegated than the ones before the twentieth century. A larger population, expanded industry and greater production have exposed man to many more hazards than before. The incidence of mental injury in today's society can be expected to be more frequent than before. As White says: 'mental injury was the stuff of "real" life in twentieth century America and hence the stuff of tort law'.[163] It is no surprise, therefore, that when Prosser called the infliction of mental distress 'the birth of a new tort',[164] he was acutely aware of the reluctance of the courts to consider mental distress as a damage or harm, and thus regard its infliction as a tort. Whether mental distress causes damage and whether it can be assessed is worthy of discussion.

In the area of tortious liability, it cannot be disputed that an imbalance of a person's mental equilibrium is inextricably related to fear. If one looks at a definition of 'fear', its relationship with pain of mind caused by a civil wrong becomes immediately apparent: 'The word 'fear' comes from the old English 'Faer' for sudden calamity or danger and was later used to describe the emotion of uneasiness caused by the sense of impending danger',[165] which is 'A normal response to active or imagined threat in higher animals and comprises an outer behavioural expression, an inner feeling and accompanying physiological damage'.[166]

Much has been written, in detail on the aggression committed by the feeling of fear and anxiety on the internal organs of the human body. Fear is said to have been 'born of innumerable injuries in the course of evolution … developed into portentous foreshadowing of possible injury … capable of arousing in the body, all of the offensive and defensive activities that favour the survival of the organism'.[167]

Emotional agitation, anxiety or fear is known to bring about an imbalance in the digestive process,[168] dryness of the mouth,[169] an increase in blood sugar[170] and a general disruption of the internal organs of the human body. This feeling of discomfort, even though temporary, is a positively unpleasant experience.[171]

The observations made so far by medical authorities seem to recognize clearly the deleterious effects of pain of mind. There is no justification, therefore, for rejecting this notion *in limine*, as being beyond human perception. However, it is difficult to reject totally the point made by the courts in the United States that mental distress, when inflicted, should not be recognized as an actionable tort, as it is difficult to prove and therefore would give rise to arbitrary and frivolous suits. The notion of mental distress, even though easily recognizable as damage, has to be considered with care. The plaintiff's case has to be viewed with circumspection, which could be done by imposing stringent standards of proof of injury on the plaintiff.

Although the early view taken by the courts that the infliction of mental distress should not be entertained at all owing to its vagueness, was totally acceptable to them in the context of the time it was followed, modern science, which has drawn a distinct relationship between the human mind and the body, has proved the view to be inconsistent with the needs of the present time. At the present time, the United States courts have veered from the original state of apprehension they were in, and have recognized mental distress as an injury, while setting standards of proof to be complied with by the plaintiff in order that the defendant be equally protected. This approach is both progressive and reasonable, although an overt emphasis on the protection of the defendant can easily act to the detriment of the plaintiff's case.

Legal theory and mental distress

The early view taken by the courts in the United States, that mental injury is incapable of being visualized or proved, was the result of the influence of English common law.[172] Heavy reliance was placed by the English courts in the tenth century on the fact that mental injury was beyond the realm of human understanding. Therefore, although not mentioned in specific language, it is evident that the courts, acknowledging the futility of defining mental distress as damage, attributed to the tortfeasor the same quality of being unable to realize and foresee the distinct mental injury that he could cause one who is injured by him. One can only surmise that it had been considered logical that if the courts could not identify mental distress as damage, the tortfeasor certainly could not either. Therefore, originally, as a tortfeasor could not be expected to be conscious of the possibility of mental injury which his victim might suffer, he would not be held liable unless he actually intended the mental injury, or was conscious that his act would result in causing the victim pain of mind that would lead to an observable physical injury. The courts have been concerned with two main problems whether physical injury should necessarily follow mental injury and whether such mental injury should be intentionally caused for it to be recognized as damage. To both these questions, the answer has been in the affirmative.

Although Prosser dealt only with the intentional infliction of mental distress,[173] he was quite emphatic that mental distress is similar to physical damage. His statement was that 'mental suffering is no less a real injury than physical pain ... and it is ... the business of the courts to make precedent where a wrong calls for redress'.[174] One of the earliest in England to observe the significance of mental distress as a positive injury, was Kennedy J, when he said: 'I should not be surprised if the surgeon or the physiologist told me that nervous shock is or may be in itself an injurious affection of the physical organism.'[175] This statement is an acknowledgment that mental injury may lead directly to physical injury which, though not externally visible, may be evident to a trained medical mind. However, it is interesting to note that such opinion did not radically change the attitude of the courts in this respect. The basic difficulty was that the conventional view of tort liability could not be shaken. The commission of a tort had to be ascertainable externally. Judges, being laymen from the medical point of view, have been consistently hesitant to adjudicate upon anything which was not apparent or proven on an empirical basis. While it is true that the effects of mental injury could not be scientifically proved by way of a general test, the overwhelming opinion of medical science should have at least made the courts acknowledge the plausibility of what was stated. This makes the judicial approach on this subject a trifle disconcerting.

Once the courts recognize that mental distress *per se* is an actionable wrong when inflicted, they can devise a viable basis for determining who is entitled to damages. The guidelines for awarding damages and the role played by the courts form the substance of this work. For the present, it can be stated that, by adopting a rigid attitude towards the infliction of mental distress, the courts do not exhibit a full appreciation of mental distress as an injury.

Failure to accord recognition to the infliction of mental distress as an actionable injury raises the interesting point whether it would constitute a violation of a fundamental human right in the context of American society. It cannot be doubted that the fundamental rights of man in the United States are, the right of personal liberty and security, reputation and property,[176] the invasion of which constitutes a tort. It is fair to assume that no court will deny this principle. If this be so, it seems clear that the infliction of pain of mind, under any circumstances, is an erosion of the right to liberty and security. To establish, therefore, that mental distress when inflicted upon a person can be regarded as a tort, the only element needed seems to be to ascertain definitely that mental distress ensued from a particular act. This should be done with caution.

That a tort is a wrong committed against a person is undisputed. To what extent this definition can be applied is seen in the statement that 'particular torts, as Trespass or Violence, Defamation, Nuisance and the like can be defined well enough, but the term "tort" is also used to denote wrong in general. It includes the unclassified residuum as well as specific definable wrongs'.[177] The infliction of mental distress falls into the 'unclassified residuum' and is certainly a wrong. Though not often, it has been judicially recognized that mental distress is synonymous with a state of anxiety caused by stress. Stanford J said, 'mental distress ... includes sorrow and grief'.[178] to which Rainey J added humiliation, mortification and shame as sensibilities of the mind which show mental distress.[179] This view is seen in one instance where a person who was subjected to a state of intense worry was held to be suffering from mental distress.[180] On the one hand, it is evident that anxiety induced by stress in any form is both an injury and an infringement of a right. On the other, the courts definitely stand circumscribed, as they have not been able to visualize the damage and assess it. It is a dichotomy difficult to resolve. The only way out of this tangle is for the courts to view mental injury as a definite injury, on the following lines.

It is a common human feature to undergo a mental reaction under stress. For instance, if a person is involved in an accident directly, or indirectly by witnessing the accident, the thought process of that person will be far from pleasant. The thoughts that run through his mind threaten his sense of security. Therefore a person who causes the accident commits a wrong against anyone who is either directly involved in it or who witnesses it and is shocked by what he sees. However, it does not necessarily mean that liability attaches in respect of everyone in the vicinity of the accident. A clear burden of proof should rest on the plaintiff to show that he in fact suffered mental injury as a result of an act of the defendant.

A gradual awakening to the problem which veered away from the initial attitude of regarding the infliction of mental distress along the lines of the English common law, which rejected the notion as being abstract and vague, was seen with the emergence of American Realist thinking. It brought out new perspectives on the concept of tort. This was done by acknowledging that the dispensation of justice was dependent, if not totally, to some extent at least, on allied disciplines. Medical science, economics and technology were used to deduce facts which were outside the purview of the law. In this light, mental distress ceased to be vague. It was found that mental distress could be assessed. The functions of Realism in the context of tort law have been subsumed in the statement: 'realism, as we have seen, reflected an enhanced Twentieth Century awareness of the psychological dimensions of human behaviour. An awareness that was limited to a growing interest in the explanatory powers of behavioural sciences.'[181]

The infliction of mental distress has been recognized by writers as an actionable wrong for a considerable period of time. The emphasis so far has been on the intention of the person who causes it. In fact, legal thinking has not been generally used to associate the infliction of mental distress with an unintentional act. This was due to regarding the human mind as totally unrelated to the functions of the human body. A duty not to upset the mental stability of a person to his detriment does not seem to tie up with the duty of care not to injure one's neighbour,[182] the fundamental premise on which negligence is based. As a result of this, the majority of jurisdictions in the United States have insisted that mental distress is parasitic and should be the outcome of an intentional act causing visible physical injury. Yet there are some jurisdictions which recognize the infliction of mental distress *per se* as actionable. This has been done with no uniformity; courts have digressed from one concept to another, ranging from foreseeability in negligence[183] to the extreme measure of imposing strict liability.[184] The profusion of legal writing, which has dealt mostly with the principles of negligence as applicable to the infliction of mental distress, and the general policy laid down in most states to award damages in tort to the most deserving, have left the courts worse confounded. To inquire into this situation, the judicial trends which evolved into the existing position have to be traced.

It is incontrovertible that in a discussion of whether mental injury is a 'wounding' or 'bodily injury', as reflected in the Warsaw Convention, a 'personal injury', as referred to in the Guatemala City Protocol,[185] or *a fortiori* a 'lésion corporelle', as appearing in the French text of the Convention, its nature has to be both medically and forensically determined in order that the concept of mental distress be assigned its place in the Convention. No judge could presume to comprehend the nature of mental injury in all its pathological and medical connotations – a necessity if a juridical basis for mental injury were to be determined under the Warsaw System.

Medical jurisprudence is greatly assisted by the pioneering research of Sigmund Freud, who first analysed mental injury and traced its origins to a combination of fear and anxiety that caused physical changes in the human body.[186] It is now well established from a medical standpoint (if not from a medical-jurisprudence standpoint) that fear and anxiety cause 'unpleasant subjective feelings of terror, a pounding heart, muscular tenseness, exaggerated startle, dryness at the throat and mouth, a sinking feeling in the stomach, nausea, perspiration, an urge to urinate and maybe to defecate ... difficulty in breathing etc.'[187]

Forensically speaking, the terms 'bodily injury', 'wounding' and 'lésion corporelle' have been obfuscated by the preconceived juridical notion that there is a strict difference between mental and bodily injury. The confusion seems to have been worse confounded by the interpretation of the French term 'lésion corporelle' as strictly bodily injury (which indeed it may well be) and therefore the erroneous basis of the two being mutually exclusive had prevailed in some instances. *Burnett* v. *Trans World Airlines*[188] is one such case where the court held that the French version of the Convention should prevail and therefore only a bodily injury (and not mental injury) must be considered as compensable. Although the case of *Rosman* v. *Trans World Airlines*[189] later rejected this view, that the French text prevails as the primal document, its ultimate decision was that mental injury *per se* was not compensable under Article 17 of the Convention. The courts in this line of cases seem to have adopted the archaic views of *Lynch* v. *Knight*,[190] without consulting the prevalent findings of forensic medicine. A second line of thinking emerged in the case of *Husserl* v. *Swiss Air Transport Co.*,[191] where the court held that mental injury was 'included' in bodily injury, claiming that the words 'bodily injury' in the Convention really covered mental injury. Here, again, the court refused to identify a medical similarity between the two terms but rather, went on to read the words 'mental injury' into the Convention.[192] Miller concludes that, if a court adopts the line of thinking in the *Husserl* and *Karfunkel* decisions, a plaintiff will recover for mental distress, while, if the *Rosman* decision were to be followed, no award of damages would ensue.

The operative point here is not whether the French text prevails over the English translation of the Convention. Nor is it, for that matter, which of the two lines of the *cursus curiae* is acceptable. The matter at issue is whether mental injury is actually a 'physical injury' in a medical sense. If this question is decided in the affirmative, there will be no need to sustain the debates that have prevailed over the thread of cases that have run through this contentious issue.

It is interesting to note that, in the case of *Floyd* v. *Eastern Airlines*,[193] the Eleventh Circuit Court of Appeals of New York examined 'lésion corporelle' in the original French text and decided that the legislative history of the Convention and the case law admitted of mental injury, even without accompanying physical injury, being compensable under Article 17. This is the only early instance of a court transcending the bounds of judicial parochialism and actually recognizing that there are other fields of human expertise that become relevant in the adjudication of human disputes. Unfortunately, however, the Supreme Court in *Eastern Airlines Inc.* v. *Floyd*[194] reversed this decision.

Mankiewicz, in a well reasoned and *au fait* paper, refers to the concept of 'personal injury' in the Guatemala Protocol (which was also suggested at the Hague Protocol 1955), and suggests a viable compromise: 'The legislative history of Article 17 compels the conclusion that, at least as far as American courts are concerned, the expression "lésion corporelle" should be understood to mean "personal injury".'[195] It is somewhat disturbing that some recent cases have still held on to the need for accompanying physical injury in order for emotional injury to be compensable. In the 1997 Australian case of *Kotsambasis* v. *Singapore Airlines*,[196] the New South Wales Court of Appeal followed the *Floyd* decision and held that, without accompanying bodily injury, the plaintiff could not recover for pure psychological injury. The plaintiff in this case had claimed that she had suffered acute nervous shock and feared for her life following a fire which broke out in the engine of the aircraft in which she was travelling, while at Athens Airport. The Court of Appeal went on the basis that the signatory states to the Warsaw Convention, in 1929, had no specific intent to include pure psychological or emotional distress within the purview of Article 17 of the Convention.[197] The Court of Appeals in the *Kotsambasis* case disagreed with the lower court judges' finding with an earlier Australian decision,[198] which was in the appellate process at the time the *Kotsambasis* case was being decided. Although the New South Wales Court of Appeal conclusively decided at the appeal of the *Georgopoulos* case that pure mental distress was comparable, without there being a need for accompanying physical injury, the *Kotsambasis* decision overruled it.

In the United States, although few instances of judicial determination which follows *Eastern Airline Inc.* v. *Floyd*[199] support the view that plaintiffs could recover only for physical injuries and for emotional injuries flowing from those injuries,[200] the 1996 decision regarding the case of *Zicherman* v. *Korean Airlines Co. Ltd*[201] gave the United States Supreme Court the opportunity to confirm that the Warsaw Convention itself contained no specific or particular preclusion from recovering compensation from any damages, be it physical or mental. The *Zicherman* decision allowed the plaintiff to claim for 'legally cognizable harm' to be determined by local law in accordance with otherwise applicable choice of law principles. A year later, the 1997 decision of the *Roselawn* case[202] held with the Supreme Court findings in the *Zickerman* case, stating: 'Article 17 does not say that a carrier will only be liable for damage caused by a bodily injury, or that passengers can only recover for mental injuries if they are caused by bodily injuries'.[203]

The aviation community has now reached a stage where the *cursus curiae* at common law such as the *Floyd* and *Zicherman* decisions will be moot when the *ICAO Convention for the Unification of Certain Rules for International Carriage by Air*, adopted in 1998, becomes effective. This Convention, once in force, will blaze a new trail, and provide the judiciary with the travaux préparatoires of the Conference as resource material. Courts will no longer have to inquire as to the intent of the makers of the original Warsaw Convention of 1929, since the 1999 ICAO Convention will pre-empt its predecessor.

In terms of the element of 'mental injury', it is very clear that the working papers of the Study Group which was appointed by the ICAO Court in November 1995 for the specific purpose of developing a mechanism written into the framework of ICAO to accelerate the modernization of the Warsaw System, are explicit in reflecting the Group's intentions. Vijay Poonoosamy, the Rapporteur of the Study Group, in his report states:

> the expression 'personal injury' would open the door to non-physical personal injuries such as slander, libel, discrimination, fear, fright and apprehension and this could be neither desirable nor acceptable. Use of 'bodily injury' would be more acceptable but would exclude mental injuries such as shock. Recent Court decisions in the U.S. demonstrate how difficult an area this is and a clear statement must be agreed upon which is not limitless in scope. Since it would be clearly fair and equitable to compensate for impairment of health (i.e. both physical and mental/psychic injuries) it may be preferable to define personal injury as such.[204]

It is interesting to note that the Rapporteur, on behalf of the ICAO Study Group, categorizes fear, fright and apprehension, which are symptoms of injury that bring about physical results as shown in the scientific evidence at the introduction of this discussion, as non-physical 'injuries'. He then goes on to identify 'shock' as a mental injury.

The ICAO Legal Committee, which examined the report of the Study Group, retained the words 'mental injury' in Article 16 of the ICAO Draft Convention.[205] However, final versions of the Draft Convention,[206] which was the document in issue at the May 1999 Diplomatic Conference at ICAO, gave Article 16 of the Draft Convention as follows:

Article 16.1

> The carrier is liable for damage sustained in case of death or bodily injury of a passenger upon condition only that the accident which caused the death or injury took place onboard the aircraft or in the course of any of the operations of embarking or disembarking. However, the carrier is not liable to the extent that the death or injury resulted from the state of health of the passenger.[207]

The Convention of 1999 has adopted this provision without the last sentence. Both in the draft, and in the final version, the words 'personal' and 'or mental' have been stricken out of the original phrase, 'personal bodily or mental injury', making it incontrovertible that the new Convention does not intend to encompass mental injury as a compensable element in Article 16. This exclusion, ipso facto, would give the courts clear direction as to the way to proceed in an adjudication involving mental injury in the carriage by air of a person, except that it is not clear whether by the exclusion of the words 'mental injury', the Convention also wished to exclude 'the impairment of mental health', which can be imputed as being inclusionary in the working papers of the ICAO Study Groups. It would not be surprising if this dichotomy were to create, in the future, two schools of judicial thought, as indeed existed under the 1929 Warsaw Convention and its Protocols.

There could also well be a line of reasoning, as in the *Zicherman* case, which would insist on interpreting 'bodily injury' as extending to 'legally cognizable harm' thereby extending the phrase to mental injury. There is no doubt that medical science has clearly identified mental disturbance. Modern science has debunked the legal attitude which was brought about by the requirement that physical injury is an essential prerequisite of mental injury. It is now believed by medical science that the mental injury that a victim suffers can be an extreme form. Although it is caused by fear, in most cases it is not mere fright or nervous shock but also an extreme form of neurosis[208] which follows the traumatic event of an accident. Neurosis in its extreme form is a psychogenic disorder following a psychic injury with or without physical harm.[209] It results in considerable impairment of ability to function in ordinary life. Generally, it is precipitated by a traumatic incident and is solely due to psychological reactions, which makes external physical injury a totally unrelated factor.

It is not surprising that, as far back as 1939, the courts pronounced that any person 'needs the privilege of being careless whether he inflicts mental injury to another or not'.[210] The courts viewed mental injury as no redressable injury. The unfortunate thing is that, although in many areas of the law, academic opinion and judicial decisions have been symbiotic, the courts did not heed the comments of Prosser,[211] Bohlen[212] and many others[213] who, at an early stage, recognized mental injury as an independent injury which infringes the interest of peace of mind. The only conclusion that can be reached is that the courts have not taken the trouble to seek a definition for mental injury and this has made their treatment of the injury misguided and often erroneous. As has been pointed our earlier, a minority of jurisdictions have, notwithstanding this general attitude, been courageous enough to say that it is a definite and identifiable injury.

The courts should primarily consider the meaning and purpose of the law when dealing with mental injury and accident liability. To say that it is the business of the law to remedy wrongs that deserve it[214] is a legal platitude. If the injury suffered by a plaintiff is proved by connecting it to an accident, there is no doubt that the injury is a wrong that needs correction by way of awarding damages to the plaintiff. There is little room for doubt that most common law courts, as indeed did the court in *King*'s case, would readily regard PTSD, which is a relatively new phenomenon (earlier referred to by the medical profession as 'whiplash' injuries) as a legally cognizable harm *per se*. PTSD excludes mental injury caused as a result of a person's death by natural causes (such as witnessing the death of a family member under natural circumstances). It includes mental injury or distress caused by witnessing sudden events such as accidents, natural disasters and instances of armed combat. Typical symptoms of PTSD are recurrent and persistent experiencing of an event in question; exclusion of the outside world when experiencing such recurrences of events in one's mind; avoidance of circumstances needing change; and increased discombobulation and disturbance of mind, resulting in such experiences as lack of sleep and temper tantrums.[215] The *facta probanda*, or elements of proof needed to establish PTSD are, in an aircraft accident; the fact that the claimant is suffering from PTSD; such PTSD has been brought about by shock caused by experiencing the event of an accident or other incident calculated to induce such a psychiatric disorder; and the close proximity of the claimant to the accident site.

The issue as to whether the courts would associate PTSD with 'bodily injury' as envisioned in the present Warsaw structure or even the new regime reflected in the Montreal Convention of 1999, would largely depend on the extent to which courts would be ready to embrace the compelling scientific findings with regard to mental distress and its application within the term 'bodily injury'.

In the United States, torts became a distinct area of the law only in the late nineteenth century. It has been regarded as a flexible discipline where rigid distinctions are impossible to make. Inflexible principles and conservatism have no place in the rapidly evolving tort law in America.[216] One writer[217] has aptly commented that, owing to this progressive evolution of tort law, the common law in time to come would entertain mental distress actions freely. The immunities given to the injurer under fault liability would gradually disappear. The reason for this is quite clear. In a civil wrong such as a tort, the law now seeks to correct a wrong rather than punish a wrongdoer. For this purpose, there is no need to depend on fault liability as the sole criterion of deciding an action in mental distress. The only thing necessary is to determine that the victim is free of fault and that the defendant was responsible in some way for the injury caused. The law itself on this matter should be based heavily on social welfare. It is inevitable that, eventually, the courts will follow this trend, taking into account social policy and the interests of society as a whole, and compensate injury, whether mental or physical, in an appropriate manner.

Interpretation of the Warsaw Convention

It was the contention of the Court of Appeal that, since the Warsaw Convention used the words 'bodily injury', it was not for the court to import other terminology into the wording of the Convention. The court went on the basis that a change in the Convention should be effected by the parties to the Convention and, if indeed it is the intention of the parties to change the Convention, they, and not the courts, had the power to do it. This general principle is an accurate statement of international legal practice. Article 31 of the Vienna Convention on the Law of Treaties, 1969, stipulates that a treaty shall be interpreted in good faith in accordance with the ordinary meaning to be given to the terms of the treaty in their context and in the light of its object and purpose. In giving effect to this fundamental principle, the Court of Appeal has followed the approach, in the court's own words:

> The effect of an international convention is, necessarily, that the agreement it contains will 'mark time' in accordance with its terms. Insofar as developments of individual domestic laws render it outmoded, the remedy is to amend it. Such amendment in relation to Article 17 was considered, but not pursued, when the Montreal Convention was negotiated.[218]

Here, the court seems to say that, since the new Montreal Convention did not explicitly include the words 'mental injury', the parties to the Convention intended not to pursue the issue.

However, this was not the case. As the legal history of the Montreal Convention shows, the reason why 'mental injury' was not explicitly included in the Convention was that there was no need to do so, as some jurisdictions already included 'mental injury' within bodily injury. The Montreal Convention, by the very fact that it does not mention 'mental injury' leaves room for jurisdictions to read mental injury into the broader scope of bodily injury if they so wish.

A more enlightened approach would have been for the court to have inquired into the nature of mental injury. There is no mention of the nature of mental injury whatsoever in the decision. Nor is there any consideration as to whether there is any scientific basis recognizing the physical ramifications of mental injury. The court seemed to have followed the somewhat antiquated presumption that mental injury and bodily injury are mutually exclusive, and that is the end of the debate.

Article 31.4 of the Vienna Convention on the Law of Treaties provides that 'a special meaning shall be given to a term if it is established that the parties so intended'. This provision, when applied to 'bodily injury', precisely means that the parties intended only bodily injury to be considered under the Convention. But does it necessarily follow, as the court seemed to think, that the founding fathers exclusively meant what was perceived then as bodily injury. Would it be logical to think that they, in their wisdom, would have intended to preclude other categories of injuries, then not thought of owing to the lack of scientific data, from being considered as bodily injuries for over 75 years?

The first principle incorporated in Article 31 of the Vienna Convention, that a treaty shall be interpreted in good faith in accordance with the ordinary meaning given to the terms of the treaty, brings to bear the need to emphasize the ordinary sense of terminology. An example of terminology in its ordinary sense was given by the Permanent Court of International Justice in 1925, when it said that 'postal service' should be interpreted as 'the normal functions of "postal service"' and should not be confined to the operation of a postal service in a given area.[219] This approach exemplifies what is now known as the 'textual approach', which invokes the need to integrate the meaning of terms in the context of the treaty as a whole and ensure contemporaneity. There is also the 'teleological approach' which admits of courts interpreting terminology further than their 'textual' context. Here the court would determine what the objects and purposes are of certain terminology in order to obviate ambiguities of intent. There is also the more radical teleological approach where the courts could 'import' substance necessary to give effect to the purposes of a treaty. Ian Brownlie suggests that this radical approach may involve a judicial implementation of purposes in a fashion not contemplated by parties to a treaty.[220] Brownlie is of the view that the textual approach, at the same time, often leaves the decision maker with options in practice, making it difficult to keep considerations of policy outside the scope of interpretation carried out, since many issues of interpretation are not narrow technicalities, but require an evolutionary approach.[221]

The teleological approach, although having its own shortcomings, cannot be totally discarded, as was done in the *Morris* case by the Court of Appeal, considering the constructive role the approach could play in the aspect of judicial legislation. This is particularly so in the issue of interpretation of the Warsaw Convention's 'bodily injury', which did not go through detailed discussion during the Warsaw Conference preceding the adoption of the Convention. What did get mentioned was the overall statement by the President of the Conference Mr Lutostanski: 'The great past men call on the living to pursue their work. And we are gathered in order to improve life, in order to render a legal text that daily life urgently requires.'[222] This statement, coupled with the observation of the Delegate of France, M Ripert, that 'at the present time, those who travel by air have no need of protection' goes to show that the founding fathers' perception of an airline passenger in 1928 was completely at variance with the risks faced by the susceptible airline passenger of today, and that it was their intention to create a legal instrument that would remain vibrant in daily life. Therefore it certainly can be inferred that they did not intend to freeze the Warsaw Convention for nearly 75 years.

The Court of Appeal, particularly in the context of existing jurisprudence reflected in the *Daddon* and *King* cases, could have done well in inquiring whether there was sufficient scientific evidence to consider mental injury as a bodily injury. The court should also have examined closely the minutes of the Warsaw Conference in order to determine whether there was a discussion on the nature of bodily injury during the Conference. Had it done so, the court would have discovered that the minutes of the Conference do not reflect any discussion on bodily injury, leaving room for modern science and daily exigencies to take effect. This exercise would have at least provided the court with the overall flavour of the Conference and the intent of the founding fathers. Another disconcerting feature in the judgment is the absolute absence of any discussion as to whether, in modern jurisprudence, judicial legislation was a possibility, given the lapse of nearly 75 years. Instead, the court seems to have taken the easy way out and relied entirely on the textual approach, when there was so much research into the workings of the Convention and precedent on the teleological approach available. This is a pity.

Wilful misconduct

Whatever may be the relationship between the flight attendant and passenger, on the one hand, and flight attendant and pilot, on the other, both relationships have a common denominator. In accidents caused as a direct or indirect result of the flight attendant's conduct – be it an injury to a passenger or aircraft accident precipitated by the conduct of the flight attendant affecting pilot performance – the legal consequences of air carrier liability would revolve round whether the act of the flight attendant or the pilot, as the case may be, was tantamount to wilful misconduct on the part of the carrier.

In the 1994 case of *Baba* v. *Compagnie National Air France*,[223] in which the Federal Courts of Washington examined a case relating to damage caused by rain water to persian rugs which were entrusted to a carrier for transport, the court considered evidence presented that the carrier had disregarded its own cargo handling regulations as well as plain common sense. Following the interpretation of wilful misconduct adopted by *In re Korean Airlines Disaster of September 1 1983*,[224] which established that 'Wilful misconduct is the intentional performance of an act with knowledge that the act will probably result in an injury or damage, or in some manner as to imply reckless disregard of the consequences of its performance',[225] the court noted that it was also clear that a combination of factors can, taken together, amount to wilful misconduct. The court further observed that only the act needs to be intended, not the resulting injury or the wrongfulness of the act. Another significant finding of the court in this case was that evidence of wilful misconduct could be drawn from the determination of whether the carrier or its servants followed regulations adopted by the carrier in performing the alleged act. If regulations of the carrier were not followed, the court concluded that ipso facto such would reflect wilful misconduct on the part of the carrier.

Strict liability or fault liability?

The question of whether strict liability or fault liability should obtain in the realm of air carrier liability becomes compelling in the context of considering the conduct of servants of the carrier in issues of liability. Clearly, in such issues of litigation where the conduct of an individual is a causative factor of the accident in question, issues of negligence or wilful misconduct would be of paramount consideration in influencing adjudicators to view fault liability as a factor for consideration.

Rationales for the limitation of liability in private air law had been discussed by Drion in 1954,[226] where he discussed nine reasons. These reasons are given elsewhere.[227] The operative question is whether private air law needs the concept of limited liability or whether another system could be recommended. The most compelling arguments for the limitation of liability in private air law are that it protects the financially weak aviation industry, unifies private air law against draconian domestic laws and expedites the payment of compensation. It is interesting to analyse these concepts in today's aviation context. We live in a world where complex litigation issues emerge, carefully thought out by contingency fee lawyers who have an inexplicable capacity to produce a variety of defendants out of a hat. For instance, now, there is a conscious awareness that there are co-liable parties: manufacturers of component parts, air traffic controllers and even government agencies such as airport authorities. Would it be fair to limit the liability of the carrier and expose these three categories of defendants to unlimited liability? There may also be the instance where the deceased or injured person may have had enormous capacity to earn during his working life, which would be interrupted or terminated by an air accident. Does it mean that such a defendant settles for a limited sum of money as compensation and bears his losses? Professor Bin Cheng claims that the 100 000 SDRs of the Montreal System is woefully inadequate and implies that a higher limit should be considered, or the possibility of breakability of the limits should be endorsed, on the lines of the Warsaw Convention.[228]

It is prudent to approach this question with due emphasis laid on the economic ramifications of this strictly legal consideration since, at its core, the question addresses not principles of legal rectitude, nor issues of justice, but matters of financial interest to the parties concerned. It is inevitable, therefore, to consider the effect of limitation of liability as against unlimited liability and to rationalize between the two and arrive at a synthesis of the concepts or (if possible), a totally new concept. Therefore a consideration of the Warsaw Convention, its principles of limitation of liability as coupled with unlimited liability in the event of gross negligence of the carrier; the Montreal Protocols with their strict liability and higher limits of liability with no possibility to accommodate unlimited liability under any circumstances; and a pure instance of general liability with no inhibitions whatever, are alternatives that warrant discussion. Of course, it is needless to say that these three alternatives would be viewed from the standpoint of the plaintiff passenger or his dependant and the defendant airline. The operative theme of this inquiry would be money and not complex legal issues, since it is money that both parties are ultimately interested in.

It is incontrovertible that aviation insurers, when faced with increasing levels of claims and declining premium income, will naturally increase their policy deductibles and seek to incorporate exclusions of cover. The aviation insurance market increasingly feels that there is no closeness at all between the underwriters and brokers, on the one hand, and the insured (airline), on the other.[229] One commentator recommends either a substantial increase in voluntary limits of liability or the total abandonment of limiting air carrier liability, implying that either would benefit both the plaintiff and the defendant.[230] Peter Martin suggests that the best future for the Warsaw System would be the abandonment of limitations.[231] He states:

> There are very good reasons for imposing on carriers at least a very high standard of care, and even strict liability. Strict liability without limitations already applies in many States to third party liability to persons other than passengers and that is generally believed to be right ... why should a passenger, therefore, be in a worse position than a person or owners of property on the ground?[232]

Insurance lawyers obviously need higher liability limits and specificity in this area. The steady disintegration of the Warsaw System, which is mainly attributable to its incompetence in providing for satisfactory compensatory limits, has been proved by figures released by the Rand Corporation showing that, in a cross-section of cases studied, Warsaw–Montreal tickets obtained a per capita compensation of US$ 184 000, while non-Warsaw–Montreal tickets had received double this amount. This amount has increased further over the years, demonstrating that the Warsaw limits are being rapidly left behind.[233] It is clear therefore that the Warsaw limits must be extended, and the first step towards this goal is the ratification by states of the Montreal Protocols. It is also imperative that the scope of the Convention be extended to third parties such as air traffic controllers and manufacturers of component parts of aircraft to seek consistency and to give the insurance market a clear picture and more accurate assessment. By bringing these parties under the Warsaw umbrella, both the plaintiff and the defendant would be well served, in that the plaintiff would be assured of quick settlement and the defendant would be comfortable with the thought that his liability is limited. This could also preclude contingency fee appearances by lawyers.

The most appropriate step to take at this juncture would be for states to ratify the Montreal Protocols, considering the rapidly growing airline fleets and the even more rapid increases in traffic potential. Limitation of liability should be retained at least for now, as there has to be immediate protection of all concerned with the aviation industry, while, at the same time, maintaining a balance with the interest of the plaintiff, who would be assured of a reasonable sum in compensation without the hassle of litigation with third parties, such as manufacturers.

It is inevitable that, when one assesses the unification process of the Warsaw System, one has to view the package offered by the Montreal Protocols as one which is both clearly presented and meticulously thought out, taking into consideration the many grey areas such as the breakability of the limit of liability, the uncertainty that a genuinely aggrieved plaintiff feels and the unrealistic compensation offered. The only factor lacking is the action needed by the states concerned to ratify these instruments as soon as possible.

Compensable limits

In November 1992, all international air carriers of Japan amended their conditions of carriage to accord with directives of the Ministry of Transport of Japan. These amendments waived passenger liability limits in international carriage by air as stipulated in the Warsaw Convention *per se* and as amended by the Hague Protocol of 1955. Accordingly, the Japanese carriers waived their right to invoke liability limits under the Convention's Article 20(1) for claims under 100 000 SDR for passenger injuries and deaths. In other words, the Japanese carriers waived their right under this category of claim to prove the absence of fault in order to rebut the presumption of liability imposed by the Convention under Article 17. This made the carriers of Japan strictly liable for claims under 100 000 SDR. As for claims above 100 000 SDR, the limitation of liability would be waived and fault would be presumed but rebuttable, as in the original Convention. Professor Bin Cheng has commented:

> This brave and enlightened initiative on the part of the Japanese airlines, in being the first to remove the limit on carriers' liability for passenger death or injury … represents a historic landmark in the evolution of the Warsaw System. It provides an unmistakable signal to all other airlines and governments that it is now time to give up the pathetic struggle to bring life to the dismal 1971 Guatemala City Protocol in the form of the Montreal Additional Protocol No. 3 (MAP3). It should also hasten the end of what is in effect an international cartel, that is already in tatters, of low compensation limit.[234]

George N. Tompkins Jr endorses the Bin Cheng view and goes a step further in examining the Japanese amendments as suitable for the United States:

> The Japanese Initiative approach presents the simple solution to the problem which has caused all of the perceived ills of the Warsaw liability system. The simplicity of the approach is emphasised by the fact that no international convention or agreement would be required to adopt and put into place the Japanese Initiative approach in the United States … The focus of current and future attention, therefore, should be upon the Japanese Initiative approach and how to make it adaptable and acceptable in the United States and presumably, thereafter, throughout the aviation world.[235]

Japan has publicly stated that it is totally dedicated to the preservation of the Warsaw System on the basis that the system eliminates 'choice of law' problems and retains unifying principles of liability. The Japanese Initiative approach complements the Warsaw System in that compensation is automatically guaranteed under the Initiative approach, without the claimant having to produce his passenger ticket. Also compensation is assured without distinction as to origin, destination or nationality of the passenger concerned.[236]

Against the backdrop of a European initiative taken by the European Civil Aviation Conference (ECAC) urging member states of ECAC to participate in a

European Intercarrier Arrangement setting up a new special contract which would contain liability limits of at least 250 000 SDR, the International Air Transport Association (IATA) convened its Airline Liability Conference in Washington DC in June 1995. The conference concluded, inter alia, that the Warsaw Convention system must be preserved; however, the existing passenger liability limits for international carriage by air are grossly inadequate in many jurisdictions and should be improved as a matter of urgency, and therefore governments were urged at the same time through the International Civil Aviation Organization (ICAO), and in consultation with airlines, to act urgently to update the Warsaw Convention system, including liability issues.

The Conference also set up two working groups to assess and report on a suitable liability package and appropriate and effective measures to secure complete compensation for passengers. The findings of these working groups have resulted in agreement among IATA members to prepare a new inter-carrier agreement, to replace the Montreal Agreement of 1966, which will include the following elements:

a) full compensatory damages, with no fixed liability figure;
b) no explicit waiver of the carrier's defences under the Warsaw/Hague system;
c) explicit reservation of the carrier's rights against third parties; and
d) promotion of widespread implementation of the Agreement by the airlines.

The IATA draft inter-carrier agreement, therefore, inter alia, provides for a single universal system without specified limits; the award of recoverable compensable damages to be in accordance with the law of domicile of the passenger; and an 'umbrella accord' which would give carriers maximum flexibility to adjust their conditions of carriage, taking into account applicable government regulations.

The 31st Session of the ICAO Assembly, which held its deliberations from 29 September to 4 October 1995, considered the developments generated by the IATA conference of June 1995 and observed that, although in the short term new limits might be accomplished through an inter-carrier agreement, most states may need a more substantive approach such as the adoption of a new protocol under the Warsaw system. Accordingly, the Assembly decided to direct the ICAO Council to continue its efforts to modernize the Warsaw System as expeditiously as possible. The Assembly also urged states to ratify Montreal Protocol No. 4, independently of the Additional Montreal Protocol No. 3.[237]

The role of the flight attendant in air carrier liability hinges upon whether or not the carrier could prove that it took necessary precautions to avoid causing injury or death to a passenger which may have been caused by the conduct of its cabin crew. Under the present liability regime, therefore, a carrier is prima facie liable up to prescribed limits and, if it proves prudence in its professional conduct, it could avoid liability or seek mitigation thereof. If on the other hand, the plaintiff proves wilful misconduct, such limits could be transgressed, leading to unlimited liability of the carrier. Under the proposed unlimited liability scheme within the Japanese Initiative approach and under the IATA umbrella, however, the question of wilful misconduct of the carrier is obviated in the context of limitation of liability, in that the latter would not exist. The liability of the carrier would then hinge on the exception to liability which is based on the principle of good conduct, which the Warsaw System identifies as the taking of due measures and precautions by the carrier to ensure the avoidance of death or injury to a passenger or the impossibility of taking such precautions. In this sense, emerging trends in air carrier liability would hinge heavily on the specific conduct of airline crew. The conduct of flight attendants would therefore be subject to more minute judicial scrutiny under such a system.

SEARCH AND RESCUE OF AIRCRAFT AND PASSENGERS

After the events of 11 September 2001, it is only natural to assume that there is heightened awareness of the possibility of aircraft being used as weapons of destruction in the future. From a social and political perspective, the world has to prepare for eventualities leading up to search and rescue of aircraft that may need to be located without loss of time and the passengers and crew rescued. There are already two international treaties on the subject, although one, the Brussels Convention of 1938,[238] has unfortunately not been ratified by the requisite number of States and has therefore not come into effect. The Brussels Convention contemplated only assistance and salvage operations at sea. The other Convention is Chicago Convention of 1944 , which requires contracting states of the International Civil Aviation Organization[240] to fulfil their obligations under Article 25, which provides:

> Each Contracting State undertakes to provide such measures of assistance to aircraft in distress in its territory as it may find practicable, and to permit, subject to control by its own authorities, the owners of aircraft or authorities of the State in which the aircraft is registered to provide such measures of assistance as may be necessitated by the circumstances. Each Contracting State, when undertaking search for missing aircraft, will collaborate in coordinated measures which may be recommended from time to time pursuant to this Convention.

Annex 12 to the Chicago Convention elaborates on this fundamental requirement by qualifying that contracting states shall arrange for the establishment and provision of search and rescue (SAR) services within their territories on a 24-hour basis.[241] Contracting states are further requested to delineate the SAR process under the Annex on the basis of regional air navigation agreements[242] and provide such services on a regional basis without overlap.[243] A search and rescue region has been defined in the Annex as 'an area of defined dimensions within which SAR service is provided'.

The dilemma facing many states extending both to airports and to airlines, relates to the lack of rapid response, adequate equipment and well-trained crews, all of which are critical to passenger survival in the event of an aircraft disaster. Although most states are particularly mindful of these compelling needs, they are by no means confined to a particular region. An example of this crisis can be provided by the 1980 incident of a Saudi Arabian Airlines L-1011 catching fire shortly after leaving Riyadh Airport. Although the pilot turned back for an emergency landing and made a perfect touchdown, nearly 30 minutes passed before firemen managed to go in, by which time all passengers and crew had perished. This could have been a survivable accident.[244] To the contrary, a hijacking incident involving a Boeing 767 aircraft on the shores of Comoros, in November 1996, when the aircraft crashed owing to lack of fuel, showed how spontaneous reaction from even non-trained professionals at rescue efforts could help. In this instance, the quick response of tourists at the scene ensured that 51 of the 175 passengers on board were saved.[245]

This section will outline principles of responsibility of states and political, economic and humanitarian consequences pertaining to search and rescue of aircraft within their territorial boundaries.[246]

Political issues

Annex 12 to the Chicago Convention requires contracting states to coordinate their SAR organizations with those of neighbouring contracting states,[247] with a recommendation that such states should, whenever necessary, coordinate their SAR operations with those of neighbouring states[248] and develop common SAR procedures to facilitate coordination of SAR operations with those of neighbouring states.[249] These provisions collectively call upon all contracting states to bond together in coordinating both their SAR organizations and operations.

At the 32nd Session of the Assembly, held in 1998, ICAO adopted Resolution A32-14, Appendix O which addresses the provision of SAR services. This resolution refers to Article 25 of the Convention in which each contracting state undertakes to provide such measures of assistance to aircraft in distress in its territory as it may find practicable and to collaborate in coordinated measures which may be recommended from time to time pursuant to the Convention.

The resolution mentions Annex 12 to the Convention which contains specifications relating to the establishment and provision of SAR services within the territories of contracting states as well as within areas over the high seas. The resolution recognizes that Annex 12 specifies that those portions of the high seas where SAR services will be provided shall be determined on the basis of regional air navigation agreements, which are agreements approved by the Council normally on the advice of regional air navigation meetings. Annex 12 also recommends that boundaries of SAR regions should, insofar as is practicable, be coincident with the boundaries of corresponding flight information regions.

Article 69 of the Convention, which is also outlined in the resolution, specifies that, if the Council is of the opinion that the air navigation services of a contracting state are not reasonably adequate for the safe operation of international air services, present or contemplated, the Council shall consult with the state directly concerned, and other states affected, with a view to finding means by which the situation may be remedied, and may make recommendations for that purpose; and that the air navigation services referred to in Article 69 of the Convention include, inter alia, SAR services.

In taking into consideration the above facts, the Assembly resolves in A32-14 that the boundaries of SAR regions, whether over states' territories or over the high seas, shall be determined on the basis of technical and operational considerations, including the desirability of coincident flight information regions and SAR regions, with the aim of ensuring optimum efficiency with the least overall cost. If any SAR regions need to extend over the territories of two or more states, or parts thereof, agreement thereon should be negotiated between the states concerned.

The resolution also calls upon the providing state, in implementing SAR services over the territory of the delegating state, to do so in accordance with the requirements of the delegating state, which shall establish and maintain in operation such facilities and services for the use of the providing state as are mutually agreed to be necessary. Any delegation of responsibility by one state to another or any assignment of responsibility over the high seas shall be limited to technical and operational functions pertaining to the provision of SAR services in the area concerned. Remedies to any inadequacies in the provision of efficient SAR services, particularly over the high seas, should be sought through negotiations with states which may be able to give operational or financial assistance in SAR operations, with a view to concluding agreements to that effect.

Furthermore, the resolution declares that any contracting state which delegates to another state the responsibility for providing SAR services within its territory does so without derogation of its sovereignty; and the approval by Council of regional air navigation agreements relating to the provision by a state of SAR services within areas over the high seas does not imply recognition of sovereignty of that state over the area concerned.

It is also stated in the resolution that contracting states should, in cooperation with other states and the organization, seek the most efficient delineation of SAR regions and consider, as necessary, pooling available resources or establishing jointly a single SAR organization to be responsible for the provision of SAR services within areas extending over the territories of two or more states or over the high seas.

Finally, the resolution calls on the Council to encourage states whose air coverage of the SAR regions for which they are responsible cannot be ensured because of a lack of adequate facilities to request assistance from other states to remedy the situation and to negotiate agreements with appropriate states regarding the assistance to be provided during SAR operations.

The legal validity of Resolution A32-14, as substantive law recognized under public international law, and therefore binding on states, is a relevant issue if the obligations of states in search and rescue are to be determined. All resolutions adopted within the United Nations' framework embody declarations of principles and rules of international law. They are particularly compelling when adopted without dissent. Article 38 of the Statute of the International Court of Justice cites, as a source of public international law, 'general principles of law recognized by civilized nations', into which category resolutions adopted by the United Nations could well fall.

Legal experts have consistently argued that resolutions could be authoritative evidence of binding international law on the grounds that such resolutions or declara-tions could be considered authentic interpretations of the United Nations Charter agreed by all parties. They have also adduced reasons for recognizing resolutions adopted within the United Nations' system as affirmations of recognized customary law and as expressions of general principles of law recognized by states. Some confirmation of these arguments has been given by the International Court of Justice when the sourt, over a period of years, recognized the force of several declarations adopted within the United Nations.[250]

In practical application, however, non-observance by states purportedly bound by such resolutions would render such states destitute of the desired legal effect. This would essentially be the case if there were negative votes or reservations attached to an Assembly resolution. In the case of A32-14, however, there is no question of reservation as the resolution was adopted by consensus.

The real utility of an Assembly resolution lies in the fact that primarily it supplements the absence of law in a given area by filling a legal lacuna that has not been filled by a formal legislative process. Treaty lawmaking is often long-winded and involves a cumbersome process. A resolution offers a 'quick fix' while embodying principles in a declaration that introduces legitimacy and validity to a given principle or group of principles. In this context, it would be correct to assume that the ICAO Standards and Recommended Practices (SARPs) on the subject of the implementation of Annex 12 are of equal persuasion. Together, the resolution and SARPs have a clear and substantial impact, reflecting the meticulous and thoughtful work that has gone with the development of these instruments and recognized the importance of safety and efficiency of civil aviation.[251]

In the case of the Africa–Indian Ocean Region, the ICAO Regional Air Navigation Plan,[252] in Part V, addresses issues of search and rescue by pointing to the provisions of the ICAO Search and Rescue Manual (Doc. 7333), referring in particular to the need for aircraft to carry specified equipment,[253] carry out paper and communications exercises[254] and, more importantly, for the need for states to pool their resources and provide mutual assistance in the case of SAR operations. The plan calls for precise agreements between states to implement these measures.[255] The ICAO regional plan also calls upon states, in order to ensure compatibility between aeronautical and maritime search and rescue regions (SRRs), and aeronautical search and rescue authorities, to maintain close liaison with their maritime counterparts and the International Maritime Organization (IMO).

In 1985, ICAO signed a memorandum of understanding (MOU) with the IMO concerning cooperation in respect of safety of aircraft operations to and from ships and other marine vehicles and of aeronautical and maritime SAR activities. Both ICAO and IMO signed this understanding with a view to ensuring the best possible coordination of activities between the organizations in matters concerned with the safety of aircraft operations to and from ships and other marine vehicles and with aeronautical and maritime search and rescue operations, agreeing to make arrangements for consultations between the secretariats of the two organizations in regard to these matters, with a view to ensuring consistency or compatibility between services and procedures in all cases where joint efforts or close cooperation may be required and in order to avoid any unnecessary duplication of efforts by them.

In determining the allocation of responsibilities of the two organizations to ensure safety of aircraft operations to and from ships and other marine vehicles, the following principles are applied:

a) All matters which are directly connected with the design, construction, equipment and operation of aircraft in general, and of helicopters in particular, should be regarded as falling primarily within the field of responsibility of ICAO.

b) All matters which are directly connected with the design, construction and equipment of ships and other marine vehicles and their operation should be regarded as falling primarily within the field of responsibility of IMO.

c) Matters which do not fall clearly within sub-paragraphs (a) or (b) above should be regarded as the responsibility of both organizations and dealt with by appropriate collaboration between them.

In determining the allocation of responsibilities of the two organizations in respect of search and rescue in maritime areas, the following principles are applied:

a) All matters which are directly connected with search and rescue by aircraft in general, and with air search and rescue facilities and operating procedures in particular, should be regarded as falling primarily within the field of responsibility of ICAO.

b) All matters which are directly connected with search and rescue by marine craft in general, and with marine search and rescue facilities and operating procedures in particular, should be regarded as falling primarily within the field of responsibility of IMO.

c) Matters which do not fall clearly within sub-paragraphs (a) and (b) above should be regarded as the responsibility of both organizations and dealt with by appropriate collaboration between them.

The MOU also provides that any draft amendment to Annex 12 'Search and Rescue' to the Convention on International Civil Aviation being considered by ICAO or any amendment to the Technical Annex to the International Convention on Maritime Search and Rescue, 1979, being considered by IMO and related to matters covered by this MOU will be communicated by the organization proposing the amendment to the other organization. Similarly, draft amendments to the ICAO SAR Manual or to the IMO SAR Manual which are related to matters covered by this MOU will be communicated in due time to the other organization with a view to keeping both Manuals aligned as closely as possible.

The consultations referred to above should also take place in respect of matters falling primarily within the responsibility of one or the other organization, so that each organization may, when it deems it necessary, safeguard its responsibilities and interests in these matters and thereby ensure effective cooperative action, whether carried out by one or the other or both organizations. In practice, the two secretariats are required to take all available steps to ensure that consultations are undertaken before either organization proceeds to take definitive action on matters subject to this MOU. The two secretariats are also expected to make available to each other relevant information and documentation prepared for meetings at which matters covered by this MOU are to be considered. Both organizations have also agreed to take appropriate steps to ensure that relevant advice from other organizations and bodies is made available in matters covered by this MOU, in accordance with the regulations and procedures of the respective signatory organization.

All the above-mentioned documents bring to bear the compelling need for the critical link between the legislative nature of the documentation and implementation: state responsibility. All the lawmaking and guidance material, declarations and resolutions would be destitute of effect if there was no element of state responsibility to give legitimacy to the instrument by complying with and adhering to the instruments. When discussing principles of state responsibility in the field of search and rescue, it is an incontrovertible fact that the provisions of the Chicago Convention, which is an international treaty, are binding on contracting states to the Convention and therefore are principles of public international law. The International Court of Justice (ICJ), in the *North Sea Continental Shelf Case*,[256] held that legal principles that are incorporated in treaties, such as the 'common interest' principle, become customary international law by virtue of Article 38 of the 1969 Vienna Convention on the Law of Treaties.[257] Article 38 recognizes that a rule set forth in a treaty will become binding upon a third state as a customary rule of international law if it is generally recognized by the states concerned as such. Obligations arising from *jus cogens* are considered applicable *erga omnes*, which would mean that states using space technology owe a duty of care to the world at large in the provision of such technology. The ICJ, in the *Barcelona Traction Case*, held:

> An essential distinction should be drawn between the obligations of a State towards the international community as a whole, and those arising *vis-à-vis* another State in the field of diplomatic protection. By their very nature, the former are the concerns of all States. In view of the importance of the rights involved, all States can be held to have a legal interest in their protection; they are obligations *erga omnes*.[258]

The International Law Commission has observed of the ICJ decision: 'In the Court's view, there are in fact a number, albeit limited, of international obligations which, by reason of their importance to the international community as a whole, are – unlike others – obligations in respect of which all States have legal interest.'[259] The views of the ICJ and of the International Law Commission, which has supported the approach taken by the ICJ, give rise to two possible conclusions relating to *jus cogens* and its resultant obligations *erga omnes*:

a) obligations *erga omnes* affect all states and thus cannot be made inapplicable to a state or group of states by an exclusive clause in a treaty or other document reflecting legal obligations without the consent of the international community as a whole;
b) obligations *erga omnes* pre-empt other obligations which may be incompatible with them.

Some examples of obligations *erga omnes* cited by the ICJ are prohibition of acts of aggression, genocide, slavery and discrimination.[260] It is indeed worthy of note that all these obligations are derivatives of norms which are *jus cogens* at international law.

International responsibility relates both to breaches of treaty provisions and to other breaches of legal duty. In the *Spanish Zone of Morocco Claims* case, Justice Huber observed: 'Responsibility is the necessary corollary of a right. All rights of an international character involve international responsibility. If the obligation in question is not met, responsibility entails the duty to make reparation.'[261] It is also now recognized as a principle of international law that the breach of a duty involves an obligation to make reparation appropriately and adequately. This reparation is regarded as the indispensable complement of a failure to apply a convention and is applied as an inarticulate premise that need not be stated in the breached convention itself.[262] The ICJ affirmed this principle in 1949 in the *Corfu Channel Case*,[263] by holding that Albania was liable under international law to pay compensation to the United Kingdom for not warning that Albania had laid mines in Albanian waters which caused explosions, damaging ships belonging to the United Kingdom. Since the treaty law provisions of liability and the general principles of international law as discussed complement each other in endorsing the liability of states to compensate for damage caused by space objects, there is no contention as to whether, in the use of nuclear power sources in outer space, damage caused by space objects or use thereof would not go uncompensated. The rationale for the award of compensation is explicitly included in Article XII of the Liability Convention, which requires that the person aggrieved or injured should be restored (by the award of compensation to him) to the condition in which he would have been if the damage had not occurred. Furthermore, under the principles of international law, moral damages based on pain, suffering and humiliation, as well as on other considerations, are considered recoverable.[264]

The sense of international responsibility that the United Nations ascribed to itself had reached a heady stage at this point, where the role of international law in international human conduct was perceived to be primary and above the authority of states. In its Report to the General Assembly, the International Law Commission recommended a draft provision which required: 'Every State has the duty to conduct its relations with other States in accordance with international law and with the principle that the sovereignty of each State is subject to the supremacy of international law.'[265] This principle, which forms a cornerstone of international conduct by states, provides the basis for strengthening international comity and regulating the conduct of states both internally – within their territories – and externally, towards other states. States are effectively precluded by this principle from pursuing their own interests untrammelled and with disregard to principles established by international law.

Economic issues

Economic aspects of SAR operations related to aviation have been on the agenda of ICAO for a considerable time. At ICAO's Conference on the Economics of Airports and Air Navigation Services (ANSConf 2000) held in Montreal from 19 to 28 June 2000, the Conference considered that, in 1996, a recommendation had been made, by an ICAO Air Navigation Services Economics Panel, that existing policy be amended to allow for costs of SAR services performed by establishments other than permanent civil establishments such as the military, to be included in the cost basis for air navigation services charges. The ICAO Council had not approved the panel's recommendations pending a secretariat study of the implications concerned. A subsequent survey carried out by the ICAO Secretariat of Contracting States had resulted in only a limited number of responses, precluding a conclusion as to the wishes of states on this issue. The Conference therefore agreed that there was a need for follow-up of the secretariat study, as well as information from many states that had not responded to the survey in the first instance.[266]

The Secretariat drew attention to the humanitarian aspects of SAR operations where states did not wish to charge for services rendered spontaneously and on an emergency basis. The Conference noted that, under the International Convention on Maritime Search and Rescue, states were obligated to render gratuitous assistance to any person in distress and that there was no attendant cost-recovery mechanism in SAR in the maritime field. On the basis of the above deliberations, the Conference recommended that ICAO undertake further study as to the position of states and the implications of amending ICAO policy with regard to recovery of costs for civil aviation related to SAR services provided by other than permanent civil establishments.[267] As for further work on the subject, the Conference recommended that ICAO develop guidance on the establishment of organizations at the regional level for SAR activities and conduct a study on the establishment of regional or subregional SAR mechanisms and how they might be funded as regards civil aviation.[268]

ICAO's policies on charges for airports and air navigation services were revised consequent to ANSConf 2000. These policies were published by ICAO in 2001.[269] As a fundamental principle, the Council considers that, where air navigation services are provided for international use, the providers may require the users to pay their share of the related costs; at the same time, international civil aviation should not be asked to meet costs that are not properly allocatable to it. The Council therefore encourages states to maintain accounts for the air navigation services they provide in a manner which ensures that air navigation services charges levied on international civil aviation are properly cost-based.

The Council also considers that an equitable cost recovery system could proceed from an accounting of total air navigation services costs incurred on behalf of aeronautical users, to an allocation of these costs among categories of users, and finally to the development of a charging or pricing policy system. In determining the total costs to be paid for by charges on international air services, the list in Appendix 2 of the document may serve as a general guide to the facilities and services to be taken into account.[270] Moreover, the Council specifically recommends that states consider the application, where appropriate, of internationally accepted accounting standards for providers of air navigation services that maintain separate accounts.

It is recommended that, when establishing the cost basis for air navigation services charges, the cost to be shared is the full cost of providing the air navigation services, including appropriate amounts for cost of capital and depreciation of assets, as well as the costs of maintenance, operation, management and administration. The costs to be taken into account should be those assessed in relation to the facilities and services, including satellite services, provided for and implemented under the ICAO Regional Air Navigation Plan(s), supplemented where necessary pursuant to recommendations made by the relevant ICAO Regional Air Navigation Meeting, as approved by the Council. Any other facilities and services, unless provided at the request of operators, should be excluded, as should the cost of facilities or services provided on contract or by the carriers themselves, as well as any excessive construction, operation or maintenance expenditures. The cost of air navigation services provided during the approach and aerodrome phase of aircraft operations should be identified separately, and so should the costs of providing aeronautical meteorological service, when possible. Air navigation services may produce sufficient revenues to exceed all direct and indirect operating costs and so provide for a return on assets (before tax and cost of capital) to contribute towards necessary capital improvements.

In determining the costs to be recovered from users, government may choose to recover less than full costs in recognition of local, regional or national benefits. It is for each state to decide for itself whether, when, and at what level any air navigation services charges should be imposed, and it is recognized that states in developing regions of the world, where financing the installation and maintenance of air navigation services is difficult, are particularly justified in asking the international air carriers to contribute through user charges towards bearing a fair share of the cost of the services. The approach towards the recovery of full costs should be a gradual progression.

The Council recommends that the allocation of the costs of air navigation services among aeronautical users be carried out in a manner equitable to all users. The proportions of cost attributable to international civil aviation and other utilization of the facilities and services (including domestic civil aviation, state or other exempted aircraft, and non-aeronautical users) should be determined in such a way as to ensure that no users are burdened with costs not properly allocatable to them according to sound accounting principles. The Council also recommends that states should acquire basic utilization data in respect of air navigation services, including the number of flights by category of user (air transport, general aviation, and other) in both domestic and international operations, and other data such as the distance flown and aircraft type or weight, where such information is relevant to the allocation of costs and the cost recovery system.[271]

The Council further recommends that states should ensure that systems used for charging for air navigation services are established so that any charging system should, so far as possible, be simple, equitable and, with regard to route air navigation services charges, suitable for general application at least on a regional basis. The administrative cost of collecting charges should not exceed a reasonable proportion of the charges collected. The charges should not be imposed in such a way as to discourage the use of facilities and services necessary for safety or the introduction of new aids and techniques. The facilities or services provided for in the ICAO Regional Air Navigation Plan(s) or in any recommendations of the relevant ICAO Regional Air Navigation Meeting as approved by the Council are, however, considered to be necessary for general safety and efficiency. Charges should be determined on the basis of sound accounting principles and may reflect, as required, other economic principles, provided that these are in conformity with Article 15 of the Convention on International Civil Aviation and other principles in this document. The system of charges must be non-discriminatory both between foreign users and those having the nationality of the state or states responsible for providing the air navigation services and engaged in similar international operations, and between two or more foreign users. Where any preferential charges, special rebates or other kinds of reduction in charges normally payable in respect of air navigation services are extended to particular categories of users, governments should ensure, so far as is practicable, that any resultant under-recovery of costs properly allocatable to the users concerned is not shouldered by other users. Any charging system should take into account the cost of providing air navigation services and the effectiveness of the services rendered. The charging system should be introduced in such a fashion as to take account of the economic and financial situation of the users directly affected, on the one hand, and that of the provider state or states, on the other. Charges should be levied in such a way that no facility or service is charged twice with respect to the same utilization. In cases where certain facilities or services have a dual utilization (for example, approach and aerodrome control, as well as en route air traffic control), their cost should be equitably distributed in the charges concerned. The charges levied on international general aviation should be assessed in a reasonable manner, having regard to the cost of the facilities needed and used and the goal of promoting the sound development of international civil aviation as a whole.

Humanitarian issues

Search and rescue operations conducted gratuitously and with intent to save human lives and property are what legal commentators call 'humanitarian intervention', which is considered to be a basic moral response of one human being to another, to save the latter's life. One definition identifies: 'humanitarian intervention as the proportionate transboundary help, including forcible help, provided by governments to individuals in another State who are being denied basic human rights and who themselves would be rationally willing to revolt against their oppressive government'.[272] The general principle of intervention for the provision of relief on moral grounds has been subject to a great degree of intellectual polarization. One view is that, if human beings are dying, one has got to help at all costs.[273] The other is that the mere act of treating humanitarian intervention as an extant legal doctrine would be to erode the applicable provision of the United Nations Charter on recourse to force. The latter view, which discourages humanitarian intervention, is substantiated by the following arguments:

1. the good Samaritan must fight for the right to perform his act of humanitarian intervention and may end up causing more injury than he averts;
2. the authorization for forceful and unilateral humanitarian assistance may be abused;
3. unilateral recourse to force even for genuinely humanitarian purposes may heighten expectations of violence within the international system and concomitantly erode the psychological constraints on the use of force for other purposes.[274]

The essence of intervention is compulsion. Compulsion could take place through the use of force, armed or otherwise. The legal question, with regard to the inviolability of the sovereignty of a state, is not whether the intervention concerned was an armed or unarmed one, but whether it was effected unilaterally under compulsion or threat by the intervening state.[275] Starke is inclined to stretch the principle of sovereignty to accommodate external involvement by a state in the affairs of another in special circumstances:

'Sovereignty' has a much more restricted meaning today than in the eighteenth and nineteenth centuries when, with the emergence of powerful highly nationalised States, few limits on State autonomy were acknowledged. At the present time there is hardly a State which, in the interests of the international community, has not accepted restrictions on its liberty of action. Thus most States are members of the United Nations and the International Labour Organization (ILO), in relation to which they have undertaken obligations limiting their unfettered discretion in matters of international policy. Therefore, it is probably more accurate today to say that the sovereignty of a State means the *residuum* of power which it possesses within the confines laid down by international law. It is of interest to note that this conception resembles the doctrine of early writers on international, law, who treated the State as subordinate to the law of nations, then identified as part of the wider 'law of nature'.[276]

Oppenheim holds a similar view that the 'traditional' law of humanity is incorporated into modern international law. He views this attitude as 'recognition of the supremacy of the law of humanity over the law of the sovereign State when enacted or applied in violation of human rights in a manner that may justly be held to shock the conscience of mankind'.[277] Some authorities in international law also believe that intervention should, if absolutely necessary, be effected when there is cogent evidence of a breakdown in the minimum guarantees of humanity.[278] Accordingly, it may be argued that any act of intervention aimed at saving the lives of human beings who are in danger would be legally and morally justifiable. Fernando Teson[279] argues that, since the ultimate justification for the existence of states is the protection and enforcement of the natural rights of the citizens, a government that engages in substantial violations of human rights betrays the very purpose for which it exists and so forfeits not only its domestic legitimacy, but its international legitimacy as well. He goes on to say:

I suggest that, from an ethical standpoint, the rights of States under international law are properly derived from individual rights. I therefore reject the notion that States have any autonomous moral standing – that they hold international rights that are independent from the rights of individuals who populate the State.[280]

Schwarzenberger analyses the concept somewhat clinically and concludes that, in the absence of an international *jus cogens* which corresponds to municipal *jus cogens* of advanced communities, where the latter prevents the worst excesses of inequality of power, the supremacy of the rule of force would prevail.[281]

There is also a contrasting view that humanitarian intervention is generally resorted to by states only in instances of serious abuses of human rights by one state upon its people or others. Michael Akehurst argues that, if a state intervenes forcibly on the territory of another in order to protect the local population from serious human violations, such an armed intervention could inevitably constitute a temporary violation de facto of the territorial integrity of the latter state, and to an extent of its political independence, if carried out against its wishes.[282] Akehurst goes on to assert: 'Any humanitarian intervention, however limited, constitutes a temporary violation of the target State's political independence and territorial integrity if it is carried out against the State's wishes.'[283]

The doctrine of humanitarian intervention is thought of by some commentators as an invention of strategy to circumvent the strong *jus cogens* nature of the principle of sovereignty and inviolability of states which Akehurst refers to. Brownlie is of the view that states have generally invoked the doctrine to give support to their commercial and strategic considerations.[284] The United Kingdom legislature recently considered the view of the British minister of state who was of the view, 'When members of the United Nations act in a forcible manner either they should do so within and under the authority of the United Nations or that which they do should be authorised by the principles of international law'.[285] Clearly, this statement establishes the view that international law in the context of intervention is *jus cogens*. The British

Foreign Office has supported this position in the following language: 'the best case that can be made in support of humanitarian intervention is that it cannot be said to be unambiguously illegal ... but the overwhelming majority of contemporary legal opinion comes down against the existence of a right of humanitarian intervention'.[286]

Despite this strong alignment towards *anti*-humanitarian intervention, it is believed that there is a school of thought within the British legislature that is prepared to accept unilateral intervention as justifiable under customary international law in cases of 'extreme humanitarian need'.[287] The author supports the view that, despite these divergent views, the non-intervention principle remains sacrosanct as a modern postulate of international law and deviations from the principle, although recognized as ethical and moral in certain instances by scholars, would be justified only in extreme cases.[288]

The essence of search and rescue operations in aviation is cooperation, which is embodied as a fundamental principle in the Preamble to the Chicago Convention which states, inter alia, that it is desirable to avoid friction and to promote that cooperation between nations and peoples upon which the peace of the world depends. At the root of international cooperation is the element of assistance, and in this sense the maritime regulations which admit of gratuitous help are both significant and laudable. Although it is not the intention of this section to recommend that all search and rescue operations be gratuitous, it certainly behoves the community of states to encourage all states who are in a position to give assistance without charge to do so. Humanitarian assistance is an integral element of diplomatic unity and coexistence.

THE THREAT OF INVASIVE ALIEN SPECIES

The brown tree snake (*Boiga irregularis*) which managed to hitchhike its way on military aircraft to Guam shortly after World War II, has caused extensive damage to the biodiversity of the island by devouring its bird population. Broadly defined, 'biodiversity' is the variety of all living things and their interactions. Biosafety is the coexistence of ecosystems and habitats without disturbance. In this context the brown tree snake is an invasive alien species which is a threat to the biosafety of the habitat and ecosystem it invades. An alien species – a species, sub-species or lower taxon, occurring as a result of a human agency in an area or ecosystem in which it is not active – becomes invasive when it colonizes natural or semi-natural ecosystems and threatens native biodiversity.[289]

Alien species can be introduced to a habitat or ecosystem unintentionally or intentionally. In the former instance, the introduction occurs as an adjunct to human activity such as trade and tourism. Intentional introduction of alien species usually occurs when production industries such as agriculture, horticulture, forestry and aquiculture import organisms for biological control purposes. Either way, whether intentionally or unintentionally, civil aviation may be instrumental as a medium of carriage of this environmental threat, although there is no evidence through documentation indicating a universal problem in civil aviation at the present time.

Biodiversity serves humanity in producing goods and services for fundamental human needs such as clean air, fresh water, food, medicines and shelter. It also provides people with essential recreation and spiritual enjoyment. After habitat destruction, invasive alien species are the most significant threat to biological diversity, over and above such threats as the overuse of resources, pollution and global climate change.

The Convention on Biological Diversity (CBD) of 1992,[290] one of the pre-eminent international treaties addressing the threat of invasive alien species, requires each party, as per Article 8(*h*) to prevent the introduction of, control or eradicate such alien species as threaten ecosystems, habitat or species. The Convention's subsidiary Body on Scientific, Technical and Technological Advice, which met in Montreal from 31 January to 4 February 2000, urged parties to apply the principles of Article 8(*h*) of the Convention and, at its latest meeting, also held in Montreal, in March 2001, adopted a set of recommendations and guiding principles to assist states with the implementation of this provision. The meeting also brought to bear the need for research and assessment on various subjects, including the pathways for aircraft and ships by which invasive alien species might be introduced. The Global Invasive Species Programme (GISP), a non-governmental organization working with the CBD, established in 1996, is working on assembling and making available best practices for the prevention and management of invasive alien species and seeking to stimulate the development of new tools in science, policy, information and education for use by states and organizations addressing the problem.

It is now recognized that special care should be taken to prevent introduced species from crossing the borders of neighbouring states. In the event of such occurrence, or where such an eventuality is probable, the affected state must promptly be warned, and consultations should be held in order to institute adequate measures. In the event of the carriage of an invasive alien species by air, inasmuch as states may require mechanisms to integrate policy recommendations from environmental, biological, management and external international sources for decision making, so do airlines have to bear some responsibility for being aware of their own part in assisting affected states if their aircraft have been used for the transport of invasive alien species, whether through the regular process of air transport as goods or without their knowledge.

Already there are various preventive measures in civil aviation that may assist in obviating the problem. Passengers and cargo subject to air carriage are sent through stringent quarantine and control measures at entry and departure points, such controls being administered by the public authorities of each contracting state. Also disinsection and disinfection of the aircraft are carried out in order to prevent unintentional introduction of invasive insects and micro organisms, respectively. However, these measures do not cover species larger than insects which may, like the brown tree snake, hitchhike on aircraft from one habitat to another.

Invasive alien species are deeply woven into the fabric of modern life and are a critical element in the context of modern economic globalization and its integral media of trade, transport, travel and tourism.[291] The linkage between this phenomenon and invasion pathways of species is arguably the most critical dimension of the problem. In this equation, notably the more substantial responsibility lies with states, in educating the public in identifying values of environmental sustainability with the big picture of international financing, transnational business and multi-media marketing; identifying measures that may work within existing value systems; and using risk assessment procedures. There is some responsibility that vests with airlines, starting with building awareness of the problem within the airline community and extending to the various exigencies involved in the carriage of goods that may carry the threat of invasive alien species.

Regulatory issues

During the 32nd Session of the ICAO Assembly, held in 1998, four states[292] presented a draft resolution to the Assembly, calculated to bring about action by ICAO to counter the threat posed through civil aviation of species which were not indigenous to a particular area and which could affect adversely the biodiversity of a new environment to which they were transported. The Assembly adopted Resolution A32-9 in response to this request, which essentially called upon the ICAO Council to work with other organizations of the United Nations in reducing the risk of potentially invasive alien species being introduced to areas outside their natural range and to report on work carried out in this regard at the 33rd Session of the Assembly.

The ICAO Secretariat, in conducting preparatory work on this request, contacted the International Maritime Organization (IMO) in order to seek the IMO's experience in solving problems relating to the introduction of invasive alien species outside their natural range. The IMO's response was that alien life forms travelling across the oceans in the ballast water of ships have, over sustained periods of time, caused acute problems for the marine environment, human health and public property. After much work, including participation in the Sixth Session of the Subsidiary Body on Scientific, Technical and Technological Advice (SBSTTA/6) of the Convention on Biological Diversity held in March 2001, the Council submitted its report[293] to the 33rd Session of the ICAO Assembly, held from 25 September to 5 October 2001, which included a draft resolution to supersede Resolution A32-9. The new Resolution[294] urges all contracting states to support one another's efforts to reduce the risk of introducing, through civil air transportation, potentially invasive alien species to places outside their natural range; requests the ICAO Council to continue to work with the appropriate concerned organizations to identify approaches that ICAO might take in helping to reduce the risk of introducing potentially invasive alien species to areas outside their natural range; and requests the ICAO Council to submit its report on the implementation of work at the next Ordinary Session of the Assembly, to be held in 2004.

In considering this recent ICAO measure in its regulatory context, one must necessarily address the existing legal framework both under the Convention on International Civil Aviation (Chicago Convention) of 1944,[295] which governs legal and regulatory principles of international civil aviation, and the Convention on Biological Diversity of 1992, which governs the general area of the spread of invasive alien species. The conventions hit common ground on one fundamental postulate – that which pertains to the introduction of laws and regulations to curb the threat. The Chicago Convention, in Article 23, empowers and requires states to promulgate provisions for Customs and immigration procedures, while the Convention on Biological Diversity, in its Article 8(k), requires contracting parties to develop or maintain necessary legislation and/or other regulatory provisions for the protection of threatened species and populations. The latter Convention, by Article 22, also provides that the provisions of the Convention shall not affect the rights and obligations of any contracting party deriving from any international agreement, except where the exercise of these rights and obligations would cause serious damage or threat to biological diversity.

Assembly Resolution A32-9,[296] adopted at the 32nd Session of the ICAO Assembly in 1998, while recognizing global concern of contracting states regarding such environmental problems as aircraft engine emissions, the depletion of the ozone layer, aircraft noise, and tobacco smoke in aircraft cabins, requests the ICAO Council to work with other United Nations organizations to identify approaches that ICAO might take in helping to reduce the risk of introducing potentially invasive alien species to areas outside their natural range. This measure is taken in view of the recognized responsibility of contracting states to achieve maximum compatibility between civil aviation operations and the quality of the human environment.

Insofar as civil aviation is concerned, intentional introduction of alien species does not affect carriage by air, since many stringent standards are already in place to check alien species and their migration, particularly if they could prove to be invasive after introduction to their new habitat. It is the unintentional carriage of alien species, such as the brown tree snake, already mentioned, that is of primary concern to civil aviation. Be that as it may, Resolution A32-9 imposes an obligation on ICAO to cooperate with other international organizations and bodies in taking measures to counter the threat of invasive alien species. To this extent, ICAO needs to liaise vigorously with those organizations which could provide ICAO with a list of possible invasive alien species in order to make the contracting states of ICAO aware of the inherent dangers involved in carrying alien species by air. More importantly, ICAO could, in the event that such a list is available, reconsider the carriage by air provisions relevant to the issue, as embodied in the various annexes to the Chicago Convention.

Annex 18 defines 'dangerous goods' as 'articles or substances, which are capable of posing significant risk to health, safety or property when transported by air'.[297] This definition incontrovertibly restricts harm envisaged to transportation by air and links the damage to the fact of transportation. The words 'when transported by air' would usually mean that the harm would be caused when the goods were being transported. As such, it is arguable that the carriage of species that could turn invasive after the fact of transportation, such as in the case of invasive alien species, could not fall under the definition of dangerous goods within the parameters of Annex 9. Another argument against linking the carriage by air of species that may turn invasive to the definition of dangerous goods is that Annex 18 identifies risks to health, safety or property as the effects of transportation of dangerous goods. Whether a danger to the biodiversity of an ecosystem is a safety issue is arguable in the context envisaged in the Annex, which essentially aims at safety of flight.

The Annex does not have an inclusive list of dangerous goods, except in Standard 4.2, which lists articles and substances that are identified in the technical instructions as being forbidden for transport in normal circumstances, and infected live animals. However, one of the fundamental articles that may detract from linking invasive alien species to Annex 18 is that invasive alien species are not 'invasive' from the outset, but become invasive after settling in their new habitat. Consequently, identifying such species, whose nomenclature is dependent on their behavioural patterns, as dangerous goods carried in an aircraft, would be inconsistent with the provisions of Annex 18.

The situation could, of course, be different if there could be some definite identification between species carried by air and the environment in which they will be, with definite and proven evidence that the carriage by air of such species to such environment would definitely result in the species turning invasive. Even in such an instance, the issue as to whether damage caused to the ecosystem and biosafety concerned could be categorized as a threat to safety in an aeronautical sense becomes academic.

LEGAL ASPECTS

There are no explicit legal treaties or provisions specifying liability of a carrier for the carriage of animals or substances which may prove to affect the environment of the territory into which such carriage takes place. However, it would be fair to say that liability would lie based on the principles of responsibility both of the states concerned who are expected to enact regulations under the Chicago Convention and the air carriers concerned who may be bound by such regulations.

The existence of responsibility, as a legal duty, is now widely recognized as a general principle of public international law, and is a concomitant of substantive legal norms and the premise that acts and omissions may be categorized as illegal according to the element of responsibility they carry.

Although there is clearly no global linkage between invasive alien species and civil aviation, there are undisputably explicit legal provisions at public international law which impel both states and air carriers to be aware of the dangers of the carriage of potentially dangerous environmental and safety hazards into the territory of a state. ICAO has taken the initiative in sensing this awareness and aligning itself with other organizations in collecting information and data that could be of assistance in eradicating the menace of the invasive alien species. This is yet another area which will need the constant vigilance of the aviation community, which should consider this threat as a crucial issue concerning civil aviation.

NOTES

1   John B. Young, 'A Look at Privacy', John B. Young (ed.), *Privacy*, New York: Wiley and Sons, 1978, p. 1.
2   S.D. Warren and L.D. Brandies, 'The Right of Privacy', *Harvard Law Review*, 4, 1890, 193.
3   As far back as 1973, it was claimed that 10 reels, each containing 1500 metres of tape 2·5 centimetres wide, could store a 20-page dossier on every man, woman and child in the world. See R.V. Jones, *Some Threats of Technology to Privacy, Privacy and Human Rights*, A.H. Robertson (ed.) (presented at the Third Colloquy about the European Convention on Human Rights, Brussels, 30 September–3 October 1970), Manchester University Press, 1973.

4   A.F. Westin, *Privacy and Freedom*, 2nd edn, London: Bodley Head, 1970, p. 124.

5   Lance J. Hoffman (ed.), *Computers and Privacy in the Next Decade*, New York: Academic Press, 1980, p. 142.

6   See, generally, G. Orwell, *Nineteen Eighty-four*, Oxford: Clarendon Press, 1984.

7   For a detailed analysis of the implications of credit cards with respect to the right of privacy, see S.L. Nock, *The Costs of Privacy*, New York: Aldine De Gryter, 1993, p. 43.

8   The paramount importance of airline computer reservation system records is reflected in the world-renowned cases *Libyan Arab Jamahiriya* v. *United Kingdom* and *Libyan Arab Jamahiriya* v. *United States of America* regarding the PANAM 103 accident at Lockerbie, Scotland in 1988, where the International Court of Justice requested air carriers to submit to the court the defendants' flight information and reservation details. See International Court of Justice. News Release 99/36, 'Questions of Interpretation and Application of the 1971 Montreal Convention arising from the Aerial Incident at Lockerbie' (1 July 1999), online: <*http://www.icj-cij.org/icjwww/idocket/iluk/iluk2frame.html*> (date accessed: 14 July 2000). In a similar vein, Arthur R. Miller describes the significance of airline computer reservation system records when dealing with federal, state, local and other types of investigations where these dossiers could provide valuable information. See A.R. Miller, *The Assault on Privacy*, Ann Arbor, Michigan: The University of Michigan Press, 1971, p. 42.

9   See G.G. Scott, *Mind Your Own Business – The Battle for Personal Privacy*, New York: Insight Books, 1995, p. 307; D. Burnham, *The Rise of the Computer State*, New York: Random House, 1983, p. 20. *A contrario* to the argument supported in this thesis that the advancement of technology directly affects the intimacy of individuals, US Circuit Judge Richard Posner favours the idea that other factors, such as urbanization, income and mobility development have particularly weakened the information control that, for instance, the government has over individuals: this denotes that individuals' privacy has increased. See R. Posner, 'The Right of Privacy', *Ga. L. Rev.*, 12(3), 1978, 409.

10   The text reads: 'No one shall be subjected to arbitrary interference with his privacy, family, home or correspondence, nor to attacks upon his honour and reputation. Everyone has the right to the protection of the law against such interference or attacks.' See Universal Declaration of Human Rights. GA Res. 217(III), 10 December 1948, Art. 12.

11   See International Covenant on Civil and Political Rights, GA Res. 2200(XXI), 16 December 1966, Art. 17; American Declaration on the Rights and Duties of the Man (1948), Art. 5; American Convention on Human Rights, 22 November 1969, San Jose, Costa Rica, Art. 11; Convention for the Protection of Migrant Workers, A/RES/45/158, 25 February 1991, Art. 14; United Nations Convention on Protection of the Child, GA Res. 44/25, 12 December 1989, Art. 16.

12   See P.M. Regan, *Legislating Privacy*, Chapel Hill, North Carolina: The University of North Caroline Press, 1995, p. 33; P.A. Freund, 'Privacy: One Concept or Many', in J.R. Pennnock and J.W. Chapman (eds), *Privacy*, New York: Atherton Press, 1971, p. 182.

13   In this case, the US Supreme Court acknowledged the right of women to have abortions, on the grounds that the federal government could not interfere within her 'decisional privacy' sphere. See *Roe* v. *Wade*, 410 U.S. 113 (1973). See also F.H. Cate, *Privacy in the Information Age*, Washington, DC: Brookings Institution Press, 1997, p. 49; also W. Zelermyer, *Invasion of Privacy*, Syracuse: Syracuse University Press, 1959, p. 16.

14   In a remarkable case concerning the legality of a national census scheduled by the authorities, the German Constitutional court connected the individual's liberty and the personal data processing of the intended census, to rule that, if the individuals do not know for what purposes and who is collecting the data, that situation will eventually create an abdication of the individual's rights to the processor's command, 'which cannot be tolerated in a democratic society'. See S. Simitis, 'From the Market to the Polis: The

EC Directive on the protection for Personal Data', *Iowa L. Rev.*, 80, 1995, 447–8. See also S. Hoffer, *World Cyberspace Law*, Juris Publishing, 2000, 8.1.; R. Gavison, 'Privacy and the Limits of the Law', *Yale L. J.*, 89, 1980, 421.

15 See T.M. Cooley, *A Treatise on the Law of Torts*, 2nd edn, Chicago: Callaghan, 1888, cited in S.D. Warren and L.D. Brandeis, 'The Right of Privacy', *Harv. L. Rev.*, 4 (5), 1980, 195.

16 Although the definition of privacy as the 'Right to be alone' is often erroneously attributed to Warren and Brandeis. Additionally, the concept of privacy as 'the right to be let alone', and 'the right most valued by civilized man' was embraced by US courts in the landmark dissenting opinion of Justice Louis D. Brandeis in *Olmstead* v. *United States*. See *Olmstead* v. *United States*, 277 U.S. 438, 478 (1928) (hereinafter *Olmstead*).

17 See A. Westin, *Privacy and Freedom*, New York: Atheneum, 1967, 368. For a similar conceptualization of privacy, see C. Fried, 'Privacy: Economics and Ethics: A Comment on Posner', *Ga. L. Rev.*, 12, 1978, 425.

18 See J.R. Reidenberg, 'Data Protection Law and the European Union's Directive: The Challenge for the United States: Setting Standards for Fair Information Practice in the U.S. Private Sector', *Iowa L. Rev.*, 80, 1995, 498.

19 The term 'data protection' has been translated from the German word *Datenschutz*, referring to a set of policies seeking to regulate the collection, storage, use and transfer of personal information. See C.J. Bennet, *Regulating Privacy*, Ithaca, New York: Cornell University Press, 1992, p. 13.

20 *Supra*, note 14, 'From the Market to the Polis'.

21 489 U.S. 749 at 763 (1988).

22 See A. Simmel, 'Privacy Is Not an Isolated Freedom', in J.R. Pennnock and J.W. Chapman, (eds), *Privacy*, New York: Atherton Press, 1971, p. 71.

23 See A. Halpin, *Rights & Law Analysis & Theory*, Oxford: Hart Publishing, 1997, p. 111. See also L.G. Foschio, 'Motor Vehicle Records: Balancing Individual Privacy and the Public's Legitimate Need to Know' in T.R. Kuferman (ed.), *Privacy and Publicity*, London: Meckler, 1990, p. 35. For a comprehensive study on the conflictive interest on privacy and the mass media and the freedom of speech, see D.R. Pember, *Privacy and the Press*, Seattle: University of Washington Press, 1972, p. 227; J.B. Prowda, 'A Layer's Ramble Down the Information Superhighway: Privacy and Security of Data', *Fordham L. Rev.*, 64, 1995, 738 at 769. See also J. Montgomery Curtis Memorial Seminar, *The Public, Privacy and the Press: Have the Media Gone Too Far?*, American Press Institute, 1992, p. 2.

24 *Supra*, note 15.

25 Apparently the concern of Samuel Warren for privacy was born when his wife's entertainment activities were scandalized by the emerging Bostonian yellow press. See Miller, *Air Carrier's Liability Under the Warren System*, Sydney: Butterworths, p. 170. For a good study on colonial privacy in New England, see generally D.H. Flaherty, *Privacy in Colonial New England*, Charlottesville: University Press of Virginia, 1972, p. 164.

26 The former Privacy Commissioner of British Columbia, Canada, has asserted that privacy was originally a 'non-legal concept'. See D.H. Flaherty, 'On the Utility of Constitutional Rights to Privacy and Data Protection', *Case W. Res.*, 41, 1991, 835.

27 The US Supreme Court has strongly affirmed that the US Constitution does not grant privacy rights to private individuals among themselves, thus leading to its resolution to the law of torts. See *Prudential Insurance Co.* v. *Cheek*, 259 U.S. 530 at 543 (1922).

28 See F.H. Cate, *Privacy in the Information Age*, *supra*, note 13. Washington, DC: Brookings Institution Press, 1997, p. 49. See also W. Zelermyer, *Invasion of Privacy*, *supra*, note 13.

29 See I.J. Lloyd, *Information Technology Law*, London: Butterworths, 1997, p. 38.

30 For an interesting business guidelines compromise with respect to the privacy of customers, see Direct Marketing Association, 'Privacy Promise Member Compliance

Guide – Keeping Our Privacy Promise to Consumers' online:
<*http://www.the-dma.org/library/privacy/privacypromise.shtml*> (date accessed: 13 July 2000).

31   See J.R. Reinberger, *supra*, note 18, 515.

32   See J.R. Reidenberg, 'Restoring Americans' Privacy in Electronic Commerce', *Berkeley Tech. L. J.*, 14, 1999, 792; R.M. Gellman, 'Fragment, Incomplete, and Discontinuous: The Failure of Federal Privacy Regulatory Proposals and Institutions', *Software L. J.*, 6, 1993, 199; M.E. Budnitz, 'Privacy Protection for Consumer Transactions in Electronic Commerce: Why Self-Regulation is Inadequate', *South Carolina L. Rev.*, 49, 1998, 860 (expressing the opinion that although acknowledging the serious threats to the privacy of consumers, the US government has decided to adopt an industry self-regulation approach conflicting with the EC Directive); P. Mell, 'A Hitchhiker's Guide To Trans-Border Data Exchanges Between EU Member States and the United States under the European Union Directive on the Protection of Personal Information' *Pace Int'l L. Rev.*, 9, 1991, 182; J.M. Myers, 'Creating Data Protection Legislation in the United States: An Examination of Current Legislation in the European Union, Spain and the United States', *Case W. Res. J. Int'l L.*, 29, 1997, 146.

33   See generally J. Rule et al., *The Politics of Privacy*, New York: Elsevier, 1980.

34   United States, Constitution, First Amendment.

35   In this regard, Fred H. Cate has written:
the U.S. approach to information privacy inevitably results in some harm to individual's privacy, reputations, and sensibilities, but it reflects a constitutional calculation that such harm is less threatening to the body politic than the harm associated with centralised privacy protection, government interference with the information flows necessary to sustain democracies and markets, and the growing ineffectiveness of omnibus legal controls in the face of the widespread proliferation of powerful information technologies. F.H. Cate, 'The Changing Face of Privacy Protection in the European Union and the United States', *Ind. L. Rev.*, 33, 1999, 231.

36   *Supra*, note 9.

37   See P. Samuelson, 'A New Kind of Privacy? Regulating Uses of Personal Data in the Global Information Economy', review of '*Data Privacy Law, Study of United States Data Protection* by P.M. Schwartz & J.R. Reidemberg', *Cal. L. Rev.*, 87, 1999, 763.

38   Originally the law solely provided a remedy for physical interference with the life and property of the individual. See M.L. Erns and A.U. Schwartz, *Privacy – The Right to Be Let Alone*, New York: Macmillan, 1962, p. 47.

39   *Supra*, note 13.

40   See D.R. Tan, 'Personal Privacy in the Information Age: Comparison of Internet Data Protection Regulations in the United States and the European Union', *Loy. L.A. Int'l & Comp. L. J.*, 21, 1999, 664.

41   See United States, Constitution, First Amendment.

42   Ibid., Third Amendment.

43   At the outset, the Fourth Amendment was envisaged as a safeguard to protect private property interests against the abuse of the federal government, a situation that was frequent during colonial times. The concept was later extended to include privacy. See D.E. Lively, *Landmark Supreme Court Cases*, Westport, Connecticut: Greenwood Press, 1999, p. 277. The full text of the amendment reads as follows:
'The right of the people to be secure in their persons, houses, papers, and effects, against unreasonable searches and seizures, shall not be violated, and no Warrants shall issue, but upon probable cause, supported by Oath or affirmation, and particularly describing the place to be searched, and the persons or things to be seized.' United States, Constitution, Fourth Amendment.

44   Ibid., Fourteenth Amendment.

45 *Supra*, note 16.
46 See B. Schwartz, *A Commentary on the Constitution of the United States*, vol. I, New York: Macmillan, 1968, p. 171.
47 *Supra*, note 16. The same rationale was later adopted in *Goldman* v. *United States*, 316 U.S. 129 (1942).
48 *Olmstead* included the secret activities of alcohol smugglers, who were intercepted by the police. The ruling of the court came when the prohibition of alcohol was at its peak. Owing to the fact that the smuggling of alcohol became a major concern for the US authorities and the media itself, it is likely that the court was influenced by those factors.
49 See *Griswold* v. *Connecticut*, 381 U.S. 479 (1965) (hereinafter *Griswold*). The case involved the claim of a couple against a statute of the State of Connecticut prohibiting the giving of contraceptive information. The court ruled in favour of the couple, granting the 'marital right of privacy'; however, the court failed to define such a right. See W. Page Keeton (ed.), *Prosser and Keeton on Torts*, 5th edn, St. Paul, Minnesota: West Publishing, 1984, p. 867.
50 *Griswold*, at 484. The principle of constitutionally protected areas of privacy was adopted, inter alia, in *Silverman* v. *United States*, 365 U.S. 505 (1961); *Lopez* v. *United States*, 373 U.S. 427 (1963); *Berger* v. *New York*, 388 U.S. 41 (1967).
51 See *Katz* v. *United States*, 389 U.S. 347 (1967). The same rationale was adopted by the US Supreme Court in *Terry* v. *Ohio*, 392 U.S. 1 at 9 (1968).
52 The case involved the wiretapping of a telephone conversation that an individual conducted from a public telephone booth, where a recording device was attached. See also C.J. Antieau, *Modern Constitutional Law*, vol. I, San Francisco: Brancroft Whitney Company, 1969, p. 160.
53 See *Smith* v. *Maryland (State of)*, 442 U.S. 735 (1979). The same reasoning was held in *Bond* v. *United States*, 120 S. Ct. 1462 (2000) (hereinafter *Bond*) and *California (State of)* v. *Ciraolo*, 476 U.S. 207 (1986).
54 A pen register tape was later defined as 'a device which records or decodes electronic or other impulses which identify the numbers dialled or otherwise transmitted on the telephone line to which such device is attached'. See 18 U.S.C. § 3127 (3) (1994).
55 See note 53, *supra*.
56 See J.H.F. Shattuck, *Rights of Privacy*, Skokie, Illinois: National Textbook Company, 1977, 19.
57 *Supra*, note 53. Furthermore, in *U.S.* v. *Smith*, 91-5077 (5th Cir. 1992), involving a case of interception of cordless phone conversation, the claim was denied on the basis that the plaintiff failed to introduce evidence that his subjective expectation of privacy was reasonable.
58 See *Whalen* v. *Roe*, 429 U.S. 589 (1977).
59 See generally A.M. Jurevic, ' When Technology and Health Care Collide: Issues with Electronic Medical Records and Electronic Mail', *Univ. of Missouri at Kansas City L. Rev.*, 66, 1998, 809.
60 See *Iacobucci* v. *Newport (City of)*, 785 F. 2d. 1354 (6th Cir. 1986). Similar decisions were previously given in *Thom* v. *New York Stock Exchange*, 306 F. Supp. 1002 (S.D.N.Y. 1969); *Miller* v. *New York Stock Exchange*, 425 F. 2d. 1074 (2nd Cir. 1970).
61 See *Perkey* v. *Department of Motor Vehicles*, 42 Cal. 3d. 185 (1986).
62 See *Skinner* v. *Railway Labour Executives Association*, 489 U.S. 602 (1989).
63 See *Vernonia* v. *Wayne Acton*, 513 U.S. 1145 (1995).
64 For a comprehensive examination of the conflictive interest between privacy and public safety in drug testing cases, see J. Wagner Decew, *In Pursuit of Privacy*, Ithaca, New York: Cornell University Press, 1997, p. 125.

65   See Convention for the Protection of Human Rights and Fundamental Freedoms, 4
      November 1950, 213 U.N.T.S. 221 at 223, Eur. T.S. 5, Art. 8.
66   See also D. Feldman, 'Privacy-related Rights and their Social Value', in P. Birks (ed.),
      Privacy and Loyalty, Oxford: Clarendon Press, 1997, p. 28.
67   The European authorities have long expressed concern about the possible implications
      for the individual's privacy caused by the advance of technology. Hence the Committee
      of Experts on Human Rights reported in 1970 that the existing legal framework was
      inadequate to protect privacy rights. See I.J. Lloyd, *supra*, note 29, p. 45.
68   The German state of Hesse passed the first legislation in Europe addressing privacy data
      protection in 1970. Later, Sweden passed the Data Act of 1973; Germany enacted the
      Federal Data Protection Act in 1977; France passed the Law on Informatics, Data Banks
      and Freedoms; and Austria endorsed the Data Protection Act, both in 1978; finally Great
      Britain established the Data Protection Act of 1984. See V. Mayer-Schonberger, 'Trans-
      Atlantic Information Privacy Legislation and Rational Choice Theory', *George Wash. L.
      Rev.*, 67, 1999, 1316. See generally J.A.L. Sterling, *The Data Protection Act 1984*, 2nd
      edn, Bicester, Oxfordshire: CCD Editions Limited, 1984; J. Freese, 'Seven Years of
      Swedish Data Legislation – Analysis of Impact and Trend for the Future', *Informatics et
      Protection de la Personality*, Saint-Paul Fribourg: Editions Universités Fribourg Suisse,
      1981, p. 69; J. Veau, *Le Droit Au Respect De La Vie Praevia*, Brussels: Presses
      Universités de Namur, 1974, p. 19; R. Wacks, *Personal Information*, Oxford: Clarendon
      Press, 1989, p. 39; D.H. Flaherty, *Protecting Privacy in Surveillance Societies*, Chapel
      Hill, North Carolina: The University of North Carolina Press, 1989; F. Rigaux et al.,
      LaVie Praevia, une liberté parmi les autres?, Brussels: Maison Larcier, 1992; P. Seipel
      (ed.), *From Data Protection to Knowledge Machines*, Deventer: Kluwer Law and
      Taxation Publishers, 1990; Y. Poullet, 'Data Protection between Property and Liberties',
      in H.W.K. Kaspersen and A. Oskamp (eds), *Amongst Friends in Computers and Law –
      A Collection of Essays in Remembrance of Guy Vandenberghe*, Deventer: Kluwer Law
      and Taxation Publishers, 1990, p. 161.
69   See Council of Europe, Convention for the Protection of Individuals with Regard to
      Automatic Processing of Personal Data, Europ. T.S. No. 108 (28 January 1981)
      (hereinafter European Convention). Later, the EC Commission recommended that states
      adopt the aforesaid Convention, understanding that the establishment of the common
      market calls for an extensive standardization of the conditions obtaining in relation to data
      processing at the European level. The rationale of the European efforts lies in the fact that
      data protection is desirable so that there can be free movement of data and information
      across frontiers and in order to prevent unequal conditions of competition and the
      consequent distortion of the common market. See EC, Commission Recommendation of
      29 July 1981 relating to the Council of Europe Convention for the protection of individuals
      with regard to automatic processing of personal data [1981] O.J.L. 246/31.
70   See also EC, *Explanatory report on the Convention for the Protection of Individuals with
      regard to Automatic Processing of Personal Data*, Strasbourg, 1981; *New technologies:
      a challenge to privacy protection?*, Strasbourg, 1989. See generally EC, *Protection of
      personal data used for social security purposes*, Strasbourg, 1986.
71   See P.P. Swire and R.F. Litan, *None of Your Business*, Washington, DC: Brookings
      Institution Press, 1998, p. 24.
72   The term 'data protection' has been highly criticized among scholars for giving the
      connotation that what is really protected is the information rather than its subjects. See
      I.J. Lloyd, *Information Technology Law*, London: Butterworths, 1997, p. 38.
73   See EC, Directive 95/46 EC of the European Parliament and of the Council of 24
      October 1995 on the protection of individuals with regard to the processing of personal
      data and on the free movement of such data, [1995] O.J.L. 281/31 (hereinafter EC
      Directive).

74 The competency of the directive, found in Article 7(*a*), lies in the European Union, which aims at promoting the free movement of goods, persons, services and capital; therefore it is envisaged that personal data should flow freely from one member state to another, but it also acknowledges the necessity to safeguard the rights of individuals in accordance with the Convention for the Protection of Human Rights and Fundamental Freedoms, 4 November 1950, 213 U.N.T.S. 221 at 223, Eur. T.S. 5, Art. 8. See Treaty Establishing the European Union, 448.

75 In a remarkable case concerning the legality of a national census scheduled by the authorities, the German Constitutional court connected the individual's liberty and the personal data processing of the intended census, to rule that, if the individuals do not know for what purposes and who is collecting the data, that situation will eventually create an abdication of the individual's rights to the processor's command, 'which cannot be tolerated in a democratic society'. See S. Simitis, 'From the Market to the Polis: The EC Directive on the protection for Personal Data', *Iowa L. Rev.*, 80, 1995, 447–8.

76 It is worth mentioning that the protection of privacy rights of legal persons falls outside the scope of the directive. See EC Directive, *supra*, note 73, Art. 1.

77 According to the definitions contained in the directive, the term 'personal data' refers to 'any information relating to an identified or identifiable natural person', clarifying that an identifiable person is 'someone who can be identified, directly or by reference to an identification number or to one or more factors specific to his physical, psychological, mental, economic, cultural or social identity'. See EC Directive, *supra*, note 73, Art. 2(*a*).

78 See P. Samuelson, 'A New Kind of Privacy? Regulating Uses of Personal Data in the Global Information Economy'; review of *Data Privacy Law, Study of United States Data Protection* by P.M. Schwartz and J.R. Reidemberg, *Cal. L. Rev.*, 87, 1999, 763.

79 The term 'processing of personal data' is referred as 'any operation or set of operations which is performed upon personal data, whether or not by automatic means, such as collection, recording, organization, storage, adaptation or alteration, retrieval, consultation, use disclosure by transmission, dissemination or otherwise making available, alignment or combination, blocking, erasure or destruction' (EC Directive, *supra*, note 73, Art. 2 (*b*)).

80 A filing system means 'any structured set of personal data which are accessible according to specific criteria, whether centralised, decentralised or dispersed on a functional or geographical basis' ibid., Art. 2(*c*).

81 See ibid., Art. 3. Some commentators have already expressed profound concern about the fact that sometimes it can be extremely difficult to distinguish between purely personal or household activity and the normal endeavours individuals undertake through the normal course of their labour activities. For instance, the use of a laptop could best illustrate the complexity of the scenario. See P.P. Swire and R.E. Litan, *None of Your Business*, Washington, DC: Brookings Institution Press, 1998, p. 70.

82 The term 'controller' is defined as: 'a natural or legal person, public authority, agency or any other body which alone or jointly with others determines the purposes and means of the processing of personal data'. See EC Directive, *supra*, note 73, Art. 2(*d*). From the language of the provision, it is clear that the EC Directive is applicable to both private organizations and government agencies that process personal data of individuals.

83 See ibid., Art. 4.

84 See Swire and Litan, *supra*, note 81, 132.

85 As a matter of fact, negotiations are under way between Amadeus corporate executives and the European authorities in order to reach an agreement viable for both parties. See Swire and Litan, *supra*, note 81, p. 133.

86 See ibid., Art. 10.

87 For details of the machine-readable passport and its development in the International Civil Aviation Organization, see, R.I.R. Abeyratne, 'The Development of the

Machine Readable Passport and Visa and the Legal Rights of the Data Subject', *Annals of Air & Space Law/Annales de Droit Aérien et Spatial*, XVII, pt II, 1992, pp. 1–31, at 22.

88 See note 73, *supra*. Similarly, numerous other countries, such as Argentina, Brazil, Paraguay and Colombia, concede the right of access to the information the government and its agencies have on the data subject through the legal institution of the *Habeas Data* as a cause of action, which translated from Latin means 'bring me the data'. In some countries the *Habeas Data* has been extended to include processing of personal data by private parties, although the latter constitutes a constant doctrinal debate among scholars. It was first established in the Portuguese Constitution of 1976, then adopted by the Spanish in 1978, and subsequently by a large number of countries, particularly in South America. See J.A. Moreno Rufinelli, *Nuevas Instituciones de la Constitución Nacional*, (Asunción: Intercontinental Editora, 1996, p. 145. See also Constitutional Act. 1994 (Argentina), Art. 43; Constitutional Act. 1976 (Portugal), Art. 35; Constitutional Act. 1978 (Spain), Art. 18(4); Constitutional Act. 1991 (Colombia), Art. 25; Constitutional Act. 1992 (Paraguay), Art. 135.

89 EC Directive, Art. 12(*b*).

90 See ibid., Art. 14.

91 See M.P. Roch, 'Filling the Void of Data Protection in the United States: Following the European Example', *Computer & High Tech. L. J.*, 12, 1996, 83.

92 See EC Directive, *supra*, note 80, Art. 16.

93 See ibid., Art. 17.

94 See ibid., Art. 28(1). For instance, the controller or his representative must inform the supervisory authority before carrying out wholly or partly any automatic processing of personal data, which, applied to the air transport sector, means that each incumbent in the business must first identify who is the controller of the personal data, to notify the supervisory authority later in its respective country. See ibid., Art. 18. The contents of the notification should include the name and address of the controller and of his representative, the purpose of processing, a description of the categories of the data relating to the data subject, the recipient of the categories, and any proposed transfers of data to third countries. See ibid., Art. 19.

95 See ibid., Art. 22.

96 See ibid., Art. 23.

97 See ibid., Art. 24.

98 See EC, *Handbook on cost-effective compliance with Directive 95/46/EC* (Annex to the Annual Report of 1998 of the working party established by Article 29 of Directive 95/46/EC), p. 58 (hereinafter *EC Handbook*).

99 Lance J. Hoffman (ed.), *Computers and Privacy in the Next Decade*, London: Tolley, 1988, 146.

100 *Collin Mellors, Governments and the Individual – Their Secrecy and His Privacy*, cited in, John B.Young (ed.), *A Look at Privacy*, New York: Wiley & Sons, 1978, p. 94.

101 *Air Letter*, Wednesday, 17 August 1994, no. 13,060, p. 1.

102 Rebecca D. Chute, 'On a Collision Course', *Air Line Pilot*, March 1995, p. 20.

103 Ibid.

104 *Pasinato* v. *American Airlines, Inc.*, No. 93 C 1510, 1994 Westlaw 171522 (N.D. Ill., 2 May 1994). For a more detailed report and analysis of this case, see *Lloyd's Aviation Law*, 13(11), 1 June 1994, pp. 4–5.

105 Convention for the Unification of Certain Rules Relating to International Carriage by Air, signed at Warsaw on 12 October 1929. Hereafter referred to as the Convention.

106 Ibid., Article 3.1.

107 Ibid., Article 3.2.

108 Halsbury states that the word 'accident' excludes the operation of natural causes such as

old age, congenital diseases or insidious diseases, or the natural progression of some constitutional, physical or mental defect (Halsbury, *Laws of England*, 3rd edn, vol. 22, para. 585, p. 293). The case of *Fenton* v. *Thorley and Co. Ltd*, 1903 A.C. 443, qualified this somewhat restrictive definition of the word 'accident' when Lord Lindley said: 'the word "accident" is not a technical legal term with a clearly defined meaning. Speaking generally, but with reference to legal liabilities, an accident means any unintended occurrence which produces hurt or loss'. Ibid., at 453. A later case, *The Board of Management of Trim Joint School* v. *Kelly*, 1914 A.C. 667, held that an intentional act of third parties could also be considered an 'accident' at common law.

109 Annex 13, Convention on International Civil Aviation 1944.
110 Shawcross and Beaumont, *Air Law*, 4th edn, re-issue, 1988, VII, 153.
111 105 S. Ct. 1338 (1985).
112 Ibid.
113 580 F. 2d. 1193 (3rd Cir. 1978).
114 Ibid., at 1052.
115 *Husserl* v. *Swiss Air Transport Co. Ltd*, 485 F. 2d. 1240, (2nd Cir. 1975); *Day* v. *Trans World Airlines Inc.*, 528 F. 2d. 31 (2nd Cir. 1975); *Evangelinos* v. *Trans World Airlines Inc.*, 550 F. 2d. 152 (3rd Cir. 1976); *Salerno* v. *Pan American World Airways*, 19 Avi. 17 705 (S.D.N.Y. 1985).
116 86 A.D. 2d. 658.
117 This test is the result of decisions in *Day* v. *Trans World Airlines Inc.*, 528 F. 2d. 31 (2nd Cir. 1975) and *Evangelinos* v. *Trans World Airlines Inc.*, 550 F. 2d. 152 (2nd Cir. 1977).
118 Article 17 of the Warsaw Convention states: 'the carrier shall be liable for damage sustained in the event of the death or wounding of a passenger, if the accident which caused the damage so sustained took place on board the aircraft or in the course of any of the operations of embarking or disembarking'.
119 Ibid.,
120 *Husserl* v. *Swiss Air Transport Co. Ltd*, 388 F. Supp. 1238 (S.D.N.Y. 1975).
121 *Scarf* v. *Trans World Airlines Inc.*, 4 Avi. 17 795 (S.D.N.Y. 1955). Also *Chutter* v. *K.L.M. Royal Dutch Airlines*, 132 F. Supp. 611 (S.D.N.Y. 1954).
122 *Adler* v. *Austrian Airlines*, 78 S.C. Eu. 564 at 568.
123 22 Av. Cas. (CCH 17,731 S.D.N.Y. 1990). Also cited in 900 F. 2d. at p. 10.
124 22 Av. Cas. (CCH 17,639 S.D.N.Y. 1989).
125 No. 83-5540 (ND-Cal. 1984).
126 Ibid., 5543.
127 *Knoll* v. *Trans World Airlines Inc.*, 528 F. 2d. 31 (2nd Cir. 1975).
128 *Supra*, note. 117.
129 Analysed in *Buonocore*, 900 F. 2d. at 10.
130 45 F. 3d. 435, 1995.
131 Ibid.
132 *Quinn* v. *Canadian Airlines International Ltd.*, Ontario Court, General Division, 18 O.R. (2d) 326, (rendered 30 May 1994), reported in *Lloyd's Aviation Law*, 13(17), 1 September, 1994, 1–2.
133 Ibid., 351–2.
134 *Supra*, note 104, at 5.
135 *In re Korean Airlines Disaster of September 1 1983*, 932 F. 2d. 1475 (D.C. Cir.), cert. denied, 112 S. Ct. 616 (1991).
136 Ibid.
137 Definition given in *In re Korean Airlines Disaster*, *supra*, note 135, at 1479.
138 See *Lloyd's Aviation Law*, 13(11), 1 June 1994, 1–3.
139 14 F. 3d. 1410 (9th Cir. 1994).
140 853 F. Supp. 30 (D. Mass. 1994).

141 See E.L. Wiener, 'Cockpit Automation', in E.L. Wiener and D.C. Nagel, *Human Factors in Aviation*, San Diego: Academic Press, 1988, pp. 433–59.

142 Rebecca D. Schute, 'Cockpit–Cabin Communication: I. A Tale of Two Cultures', *The International Journal of Aviation Psychology*, 5(3), 1995, 258.

143 Cited in V. P. Moshansky, *Commission of Inquiry into the Air Ontario Crash at Dryden, Ontario*, Toronto: Minister of Supply and Services, 1992, p.1087.

144 See M.J. Vandermark, 'Should Flight Attendants be Included in CRM Training?' A Discussion of Major Air Carriers' Approach to Total Crew Training', *The International Journal of Aviation Psychology*, 1, 1991, pp. 87–94. See also A. Merritt, 'Human Factors on the Flight Deck; the Influence of National Culture', paper presented at the Seventh International Symposium on Aviation Psychology, Columbus, Ohio, April 1993.

145 Convention for the Unification of Certain Rules Relating to International Carriage by Air, signed at Warsaw on 12 October 1929. See *Annals of Air & Space Law*, XVIII, 1993, pt 11, 323 for text of the Convention.

146 [1980] 2 All E.R. 696.

147 Ibid., at 704, also [1981] A.C. 251 at 279.

148 Ibid.

149 [1997] 1 All E.R. 193 at 102, also [1997] A.C. 430 at 442.

150 *Landress* v. *Phoenix Mutual Life Ins. Co.* (1934) 291 U.S. 491; *Air France* v. *Saks* (1985) 470 U.S. 392.

151 *Daddon* v. *Air France*, [1984] Shawcross & Beaumont Aviation Reports, VII/141.

152 [2000] 1 *Lloyd's Rep*. 95.

153 17 April 1991, 23 Avi. 17 367.

154 358 N.Y.S. 2d. 97 (1974), 13 Avi. 17 231.

155 368 F. Supp. 1152 (1973), 12 Avi. 18 405.

156 For a detailed discussion on this subject, see Caroline Desbiens, 'Air Carrier's Liability for Emotional Distress Under Article 17 of the Warsaw Convention: Can it Still be Invoked?', *Annals of Air and Space Law*, XVII, pt II, 1992, pp. 159–66.

157 (D.C.N.Y. 1972) 351 F. Supp. 702.

158 See *Lynch* v. *Knight* (1861) 9 H.L.C. 577, at 598 where Lord Wensleydale said: 'Mental pain or anxiety the law cannot value, and does not pretend to redress, when the unlawful act complained of causes that alone'.

159 Hereafter, injury to the human mind, mental distress, pain of mind, emotional distress and other similar references mean any influence on the human mind which would temporarily or permanently upset the mental stability of a person, sufficiently to cause discomfort to the mind.

160 Hereinafter referred to as the United States.

161 G.E. White, *Tort Law in America* (1980), XI.

162 See W. Prosser, *Handbook of the Law of Torts*, 4th edn, 1971; also, Prosser, 'Intentional Infliction of Mental Suffering – A New Tort', *Michigan Law Review*, 37, 1939, 874; G.E. White, *supra*, note 161, 102.

163 See G.E. White, *supra*, notes 161, 102, 103.

164 See *Michigan Law Review*, 37, 1939, 874.

165 I.M. Marks, *Fears and Phobias* (1969) 1.

166 Ibid.

167 *Boston Medical and Surgical Journal*, CL XIII, 1910, 893.

168 W.B. Cannon, *Bodily Changes in Pain, Hunger, Fear and Rage*, 1932, 253–4.

169 Ibid., 325–6.

170 W.B. Cannon, *The Wisdom of the Human Body*, 1967, p. 276.

171 For internal changes causing discomfort, see generally, 'The Physiology of Emotions', *Report of the Third Annual Symposium of the Kaiser Foundation Hospitals, Northern California*, 1961, 17-15.

172 The attitude is typified by the strong approach taken in *Lynch* v. *Knight*, *supra*, note 158.
173 See W. Prosser, *Handbook of the Law of Torts*, 4th edn, p. 328.
174 Ibid.
175 *Dulieu* v. *White* (1901) 2 K.B. 669, at 677.
176 Jeremiah Smith, 'Torts Without Names', *University of Pennsylvania Law Review*, 69, 1920–21, 91.
177 Street, Introduction, *Foundations of Legal Liability*, pp. XXV–XXVI.
178 *Davis* v. *Hill*, 291 S.W. (1927) 681, at 684.
179 *International & G.N.R. Co.* v. *Hood*, 118 S.W. (1909) 1119, at 1122.
180 *Waller* v. *Keller*, 218 S.W. (1920) 792, at 794.
181 G.E. White, *supra*, note 161, 103.
182 See *Donoughue* v. *Stevenson*, 1932 A.C. 562.
183 See *Dillon* v. *Legg*, 69 Cal. Rptr. 72.
184 See *Shepard* v. *Superior Court*, 142 Cal. Rptr. 612.
185 Protocol to Amend the Warsaw Convention signed at Guatemala City, 1971, hereafter referred to as the Guatemala Protocol.
186 S. Freud, *Inhibitions, Symptoms and Anxiety*, 1959, p.12. Sigmund Freud indicated here that, while fear *per se* was identified as neurotic anxiety, a combination of fear with anxiety produced mental injury, which he said was the result of unrecognized internal sources of threat that produced adverse physical changes in the human body. See also C.E. Izard, and S.S. Tompkins, *Anxiety and Behaviour*, 1966, p. 125; C.D. Spielberger, *Anxiety – Current Trends in Theory and Research*, vol. 2, 1972, p. 263; R. May, *Meaning of Anxiety*, 1950, p. 53; 'The Physiology of Emotions', *Report of the Third Annual Symposium of The Kaiser Foundation Hospitals, Northern California*, 1961, pp. 15–16; F. Dunbar, *Emotions and Bodily Changes*, 4th edn, 1954, p. 685, who give similar views on the pathological effects of mental distress on the human body.
187 Isaacz M. Marks, *supra*, note 165. The experience of fear and anxiety is known to cause a person to bend his body, jerk his head forward, blink his eyes: see R. May, *supra*, note 186, pp. 46-48. *The Psychosomatic Journal of the American Medical Association* in 1947, p. 1527, recorded that half the cases of acute illnesses and recovery problems are attributable to the mental state of the patient. Anxiety is also known to bring about an imbalance in the digestive process: see W.B. Cannon, *supra*, note 168. W.B. Cannon, in his book, *Wisdom of the Human Body*, *supra*, note 170, 276, states that mental distress would increase blood sugar levels of a subject, bringing about a positively unpleasant experience.
188 12 Avi. 17 603 (S.D.N.Y. 1975).
189 3 Avi. 17 231 (N.Y. Ct. App. 1974).
190 *Supra*, note 158.
191 13 Avi. 17 603 (S.D. N.Y. 1975).
192 This somewhat parochial view was followed in the cases of *Karfunkel* v. *Air France*, 14 Avi. 17 674 (S.D.N.Y. 1977) and *Krystal* v. *British Overseas Airways Corporation*, 14 Avi. 17 128 (C.D. Cal. 1975). Also *Herman* v. *TWA*, 12 Avi. 17 304 (1972) and *Palagonia* v. *TWA*, 13 Avi. 17 478(1974) were two further instances of mental injury being 'included' in the rubric of physical injury.
193 872 F. 2d. 1462 (11th Cir. 1989).
194 (1991) 499 U.S. 530.
195 Rene H. Mankiewicz, 'The Application of Article 17 of the Warsaw Convention to Mental Suffering Not Related to Physical Injury', *Annals of Air & Space Law*, IV, 1979, 192.
196 See David B. Johnston, 'Australian Court Holds that Damages for Pure Psychological Injury are not Recoverable in Warsaw Convention Cases', *Aviation Insurance and Law*, 16(9), September 1997, p. 166.

197 Ibid.
198 *Georgopoulos* v. *America Airlines* [1994] I.A.S.L.R. 38 (N.S.W. Sup. Ct.).
199 *Supra*, note 194.
200 See *Jack* v. *Transworld Airlines, Inc.*, 854 F. Supp. 654 (N.W.Cal. 1994); *Burnett* v. *Transworld*, Inc. 975 F. 2d. 35; Also *Tseng* v. *El Al Israeli Airlines Ltd*, 919 F. Supp. 155 (S.D.N.Y. 1996).
201 11b. S. Ct. 629 (1996).
202 *In re Aircraft Disaster Near Roselawn, Indiana on October 31, 1994*, 954 F. Supp. 175 (N.D. Ill. 1997).
203 Ibid., at 179.
204 'The Modernization of the "Warsaw System" – The ICAO Draft Convention on the Liability of the Air Carrier', *The Aviation Quarterly*, pt 5, July 1997, pp. 298–9.
205 Ibid., p. 313.
206 Draft Convention for the Unification of Certain Rules for International Carriage by Air, Reference Text, DCW Doc. No. 5. 5/3/99, Montreal: ICAO.
207 Ibid., p. 8.
208 See J.M. Hart, 'Neurosis Following Trauma', *Cumberland Law Review*, 8, 495.
209 Ibid., 497.
210 *Clark* v. *Associate Retail Credit Men*, 105 F. 2d. 62, at 64.
211 See Prosser, *Handbook of the Law of Torts*, 4th edn, 1971, p. 327.
212 Bohlen, *Am. L. Reg.*, 51, 1902, N.S., 141.
213 See Harper and McNeely, *Wis. L. R.*, 1983, 426; Goodrich, *Michigan L. R.*, 20, 1922, 497; Magruder, *Harvard L. R.*, 49, 1936, 1033.
214 W. Prosser, *supra*, note 211, 54.
215 See Mark Franklin, 'Liability in Negligence for Post Traumatic Stress Disorder', *The Aviation Quarterly*, pt 3, January 1997, p. 173.
216 N. Green, *Proximate and Remote Cause* (in essays) at 1.
217 W.H. Pedrick, 'Does Tort Law Have A Future ?', *Ohio S. L. J.*, 39, 784.
218 *Morris* v. *KLM* [2001] 3 All E.R. 126 at 143.
219 *Polish Service in Danzig Case* (1925) P.C.I.J., Ser. B No. 11 at p. 37. For similar approaches, see the *Eastern Greenland Case* (1933) P.C.I.J. Ser. A/B No. 53 at p. 49, and US–Italy Arbitration, *Interpretation of Air Transport Services Agreement*, RIAA XVI 75, p. 91.
220 Ian Brownlie, *Principles of Public International Law*, 4th edn, Oxford: Clarendon Press, 1992, p. 632.
221 Ibid.
222 Second International Conference on Private Aeronautical Law, Warsaw, 4–12 October, 1929, *Minutes*, translated by Robert S. Horner and Didier Legrez, Rothman & Co., 1975, p. 13.
223 866 F. Supp. 588 (D.D.C. 1994).
224 932 F. 2d. 1475, 1479 (D.C. Cir. 1991).
225 Ibid.
226 H. Drion, *Limitation of Liabilities in International Air Law*, The Hague: Martinus Nijhoff, 1954, p. 12.
227 Ibid., p. 64.
228 Bin Cheng, 'What is Wrong with the Montreal Additional Protocol No. 3?', *Air Law*, XIV(6), 1989, 232.
229 D.A. Kilbride, 'Six Decades of Insuring Liability Under Warsaw', *Air Law*, XIV(4/5) 1989, 191.
230 Ibid., 192.
231 Peter Martin, '50 Years of the Warsaw Convention: A Practical Man's Guide', *Annals of Air & Space Law*, IV, 1979, 248.

232 Ibid.
233 Werner Guldimann, 'A Future System of Liability in Air Carriage', *Annals of Air & Space Law*, 1991, 96.
234 Bin Cheng, 'Limit on Air Carriers' Liability for Passenger Injury or Death: The Rising Sun Eclipses Guatemala City and Montreal – USA, Quo Vadis?', *Lloyd's Aviation Law*, 13(10), 15 May 1994.
235 George N. Tompkins Jr, 'The Case for the Japanese Initiative Approach in the United States', *Lloyd's Aviation Law*, 13(23), 1 December 1994, 4–5. See also, generally, Koichi Abe, 'The Warsaw Convention and the Waiver of Limitations of Liability by the Airlines of Japan', *Lloyd's Aviation Law*, 12(12), 15 June 1993, 1.
236 Opening Statement of Japan Airlines Delivered by Koichi Abe, Vice President, Legal Affairs, at the International Air Transport Association, Airline Liability Conference, 19–27 June 1995 (Washington, DC). See ALC – Item 7, WP 21, Doc. II, pp. 2–4.
237 See ICAO papers, A31-WP/224, P/57, 'Report on Agenda Item 36.2', 36.2-3.
238 Convention for the Unification of Certain Rules Relating to Assistance and Salvage of Aircraft at Sea, Brussels, 29 September 1938.
239 Convention on International Civil Aviation, signed at Chicago on 7 December 1944. See ICAO Doc. 7300/8, 8th edn, 2000.
240 The International Civil Aviation Organization (ICAO), is a specialized agency of the United Nations responsible for the regulation of international civil aviation. ICAO, which has a membership of 187 states, was created by the Chicago Convention.
241 Annex 12 to the Convention on International Civil Aviation, 'Search and Rescue', 6th edn, March 1975, Standard 2.1.1.
242 Ibid., Standard 2.1.1.1.
243 Ibid., Standard 2.2.1: boundaries of search and rescue regions should, insofar as is practicable, be coincident with the boundaries of corresponding flight information regions. See Recommendation 2.2.1.1 of Annex 12.
244 David Morrow, 'Preparing for Disaster', *Airport Support*, April 1995, p. 29.
245 Report in FAZ No. 275/1996 (25 November 1996), p. 9.
246 It is not the intention of this discussion to address issues pertaining to rights in recovery of costs incurred in search and rescue of aircraft and passengers. For this aspect of SAR, see Andreas Kadletz, 'Rescue and Salvage of Aircraft', ZLW 46. Jg 2/1997, 209–16.
247 Standard 3.1.1.
248 Recommendation 3.1.2.
249 Recommendation 3.1.2.1.
250 Advisory Opinions on Western Sahara, 1975 *I.C.J. Rep.* 12 (16 October); Legal Consequences for States of the Continued Presence of South Africa in Namibia (South West Africa) notwithstanding Security Council Resolution 276 (1970), 1971 *I.C.J. Rep* 16 (21 June).
251 See *The United Nations and International Law*, Christopher C. Joyner (ed.), Cambridge University Press, 1997, p. 84.
252 Air Navigation Plan – Africa–Indian Ocean Region, Doc. 7474.
253 Ibid., 3.1.
254 Ibid., 3.3(*a*).
255 Ibid., 4.1.
256 *I.C.J. Rep.*, 1970, 32.
257 *Vienna Convention on the Law of Treaties*, United Nations General Assembly document A/CONF.39/27, 23 May 1969.
258 *Barcelona Traction, Light and Power Company Limited*, *I.C.J. Rep.*, 1974, 269–70.
259 *Yearbook of International Law Commission*, 1976, vol. II, pt one, p. 29.
260 *I.C.J. Rep.*, 1970, 32.

261 1925 R.I.A.A. ii 615, at 641.
262 *In Re. Chorzow Factory (Jurisdiction) Case*, (1927) P.C.I.J., Ser. A, No. 9, at 21.
263 *I.C.J. Rep.*, 1949, 23.
264 Carl Q. Christol, *Space Law Past, Present and Future*, Deventer: Kluwer Law and Taxation Publishers, 1991, p. 231.
265 *Report of the International Law Commission to the General Assembly on the Work of the 1st Session*, A/CN.4/13, 9 June 1949, p. 21.
266 See 'Report of the Conference on the Economics of Airports and Air Navigation Services', Montreal, 19–28 June 2000, Doc. 9764 ANSConf 2000, p. 37.
267 Ibid., Recommendation 23, p. 38.
268 Ibid., Recommendation 24, p. 38.
269 See 'ICAO's Policies on Charges for Airports and Air Navigation Services', 6th edn, 2001, Doc. 9082/6.
270 Guidance on accounting contained in the *Airport Economics Manual* (Doc. 9562) and the *Manual on Air Navigation Services Economics* (Doc. 9161) may be found useful in this general context.
271 Guidance on cost allocation is contained in the *Manual on Air Navigation Services Economics* (Doc. 9161), and the *Airport Economics Manual* (Doc. 9562), although states use any accounting approach they consider meets their particular requirements.
272 Fernando R. Teson, *Humanitarian Intervention: An Inquiry into Law and Morality*, Dobbs Ferry, New York: Transnational Publishers, 1956, p. 5.
273 See letter to the editor by Professor Leff, Yale Law School, *New York Times*, 4 October 1968, p. 46, col. 3, cited in *Humanitarian Intervention and the United Nations*, Richard B. Lillich (ed.), Charlottesville: University Press of Virginia, 1973, p. 151.
274 The principle of non-intervention has been strongly espoused in order that sovereignty of a state be retained as sacrosanct. See B. Vattel, *Le droit des gens*, bk II, ch. V, (ed.) F. Scott, 1916, p. 135; also, R. Hall, *International Law*, Higgins, 8th edn, 1924, p. 343; O. Lawrence, *Principles of International Law*, Winfield, 7th edn, 1923, p. 126.
275 F.X. de Lima, *Intervention in International Law*, Den Haag: Vitgeverij Pax Nederland, 1971, p. 16.
276 J.G. Starke, *An Introduction to International Law*, 7th edn, London: Butterworths, 1977 p. 106.
277 Oppenheim, *International Law*, vol. 1, H. Lauterpacht, 8th edn, 1955, pp. 312.
278 Hall, *supra*, note 274, 343; Lawrence, *supra*, note 274, pp. 126, 132; D. Hyde, *International Law*, vol. 1, 2nd review, 1945, p. 253. *Stowell's Intervention at International Law*, 1921, pp. 126, 350; also Wehberg, 'La Guerre Civile et le Droit International', Hague Recueil, 63, 1938, 115.
279 *Supra*, note 272, p. 15.
280 Ibid., 16.
281 Georg Schwarzenberger, *International Law and Order*, London: Stevens and Sons, 1971 p. 63.
282 Michael Akehurst, 'The Use of Force to Protect Nationals Abroad', *Int. Rel.*, 5, 1977, p. 16.
283 Michael Akehurst, 'Humanitarian Intervention', in H. Bull (ed.), *Intervention in World Politics*, 1984, p. 105.
284 I. Brownlie, *International Law and the Use of Force by States*, 1963, pp. 338–40.
285 *Hansard*, H.C, vol. 219, col. 784 (23 February 1993).
286 U.K.M.I.L. (1986) 57 *B.Y.I.L.* 619.
287 See 'Current Developments: International Law', A.V. Lowe and Colin Warbrick (eds), *I.C.L.Q.*, vol. 42, pt 4, October 1993, 944.
288 See R.J. Vincent, *Non-intervention and International Order*, Princeton, NJ: Princeton University Press, 1974, p. 313.

289 See 'Extract from the Draft IUCN Guidelines for the Prevention of Biodiversity Loss due to Biological Invasion', compiled by Mick Clout, Sarah Lowe and the IUCN/SSC Invasive Species Specialist Group, October 1996, p. 2. At the 33rd Session of the ICAO Assembly, the Assembly noted the definition of invasive alien species to be 'a group of organisms – plant or animal, large or small – with unique characteristics, which have been relocated outside their normal distribution or natural range, and having become established in their natural environment, threaten one or more species which are native to that environment'. See A33/WP/11, EC/6, 25/5/01.

290 The CBD was adopted under the umbrella of the United Nations Convention on Environment and Development (UNCED), held in Rio de Janeiro, 3–14 June 1992, which was a milestone in environmental treaty making. For the text of the CBD, see *ILM*, 31, 1997, 818.

291 Jeffrey A. McNeeley, 'Human Dimensions of Invasive Alien Species', *CBD News*, Vol. 1(1), January/March 2001, 1–3.

292 Australia, Canada, Norway and the United States.

293 A33-WP/11, EC/6, 25/5/01.

294 Ibid., Appendix.

295 ICAO Doc. 7300/8, 2000.

296 'Assembly Resolution in Force', Doc. 9730, ICAO, Montreal, pp. 1–41.

297 'Annex 18 to the convention on international civil Aviation (The Safe Transport of Dangerous Goods by Air)', 2nd edn, July 1989, Chapter 1, 'Definitions'.

Chapter 4

The Insurance Crisis

INTRODUCTION

Following the events of 11 September 2001, where civil aircraft were used as weapons of destruction, aviation insurers gave seven days' notice on 17 September that war risk third party liability coverage according to policy terms applying to the write-back coverage for war, hijacking and other perils would be withdrawn. The most compelling reason for the cancellations was the emergence of an exposure in terms of third party bodily injury and property damage that was unquantifiable. The International Union of Aviation Underwriters (IUAU) has assessed that the total losses in respect of third party bodily injury and property damage caused by these events could exceed the previous greatest single catastrophic loss of US$20 billion caused by Hurricane Andrew in 1992 by a significant margin.[1]

Coverage provided by airline insurance policies regarding perils other than third party liability for war risks have not been affected by this cancellation. War and allied perils coverage with regard to passengers have been left unchanged but the uncertainty created by the events hes made it essential to circumscribe coverage for third party losses at a maximum of US$50 million. Although premiums were increasing as a result of a sustained period of unprofitable trading in the insurance market, the events themselves triggered accelerated premium increases both in order to assist markets to revive from the bout of unprofitable trading and to create a reasonably adequate premium base for future exigencies of the nature of the catastrophes of September 2001.

In general terms, the price to be paid to revive or reinstate adequate coverage for third party war risk coverage would cost the airlines an additional premium of US$1·25 per passenger carried. If airlines were to purchase coverage for limits of US$950 million in excess of the already available US$50 million, they would have to pay US$1·85 per passenger carried. In view of the fact that the airports, refuellers, ground handlers and other service providers in the aviation industry contribute to an accumulation of risk, since many of them may serve a particular airline at one location, underwriters were disinclined to offer coverage for these providers. However, many insurers have shown willingness to extend coverage for an additional US$100 million over the US$50 million coverage already provided.[2]

Both the International Civil Aviation Organization (ICAO) and the International Air Transport Association (IATA) have stringently and correctly maintained that there is an inherent role to be played by governments in the event of war risk claims. IATA has justifiably claimed, in a well reasoned argument,[3] that a new international regime must provide for governments to agree to act as a multilateral guarantor covering terrorist actions against airlines in any part of the world. IATA has requested that any solution to the insurance crisis be widely available to international aviation shareholders, be reasonably affordable, provide for long-term stability even in the event of terrorist acts, and recognize the inherent role of governments in the event of war risk claims.

The above remarks were made at the First Meeting of the ICAO War Risk Insurance Working Group, held in Montreal in December 2001. This working group was appointed by the ICAO Council in response to ICAO Assembly Resolution A33-20,[4] adopted at the 33rd Session of the Assembly in September/October 2001. This resolution urges contracting states to work together to develop a non-enduring and coordinated approach to the important problem of providing assistance to airline operators and to other service providers in the field of aviation war risk insurance. Towards achieving this objective, the Assembly directed the Council to urgently establish a special group to consider the issues referred to above and to report back to Council with recommendations as soon as possible. The resolution also broadens ICAO's mandate by inviting the Council and the secretary-general to take any other measures considered necessary or desirable.

At the second meeting of the Working Group, held in Montreal from 18 to 20 January 2002, the London Market Brokers Committee (LMBC) presented a medium-term scheme to cover airlines against war risk liabilities. The scheme envisions the formation of a company, the board of directors of which shall include representatives of participating states, ICAO and participating aviation and insurance industries. The company would offer third party war risk liability cover up to US$1·5 billion in excess of US$50 million per insured. This cover will be non-cancellable and apply per occurrence and per aircraft where multiple aircraft are involved. The insurance cover to be provided by the company would be available to the entire aviation sector and include domestic and international operations as well as equipment lessors, financiers and manufacturers of each state that joins the scheme.

The scheme so outlined offers a continuous cover of aviation war and other perils liability insurance based on clauses AVN 52D and AVN 52F (which generally exclude coverage of war risk liability with a write-back possibility). The scheme also admits of a full review by participating contracting states, to be undertaken at its fifth anniversary, with an option to cancel or suspend the scheme 90 days thereafter. Participating states would act as guarantors or 'reinsurers of last resort' through a legal agreement with the insurance company. In the event of a claim, the contributions of participating states would be pro-rated on the basis of their ICAO assessments. Each state's maximum liability under the scheme would be capped. The total cap, if all ICAO states participate in the scheme, is expected to be US$15 billion (therefore, for example, if only 50 per cent of ICAO contracting states participate, the total cap were be US$7·5 billion). The maximum exposure of each state, in any given instance, would be its ICAO assessment percentage of the total cap as it may apply, depending on the participation of states in the scheme, as outlined above.

Premiums will be collected from the insured in order to build a reinsurance pool to meet claims under the policies. This pool will obviate the need for participating states to make cash contributions to the company in the event of a claim. The total amount of premiums to be collected in the first year is set at US$850 million (equivalent to 50 cents per passenger segment based on total passenger segments of 1·7 billion). The premiums for subsequent years would be kept at approximately the same level, provided there were no losses. Although some members argued that the US$0·50 per passenger charge was not an equitable measurement for the collection of the premium (as the numbers carried per flight may differ and smaller aircraft may not necessarily be considered as much a threat as weapons of destruction as the larger aircraft which have larger capacity), the group decided to work on the basis of US$0·50 per passenger as this was considered to be the only workable means of premium funding.

The principle of state responsibility in supporting their air carriers' war risk third party insurance coverage commitments has become quite pervasive, under the argument that liability for third party damage, be it personal or involving destruction of property, is not a commercial issue under war risk coverage. Where this reasoning is applied to the events of 11 September 2001, where people had been cleared for carriage by air by a security system for which the state was responsible, it becomes clear that an air carrier should not technically be held responsible for events such as those of 11 September.

At the First Meeting of the ICAO Working Group on War Risk Third Party Insurance, the International Coordinating Council of Aerospace Industries Associations (ICCAIA) proposed a draft convention on losses and damages to third parties and property caused by unlawful seizure, terrorism or war,[5] Article 5 of which, addressing issues of obligations of state with security responsibility, provides that, following a hostile act against aviation causing loss or damage to any third party or third party property, the state with security responsibility shall pay to a reinsurance fund already established an amount equal to that payable by the fund in connection with that act. The draft convention also provides for joint responsibility in this region if more than one state is involved.

The present discussion will address the issue of the extent to which principles of state responsibility can be applied to the provision of third party war risk coverage in air transport.

INSURING AIR TRANSPORT

In the context of these discussions, it is necessary to examine the nature of insurance and the manner in which it fits into the regulatory regime governing air transport. Insurance, in general terms, is primarily designed to protect the insured against loss or damage caused by unforeseen or unexpected future events, which cannot be predicted or otherwise guarded against.[6] This definition is equally applicable to air transport, where liability insurance protects the insured against liability arising from loss or damage, including injury or death to passengers and third parties.[7] In view of the extremely high risk posed by war and associated risks which encompass hijacking and acts of terrorism, an express exclusion is usually incorporated in the insurance policy of a carrier, which is known as AVN 48B,[8] as used in the London insurance market. However, certain risks excluded by this clause can be 'written back' into the policy in return for an increased or additional premium. In the case of liability insurance, all excluded rules may be written back with the exclusion of hostile detonation or explosion of a nuclear weapon.

It is arguable that, when applying the above definition, insurance can be identified as a commercial or economic exigency affecting the air carrier as a reimbursement of a loss incurred. On this basis one may ask whether insurance coverage or lack thereof directly affects the operators of a carrier, particularly in the context of a war situation.

The Preamble to the Convention on International Civil Aviation[9] reflects agreement of the contracting states on the development of international air transport in a safe and orderly manner and on its operation being sound and economical. Article 4 of the Convention acknowledges each contracting state's agreement not to use civil aviation for any purpose inconsistent with the aims of the Convention. In the specific context of this discussion, two issues emerge: whether there is an implied obligation on the part of contracting states to ensure that civil aviation is not used for any purpose inconsistent with the aims of the Convention, and what the aims of the Convention are. At the Chicago Conference of 1944 which gave rise to the Convention, Article 4 was originally intended to read as follows:

> In case of war, the provisions of this Convention shall not affect the freedom of action of any of the member States affected, whether as belligerents or as neutrals. The same principle shall apply in the case of any member State which declares a state of national emergency and notifies the fact to the Council'.[10]

Of course, the draft did not survive the Conference and was changed textually. However, it does not fail to give an indication of the general approach taken by the pioneers of regulation, that, in a war situation, a contracting state may not be obligated to honour the aims of the Convention, which, as stated above, are that civil aviation may be developed in a safe and orderly manner and international air transport services may be established on the basis of equality of opportunity and operated soundly and economically.

If one were to argue that the Chicago Convention imposes an implicit obligation on contracting states to ensure that insurance coverage be maintained, as a part of the overall obligation to ensure that air transport services are operated soundly and economically, what happens in a war situation?[11] Could states absolve themselves of this obligation as per the original approach taken on Article 4 of the Convention? If, on the other hand, the current text of Article 4 – that states should ensure that civil aviation should not be used for any purpose inconsistent with the aims of the Convention – were to be taken literally, should states ensure the security of aircraft and, if so, if a state is found to be responsible for an event which violates the principle enshrined in Article 4, should that state be held responsible for the continued operation of air services by the carrier affected?

The problem of 'misuse of civil aviation', 'improper use of civil aviation', 'undue use of civil aviation' or 'criminal use of civil aviation' was raised by several delegations at the 25th Session (Extraordinary) of the ICAO Assembly in April/May 1984 and was mentioned by several representatives on the Council in the context of discussions on the proposed amendment of Annex 2 to the Convention on International Civil Aviation with respect to interception of civil aircraft. In that context, several representatives expressed concern that necessary procedures must be foreseen to prevent the use of civil aviation for unlawful purposes, in particular for drug trafficking, which is more and more generally recognized as a serious crime against humanity. The problem to be addressed is essentially how to reconcile the protection of civil aircraft in situations of interception with the protection of the law and order of states concerned and with the enforcement of such applicable laws. The scope of the problem encompasses in particular the concern of several states about whether Article 3*bis* of the Chicago Convention and the amended Annex 2 leave sufficient safeguards for States to prevent, prosecute and punish any deliberate use of civil aircraft for unlawful purposes.

Article 3*bis* provides inter alia that every state must refrain from resorting to the use of weapons against civil aircraft in flight. The worlds 'refrain from' do not provide the provision with the necessary strength, as it does not explicitly prohibit the use of weapons against aircraft in flight. Article 4 of the Chicago Convention is the only provision in the Convention explicitly using the words 'misuse of civil aviation'; even there, however, the expression is used only in the heading (in fact, in the margin in the original signature copy) and not in the substantive text of the article. The first paragraph of the Preamble to the Convention refers to 'abuse' of international civil aviation, without any attempt at a definition of that term.

Article 4 of the Convention has never been the subject of nor involved in a decision or interpretation either by the Assembly or the Council. The drafting history of this article indicates that the underlying intent of Article 4 was to prevent the use of civil aviation by states for purposes which might create a threat to the security of other nations. The intent of Article 4 originated in the Canadian 'Preliminary Draft' which stated as one of the purposes of ICAO (or Provisional ICAO, as was then envisaged), the future organization as being 'to avert the possibility of the misuse of civil aviation creating a threat to the security of nations and to make the most effective contribution to the establishment and maintenance of a permanent system of general security'. In the further drafting development ('Tripartite Proposal' presented to the conference by the delegations of the United States, United Kingdom and Canada) the wording was changed to read: 'Each member State rejects the use of civil air transport as an instrument of national policy in international relations.' This wording practically repeated the text of the Treaty for the Renunciation of War of 27 August 1928 (commonly known as the Briand–Kellog Pact) in which the signatories renounced war 'as an instrument of national policy in their mutual relations'. The words 'purposes inconsistent with the aims of this Convention' in Article 4 therefore essentially mean 'threats to the general security'.

Article 4 does not offer any solution to the problem of 'misuse of civil aviation' within the scope of the status of an aircraft which is used for criminal purposes or other unlawful purposes.

The Chicago Convention in general does not contain any provisions which would foresee the specific situations when an aircraft is used for or involved in criminal activities or other activities violating the law and public order of the state. However, there are numerous provisions in the Convention which offer effective safeguards to states that their applicable laws and public order are observed by foreign aircraft (with respect to aircraft of its own registry, the state concerned has unrestricted jurisdiction). Articles 11, 12 and 13 of the Convention in essence confirm the rule of general international law that foreign aircraft, its crew, passengers and cargo do not enjoy any 'extraterritorial' status while in the airspace or on the ground of another state; such aircraft are fully subject to the applicable laws of the state concerned. Under the Convention, the state may require the landing of a foreign aircraft involved in non-scheduled flight (Article 5), may prohibit or restrict foreign aircraft from flying over certain parts of its territory or over the whole territory (Article 9), may require landing of foreign aircraft at a designated customs airport (Article 10), may search the foreign aircraft (Article 16) and may regulate or prohibit the carriage of certain articles in or above its territory (Article 35(*b*)).

It is submitted that all states possess within the existing framework of the Chicago Convention full jurisdiction in the application of their respective laws to prevent or prohibit the use of civil aircraft for unlawful purposes. The practical problem therefore does not appear to arise in the field of the applicability of particular laws but in the field of practical enforcement of such laws with respect to aircraft, particularly aircraft in flight.

The practical enforcement of legal obligations involves a legal procedure which in the case of criminal acts would include the arrest and taking into custody of the suspected offender, collection and presentation of pertinent evidence, judicial evaluation of the evidence and evaluation of the points of defence, judicial conviction, sentencing and execution of the judgment. All aspects of such legal procedure are governed by *lex fori*, that is, the domestic law of the court seized of the case. That law would determine, inter alia, what degree of force (including the possible use of weapons) may be legally employed in the process of arrest of the suspected offender; as a rule, that level of force is to be proportionate and adequate to the level of public danger created by the suspected offender and by the level of force used by the suspected offender in resisting arrest.

The only legal provision available in terms of international treaty law on the subject of responsibility for third party liability of air carriers is contained in the Convention on Damage Caused by Foreign Aircraft to Third Parties on the Surface, signed in Rome in 1952, Article 15 of which provides that any contracting state may require that the operator of an aircraft registered in another contracting state shall be insured in respect of this liability for damage sustained in its territory for which a right to compensation exists by means of insurance up to the limits applicable according to the relevant requirements of the Convention. There is provision in the Convention that, instead of insurance, one of the securities acceptable would be a guarantee given by the contracting state where the aircraft is registered, if that state undertakes that it will not claim immunity from suit in respect of that guarantee.[12]

RESPONSIBILITY OF STATES

States have clearly assumed responsibility for the operation of air services by their national carriers and the circumstances, rules and regulations under which they are carried out. This is evidenced in the bilateral air services agreements signed by and between states laying down principles and conditions of operations. States are also responsible for the provision of security within their territories. Arguably, states should then be responsible for the clearance of passengers for air carriage when such passengers embark within their territories. If such were the case, air carriers should not be required to face fiscal responsibility for breaches of security that impede their aircraft and third parties and property on the ground who may be injured as a result of such breaches.

The applicable legal procedure is determined by the sovereign states and 'the general principles of law recognized by civilized nations' as reflected in Article 38, 1(c) of the Statute of the International Court of Justice. These are elements of the general international law, including the general concept of human rights and specifically the protection of human life, presumption of innocence in criminal procedure, and so on. The principles of modern general international law in this field reflect the requirement of 'due process' in the procedure for the enforcement of laws.

Problems of interception of and other enforcement measures with respect to a civil aircraft in flight are directly addressed in Article 3*bis* of the Chicago Convention[13] adopted by unanimous consensus on 10 May 1984 by the 25th Session (Extraordinary) of the ICAO Assembly. The drafting history of this article supports the conclusion that Article 3*bis* is declaratory of the existing general international law with respect to the following elements:

a) obligation of states to refrain from resorting to the use of weapons against civil aircraft in flight;
b) obligation, in case of interception, not to endanger the lives of persons on board and the safety of aircraft; and
c) right of states to require landing at a designated airport of a civil aircraft flying above its territory without authority or if there are reasonable grounds to conclude that it is being used for any purpose inconsistent with the aims of the Convention.

While Article 3*bis* accepted in paragraphs (*b*) and (*d*) the terminology 'for any purpose inconsistent with the aims of the Convention' exactly as it is used in Article 4 of the Convention, the drafting history indicates conclusively that the scope of the phrase is different in Article 3*bis* than in Article 4 (see paragraph 3.3 above). At the 25th Session (Extraordinary) of the Assembly, this phrase was meant to cover not only violations of the 'aims' of the Chicago Convention as spelled out in the Preamble to the Convention and in its Article 44 (which deals with the aims and objectives of the organization rather than the Convention), but any violation of the law and public order of the state concerned. In the assembly discussions, specific references were made to transport of illicit drugs, contraband, gun running, illegal transport of persons and any other common crimes.

It should be stressed that the scope of applicability of Article 3*bis* is subject to significant restrictions; the protection of this article is reserved only to

a) 'civil aircraft'; consequently, 'state aircraft' would not enjoy the same protection; and
b) civil aircraft 'in flight'. While the Convention does not define the concept 'in flight', it is likely that this phrase will be interpreted in harmony with the Rome Convention on Damage Caused by Foreign Aircraft to Third Parties on the Surface of 1952 (Article 1, paragraph 2) and the Tokyo Convention of 1963 (Article 1, paragraph 3). An aircraft shall be deemed to be in flight from the moment when power is applied for the purpose of take-off until the moment when the landing run ends. Consequently, aircraft which are not 'in flight' do not enjoy the special protection of Article 3*bis*.

It is also submitted that the protection of Article 3*bis* is reserved to 'foreign' aircraft and does not include aircraft of the state's own registration. After discussions in the Executive Committee of the Assembly, the reference to aircraft 'of the other contracting State' was dropped for the specific reason that the protection was to be recognized as mandatory with respect to aircraft, whether belonging to contracting or to non-contracting states. At no stage of the deliberations and drafting did the Assembly (in the plenary, in the executive committee or in the working group) contemplate regulation of the status of an aircraft in relation to the state of its own registration; such regulation would have exceeded the scope of the Convention, which deals with international civil aviation. Again, the purpose of the Chicago Convention is to establish conventional rules of conduct in the mutual relations of sovereign states but not to govern matters of their exclusive domestic jurisdiction. Consequently, Article 3*bis* will not apply to the treatment of aircraft by the states of their registration. This conclusion does not imply that a state is free to treat aircraft of its own registration without regard to any rules of international law; other sources of international law (such as the International Covenants on Human Rights) may be relevant for the conduct of states (protection of the right to life, requirement of due legal process, presumption of innocence, and so on).

When requiring the landing of a civil aircraft flying above its territory, or when issuing other instructions to the aircraft to put an end to a 'violation', contracting states may resort to any appropriate means consistent with relevant rules of international law, including the Chicago Convention and, specifically, paragraph (*a*) of Article 3*bis*. Consequently, Article 3*bis* does not exclude enforcement against foreign aircraft in flight, does not rule out the use of adequate and proportionate force and does not rule out interception as such. Any act of interception or other enforcement measure not involving the use of weapons against civil aircraft in flight and not endangering the lives of persons on board and the safety of flight is legitimate and acceptable. Any interception procedures consistent with the applicable Standards and Recommended Practices adopted by the Council of ICAO pursuant to Articles 37, 54(1) and 90 of the Chicago Convention would be 'consistent with relevant rules of international law'.

Two additional provisions of Article 3*bis* are likely to deter the occurrences of 'misuse' of civil aviation. Firstly, civil aircraft are unconditionally obliged to comply with an order to land or other instruction; contracting states are accepting, under paragraph (*c*) of Article 3*bis*, an obligation to establish all necessary provisions in the national law or regulations to make such compliance mandatory for aircraft of their registration or operated by an operator having his principal place of business or permanent residence in that state. Contracting states are also accepting an obligation to make violation of such laws or regulations punishable by severe penalties and to submit the case to their competent authorities. This provision may offer a practical safeguard that no violators would go unpunished; even if they were to escape from the jurisdiction of the state where the unlawful act was committed, they should be prosecuted and punished by the state of the registration of the aircraft; in practical application this provision may be reinforced by existing or future arrangements for extradition of offenders.

Secondly, all contracting states are accepting an unconditional obligation to take appropriate measures to prohibit any deliberate 'misuse' of any civil aircraft of their registration or operated by an operator having his principal place of business or permanent residence in that state. Legislative implementation of such a prohibition will no doubt be accompanied by appropriate penalties.

States can exercise criminal jurisdiction over foreign aircraft in flight over their territory as well as over the territory not subject to sovereignty of any state (such as the high seas) also under the conditions set forth in the Tokyo Convention of 1963.[14] Article 4 of that Convention permits 'interference' with an aircraft in flight in order to exercise criminal jurisdiction over an offence committed on board in the following cases:

a) the offence has effect on the territory of such state;
b) the offence has been committed by or against a national or permanent resident of such state;
c) the offence is against the security of such state;
d) the offence consists of a breach of any rules or regulations relating to the flight or manoeuvre of aircraft in force in such state; and
e) the exercise of jurisdiction is necessary to ensure the observance of any obligation of such state under a multilateral international agreement.

Since the Tokyo Convention has been accepted by many of ICAO's contracting states, this provision represents an important additional clarification to Article 3*bis* of the Chicago Convention with respect to the interpretation of the term 'any purpose inconsistent with the aims of this Convention'. It is submitted that any offence foreseen in Article 4 of the Tokyo Convention gives the right to the state concerned to 'interfere', that is, to require the landing of the aircraft or give the aircraft other instructions and to resort to proportionate and adequate use of force against such aircraft. The United Nations Convention on the Law of the Sea does not foresee the right of hot pursuit of aircraft; the target of hot pursuit may be exclusively a ship but the procedures of hot pursuit may be effected by an aircraft (Article 111, paragraph 6).

The study of the problem of 'misuse' of civil aviation and of its consequences for law enforcement with respect to civil aircraft in flight leads to the following conclusions.

a) Although the term 'misuse of civil aviation' is a legally imprecise term which has no firm basis in the Convention on International Civil Aviation apart from the title of Article 4, it still reflects the overall threat posed by unlawful interference with civil aviation.
b) The phrase 'any purpose inconsistent with the aims of this Convention' has historically a different meaning in Article 4 of the Convention and in paragraphs (*b*) and (*d*) of Article 3*bis*.
c) The concept of 'misuse of civil aircraft' should best be referred to as 'deliberate use of civil aircraft for unlawful purposes'.
d) The Chicago Convention contains effective provisions safeguarding full jurisdiction of states to prevent or prohibit the use of foreign aircraft for unlawful purposes in their territory.

The above conclusions may be drawn upon to use the relevant provisions of the Chicago Convention as a basis to formulate other legal documents that would enforce more stringent control over this offence. Some recommendations as to the measures that could be adopted in this regard follow in the concluding chapter.

The provisions of the Chicago Convention, which is an international treaty, are binding on contracting states to the Convention and therefore are priciples of public international law. The International Court of Justice (ICJ), in the *North Sea Continental Shelf Case*,[15] held that legal principles that are incorporated in treaties, such as the 'common interest' principle, become customary international law by virtue of Article 38 of the 1969 Vienna Convention on the Law of Treaties.[16] Article 38 recognizes that a rule set forth in a treaty would become binding upon a third state as a customary rule of international law if it is generally recognized by the states concerned as such. Obligations arising from *jus cogens* are considered applicable *erga omnes*, which would mean that states using space technology owe a duty of care to the world at large in the provision of such technology. The ICJ in the *Barcelona Traction Case* held:

> An essential distinction should be drawn between the obligations of a State towards the international community as a whole, and those arising vis à vis another State in the field of diplomatic protection. By their very nature, the former are the concerns of all States. In view of the importance of the rights involved, all States can be held to have a legal interest in their protection; they are obligations *erga omnes*.[17]

The International Law Commission has observed of the ICJ decision: 'In the Court's view, there are in fact a number, albeit limited, of international obligations which, by reason of their importance to the international community as a whole, are – unlike others – obligations in respect of which all States have legal interest.'[18] The views of the ICJ and the International Law Commission, which has supported the approach taken by the ICJ, give rise to two possible conclusions relating to *jus cogens* and its resultant obligations *erga omnes*: (a) obligations *erga omnes* affect all states and thus cannot be made inapplicable to a state or group of states by an exclusive clause in a treaty or other document reflecting legal obligations without the consent of the international community as a whole; and (b) obligations *erga omnes* pre-empt other obligations which may be incompatible with them.

Some examples of obligations *erga omnes* cited by the ICJ are prohibition of acts of aggression, genocide, slavery and discrimination.[19] It is indeed worthy of note that all these obligations are derivatives of norms which are *jus cogens* at international law. International responsibility relates both to breaches of treaty provisions and to other breaches of legal duty. In the *Spanish Zone of Morocco Claims* case, Justice Huber observed: 'Responsibility is the necessary corollary of a right. All rights of an international character involve international responsibility. If the obligation in question is not met, responsibility entails the duty to make reparation.'[20]

It is also now recognized as a principle of international law that the breach of a duty involves an obligation to make reparation appropriately and adequately. This reparation is regarded as the indispensable complement of a failure to apply a convention and is applied as an inarticulate premise that need not be stated in the breached convention itself.[21] The ICJ affirmed this principle in 1949 in the *Corfu Channel Case*[22] by holding that Albania was responsible under international law to pay compensation to the United Kingdom for not warning that Albania had laid mines in Albanian waters which caused explosions, damaging ships belonging to the United Kingdom. Since the treaty law provisions of liability and the general principles of international law as discussed complement each other in endorsing the liability of states to compensate for damage caused by space objects, there is no contention as to whether, in the use of nuclear power sources in outer space, damage caused by the uses of space objects or use thereof would not go uncompensated.

The sense of international responsibility that the United Nations ascribed to itself had reached a heady stage at this point, where the role of international law in international human conduct was perceived to be primary and above the authority of states. In its Report to the General Assembly, the International Law Commission recommended a draft provision which required: 'Every State has the duty to conduct its relations with other States in accordance with international law and with the principle that the sovereignty of each State is subject to the supremacy of international law.'[23] This principle, which forms a cornerstone of international conduct by states, provides the basis for strengthening international comity and regulating the conduct of states both internally – within their territories – and externally, towards other states. States are effectively precluded by this principle from pursuing their own interests untrammelled and with disregard to principles established by international law.

State responsibility is accepted in modern parlance as an established principle of public international law. This principle is based on both substantive rules of law and the imputability to a state of acts and omissions of that state that may be categorized as legally reprehensible or illegal by reference to established norms and rules identifying rights and duties.[24] The notion of *culpa*, is often used to denote blameworthiness predicated upon reasonable foreseeability or foresight without consequences. *Culpa* is generally not a condition of liability *per se*, but in certain contexts it may be imputed to a state whose officials are negligent in not foreseeing the consequences of their acts or omissions. In such instances a causal nexus has of necessity to be established between the act or omission and the result. In the *Lighthouse* arbitration, which was undertaken in 1956 by the Permanent Court of International Justice, the court held that damage should be a foreseeable and normal consequence of an act or omission.[25] In instances where a state engages in lawful practices, responsibility may be attributed to a state for lack of diligence.[26] This principle is borne out by the fundamental judicial acceptance that the state bears an international responsibility for all acts committed by its officials or its organs which are delictual or tortuous according to principles of public international law.[27] In order that this objective criterion of responsibility be applied, it is important to determine that officials act as authorized officials or instrumentalities of state, or that in so acting or omitting to act they use powers or measures appropriate to their official character.

In the event of localized violence or mob attacks, contrived and substantial neglect to take the necessary and reasonable precautions to avoid damage or prevent injury would be tantamount to official indifference and would create responsibility for damage to persons and property, particularly if interests are vested in foreign hands.

The aviation industry is posed a unique challenge by the need for its credibility to be restored with the insurance industry, at least partially, if not totally. The cost of this challenge to airlines may be considerable. The civil aviation sector is of considerable dimensions, and the airlines are integrated from an information technology (IT) standpoint to airports, ground handling, avionics and engineering, air traffic control and maintenance in their daily operations. This means that the IT requirements of each of these sectors, however varied and multifarious, have to mesh together for security and safety purposes in order that airlines perform their task of carrying passengers and freight without mishap.

Aviation insurers will certainly be concerned as to how their insured are going to handle the credibility challenge. Any flaw in the preparation of the insured – the airlines – in fixing the problem has direct potential ramifications for the insurance industry, who will have to pay up claims resulting from safety related incidents and accidents involving aircraft.

There is a strong possibility that the insurance industry will require states to show that they exercised due diligence or, in other words, adequately dispensed with the duty of care they owed to the consumer in addressing the problem and solving it. In this context, legal principles applicable to states and their instrumentalities responsible for providing preventive measures to ensure security would be analogous to those applicable to professionals who profess special skills, such as medical doctors, and the diligence and care required of such a category would be objectively assessed at a higher level than that which is required of the common man. At common law, therefore, the jurisprudence related to medical malpractice would be a distinct analogy and principles enunciated therein would serve as a yardstick in instances where state responsibility is assessed.

Under English law, the burden of proving negligence rests on the plaintiff. He has to prove that the defendant was negligent and that such negligence resulted in the loss or injury alleged. English law knows no sharp categories of care and a degree of care and diligence which a defendant must exercise corresponds to the degree of negligence for which he is responsible,[28] and the defendant must do what is reasonable in the circumstances. A good example is the case of *Marshall* v. *Lindsay*,[29] which held that a defendant who is charged with professional negligence can clear himself if he shows that he acted in accordance with general or approved practice. A 1953 decision[30] had held that the competent practitioner would know when a case is beyond his or her skill and thereupon it would become his or her duty either to call in a more skilled person or to order removal of the patient to a hospital where skilled treatment is available. The case had also held that when a consultant takes over the responsibility for the treatment of a patient, it is a defence in favour of that consultant to show that he had acted on the specific instructions given to him or her by another consultant. This principle would indeed be persuasive authority in the case of computer consultants hired by the aviation industry to correct the millennium problem.

It can also be observed that, in strict legal analysis, negligence means more than heedless or careless conduct, whether in omission or commission; it properly connotes a breach of duty, which causes damage to the person to whom the duty was owing. However, a doctor failing to diagnose a disease cannot excuse himself by showing that he acted to the best of his skill if a reasonable doctor would have diagnosed it.[31] The civil liability of medical professionals towards their patients is compendiously stated in *R*. v. *Bateman*,[32] as follows:

> if a person holds himself out as possessing special skill and knowledge and he is consulted as possessing such skill and knowledge, by or on behalf of a patient, he

owes a duty to the patient to use due caution in undertaking the treatment. If he accepts the responsibility and undertakes the treatment and the patient submits to his direction and treatment accordingly, he owes a duty to the patient to use diligence, care, knowledge, skill and caution in administering the treatment. No contractual relation is necessary, nor is it necessary that the service be rendered for reward ... The law requires a fair and reasonable standard of care and competence. This standard must be reached in all the matters above mentioned. If the patient's death has been caused by the defendant's indolence or carelessness, it will not avail to show that he had sufficient knowledge; nor will it avail to prove that he was diligent in attendance, if the patient has been killed by his gross ignorance and unskilfulness ... As regards cases where incompetence is alleged, it is only necessary to say that the unqualified practitioner cannot claim to be measured by any lower standard than that which is applied to a qualified man. There may be recklessness in undertaking the treatment and recklessness in the conduct of it. It is, no doubt, conceivable that a qualified man may be held liable for recklessly undertaking a case which he knew, or should have known, to be beyond his powers, or for making his patient the subject of reckless experiment. Such cases are likely to be rare.[33]

The primary question therefore is whether, in all the circumstances, the defendant acted with the skill and competence to be expected of a person undertaking the particular activity and professing his specific skill.

One of the difficulties that may be encountered in the determination of professional negligence is whether there are specific established norms within a particular jurisdiction which recognizes what constitutes established proper professional practice. The classic statement of the governing principles is to be found in the direction to the jury given by McNair J in *Bolam* v. *Friern Hospital Management Committee*:[34]

where you get a situation which involves the use of some special skill or competence, then the test whether there has been negligence or not is not the test of the man on top of the Clapham omnibus, because he has not got this special skill. The test is the standard of the ordinary skilled man exercising and professing to have that special skill. A man need not possess the highest expert skill at the risk of being found negligent. It is well established law that it is sufficient if he exercises the ordinary skill of an ordinary competent man exercising that particular art ... there may be one or more perfectly proper standards; and if a medical man conforms with one of those proper standards then he is not negligent ... a mere personal belief that a particular technique is best is no defence unless that belief is based on reasonable grounds ... a doctor is not negligent if he is acting in accordance with ... a practice (accepted as proper by a responsible body of medical men skilled in that particular art), merely because there is a body of opinion that takes a contrary view. At the same time, that does not mean that a medical man can obstinately and pigheadedly carry on with some old technique if it has been proved to be contrary to what is really substantially the whole of informed medical opinion.[35]

The *Bolam* test has been applied to every exercise of professional skill and judgment. The courts have rejected attempts to categorize professional tasks by subdividing them for the purpose of ignoring the *Bolam* case in particular contexts.[36] The test is not merely confined to cases relating to highly technical skills.[37] The *Bolam* case has received approval in Parliament,[38] the House of Lords[39] and the Privy Council.[40]

The House of Lords, in *Whitehouse* v. *Jordan*,[41] rejected the idea that mere errors of judgment cannot amount to negligence.[42] Lord Fraser observed:

> merely to describe something as an error of judgement tells us nothing about whether it is negligent or not. The true position is that an error of judgement may, or may not, be negligent; it depends on the nature of the error. If it is one that would not have been made by a reasonable competent professional man professing to have the standard and type of skill that the defendant held himself out as having, and acting with ordinary care, then it is negligent.[43]

In this context the position of the English common law is of great significance to the position of the aviation industry in the context of the millennium bug.

It is generally recognized that in determinations of negligence on the part of medical practitioners, the defendant must exhibit the degree of skill which a member of the public would expect from a person in his position. Pressures on her for which he is in no way responsible will not detract from guilt for an error on his part.

Moral responsibility and incompetence are generally considered mutually exclusive from negligence. In *Wilsher* v. *Essex Area Health Authority*,[44] the medical staff of a hospital was considered negligent for making an error in administering too much oxygen to a baby, who, as a consequence of excessive oxygen, became blind. The plaintiff was an infant child who was born prematurely suffering from various illnesses, including oxygen deficiency. His prospects of survival were considered to be poor and he was placed in the 24-hour special care baby unit at the hospital where he was born. The unit was staffed by a medical team, consisting of two consultants, a senior registrar, several junior doctors and trained nurses. While the plaintiff was in the unit a junior and inexperienced doctor monitoring the oxygen in the plaintiff's bloodstream mistakenly inserted a catheter into a vein rather than an artery but then asked the senior registrar to check what he had done. The registrar failed to see the mistake and some hours later, when replacing the catheter, did exactly the same thing himself.

Mustill L J observed:

> This appeal raises three questions of law relating to the allegation that the defendants are liable for breach of duty. (1) What is the nature of the cause of action on which the plaintiff relies? (2) What standard of care was demanded of those members of the medical and nursing staff who are said to have been negligent? (3) On whom rests the burden of proof in relation to the allegation of negligence?

His Lordship also quoted with approval the *Bolam* case:

> a doctor who adopts a practice accepted as proper by a responsible body of medical men skilled in the relevant branch of medicine is not to be taken as negligent merely because there is a contrary view. Although this principle may have some bearing on the later episodes, it can have nothing to do with the first episode, for, although there were witnesses who regarded it as excusable in a young doctor not to know about the significance of the loop and its absence, there was no body of medical opinion which could regard it as appropriate to overlook the indications given by the X-rays as to the position of the catheter. The doctors made a mistake, although not necessarily a culpable one.[45]

Errors of judgment are often the fundamental basis for negligence at English law. In *Whitehouse* v. *Jordan*,[46] the plaintiff, who was born in 1970 with severe brain damage, brought an action against, inter alia the first defendant, a senior registrar at the time of his birth, and the hospital authority, claiming that the damage had been caused by the first defendant's professional negligence. The principal allegations of negligence were that in the course of carrying out a 'trial of forceps delivery' the first defendant had pulled too long and too strongly on the plaintiff's head, thereby causing the brain damage. At the trial, the mother of the plaintiff said that, when the forceps had been applied, it had felt like a deadened electric shock that lifted her hips off the (delivery) bed. Both the first defendant and the doctor who had assisted him denied that she had been lifted off the bed or that the first defendant had pulled violently with the forceps. The first defendant denied that the plaintiff's head had been wedged or stuck.

Lord Wilberforce observed:

> first, it is necessary, in order to establish liability of, and to obtain an award of compensation against, a doctor or a hospital that there has been negligence in law. There is in this field no liability without proof of fault. Secondly, there are strict limitations upon this power of an appeal court to reverse the decision of the judge on an issue of fact.[47]

A significant consideration relating to the plaintiff's burden of proof of the defendant's negligence is that, if the evidence is equally balanced so that there is no balance of probability in favour of the plaintiff's contention of negligence, his action fails. In other words, if it is not clear whether the injury complained of may have occurred without carelessness on the part of the defendant, the plaintiff will not be considered as having discharged his burden of proof. The 1983 case of *Ashcroft* v. *Mersey Regional Health Authority*[48] concerned a case where, on 20 January 1978, the plaintiff submitted herself to an operation on her left ear. It was performed by a surgeon of long experience, great skill and the highest reputation. The operation proved to be disastrous, for the plaintiff was left with a partial paralysis of the left side of the face, an injury for which she claimed damages alleging that the operation was carried out negligently. The paralysis was caused by damage to the facial nerve. Kilner Brown J observed:

> Where an injury is caused which never should have been caused, common sense and natural justice indicate that some degree of compensation ought to be paid by someone. As the law stands, in order to obtain compensation an injured person is compelled to allege negligence against a surgeon who may, as in this case, be a careful, dedicated person of the highest skill and reputation. If ever there was a case in which some reasonable compromise was called for, which would provide some amount of solace for the injured person and avoid the pillorying of a distinguished surgeon, this was such a case,[49] the proposition that an error of judgement by a medical man is not negligence is an inaccurate statement of the law. It may be; it may not. The question for consideration is whether on a balance of probabilities it has been established that a professional man has failed to exercise the care required of a man possessing and professing special skill in circumstances which require the exercise of that special skill. If there is an added burden, such burden does not rest on the person alleging negligence; on the contrary, it could be said that the more skilled a person is the more the care that is expected of him.[50]

A fundamental principle in the common law with regard to professional negligence is that, when a professional lacks the skill and experience to deal with a particular case, or he realizes the possibility of his client being adversely affected by that professional's work which should be referred to a specialist practising in the field related to that work, he should refer the matter to someone who is competent to deal with it. In the 1952 case of *Payne* v. *St. Helier Group Hospital Management Committee*,[51] Donovan J held that a medical officer who incorrectly diagnosed a disease was negligent in that he had failed to refer the patient to a consultant medical practitioner.

However, the above principle is tempered with the premise that, if a professional acts in accordance with general and approved practices of the profession, that will indeed constitute a good defence to a claim in negligence. In the Canadian Case of *Vancouver General Hospital* v. *McDaniel*,[52] the Privy Council reversed the decision of the Court of Appeal of British Columbia which imputed negligence to a hospital for allowing a small group of patients to be in a room with the plaintiff – a diphtheria patient who contracted smallpox thereafter. The Privy Council held:

> a defendant charged with negligence can clear his name if he shows that he has acted in accordance with general and approved practice. The appellants, in his Lordship's opinion, even if the onus rested on them of doing this, have in this case done so by a weight of evidence that cannot be ignored.[53]

The 1955 case of *Hunter* v. *Hanley*[54] established three criteria which determine a doctor's deviation from normal practice: (a) it must be proved that there is a usual and normal practice; (b) it must be proved that the defendant had not adopted that practice; and (c) it must be established that the course the doctor adopted is one which no professional man of ordinary skill would have taken if he had been acting with ordinary care.[55] A proper examination of the patient, particularly if the patient had not been seen earlier by a doctor for the ailment complained of, is a basic responsibility which would fall in the first category of usual and normal practice.[56] A wrong diagnosis, if proved, or failure to refer a patient to another physician where necessary, would fit into the third category. Caution must be exercised, however, in determining whether the doctor could have, according to her skill, knowledge and experience, diagnosed a disease correctly, as in the case of *Sadler* v. *Henry*,[57] where Cassels J held that the defendant medical practitioner was not negligent in failing to diagnose localized meningitis, since there were no signs or symptoms which could reasonably have led him to suspect that condition.

Of comparative interest to the legal liability of the aviation industry would be the area of tortuous liability relating to medical malpractice in the United States. Malpractice is defined as bad or unskilful practice on the part of a physician or surgeon resulting in injury to a patient,[58] or the failure of a physician to exercise the required degree of care, skill and diligence; or the treatment by a surgeon or physician in a manner contrary to accepted rules and with injuries resulting to a patient. The law relating to malpractice is based on three elements: the professional relationship of physician and patient; departure of the physician from some professional duty that he owed the patient; and the link of such departure of duty to the proximate cause of injury.

In an instance where the physician is a specialist, she is bound to exercise a degree of skill and knowledge which is usually possessed by similar specialists. Such skill and knowledge is expected to be of a higher level than that which is possessed by the general practitioner. Where the doctor is a specialist, she is bound to exercise that degree of skill and knowledge which is ordinarily possessed by similar specialists, and not merely the degree of skill and knowledge of a general practitioner.[59] This rule is well stated in *Corpus Juris Secundum*:[60]

A physician holding himself out as having special knowledge and skill in the treatment of a particular organ, disease or type of injury is bound to bring to the discharge of his duty to a patient employing him as such specialist, not merely the average degree of skill possessed by general practitioners, but that special degree of skill and knowledge possessed by physicians who devote special study and attention to the treatment of such organ, disease or injury, regard being had to the state of scientific knowledge at the time.

Similarly, a general practitioner who undertakes to treat a case which clearly lies within the field of a special branch of medicine will be held liable for failure to use skill equal to that of a specialist.[61]

The fundamental principle of professional conduct obtaining in the United States is that the physician is in a position of trust and confidence as regards his patient, and it is his duty to act with the utmost good faith towards the patient. If she knows that she cannot accomplish a cure, or that the treatment adopted will probably be of no benefit, it is her duty to advise her patient of these facts.[62] In *Waltuck* v. *Poushter*,[63] it was held incorrect to dismiss the complaint where the proof was that the defendant was called to the decedent's home and treated her for complaints of malaise, head pains, high temperature and blood in her left ear. He was called *later* that day and advised that her condition had *worsened*. Yet he made no effort at treatment or to contact a *specialist* to evaluate her symptoms. She then died of meningitis. It was held that a jury could find that his professional knowledge should have alerted him to the possible consequences of his failure to treat the complaints or perceive the seriousness of the plaintiff's condition.

It is one of the fundamental duties of a physician to make a properly skilful and careful diagnosis of the ailment of a patient, and if she fails to bring to that diagnosis the proper degree of skill and care and makes an incorrect diagnosis, she may be held liable to the patient.[64] Furthermore, the physician must inform herself by the proper tests and examinations of the condition of her patient to undergo a proposed treatment or operation, so that she may intelligently exercise the skill of her calling.[65] The duty of exercising reasonable skill and diligence includes not only the diagnosis and treatment, but also the giving of proper instructions to her patient in relation to conduct, exercise and the use of an injured limb.[66]

Another area of common law which brings to bear an interesting analogy in the law of negligence and due diligence is the Roman Dutch law. Under Roman Dutch law negligence falls within the purview of the ancient *lex Aquilian* concept of 'culpa' which is established objectively. The question for the courts is not what a tortfeasor was thinking or not thinking about, expecting or not expecting, but whether his behaviour was or was not such as is demanded of a prudent person under given circumstances. Negligence, therefore, may be defined as conduct which involves an unreasonable risk of harm to others.

The notion of duty of care is essentially an English common law principle, and Roman Dutch jurist McKerron cites with approval the dictum of Lord McMillan in *Bourhill* v. *Young*:[67]

> The duty to take care is the duty to avoid doing or omitting to do anything the doing or omitting to do which may have as its reasonable and probable consequence injury to others, and the duty is owed to those to whom injury may reasonably and probably be anticipated if the duty is not observed.[68]

In the 1934 case of *Perlman* v. *Zoutendyk*,[69] Watermeyer J delivered a watershed decision which established the essence of professional negligence. The case involved an instance where a sworn appraiser had issued a certificate of valuation with the knowledge that it would be used for the purpose of inducing someone to lend money on the property valued. The court held:

> in Roman Dutch law the duty to exercise reasonable care arises wherever the defendant whose act is complained of should reasonably have foreseen probability of harm being caused by his act to another person, except, perhaps in those cases in which the act complained of can be said to be justified or exercised.[70]

The above dictum in the *Perlman* case, when compared with that of *Bourhill* v. *Young* above, reflects that duty of care is a common feature in both the Roman Dutch law and English common law. The Roman Dutch law requires two distinct questions to be answered: (a) what was the standard of care required of the tortfeasor at the time the alleged tortuous act was committed, and (b) did the conduct of the tortfeasor comply with that standard? One of the methods that the courts have employed in answering these questions is to place themselves, as nearly as they can, in the position of the tortfeasor at the time when the act was committed and judge whether ordinary care which can reasonably be expected from a reasonable person under all circumstances was shown by the tortfeasor.[71] It is arguable, therefore, that this fundamental premise would be extended by jurisdictions which follow the Roman Dutch law to instances of professional negligence.

One of the most significant aspects of Roman Dutch law principles regarding professional negligence is the maxim *imperitia culpae adnumeratur* which establishes that negligence is not determined by the lack of skill of the tortfeasor but in his undertaking work without skill. Therefore, where a person engages in a profession or occupation which calls for special skill, the degree of skill which is required is that reasonably to be expected of a person engaged in such profession or occupation. Innes C J observed: 'the Court will have regard to the general level of skill and diligence possessed and exercised at the time by the members of the branch of the profession to which the practitioner belongs'.[72]

Under Roman Dutch law, the burden of proving negligence – on a preponderance of probability – rests with the plaintiff. Proof must be adduced not only to show the defendant's negligence, but also to draw a link between the defendant's negligence and the harm caused. Wherever direct evidence of the defendant's negligence is not available, negligence may be established by inference of facts.

Moreover, the plaintiff need not demonstrate his case; the court is entitled to act on a balance of probabilities.

Therefore, under the Roman Dutch law as in English law and American law, it can be said that, when considered as an objective fact, negligence may be defined as conduct which involves an unreasonable risk of harm to others. It is the failure in given circumstances to exercise that degree of care which the circumstances demand. A requisite of liability in negligence is the breach of duty to the plaintiff.

CONCLUSION

It is incontrovertible that responsibility for the provision of security in municipal and international human activity lies within the state which has control over that activity. In ensuring aviation security, this responsibility devolves upon the state, both through the public international law of treaties and through other established legal principles, as demonstrated earlier in this chapter. Although there has been no explicit nexus drawn between a requirement for a state to provide insurance coverage for an activity in order that it may keep going and the overall responsibility of a state to ensure that any activity for which that state is reponsible, such as ensuring that security within its territory is carried out without hindrance, there is certainly room for persuasive argumentation that airlines cannot be expected to provide for insurance against war risks over which they may not have sufficient control. As to how far states are responsible for providing indemnities to air carriers against grounding of aircraft owing to non-existence of coverage, it is a subject that needs qualification on a more empirical basis.

NOTES

1   See SGWA/1-IP/4, 5/12/01, Comments of IUAU, ICAO Special Group on Aviation War Risk (SGW1), First Meeting, Montreal, 6 to 7 December 2001, p. 2.
2   Ibid.
3   SGW1/1-WP/4, 5/12/01 – Comments of IATA, Special Group on Aviation War Risk Insurance, First Meeting, Montreal, 6 to 7 December 2001, p. 2.
4   A33-20, Coordinated Approach in Providing Assistance in the field of War Risk Insurance, Resolutions Adopted by the Assembly, 33rd Session, Montreal, 25 September–5 October 2001, Provisional Edition, October 2001, p. 86.
5   SGW1/1-WP/3, Appendix.
6   Rod D. Margo, 'Aspects of Insurance in Aviation Finance', *Journal of Air Law & Commerce*, 62(2), 1996, p. 428.
7   Ibid., p. 429.
8   AVN48B excludes risks of war, invasion, hostilities, civil war, rebellion, revolution, insurrection, martial law, hostile detonation of atomic weapons, strikes, riots, civil commotions or labour disturbances, acts of a political or terrorist nature, sabotage, confiscation, nationalization, seizure and hijacking.
9   Convention on International Civil Aviation, signed at Chicago on 7 December 1944. See ICAO Doc. 7300/8.
10 Proceedings of the International Civil Aviation Conference, Chicago, Illinois, 1 November–7 December, 1944, vol. 1, p. 661.

11 For insurance purposes, there is no absolute necessity for there to be a formal declaration of war. See *Kawasaki Kissen Kbushiki Kaisha of Kobe* v. *Bantham Steamship Company Ltd* [1939] 2KB544 at 556.

12 Convention on Damage Caused by Foreign Aircraft to Third Parties on the Surface, signed in Rome on 7 October 1952, ICAO Doc. 7364, Article 15(4)(c).

13 *Supra*, Note 9.

14 Convention on Offences and Certain Other Acts Committed on Board Aircraft, signed at Tokyo on 14 September 1963, ICAO Doc. 8364.

15 *I.C.J. Rep.*, 1970, at 32.

16 Vienna Convention on the Law of Treaties, United Nations General Assembly Document A/CONF.39/27, 23 May 1969.

17 *Barcelona Traction, Light and Power Company Limited*, *I.C.J. Reports*, 1974, 253, at 269–70.

18 *Yearbook of International Law Commission*, 1976, vol. II, pt One, p. 29.

19 *I.C.J. Rep.*, 1970, at 32.

20 *1925 R.I.A.A. ii*, 615 at 641.

21 *In Re Chorzow Factory (Jurisdiction) Case*, (1927) P.C.I.J., Ser. A, No. 9, at 21.

22 *I.C.J. Rep.* (1949), 4, at 23.

23 *Report of the International Law Commission to the General Assembly on the Work of the 1st Session*, A/CN.4/13, June 9 1949, p. 21.

24 See Ian Brownlie, *Principles of Public International Law*, 4th edn, Oxford: Clarendon Press, 1992.

25 RIAA xii 217–18; I.L.R. 23 (1956), pp. 352–3.

26 *In re Rizzo*, I.L.R. 22 (1955), 322.

27 The *Caire* claim, (1929) R.I.A.A.V., p. 530.

28 *Giblin* v. *McMullen* (1869) L.R. 2 P.G. 317 at 337, *per* Law, Chelmsford

29 1935 1 K.B. 516.

30 *Pudney* v. *Union Castle Mail S.S. Ltd*, 1953 *Lloyd's Rep*. 73.

31 *Street on Torts*, Margaret Brazer ed., London: Butterworth, 1982, p. 205

32 (1925) 94 L.J.K.B. 791, see *Akerele* v. *The King* [1943] A.C. 255, also the article, 'The negligent doctor' (Linden) 11 *Osgoode Hall L. J.* 31.

32 Ibid., at 798.

34 [1957] 2 All E.R. 118, [1957] 1 W.L.R. 582, at 586–7

35 Ibid.

36 *Gold* v. *Haringey Health Authority* [1988] 8 C&P 475.

37 *Alchemy (International) Ltd* v. *Tattersalls Ltd* [1985] 2 E.G.L.R. 17.

38 Congenital Disabilities (Civil Liability) Act 1976, s.1(5).

39 *Whitehouse* v. *Jordan* [1981] 1 All E.R. 267, [1981] 1 W.L.R. 246, HL; *Maynard* v. *West Midlands Regional Health Authority* [1985] 1 All E.R. 635, [1982] 1 All E.R. 634, HL; *Sidaway* v. *Bethlem Royal Hospital and the Maudsley Hospital Governors* [1985] A.C. 871, [1985] 1 All E.R. 643, H.L.

40 *Chin Keow* v. *Government of Malaysia* [1967] 1 W.L.R. 813, P.C.

41 [1981] 1 All E.R. 267, at 276, Also [1981] 1 W.L.R. 246 at 258.

42 An argument to this effect had been put forward by Lord Denning MR in the Court of Appeal [1980] 1 All E.R. 650, at 658, CA. Lord Denning was concerned that there might be an explosion of medical malpractice claims if the courts did not reduce the standard of care applicable to professional persons.

43 [1981] 1 W.L.R. 247.

44 (1987) Q.B. 730. Also (1986) 3 All E.R. 801.

45 (1986) 3 All E.R. 801 at 812.

46 (1981) 1 W.L.R. 246.

47 Ibid., at 258.

48   [1983] 2 All E.R. 245 affd. 1985 2 All E.R. 96.
49   Ibid., at p. 246.
50   Ibid., at p. 247.
51   [1952] *C.L.Y.B.*, 2442.
52   [1935] 152 L.T.R. 56.
53   Ibid., at pp. 57–8.
54   1955 S.C. 200.
55   Ibid., at p. 206.
56   See *Barnett* v. *Chelsea & Kensington Hospital Management Committee* [1969] 1 Q.B. 428, and *Kavanaugh* v. *Abramson* (1964) 108 S.J. 320.
57   [1954] I.B.M.J. 1331.
58   Charles Kramer, *Medical Malpractice*, New York City: Practicing Law Institute, 1976, p. 6
59   *Beach* v. *Chollet*, 120 Ohio St. 449, 166 N.E. 415 (1928).
60   70 *C.J.S.*, Physicians and Surgeons, para. 41.
61   Herzog, *Medical Jurisprudence* (1931, p. 157); Gordon, Turner & Price, *Medical Jurisprudence*, (1953, p. 121); In *Monahan* v. *Devinny*, 223 App. Div. 547, 229 N.Y.S. 60 (3rd Dept 1928), the defendants were *chiropractors* who treated the plaintiff unskilfully, as a result of which he became paralysed. The court held that the defendants were illegally practising medicine in violation of the Education Law so that 'in an action of this kind they must be held to the same standards of skill and care as prevail amongst those who are licensed.' *N.Y. Educ. Law*, para. 6501, subd. 4, defines the practice of medicine: 'A person practices medicine within the meaning of this discussion, except as hereinafter stated, who holds himself out as being able to diagnose, treat, operate or prescribe for any human disease, pain, injury, deformity or physical condition, and who shall either offer or undertake, by any means or method, to diagnose, treat, operate or prescribe for any human disease, pain, injury, deformity or physical condition.'
62   Regan, *Doctor, Patient and the Law* (1950, p. 34); *Benson* v. *Dean* 232 N.Y. 52, 133 N.E. 125 (1921). S. Stryker, *Courts and Doctors*, London: Butterworths, 1964, p. 9 states: 'The relationship of patient and physician is to the highest possible degree a fiduciary one, involving every element of trust and confidence.' The American Medical Association, *Principles of Medical Ethics*, para. 8 provides, 'A physician should seek consultation upon request, in doubtful or difficult cases, or whenever it appears that the quality of medical service may be enhanced thereby.' See also Annot, 'Duty to send patient to specialist', 132 *A.L.R.*, 392 (1949).
63   42 A.D. 2d 673, 344 N.Y.S. 2d 369 (4th Dept 1973).
64   41 Am. Jur., *Physician and Surgeon*, para. 95.
65   41 Am. Jur., *Physician and Surgeon*, para. 94.
66   *Pike* v. *Honsinger*, 155 N.Y. 201, 49 N.E. 760 (1898).
67   [1942], 2 All E.R. 396, at 402.
68   R.M. McKerron, *The Law of Delict*, 7th edn, Capetown: Juta & Co., 1971, p. 26.
69   1934 C.P.D. 151.
70   Ibid., at 154.
71   *S.A.R.* v. *Bardekber*, 1934 A.D. 473 at 480, *per* Wessels C J.
72   *Van Wyk* v. *Lewis*, 1924 A.D. 438, at 444.

Chapter 5

The Environmental Crisis

AIR TRANSPORT AND SUSTAINABLE DEVELOPMENT

Introduction

The emissions of aircraft engines are similar in nature to other fossil fuel combustion emissions. The only difference between them is that aircraft emissions are released in high altitude, affecting the environment and local air quality. The most serious concern lies in the impact of these emissions on climate change, which has prompted the Kyoto Protocol (1997)[1] to the United Nations Framework on Climate Change (UNFCC) to require developed countries in particular to reduce their collective greenhouse gas emissions by 5 per cent by the period 2005–12,[2] with 1990 as a benchmark.

The other environmental concern pertaining to aviation is aircraft engine noise which has highlighted the compelling need to certify aircraft according to noise certificates in order to ensure that the latest available noise reduction techniques are incorporated into modern aircraft design. Both aspects of environmental pollution can be encapsulated within the broad rubric of 'sustainable development' – a concept spawned in the 1980s, notably by OECD, and subsequently endorsed in 1987 by the Brundtland Report published by the World Commission on Environment and Development.[3] Simplistically put, sustainable development can be identified as the process which, while bringing about development, does so without adversely affecting the interests of future generations and their needs.

The aviation industry plays a significant role in the activities of the global economy and has a substantial input upon the economic development of nations. The industry is composed of suppliers and operators of aircraft, fuel suppliers, aircraft component manufacturers, and airports and air navigation service providers. The commercial airline industry relies heavily on support rendered by airports and air navigation service providers in its attempt to alleviate the serious airport congestion problems currently posed. These problems are a result of the rapid expansion of the air transport industry and the demand for increasing air transport services. From a regulatory perspective, the International Civil Aviation Organization (ICAO), both through its Committee on Aviation Environmental Protection (CAEP), which ICAO commissioned (at its 32nd Session of the Assembly in 1998 to study policy options to limit or reduce the greenhouse gas emissions from civil aviation), and by astute diplomacy and sustained effort towards sustainable development of aviation, has worked diligently towards ensuring environmental protection in civil aviation. It is expected that total fuel use will increase 6 per cent per year between 1990 and 2015, whereas total aviation fuel use, including passenger, freight and military requirements, is projected to increase by 3 per cent per year.[4]

One of ICAO's initiatives in this regard was to request a special report on aviation and the global atmosphere from the Intergovernmental Panel on Climate Change (IPCC) which was released in 1999. According to this report, there is an estimated 3·5 per cent contribution by aircraft to the total radiative forcing resulting from all human activities.[5] The report also predicted that global passenger air travel, as a measure in revenue passenger kilometres, is projected to grow by about 5 per cent per year.

Current air transport statistics

In order to obtain a clear perspective on the potential of the aviation industry to affect the global environment adversely, it becomes necessary to examine the dimensions of air transport and its contribution to the world economy. The ICAO *Annual Report of the Council* for the year ending 31 December 2001 indicates that in 2001, the world economy witnessed a sharp slowdown in growth in almost all major regions. The world gross domestic product (GDP) grew by approximately 2·5 per cent in real terms. For the industrialized countries, GDP grew only by 1·2 per cent; the North American economy showing economic growth of about 1·2 per cent, almost 3 percentage points lower than the previous year. GDP growth for developing countries amounted to about 4 per cent, some 1·7 per cent lower than in the year 2000.[6] International tourism decreased in 2001 by an estimated 1·3 per cent, owing to the events of 11 September and the weakening of the economies of the major tourism-generating markets. The World Tourism Organization (WTO) estimates that almost 690 million tourists travelled to foreign countries in 2001.

According to the *Annual Report of the Council*, available statistics pertaining to air transport in 2001 show that the total scheduled traffic carried by the airlines of the 187 contracting states of ICAO amounted to about 1621 million passengers and some 29 million tonnes of freight. Reported monthly figures suggest that, up to September 2001, there had been little change in overall passenger/freight/mail tonne-kilometres performed over the same period in 2000, a small growth in passenger traffic being countered by a significant decrease in freight traffic. However, following the events of 11 September, data for the entire year 2001 indicate that total traffic decreased some 4 per cent compared to 2000 and international tonne-kilometres by some 5 per cent, the first annual decrease in these figures since 1991.

In 2001, the overall capacity was reduced, but at a lower rate than the decrease in traffic. Hence, the average passenger and weight load factors on total scheduled services (domestic plus international) decreased to 69 and 59 per cent, respectively. On a regional basis, some 35 per cent of the total traffic volume (passengers/freight/mail) was carried by North American airlines. European airlines carried 28 per cent, Asia/Pacific airlines 27 per cent, Latin American and the Caribbean airlines and Middle East airlines 4 per cent each and African airlines 2 per cent. Data for individual countries indicate that in 2001 about 43 per cent of the total volume of scheduled passenger, freight and mail traffic was accounted for by the airlines of the United States, Japan and the United Kingdom (32, 6 and 5 per cent respectively). On international services, almost 37 per cent of all traffic was carried by the airlines of the United States, the United Kingdom, Germany and Japan (17, 7, 7 and 6 per cent, respectively).[7]

On the basis of schedules published in multilateral airline schedule guides, the *Annual Report of the Council* of ICAO estimates that at the end of 2001 there were some 781 air carriers worldwide providing scheduled passenger services (international and/or domestic) and about 113 operating scheduled all-freight services. Compared with the same period in 2000, this represents a net overall increase of 87 air carriers.

The trend of privatization of government-owned airlines continued in 2001. In several cases, however, privatization plans were deferred or postponed because of the complexities encountered in the process or the economic situation of the airlines concerned, or owing to other circumstances. In contrast to the general trend, government shareholdings in several privatized carriers were increased in order to rescue the carriers from imminent collapse.

Where is air transport headed?

Although 2002 was a difficult year for the air transport industry, whose prosperity declined, 2003 threatened to be even more challenging. This is mostly due to airlines taking more courageous and calculated risks towards higher yield in response to trends in economic and global security. Although this should prove beneficial in the long term, the sense of uncertainty that prevails in 2003 will affect the supply of air transport services if only in response to the natural apprehension of uncertainty about getting a short-term return on investments. Since individual airlines are being increasingly challenged to deliver improved results in 2003, the world is faced with a trend towards increasing supply of air transport services, bringing with it an ominous dimension of concern for the environment and the compelling need for the industry to move towards sustainability within its own parameters of development. The significance of this reality is brought out by the fourth principle of the Declaration of the June 1992 Rio Summit,[8] which states that, in order to achieve sustainable development, environmental protection must constitute an integral part of the development process and cannot be considered in isolation from it.[9] The integral link between development and environmental protection, with a view to ensuring sustainable development, was developed as early as 1972, when member countries of the European Economic Community, through their heads of state, endorsed the view that economic development must intrinsically be proportionate to improvement in the quality of life.[10]

This section will assess the need for an overall conceptual approach in order to ensure that developments in air transport and its contribution to the global economy of necessity relate to overall sustainable development in global terms.

Sustainable development and air transport: a workable framework?

What is sustainable development ?

Essentially, the term 'sustainable development' in the context of environmental protection means 'development which the environment can sustain without being polluted'. The term has its genesis in the Rio Summit, whose priorities included, along with sustainable growth, efficient use of resources, protection of human health and protection of global and regional resources, including the atmosphere.

For the above purposes, member states of the United Nations agreed at the conference to establish a new Commission for Sustainable Development.

Sustainable development is now internationally managed by the primary United Nations regulatory body on the environment – the UN Environmental Programme (UNEP) – which addresses the subject of sustainable development in three component elements:

a. environmental assessment: through evaluation and review, research and monitoring and the exchange of views on the environment;
b. environmental management: through comprehensive planning that takes into account the effects of the acts of humans on the environment; and
c. supporting measures: through education, training and public information and also through financial assistance and organizational arrangements.

The expectations placed upon and the tasks assigned to UNEP by the international community confirm UNEP's approach of positioning the environment in the broader context of sustainable development. UNEP's mandate is consistent with the conclusion that the environment cannot be viewed in isolation and needs to be managed within the integrated context of sustainable development. This approach was confirmed by the global community at the United Nations Conference on Environment and Development (UNCED).

The main objective of the World Summit on Sustainable Development, which was held in Johannesburg from 26 August to 4 September 2002, was to hold a ten-year review of the Rio Summit in order to re-energize the existing global commitment to sustainable development.[11] The deliberations of the Johannesburg Summit resulted in the adoption of two documents, the Johannesburg Declaration[12] (the Declaration) and the Plan of Implementation.[13] The Declaration, while drawing on the rich history of global environmental protection measures, reconfirmed the world's commitment to sustainable development through multilateral solution seeking and implementation. The three fundamental foundations of sustainable development, as endorsed by the Declaration, are poverty eradication, change of consumption and production patterns, and protection and management of the natural resource base. Of these, consumption, production and protection of nature are critical for air transport, and in this context the Plan of Implementation's recognition of the foundations mentioned in the Declaration, as 'the overarching objectives of, and essential requirements for, sustainable development' emphasizes the intrinsic relevance of both the Declaration and Plan of Implementation to air transport.

The Johannesburg Summit also emphasized the concept of partnerships between governments, while giving a large boost to business and civil society in the Summit and the Plan of Implementation. Over 220 partnerships (with $235 million in resources) were identified in advance of the Summit and around 60 partnerships were announced during the Summit by a variety of countries. The Summit also pledged its efforts towards improving access to reliable, affordable, economically viable, socially acceptable and environmentally sound energy services and resources, sufficient to achieve the Millennium Development Goals,[14] including the goal of halving the proportion of people in poverty by 2015.

A workable framework

The fundamental starting point for any discussion on sustainable development is the prospect of the world population doubling in size at the end of the current century to 10 billion, at the rate of increase of 95 million per year.[15] Human population will remain the key indicator acting as a variable in determining the exploitative use of resources which will include a rapid consumption of non-renewable resources as well as the exhaustive use of renewable resources beyond the scope of their regenerative capacity. In this context, the failure of a society to generate a solution to the particular problem of consumption in excess of available resources would result in what is termed 'market failure'. Market failure occurs when economic activity is undertaken without a full realization or study of its impact on the sustainability of the environment in which that activity takes place.

The ICAO Assembly, at its 33rd Session held in September/October 2001, adopted Resolution A33-7 (Consolidated Statement of Continuing ICAO Policies and Practices related to Environmental Protection) which recognizes the preamble to the Convention on International Civil Aviation providing that the future development of international civil aviation can greatly help to create and preserve friendship and understanding among the nations and peoples of the world. Article 44 of the Chicago Convention states that ICAO should develop the principles and techniques of international air navigation and foster the planning and development of international air transport so as to meet the needs of the peoples of the world for safe, regular, efficient and economical air transport.

Resolution A33-7 also recognizes that many of the adverse environmental effects of civil aviation activity can be reduced by the application of integrated measures embracing technological improvements, appropriate operating procedures, proper organization of air traffic and the appropriate use of airport planning, land-use planning and management, and market-based measures. In accordance with the Resolution, and in fulfilling its role, ICAO strives to achieve a balance between the benefit accruing to the world community through civil aviation and the harm caused to the environment in certain areas through the progressive advancement of civil aviation. ICAO is conscious of (and will continue to take into account) the adverse environmental impacts that may be related to civil aviation activity and of its responsibility and that of its contracting states to achieve maximum compatibility between the safe and orderly development of civil aviation and the quality of the environment.

In compliance with the objective of the Resolution, which is to ensure that regulation in aviation and environmental protection will maintain the essential balance between advancement of the aviation industry and sustainable development, the Council of ICAO will continue to pursue all civil aviation matters related to the environment and also maintain the initiative in developing policy guidance on these matters, and not leave such initiatives to other organizations. Also, in the spirit of A33-7, states have pledged to continue their active support for ICAO's environment-related activities on all appropriate occasions.

The philosophical approach of Resolution A33-7 is a sound one in that it takes cognizance of the basic principle that environmental degradation is primarily caused by externalities which arise when a decision of some economic agent, such as a government or state instrumentality, affect other economic agents which are not factored into the overall equation of development. A classic example of environmental degradation in the field of aviation would be when a state takes a decision to adopt an open skies policy in order to attract tourism into its territory, resulting in a proliferation of air services into the country. Although in financial and economic terms such a measure would be profitable, the volume of environmental degradation in the country (particularly in the vicinity of the airports) would increase exponentially. There have been numerous analogies to this example, one being the case of Indonesia. The Indonesian government taxed and later banned the import of timber, with a view to giving a boost to domestic sectors using timber as an element of production. This subsidy, although buttressing the local timber industry's economy, resulted in massive deforestation in the country as a result of local lumber enterprises trying to keep up with the evolving demand for timber products with the supply of local timber resources.[16] One must realize of course that trade per se is not a causative factor in environmental degradation but remains merely a contributory factor. It is in this sense that trade in air transport services, and in particular market access by air carriers, must be viewed as being potentially contributory to environmental degradation if trade aspects are not viewed by economic agents in conjunction with the environment.

The conceptual structure of Resolution A33-7 also lends itself well to recognizing that, although economics and ecology have been mutually exclusive from a historical perspective, this perception has now changed, underscoring the current need to integrate the two, bringing together the complex and multidimensional issues involved. Within the context of the air transport field, this merger has to be viewed on the basis that neither trade liberalization – which is the current trend in air transport market access – nor environmental protection is an end in itself, but remains a means towards achieving a harmonious blending of the elements of development and restraint contemporaneously so that sustainable development is ensured.

It is incontrovertible that, in recent times, there has been confluence of global community awareness of the significance of the interrelationship between trade and environment. Unfortunately, although this fact has emerged in sectors such as energy and agriculture, it has not permeated the air transport industry sufficiently for a cohesive and composite philosophy to emerge in trade and environment. The award of market access, open skies exchanges and trade reciprocity stands isolated from environmental impact studies that may be necessary to maintain an overall balance. Even though some may argue that the contribution of aviation to environmental degradation is negligible, and that economic prospects for air transport are gloomy at best, there is no room for doubt that prudence would dictate the need for a multilateral approach to the integration of trade and the environment in a mutually supportive manner. Air transport needs a predictable multilateral trading system in order to ensure sustainable development for developed and developing countries alike.

The United Nations scientific and technical information system has as its objective the accumulation and improvement of reliable and comparable scientific and technical information about environmental issues and the development and application of means of collecting, storing, retrieving and processing such information that will make it readily available to decision makers and specialists.[17] Industry and transport is one area within the purview of UNEP, which has a mandate to support the improvement of methodologies for analysing the relationship between environment and development of procedures for incorporating environmental considerations into development policies, planning and administration.[18] Be that as it may, the exclusive mandate given to ICAO by the Chicago Convention of 1944 to regulate on aviation issues, coupled with exclusive and explicit recognition in the 1997 Kyoto Protocol to UNFCC, that ICAO will be the regulatory body in charge of aviation and environmental issues pertaining to climate change, imposes on ICAO a certain exclusive mandate under the United Nations umbrella to be responsible for regulatory issues relating to aviation and the environment. It is in this context that one should examine the issue of air transport and environment having a common framework for sustainable development.

The infrastructure for a global framework for air transport resides with ICAO, in particular with the recognition given to ICAO by the Kyoto Protocol, even if only in the area of engine emissions. The Chicago Convention, being the fundamental statutory instrument which lays down ICAO's mandate and purpose, endorses ICAO's role in Article 44 of the Convention, devolving responsibility on the Organization to develop principles and techniques of air navigation and to foster the planning and development of international air transport so as, inter alia, to ensure the safe and orderly growth of international civil aviation throughout the world; meet the needs of the peoples of the world for safe, regular, efficient and economical air transport,[19] and promote generally the development of all aspects of international civil aeronautics.[20]

Taking into consideration that trade in market access pertaining to air transport services is not under the umbrella of the World Trade Organization, the regulation of market access has to endeavour consistently to obviate unsustainable patterns of economic activity which may exacerbate problems of pollution and resource depletion. In this respect, ICAO has already initiated externalities such as incorporating emissions trading as a market-based option,[21] although such initiatives, including the introduction of sustainable processes of environmental taxation, proceed at different levels of progress and speed in different countries.[22]

ICAO has also taken sustained action over the past decade to adopt regulatory measures in the areas of engine emissions and noise. For example, in following up revisions made by the Council in June 2001, the 33rd Session of the Assembly adopted Resolution A33-7, and urged contracting states to adopt a balanced approach to noise management, taking full account of ICAO guidance, applicable legal obligations, existing agreements, current laws and established policies, all to be given due consideration when addressing noise problems at international airports. Contracting states are urged to adopt appropriate mechanisms in implementing this balanced approach: notably, in establishing a transparent process based on objective, measurable criteria for the assessment of the noise problem; in evaluating likely costs and benefits of various measures with a view to achieving maximum environmental benefit; and in providing for dissemination of the evaluation results that may be used in consultation with stakeholders and in dispute resolutions.

Resolution A33-7 also addressed growing concerns about environmental problems in the atmosphere such as global warming and depletion of the ozone layer, noting that the Agenda 21 action plan adopted by the 1992 United Nations Conference on Environment and Development calls on governments to address these problems with the cooperation of relevant United Nations bodies. Particular reference is made to the Kyoto Protocol which recognizes ICAO as the primary body responsible for the regulation of aviation-related environmental issues on aircraft engine emission, and which calls upon developed countries to pursue limitation or reduction of greenhouse gases from 'aviation bunker fuels' working through ICAO.

The Assembly recognized that market-based measures are policy tools that are designed to achieve environmental goals at a lower cost and in a more flexible manner than traditional regulatory measures. Particularly in the context of controlling greenhouse gas emissions, the Assembly recognized that there has been increasing recognition by governments of the need for each economic sector to pay the full cost of the environmental damage it causes and market-based measures for protecting the environment were particularly relevant in this regard. It was the Assembly's view that any charges imposed, based on the costs of the mitigating or environmental impact of aircraft engine emissions to the extent that such costs can be properly identified and directly attributable to air transport, should be applicable only insofar as they are consistent with Article 15 of the Chicago Convention and ICAO's policies on taxes and charges.[23] The Assembly noted with approval analyses conducted by CAEP, showing that an open emissions trading system, whereby the total amount of emissions would be capped and allowances in the form of permits to emit carbon dioxide could be bought and sold to meet emission reduction objectives, was a cost-effective measure to limit or reduce carbon dioxide emitted by civil aviation, particularly in the long term. Short-term voluntary measures, where industry and governments agree to a target and/or to a set of actions to reduce emissions, would serve as a first step towards such long-term measures.

Although, admittedly, economic activity in air transport, particularly in the movement of aircraft between states' territories, does not portend catastrophic environmental consequences on a short-term basis, it is now opportune to address trade in air transport and its effect on global environmental welfare as a composite whole, rather than retain the status quo of a bifurcated group of interests. In this context it might be a useful exercise to commission a study to assess the two areas and their synergies.

Conclusion

The most critical factor that adversely affects environmental protection is the fact that the global political structure which is based on the primacy of states as sovereign entities has created conditions detrimental to sustainable development. The significance of the demographic structure of the world and its varied political interests underscore the inevitable emergence of a dichotomy between exponential increases in population, the needs thereof and the limited resource base available for development to meet such needs. Therefore sustainable development must, as a necessity, be addressed within the context of balancing population and natural resources.[24] It is within these parameters that a study should make an assessment of whether air transport, in its different trade dimensions, is a distinct threat to sustainable development.

LEGAL AND REGULATORY ISSUES

At the 33rd Session of the Assembly of the International Civil Aviation Organization (ICAO),[25] held in Montreal from 25 September to 5 October 2001, a resolution was adopted containing a consolidated statement of continuing policies and practices related to environmental protection.[26] This resolution was a response to the need to incorporate new ICAO policies and guidance material regarding aircraft noise and other developments in that field since the 32nd Session, held in 1998, in particular, to achieve a balanced approach to noise management. The Resolution also addressed, inter alia, the issue of aircraft engine emissions, including an increased and improved understanding of emissions, notably a possible means of limiting or reducing greenhouse gases from aviation.

Over the past decade, there has been continuing awareness that aviation may contribute to adverse environmental impacts on the world and that it behoves the world aviation community to achieve maximum compatibility between the safe and orderly development of civil aviation and the quality of the environment. This is particularly significant in the context of ICAO's role in developing international air transport so as to meet the needs of the peoples to ensure safe, regular, efficient and economical air transport.[27] The philosophy of Resolution A33-7 is based on the fact that adverse environmental effects of civil aviation activity can be reduced by integrated measures embracing technological developments, proper operating procedures, appropriate organization of air traffic and strategic use of airport planning, land use planning and market-based measures. ICAO's role, in this delicately balanced operation, is to strive to achieve harmony between the benefit occurring to the world community through civil aviation and the harm caused to the environment in certain key areas through the progressive advancement of civil aviation.

AIRCRAFT NOISE

With regard to aircraft noise, the resolution, in Appendix B, makes reference to Annex 16 to the Convention on International Civil Aviation (Chicago Convention),[28] which contains noise certification standards for subsonic aircraft, and ICAO's 'Policies on Charges for Airports and Air Navigation Services' (Doc. 9082), which has policy guidance on noise-related charges. In the context of these documents, and particularly with regard to more stringent aircraft noise standards adopted by the ICAO Council in June 2001 for inclusion in Annex 16, the Assembly requested the Council to continue with vigour the work related to the development of Standards, Recommended Practices and Procedures and ensure that work conducted by the Council's Committee on Aviation Environmental Protection (CAEP) continues expeditiously in order that appropriate solutions can be developed as soon as possible.

In following up on revisions made by the Council in June 2001, the Assembly, through the resolution, urged contracting states to adopt a balanced approach to noise management, taking full account of ICAO guidance, applicable legal obligations, existing agreements, current laws and established policies, all to be given due consideration when addressing noise problems at international airports. Contracting states are urged to adopt appropriate mechanisms in implementing this balanced approach, notably in establishing a transparent process based on objective, measurable criteria for the assessment of the noise problem; in evaluating likely costs and benefits of various measures with a view to achieving maximum environmental benefit; and in providing for dissemination of the evaluation results that may be used in consultation with stakeholders and dispute resolutions.

As part of the balanced approach, Resolution A33-7 encourages states, inter alia, to conduct studies, support research and technology programmes aimed at reducing noise at source and to work closely with each other to ensure that their noise management programmes are harmonized, taking into consideration the particular economic exigencies of developing countries and also taking particular care not to derogate the non-discrimination principle enshrined in Article 15 of the Chicago Convention.[29]

Resolution A33-7, in Appendix D, urges contracting states not to introduce any phase-outs of subsonic jet aircraft which exceed noise levels contained in Volume 1 of Annex 16 to the Chicago Convention before giving consideration to a clear determination as to whether normal attrition of existing fleets of such aircraft will provide the necessary protection of noise climates around airports and whether necessary protection can be achieved by regulators preventing their operations from adding such aircraft to their fleets through either purchase, or lease/charter/ interchange, or alternatively by incentives to accelerate fleet modernization. Before phasing out subsonic aircraft that may exceed the above mentioned noise levels, the resolution also calls upon contracting states to give careful thought to whether alternatively effective noise management can be achieved by applying regulations preventing operations of such aircraft through restrictions limited to airports and runways, the use of which has been identified and declared by these states as generating noise problems and limited to time periods when greater noise disturbance is caused. Finally, contracting states are called upon to consider implications of any restrictions for other states concerned, through consultation and reasonable notification of the application of restrictions.

One of the most significant achievements of Resolution A33-7 lies in the skilful balance achieved in offering a compromise to contracting states which, despite the above-mentioned criteria, decide to phase out aircraft which comply with noise certificates standards in Volume 1, Chapter 2 of Annex 16 but which exceed the noise levels in Volume 1, Chapter 3 of Annex 16. This compromise recommends that such states frame any restrictions so that Chapter 2 compliant aircraft of an individual operator which are operating at present to their territories may be withdrawn from such operations gradually, over a period of not less than seven years. The resolution also requests contracting states not to restrict before the end of the above period the operations of any aircraft less than 25 years after the date of issue of its first individual certificates of airworthiness, and not to restrict before the end of the period the operations of any currently existing wide-body aircraft or of any fitted with engines that have a by-pass ratio higher than two to one. Contracting states are required to inform ICAO, as well as the other states concerned, of all restrictions imposed.

Finally, the resolution urges states not to introduce measures to phase out aircraft which comply, through original certification or recertification, with the noise certification standards in Volume 1, Chapter 3 or 4, of Annex 16 and, in particular, not to impose any operating restrictions on Chapter 3-compliant aircraft, except as part of the balanced approach to noise management developed by ICAO and in accordance with Appendices C and E to the resolution which address issues pertaining to phase-out of subsonic aircraft and local noise-related operations at airports.

Background to noise regulation

It is imperative that, for there to be a meaningful discussion on aircraft noise regulation, the various noise regulations referred to in A33-7 be identified. In order to discuss these regulations, one has to go back in time to the origins of noise regulation in ICAO. The ICAO Assembly has adopted several resolutions concerning aviation and the environment. At its 22nd Assembly held in September/October 1977, the ICAO Assembly adopted Resolution A22-12 which recognized, inter alia, the following:

1) advancing technology has caused aviation to become a significant influence on the environment;
2) many of the adverse environmental effects of civil aviation activity can be reduced by the application of integrated measures embracing technological improvements, appropriate noise abatement operating procedures, proper organization of air traffic and the appropriate use of airport planning and land use control mechanisms;
3) other international organizations are becoming involved in activities relating to noise abatement policies; and
4) in fulfilling its role, ICAO strives to achieve a balance between the benefit accruing to the world community through civil aviation and the harm caused to the human environment in certain areas through the progressive advancement of civil aviation.

The Assembly therefore declared:

1) that ICAO is conscious of the adverse environmental impacts that may be related to aircraft activity and of its responsibility and that of its contracting states to achieve maximum compatibility between the safe and orderly development of civil aviation and the quality of the human environment; and
2) that the Council should maintain its vigilance in the pursuit of aviation interests related to the human environment and also maintain the initiative in developing policy guidance on all aviation matters related to the human environment, and not leave such initiatives to other organizations.

The Assembly also invited states to continue their active support for ICAO's Action Programme Regarding the Environment on all appropriate occasions as their participation in civil aviation's contribution to the United Nations Environment Programme (UNEP) and authorized the ICAO Council, if and when it deems this desirable, to enter into cooperative arrangements with the United Nations Environment Programme for the execution of environmental projects financed by the United Nations Environment Fund. The Assembly urged states to refrain from unilateral measures that would be harmful to the development of international civil aviation.

At the same session, the Assembly adopted Resolution A22-13 on airports and the environment, observing, inter alia, that:

1) the compatibility between the airport and its environment was one of the elements to be taken into account in long-term systems planning;
2) the problem of aircraft noise in the vicinity of many of the world's airports continued to arouse public concern and required appropriate action; and
3) the introduction of future aircraft types could increase and aggravate this noise unless action was taken to alleviate the situation.

The Assembly therefore requested the Council to continue its work on establishing Standards and Recommended Practices relating to the alleviation of the problem and urged contracting states to adopt, where appropriate, the ICAO measures and procedures applicable.

In the following session (September/October 1980), the Assembly adopted Resolution A23-10 on aircraft noise and engine emissions from subsonic aircraft and requested contracting states not to allow the operation of foreign registered subsonic jet planes that did not conform to ICAO's specifications on noise certification standards as specified in Annex 16 until 1 January 1988.[30] At the 28th Assembly Sessions held in October 1990, the ICAO Assembly observed that while certification standards for subsonic jet aircraft noise levels are specified in Volume 1, Chapter 2 and Chapter 3, of Annex 16 and that environmental problems due to aircraft noise continued to exist in the neighbourhood of many international airports, some states were consequently considering restrictions on the operations of aircraft which exceed the noise levels in Volume I, Chapter 3, of Annex 16. The Assembly also recognized that the noise standards in Annex 16 were not intended to introduce operating restrictions on aircraft and that operating restrictions on existing aircraft would increase the costs of airlines and would impose a heavy economic burden, particularly on those airlines which do not have the financial resources to re-equip their fleets. Therefore, considering that resolution of problems due to aircraft noise must be based on the mutual recognition of the difficulties encountered by states and a balance among their different concerns, the Assembly, by Resolution A28-3, urged states not to introduce any new operating restrictions on aircraft which exceed the noise levels in Volume I, Chapter 3, of Annex 16 before considering

a) whether the normal attrition of existing fleets of such aircraft will provide the necessary protection of noise climates around their airports;
b) whether the necessary protection can be achieved by regulations preventing their operators from adding such aircraft to their fleets through either purchase, or lease/charter/interchange, or alternatively by incentives to accelerate fleet modernization;
c) whether the necessary protection can be achieved through restrictions limited to airports and runways the use of which has been identified and declared by them as generating noise problems and limited to time periods when greater noise disturbance is caused; and

d) the implications of any restrictions for other states concerned, consulting these states and giving them reasonable notice of intention.

The Assembly further urged states

a) to frame any restrictions so that Chapter 2-compliant aircraft of an individual operator which are currently operating to their territories may be withdrawn from these operations gradually over a period of not less than seven years;
b) not to begin the above phase-in period for any restrictions before 1 April 1995;
c) not to restrict before the end of the phase-in period the operations of any aircraft less than 25 years after the date of issue of its first individual certificate of airworthiness;
d) not to restrict before the end of the phase-in period the operations of any currently existing wide-body aircraft or of any fitted with high by-pass ratio engines;
e) to apply any restrictions consistently with the non-discrimination principle in Article 15 of the Chicago Convention so as to give foreign operators at least as favourable treatment as their own operators at the same airports; and
f) to inform ICAO, as well as the other states concerned, of all restrictions imposed.

The Assembly also strongly encouraged states to continue to cooperate bilaterally, regionally and inter-regionally with a view to (a) alleviating the noise burden on communities around airports without imposing severe economic hardship on aircraft operators; and (b) taking into account the problems of operators of developing countries with regard to Chapter 2 aircraft currently on their register, where they cannot be replaced before the end of the phase-in period, provided that there is proof of a purchase order or leasing contract placed for a replacement Chapter 3-compliant aircraft and the first date of delivery of the aircraft has been accepted.

The Assembly, while urging states, if and when any new noise certification standards are introduced which are more stringent than those in Volume I, Chapter 3, of Annex 16, not to impose any operating restrictions on Chapter 3-compliant aircraft, urged the Council to promote and states to develop an integrated approach to the problem of aircraft noise, including land-use planning procedures around international airports, so that any residential, industrial or other land use that might be adversely affected by aircraft noise is minimal. The Assembly further urged states to assist aircraft operators in their efforts to accelerate fleet modernization and thereby prevent obstacles and permit all states to have access to lease or purchase aircraft compliant with Chapter 3, including the provision of multilateral technical assistance where appropriate. This resolution superseded Resolution A23-10, which was discussed above.

Resolution A28-3 represents a cautious balance between the concerns of the aircraft manufacturers, the airline industry and developing states who do not wish to lose, in the near future, the services of Chapter 2 aircraft which are already in use and service. Although aircraft manufactured prior to October 1977 that are included in Chapter 2 of Annex 16 and called 'Chapter 2 aircraft' are required to be phased out, the compromise in Resolution A28-3 allowed states that had noise problems at airports to start phasing out operations by Chapter 2 aircraft from the year 1995 and to have all of them withdrawn by the year 2002, with some exceptions. The resolution envisaged that, by the year 2002, only aircraft manufactured after October 1977 and described in Chapter 3 of Annex 16 (called 'Chapter 3 aircraft') would be in operation. Following this resolution, a number of developed states have already started to phase out Chapter 2 aircraft, while giving due recognition to the compromise reached in Resolution A28-3.

At its 32nd Assembly, held in September 1998, Assembly Resolution A32-8[31] containing a consolidated statement of continuing ICAO policies and practices related to environmental protection was adopted, making current the regulatory policies relating to aviation and the environment. Appendix B to the Resolution cites Annex 16, Volume 1, as comprising, inter alia, noise certification standards for future subsonic aircraft and mentions that aircraft manufacturers and operators need to note that future generations of aircraft have to be so designed as to operate efficiently and with the least possible environmental disturbance. Appendix C calls upon contracting states and international organizations to recognize the leading role of ICAO in dealing with aircraft noise and requests the former to work closely together to ensure the greatest harmonization of work in the area of environmental protection as related to air transport. In Appendix G, which relates to the problem of sonic boom, the Assembly reaffirms the importance attached to ameliorating problems caused to the public by sonic boom as a result of supersonic flight and invites states involved in the manufacture of supersonic aircraft to furnish ICAO with proposals that would meet specifications established by ICAO on the subject.

The most topical issue addressed by Resolution A32-8 is in its Appendix D, which, whilst reiterating the time limits specified for the phasing out of Chapter 2 aircraft and related dates, strongly encourages states to continue to cooperate bilaterally, regionally and inter-regionally, with a view to alleviating the noise burden on communities and also to take into account the problems that may be faced by some operators in phasing out their Chapter 2 aircraft before the end of the period specified. The resolution also urges states, if and when any noise certification standards are introduced which are more stringent than those in Volume 1, Chapter 3, of Annex 16, not to impose any operating restrictions on Chapter 3-compliant aircraft. More importantly, states are urged to assist operators in their efforts at fleet modernization with a view to preventing obstacles and to permit all states to have access to lease or purchase aircraft compliant with Chapter 3.

The qualification in Resolution A32-8 seemingly admits of Chapter 2 aircraft which are converted to be compliant with Chapter 3 noise levels being considered for operation at least until 1 April 2002. The resolution urges states to consider the difficulties faced by operators of Chapter 2 aircraft who are unable to make them Chapter 3-compliant by the given date, implying that it would be in the economic interests of such operators to be given additional time in order to make the necessary replacements. Chapter 2 aircraft could be made Chapter 3-compliant whereby the aircraft can be re-certified to Chapter 3 standards through re-engining or 'hush kitting'. Chapter 2 aircraft which are likely to be re-engined or hush-kitted are Boeing 727s and 737s, DC-9s, BAC1-11s and some Boeing 747-100s that need hush-kitting.

There is an attempt on the part of the European Union to limit and eventually eliminate Chapter 3-compliant aircraft from operating within countries of the European Union. This ban would also be calculated to affect the importation of such aircraft into the region. Legislation passed by the Union in April 1999 was intended to bar Chapter 3-compliant aircraft from European registries from 4 May 2000 (originally 1 April 1999, which is three years before the date specified in Resolution A32-8, namely, 1 April 2002) and to prohibit their operation into the countries of the European Union after 1 April 2002. Such action has been reportedly criticized by the Air Transport Association, which claims that the inflexibility of such a deadline 'will severely undercut, if not destroy entirely, ICAO's efforts to address environmental issues on a uniform international basis'.[32]

The action of the European Union seeks justification on the basis that the exponential air traffic growth in Europe will increase noise around European airports, requiring stringent noise standards. A related fear is reportedly that hush-kitted aircraft, which are rare in Europe, will find a new home in the Continent. Unlike the situation in Europe, airlines in the United States have been somewhat prolific in the use of hush-kits in aircraft[33] and many US carriers operate Stage 2 hush-kitted aircraft into Europe and have even based equipment in the Continent. At the time of writing, although the US State Department had reacted forcefully to the European Union's hush-kitted aircraft ban, the application of which was extended by the Union until May 2000, it was reported that both the United States and the European Union were working together on a possible new ICAO Standard (presumably to be called Chapter 4).[34]

The issue is a 'double-edged sword' involving two distinct disciplines. As discussed earlier, the European contention is based on the strictly legal issue of noise pollution and overtones of the tort of nuisance committed by operators whose aircraft are not compliant with Chapter 3 standards to the satisfaction of the European Union. Others who oppose what they claim to be a premature enforcement of ICAO standards, as contained in Resolution A32-8, argue that the European hush-kit rule would cost the manufacturing industry significant losses. It is reported that the US industry would lose $2 billion if the ban was enforced in Europe as scheduled.[35]

It was against this backdrop that the 33rd ICAO Assembly considered the noise issue and adopted A33-7.

AIRCRAFT ENGINE EMISSIONS

Resolution A33-7 also addressed growing concerns about environmental problems in the atmosphere such as global warming and depletion of the ozone layer, noting that the Agenda 21 action plan adopted by the 1992 United Nations Conference on Environment and Development calls on governments to address these problems with the cooperation of relevant United Nations bodies. Particular mention is made of the Kyoto Protocol, adopted by the Conference of the Parties to the United Nations Framework Convention on Climate Change (UNFCCC) in December 1997 (referred to in some detail later on) which recognizes ICAO as the primary body responsible for the regulation of aviation-related environmental issues on aircraft engine emission, and which calls upon developed countries to pursue limitation or reduction of greenhouse gases from 'aviation bunker fuels' working through ICAO.

The Assembly recognized that market-based measures, which will be described in some detail below, are policy tools that are designed to achieve environmental goals at a lower cost and in a more flexible manner than traditional regulatory measures. Particularly in the context of controlling greenhouse gas emissions, the Assembly recognized that there has been increasing recognition by governments of the need for each economic sector to pay the full cost of the environmental damage it causes and market-based measures for protecting the environment were particularly relevant in this regard. It was the Assembly's view that any charges imposed, based on the costs of the mitigating of environmental impact of aircraft engine emissions, to the extent that such costs can be properly identified and directly attributable to air transport, should be applicable only insofar as they are consistent with Article 15 of the Chicago Convention and ICAO's policies on taxes and charges.[36] The Assembly noted with approval analyses conducted by CAEP suggesting that an open emissions trading system, whereby the total amount of emissions would be capped and allowances in the form of permits to emit carbon dioxide could be bought and sold to meet emission reduction objectives, was a cost-effective measure to limit or reduce carbon dioxide emitted by civil aviation, particularly in the long-term. Short-term voluntary measures, where industry and governments agree to a target and/or to a set of actions to reduce emissions, would serve as a first step towards such long-term measures.

The Assembly required the Council of ICAO to develop guidance for states on the application of market-based measures aimed at reducing or limiting the environmental impact of aircraft engine emissions, particularly with respect to mitigating the impact of aviation on climate changes. Above all, contracting states and the Council are encouraged through Resolution A33-7 to take into account the interests of all parties concerned, to evaluate the costs and benefits of various measures with the goal of addressing aircraft engine emissions in the most cost-effective manner and to adopt actions consistent with ICAO policies. The Assembly endorsed the development of an open emissions trading system for international aviation and requested the Council to develop guidelines for open emissions trading for international aviation, as a matter of priority.

In making its recommendations and requests, the Assembly took into consideration the work of the CAEP which, at its Fifth Meeting (CAEP/5), held from 8 to 17 January 2001, identified market-based measures as being policy tools that are designed to achieve environmental goals at a lower cost and in a more flexible manner than traditional regulatory measures. CAEP considered three types of measures: emissions-related levies: generically, referring to charges and taxes; emissions trading: a system whereby the total amount of emissions would be capped and allowances in the form of permits could be bought and sold to meet emission reduction objectives; and voluntary measures: mechanisms under which industry and governments agree to a target and/or a set of actions to reduce emissions.

Under emission-related levies, three options were considered by CAEP: a fuel (or en route emissions) tax with revenue going to the national treasury, a revenue-neutral aircraft efficiency charge, and an en route emissions charge with revenue returned to the aviation sector. The main findings of the analysis conducted by CAEP on these three options are that, in the context of a fuel tax, it raises legal issues concerning air services agreements and ICAO policies and, if not applied worldwide, could cause tankering practices (by which aircraft would carry extra fuel for later segments rather than purchasing the fuel locally). With regard to a revenue-neutral charge, CAEP felt that it would be consistent with ICAO policies but would require an acceptable method to be developed for defining aircraft efficiency, and could not be implemented in those areas which do not have en route charges. An en route emissions charge would be consistent with ICAO policies, assuming that revenues were recycled to the aviation sector, but, if not applied worldwide, could raise equity and competitiveness issues and would necessitate further guidance for the use and distribution of the revenue collected.

In designing an emissions-trading regime, it was the view of CAEP that the key issues are the scope of trading (that is open trading across sectors, or closed trading within the aviation sector alone) and the distribution of emission permits or allowances (that is, grandfathering, based on past or current use, or auctioning through a bidding process). Since such a system is untested for aviation, there would need to be rules for participation and the establishment of administrative mechanisms for recording trades and monitoring and ensuring compliance.

As for voluntary measures, CAEP advised the ICAO Council that an industry initiative, where a set of actions and/or a target to be met whould be proposed, based on a negotiated agreement between industry and government to take a set of actions, and/or to achieve a specific emission target, and a hybrid option, under which one of the two above-mentioned options is used in conjunction with another market-based measure.

The main findings were that voluntary measures alone cannot achieve an ambitious emission reduction target. They would have to be used in conjunction with other measures. In addition, these voluntary measures allow industry to enhance its ability to undertake activities related to 'capability building'. They are primarily looked at as transitional measures. A key issue is the need to ensure that any such action would be to the advantage of the participants if market-based or other regulatory measures were imposed at a later date.

CAEP/5 concluded that a closed emissions trading system does not show cost–benefit results to justify further consideration, and felt that an open emissions trading system would be a cost-effective solution for CO^2 emission reductions in the long term, but cannot be implemented until the Kyoto Protocol has entered into force and an emissions cap has been agreed. Further work is necessary to develop an emissions-trading system and to study the consequences for developing countries; and ICAO should continue to play a leadership role, particularly in the development of proposals for caps, consistent with the responsibility given to ICAO in Article 2.2 of the Kyoto Protocol.

Emissions trading as a market-based measure

The essential philosophy of emissions trading in environmental protection is based on a certain flexibility allowed market forces to reach the lowest cost involved in an operation while at the same time achieving an environmental target which has been already set. The word 'trading' correctly denotes an exchange, and when applied to the aviation context means a certain trade-off between airlines whose fleets pollute more than others and low polluting airlines. The trade-off could take the form of a 'purchase' by the high-polluting airline of the reduction level of a low-polluting airline. Emissions trading would encourage airlines to seek innovation in technology and to reduce their emission levels.

Emissions trading of levels of pollution between airlines differs fundamentally with the existing expectation of each airline maintaining a standard level of emission by its aircraft. When airlines trade emission levels, the rates at which their aircraft pollute the atmosphere will be taken as a whole and applicable to a whole fleet, so that an airline which is above its permitted pollution level could join with another airline which is below the standard level of pollution required of it, thus making the average pollution between the two more acceptable than if taken individually. This mechanism encourages a low-polluting airline to achieve even lower standards, in order to trade its levels with high-polluting airlines.

The Third Conference of the Parties to the United Nations Framework Convention on Climate Change (Climate Change Convention)[37] was held from 1 to 11 December 1997 at Kyoto, Japan. Significantly, the states parties to the Convention adopted a protocol (Kyoto Protocol)[38] on 11 December 1997 under which industrialized countries have agreed to reduce their collective emissions of six greenhouse gases[39] by at least 5 per cent by 2008–12. Ambassador Raul Estrada-Oyuela, who had chaired the Committee of the Whole established by the Conference to facilitate the negotiation of a Protocol text, expressed the view that the agreement will have a real impact on the problem of greenhouse gas emissions and that 11 December 1997 should be remembered as the 'Day of the Atmosphere'.[40]

The Kyoto Protocol, in Article 1(*a*) (*v*) calls on each state party to achieve progressive phasing out of market imperfections, fiscal incentives, tax and duty exemptions and subsidies in all greenhouse gas-emitting sectors that run counter to the objective of the Convention and application of market instruments. The subject of emissions leading to trading is addressed initially in Article 3 of the Protocol, which requires states parties to ensure that their aggregate anthropogenic carbon dioxide-equivalent emissions of the greenhouse gases listed in Annex A do not exceed their assigned amounts, calculated pursuant to their quantified emission limitation and reduction commitments inscribed in Annex B. The provision also requires states parties to the Protocol to reduce their overall emissions of greenhouse gases by at least 5 per cent below 1990 levels in the commitment period 2008 to 2012. Article 3(6) goes further, in providing that states parties shall be allowed a certain degree of flexibility in implementation of Article 3 and the reduction of their emission standards.

The subject of emissions trading is explicitly addressed in Article 6, which states that, for the purpose of meeting its commitments under Article 3, any party included in Annex 1 may transfer to or acquire from any other such party emission reduction units resulting from projects aimed at reducing anthropogenic emissions by sources or enhancing anthropogenic removals by sinks of greenhouse gases in any sector of the economy provided the parties concerned approve of such trading and, inter alia, such trading actually results in a reduction in emission by sources.

Article 17 sets out that the Conference of the Parties shall define the relevant principles, modalities, rules and guidelines, in particular for verification, reporting and accountability for emissions trading. It also provides that the parties included in Annex B to the Protocol may participate in emissions trading for the purposes of fulfilling their commitments under Article 3. Such trading shall be supplemental to domestic actions for the purpose of meeting qualified emission limitation and reduction commitments under Article 3.[41]

Once the Protocol has entered into force,[42] Annex I parties must submit an annual inventory of emissions to the Convention Secretariat,[43] enabling expert review teams to provide a full assessment of such parties' compliance with the Protocol.[44] These expert assessments will be reviewed by the Conference of the Parties serving as the meeting of the parties to the Protocol,[45] which will adopt decisions on implementation.[46]

Article 12 of the Protocol is also noteworthy in that it defines a clean development mechanism (CDM) which introduces the concept of joint implementation by a developed country and a developing country.[47] The mechanism admits of the advantage afforded to the parties concerned, with developed countries gaining the benefit of the partnerships in emissions trading with developing countries which are more cost-effective in financing such projects. The CDM achieves the dual goal of enabling developing countries to operate projects which result in emission reductions which contribute to the objectives of the UNFCCC,[48] and also enabling countries specified in Annex I of the Kyoto Protocol which finance such projects through the CDM to use emissions reductions to reduce their own emissions in toto.[49]

The mechanism is supervised by an executive board and the responsibility for establishing procedures to make certain that proper verification of projects is achieved in a transparent manner devolves upon the Conference of the Parties to the Protocol.[50] By virtue of Articles 12(10) and 3(12), Annex I countries could contribute to their own emission reduction targets under the Protocol by using emission reductions from jointly implemented projects under the CDM during the period 2000–2008.

A watershed provision of the Kyoto Protocol lies in Article 2.2 which stipulates that parties included in Annex II shall pursue limitation or reduction of emissions of greenhouse gases not controlled by the Montreal Protocol[51] from aviation and marine bunker fuels, working through the International Civil Aviation Organization and the International Maritime Organization, respectively. This lays the regulatory responsibility for emissions trading with regard to aircraft engine emissions squarely on ICAO.

Resolution A32-8 of ICAO, referred to earlier, and containing a consolidated statement of continuing ICAO policies and practices related to environmental protection, urges states to refrain from unilateral environmental measures that would be harmful to the development of international civil aviation. On the subject of aircraft engine emissions, the resolution, in its Appendix F, makes mention of the fact that the Kyoto Protocol calls for developed countries to pursue limitation or reduction of greenhouse gases from aviation bunker fuels, working through ICAO, and invokes Appendix A, which calls upon the ICAO Council to maintain the initiative in developing policy guidance on all aviation matters related to the environment and not leave such initiatives to other organizations.

Appendix H of A32-8 refers to ICAO's policies on charges and taxes[52] and the policy statement issued by the ICAO Council on 9 December 1996 in the form of a Council resolution of an interim nature, and urges states to follow the current guidance of the Council on emission-related levies. The Council is similarly exhorted by the Assembly, through A32-8, to continue to pursue the question of emission-related levies with a view to reaching a conclusion prior to the next ordinary session of the Assembly in 2001.

The policy statement of the Council dated 9 December 1996 takes into consideration the fact that a number of states consider it desirable to use a levy to reflect environmental costs associated with air transport, while other states do not consider it appropriate to impose such a levy under the present circumstances. The Council goes on to state that it considers the development of an internationally agreed environmental charge or tax on air transport that all states would be expected to impose would appear not to be practicable at the present time, given the differing views of states and the significant organization and practical implementation problems that would be likely to arise.

According to the Council Statement, ICAO is seeking to identify a rational common basis on which states wishing to introduce environmental levies on air transport could do so. The Council strongly recommends in its statement that any environmental reviews on air transport which states may introduce should be in the form of charges rather than taxes and that the funds collected should be applied in the first instance to mitigating the environmental impact of aircraft engine emissions, for example by (a) addressing the specific damage caused by these emissions, if that can be identified, (b) funding scientific research into their environmental impact, or (c) funding research aimed at reducing their environmental impact, through developments in technology and new approaches to aircraft operations.

Finally, the Council urges states that are considering the introduction of emission-related charges to take into account the non-discrimination principle in Article 15 of the Convention on International Civil Aviation and the work in progress within ICAO and, in the meantime, to be guided by the general principles in the 'Statements by the Council to contracting States on Charges for Airports and Air Navigation Services' (Doc. 9082/4) and the following principles adapted from those agreed by the 31st Session of the ICAO assembly: that there should be no fiscal aims behind the charges, the charges should be related to costs, and the charges should not discriminate against air transport compared with other modes of transport.

CAEP, at its 4th meeting (CAEP/4) held in April 1998, identified as an integral part of its work programme the need to address emissions inventories for future scientific assessments; long-term emissions burden estimates used for quantifying benefits of regulatory charges; and the effectiveness of operational measures to reduce aircraft emissions or their effect on the atmosphere.[53] The meeting also noted that further work on market-based options for reducing emissions was necessary.

The CAEP/4 Report, which was considered by the 32nd Session of the ICAO Assembly, presented a study on emissions-related levies which was quite extensive. CAEP/4 basically envisioned four options for levies: a fuel levy; a ticket levy; a route levy and an airport levy. With regard to the application of a levy, the report considered a revenue neutral application, a general taxation application, a levy application based on a preventive-cost approach and an application involving paying damages or compensation for third party injury. The report also considered the efficacy of each levy option and application as well as implementation aspects of environmental levies both in the context of their relation to levy collection and as to the application of levies. As a pivotal point to the whole exercise, CAEP/4 examined the role of ICAO with regard to such levies.

The 33rd Session of the Assembly, in considering the work of both CAEP/4 and CAEP/5, endorsed the development of an open emissions trading system for international civil aviation and requested the Council to develop, as a matter of priority, guidelines for open emissions trading for international aviation focusing on establishing the structural and legal basis for aviation's participation in an open trading system, and including key elements such as reporting, monitoring and compliance, while proving flexibility to the maximum extent possible consistent with the UNFCCC process.

There is no room for doubt that development in aviation and the environment over the years has now led the international community in general, and the aviation community in particular, to a crossroads, where a formula delicately balanced between market demand and sustainability has to be reached. This is indeed true in the contexts of both aircraft noise and engine emissions. As for market demand, it is incontrovertible that, notwithstanding the short-term effects that may be felt as a result of recent setbacks, economic analysts are of the view that air transport is still the most expensive of all modes of transport (road, rail, air and sea) to operate in terms of per kilogram of mass carried.[54] This essentially means that commercial air transport is predominantly offered to the high-value/high-yield end of the market, that is, to the business community, the tourism industry and the time-critical freight industry dealing with overnight documents and high-value/highly perishable items.

The total scheduled traffic (domestic and international) carried by the airlines of contracting states of ICAO in 1999 is estimated to have been at about 369 billion tonne-kilometres performed, an increase of about 6 per cent over 1998.[55] The airlines of these states carried a total of 1558 million passengers and some 28 million tonnes of freight in 1999. The freight figure compares with 26 million tonnes carried in 1998.[56] Compared with previous years, the carriage of international freight showed an increase of 9 per cent in 1999.

ICAO records that between 1989 and 1998 the reported number of commercial aircraft in service increased by about 60 per cent, from 11 253 to 18 139 aircraft. In 1998, 1463 jet aircraft were ordered, compared with 1309 in 1997, and 929 were delivered compared with 674 aircraft in 1997. In 1998, the total scheduled traffic carried by airlines of the 185 contracting states of ICAO amounted to a total of about 1462 million passengers and about 26 million tonnes of freight. In the years 1988–99, the total tonne-kilometres performed, or in other words, total scheduled airline traffic, grew at an annual rate of 5·2 per cent.[57] Passenger kilometres growth during this decade was 4·6 per cent and freight tonne-kilometres growth was 6·6 per cent for the same period.[58] These figures[59] are reflective of the rapidly increasing frequency of aircraft movements at airports, calling for drastic management of aircraft movements in terms of noise and airport capacity.

With regard to sustainability, the regulators of the environmental impact of aviation will necessarily have to bear in mind the vibrant significance of the balanced approach suggested by Resolution A33-7. Essentially, the term 'sustainable development' in the context of environmental protection means 'development which the environment can sustain without being polluted'. The notion that the environment is an inextricable and integral part of sustainable development and that environmental issues were not *sui generis* or 'stand-alone' issues but were incontrovertibly linked to their economic, political and social contexts is critical in the context of aviation and environmental protection. Environmental issues are the necessary corollaries to social processes and should be addressed on the basis of equity, care for nature and natural resources and development of society.

Environmental management is therefore the key to effective sustainable development. This should involve a necessary diversion from the mere cleaning up or repairing of damage to being a sustained social activity which brings to bear the need to force development to keep pace with the environmental equilibrium and stability of the world.

Another integral part of sustainable development is economics, and it is in this broad context that a link can be drawn between sustainability and market demand in the field of commercial aviation. Economics not only plays a key role in societal decision making, but it also integrates environmental issues with distribution, ownership and control, identifying economic development and social issues as major elements in the management of a society. Another aspect of the role of economics in sustainable development is reflected in the very nature of sustainable development itself, in that it requires a delicate balance between the needs of the present generation and the long-term environmental well-being of a society. If, for instance, the alienation of environmental assets were to enrich the present generation, but would adversely affect future generations, the management of this dichotomy could be addressed by considering, primarily, the economic implications of unsustainable development.

Another factor which influences sustainable development is globalization, which calls for intervention at international level to ensure that development could be sustained environmentally. In this context, in addition to the implementation of international environmental agreements, it becomes necessary to analyse critically the impact of the global economy and the liberalization of trade on environmental issues.

In any aspect of trade, including trade related to the aviation industry, any bifurcation of environment and sustainable development becomes arbitrary and cosmetic. With this in view, sustainable development in aviation should be internationally managed in three component elements:

a) environmental assessment: through evaluation and review, research and monitoring and the exchange of views on the environment;
b) environmental management: through comprehensive planning that takes into account the effects of the acts of humans on the environment; and
c) supporting measures: through education, training and public information and also through financial assistance and organizational arrangements.

Any balanced approach towards environmental management should essentially be based on these guidelines.

BIRD STRIKES AGAINST AIRCRAFT

Introduction

A bird strike is deemed to have occurred whenever a pilot reports a bird strike, aircraft maintenance personnel identify some damage to an aircraft which they can attribute to a bird strike, ground personnel report seeing an aircraft hit one or more birds in flight, or bird remains, whether in full or part, are found on an airside pavement area or within 200 feet of a runway, unless another reason for the bird's death is identified. The first fatal aircraft accident involving a bird strike is reported to have occurred in 1912.[60] The Bird Strike Committee of the United States reports that, since 1960, about 400 aircraft have been destroyed and over 370 people killed in the United States as a result of bird or other wildlife strikes.[61] It is also reported that more than half of bird strike accidents occur at less than 100 feet (30 metres) above the ground, although strikes have been reported as high as 37 000 feet above ground, the highest recorded being at 54 000 feet.[62] The Civil Aviation Administration (CAA) of the United Kingdom has estimated that UK registered aircraft of over 12 500 pounds (5 700 kg) strike a bird about once every one thousand flights.[63] The International Civil Aviation Organization (ICAO), which, through its Bird Strike Information System, provides an analysis of bird strike reports that are received from different countries, has recorded that there were over 25 000 bird strikes reported on civil aircraft from 1988 to 1992.[64]

Bird strikes are therefore by no means rare occurrences in civil aviation. They can cause serious damage to aircraft, as is evidenced by the fact that , since 1975 in the United States alone, five large jet aircraft have encountered major accidents consequent upon bird strikes which, in one instance, resulted in the death of nearly three dozen people. A popular misconception, that a minor accident caused by a bird strike would not have serious financial implications, has prompted the publication of several information papers by commentators focusing on the fact that even minor damage can lead to significant costs. Even if a pair of fan blades have to be replaced as a result of such incidents, the add-on costs, in addition to replacement costs and labour, such as costs involving the grounding of the aircraft for repair and redirection of passengers, would be considerable. The FAA has estimated that during the 1990–99 decade, bird strikes cost civil aviation over $390 million per year in the United States.[65] Additionally, minor damage to aircraft may come within deductible limits of standard aircraft insurance coverage, or may not be covered in the insurance policy, obliging the airline concerned to absorb direct and indirect costs of such damage.[66]

Industry experts have issued a serious warning that flocks of birds, particularly migrating flocks of large Canada geese, could be the cause of aircraft accidents and passenger fatalities if preventive measures are not taken.[67] Two major US air carriers, Northwest and United, have reported 200 to 300 bird strikes a year on average. A notable incident in this report is the $23 million damage sustained by a Northwest Airlines aircraft when birds were ingested into one of its engines.

The issue of bird strikes takes on an added dimension by affecting social and policy issues which are not strictly linked to air transport. The key area of environmental protection – particularly in the fields of wildlife policy and habitat management –

brings to bear issues of state responsibility for national policy as well as a commitment towards maintaining the biodiversity of the ecosystem. An example of dire consequences of a bird strike is the instance of a Boeing 747 aircraft departing Los Angeles Airport in late August 2000, which had to dump 83 tons of fuel to land safely after a bird strike.[68]

All of this raises the question of accountability: who is responsible for preventing bird strikes against aircraft? The initial answer to the question lies in the element of control exercised in a particular jurisdiction in the vicinity of the site of the accident. The airport is a key player in this equation, as would be an air traffic control authority, albeit to a lesser extent, particularly in instances of failure to warn aircraft of possible bird hazards. The state in whose territory the accident takes place would be called upon to answer whether it had a successful wildlife programme in place. However, in the ultimate analysis, the airport authorities would be held liable as they owe aircraft operators the common duty of care of ensuring that the latters' aircraft are afforded basic safety from bird hazards. Therefore the onus of responsibility to avoid bird strikes depends very much on the airport authorities as a few significant instances at adjudication show, with a focus on exculpation of any airport that shows such mechanisms as bird control systems in operation and trained staff to deal with the problem of wildlife hazards in the airfield were in operation.

Issues of liability which primarily fall within the purview of the airport concerned can be viewed in two ways. The first is state liability and responsibility when the airport concerned is an instrumentality of state or is government-owned and -controlled. The second is the liability of the airport itself, when such airport is an autonomous entity, either through the process of privatization, which is increasing in popularity at the present time, or through some other measure that accords independent financial ownership to the airport. This discussion will address liability issues within those two broad areas of control.

Regulatory initiative of ICAO

At its Sixth European–Mediterranean Regional Air Navigation Meeting, held in Geneva from 2 to 27 November 1971, ICAO considered bird hazards to aircraft operations, particularly in the context of possible measures that could be taken to minimize the risk of collision in all phases of flight between aircraft and birds. The meeting therefore considered the possible development of measures to be applied in this regard.[69] Consequently, the Air Navigation Commission of ICAO requested the Secretary General of ICAO to examine the issue further and submit recommendations to the Commission.[70] As a result, in 1973, at the ICAO Asia/Pacific Regional Air Navigation Meeting held in Honolulu, the meeting adopted Recommendation 6/5, which requested:

a) that each state organize a national bird strike committee to investigate the measures to be taken at the aerodromes within the state to reduce the bird hazards;
b) that the states within the region join together in the formation of a regional bird strike committee with the objective of providing assistance and guidance to each other in reducing the bird hazard; and
c) that ICAO lend its support to the formation and activities of the regional bird strike committee.[71]

Although this recommendation was proactive, it was a little too ahead of its time, as was later found by the Air Navigation Committee, after ICAO had held a workshop for contracting states on the subject of establishing national bird strike committees in such states. It did not appear at that time that measures to reduce bird strikes at airports in states, particularly in the Asia/Pacific region, would lead to a massive international cooperative effort towards reducing the incidence of bird strikes.[72]

ICAO's efforts at regulation in this particular field date back to 29 May 1951, when the Council of ICAO first adopted Standards and Recommended Practices for Aerodromes, adopting Annex 14 (Aerodromes) to the Convention on International Civil Aviation,[73] signed at Chicago on 7 December 1944. This Convention, by its Article 37, requires that each contracting state undertake to collaborate in securing the highest practicable degree of uniformity in regulations, standards, procedures and organization in relation to aircraft, personnel, airways and auxiliary services in all matters in which such uniformity will facilitate and improve air navigation. To this end, ICAO is mandated by Article 37 to adopt and amend from time to time, as may be necessary, international standards and recommended practices pertaining to 11 key areas of civil aviation, one of which pertains to characteristics of airports and landing areas.[74]

Accordingly, Annex 14 on Aerodromes, in Chapter 9, contains three recommendations pertaining to bird strike reduction. The first recommendation calls for a bird strike hazard on, or in the vicinity of, an aerodrome to be assessed through the establishment of a national procedure for recording and reporting bird strikes on aircraft and the collection of information from aircraft operators, airport personnel and so on on the presence of birds on or around an aerodrome.[75] The Annex also recommends that, when a bird strike hazard is identified at an aerodrome, the appropriate authority should take action to decrease the number of birds constituting a potential hazard to aircraft operators by adopting measures for discouraging their presence on, or in the vicinity of, an aerodrome.[76] The final recommendation of the Annex urges that garbage disposal dumps or any such other feature attracting birds on or in the vicinity of an aerodrome be eliminated or their establishment prevented, unless studies indicate that such disposal units are unlikely to be conducing to bird activity and a bird hazard problem.[77]

Recommendation 9.5.2, which encourages measures to be taken towards discouraging bird activity within the vicinity of an aerodrome, is given effect to in guidance material formulated by ICAO in the form of provisions in the *Airport Services Manual*,[78] Part 3 of which is dedicated to bird control and reduction. The manual gives detailed guidance to States on how to organize a National Committee and lays out the roles and responsibilities of a control programme. Chapter 4 of the Manual is particularly significant, in that it gives a detailed breakdown on how to organize an airport bird strike control programme. This calls for a very integrated approach to be evolved and developed to control bird activity at airports. Communications between field personnel and air traffic controllers, allocation of monies for bird control and assistance of aircraft operators in coordinating a concerted effort are some measures recommended. There is also a separate chapter on environment management and site modification, together with segments on dispersal methods, incompatible land use around airports, evaluation of wildlife control programmes and staffing airport bird control programmes being given special chapter treatment. Another ICAO document which lends itself to alleviating bird hazards at airports is the *Airport Planning Manual* which contains, inter alia, an appendix providing a land use table for bird hazard considerations.[79]

There are also other compelling factors that any airport administration should take into account when planning for the injection of additional aircraft capacity. These are the responses of the international community in the form of Standards and Recommended Practices as promulgated by ICAO, in order that international civil aviation retains a certain consistency and uniformity in its global activity. For instance, the *Airport Planning Manual*,[80] in two parts, sets out in detail all aspects of airport planning. ICAO has, in this document, developed a master planning process which involves plans, programmes and stringent policy that go to make a viable airport. The document serves as a basis for providing for the orderly and timely development of an airport adequate to meet the present and future air transportation needs of an area or state.[81] The manual starts from the fact that early aviation history recognized the need for some public control of land in the vicinity of an airport,[82] and bifurcates this need to reflect airport needs, that is, obstacle limitation areas, future airport development and so on, and the need to ensure minimal interference with the environment and the public.[83] By this dual approach, ICAO has introduced a whole new area of thought into airport development. What was once a concern merely to provide easy facilities for the fluid movement of air traffic has now become in addition an ecological concern. By this process, airport development now falls into three main areas: (a) the development of airport capacity and facilities, (b) the balancing of airport development with necessary security measures, and, (c) the balancing of airport development with ecology, that is, city planning, noise pollution avoidance and so on. The ICAO *Airport Planning Manual* ensures a balance between airport development and ecological considerations.

On an examination of the foregoing discussions no one could say that the problem has not been perceived so far; *a fortiori*, no one could even say that those responsible for the alleviation of the problem have not attempted to solve it. What now remains to be done is to examine the most proper manner in which to approach the problem of bird hazards. There is no doubt that the planners can take off from where we are at present. However, any future planning by individual states on the expansion of their airport programmes would have to be done with the primary consideration that 'Looking to the immediate future, air transport will require new forms of international cooperation in technical and economic areas.'[84]

The cooperation referred to in technical and economic areas would have to be further expanded to include safety and ecological factors in the technical field and all economic research in city planning and infrastructural development in the economic field. These studies would have to be done in the form of committed and in-depth country studies by individual states taking into consideration futuristic studies of a country's outlook and the financial outlay that the country would be prepared to make for an airport expansion programme. The outcome of these studies could then form legislation for the planning of airports in a state. Such legislation would present, for the first time, a cohesive and enforceable set of laws in that state that would meet the airport congestion problem.

Although the concept of airport planning laws can be summed up easily, as above, the three broad areas of ecology, safety and and infrastructural planning need a sustained approach of study before such are incorporated into laws. For a start, ICAO's *Airport Planning Manual* is geared to provide information and guidance to those responsible for airport planning,[85] where information on a comprehensive list of planning subjects such as sizes and types of projects,[86] task identification,[87] preparation of manpower and cost budgets,[88] selection of consultants[89] and standard contract provisions[90] are given. With these guidelines, each state can start its planning process.

Legal issues

ICAO's extensive regulatory guidance impels contracting states to take adequate measures to adopt clear and cogent national policy towards a bird strike control programme and also assume responsibility for liability arising out of accidents if they are responsible for providing aeronautical and airport services to aircraft operations. Principles of state responsibility, *inter se*, are now clearly entrenched in public international law.

State Liability   The fundamental postulate which establishes a global legal basis for the provision of airports is contained in Article 28 of the Convention on International Civil Aviation,[91] which provides that each contracting state undertakes, as far as is practicable, to provide in its territory, airports, radio services, meteorological services and other air navigational facilities to facilitate international air navigation in accordance with the standards and practices recommended or established from time to time, pursuant to the Convention. In addition, the Chicago Convention also stipulates, inter alia, that every aircraft which enters the territory of a state shall, if the regulations of that state so dictate, land at an airport designated by that state for purposes of Customs and other examination.[92] Each contracting state to the Chicago Convention could also, subject to the provisions of the Convention, designate to an aircraft which passes through the airspace over the territory of the State and another state the route it may follow within the territory of the state concerned and the airports it may use within the territory of the state.[93]

An airport, whether publicly owned and operated or privately owned and operated, has to follow a prescribed policy with regard to the recovery of costs incurred in providing airport and air navigation services. This policy is enshrined in Article 15 of the Chicago Convention, which requires that a state is obligated not to impose higher charges on aircraft of another state engaged in international operations than those paid by its national aircraft engaged in similar international operations. This charges policy is a universal one applying to any type of airport, whether public or private, since the regulation of airports within the territory of a state is usually the responsibility of that state concerned.

The United Nations General Assembly, at its 93rd Plenary Session in December 1992, endorsed privatization in the context of economic restructuring, economic growth and sustainable development. By Assembly Resolution A47/171, the General Assembly, while noting, inter alia, that many countries were attaching growing importance, in the context of their economic restructuring policies, to the privatization of enterprises, urged member states to support when requested the national efforts of states in implementing privatization. In 1993, the General Assembly followed up its stance on privatization by adopting Resolution A48/180 which, inter alia, requested the Secretary General to strengthen the activities of the United Nations system related to the promotion of entrepreneurship and to the implementation of privatization programmes.

On the specific issue of airport privatization, the Latin American Civil Aviation Commission (LACAC), at its Thirteenth Ordinary Assembly held in Chile in July 1998, adopted Recommendation A13-4 which recognized, inter alia, that airport privatization was becoming more prevalent in the Latin American region and that the process of privatization involves a detailed analysis of different factors. Accordingly, the Assembly recommended that the LACAC member states consider the following issues, in order to obtain the best results from the privatization process:

a) Define the role of the state and the responsibilities it must fulfil in order to guarantee the rights of users, as well as airport security and operational safety, in accordance with international standards in force.

b) Consider the convenience of maintaining public ownership of airports, granting concessions for suitable periods of time in keeping with investments made.

c) Clearly establish the required infrastructure, whose costs the state and/or the users will be willing to recognize, avoiding surpluses or deficiencies which may be detrimental to them.

d) Determine the services to be transferred to the private sector and those which will remain in the hands of the state, describing the standards to be used in defining the quality of the services provided.

e) As much as possible, aim at establishing a competitive environment for providers of the various services, seeking mechanisms such as public tenders. Maximum allowable rates should be established for monopolistic services.

f) Define the financing of the air transport sector, deciding whether higher-income airports should support economically the less profitable ones or those working at a loss, in order to maintain a self-financed airport network compatible with national civil aviation needs.

g) The contract between the state and private airport service operators must be the result of an open public tender where the required conditions, evaluation formulae and criteria to be used to award the contract must be clearly established and made known to all interested parties, in an absolutely transparent way.

h) Reserve the right to implement the relevant measures to follow up , and maintain, operational control over the concession contract.

i) Pay special attention to the contract termination clause for its timely enforcement in case of non-compliance and recovery of the relevant value.

j) The Civil Aviation Administrations should actively participate in all privatization processes.

The privatization process would usually involve a sustained consultation period between the parties, particularly involving the fundamental issue of the exact mode of privatization involved. Some of the options which may be considered are the creation of a new corporation whereby existing assets could be vested in the new entity and be floated publicly. Privatization could also be partial, involving just some assets of the enterprise. There might also be a full public share floatation of the enterprise or a management buyout structure where a company could provide backing finance in order to take the airport concerned into the private sector. There could also be a joint venture arrangement in airport privatization where private sector and government could share their equity involvements.

At the implementation stage of the privatization process, a tremendous amount of information is usually exchanged, particularly between the owners of the enterprise and the investors. Such information should demonstrate the legal rights of the parties and stipulate the rights and liabilities that would remain as residual rights and obligations of the state. A privatization process, whether it be by concession or trade sale, would also entail a complex series of negotiations and contractual wrangling. Competing companies would bid against each other for the enterprise being offered for privatization.

It is incontrovertible that the responsibility of the state is not extinguished merely because an airport is made subject to private ownership or private management control. In international air transport, the mere fact that the state has to provide airport services under Article 28 of the Chicago Convention, and indeed designate airports within its territory for landing purposes as per Articles 10 and 68, imposes legal responsibility upon the state to be accountable at public international law for any liability incurred as a result of action on the part of airports within its territory.

Liability of the state at common law is best exemplified by the legal process of the United Kingdom. At private law involving issues of state liability and responsibility, the perennial adage that 'the king can do no wrong' extended from immunity of the sovereign to cover actions of the central government and its servants when acting within the scope of their employment. This immunity was more focused on exemption from tortuous liability than on contractual liability and obviated the state's exposure to compensatory damages arising out of injury. There was, however, no bar to imposing personal liability of civil servants and in 1765, the British government agreed to pay, *ex gratia*, damages awarded against one of its servants.[94] In the 1946 case of *Adams* v. *Naylor*,[95] the principle of *ex gratia* payment was rejected, giving way to the enactment in Britain of the Crown Proceedings Act of 1947, which allowed a plaintiff the right to take up a matter involving Crown liability directly in the courts of law. The Act did not apply to members of the armed forces, which essentially meant that if an airport were to be manned by the armed forces, there would be no Crown liability for acts committed officially by the airport management concerned.

Liability of the airport as an autonomous entity   Irrespective of the responsibility of a state with regard to airports within its territories, which is founded both at customary international law and at private law for liability incurred by airports, a privately run airport may incur tortuous liability on a private basis, as the occupier of the premises. Legal liability of airports run by private entities would be liable to the various users of airports, including air carriers, and to non-users who may be outside the premises of the airport but be injured by the activities of the airport. A good example of the latter is damage caused by environmental pollution through noise within the vicinity of the airport.

In the instance of a privately managed airport where the entity charged with managing airport services is located within the airport premises, such an entity would be considered as a legal occupier for purposes of liability. The leading case which expands the definition of 'occupier' is the House of Lords decision in *Wheat v. E. Lacon & Co. Ltd*,[96] where the defendants owned a public house of which R was their manager. R and his wife were allowed by agreement to live in the upper floor, access to which was by a door separate from the licensed premises. Mrs R was allowed to take paying guests on the upper floor. An accident was sustained by a paying guest on the staircase leading to the upper floor. It was held that the defendants were occupiers of the upper floor. Mr R was only a licensee of that part, and the defendants had enough residuary control to be treated as occupiers. In fact the defendants, Mr R and Mrs R, were all occupiers.

The case recognizes three principles: that there may be two or more occupiers at one time;[97] that exclusive occupation is not required; and that the test is whether a person has some degree of control associated with and arising from his presence in and use of or activity in the premises. The following principles, enunciated by earlier decisions, that a concessionaire without a lease in a fairground is an occupier;[98] a contractor converting a ship into a troopship in dry dock occupies the ship;[99] and a local authority which has requisitioned a house[100] is an occupier (even in respect of those parts of the house in which it is allowing homeless persons to live)[101] are also valid.

Although the *Wheat* case contains a decision on the meaning of 'occupier' for the purposes of the Occupiers' Liability Act, 1957 of the United Kingdom, the judgments following the case show that it applies to all cases, whether at common law or under that Act, or the Occupiers' Liability Act 1984 which now regulates occupiers' duties to trespassers, where it is necessary to determine the duty of care owed by occupiers to entrants.

The Occupiers' Liability Act, 1957 was enacted to give effect to the recommendations of the Law Reform Committee[102] and to eliminate the confusion that had clouded the common law rules on liability to entrants on premises. The rules enacted by sections 2 and 3 of the Act 'have effect, in place of the rules of the common law, to regulate the duty which an occupier of premises owes to his visitors in respect of dangers due to the state of the premises or to things done or omitted to be done on them'.[103]

At common law, it was necessary to distinguish between invitees, licensees and other entrants on premises. The approximate distinction was that an invitee was requested to enter the premises in the interest of the occupier, whereas a licensee was merely permitted to enter. 'Visitors' for the purposes of the Act are those persons who were invitees or licensees at common law:

> The common duty of care of an occupier is a duty to take such care as in all the circumstances of the case is reasonable to see that the visitor will be reasonably safe in using the premises for the purposes for which he is invited or permitted by the occupier to be there.[104]

If the entrant does not use the premises for that purpose which entitles him to be there, no duty is owed to him under the 1957 Act and any remedy which he might have would be regulated by the 1984 Act on the duty owed to trespassers.

Those entering as of right are not 'invited or permitted' by the occupier for any purpose. Section 2(6) of the Act nonetheless makes the common law duty extend to them by providing that 'persons who enter premises for any purpose in the exercise of a right conferred by law are to be treated as permitted by the occupier to be there for that purpose, whether they in fact have his permission or not'. Section 2(6) does not extend the category of visitors beyond the common law definition – it merely extends the circumstances when a visitor will be owed the common-law duty of care by providing that visitors who enter for any purpose in the exercise of a right conferred by law are to be treated as permitted by the occupier to be there for that purpose.[105]

Whether the standard required by the common duty of care has been attained in a case involving liability of an airport authority is a question of fact and the important issues will be resolved by inference rather than on primary facts. The circumstances relevant would include the degree of care, and want of care, which would ordinarily be looked for in a visitor, on the following basis: (a) an occupier must expect children to be less careful than adults; and (b) an occupier may expect that a person, in the exercise of his calling, will appreciate and guard against any special risks ordinarily incident to it, so far as the occupier leaves him free to do so.[106] These principles reiterate existing rules of common law, and therefore support the view that in deciding the countless issues of fact which will arise in applying the 'common duty of care', it will be proper to consider cases decided before the Act as guides (but certainly no more than guides) in interpreting the duty where no unambiguous rule is laid down in the Act itself.

One of the most significant principles at common law on occupier's liability is the consideration of the child visitor. In deciding whether there is a danger, an occupier, such as an airport authority must especially consider the physical and mental powers of a child visitor on the basis that what is not a danger to an adult may be a danger to a child.[107] And this may be so because of the allurement or property of temptation, to a child, of some condition on the land.[108] In determining the standard of care owed to a child who is not accompanied by a guardian, it will be material to inquire whether, in the circumstances, the occupier could reasonably have expected the presence of the infant unaccompanied.[109]

At common law, an occupier discharged his duty to a visitor by a warning sufficient to convey to the visitor full knowledge of the nature and extent of the danger. That rule is changed by section 2(4)(a) of the Act,[110] which provides that, where damage is caused to a visitor by a danger[111] of which he had been warned by the occupier, the warning is not to be treated without more as absolving the occupier from liability, unless in all the circumstances it was enough to enable the visitor to be reasonably safe.

For example, the farmer who warns the veterinary surgeon whom he has summoned to the farm at night to attend a sick cow by saying, 'Be careful how you go down the yard or you may fall into a tank', or the railway company which warns of the dangerous roof over what is the sole approach to the ticket office, can no longer absolve themselves from liability by that warning alone. On the other hand, where a customer does not heed the warning of a shopkeeper not to go to the far end of the shop because there is a dangerous hole, it might presumably be held in all the circumstances that the common duty of care owed to him under the Act has been discharged. If the defendant does not know of the danger he cannot rely on section 2(4)(*a*), although he may still have a defence under section 2(1).[112]

Assumption of risk   The common duty of care does not impose on an occupier any obligation to a visitor in respect of risks willingly accepted as his by the visitor (the question whether a risk is so accepted should be decided on the same principles as in other cases in which one person owes a duty of care to another).[113] According to the ordinary principles of negligence, a defendant breaches no duty of care towards a plaintiff who has voluntarily assumed the risk.

At common law no duty of care was owed to a visitor who had full knowledge of the nature and extent of the danger.[114] Knowledge is not specifically mentioned as a relevant circumstance in determining whether the common duty of care has been discharged. But since the Act expressly provides that voluntary assumption of a risk discharges the duty of care, its silence about the effect of mere knowledge of the risk makes it clear that knowledge on the part of the visitor in itself no longer serves to discharge the duty of care. Yet the visitor's knowledge of the danger remains relevant in deciding whether in all the circumstances it was enough to enable him to be reasonably safe.[115]

Liability towards neighbours   The risk created by dangers caused by the defective state of premises is not confined to entrants to those premises. Slates falling from roofs, crumbling walls and dangerous activities carried out on premises are just a few examples of risks as likely to endanger passers-by on the highway, or persons on adjoining premises, as to injure persons actually on the occupier's premises. The circumstances in which a duty of care is owed to such persons by the occupier of premises therefore warrant brief consideration.

An action in nuisance, derived from public nuisance, often lies at the instance of those injured on a highway as a result of harmful conditions on adjoining land. Because of this historical anomaly, in a large number of situations a plaintiff may now sue either in negligence or in nuisance (or, as often happens, in both) for personal injuries; and yet the law is the same whichever tort is relied on. In several House of Lords cases, it has been a matter of indifference whether the case was decided in negligence or in nuisance, both of which were pleaded.[116] Often it seems quite fortuitous which tort is relied on: if, for instance, some act of negligent omission stands out, the claim will often be negligence. The 1948 decision in *Holling* v. *Yorkshire Traction Co. Ltd* is a typical example of this ambivalence:

> The defendants emitted so much steam and smoke on to the highway from their adjoining factory that the view was obscured and two vehicles collided, killing the plaintiff, who was on the highway. It was held to be negligence on the part of the defendant to fail to post a man at each end of the affected area. They were also held liable in nuisance.[117]

Accordingly, there is no room for doubt that the ordinary principles of negligence can be applied where highway users are injured because of harmful operations being carried out there.[118]

Occupiers are also under a general duty to take reasonable care to prevent dangers existing on their premises from damaging persons or property on adjoining premises.[119] This is so whether the danger arises from disrepair on the premises, or some natural or man-made hazard, for example fire caused by lightning striking a tree.[120] It has been held that where adjoining properties have mutual rights of support, an occupier who negligently allows a property to fall into dereliction so as to damage the adjoining premises is liable in negligence as well as in nuisance.[121] There are two issues of particular difficulty affecting the duties of care owed *inter se* by occupiers of adjoining premises.

First, where a plaintiff tenant sues his landlord for damage resulting from the defective state of repair of premises retained by the landlord the case law is somewhat ambivalent. The facts in *Cunard* v. *Antifyre Ltd*[122] were that some defective roofing and guttering, which formed part of the premises retained by the defendant landlord, fell into a part of the premises let by him to the plaintiff tenant. As a result, his wife was injured and his goods were damaged. Damages in general negligence were awarded to both the tenant and his wife.

However, in *Cheater* v. *Cater*,[123] the Court of Appeal had held earlier that a landlord, who had let a field to a tenant at a time when there was a yew tree on the adjoining premises retained by the landlord, was not liable in negligence when the tenant's horse died through eating leaves from that tree which was then in the same state as at the date of the lease. The Court of Appeal in *Shirvell* v. *Hackwood Estates Co. Ltd*,[124] a later case, questioned *Cunard* v. *Antifyre Ltd* and held that a workman of a tenant could not recover in negligence from the landlord whose tree on adjoining land fell on him. In *Taylor* v. *Liverpool Corpn*, the plaintiff, the daughter of a tenant of one of the defendant landlords' flats, was injured by the fall of a chimney stack belonging to these flats into the yard adjoining the premises. The landlords had negligently maintained this chimney, which formed part of the building retained by them.[125] Stable J found for the plaintiff in negligence, following *Cunard* v. *Antifyre Ltd*, and distinguishing *Cheater* v. *Cater* on the ground that the tenant had there impliedly agreed to take the risk in respect of danger existing on the premises at that time. His Lordship treated the observations in *Shirvell*'s case as *obiter* on the ground that no negligence had in any event occurred. The above notwithstanding, the principle in the *Cunard* case is more plausible than one which gives the landlord blanket immunity.

The two leading aircraft manufacturers, Boeing and Airbus Industrie, have forecast exponential growth in air traffic in the long term, necessitating a steadily increasing need for capacity and services. While Airbus industrie has estimated that 13 000 new aircraft will be needed, at a value of US$1·2 trillion by the year 2020,[126] Boeing has made a more liberal estimate of 18 406 new aircraft, valued at US$1·25 trillion over the same period.[127] The International Civil Aviation Organization has forecast an annual growth rate in air transport in excess of 5 per cent over the next 10 years.[128] This expected growth will involve larger investment requirements, inter alia, in airport and aerodrome infrastructure, including infrastructural investment for ensuring safety of flight.

Bird strikes have varied connotations, in terms of the post accident economic, environmental and safety implications involved. From an economic perspective, where a bird strike damages an aircraft, apart from direct costs, such as repair and replace-ment costs, which are not too difficult to quantify, there are also indirect costs involved, relating to delays, rerouting of passengers, non-productivity of an unserviceable aircraft, accommodation of passengers and so on. As for environmental factors, such as those brought about by the jettisoning of fuel after an aircraft is debilitated by a bird strike, in view of the infrequent occurrences, they should primarily be viewed from a trade perspective, as to whether environmental concerns are sufficiently significant to be placed alongside economic and safety issues. The symbiosis of trade and the environment emerged as a critical issue for trade negotiators in the last stages of the Uruguay Round of discussions.[129] At these discussions the focus remained on two approaches to the issue. The first approach was from the essentially pro-environment groups, who considered that those involved in international trade are primarily interested in the movement of their goods and therefore were not concerned about the environmental implications of their trading activities. The second approach was based on the belief that increased trading activity enhanced possibilities of solving environmental problems. This trend of thinking leaned towards sanctions being introduced against environmentally detrimental trading activity, using GATT (later WTO) as a tool of implementation. The official statement issued in support of the latter approach, which was not supported initially by the majority of states at the Uruguay Round, stated:

> GATT Contracting Parties believe that the successful conclusion of the Uruguay Round was an important step towards creating the conditions for sustainable development. Trade liberalization and the maintenance of an open, non-discriminatory trading system are key elements of the follow up to UNCED (United Nations Conference on the Environment).[130]

Developing countries, however, were reluctant to embrace the idea of using trading sanctions towards environmental protection, as their main priority remained development, and they were not fully convinced that already scarce resources should be deployed for purposes of protecting the environment. Being a new challenge and still esoteric, environmental protection was viewed in the context of trade liberalization by the developing states in the following manner:

> For developing countries, where poverty is the number one policy preoccupation and the most important obstacle to better environmental protection, global trade liberalization, coupled with financial and technological transfers, is essential for promoting sustainable development.[131]

Multilateral lending institutions such as the World Bank and the International Monetary Fund are beginning to lay more emphasis on the environmental impact of projects funded by them. However, in the ultimate analysis, both international trade and environmental protection are key issues for development, and they should be viewed as tools that could result in a 'win–win situation' for the parties concerned.

The most important issue – safety – calls for vigilance from the international community, given the enormity of the threat to aviation safety posed by bird hazards, particularly in view of forecasts of increased air transport demand in the future. Safety is the primary concern of the world aviation community at the present time. This is not only because the fundamental postulates of the Chicago Convention of 1944[132] call for the safe and orderly development of international civil aviation[133] and mandate ICAO to ensure the safe and orderly growth of international civil aviation throughout the world,[134] but also because the aviation world faces a critical era where, in the words of Dr Assad Kotaite, President of the ICAO Council, 'the international aviation community cannot afford to relax its vigilance ... ICAO would continue to take timely action to ensure safety and security standards are in effect, and that deficiencies are properly and efficiently addressed'.[135]

The most relevant provision in the Chicago Convention which affects the subject of safety, particularly in the context of bird strikes against aircraft, is Article 12, which requires each contracting state to maintain uniform aviation regulations in conformity, to the greatest possible extent, with those established under the Convention. Incontrovertibly, such a responsibility should fall on the entire world civil aviation community. As mentioned earlier, the methodology for this proposition is already in place, in the nature of ICAO Standards and Recommended Practices (SARPs). The solution, however, is elusive, purely because ICAO SARPs do not have absolute powers of enforceability under international law.

Basically, ICAO promulgates its SARPs through its 18 Annexes to the Chicago Convention, one of which, Annex 14, contains key provisions on bird strike avoidance. Article 54(l) of the Chicago Convention prescribes the adoption of international Standards and Recommended Practices and their designation in Annexes to the Convention, while notifying all contracting states of the action taken. The fundamental question which has to be addressed *in limine*, in the consideration of the effectiveness of ICAO's SARPs, is whether SARPs are legislative in character. If the answer is in the affirmative, then, at least theoretically, one can insist upon adherence to SARPs by states.

The adoption of SARPS was considered a priority by the ICAO Council in its Second Session (2 September to 12 December 1947),[136] which attempted to obviate any delays to the adoption of SARPs on air navigation as required by the First Assembly of ICAO.[137] SARPs inevitably take two forms: a negative form, for example, that states shall not impose more than certain maximum requirements; and a positive form, such as that states shall take certain steps as prescribed by the ICAO Annexes.[138]

As has already been mentioned, Article 37 of the Convention obtains the undertaking of each contracting state to collaborate in securing the highest practical degree of uniformity in regulations, standards, procedures and organization in relation to international civil aviation in all matters in which such uniformity will facilitate and improve air navigation. Article 38 obligates all contracting states to the Convention to inform ICAO immediately if they are unable to comply with any such international standard or procedure and to notify differences between their own practices and those prescribed by ICAO. In the case of amendments to international standards, any state which does not make the appropriate amendment to its own regulations or practices shall give notice to the Council of ICAO within 60 days of the adoption of the said amendment to the international standard or indicate the action which it proposes to take.

There is no room for doubt that the Annexes to the Convention or parts thereof lay down rules of conduct both directly and analogically. In fact, although there is a conception based on a foundation of practicality that ICAO's international standards that are identified by the words 'contracting states shall' have a mandatory flavour (imputed by the word 'shall') while recommended practices identified by the words 'contracting states may' have only an advisory and recommendatory connotation (imputed by the word 'may'), it is interesting that at least one ICAO document requires states, under Article 38 of the Convention, to notify ICAO of all significant differences from both standards and recommended practices, thus making all SARPS regulatory in nature.[139]

Another strong factor that reflects the overall ability and power of the Council to prescribe civil rules of conduct (and therefore legislate) on a strict interpretation of the word is that, in Article 22 of the Convention, each contracting state agrees to adopt all practical measures through the issuance of special regulations or otherwise, to facilitate and expedite air navigation. It is clear that this provision can be regarded as an incontrovertible rule of conduct that responds to the requirement in Article 54(1) of the Convention. Furthermore, the mandatory nature of Article 90 of the Convention – that an Annex or amendment thereto shall become effective within three months after it is submitted by the ICAO Council to contracting states – is yet another pronouncement on the power of the Council to prescribe rules of state conduct in matters of international civil aviation. *A fortiori*, it is arguable that the ICAO Council is seen not only to possess the attribute of 'jurisfaction' (the power to make rules of conduct) but also that of 'jurisaction' (the power to enforce its own rules of conduct). The latter attribute can be seen where the Convention obtains the undertaking of contracting states not to allow airlines to operate through their air space if the Council decides that the airline concerned is not conforming to a final decision rendered by the Council on a matter that concerns the operation of an international airline.[140] This is particularly applicable when such airline is found not to conform to the provisions of Annex 2 to the Convention that derives its validity from Article 12 of the Convention relating to rules of the air.[141] In fact, it is very relevant that Annex 2, the responsibility for the promulgation of which devolves upon the Council by virtue of Article 54(1), sets mandatory rules of the air, making the existence of the legislative powers of the Council an unequivocal and irrefutable fact.

Academic and professional opinion also favours the view that, in a practical sense, the ICAO Council does have legislative powers. Professor Michael Milde says:

> The Chicago Convention, as any other legal instrument, provides only a general legal framework which is given true life only in the practical implementation of its provisions. Thus, for example, Article 37 of the Convention relating to the adoption of international standards and recommended procedures would be a very hollow and meaningless provision without active involvement of all contracting States, Panels, Regional and Divisional Meetings, deliberations in the Air Navigation Commission and final adoption of the standards by the Council. Similarly, provisions of Article 12 relating to the rules of the air applicable over the high seas, Articles 17 to 20 on the nationality of aircraft, Article 22 on facilitation, Article 26 on the investigation of accidents, etc., would be meaningless without appropriate implementation in the respective Annexes. On the same level is the provision of the last sentence of Article 77 relating to the determination by the Council in what manner the provisions of the Convention relating to nationality of aircraft shall apply to aircraft operated by international operating agencies.[142]

Professor Milde concludes that ICAO has regulatory and quasi-legislative functions in the technical field and plays a consultative and advisory role in the economic sphere.[143] A similar view had earlier been expressed by Buergenthal, who states:

> the manner in which the International Civil Aviation organization has exercised its regulatory functions in matters relating to the safety of international air navigation and the facilitation of international air transport provides a fascinating example of international law making ... the Organization has consequently not had to contend with any of the post war ideological differences that have impeded international law making on politically sensitive issues.[144]

Paul Stephen Dempsey endorses, in a somewhat conservative manner, the view that ICAO has the ability to make regulations, when he states: 'In addition to the comprehensive, but largely dormant adjudicative enforcement held by ICAO under Articles 84–88 of the Chicago Convention, the Agency also has a solid foundation for enhanced participation in economic regulatory aspects of international aviation in Article 44, as well as the Convention's Preamble.'[145]

Another significant attribute of the legislative capabilities of the ICAO Council is its ability to adopt technical standards as Annexes to the Convention without going through a lengthy process of ratification.[146] Eugene Sochor refers to the Council as a powerful and visible body in international aviation.[147] It is interesting, however, to note that although, by definition, the ICAO Council has been considered by some as unable to deal with strictly legal matters since other important matters come within its purview,[148] this does not derogate the compelling facts that reflect the distinct law-making abilities of ICAO. Should this not be true, the functions that the Convention assigns to ICAO in Article 44 – that ICAO's aims and objectives are 'to develop the principles and techniques of international air navigation and to foster the planning and development of international air transport' – would be rendered destitute of effect.

The above discussion makes it clear that the Chicago Convention has, through the Assembly and Council of ICAO, legitimately and according to customary international law, created a regulatory framework through its Annexes legally to implement its policy. The measures taken by the Assembly in promulgating the SARPS of ICAO in order that states may not find practical and philosophical difficulties in implementing such, together with the fact that the 18 Annexes ensure the establishment of a uniform regulatory structure in international civil aviation, thus bringing ICAO member states under one regulatory umbrella, are typical of the principles of customary international law. In the face of such compelling evidence, the fact that Article 54(l) of the Chicago Convention provides that the Annexes are named as such for convenience becomes irrelevant at law.

NOTES

1   Kyoto Protocol to the Framework Convention on Climate Change (1998) 37 *I.L.M.* 22.
2   Report of the Committee on Aviation Environmental Protection, Fifth Meeting, Montreal, 8–17 January 2001, ICAO Doc. 9777, CAEP/5 at p. 1A-1
3   Brundtland et al., *Our Common Future*, London: Oxford University Press, 1987. This

report outlines the findings of the World Commission on Environment and Development (WCED) on the state of the world environment to set an agenda for change.

4   Ibid.

5   Intergovernmental Panel on Climate Change, *Aviation and the Global Atmosphere*, Cambridge: Cambridge University Press, 1999, p.4.

6   In 2001, Africa's economy achieved a 3·7 per cent GDP increase. The aggregate economy of the region with the largest share of the world economy, Asia and the Pacific, grew by some 3·6 per cent in 2001, above the world average. Europe achieved an average GDP growth of 1·9 per cent, almost half of the growth rate of the previous year. The Central and Eastern European economies grew by around 3 per cent. The countries of the Commonwealth of Independent States (CIS) showed significant GDP growth, averaging about 6·2 per cent, but about 2 per cent lower than the previous year. Latin America and the Caribbean region were adversely affected both by the slowdown in the global economy and by the financial crisis in Argentina. As a result, the region's GDP growth slowed down to 0·7 per cent, about 3 percentage points lower than the previous year. Linked to the fall in oil prices, the Middle East region's economy grew only by about 4·5 per cent, down almost 1 percentage point from the previous year. In 2001, the 25 largest airports in the world handled some 1030 million passengers, according to preliminary estimates. During the same period, the airports concerned (16 of which are located in North America, six in Europe and three in Asia) also handled some 11 million commercial air transport movements. *See Annual Report of The Council 2001*, ICAO Doc. 9786, ch. I.

7   Ibid. Between 1992 and 2001, the reported number of commercial air transport aircraft in service increased by about 39 per cent, from 14 919 to 20 771 (excluding aircraft with a maximum take-off mass of less than 9000 kg). Within these totals, turbojet aircraft numbers increased by about 35 per cent, from 12 008 to 16 229, over the same period. In 2001, 990 jet aircraft were ordered (compared with 1553 in 2000) and 1219 aircraft were delivered (compared with 1009 in 2000). The backlog of unfilled orders at the end of 2001 was 3799 aircraft, compared with 3649 at the end of 2000. The financial commitment in terms of jet aircraft orders placed with the major aircraft manufacturers in 2001 is estimated to be about 69 billion dollars. The number of turboprop and piston aircraft ordered in 2001 was 89, and 109 aircraft were delivered during the year.

8   1992 United Nations Conference on Environment and Development (Rio Summit).

9   See. P.W. Birnie and A. Boyle, *Basic Documents on International Law and the Environment*, Oxford: Clarendon Press, p. 6.

10   See 'Purpose for a Resolution of the Council of European Communities on a Community Programme of Policy and Action in relation to the Environment and Sustainable Development', a document released in 1992 which quotes the 1972 endorsement. (Brussels, 30 March 1992, Doc. COM(92) 23 final, vol. II, p. 19.)

11   See United Nations General Assembly (UNGA) Resolution 55/199.

12   For the text of the Declaration, see Johannesburg Declaration on Sustainable Development (2002), A/CONF.199/1.6 <http://www.johannesburgsummit.org/html/documents/summit_docs/1009wssd_pol_declaration.doc>.

13   See World Summit on Sustainable Development Plan of Implementation (2002) <http://www.johannesburgsummit.org/html/documents/summit_docs/2309_planfinal.pdf>.

14   At its 5th Session in September 2000, the United Nations adopted Resolution A55/2 United Nations Millennium Declaration which recognizes that states have a collective responsibility to uphold the principles of human dignity, equality and equity at the global level, notwithstanding their separate responsibilities. The Resolution reaffirmed states' commitment to the United Nations Charter and its relevance and capacity to inspire nations and peoples. The Resolution called, inter alia, for shared responsibility for managing worldwide economic and social development.

15   Renata Serra, 'The Causes of Environmental Degradation', Timothy M. Swanson (ed.),

The Economics of Environmental Degradation, Cheltenham: Edward Elgar, 1996, pp. 82 and 87.

16 See C.A. Primo Braga, 'Tropical Forests and Trade Policy: The Case of Indonesia and Brazil', P. Low (ed.), *International Trade and the Environment*, Discussion Paper No. 159, World Bank: Washington, DC, 1992, pp. 173–94.

17 UNEP (1988), *Annual Report of the Executive Director*, UN Doc. UNEP/GC 15/4 (1989) at p. 54.

18 UNEP/GCSS. 1/7/add.1 (Nairobi, 1988) at p. 91.

19 Ibid., Article 44(*d*).

20 Ibid., Article 44(*i*).

21 See R.I.R. Abeyratne, 'Emissions Trading As a Market-based Option in Air Transport – Contractual Issues', *Environmental Policy and Law*, 29(5), November 1999, pp. 226–35.

22 Duncan Brack, *International Trade and the Montreal Protocol*, London: Earthscan Publications, 1996, p.2

23 ICAO's policies on taxes and charges are contained in Doc. 8632. These policies recommend, *inter alia*, the reciprocal exemption from all taxes levied on fuel taken on board by aircraft in connection with international air services, and reduction, to the fullest possible extent, or elimination of taxes related to the sale or use of international air transport.

24 UNFPA/Norman Myers, *Population, Resources and the Environment: The Critical Challenges*, New York: UN Population Fund, 1991, p. 5.

25 The International Civil Aviation Organization is a specialized agency of the United Nations charged with regulating international civil aviation. ICAO has 187 contracting states.

26 See ICAO Resolution A33-7, 'Consolidated Statement of Continuing ICAO Policies and Practices related to Environmental Protection', *Resolutions Adopted by the Assembly*, Provisional Edition, October 2001, p. 15.

27 See 'Convention on International Civil Aviation', Doc. 7300/8, 8th edn, 2000, Article 44(*d*).

28 *Supra*, note 27.

29 Article 15, inter alia, generally requires that any charges that may be imposed or permitted to be imposed by a contracting state for the use of airports and air navigation facilities by aircraft shall not be higher than those that are payable by national aircraft of the state imposing such charges.

30 See 'Assembly Resolutions in Force' (as of 6 October 1989), ICAO Doc. 9558, at II-18.

31 'Assembly Resolutions in Force', (as of 2 October 1998), ICAO Doc. 9730, Montreal: ICAO, at I–36.

32 Perry Flint, 'Breaking the Sound Barrier', *Air Transport World*, 3, March 1999, p. 29.

33 It was reported that American Airlines is installing the Raisbeck System on 52 B 727 aircraft and hush-kitting 20 more. United is installing hush-kits on 75 B 727 aircraft and 24 B 737-200s. Delta is hush-kitting 104 727s and 54 737-200s. Southwest, TWA, Alaska Airlines and US Airways are other carriers who plan to hush-kit their Chapter 2 aircraft. See Perry Flint, *supra*, note 32, p. 34.

34 David Esler, 'The Latest Noise about Noise', *Business and Commercial Aviation*, December 1999, p. 53.

35 'Europe Considers Delaying Hushkit Ban', *Aviation Daily*, Thursday 7 October 1999, p. 1.

36 ICAO's policies on taxes and charges are contained in Doc. 8632. These policies recommend, inter alia, the reciprocal exemption from all taxes levied on fuel taken on board by aircraft in connection with international air services, and reduction to the fullest possible extent, or elimination, of taxes related to the sale or use of international air transport.

37 (1992) 31 I.L.M. 849. On the negotiations and text of the Climate Change Convention, see D. Bodansky, 'The United Nations Framework Convention on Climate Change: A

Commentary', *Yale J. Int'l L.*, 18, 1993, 451–558. See also J. Barrett, 'The Negotiation and Drafting of the Climate Change Convention', in R. Churchill and D. Freestone (eds), *International Law and Global Climate Change*, 1991, pp. 183–200.

38 Kyoto Protocol to the United Nations Framework Convention on Climate Change, UN Doc. FCCC/CP/1997/L.7/Add.1.

39 Carbon dioxide, methane, nitrous oxide, hydrofluorocarbons, perfluorocarbons and sulphur hexafluoride.

40 UN Environment Programme (UNEP) press release, 11 December 1997.

41 The subject of emissions trading falls within the purview of the Intergovernmental Panel on Climate Change (IPCC), which was established in 1988 by the World Meteorological Organization and the United Nations' Environment Programme (UNEP) to assess the scientific basis and impact of climate change. The IPCC's first scientific report was published in 1990 and recommended the negotiation of a framework convention to combat global warming. The United Nations Framework Convention on Climate Change (UNFCCC) was adopted on 9 May 1992 and the treaty entered into force on 21 March 1994. This discussion, being a legal one, will not address details of these bodies. For an extensive treatment of the IPCC's work and the UNFCC, see 'Global Warming and the Kyoto Protocol', Colin Warbrick and Dominic McGoldric (eds), *ICLQ*, 47, April 1998, pp. 446–62.

42 The Protocol will enter into force 90 days after 'not less than 55 Parties to the [Climate Change] Convention, incorporating Parties included in Annex 1 which accounted in total for at least 55% of the total carbon dioxide emissions for 1990 of the Parties included in Annex 1' have ratified Art. 24 of the Protocol.

43 Ibid., Art.7(1). The Secretariat is located in Bonn, Germany. Its postal address is P.O. Box 260 124, D-53153, Bonn, Germany.

44 Ibid., Art. 8 (1).

45 Ibid., Art. 8 (5). When the Conference of the Parties meets as the meeting of Parties to the Protocol, those states that are party to the Convention but not to the Protocol may participate but only as non-voting observers (Art. 13(1) and (2)). Parties to the Protocol will meet annually (Art. 13(6)) to review the implementation of the Protocol (Art. 13(4)).

46 Ibid., Art. 8 (6).

47 See J.K. Parikh, 'Joint Implementation and North South Cooperation for Climate Change', *International Environmental Affairs*, 7 (1), 1995, pp. 22–41.

48 *Supra*, note 41.

49 See Article 12(3) of the Kyoto Protocol.

50 Art. 8 of the Protocol.

51 'Montreal Protocol on Substances that Deplete the Ozone Layer', *I.L.M.* 26, 1987, 1550. The Montreal Protocol controls gases such as chlorofluorocarbons, which not only have ozone depleting characteristics but also contribute to the greenhouse effect. The Kyoto Protocol, by explicitly excluding the Montreal Protocol's role in ICAO's mandate, has included carbon dioxide, nitrogen oxides and compounds of sulphur emissions in ICAO's purview.

52 As contained in Doc. 9082, 'Statements by the Council to Contracting States on Charges for Airports and Air Navigation Services' and Doc. 8632, 'ICAO Policies on Taxation in the Field of International Air Transport'.

53 CAEP/4, Committee on Aviation Environmental Protection, Fourth Meeting, Montreal, 6–8 April 1998, Montreal: ICAO, pp. i–8.

54 'The Supply of Air Freight Capacity to Asian Markets', Working Paper 42, Bureau of Transport Economics, Commonwealth of Australia, 2001, at p. 1.

55 'The World of Civil Aviation 1999–2002', ICAO Circular 279-AT/116, Montreal: ICAO, p. 27.

56 Ibid.

57 *The World of Civil Aviation 1999–2002, supra*, note 55, para. 5.11
58 Ibid.
59 The above figures were extracted from the *Annual Report of the Council*, (1998, Montreal: ICAO, Doc. 9732, p. 6.
60 Hans Blokpoel, *Bird Hazards to Aircraft*, Toronto: Clark, Irwin and Company, 1976, p. xiii.
61 See <*http://www.birdstrike.org/risk/threat.htm*>. Statistics from the Federal Aviation Administration (FAA) estimate that there were over 33 000 bird strike incidents reported to civil aircraft between 1999 and 2000, 15 per cent of which resulted in accidents.
62 Ibid.
63 Ibid.
64 See <*http://www.birdstrike.org/commlink/top_ten.htm*>.
65 Ibid.
66 For more information on aircraft engine and full repair resulting from a bird strike, see Blokpoel, *supra*, note 60, p. 34.
67 Dennis Blank, 'Rising Geese Numbers Increase Accident Threat', *Flight International*, 15–21 August 2000, p. 11.
68 <*http://www/birdstrike.org*>, op. cit., p. 3.
69 See 'Report of the Sixth European–Mediterranean Regional Air Navigation Meeting, Geneva, 2–27 November 1971', doc. 8994, EUM/VI at 9–30.
70 Ibid., Recommendations 16/16 and 16/17; also AN-WP/4390, 10/2/75.
71 See AN-WP/4810, 23/5/78, p. 1.
72 Ibid., at p. 1.
73 'Convention on International Civil Aviation' (Chicago Convention), signed at Chicago on 7 December 1944, Doc. 7300/8, 8th edn, 2000.
74 Ibid., Art. 37(*b*).
75 Annex 14, Aerodromes, Volume 1, Aerodrome Design and Operations, 3rd edn, July 1999, Recommendation 9.5.1.
76 Ibid., Recommendation 9.5.2.
77 Recommendation 9.5.3.
78 *Airport Services Manual*, Doc. 9137, AN/598 pt 3, 3rd edn, 1991.
79 *Airport Planning Manual*, Doc 9184, AN/902, pt 2, 'Land Use and Environmental Control', 2nd edn, 1985.
80 Doc. 9184-AN/902, pts 1 and 2.
81 Ibid., pt 1, 2.9.1(*a*).
82 Ibid., pt 2, 1.3.1.
83 Ibid., 1.3.2.
84 Eugene Sochor, 'From the DC 3 to Hypersonic Flight: ICAO in a Changing Environment', *Journal of Air Law and Commerce*, 55(2), 1989, 408.
85 *Airport Planning Manual*, Doc. 9184-AN/902, pt 3.
86 Ibid., 1.3.1–1.3.5.
87 Ibid., ch. 2.2.1.
88 Ibid., 2.4.
89 Ibid., 3.1.
90 Ibid., appendix.
91 Convention on International Civil Aviation, *supra*, note 48.
92 Ibid., Art. 10.
93 Ibid., Art. 68.
94 *Entick* v. *Carrington* (1765) 19 St. Tr. 1030.
95 [1946] A.C. 543.
96 [1966] A.C. 552, [1966] 1 All E.R. 582, HL.
97 In *Fisher* v. *CHT Ltd (No 2)* [1966] 1 All E.R. 88, CA, the owners of a club and the

defendants who ran a restaurant in the club under licence from the club were both held to be occupiers. In *AMF International Ltd*. v. *Magnet Bowling Ltd* [1968] 2 All E.R. 789, a contractor (as well as the owner) was an occupier of the whole building although part of the building was separated by a screen beyond which he went only to attend to heating and lighting. It is doubtful whether someone who has granted a right of way occupies that right of way: see *Holden* v. *White* [1982] Q.B. 679, [1982] 2 All E.R. 328, CA. A highway authority which owns the land but has not adopted the highway is not an occupier of the highway: see *Holmes* v. *Norfolk County Council* (1981) 131 N.L.J. 401. A highway authority does not occupy a footpath on land owned by another although it has a statutory obligation to maintain it: see *Whiting* v. *Hillingdon London Borough Council* (1970) 68 L.G.R. 437.

98   *Humphreys* v. *Dreamland (Margate) Ltd*. [1930] All E.R. Rep. 327, HL.

99   *Hartwell* v. *Grayson Rollo and Clover Docks Ltd*. [1947] K.B. 901, C.A. However, a contractor merely painting a house is not an occupier: see *Page* v. *Read* (1984) 134 N.L.J. 723.

100 *Hawkins* v. *Coulsdon and Purley UDC* [1954] 1 Q.B. 319, [1954] 1 All E.R. 97 C.A.

101 *Greene* v. *Chelsea Borough Council* [1954] 2 Q.B. 127, [1954] 2 All E.R. 318, C.A. See also *Harris* v. *Birkenhead Corporation* [1976] 1 All E.R. 341, C.A, where a local authority, having acquired a house by compulsory purchase, occupies it even before its staff enter it.

102 Cmd 9305.

103 Section 1.

104 Section 2(2) of the Occupier's Liability Act, 1957.

105 *Greenhalgh* v. *British Railways Board* [1969] 2 Q.B. 286, [1969] 2 All E.R. 114, C.A., *per* Lord Denning M R at 292–3.

106 Section 2(3).

107 *Cooke* v. *Midland Great Western Rly of Ireland* [1909] A.C. 229 at 238 (*per* Lord Atkinson), H.L.; also *Gough* v. *National Coal Board* [1954] 1 Q.B. 191, [1953] 2 All E.R. 1283, C.A. The cases are legion but they all turn on their particular facts, such as *Williams* v. *Cardiff Corporation* [1950] 1 K.B. 514 [1950] 1 All E.R. 250, C.A. (a grassy slope with broken glass at the foot is a trap for a four-year-old child). The principle stated in the text also applied at common law in the case of adults suffering from mental or physical handicap and, it is submitted, will continue to apply to them under the Act.

108 See *Glasgow Corporation* v. *Taylor* [1922] 1 A.C. 44 H.L. which concerned liability for brightly coloured poisoned berries in a park and within easy reach of the child. The decision can be contrasted with D (*a minor*) v. *Department of Environment (NI)* [1992] 4 B.N.I.L. 117, where there was no liability when a six-year-old climbed a tree and fell out.

109 See *Phipps* v. *Rochester Corporation* [1955] 1 Q.B. 450, [1955] 1 All E.R. 129, containing an excellent review by Devlin J of the rights of child visitors which was applied in *Simkiss* v. *Rhondda Borough Council* (1982) 81 L.G.R. 460, C.A.

110 *Roles* v. *Nathan* [1963] 2 All E.R. 908, C.A.

111 Here it is valid to consider whether 'danger' means the peril or the thing which creates the peril.

112 *White* v. *Blackmore* [1972] 2 Q.B. 651, [1972] 3 All E.R. 158, C.A.

113 Section 2(5).

114 *London Graving Dock Co. Ltd* v. *Horton* [1951] A.C. 737, [1951] 2 All E.R. 1, H.L.

115 *Bunker* v. *Charles Brand & Son Ltd* [1969] 2 Q.B. 480, [1969] 2 All E.R. 59. See also *McMillan* v. *Lord Advocate* 1991 S.L.T. 150n.

116 *Longhurst* v. *Metropolitan Water Board* [1948] 2 All E.R. 834, H.L; *Caminer* v. *Northern and London Investment Trust Ltd* [1951] A.C. 88 [1950] 2 All E.R. 486; *Bolton* v. *Stone* [1951] A.C. 850 [1951] All E.R. 1078, H.L. Sometimes it is not clear on which tort a

judgment is based. See Denning LJ in *Mint* v. *Good* [1951] 1 K.B. 517 at 526 [1950] 2 All E.R. 1159 at 1168, C.A.

117 [1948] 2 All E.R. 662; cf. *Wheeler* v. *Morris* (1915) 84 L.J.K.B. 1435, C.A.

118 For example, *Hilder* v. *Associated Portland Cement Manufacturers Ltd* [1961] 3 All E.R. 709 [1961] 1 W.L.R. 1434. In this case the defendant occupiers of a field allowed children to play football in the field and were held liable to a motor-cyclist who, when driving along the adjoining highway, was knocked off his machine by a ball kicked by the children from the field.

119 *Hughes* v. *Percival* (1883) 8 App. Cas. 443, H.L.: the premises for the benefit of which the present rule applies are those in respect of which someone other than the defendant has a vested interest in possession. Also *Murphy* v. *Brentwood District Council* [1990] 2 All E.R. 908 and 926 (*per* Lord Bridge).

120 *Goldman* v. *Hargrave* [1907] 1 A.C. 645 [1966] 2 All E.R. 989, P.C. Water normally percolates from the defendant's land to the plaintiff's, and the defendant pumps out the water from his land, and by so stopping the subterranean flow causes settlement damage to the plaintiff's land. The plaintiff has no remedy, because the defendant has no duty to adjoining occupiers in respect of percolating water; *Langbrook Properties Ltd* v. *Surrey County Council* [1969] 3 All E.R. 1424, [1970] 1 W.L.R. 161.

121 *Bradburn* v. *Lindsay* [1983] 2 All E.R. 408.

122 [1933] 1 K.B. 551; the principle on which this case was based was approved *obiter* by Parcq J in *Bishop* v. *Consolidated London Properties Ltd* (1933) 102 L.J.K.B. 257, at 262.

123 [1918] 1 K.B. 247, CA (not cited in *Cunard* v. *Antifyre Ltd*).

124 [1938] 2 K.B. 577 at 594-5 (per Greer L J) [1938] 2 All E.R. 1, C.A.

125 [1939] 3 All E.R. 329.

126 Airbus Industrie, *1998 Global Forecast*, p. 4. This forecast can be viewed at <*http://www.Airbus.com*>.

127 The Boeing Company, *1998 Current Market Outlook*, p. 42. According to the Boeing forecast, the world fleet is expected to more than double by 2020, with total fleet size growing to 32 954 aircraft. Over the 20-year forecast period, 5053 aircraft will be retired from active commercial service and will be replaced. An additional 18 406 airplanes will be needed to fill capacity demand. See <*http://www.Boeing.com*>.

128 *Annual Report of the Council*, ICAO Doc. 9770, p.1; also, 'Airline Financial Results Remain Positive in 2002 Despite Soaring Fuel Prices', *ICAO News Release*, PIO 05/01.

129 'General Agreements on Tariffs and Trade, Multilateral Trade Negotiations' Final Act Embodying the Results of the Uruguay Round of Trade Negotiations' (done at Marrakesh, 15 April 1994, 33 *I.L.M.* 1125 (1994), Annex 1B, Part II Article II.

130 *Report of the GATT Secretariat to the Second Meeting on Sustainable Development*, 16–31 May 1994, Let/1873, 94-0438.

131 'Note by the GATT Secretariat prepared for the Second Meeting of the Commission on Sustainable Development', included in the report cited *supra*, note 127.

132 'Convention on International Civil Aviation', *supra*, note 70..

133 Ibid., Preamble, p. 1.

134 Ibid., Article 44(*a*).

135 ITA Press Release, 284, p. 10.

136 'Proceedings of the Council 2nd Session, 2 September–12 December 1947', Doc 7248 – C/839 at 44–5.

137 ICAO Resolutions A-13 and A-33, which resolved that SARPS relating to the efficient and safe regulation of international air navigation be adopted.

138 ICAO Annex 9, 'Facilitation', 9th edn, July 1990, Foreword.

139 *Aeronautical Information Services Manual*, ICAO Doc. 8126-0 AN/872/3. ICAO Resolution A 1-31 defines a Standard as any specification for physical characteristics 'the

uniform application of which is recognized as necessary ... and one that States will conform to'. The same resolution describes a Recommended Practice as any specification for physical characteristics 'which is recognized as desirable ... and one that member States will endeavour to conform to'. T Buergenthal, *Law Making in the International Civil Aviation Organization*, New York: Law Book Co.,1969, p. 10, also cites the definitions given in ICAO's Annex 9 of SARPS.

140 Art. 86 of the Convention.

141 Art. 12 stipulates that over the high seas, the rules in force shall be those established under the Convention, and each contracting state undertakes to ensure the prosecution of all persons violating the applicable regulations.

142 Michael Milde, 'The Chicago Convention – After Forty Years', *Annals of Air & Space Law*, IX, 1987, p. 126. See also Jacob Schenkman, *International Civil Aviation Organization*, Geneva: Librarie E. Droz, 1955, p. 163.

143 Milde, *supra*, note 142.

144 T. Buergenthal, *Law Making in the International Civil Aviation Organization*, New York: Law Book Co., 1969, p. 9.

145 Paul Stephen Dempsey, *Law and Foreign Policy in International Aviation*, Dobbs Ferry, New York: Transnational Publishers, 1987, p. 302.

146 Eugene Sochor, *The Politics of International Aviation*, London: Macmillan, 1991, p. 58.

147 Ibid.

148 Alexander Tobolewski, 'ICAO's Legal Syndrome', *Annals of Air & Space Law*, IV, 1979, p. 359.

Chapter 6

Conclusion

There is no room for any doubt that, in international civil aviation management, international and domestic civil aviation should not be considered in mutual exclusivity when it comes to matters of aviation security. The world community will now have to establish a carefully synchronized and thoughtfully orchestrated plan of action and system of progressing towards achieving substantial enforcement of aviation security. With regard to commercial implications, the air transport industry has undergone a substantial metamorphosis following the recent attacks on America, not only through the attacks themselves, but also through the portentous threat to the liberalization of air transport and maximization of commercial opportunity. Indeed, these new events have given the air transport industry new perspective, and a new impetus to rethink aviation policy through cautious but visionary regulation, on the one hand, and prudent economic policy, on the other.

On a more short-term level, and of no less critical importance, are the insurance and security implications that have been slated for urgent discussion. Both resolutions on insurance and security have called upon ICAO to initiate work of an urgent nature. The working group on insurance will be required to make recommendations on ways in which States could assist air transport operators and service providers in providing some financial protection. On the aviation security front, the Ministerial Conference held at ICAO on 19 and 20 February 2001 needed to spell out in some detail action to be taken to combat terrorism which sees aviation as a tool of destruction. Of course, any action proposed at this Conference was calculated to amount to more than just a resolution or two to be adopted by states. The 33rd Session of the ICAO Assembly had already done that, and it now remained for the international community to come up with some urgent actions for implementation. These actions would essentially have to be implemented with full international accord and cooperation. There should not be more Conventions, protocols and other documents waiting for ratification in order that they could come into effect.

In achieving the above-mentioned management objectives, the aviation community should start by attaining a full appreciation of the potential social and economic advantages of restoring confidence in air travel worldwide. The starting point should ineluctably be in the area of regulatory management, where ICAO should be called upon to identify and analyse new emerging and potential threats to civil aviation and to formulate appropriate practical strategy to address the threats. Once threat identification is completed, effective management follow-through should involve modular application of technological tools. Available technology, such as biometric identification equipment and machine-readable travel document readers, should be put to wider and more effective use. Management databases containing personal information relevant to ensuring safety should also be used extensively on the basis that the international use of these databases in providing advance passenger information is essential as a preventive management tool. Another important preventive measure is the immediate revision of existing regulatory guidelines, including Annex 17 to the Chicago Convention.

With regard to state responsibility, states should reaffirm their responsibility for effective security management. They should ensure integrated management, through partnerships between aviation and other authorities, between government and industry, spreading out to global, regional and interregional cooperation. Critical to this exercise would be the conduct by ICAO of aviation security audits, along the lines of aviation safety audits already carried out by the organization. Procedures for assisting states in taking remedial action have to be in place with the necessary follow up and technical assistance. It is only then that an effective preventive security management system could be developed.

A critical aspect of restoring confidence in air transport and ensuring effective aviation management lies in the need for a closer look at prevention and deterrence as effective measures in countering acts of terrorism that affect aviation. The United Nations General Assembly, on 9 December 1999, adopted the International Convention for the Suppression of the Financing of Terrorism, aimed at enhancing international cooperation among states in devising and adopting effective measures for the prevention of the financing of terrorism, as well as for its suppression through the prosecution and punishment of its perpetrators.

The Convention, in its Article 2, recognizes that any person who by any means, directly or indirectly, unlawfully or wilfully, provides or collects funds with the intention that they should be used or in the knowledge that they are to be used, in full or in part, in order to carry out any act which constitutes an offence under certain named treaties, commits an offence. The treaties listed are those that are already adopted and in force and which address acts of unlawful interference with such activities as deal with air transport and maritime transport. Also cited is the International Convention for the Suppression of Terrorist Bombings, adopted by the General Assembly of the United Nations on 15 December 1997.

The Convention for the Suppression of the Financing of Terrorism also provides that, over and above the acts mentioned, providing or collecting funds for any other act intended to cause death or serious bodily injury to a civilian, or to any other person not taking an active part in the hostilities in the situation of armed conflict, when the purpose of such act, by its nature or context, is to intimidate a population, or to compel a government or an international organization to do or to abstain from doing any act, would be deemed an offence under the Convention.

The use of the word 'terrorism' in the title of the Convention brings to bear the need to examine in greater detail both the etymology and the connotations of the word in modern parlance. The term 'terrorism' is seemingly of French origin and is believed to have been first used in 1798. 'Terrorism', which originally had connotations of criminality in one's conduct, is now generally considered a system of coercive intimidation brought about by the infliction of terror or fear. The most frustrating obstacle to the control of unlawful acts against international peace is the lack of a clear definition of the offence itself. Many attempts at defining the offence have often resulted in the offence being shrouded in political or national barriers.

In 1980, the Central Intelligence Agency of the United States of America adopted a definition of terrorism which read:

Terrorism is the threat or use of violence for political purposes by individuals or groups, whether acting for or in opposition to established governmental authority, when such actions are intended to shock, stun or intimidate victims. Terrorism has involved groups seeking to overthrow specific regimes, to rectify perceived national or group grievances, or to undermine international order as an end in itself.

This all-embracing definition underscores the misapprehension that certain groups which are etched in history, such as the French Resistance of Nazi occupied France during World War II and the Contras in Nicaragua, would broadly fall within the definitive parameters of terrorism. In fact, this formula labels every act of violence as being 'terrorist', engulfing in its broad spectrum such diverse groups as the Seikigunha of Japan and the Mujahedeen of Afghanistan, although their aims, *modus operandi* and ideologies are different. James Adams prefers a narrower definition, which reads:

a terrorist is an individual or member of a group that wishes to achieve political ends using violent means, often at the cost of casualties to innocent civilians and with the support of only a minority of the people they claim to represent.

Even this definition, although narrower than the 1980 definition cited above, is not sufficiently comprehensive to cover, for instance, the terrorist who hijacks an airplane for his own personal gain. The difficulty in defining the term seems to lie in its association with political aims of the terrorist, as is found in the definition that terrorism is really 'terror inspired by violence, containing an international element that is committed by individuals or groups against non-combatants, civilians, States or internationally protected persons or entities in order to achieve political ends'.

The offence of terrorism has also been defined as one caused by 'any serious act of violence or threat thereof by an individual, whether acting alone or in association with other persons, which is directed against internationally protected persons, organizations, places, transportation or communication systems or against members of the general public for the purpose of intimidating such persons, causing injury to or the death of such persons, disrupting the activities of such international organizations, of causing loss, detriment or damage to such places or property, or of interfering with such transportation and communications systems in order to undermine friendly relations among States or among the nationals of different States or to extort concessions from States'.

It is time that terrorism was recognized as an offence that is *sui generis* and one that is not always international in nature and motivated by the political aims of the perpetrator. For the moment, if terrorism were to be regarded as the use of fear, subjugation and intimidation to disrupt the normal operations of humanity, a more specific and accurate definition could be sought, once more analysis is carried out on the subject. One must always be mindful, however, that, without a proper and universally acceptable definition, international cooperation in combating terrorism would be impossible.

A terrorist act is one which is *mala in se* or evil by nature. A terrorist is a *hostis humani generis* or common enemy of humanity. International terrorism has so far not been defined comprehensively, largely owing to the fact that, owing to its diversity of nature, the concept itself has defied precise definition. However, this does not preclude the conclusion that international terrorism involves two factors: the commission of a terrorist act by a terrorist or terrorists, and the 'international' element involved in the act or acts in question, that is, the motivation for the commission of such act or acts or the eventual goal of the terrorist should inextricably be linked with a country other than that in which the act or acts are committed. Perhaps the oldest paradigm of international terrorism is piracy, which has been recognized as an offence against the law of nations and which is seen commonly today in the offence of aerial piracy or hijacking.

Acts of international terrorism that have been committed over the past two decades are too numerous to mention. Suffice it to say that the most deleterious effect of the offence is that it exacerbates international relations and endangers international security. From the isolated incidents of the 1960s, international terrorism has progressed to becoming a concentrated assault on nations and organizations that are usually susceptible to political conflict, although politics is not always the motivation of the international terrorist. International terrorism has been recognized as embracing acts of aggression by one state on another, as well as by an individual or a group of individuals of one state on another state. The former typifies such acts as invasion, while the latter relates to such individual acts of violence as hijacking and the murder of civilians in isolated instances. In both cases, the duties of the offender state have been emphatically recognized. Such duties are to condemn such acts and take necessary action. The United Nations gave effect to this principle in 1970, when it proclaimed:

> Every State has the duty to refrain from organizing or encouraging the organization of irregular forces or armed bands, including mercenaries, for incursion into the territory of another State. Every State has the duty to refrain from organizing, instigating, assisting or participating in acts of civil strife or terrorist acts in another State or acquiescing in organized activities within its territory directed towards the commission of such acts, when the acts referred to in the present paragraph involve a threat or use of force.

The most pragmatic approach to the problem lies in identifying the parameters of the offence of international terrorism and seeking a solution to the various categories of the offence. To obtain a precise definition would be unwise, if not impossible. Once the offence and its parasitic qualities were clearly identified, it would become necessary to discuss briefly its harmful effects on the international community. It is only then that a solution could be discussed that would obviate the fear and apprehension we suffer in the face of this threat.

It is said that terrorism is a selective use of fear, subjugation and intimidation to disrupt the normal operations of society. Beyond this statement, which stands for both national and international terrorism, any attempt at a working definition of the words 'international terrorism' would entail complications. However, in seeking a solution which would lead to the control of international terrorism, it is imperative that contemporaneous instances of the infliction of terror be identified in order that they may be classified either as acts of international terrorism or as mere innocuous acts of self-defence. Broadly, acts of international terrorism may be categorized into two distinct groups. In the first category may be included what are termed 'acts of oppression', such as the invasion of one state by another. In the second category are acts which are deviously claimed to be 'acts of defence'. While the former is self-explanatory, the latter – by far the more common in modern society – can be identified in four separate forms of manifestation:

a) acts claimed to be committed in self-defence and in pursuance of self-determination to circumvent oppression;
b) non-violent acts committed internationally which are calculated to sabotage and destroy an established regime;
c) random acts of violence committed internationally by an individual or groups of individuals to pressurize a state or a group of individuals to succumb to the demands of terrorists; and,
d) acts committed internationally which aid and abet national terrorism.

With the exception of the first category of invasion, the others are prima facie acts of international terrorism which are essentially extensions of national terrorism. That is to say, most acts of international terrorism are a species of the genus national terrorism.

ACTS OF DEFENCE

Some states claim that internal oppression either by foreign invasion or by an internal totalitarian regime necessitates guerrilla warfare for the achievement of freedom. With more emphasis, it has been claimed that one state must not be allowed to exploit and harass another and that the physical manifestation of desire to attain freedom should not be construed as terrorism. Often such acts of self-defence prove to take extreme violent forms and manifest themselves overseas, thus giving rise to international terrorism. Acts of defence, as they are called, are common forms of international terrorism and are categorized as political violence. These acts take the form of 'acts of disruption, destruction, injury whose purpose, choice of targets or victims, surrounding circumstances, implementation and/or effects have political significance'.

Organized political groups plan strikes and acts of violence internally while extensions of these groups carry out brutal assassinations and kidnapping, and cause severe damage to property overseas. The retaliatory process which commences as a token of self-defence is transformed into terroristic violence which is totally ruthless and devoid of moral scruples. Usually, a cause which originates as dedicated to self-defence and self-determination seeks to gain the support of the people, disarm the military strength of the regime against which it rebels and, above all, seeks to strengthen itself in order that the terrorist movement may attain stability. In this instance terrorist acts seek primarily to carry out a massive propaganda campaign in the international community while at the same time concentrating more on individual instances of terrorism in populated urban areas which attract more attention than those committed in isolated areas. Advertising a cause in the international community becomes an integral part of political terrorism of this nature.

Both the international community and the governments concerned should be mindful that acts of defence can be treated as such only in instances where people defend themselves when they are attacked, and not when retaliatory measures are

taken in isolation to instil fear in the international community. To that extent, acts of
defence can be differentiated from acts of terrorism.

NON-VIOLENT ACTS

There are instances where terrorism extends to destabilizing an established regime
or a group of persons by the use of threats which are often calculated to instil fear in
the international community. Typical examples of this kind of terrorism are the
spreading of false propaganda and the invocation of threats which unhinge both the
nation or a group of persons against whom the threats are carried out and the nations
in which such acts are said to be committed. There have been instances in the past
where export consumer commodities of a nation, such as food items, have been
claimed to be poisoned in order that foreign trade between nations be precluded.
Although such acts are devoid of actual physical violence, they tend to unhinge the
economic stability of a nation, particularly if such nation depends solely on the
export of the item in question. In such instances, international terrorism assumes
proportions of great complexity and succeeds at least temporarily in disrupting the
infrastructural equilibrium of the nation against which such threat is aimed. The
government concerned is immediately placed on the defensive and attempts counter-
propaganda. In spreading propaganda of this nature, the media are the terrorist's best
friend. He uses the media of television and radio as a symbolic weapon to instil fear
in the public and to cripple the persons or government against which his attack has
been aimed. The effect of publicity on people is truly tangible, whether it pertains to
the statement of facts or whether it relates to the issuance of threats. Primarily, media
terrorism creates an emotional state of apprehension and fear in threatened groups
and, secondly, it draws world attention to the existence of the terrorists and their
cause. In both instances, the terrorist succeeds in creating a credibility gap between
his target and the rest of the world. Psychological terrorism of this nature is perhaps
the most insidious of its kind. It is certainly the most devious.

RANDOM ACTS OF VIOLENCE

A random act of violence is normally a corollary to a threat, though not necessarily
so. Often, as it happens, the international community is shocked by a despicable act
of mass murder or destruction of property which takes the world completely by
surprise. Responsibility for the act may be acknowledged later, though in many
instances no responsibility is claimed. In the latter instance when no responsibility
is claimed, the offended nation and the world at large are rendered destitute of an
immediate remedy against the offence. Even if motive is imputed to a particular
terrorist group, the exercise of sanctions becomes difficult as the international
community would not condone sanctions in the absence of concrete and cogent
evidence.

The difficulty lies largely in the fact that any terrorist act is usually carefully
planned and executed. Often one observes that the terrorist cautiously retraces his
steps, obscuring all evidence, unless he seeks publicity. The average terrorist is a

militant who employs tactics aimed at instilling fear in the minds of the international community. His acts are calculated to instil fright and paralyse the infrastructure of a state by totally exhausting the strength of his target. He further disarms his target by introducing the element of surprise to his attack. Perhaps the most outstanding element of a random attack is the psychological element where excessive and sporadic acts of violence instil both fear and psychological disorientation in a society. This in turn contributes to undermining and weakening a government's authority and control. The disruptive influence that terrorism of this kind exercises over society often creates disharmony within the political circles of a nation and unhinges the psychological behavioural pattern of an organized society. Most often the gap between the citizen and the established government, both in the state in which the act is committed and in the state against which the act is committed, is widened as the average citizen tends to regard his personal security as the most inviolate of rights that has to be protected by his government.

ACTS WHICH AID AND ABET NATIONAL TERRORISM

The fourth facet of international terrorism pertains to acts which promote national terrorism and which are committed outside the state against which the terrorist cause exists. These acts manifest themselves in the maintenance of overseas training camps for terrorists, where guerrilla warfare, techniques of assassination, destruction and sabotage are taught to terrorist groups who, after sustained training, return to their country and practise what they have learnt overseas. Such training camps are usually conducted by revolutionary groups and mercenaries at the request of terrorist organizations. A natural corollary to this trend is the collection of funds overseas for the financing of such training programmes, the purchase of arms, ammunition and explosives and the collection of monies involved in meeting the costs incurred by foreign propaganda.

Indirect acts of international terrorism such as those which aid and abet national terrorism indicate clearly that, although there is no identifiable definition of the word 'terrorism', the word itself can no longer be associated only with violent acts of aggression. In fact, recent studies reflect that any organized campaign of international terrorism involves both direct and indirect acts in equal proportion. Broadly, international terrorism embitters humanity and antagonizes one nation against another, one human being against another. The eventual consequence of the problem is aggression and even war. The main aim of use of the psychological element by the international terrorist which is by far the most obnoxious and objectionable is to polarize humans and society. However, its immediate manifestation and future development are not without features sufficient to cause grave concern to the world.

Acts of international terrorism, whether in the form of violent or non-violent acts, have clear and immediate international consequences. They are numerous in nature and warrant a separate study. However, in effect they obtain for the miscreant the same result of creating disharmony and disruption in society. The concept has grown in recent times to portend more serious problems for the international community. Those problems are worthy of comment.

Terrorism has so far not reached the proportions of being an international conspiracy, although one group may identify its objectives and purpose with another's. We have not had the misfortune of seeing all terrorist groups band together to work as a composite element. This has not happened for the reason that diverse ideologies and religions have kept each group separate. Nevertheless, there is a strong identity bond between groups and even evidence that one helps another with training and military aid, even though their causes are quite different. The link between terrorist groups is an important consideration for the world as close association between groups could strengthen a weak force and nurture it to maturity. In addition, strong and established terrorist organizations, under cover of burgeoning groups, could carry out campaigns which would cover their tracks and make identification difficult. In most actual instances, this has been found to be true and investigation has revealed that a small group, not significant enough at that time to take account of, has been responsible for an act or acts, whereas later it has been revealed that a much stronger group had masterminded the offences for its benefit. Another important feature of the growing incidence of international terrorism is the assistance the terrorists receive from the advancement of technology in communication, the manufacture of sophisticated weaponry and the proliferation of nuclear armament. In today's context, terrorism has swelled to unmanageable proportions with the use of advanced weapons of destruction. Arms control plays a vital role in the control of aggression and it naturally follows that terrorism too benefits from the availability of new modes of aggression. The vulnerability of the international community has been mainly brought about by the paucity of adequate security measures to prevent nuclear theft. With the growth of the nuclear power industry, developed nations have exposed themselves to the possibility of theft by power groups, in whose hands nuclear weapons act as threats of destruction. The most effective countermeasure that can be taken in this instance against the threat of nuclear theft is to take such effective measures as are necessary to protect the stored items and to make known to the terrorist the high risk involved in an attempt to steal such material. Ideally, any hope of theft must be obviated. This can be achieved by strengthening governmental security.

PROBLEMS OF DETERRENCE

The only deterrent that would be effective against terrorism of any nature is broadly based on success in convincing the terrorist that the risk he takes outweighs the benefits which may accrue to his cause by his act. The futility of attempting to wipe out terrorism by the use of military force or the threat of general sanction on an international level is apparent. The terrorist has to be shown that any attempt at terrorist activity would cause him and his cause more harm than good. Deterrence in this context attains fruition when effective punitive sanctions are prescribed and carried out while simultaneously the terrorist's demands are rejected. In both instances, the measures taken should be imperatively effective. It is not sufficient if such measures are merely entered into the statute books of a state or incorporated into international treaty. The international community has to be convinced that such measures are forceful and capable of being carried out.

However, deterrence does not stop at the mere imposition of effective sanctions, nor does it complete its task by the denial of terrorist demands. Perhaps the most effective method of countering terrorism is psychological warfare. The terrorist himself depends heavily on psychology. His main task is to polarize the people and the establishment. He wants popular support and a sympathetic ear. He wants a lot of people listening and watching, not a lot of people dead. Countermeasures taken against a terrorist attack, such as hostage taking, kidnapping or a threat of murder, should essentially include an effective campaign to destroy the terrorist's credibility and sincerity in the eyes of the public. Always the loyalty of the public should be won over by the target and not by the terrorist. It is only then that the terrorist's risk outweighs the benefits he obtains. To achieve this objective it must be ensured that the terrorist receives publicity detrimental to him, showing the public that, if the threatened person, group of persons or state comes to harm, the terrorist alone is responsible. Therefore the most practical measures that could be adopted to deter the spread of terrorism can be accommodated in two chronological stages:

1) measures taken before the commission of an offence, such as the effective imposition and carrying out of sanctions and the refusal to comply readily with the demands of the terrorist;
2) measures taken after the commission of the act, such as the skilful use of the media to destroy the credibility of the terrorist cause and to convince the people that the responsibility for the act devolves at all stages solely upon the terrorist.

One difficulty in exercising deterrence against terrorism in general and international terrorism in particular is that, often, the measures taken are not effective enough to convince the terrorist that, in the end, more harm would be caused to him than good. Negotiation with the terrorist in particular has to be done by professionals specially trained for the task. *A fortiori*, the media have to be handled by specialists with experience. Things would be much more difficult for the terrorist if such expertise was used. The greatest problem of deterrence is the pusillanimity of the international community in the face of terrorism and the feeble response offered by states as a composite body. The reasons for this hesitation on the part of the international community to adopt effective measures against international terrorism are by no means inexplicable. When one state supports a revolutionary cause which is aimed against another, it is quite natural that the terrorist is aware of the support he is capable of obtaining from at least one part of the already polarized world. Therein lies the problem.

THE PRACTICAL SOLUTION

The primary objective of international peace and security is the endeavour to preserve the right to life and liberty. This right is entrenched in Article 3 of the Universal Declaration of Human Rights of 1948 and is accepted today as constituting an obligation on all member states to recognize the legally and morally binding nature of the declaration. Therefore the destruction of human life and the restriction of liberty are acts committed against international law and order. International terrorism destroys both life and liberty. Indeed, there need be no doubt in our minds that international terrorism is illegal. To begin with, there should be more awareness in the world today that every human being has the inherent right to life and that the right is protected by law. Any act of terrorism, being illegal, becomes subject to law and its punitive sanctions. However, in this instance, unlike a simple instance of murder, where sanction itself may act as a deterrent, the two forces of law and sanction are not sufficient to curb terrorism. The international community should realize that the solution to terrorism lies rather in its prevention than in its cure. Therefore the problem has to be approached solely on the basis that the terrorist, on the one hand, has to be persuaded that his act may not succeed while, on the other, he has to be persuaded that, even if he succeeded in committing the act of terrorism, it would not achieve for him the desired results.

The philosophy of warfare against terrorism is therefore based on one single fact, that of convincing the terrorist that any attempt at committing a terrorist act would be fruitless and would entail for him unnecessary harm. This simple philosophy should be adopted gradually in stages with the sustained realization that each measure taken is as important as the next and that all measures should be adopted as a composite element and not as measures that are mutually exclusive. A potential terrorist can therefore be attacked in two ways: by the adoption of practical measures to discourage the commission of the act and by the adoption of such effective measures as would impose severe punitive sanctions if the act was committed.

In the first instance, self-help measures are essential. They should be adopted with careful planning and the terrorist should be made aware that the community at large are afforded the full protection of these measures:

a) the establishment of a system of intelligence which would inform the state concerned of an impending terrorist attack;
b) the establishment of counter-terrorism mechanisms which would effectively preclude such catalysts as the collection of arms, ammunition and weaponry;
c) the adoption of such practical measures of self-help and attack as are necessary in an instance of an attack;
d) the existence of the necessary machinery to retain the confidence and sympathy of the public at all times;
e) the persuasion necessary to convince the public that terrorism of any kind is evil and should not be condoned, whatever its cause.

The second instance is concerned with measures taken in the event of a terrorist act being committed. If strongly enforced with unanimity, such measures as the imposition of laws which bind all nations to view terrorist acts as crimes against humanity can be an effective deterrent. *A fortiori*, sanctions would further discourage the terrorist.

The first step that should be taken to deter terrorism is to be equipped with the expertise to detect a potential threat beforehand and to be prepared for an attack. The next is to intensify security in all susceptible areas, particularly in such places as airports and subway terminals. Surveillance of all people who are seen in such areas as are revealed to be targets of terrorist acts is imperative . There should be more awareness of the threat of terrorist activity, particularly in international airports and international bus and train terminals, where travel documents should be checked and passengers double-checked. Electronic surveillance of passports and other documents has proved to be an effective means of deterrence in this context. Perhaps the most important facet of surveillance is the use of personnel who do not reveal their identity to the public, but mingle unobtrusively with the crowds. This category of person can easily detect an irregularity without arousing suspicion and without alarming the common man. It is recommended that, together with the armed personnel, there should also be trained personnel who in all informality may work together with the security forces in such instances. Another significant requirement is the support of the people. The media should be made maximum use of to educate the common man on how to react in an emergency and also to be totally distrustful of the terrorist whose acts are calculated to evoke sympathy. The state or persons against whom the terrorist attack is launched should, at all times, use the media to convince the public that responsibility for any destruction or harm resulting from a terrorist act devolves totally on the terrorist.

Index

For Product Safety Concerns and Information please contact our EU
representative GPSR@taylorandfrancis.com Taylor & Francis Verlag GmbH,
Kaufingerstraße 24, 80331 München, Germany

Printed and bound by CPI Group (UK) Ltd, Croydon, CR0 4YY
01/05/2025
01858342-0013